The L/L Research Channeling Archives

Transcripts of the Meditation Sessions

Volume II
March 18, 1990 to March 27, 1991

| Don Elkins | Jim McCarty | Carla L. Rueckert |

Copyright © 2009 L/L Research

All rights reserved. No part of this book may be reproduced or used in any form or by any means—graphic, electronic or mechanical, including photocopying or information storage and retrieval systems—without written permission from the copyright holder.

ISBN: 978-0-945007-85-2

Published by L/L Research
Box 5195
Louisville, Kentucky 40255-0195

E-mail: contact@llresearch.org
www.llresearch.org

About the cover photo: *This photograph of Jim McCarty and Carla L. Rueckert was taken during an L/L Research channeling session on August 4, 2009, in the living room of their Louisville, Kentucky home. Jim always holds hands with Carla when she channels, following the Ra group's advice on how she can avoid any possibility of astral travel.*

Dedication

These archive volumes are dedicated to Hal and Jo Price, who faithfully and lovingly hosted this group's weekly meditation meetings from 1962 to 1975,

to Walt Rogers, whose work with the research group Man, Consciousness and Understanding of Detroit offered the information needed to begin this ongoing channeling experiment,

and to the Confederation of Angels and Planets in the Service of the Infinite Creator, for sharing their love and wisdom with us so generously through the years.

Table of Contents

Introduction 6
Year 1990 8
    March 18, 1990 9
    March 25, 1990 15
    April 1, 1990 22
    April 15, 1990 28
    April 29, 1990 34
    May 6, 1990 38
    May 13, 1990 44
    May 20, 1990 51
    May 27, 1990 55
    June 3, 1990 60
    June 4, 1990 65
    June 7, 1990 69
    June 8, 1990 72
    June 15, 1990 75
    June 17, 1990 81
    June 20, 1990 86
    June 23, 1990 92
    June 24, 1990 98
    June 29, 1990 102
    July 1, 1990 108
    July 8, 1990 115
    July 12, 1990 118
    July 15, 1990 124
    July 19, 1990 130
    July 22, 1990 133
    August 2, 1990 138
    August 5, 1990 141
    August 12, 1990 146
    September 9, 1990 152
    September 16, 1990 158
    September 20, 1990 165
    September 23, 1990 167
    September 30, 1990 173
    October 7, 1990 179
    October 14, 1990 185
    October 21, 1990 190
    October 25, 1990 198

October 28, 1990	202
November 4, 1990	207
November 8, 1990	213
November 11, 1990	219
November 15, 1990	225
November 16, 1990	230
November 17, 1990	233
November 18, 1990	237
November 25, 1990	245
November 29, 1990	251
December 2, 1990	256
December 16, 1990	261
December 30, 1990	268
Year 1991	**274**
January 6, 1991	275
January 10, 1991	282
January 13, 1991	285
January 20, 1991	291
January 24, 1991	295
January 27, 1991	299
January 31, 1991	303
February 3, 1991	306
February 8, 1991	312
February 24, 1991	316
February 28, 1991	322
February 28, 1991	323
March 1, 1991	330
March 1, 1991	337
March 2, 1991	342
March 3, 1991	350
March 3, 1991	357
March 8, 1991	367
March 10, 1991	370
March 20, 1991	375
March 22, 1991	382
March 24, 1991	386
March 27, 1991	392

Introduction

Welcome to this volume of the *L/L Research Channeling Archives*. This series of publications represents the collection of channeling sessions recorded by L/L Research during the period from the early seventies to the present day. The sessions are also available on the L/L Research website, www.llresearch.org.

Starting in the mid-1950s, Don Elkins, a professor of physics and engineering at Speed Scientific School, had begun researching the paranormal in general and UFOs in particular. Elkins was a pilot as well as a professor and he flew his small plane to meet with many of the UFO contactees of the period.

Hal Price had been a part of a UFO-contactee channeling circle in Detroit called "The Detroit Group." When Price was transferred from Detroit's Ford plant to its Louisville truck plant, mutual friends discovered that Price also was a UFO researcher and put the two men together. Hal introduced Elkins to material called *The Brown Notebook* which contained instructions on how to create a group and receive UFO contactee information. In January of 1962 they decided to put the instructions to use and began holding silent meditation meetings on Sunday nights just across the Ohio River in the southern Indiana home of Hal and his wife, Jo. This was the beginning of what was called the "Louisville Group."

I was an original member of that group, along with a dozen of Elkins' physics students. However, I did not learn to channel until 1974. Before that date, almost none of our weekly channeling sessions were recorded or transcribed. After I began improving as a channel, Elkins decided for the first time to record all the sessions and transcribe them.

During the first eighteen months or so of my studying channeling and producing material, we tended to reuse the tapes as soon as the transcriptions were finished. Since those were typewriter days, we had no record of the work that could be reopened and used again, as we do now with computers. And I used up the original and the carbon copy of my transcriptions putting together a manuscript, *Voices of the Gods*, which has not yet been published. It remains as almost the only record of Don Elkins' and my channeling of that period.

We learned from this experience to retain the original tapes of all of our sessions, and during the remainder of the seventies and through the eighties, our "Louisville Group" was prolific. The "Louisville Group" became "L/L Research" after Elkins and I published a book in 1976, *Secrets of the UFO*, using that publishing name. At first we met almost every night. In later years, we met gradually less often, and the number of sessions recorded by our group in a year accordingly went down. Eventually, the group began taking three months off from channeling during the summer. And after 2000, we began having channeling meditations only twice a month. The volume of sessions dropped to its present output of eighteen or so each year.

These sessions feature channeling from sources which call themselves members of the Confederation of Planets in the Service of the Infinite Creator. At first we enjoyed hearing from many different voices: Hatonn, Laitos, Oxal, L/Leema and Yadda being just a few of them. As I improved my tuning techniques, and became the sole senior channel in L/L Research, the number of contacts dwindled. When I began asking for "the highest and best contact which I can receive of Jesus the Christ's vibration of unconditional love in a conscious and stable manner," the entity offering its thoughts through our group was almost always Q'uo. This remains true as our group continues to channel on an ongoing basis.

The channelings are always about love and unity, enunciating "The Law of One" in one aspect or another. Seekers who are working with spiritual principles often find the material a good resource. We hope that you will as well. As time has gone on the questions have shifted somewhat, but in general the content of the channeling is metaphysical and focused on helping seekers find the love in the moment and the Creator in the love.

At first, I transcribed our channeling sessions. I got busier, as our little group became more widely known, and got hopelessly behind on transcribing. Two early transcribers who took that job off my hands were Kim

Howard and Judy Dunn, both of whom masterfully transcribed literally hundreds of sessions through the eighties and early nineties.

Then Ian Jaffray volunteered to create a web site for these transcriptions, and single-handedly unified the many different formats that the transcripts were in at that time and made them available online. This additional exposure prompted more volunteers to join the ranks of our transcribers, and now there are a dozen or so who help with this. Our thanks go out to all of these kind volunteers, early and late, who have made it possible for our webguy to make these archives available.

Around the turn of the millennium, I decided to commit to editing each session after it had been transcribed. So the later transcripts have fewer errata than the earlier ones, which are quite imperfect in places. One day, perhaps, those earlier sessions will be revisited and corrections will be made to the transcripts. It would be a large task, since there are well over 1500 channeling sessions as of this date, and counting. We apologize for the imperfections in those transcripts, and trust that you can ascertain the sense of them regardless of a mistake here and there.

Blessings, dear reader! Enjoy these "humble thoughts" from the Confederation of Planets. May they prove good companions to your spiritual seeking. ☙

For all of us at L/L Research,

Carla L. Rueckert

Louisville, Kentucky

July 16, 2009

Year 1990

March 18, 1990 to December 30, 1990

L/L Research

L/L Research is a subsidiary of Rock Creek Research & Development Laboratories, Inc.

P.O. Box 5195
Louisville, KY 40255-0195

www.llresearch.org

Rock Creek is a non-profit corporation dedicated to discovering and sharing information which may aid in the spiritual evolution of humankind.

ABOUT THE CONTENTS OF THIS TRANSCRIPT: This telepathic channeling has been taken from transcriptions of the weekly study and meditation meetings of the Rock Creek Research & Development Laboratories and L/L Research. It is offered in the hope that it may be useful to you. As the Confederation entities always make a point of saying, please use your discrimination and judgment in assessing this material. If something rings true to you, fine. If something does not resonate, please leave it behind, for neither we nor those of the Confederation would wish to be a stumbling block for any.

© 2009 L/L RESEARCH

Sunday Meditation
March 18, 1990

Group question: The question this evening is about limits. To what degree is accepting our limitations giving up, and to what degree is it freeing ourselves of unnecessary suffering?

(Carla channeling)

I am of that principle known to you as Q'uo. We greet you in the love and in the light of the one infinite One, the Creator of all, in Whose name we serve, and we bless and greet [you] and rejoice with greatest joy in being called to this beloved group. Your radiance is bright to us, and we bask in the sunshine of your desire to seek and to know, though you are vulnerable and open to pain, though you know the truth may cause you hurt, yet you seek, and you seek still, willing to bear the brunt of the truth, willing to ask past the surface of things. You are gallant friends, and we thank this group.

It is with gratitude and humility that we remind you that we are your brothers and sisters, not those infallible with authority over you of any kind, but those who wish you well, and who would give to you the best of ourselves, our feelings, our opinions, our thoughts. It is for this reason that we are awake to the cries of people such as you. It is for this reason that we come to those who seek through dreaming, through visions, through writing, and more occasionally, in those who are disciplined in their seeking, and have chosen this particular path of service through the vocal channeling, in which we are able to offer information more specific than paintings, music and poetry, though surely not more eloquent—simply more lucid and easy to penetrate.

You ask this evening a question which bears with it some dangers, and of these dangers we would speak first. To assume that one knows one's limitations and one's abilities, to assume that one has the intelligence to control one's destiny by thought and reasoning, is to assume a grandeur that you do not possess. And we say to you straight out that you who are guided by intellectual evaluations of situations, and respect for authority of any kind whatsoever, are hag-ridden and living in a nightmare.

One of the great misunderstandings of the many beautiful works man has created is the concept that man has created them by means of his reasoning, his logic, his intelligence. This is the mainstay of the culture in which you now exist. It is this over-respect for authority which one does not understand, that accepts without understanding, that is the hallmark of your desperate civilization at this time.

To whom give you authority? To those who are the priests of reason, of intellect, of logic, of hypothesis and conclusion, whether they be in the guise of those who come in the name of religion, having explained precisely by dogma and doctrine that which may be believed and that which shall not be believed, or whether one wishes to give credence to the doctors and the teachers, the scientists, the priests of reason and technology. Such is authority given to idols made of clay, for though each entity trained to be in authority, and with the feeling of being in authority felt in surety within, yet is this person fooling itself, and removing the possibility of movement in spirit. Those who follow without understanding, without seeking the heart and not the mind, are those who consign themselves to prisons made of their own mental biases: this, this and this is true, and therefore all other is false. Such concepts are comforting, for one may again relax into the structure of a prepared life path where one is aware when one is doing well and knowledgeable of one's errors as they are pointed out to one by the authority accepted.

Thus, those who ponder the meaning, the necessity and the response to limitation with the mind alone, with weights of opinion from authority without the self, are those who seek to avoid the responsibility of being, to avoid the vulnerability of making an error. The great fallacy of all authority is error. There is no error; there are only ways to learn. Some ways of learning quite clearly inform one of that which one does not wish to do again. Was this then an error which brought one to such a speedy and heartfelt conclusion?

Therefore, let us banish from our minds our own mind's power over us. See your intelligence, your logic, your intellect as a workhorse, a machine, a computer which has been trained to make choices. Realize that you need this computer, for you dwell in so rich a tapestry of sensual experience that you could not ever be aware of your entire environment in any moment whatsoever. The creation is not large enough to hold the resonance of each passing moment. All your senses are open, thirsty, vulnerable, and the intellect chooses those things of which you must be aware to avoid extinction, to maintain preservation of the physical vehicle, and to meet those needs which your biases have previously fed into the computer again and again until the computer smoothly and quickly eliminates much from your environment, so that you are only aware of a tiny, tiny portion of your own creation.

This was planned by you, not that you be so limited, in and of itself, but that you continually examine your vulnerabilities to see if the choices you have made in what you perceive of what you see is that which you wish to perceive. Allow in your daily meditative moments this question to arise within you: "Are my choices causing me to praise the one infinite Creator? Do my choices bring me joy? Do my choices open me to the glory of consciousness, to the depth and breadth of the resonances of the present moment?"

Avoid satisfaction, especially self-satisfaction, but be hungry and thirsty, for there is more to learn, more to experience, and in that learning and in that experiencing there shall be change, which is, by definition, uncomfortable, stressful, painful. It is the successful heart that is open to these things, yet aware of the power of its own abilities to forgive, to love and to accept.

Once the faculty of unnecessary judging has been removed and replaced by an eager acceptance of the rightness of that which is occurring, one may then gaze upon what one considers limitations, and it is at this point only that we speak of limitations, having warned you as carefully as possible always to avoid mental constructs and structures which predetermine the meaning of your particular experience of being limited. This is your creation, a creation of the heart and of the spirit. Yes, it is a creation of your deeper mind, but your deeper mind is your heart, not your intellect. The intellect is the animal you ride so that you do not die to this world before you have tasted of the joy of being alive.

Conditions among your people are harsh. There is much pain in joy, there is much sorrow in laughter, there is much loss in each passing moment, until finally the loss of the physical vehicle is complete. All this is illusion, and this the heart knows; the intellect does not. It presumes its own self-preservation as a given which shall continue with no foreseeable end, and to this end it bends all experience. Abandon this, if you ever embraced it, for you seek upon a dusty path that is mystery, not surety, and your limitations are as you find them, shifting, moving, transforming before you as you change in your perception of them.

A limitation is wisely accepted as the basis of evaluation of further action. When one cannot walk one finds oneself an appropriate seat. When one cannot speak, one remains silent. When one cannot understand, one embraces mystery. When one cannot move, one embraces the concept of moving motionlessness. This is a foundation acceptance that is very helpful to the heart. It is not wisdom to ignore the circumstance of the physical vehicle, for these are the limitations of which you speak, limitations of action, of movement, of energy, but this is only the basis for further waiting, waiting in patience, in quietude, in certainty of the constant inflow of inspiration, for many are those who choose to do as much as possible, regardless of the circumstances and regardless of those things done, because authority says those who do the most are worth the most. Thus, the self values activity without evaluating worth, the love one has, the joy one has in each activity, but simply assuming that to give is to be productive, to be busy, to be active.

We speak directly to this particular instrument as well as in general to all, for this instrument has recently moved through the concepts of authority, limitation, and the making of decisions and it has discovered, and you will discover, the positive and the negative necessity of the acceptance of limitations being the beginning of the true choosing of that which is good to do for the self, and that which is kind to yield to for the self. It takes more patience than many have to wait upon inspiration, for the process of waiting is the process of forgiving the self for the limitation it has, and a beginning to believe that the change that is occurring is not a limitation, but a transformation, an alteration of the path of service intended by yourself and the Creator together before this incarnational experience was ever begun.

Times of pain and limitation are those times to find rejoicing and praise and thanksgiving, for these are the signals that the Creator is especially near, and transformation of the life, new lessons, are about to appear to one who truly forgives, who truly accepts, and may sit in peace, glorying in the light of the infinite Creator, and resting in the embrace of the universe with no thought except to wait upon that transformation to declare itself within one's heart.

The rest of that which we have to say is perhaps self-evident from this point. Many are the things which may be, not given up, but released, for they are no longer a part of your path of service. A grieving process for them is understandable, yet it is time also for faith to show itself, faith without understanding, without knowledge of any kind, but only faith that things are as they should be, that love permeates this and every transaction of the incarnational experience, that there is a path of service in every changed life. Even if the changes seem more and more limiting to the mind, to the heart, that energy which has been set free from those activities released is now there to place in a new path of service, in a new way of seeing, perceiving, changing and becoming. All entities are entities in transition, just as all entities are forever perfect. You are being and you are becoming. Thus, it is folly to hold to old paths of service which seem no longer to be possible, given growing physical, mental or spiritual limitations.

Yet there are those things which still resonate to the heart in a special way, those paths of service which survive change and transformation, because so deep are they within the heart that they are part of the deep self, that which cannot and should not be denied. The one authority you heed is that authority of your own heart. And so, though sometimes limited, one may choose to press against that limitation for the purposes of service, and more than that, for the purposes of experiencing the greatest joy possible to the spirit that you are with your own biases within this incarnational experience.

If you are thirsty and there is something that slakes that spiritual thirst, and you seek still to do this, pressing against a limitation, then you are not harming yourself, but giving yourself a reason to enjoy, to accept and to rejoice in the state or condition of life in which you find yourself regardless of your limitations. How to tell the difference is not a matter for the intellect, not a matter of constant, conscious, careful choice, but a matter of loving, waiting, accepting and listening to the voice that speaks within with the authority of your deeper self saying "Send me, send me here, send me, send me here," and so you send yourself, whatever the cost may be, if it is possible, for still this feels to be part of your path of service.

You are not here, my beloved ones, to have, to hold, to collect, to sustain. You are here to learn in deeper and more resonant ways always, what it is to be of service, what it is to love. You must begin with yourself, loving, accepting, opening your vulnerable self to wear the harshness of your humanity, for you are sturdy within, you have the strength of the universe within, you abide in the Creator, and love and light are your nature. You live in union with all that there is, there is nothing to fight. A limitation is an invitation to change. Know, each time that you experience limitation, you are experiencing the chance to learn something new, to serve in a new way, to find out more about what being and becoming truly are, to discover within yourself that core of being which is the infinite One. The infinite

One is without, the infinite One is within, there is nothing but the infinite One, all is One. Cast aside fear, for your heart shall tell you in good time what choices to release, what choices to keep, and what choices to make for the first time that you may learn yet another lesson of love.

It is for this reason that you came into this world of loss and sorrow and vulnerability and pain and harshness. You came to be thirsty and hungry. You came to yearn and ache and be intensely passionate in your search for that which you know not, that which you cannot ever know, yet the search is your joy, your peace, your fulfillment and your inspiration. Limitation and change are but the hallmarks of an incarnation. Look past the agony and the anguish of that dust that you are. See yourself clearly, vessels of clay with treasures hidden within. Do not dissect your Earthly vessel. Do not agonize overmuch over its flaws, for clay will have flaws, and will eventually crumble, and be of interest only to archaeologists.

You are treasures, you are gems. Trust the process of limitation and loss to show forth to yourself, to the world and to all whom you may serve, all whom you may meet, that beautiful gem hidden within, that many-faceted, amazingly wondrous, youthful self. May you shine through that Earthly vessel. May you use misfortune in joy. May you drop away that which is busyness without undue fear, but with love and acceptance, and may you accept each change through the pain, through the difficulty of change, in perfect faith that all is well and all will be well, and you are fearless, holding up the light of consciousness to a world hungry for consciousness and far too full of the awareness of its own clay.

We are aware that what we ask you to do in such an intense way is that which you shall do perhaps reluctantly, perhaps with upset, forgetfulness and backtracking. It is inevitable, but be courageous enough to forgive yourself each time you forget your true nature. Forgive and accept yourself. You are clay …

(Side one of tape ends.)

(Carla channeling)

You will, all beings will, seem to yourselves to fail again and again, to forget your true natures again and again and be lost in the wilderness of logical thought. You will be discouraged, you will despair. Allow yourselves to make self-perceived errors, and at the end of each, as you recognize that you do not wish to be as you are, forgive immediately yourself for your despair, your fear, your cautiousness and your lack of intensity, and go forward a new person, refreshed, consoled and forgiven by the self that so you may be a refresher, a consoler, an accepter and a forgiver of others.

Whatever your limitations, do that which you love for the joy of it, and if you can no longer do it, wait, for the Creator has more joy in store for you; there will always be joy in store for you. Abide in the desert, meditate in patience, day by thirsty day, until at last you are delivered by your heart into the oasis and thirst no more, and then give all your love away in service to the one infinite Creator, and to the Creator you see in each face, beginning with your own.

We would at this time close the meditation through the one known as Jim, thanking this instrument for its willingness to speak, though fatigued. We shall now transfer this contact. We are known to you as those of Q'uo.

(Jim channeling)

I am Q'uo, and greet each again in love and light through this instrument. It is our privilege to ask if there may be queries at this time upon the subject of the evening or any other subject. Is there a query at this time?

K: You originally identified yourself as being of the principle of those known to us as those of Q'uo. Can you tell me what a principle is and if and how that differs from a social memory complex?

I am Q'uo, and am aware of your query, my sister. It is our understanding that we come to you in a blended fashion, blending those energies of what you know of as two social memory complexes which have as their origins densities of vibrations that study lessons of unity in somewhat different fashions. The blending of these two groupings of entities creates that which we call a principle, which is our approximation, or attempt, to focus energy upon a certain vibrational level that gives witness to a certain facet of the Creator. Thus, we are as those who testify as to this aspect in a fashion which is ours due to the unique blending of our energies. Thus, our reference to ourselves as that of a principle is a more specific description of our natures than is our usual giving of a name only.

Does this answer your query, my sister?

K: Yes, thank you.

I am Q'uo, and we thank you. Is there another query?

Carla: I have been facing some real changes lately, and my first impulse was to give up everything in order to give myself time to make decisions. I didn't give up anything for good, but I gave up things for the moment. When I came to the feeling of what to go on with and what to leave, I found that I had left a great deal. Where does this energy go? Do I now wait for new activity? I feel a little bit as if I'm left hanging. Is that what you talk about when you speak of patience?

I am Q'uo, and am aware of your query, my sister. This is so, for you are as each seeker is, moving within a great darkness with but the smallest of candles to illumine the places upon which you shall place your feet, one slowly after another, not ever sure that the journey has been straight, meandering, circular, or if it should be any of these things, yet you gather what information as is possible to be gathered from the small range of view provided by your consciousness within this mystery of being. You use your conscious ability to analyze, you take counsel from that subconscious nature that communicates through intuition, and you go forth.

Oftentimes there needs be readjustment of the progress, reevaluation of decisions. This is but the nature of the choice-making density. It requires that one cultivate that quality you have called the faith that progress is possible, and the will to persevere in the choosing, in the stepping forth, not ever knowing for sure whether the ground is firm, in the metaphysical sense, or if one shall find but thin air for footing.

It is well that you question, that you wonder, that you choose, even that you blunder, for in each action, thought, word and possibility, you exercise those twin steeds of will and faith. That you should move ever closer to those mundane manifestations of metaphysical principles is possible, is probable, is, in its own way, of importance, yet of the greater importance is that you partake in this dance, illumined so mysteriously, with a heart that seeks, that desires, that yearns for the Creator and for the Creator's touch within the life pattern. This builds the bridge betwixt your illusion and the absolute reality of unity. This bridge which shall hold your feet more surely than any street or ground within your illusion, this desire to know, to move into love, into unity, into harmony, fashions that which cannot be seen, but which cannot, in the metaphysical realms, be denied, for this quality of desire, fueling the faith and the will, is that portion of your being that is more real than any portion of your illusion, and more real than any error or miscalculation.

Is there a further query, my sister?

Carla: Yes, I have two. First of all, I've had a considerable amount of anger that this should be happening to me just when I was beginning to be more effective, in my own way of thinking, to the community of Christ which I serve. It seems to me—you mentioned the process of grieving, and (how) do I find a way to forgive that anger and that despair as a process of grieving which is acceptable?

I am Q'uo, and am aware of your query, my sister. To grieve for that service which has been lost, or seems so, and to find as the heart, the source of the grieving, the simple desire to serve, is an helpful process which will eventually dissolve those boundaries that one has built of the small self's estimation of service, that there might be recognized other avenues of service which may have gone unnoticed because of the narrowness of the original definition.

Thus, such grieving is a part of a process which will eventually bring one to the realization that there is nothing but service that can be rendered. There is, however, the ability to offer oneself in new ways that can be cultivated, so that the small self may see with new eyes that which is before one, for there is never the lack of opportunity to serve, there is only the inability to see that which offers itself to one at all times.

Is there a further query, my sister?

Carla: Yes, one last one. I have felt in the last couple of weeks that perhaps Jim and I could benefit at this time from being more mindful, and meditating just perhaps for five minutes or so during the day, at noon, and at supper time and at bedtime, in addition to the times that we already spend. First of all, is this a good way to stay mindful, since the times involved are short, and second of all, is it acceptable to use rituals that contain Christian words which the one known as Jim can only take as mythical? Is it ethical to do so, or do we need to write our own services?

I am Q'uo, and am aware of your query, my sister. These decisions are those which have meaning as the parties involved agree. There is no suggestion that we can give that holds more significance than the desires which each of you express. It is well to remain mindful, as you have put it, during your diurnal cycles, of the one Creator and one's seeking of the Creator, for your illusion is one which is designed to give experiences that move one in and out of the presence or the mindfulness of the one Creator, for when one seems to move away from this mindfulness, there is created within that likened unto the vacuum which pulls the consciousness back again to the seeking, to the questioning, to the asking. Then that which is learned by such questing again allows one to move outward, as it were, only to return again, and again, in what is an upward spiraling path of energy expenditure. Each entity must needs create the pattern for this spiral. That which you create has significance in your journey as it comes from your desires, rather than being imposed by any outside source such as ourselves, beyond the general recommendation that periodic rituals of remembrance, shall we say, are helpful in each entity's journey.

Is there another query, my sister?

Carla: No, thank you Q'uo.

I am Q'uo, and we thank you once again, my sister. Is there another query at this time?

Carla: Thank you for being with us tonight, Q'uo.

I am Q'uo, and we also extend our great gratitude to this group which has once again allowed us to have our beingness within your illusion, and to offer our service to those who request it. We are most grateful and rejoice at each thought, each query, and each blending of energies. We shall take our leave of this group at this time. We are those of Q'uo. Adonai, my friends. We leave you in the love and light of the one infinite Creator. ✤

Sunday Meditation
March 25, 1990

Group question: What is important in the spiritual life/search?

(Carla channeling)

I am of the principle known to you as Q'uo, and I greet you in the love and in the light of the one infinite Creator. We know that you have enjoyed the silent meditation that has come before our speaking, yet we would explain the reason for the extra time which was spent, for it applies directly to the question of that which is important when one undertakes the spiritual search.

This instrument was not receiving the full power of its considerable beingness, as its heart chakra was in part blocked, a most unusual state for this instrument. Consequently, those who greet you of the negative polarity were all too happy to say our names, and because of the lack of full power of perception this instrument was able to discern only that there was something amiss. We were not yet in contact with this instrument, and in any case, had we been or not, we could not have made the choice patiently to return and go through each step of tuning to discover the blockage. That this instrument has the humility, the patience, and the high level of trust of the self by the self in its intuition to move back and attempt only the highest and best of contacts is to the credit of this instrument and to any who would seek.

This instrument's heart chakra was in part locked into a less than full compassion for one who wished this instrument well, yet who chose to speak and act in ways this instrument could not understand, in ways that were thoughtless and hurtful. This entity has the name, S. Therefore, this instrument took the time to focus upon this relationship, to forgive, forgive the other, forgive and love the self, and realize that no harm is meant in that which causes hurt, in many, many encounters between people upon your Earth.

Some may say, indeed, that this was an orange-ray blockage, a difficulty in relationship, but because of this instrument's, shall we say, spiritual circuitry, all such imbalances are, in truth, those of green ray. When this anger, frustration and pain, feeling of betrayal and abandonment was released, there opened in the being a chakra full of unconditional love which excluded no part of humankind.

Thus, in answering the question of what is most important in the spiritual life, the spiritual search and the spiritual path, we would say absolute and rigorous honesty in evaluation of who you are, what you wish, what you will to be done, and what sort of search you wish to mount for the Creator. Many look at the relationship with the Creator as the mountain climber looks upon Everest. Like a mountain, the spiritual instinct lies within man, and its very beingness in the consciousness requires many to strive to scale it. The great fallacy is in allowing oneself the thought that when one has reached the top of the great mountain and gazed at the vistas of spirituality available to the eternal spirit, one is somehow changed. One is merely seeing a beautiful view. The reasons, the intentions and the desires of the one who climbs the mountain of spiritual seeking are all important. The success of the attainment of the peak of that mountain is a goodness qualified and biased most strongly by one's truest and deepest desires and intentions upon attempting the climb. The mountain you climb has no peak. Many, many times the spiritual adept shall find a marvelous apex of consciousness, a newer and broader view of the entire spectrum of perception and experience. This is, however, not an end, not a finality, but rather that gift which often signals a new chapter, a transfiguration, a moment of light that has shed its welcoming and loving brilliance upon the spiritual search and the spiritual seeker.

Beneath your oceans there are also extremely high peaks, extremely high mountains, yet to those of the second density who inhabit that medium of existence and take their life from the neighborhood of that which is water, we may observe that there is no attempt to climb to the peak of any mountain, for surrounding and engulfing all the topography and the geography of the underwater kingdom, one height is not seen as superior to another, nor is it related to the basic consciousness inherent in that mind/body complex.

We are not comparing you to fish. We are comparing you to those who swim in a sea of energy, consciousness and love. You may find yourself in the great valleys of your emotional ocean. There, love is. There, your path of service lies. At other times you find yourself upon the oh, so desired peak, the mountain top. You are no closer to heaven, no closer to the Creator there than at the very gates of what many have called Hell.

When one lives in an illusion which seems to give one condition importance over another, one is allowed by free will then to choose that which it will consider to be of value, and this is especially true of those who have launched themselves into what we may call, in your mythical terminology, (the) search for the holy grail. How long and dusty is the road which seems to go on forever! How few the mountain tops, and how far apart are they! Can one stay upon the mountain top forever? We assure you that if one attempts to do so one will eventually be seduced by pride, which is a killer of light. Likewise those who live in the valley, and though seeking, must admit failure after failure, are no less spiritual.

The first part or aspect of the spiritual search that needs clearly to be seen by each is that each is in an atmosphere not of air and nitrogen, oxygen, all the elements that you breathe in. You live in a sea of consciousness, a sea of energy. You do not float upon this sea, although many, many are the times we have used this simile in attempting to speak in parables about the spiritual journey. In truth you are simply within the environment of the Creator. You are everywhere, you are everywhen, you are every condition. You can improve your behavior, but it is only persistent and patient work upon the self by the self that enables one to be the athlete of the spirit that shall question again and again if necessary its readiness to act, to live and to be one through whom love may shine.

Although it is easy to say that you are not alone in this choice, in this constant series of choices and determinations which can only be subjective, the truth within the illusion is quite different. The illusion is designed to confuse you utterly. Not partially, not variably, but completely. Thus, first, in order to have a spiritual life of seeking in service to others, one must recognize one's nature, not a nature that is dependent upon its place in the geography of the human spirit, but upon its steadfast and unchanging place in the very heart of the Creator. We wish by this statement to remove from each the pride of knowledge, the arrogance of those who are faithful, the terrible wasted humility of those who feel that they have failed and will always fail to be worthy of this search.

You shall not judge yourself. You may only see, in faith, your nature, in the environment which you occupy. Your nature is something we may call love. That Creator that you seek is something that we may call purified or divine Love. Your search is in answer to instinct. With this statement would we take away the sting of judgment, pride and humility. You are an I AM. You are not an "I am a philosopher," you are not an "I am a recluse," you are not an "I am a spiritual failure." You simply are. You always have [been], you are now, and you will always be of this one gemlike nature, a crystal, fully faceted, most beautiful, unique to you and to the creation, and infinitely desirable to the Creator.

The first step in the spiritual search is to see that side of yourself and to realize that of yourself you may not, can not and will not progress. But within you lies this jewel, this brilliance, this perfection. It is within you in the valley, on the mountaintop, in feelings of unworthiness and in feelings of pride. There is nothing you can do so terrible as to remove yourself from this great love, this perfect identity, nor is there any way whatsoever, by good works, by acts of love and consciousness, by the giving and consolation that you feel flowing with you, to improve or better your condition. You are. The changes within yourself that you perceive are the subjective signs and symptoms of a search led in complete free will, to uncover within the clay of oneself that jewel of beingness, that I AM which exists within the form of bone and flesh that serves you as vehicle in your incarnation at this time. To know that you are as you are is the first and great step, the cornerstone of spiritual seeking. If you are, if the Creator is, the relationship of beingness is one of unity. You are in the Creator, the Creator in you. You and the Creator are love. The Creator is love unknown and unmanifest. You are love known and made manifest.

The second step of spiritual search, life and work is the decision of the self in all honesty and humility to attempt to lessen the opacity of the illusion of the milieu in which you live, the illusion of flesh and bone and hair in which your imperishable spirit lives for this brief incarnational period. As you find your own way to make yourself transparent, so can the love which is infinite in the Creator, but finite in any manifestation of that same Creator to speak, to bear witness, to be that messenger of hope, of abiding, of loving and of caring make of you the Creator manifest.

No one can do more than experience the fringes of the true kingdom and power and glory of love in its fullest sense. Those who feel they have the same chance of doing so as the Creator Itself have fallen into the trap of pride. Those who surrender the jar to be hollowed out and made transparent are those in whom the manifestation of love may not end, but continue infinitely. This process of choosing a way of manifesting an instinct which is inherent to all is entirely up to you. That you choose to seek in this mystery of the finite and the infinite is the cornerstone of all spiritual seeking, the bedrock of the spiritual life.

Now, there are two ways in which one may go about accelerating that movement towards the one great original Thought of love, and bringing that through consciously into manifestation in the life experience. Firstly, the work within the self must never be taken for granted. Just as this entity, which rarely has a green-ray blockage, had the humility, the patience and the determination to find and clear that which kept it from feeling correct in its attitude toward contact, so is that same patience which again and again will bring practicality, sensitivity and effectiveness to the spiritual knowing of the self [useful to you].

In meditation you begin to be acquainted with your true self. You are not this lifetime, you are not a product of the experiences of this lifetime, though many place enormous emphasis on the difficulties which have biased, within this incarnational experience, that which seems to be your nature. You are not the conglomeration of past incarnations. You are not the gifts into which you poured life within manifestation as you were born. You are love. If you think that you are a wanderer, a teacher, a healer, or even if you wish to be one who has a path of service that is obvious to others and commanding of respect, you have lost your way, for your way within yourself is to love the self, to forgive the self and to see that I AM within the self as the I AM that is consciousness and that is love.

Many, many are the stories and myths told to enable entities to move themselves into a position of realization of the true nature of the self. The final goal of all of these true spiritual paths is humility and a willingness to surrender that clay, the pride, the arrogance, the unworthiness and fear, to surrender all these emotions utterly to the power and peace of knowing that you are love. This you can know only by faith, and faith can be strengthened only through contact in silence within the self, gazing at nothing, thinking nothing, expecting nothing, allowing all distractions to fade away, condemning yourself for no thought which takes you from this condition of emptiness, but rather, giving it position to have an irrelevance to the state of mind which your heart has wrapped around you for the meditative process of learning through silence.

The other and corollary method of working to maximize the opportunities of the incarnation that one may live a life of spirituality is to allow the self as imperfect, as poorly hollowed out, as opaque as it may be, to follow each instinct of the heart. To love all others is easy to do, to love entities one at a time, very difficult indeed. We ask you to realize that loving humankind will not polarize you towards the positive service-to-others path, but will seek only to stultify and stunt your growth in spirit.

You do not have answers. There are no answers. Focus then upon the questions of the spiritual seeker. The primary question in dealing with any other entity is "How shall I love, and how may I serve?" In many, the only way available to the loving heart in offering love, is the offering itself. There must be no expectation upon the part of any that those seeds which one sows of truth subjectively understood by the self, may bear any fruit in any other but the self.

To see each entity as an entity of love is an enormous challenge within your illusion, for you cannot see that they too are love, made of love, abiding in love, and very often completely unaware of and uninterested in this primal, instinctual, inherent characteristic of humankind. This awareness cannot be forced upon any, nor should it be. How then to serve others? We ask you to listen, not to speak, for in listening you provide a loving and compassionate mirror which mirrors back to that other self which is the Creator that which that other self is doing that it would not wish to do, to allow that entity to realize that which it is not doing that it does wish to do. In listening you become a manifestation of the Christ. In listening and forgiving you have moved ever closer to the mind of Christ.

Therefore, when no one asks for your help, know that your basic and most important help is in your beingness itself, in the joy that you take, in the zest, the leaping for joy that you experience as you experience who you truly are. Be not cast down. Be merry, for to be merry in the little things and the big things of mundane existence is to express the nature of love. There is nothing ponderous about love; it is spontaneous and full of light, and you need do nothing to those who do not wish to speak with you, but only be who you are with rigorous honesty, admitting [it] to yourself each time that you jangle and are out of tune, moving then from service to others to the repairing of the self until you once again love and respect that self, finding that self worthy of being a vessel for the infinite light and love of the one Creator.

There are those who will ask you for help. Evaluate these requests carefully. Will they be of service in the spiritual seeking of that person? Or will they be worthless in the spiritual seeking of that person? Many ask to be pleased at all times by those about them, to be placated, soothed and cherished at every turn. They seek for themselves a comfort, a rest and a peace through requests of humans other than themselves. To move toward what such entities ask is sometimes that which maintains that entity in a state of spiritual anarchy, for the saving, or shall we say, the savior, is seen as that which is embodied in another. You are not another, you are the other self of that entity. You can by no means teach through pleasing others.

Upon the contrary, there are those who truly seek the Creator, and at those times may you pray fervently and heartily that you may be single-minded in your persistent effort to be hollow and transparent, that that which is infinite love may work through your oh, so mortal being.

It is said within your holy works that you need never fear [for] that which you will speak when the time comes to be of service to another. This is not so of pleasing others, but it is indeed so of serving others. Again, it is first necessary to know and love the self, for others are merely distortions of you. As you learn to nurture yourself you learn to serve and heal others. Learn that whatever their outer circumstance and appearance, you are they, and they, you. In all humility surrender that finite self and seek the jewel within, asking it, as you would ask your most beloved self in its deepest aspect, to show itself as it will, to speak as it will. This attitude shall bring about within you that attitude which you seek, the attitude which seeks to be of service in any situation.

We shall end with this thought, "What is it to serve, rather than please?" Ponder this, for upon this hangs much, and if you wish, we may speak to you again upon this subject.

We are sorry to have been long-winded, but we have observed that your recording device has tolled the bell of our sermonette to you. So we shall remove ourselves from this soapbox, that we may in all humility, and asking you to remember that we are very fallible and prone to error, and offering only our own opinions, close this instrument through our beloved brother, the one known as Jim. We thank this instrument. We thank those in the support group, for truly this group is strong in seeking, and it enables us to protect this contact in a way which heartens us. We thank each. I leave this instrument in love and light. I am known to you as Q'uo.

(Jim channeling)

I am Q'uo, and greet each again in love and light through this instrument. We are now able to offer ourselves in further querying if there be queries which yet remain. Is there a query to which we may speak?

K: You said earlier that when a person asks for help it's a good idea to evaluate that request to determine if our compliance would be helpful for that person in their spiritual search or not. In some cases there seems to be a fairly obvious difference between what would be of help to a person and what would be just pleasing them, but in other cases it is more difficult to tell. My question is, how am I to judge what is going to be helpful to a person in their spiritual search and what is not? Could you offer me some suggestions on that?

I am Q'uo, and am aware of your query, my sister. As you speak to those who request your assistance, it is well that you determine through your own intuitive nature the quality that is at the heart of the request. This is to say that one looks beyond the words spoken, beyond the information which is sought, and looks to that yearning that inspired the request. This cannot be done by mental analysis or the recalling of specific information that would meet the letter of the request. This is the nature of the process of taking no concern for what you will say when you are asked to serve, but having faith that words, deeds, feelings, will be given.

Thus, it is our suggestion that, before you seek to serve in any particular fashion that is related to a spiritual query, you take a moment with yourself to make silent your conscious mind that would rush to answer with words, and dive deeply within the silence, there to attempt to become [who] that entity [is] in the quality of its query at that moment, not who the entity has been in your mind, or who the entity should be in your mind, or might be, but who the entity is at that moment. Then, respond as you are inspired. You may of course find that there are retrievals of information that occur, memories that are utilized, analysis that is applied, as you respond to the inner inspiration. This is well, for each of you has experiences that are useful in fleshing out the concepts that are oftentimes beyond words.

Is there a further query, my sister?

K: Does this process also apply to requests for help that have no obvious relation to the spiritual quest?

I am Q'uo, and we would suggest that this is an useful means of communicating upon the level of pure idea, shall we say, for want of better terms, and can be helpful in any area of concern or inquiry.

Is there another query, my sister?

K: Not for now, thank you.

I am Q'uo, and we thank you, my sister. Is there another query?

Carla: I have one. There have been several times in my life when I had a very difficult situation, and looked at it, realizing that people were going to think I was a doormat, deciding nevertheless to continue, because I saw a spiritual principle involved. To give you a simple example, I had a boss once who had a very low opinion of herself. I could be two minutes away, rushing all away to the ringing telephone on her desk, but such was the depth of her need to feel superior that she would wait until I answered the telephone. Obviously in doing so I was pleasing her, but to my way of thinking, and this may have simply been in my head and not in my heart, I don't know, I felt I was serving her also because I was giving her a feeling that she was worth any effort I could make for her. Is this rationalization or is it thinking from the heart? Because this situation has come up repeatedly in my life, and I would like to understand the pattern.

I am Q'uo, and am aware of your query, my sister. To speak without infringement is our desire, thus we would say that it is, in the case that you have mentioned, an action which fulfills the spiritual or metaphysical prerequisite for polarization that your intention for the action is to be of service to another. Thus, the action is efficacious for you. However, it may or may not be a service to the entity that you reinforce a distorted perception of the self. This cannot be said with any certainty, for we would need to examine each entity's life pattern in order to offer more informed opinion. The desire to serve is the most important quality in any action that relates entities. The method that we suggested earlier, to take a moment to attempt within to become that entity, is a means by which this desire may perhaps be more carefully and precisely honed and utilized. However, the desire is the most important quality.

Is there at further query, my sister?

Carla: I just want to make sure I understand what you're saying. What you're saying is, my action was not necessarily of service to anyone else, but it enabled me to work on my own polarization in consciousness. Is that it?

I am Q'uo, and this is basically correct, my sister. Is there another query?

Carla: Is it wrong to please someone, or inadvisable, I should say, just for the sake of seeing them smile?

I am Q'uo, and am aware of your query, my sister. Of course, as you realize yourself, there is no right or wrong to the means by which entities interact, for each entity is the Creator that works upon Itself and reveals more of the Self in the process. All interaction offers this opportunity. It is the great dance of your illusion to offer opportunities in many and various patterns according to individual choices and idiosyncrasies. Thus are the avenues for progress multiple.

If one should desire to inspire the smile upon the face of another, it is a desire well placed, for within your illusion there is much of confusion that does not bring the smile either to the face or to the heart. Thus, it is a small gift that one may give that is a joy for each. There are, of course, ramifications to any behavior that is repeated, that each entity does well to study. This includes all behaviors, for all behaviors are the coursework of your illusion, and indicate certain tendencies that allow the insight into the deeper nature of the self. Some are well to build upon, others are well to balance. These are individual choices, as you are aware.

Is there a further query, my sister?

Carla: No, Q'uo, thank you.

I am Q'uo, and we thank you, my sister. Is there another query at this time?

(Pause)

I am Q'uo. We feel that we have spoken at length this evening in a manner which we hope has been helpful, and we thank each for not only calling for our presence in your gathering, but for the patience that each has shown, as we have offered ourselves in a lengthy manner, which often makes the physical vehicle uncomfortable as it rests in one position over the long …

Carla: May I ask a question?

I am Q'uo, and we are happy to attempt your query.

Carla: If this group studied together the information in this session and developed a further question from this session, and tried to get more continuity in the questions, would we be being of aid to your social memory complex, or group of them, to a further extent than accepting the randomized questions of those who write questions, or would it be more helpful if we kept on as we are, in terms of your service at this time?

I am Q'uo, and am aware of your query, my sister. We are filled with joy at the opportunity to speak at any gathering of this group. We have no agenda, shall we say. We have no desire to offer specific information in what you call a coherent fashion. We are happy to offer such information if we are queried in that manner. We look at the queries which are offered to us and see that they come from genuine concern. This is the most important quality for these contacts, for it is your desire for information regarding the evolutionary process that provides us with the opportunity to serve and the means by which information is drawn from us, for we answer as we are queried. Your desire is much like the magnet which draws to it the iron filing. We see each opportunity as whole and perfect in itself. We are happy to offer ourselves in any capacity as you structure either these sessions or any queries asked within them.

Do you have a further query, my sister?

Carla: No, no, please, I'm sorry I interrupted your closing. I just wanted to ask that.

I am Q'uo, and we are grateful for your queries, my sister, at all times. We are grateful for each opportunity to blend our vibrations with this group's. We are grateful that there are entities upon your planetary surface that seek information and inspiration, both in spoken words and in those thoughts and feeling-tones which are unspoken as well. We are greatly honored to be able to offer ourselves in even the smallest capacity of sending love to those that request it, and who may be quite unaware that they do indeed receive an answer to their inner queries and needs.

At this time we shall take our leave of this group. We are those known to you as Q'uo. We leave you as always in the love and in the light of the one infinite Creator. Adonai, my friends. Adonai.

Sunday Meditation
April 1, 1990

Group question: The question this evening focuses on the points of the journey rather than the goal of the journey, how we are all in a process, and at times struggling quite mightily to meet the various challenges that come our way, whether it might be sickness or monetary problems, relationship problems, finding out exactly who we are [in] different facets of our being. We tend to focus upon making some sort of resolution and judge ourselves by how well we succeed in our own eyes at solving these problems. We would like some information this evening concerning the process and how this process works, not so much in helping us to achieve a goal, but in becoming a new type of person, a new soul, a new being by going through the process, by going through the struggle, the heroic struggle.

(Carla channeling)

I am of the principle known to you as Q'uo, and greet you, my friends, in the love and in the light of the one infinite Creator, whose servants and messengers we are. We are most grateful for this opportunity to be called to your group, for the energy which each has offered, moving through this instrument, that we may have good steady contact. May we say what a pleasure and a blessing it is also for us to share with each of your vibratory patterns. As we seek together, so the blending becomes ever more harmonious, and we find great joy in the springtime that is in all of your hearts this evening, that springtime sense of renewal and of growth, of movement and rebirth, of transformation and transfiguration.

You ask us to speak of the journey of the pilgrim, of the search for the Holy Grail, of the quest for the impossible dream, of the seeking of truth in an illusion whose purpose is extraordinarily bound up in there being no perfect truths, *(inaudible)* [only] pragmatic solutions which have nothing of the ideal in them, only compromise and expediency. There are more and more such as you upon the surface of your sphere at this time that seek that which they cannot know, rather than what has given them their gadgets, their toys, their weapons of war.

Let us first examine the condition into which each of you was incarnated. Into each of your preincarnative programs there was inserted the spirit of willfulness, that is, the spirit to wander, to roam and to do as one wilt no matter what the cost to others. And in almost each life at some time there is the necessity to break free from old bonds of seeming righteousness and propriety, to seek a truer, better, more resonant and halfway remembered road upon which you have trod before. This is the road you call home. You are always on the way. See you then a tree? There is your home. Pitch your tent, drink from the spring, and move on. Within you there is a single self that seeks. The outer self in the great illusion of third density is violently bombarded at almost every turn by attempts to distract one from the contemplation and the seeking after that which you would call the pilgrim's journey.

Let us examine but two of your myths to see the basic similarities and dynamics of that cosmology into which your own personal faith is the central portion. The first is that parable so familiar to you within the works attributed to those who knew the one known as Jesus. He spoke of a prodigal son, a son who wished to take all that was his and go and have adventure, in the glory of his youth and manhood, and a fine time did he also have, till his pockets were let and empty, and he no more than swine, eating that which the pigs left behind.

What is most often forgotten in this parable was the plight of the faithful son, the one who never took a chance, the one who never did anything wrong, the brother that stayed at home and worked hard for the father. Years later, after many painful and disastrous experiences, the prodigal son, hoping to be hired on as a slave at his father's estate, limped slowly and wearily toward the great castle which had once been half his and was his no more. Yet the father saw this entity, this son, and to correct the biases of your holy work, this daughter, moving wearily towards a home that [he] no longer knew might exist, wearily hoping to find the humblest and lowest position in the household, for simply to be in the gates of his father's house was reckoned enough by the prodigal.

The prodigal was aware of the journey it had made. It was not easy upon itself, and, indeed, it had done many things seemingly amiss. Yet did the father's love respond in any way to judgment when he saw that his son, his daughter, was coming to meet him at last? No, not at all. Rather, he gathered all together for a great feast to celebrate that son, that daughter, whom he thought he had lost, and in free will could not bring back; that prodigal child who had of its own accord turned back to the father's house, not knowing the outcome, not knowing the reception, being content to be as one of the dogs at the table catching the crumbs of the meals of those worthy to sit at the high table of his lord the father. Ah, what a welcome this child received, how gloriously happy was the father that that which had been lost to him was found again.

In another of your myths the deep dark of winter is brought about as the hero is chopped up and his parts strewn so that they may not ever be found again. Deep winter dwells upon the Earth as the father is seemingly no more and chaos reigns. Yet such love has Isis that she goes about gathering up those pieces, and putting back together the great prodigal scattering of godhead. Each part within itself could be nothing; it was only as it was put together that it regained unity, and made all the people joyful, the flowers bloom anew, the leaves dance and clap their hands, and the mountains laugh with joyful abandon, for once more that which was lost had been found.

Within your culture this day, my friends, many, many are those who see spiritually oriented or metaphysically oriented groups as those whose duty it is, whose responsibility it is, and whose pleasure it is to reassure, comfort and tend to the needs of those others within the group. Each is felt to be a shepherd to all the rest, and the world becomes one great pasture, where none ever leaves the fold of the father, as the father expresses itself in each son that has stayed at home, for all that the father has is the son's also.

The comfort, the tenderness, the poignancy and the security of the pastoral sense of community cannot be gainsaid, nor would we wish to. But we address you as pilgrims. You are not of a pastoral faith, you are a pilgrim people, and you move forward into uncharted lands, strange adventures, unknown happenings. The end of your journey is something of which you know not, neither can you know at all. We, who have had some slight more experience than you, know this not at all ourselves.

So we urge each, in the beginning, to recognize the benefits of the pastoral, loving, nurturing community of seekers, but we remind you also, that each of you is a teacher to each other, each of you is a mirror held up to each other and you must hold up an honest, straightforward and fearless mirror that shows whatever is there, whether it may be called that which is spiritually desirable, or that which is considered otherwise.

The pastoral part of your community is excellent for raising the trust of each member for each other. What love is born as one listens, pardons, consoles and gives, as pilgrims who have almost nothing but give what they have to each other, companions upon a dusty path that leads they know not where, in search of an ideal in a land they know not to be ideal, in search of a hollowness of self, when they feel that self overflowing with personality and character and opinion and bias.

Can a pilgrim afford these attitudes of judgment? We say to you, no, a pilgrim cannot. It cannot judge itself, for it is merely a dusty-footed pilgrim upon a very, very long path whose ending lies at the source of all things, the home to which all strive to attain. Although you may find many, many dear companions along the way, each of you is his own pilgrim self, whole, complete, male and female together. There is no need to balance in pairs, there is no need to find balances so that your so-called yin and yang energies are balanced betwixt two entities or more, for the true balancing is done as the prodigal child turns and says, "No more, no more. I am not in a state of enjoyment or happiness, all those things I have sought with money and with debauchery have proven to be false. Let me turn now and listen to that which before I did not hear, see that which I saw before but did not perceive, and understand in my heart those things which made no intellectual sense whatsoever."

We find that the central image in each which suggests the path that is taken is that path called the path to the Holy Grail. First let us gaze at this great prize. It is a hollow, empty vessel. It waits to be filled with that which is holy. Know you not, then, that that which you seek is within you? That your cup is too full of yourself? You must spill yourself out in your pilgrim walk. You must drop bag after bag, and garment after garment, bias after bias, and prejudice after prejudice, until at last you stand, vulnerable, without the ability to defend the self, yet having no fear, for you have become empty and you wait for the grail of an Earthly self to be filled with the immediate presence of the love of the one infinite Creator.

It is difficult to speak to entities who do not see through the veil of a seemingly objective journey that is also seemingly subjective. In just the way that the creation shows itself through the telescope, but shows itself also within you, so is there the symbol of a glass waiting to be filled with love and light outside the self which may be translated into the cup of the self deliberately and sacrificially emptied day by day by day, until you have the capacity to be hollow, to be humble, and to accept the glory of love divine and imperishable. The cup of your body shall cease to be, yet if you have fashioned it lovingly enough in your thoughts, this cup shall be your metaphysical statement, the centerpiece of a tapestry woven in purity and love and desperation and desire, the tapestry of the life of a pilgrim.

We have said this before and shall say it again: we ask you above all things to be merry in your journey. It is not pleasing to the self, or to one's companions, to become so involved, so agonized about the spiritual side of the self that it simply cannot think beyond itself. Many spiritual seekers are solipsistic, and therefore not able to polarize towards the positive, for to polarize positively is to see in each face the face of love. It is not looking and searching within the self in the mirror, contemplating the navel, meditating, organizing the life, starting grand projects of spirituality. All these things are good in their place, but realize first of all that when you have become clear enough to open the heart to unconditional love it is time to empty the vessel of yourself of all that is clay and dust, and become that hollow self through which the light and the love of the one Creator may flow.

Is there an answer to the question you ask? We must tell you: if there is one, we do not know it. All we do know is that we are experiencing a journey, a journey without time, a journey without space, in the subjective sense; a journey very much in time and very much in space in your outer experience. We suggest that you study not the fortune-telling aspects of the tarot or the archetypical mind but the symbols themselves, for they show to the self that blueprint of that which any entity has the capacity to attain. Sincerity, humility and persistence, the daily, constant centering and meditation, all these humble things are those that open the self to be a pilgrim.

Stay not at home, tend not your father's flocks, until you first have discovered your own limitations, your own compassion for those whom you previously thought quite unlike yourself, for you are everyone you meet, and it is only when you have the humility to recognize yourself in all that you see that it is possible for you as a pilgrim to shine forth in each dark corner with the infinite love of the great Spirit that hovers over, around, beneath and within you. Bow to that which is within yourself. Die to that dross which keeps you from the grail. Be a pilgrim people, and exhort each other as each becomes discouraged. Listen to each other, not to change each other, but simply to listen. Trust each entity to heal itself once difficulties have been expressed.

The freedom to speak and communicate clearly is born a very hard birth by most entities who do not have within them the native trust to confide, to be open, to be foursquare against all odds and in all situations. Consequently, we ask that as you walk the dusty road you gaze at those things which you have not thought to trust before: the beating of your heart, the warmth of the sun, the rustling of the trees, the song of the birds. All these things are there to give you that which you may learn from and in which you may abide as you begin and continue an arduous yet most exciting and exhilarating journey full of epiphany, transformation and change.

There are no answers that we have to give you. We can only say that you are asking the correct questions. We cannot promise you riches, fame, security or happiness. We offer you only the dust, the coarse roads of the pilgrim, the harsh sun of the desert which is often traveled while the soul is in travail and a new soul is being born within. We offer you discomfort, the discomfort of change, and as you meditate and seek to know your own deep self, seek to deepen your trust, you shall find yourself more and more uncomfortable as you change more and more. This discomfort is a divine discomfort, an excellent discomfort, an encouraging discomfort, for it means that you are in truth prepared to change. You have allowed your rigidity of belief to melt into the malleable, impressionable thought processes which are powered by the energy gained from dropping the old programs that have been to you in some way destructive.

Each of you has a different way of destroying self-esteem within the self, a different way of rationalizing. Do not condemn yourselves, pilgrims. Move to one who is in pastoral relationship with you and speak your thoughts freely, for you are the Creator speaking to the Creator, and you must needs find entities whom you may trust to that extent, else you shall be alone and confused in the outer world. But when you have expressed yourself and have been heard, then it is time to carry on that which you have begun, the infinite processes of change and transformation.

You will always be on the way, you will never see the face of the one infinite Creator, for could you but see it, it would appear only as light, a light that would blind you. You are not ready for an unbiased look at the infinite One which broods over the universe and gazes upon Itself with a love so compassionate and so complete that there is no end to the loving you are receiving at this very moment, not simply from us, messengers of the Law of One, but from the Creator Itself, whose love sparkles in the air that you breathe, comes through the soles of your feet as you touch the earth, moves through the body enlivening, refreshing, restoring.

Once you feel so restored, remember you are a pilgrim. Pick up your staff and trudge on, for there is more to learn about love, and as long as you are in the physical body that you enjoy for this incarnation, you are gazing at your path of service not in some far off way of extreme asceticism, not in the travels from one group to another to sample the spiritual supermarket, as this instrument likes to call it. You are here to gaze upon an illusion, to come to some basic conclusions about that illusion, and that is that it is a dualistic illusion. In your heart you know there is no duality. The illusion expresses duality in every way possible. Expect your spiritual pilgrimage to be full not only of mystery but of paradox, yet go forth rejoicing, for this present moment intersects with eternity and resonates with joy and love and peace right now, this moment, and this moment, and this moment.

Be ye mindful pilgrims, be ye open to change, be ye not content to stay at home, but move into challenging and unknown ways, freely to examine, to sample and to experience the nuances of the choice that you must make in this density. Nations have made this choice, entities have made this choice. Shall you serve others or shall you serve yourself? In both nations and individuals the answer is usually that of the brother that stays at home where it is safe. Live dangerously, my friends. As this instrument would put it, die behind the wheel. In your content, find the divine discontent of one who seeks always the wider viewpoint, the clearer, more lucid expression of the gemlike self which is the Christ, the great One within. And keep your quest and your questions before you.

As you correctly surmise, the persistent quest of your ideal in an illusion which is not ideal is both foolish and the wisest thing you shall ever do within this illusion. Seek, seek ye, and what shall you find? If you knock, what shall open unto you? Pilgrims, we call you, take up your walking sticks and come along. It is a fine journey. And be very careful as to that which you seek and that which you desire, for you shall receive that which you desire.

We would like to leave this instrument at this time, as this instrument has been explaining to us again that we have outstayed our allotted time period. Pardon our prolixity. We do get wound up, do we not, in what we have to say? We feel our cup is not yet quite hollow ourselves, and we join you in your search. We thank this instrument, and we now transfer in love and in light and in the merriment of brother and sisterhood together, to the one known as Jim. I am Q'uo.

(Jim channeling)

I am Q'uo, and greet each again in love and light. At this time it is our privilege to offer ourselves in the attempt to speak to any queries which have arisen during this gathering, or to any other query which is upon the mind of those present. We would preface this offering by reminding each that we offer but that which is our opinion. Take that which is useful to you and leave behind any words which do not ring with your own truth.

Is there a query at this time?

K: I have a brief one. Could you please give me as exact a transliteration as possible of "Adonai vasu borragus," and what the origins are of those words?

I am Q'uo, and am aware of your query, my sister. These closing exaltations are from a language which some upon your planet know of as Solex Mal. These words …

We pause.

(Pause)

We apologize, there was a disturbance with this instrument. These words are those which offer a thanksgiving to the crystal pure light within each being that has called for the presence of the contact speaking through an instrument. "The lord of the light" is one literal translation of the "adonai." The "vasu" and "borragus" have meanings that are approximated by "the One who reigns within and forever." This is seen as the essence of each entity and is felt to be a fitting closing for messages which are in truth spoken from the One to the One.

Is there a further query, my sister?

K: Not for now, thank you.

I am Q'uo, and we thank you, my sister. Is there another query?

C: I have a query as to this time of year, the season, it being a time of growth and blossoming on this planet, and as to what activities and pursuits we can engage in singly and in combination with others to further the process of growth within ourselves and all that is around us.

I am Q'uo, and am aware of your query, my sister. Your planet at this time experiences each of those rhythmic cycles which you call the seasons. Within your own hemisphere there is the springing forth of new plant life as your days lengthen and warm to the greater presence of your sun body. It is a natural portion of each entity's life pattern to respond in an harmonic fashion to those seasons which paint the background of your daily round of activities. Thus, to those who are sensitive to such cycles, one may see the harvest of the fall being taken into the heart of the self to be reflected upon in the depths and cold of your winter season. This reflection and burying of seeds within then makes way for the bursting forth of new ideas, new directions, new energies and growth in that season of spring which you now begin to enjoy, to produce its own crop of nourishment for the soul in your summer season.

It is well for those who have this sensitivity to engage in the group ritual observations of the changing of the seasons so that the essence of each is understood and practiced by the individuals who bring themselves and offer themselves in group worship, rejoicing and ritual. These are the milestones of the yearly procession of each day that you walk as a pilgrim upon your journey.

As a conscious pilgrim on the journey it is within your abilities to look upon each day as complete and to see the portions of the day as yet another cycle in a somewhat shorter season, so that you are completely free to bring forth new beginnings at any moment, to share the fruit of your learning of love and compassion and wisdom and of service with any entity that may for a moment walk upon the path with you. To share the smile, the helping hand, the understanding ear in any manner with any entity is to share the best of that which is yours, the fruit of your journey thus far within this illusion.

Thus, you are creatures of free will, moved by feelings, moved by tides within your own subconscious minds, and moved by a desire within your being to know that which is called the truth, and to experience that which is love, to learn that which is wisdom, and to serve in the power of the One, which you may do at any moment, according to your renewed desire that begins with your waking from your slumber, and extends throughout your day as you travel with each of your brothers and sisters upon this same journey.

Thus, what you do is to share that which you have when it is your moment to share as you are moved by the opportunities of the day and by your own desire to expand upon the opportunities and your abilities.

Is there a further query, my sister?

C: Not at this time, thank you.

I am Q'uo, and we thank you, my sister. Is there another query?

Carla: I guess not, Q'uo. Thank you so very much for being here.

I am Q'uo, and we also offer our gratitude to each of you who have invited our presence. We rejoice at these opportunities to share our opinions and our thoughts with you. We hope that within the many, many words which we have shared this evening there might be a few which are useful to you. Go forth, my friends, and use that which is helpful in your own way to further your own journey and those of your brothers and sisters as they walk with you.

At this time we shall take our leave of this instrument and this group. We are known to you as those of Q'uo, and we leave you as always in the love and in the light of the one infinite Creator. Adonai, my friends. Adonai. ✢

L/L Research

L/L Research is a subsidiary of Rock Creek Research & Development Laboratories, Inc.

P.O. Box 5195
Louisville, KY 40255-0195

www.llresearch.org

Rock Creek is a non-profit corporation dedicated to discovering and sharing information which may aid in the spiritual evolution of humankind.

ABOUT THE CONTENTS OF THIS TRANSCRIPT: This telepathic channeling has been taken from transcriptions of the weekly study and meditation meetings of the Rock Creek Research & Development Laboratories and L/L Research. It is offered in the hope that it may be useful to you. As the Confederation entities always make a point of saying, please use your discrimination and judgment in assessing this material. If something rings true to you, fine. If something does not resonate, please leave it behind, for neither we nor those of the Confederation would wish to be a stumbling block for any.

© 2009 L/L Research

Sunday Meditation
April 15, 1990

Group question: The question this evening concerns how we find our spiritual path when we find it in a conscious fashion. How it is that we select the path that we do finally select? Are there forces or influences that come, not only from our current experience, but from childhood, from the way we first experience the world? Are there forces that come from before the incarnation? Do we set up, preincarnationally, choices or biases that eventually lead us to the path that we choose, or that eventually becomes ours? What are the forces that help us to choose our path and to follow it?

(Carla channeling)

I am Q'uo. I am known to you as Q'uo, though the name that we use we give to you only because of your fondness in the naming. We are a portion of the creation of Love, which is the one great original Thought, the Logos of the infinite Creator of us all. We wish to acknowledge entities within the Confederation of Planets in the Service of the Infinite Creator, those known as Hatonn, and those known as Latwii, and to thank them for their participation in this particular meeting, for there are those here who need the silent comfort of the sharing of vibrations with these entities. They will not be speaking, but have simply been called here in order to abide in silent meditation with some few of those present at this time, for there is great fondness and affection in some for these entities.

We thank each for calling us to speak upon the subject of the influences which affect each seeking soul's way of experiencing spiritual help. The honor is great and we are very humble, as we feel that you may have a desire to share with us our opinion. Because you so desire this, we offer to you our plea that you not take us or any but your own heart as the authority which recognizes the truth that is the truth for you. We are not infallible. We simply share opinions based on a larger range of experiences than you.

As you gaze into the memory of your childhood you see much of what was there, and you have blocked yourself from seeing many other things that were part of the childhood which you experienced. It is so that you came into this experience of incarnation with your own biases, opinions, tendencies and characteristic ways of thinking, feeling and acting. All of these things were yours within the womb before your mother ever gave birth to you. You came into this experience of incarnation a realized being who has chosen various difficulties and challenges as the means whereby you may come to a greater polarity of service, service to the Creator, service and nurturing the self as part of the Creator, and service to those entities who are your own selves, seen in a mirror.

Therefore, we cannot generalize that this or that about a certain childhood would have such and such a specific effect. Each entity is unique. There are, however, those categories of conditions which set up for the seeker the way he will visualize and perceive the road of seeking the truth. There are some few who do not wish to seek, or to know, but wish to be told what is true. Those people are not interested in what we have to say, but we wish them well. Those are the entities which accept specific guidelines such as good and evil, righteousness and sin. These are entities who are only comfortable as slaves. They do not question, they do not seek. They simply stand and believe that which is told them.

This tendency cannot be learned and is not the usual true nature of a third-density entity, but we did not wish to leave out entities such as these, for in these entities too lies a viable and beautiful link between the self and the realization of a Creator which banishes all of that which you call error or sin. To these people the blessing of simplicity is given, and they seem to a more seeking entity narrow or dogmatic, yet their way is as valid as any, if by that way they are able to open their hearts in service to others as they love the Creator and as they love the self as heir to the Creator, son and daughter of the Creator, the hands, the mouth and the energy of the Creator alive and working in your environment at this time. These are not entities upon which one should shower patronization. They simply are simple and uncomplicated entities who do not have the desire to seek further.

Most entities, and certainly those who would call us to them, have entered into this incarnational experience choosing limitations which shall be experienced during the years of youth. Perhaps the greatest stimulus towards freeing the self of mandatory belief is the simple demand that all be believed without question. The spiritual disciple will not accept an unquestioned description of the spiritual life. One who wishes to seek the truth must seek it through movement, movement and change and transformation, day by day, sunset by sunset, and moon by moon, [through the questioning] of a living, powerful, very real purveyor of truth. Each seeks the link that will link the mundane to that which is eternal.

Many entities within the childhood experience are cut off from the feeling of self-love. This is perhaps the most common of those limitations which are chosen before the incarnation, in order that the entity may experience and exercise the lesson that one is not here to be loved but to love. One is not here to be pampered, but to console others. One is not here to be praised, but to support, cherish and nurture those about one, seeing in them the infinite Creator. The inability to feel the worth of the self derives its strength, for the most part, from the childhood wherein the child is not accepted as it is, in which the child is not appreciated, feels itself not to be fully loved, feels itself to be criticized, feels itself to be unable to please those first witnesses and embodiments of the Creator, the parents.

As the parents cut the child off from the spontaneous giving and taking of love, so in the mature spiritual search the pilgrim shall find itself laden with a burden of self-doubt, and that even heavier burden of unidentified guilt, for in such a childhood one is given the feeling that one is somehow guilty, but of what, the child knows not. One is given the feeling that the child is unwanted, and there is no defense possible to that child, for in the young years of incarnation the child is too purely that spirit which incarnated into the world to have defenses against lack of self-perceived love, worth and righteousness.

The second most heavy influence upon the mature experience of the seeker is that yellow-ray experience the entity has had with what this instrument would call institutionalized religion. We use this word carefully to differentiate it from cultural religion. Each of you lives within the Christian culture. Each of you thinks in terms of the story of the one known as Jesus Christ, of the parables this entity gave, of the life this entity lived. The threads of this incarnation run so deeply within your culture that whether you be devout or atheistic, or anywhere in between those two, you are still forced to use a language of Christianity and Judeo-Christianity, because that is your cultural heritage.

This creates a very great difficulty in those who have rejected the vocabulary of institutionalized religion and have left that institution, either because they did not believe the institutionalized religion was helpful to the self, or because this religion held no interest for the self, no identity for the self, no means of expression for the self, or simply because the entity was too sensitive to the deeper, darker strains that weave their way through the Christian religious story. How dark and sad is that story, a story of an entity one with God and one with man, who must die; that entity asking us each to die each day, to give up the self each day, to be with the Creator in the small death of the personal part of the self, the ego, in order that one may more and more come to a realization of a greater self within. When it is put to an entity in specifically Christian terms, the entire experience of redemption, forgiveness and freedom is bent and twisted in such a way that many, many entities cannot at all accept this expression of redemption. Yet each seeks the experience of being forgiven.

It is one thing for a parent to act in such a way that an entity feels chronically unforgiven and unappreciated. It is a far more serious thing when an entity cannot, within the confines of its spiritual practice in that which you call Christianity, find, believe or rejoice in the experience of forgiveness and redemption. Few there are who truly believe, if they have considered it well, that they are, without some movement of the spirit within, forgiven all those things known and all those things not known which have been acts which separate us from ourselves, from each other, or from that great principle of love which is the Creator. Thus, the parents first, and the church, shall we call it, secondly, create the basic limitations upon those who seek the truth but cannot accept the particular expression and distortion of the truth of forgiveness and redemption in any language which is used within your religion.

There are many ways in which entities find a process of forgiveness, for let it be noted well that none feels truly without error. All consciousnesses are aware of their own humanity, their own clay feet, their own self-perceived error. It is part of the illusion in which you live that you experience this as part of being yourself. This is a part of yourself. In some entities, because of a childhood in which the entity was greatly loved and was given the love, the smiles, the touching, the obvious caring, the entity will far more likely be able to experience a sense of forgiveness through the forgiveness of the self by the greater self within. It is not that such entities know that they are without error, but that they have the faith given them because the sun shone upon them in the days of their youth, that the sun still shines upon them, and that there is no thing which cannot be forgiven.

How do these entities experience this forgiveness? By their forgiveness without stint or hindrance of any kind of all those with whom they come in contact. It is the self-forgiven entity which forgives others, not because he has earned forgiveness, but because he is an entity, and there is no error which may take away from that entity the truth of that entity's nature, a being of oneness with the Creator.

When the experiences of the childhood were ones in which much was unforgiven, criticized, denied or rejected, the pilgrim shall have, shall we say, the knee-jerk reaction to deal with, of a feeling of not forgiving the self. Others it may forgive, but until one has come to some deep archetypical emotion within which expresses itself to the spirit in the words, "You are forgiven, you are loved," that entity shall have a great deal of trouble loving the self, and thus, its forgiveness and compassion towards others masks a deep and abiding ache, a wound so terrible that it cannot be described, a wound of the self that will not forgive the self for being human.

All entities have help available to them. None need rely upon the self. But to those whose childhoods have been experienced as accepting and cherishing and nurturing will come those entities which are personal, speak personally to the entity, are intimate with the entity, and become the objective vision which encompasses the wall of self-forgiveness. Those who have been caused to believe that they cannot be as they are and be loved learn to behave and carry into their relationship with love an entity which behaves, rather than an entity which is as it is. In this case the same help is available, but it shall come to the entity in an impersonal form. Such impersonal forces, principles and entities, are as we, those who speak as inspiringly as possible through each instrument of the depth and resonance of the self of each of you, calling to you to call within yourself, acceptance, love and forgiveness.

You carry upon your backs, unless you forgive yourself every day, a terrible, terrible burden. The variousness of catalyst and experience among your peoples is intended and is guaranteed to create within the experience a subjective concept and opinion of the self as having come up short, of having failed in some way. Where, then, is salvation? It is within you, each of you. Roll the stone away from the tomb of low self-esteem, of self-doubt, of prejudice against the self. Think of yourself as an object other than yourself. Gaze upon the self as upon a stranger, and you will find that your opinion of yourself is changed, for you do not judge others as you judge yourself.

We are being asked by this instrument to come to a conclusion of our part of the message which we wish to offer, that comes through this instrument, as the hour, as this instrument calls it, grows late. We confess, we are talkative, and always speak overlong, according to this instrument.

We wish you to realize, each of you, that each of you has had various experiences in your youth, various experiences in those that seem to be in authority over you in a spiritual way. This has the repercussions of your own self-image, of your relationships with the Creator, with yourself and with those about you. We ask you simply to remember that it was to a man who had betrayed and denied the one known as Jesus that the one known as Jesus said, "You are my rock. That which is forgiven by you is forgiven, that which is not forgiven by you is not forgiven."

My children, each of you can be perceived as less than perfect, but each of you has an honor and a duty to perform. Love yourself, and if you do not love yourself, work to love yourself. Love the Creator more and more passionately, spending time with the Creator in silence, and love and forgive all with whom you come in contact, for you are as powerful as any other human, fallible being. There is that within you which is of the consciousness of love, and your wellness, your wholeness and the truth of your being is wrapped up in the concept of yourself as an extension of brother or sister, a fellow heir of the one infinite Creator. Forgive, console and love, the Creator, yourself and others.

As we know that we are out of time, we must end with this instrument. We ask you to remember only one thing more. You may find yourself to be incapable of creating this within yourself in a week, or a month or a year. You have eternity in which to become joyful, forgiven and redeemed by whatever objectivization, such as Jesus the Christ, you may choose, or by whatever inner guide that your own background has made better for you as a bridge to the eternity and the infinity of love.

We would at this time transfer this contact to the one known as Jim. I am known to you as Q'uo.

(Jim channeling)

I am Q'uo, and greet each in love and light through this instrument. We thank you for your patience, as it was necessary for us to pause as this instrument needed to complete the duties with the recording device. At this time we would offer ourselves in the attempt to speak to any queries which you may feel have importance for you. Again we remind you that we offer that which is but our opinion, though we offer it joyfully. Is there a query at this time?

Carla: I'll ask one, if people want to wait awhile and think. I have had several people in a wave talk to me about healing myself, as though my illness were some sort of crime, or indication of my waywardness of spirit. It is, on the contrary, my opinion of my own self, knowing my history, that is, that I died at one time of kidney failure, for about twenty seconds, that I indeed have a very healthy body that is doing amazingly well. I do not know what I can say to entities to give them comfort and to free themselves and myself from the feeling of guilt that is lain on me by those who feel that one must be bursting with physical health in order to be of mental, emotional and spiritual health. Could you comment?

I am Q'uo, and am aware of your query, my sister. We may comment in a general fashion, for we wish to share the principle. Those who offer their help, their opinion, of your situation, have the desire to serve, the basic love that propels motion and service. The vehicle, or channel through which the service is offered, is whatever framework of belief has served this entity, or any who offer their assistance. Thus, they give that which is biased, according to what they have found helpful. The manner in which you receive that which is given is determined again by your own framework of belief. You may see the offering as that which is laden with guilt. This may be the result of a distortion of either one or both of the means of perceiving. This perception of the role of guilt, then, has meaning for each in an unique manner. The weight that you give to that perception, then, is a function of …

We must pause, we are having difficulty with this instrument.

(Pause)

I am Q'uo, and we apologize for the delay. We shall continue. The perception of guilt as a portion of your condition, is merely a reflection of the …

Jim: Carla, this isn't *(inaudible)*. It doesn't feel right, I'm going to have to stop. It doesn't feel like Q'uo.

(Carla channeling)

I am Q'uo, and greet each through this instrument once again in love and light. We wish to applaud and encourage the instrument known as Jim, that this instrument's *(inaudible)* is such that there was *(inaudible)* lack of steadiness of the tuning, and although the one known as Carla was keeping the circle well guarded by means placed there by the instrument before the meditation, yet it is always well whenever in doubt to cease the communication, for it is the desire of the Confederation of the Planets, who are in service to the one Creator to offer only that highest truth that may be offered in a *(inaudible)* and secure manner.

(Inaudible) query which was posed by this instrument, as there is the difficulty of the instrument's own individual small self which has its opinion, and would in any case doubt that which we were to offer. We shall simply say that the nature of health and wellness is a nature which knows not bone nor sinew, blood or tendon, infection or disease. The health and wellness of an entity is its acceptance of itself, and its realization that all is as it should be and as it must be for the entity to be open to the lessons of love received and given in that moment.

Before we close through this instrument we would ask once more if there are any further queries?

K: My name is K *(inaudible)* weekly, and I would like for you to comment on the teaching and work of the circle that I am speaking about, particularly, could you comment upon the entity Sananda, who speaks to the circle?

I am Q'uo, and we greet you, K of St. Louis. Blessings upon you and upon your seeking. The conditions of that activity called channeling are different for each channel, and the sensitivity each channel may bring to its work is unique to that entity. Those ideas which can be used as tools and resources in the daily life are ideas inspired by love, call it what you will.

As to the name, Sananda, the Christ name has moved through many namings. There is no one name of this consciousness that may declare itself unique at this time, that is, the only entity which speaks as the principle of the master known as Jehoshua, or Jesus. We ask that you yourself listen with an open heart to the messages of the one known to you as Sananda—how many names this energy has been perceived as having, how many more shall there be. You are one, as are most who have studied the consciousness, the mind and the actions of the one known as Jesus the Christ. Listen to this entity. Seems it to speak in humility, compassion and acceptance, encouraging each to love each other? If that be so, what matters it what it call itself?

We may say specifically only that the intentness of the entity which is Christ is a consciousness which has used channels which have given over their lives to servanthood. Gaze clearly upon the face of love. There is no pride, there is no judgment, there is always love, forgiveness and healing. That which is of Christ-consciousness dares the entity to look at itself, to accept itself, and by that impossibility of self acceptance and blind faith, be healed. If the entity whom you hear has this love, this yearning, this passion and this healing, you may judge for yourself what energy or principle of the Creator this entity is. We do not give opinions positive or negative of any source, but ask each entity to use its discrimination, and always to use the light touch, the relaxed and time-consuming patience allowing ideas offered by such consciousnesses to steep and ripen within the self. By [the] fruits of these teachings shall you know the nature of him who planted the seed that blooms within yourself.

May we be of any more service to you at this time, my brother?

K: Thank you very much.

We thank you, K of St. Louis. Is there another query at this time?

K: Could you comment briefly about the connection that B and I have between each other?

I am Q'uo, and without abridging free will, we may. K is teacher to B; B teacher to K. You have the honor of being honest, and the duty to be compassionately honest, and to give to each other a true picture of each other, that together you may pull as two oxen the cart of your faith and your will to serve, not a striving to please, only, but looking always for that which may serve, never striving to limit, but searching always for that which may advance a sense of freedom.

The mated relationship, regardless of what its nature be within the legal framework of your culture, is the most powerful possible arrangement within which acceleration of the spiritual path may be done. It is also the most difficult, because intimacy is very difficult among those in a culture which teaches each entity to wear the mask and to behave in such and such a way, that the truth be only half told, or not mentioned, for to do so would cause time-consuming, heart-rending work in consciousness by both.

Thus, each who is a teacher to the other in a mated relationship must, to be the most effective partner, gaze within the self within all circumstances and within all transactions with the cleansing, purifying and healing openness of heart, never allowing difficulties to remain between the two, realizing always that difficulties will continually be between you, for you are each other's greatest catalyst for learning. Face that squarely. You shall make each other uncomfortable. That is the nature of change. And when you have a teacher, the weight of learning increases, and the discomfort increases likewise. Therefore, see the pain that you give each other with sorrow and with apology, but with the knowledge that it is a necessary portion of the learning of two who together seek most beautifully.

Is there another question, my brother?

K: Thank you. Thank you very much for increasing my insight and understanding, and I wish to give the rest of the time to someone else who may have a question.

We thank you, my brother. Is there another query at this time?

(Pause)

I am Q'uo. We are aware of your questions, and respect each for the silence that indicates that it is not now the time to ask such questions. Ponder them instead within your heart and your soul. You can answer as well as we. If you give yourself the time to allow these questions to sink deeply into your subconscious, each question shall be answered at last, by whatever means.

Your planetary sphere has a special light this day, which you call Easter and Passover within the culture in which you live. Lift up your hearts, my children, sing alleluia to new beginnings, new understanding, new perceptions of the self, new consolations and a renewal of a passionate desire to know, to love, and to express by service to others the one infinite Creator. In the love and the light of that Creator we leave you now, rejoicing with you at your Eastertide. We are those known to you as Q'uo. Adonai. Adonai vasu borragus. ☥

Sunday Meditation
April 29, 1990

Group question: No group question today. We'll take potluck.

(Carla channeling)

We are those of the principle of Q'uo, and we greet you in the love and in the light of the one infinite Creator. We thank you for the plenty of your company, for the thanksgiving of your meditation together, for the rejoicing in unity of this circle of seeking, and for the openness to hear what we have to say to you, though you are so scattered at this time that you are not able to form queries that are deeply in your heart. And we assure each of you there are queries in your heart at this time, queries that you could bring closer and closer to the surface by wishing and desiring and willing to live more and more consciously, more and more single-mindedly, to burn with passion, to hear the voice of the one infinite Creator within you, to have the enlightenment and the opening up of those things which seem closed to you because they are caught in the prison of words.

Each of you has suffered in this week, each of you has rejoiced in this week. Have you noticed? Have you grasped your life in any one moment, and turned to the central sun of your being in praise and thanksgiving and joy? Where is your joy, my children? Where is your passion? Where is your thanksgiving? You are upon a road, and each stranger that you meet may open to you the book of your life, the meaning of your moment. Do you listen to every stranger? You are strangers to yourself, each of you. Do you know how your heart yearns to dwell in joy? Do you know the passion that lies within you to follow with a single mind and a single heart that trail you can sense, that dusty road that you know is better than it feels, finer than it seems, more wonderful than it apparently could ever be? What ties you to this illusion, my children, you who are in such an advantageous position, you who have made such firm commitments?

We choose to speak of what this instrument spoke of earlier, for though this instrument knows not whence its thoughts arise, yet it is true that this instrument has opened, more than most, those passages into what may be called the frontal lobes of your brain, if you wish to give a geographical location to that portion of consciousness which is capable of faith. Because of this instrument's blind and unknowing faith, because of its insistence that there is a positive way to observe an act in each circumstance, it burns, it gives praise, it has its moments of joy, perhaps more often than some, though it too dwells completely within your illusion and is completely blind to that which it senses. It is, however, correct. You, my children, have banded together in blind faith with apparent difficulties on every side, with personality clashes, with personal difficulties that seem to make certain relationships less easy, each with personal business that seems upon the surface to cause the relationship to be that that is not unity.

So it seems to you, yet you have vowed deep within yourself to serve the infinite One together, and all your words and moods and fears and tears and problems within the illusion have absolutely no effect whatsoever upon the joy of your union within the love and the light of the service to the one infinite Creator. You have made a choice that is completely idealistic and unrealistic with regard to your circumstances. You shall not see your oneness, perhaps ever, and surely not quickly, for each of you lacks, in some way, the work that must be done to learn passion, and sureness, and stillness, and blindness.

You are not blind to your illusions. Why, why is that? We may ask all upon your grieving, weeping, agonized planet. Why can you not be blind? You know that which you see is an illusion. Even your scientists speak to you thus. Your poets have always spoken so. All have wished to burn with passion for the infinite, the divine, the ideal, the everlasting. Why do you see? Why do you open your eyes and allow yourselves to be pulled into an illusion that you are so aware of as an illusion?

The answer is very simple. You are doing what you are supposed to do. Were you able to be blind to this illusion and awake to joy, you would not, nor should you, be here, dwelling in this illusion, learning and suffering and changing and transforming yourself, day by day, step by weary and seemingly plodding step. You have come here and have given up your true sight, and so you do not find your blindness a virtue. This is the forgetting, this is the veil, this is birth into an illusion, and you have plunged yourself into its icy waters, because in your courage you have wished to become better, to become more single-minded, to find more courage, to burn brighter, to have more passion and more single-mindedness in love of the one infinite Idea or Thought that is Love itself.

So, do not in any way cause yourself to criticize yourself, discourage, doubt or complain about yourself. No matter what it may seem that your lacks are, you have chosen them, bravely, knowing the pain you would endure by your blindness. In such blindness the ideas of one who has faith, such as this instrument, often sound unrealistic in the extreme. Nor is this instrument at all infallible, yet in this particular statement, that you who have banded together to serve and have called yourself L/L are indeed one, [she offers an accurate translation of our concept]. We do not know if you shall ever have the joy and the thanksgiving and the harmony that you would wish. The combination is more difficult, the problems each has more serious. Each is unbalanced in a different way. The group, upon the mundane level, functions in love and light often by refraining from speaking. This may seem like a mistake. Is it not good to correct each other's faults? Is it not good to share the mirror, and say, "Gaze, gaze upon this mirror, look honestly into what you are saying and doing. Let me help you see yourself better." This is what each is to do with the other in relationship. Yet, how often have each of you chosen not to speak, and why? Have you wondered, you who so often do speak, and right clearly, mirroring each other?

As L/L, you have stubbornly and blindly refrained, not out of fear, not out of a lack of ability, but you have allowed your surface to remain calm, and though in each there is difficulty, judgment, disappointment, unhappiness and confusion, you carry it as your own baggage and do not mirror it to each other. Although in your personal relationships you very well may, and so you must, as L/L, you have given the best of yourselves. Are you aware of this? No, my children, you have not known, but have only felt your way. You are blind, and so this must be. Trust in this blindness, trust in your feelings. Do not doubt, for one second, ever, your intuitions regarding this particular commitment to service to others.

Each of you gives up and sacrifices much to serve. When a group serves together each sacrifices in order to harmonize with others. This is known, but not appreciated. You do not give yourselves credit, for you suffer for a grand and wonderful purpose, and the harmony you create, though created in blind faith and confusion, is the brightest light you may shine as a nascent, inchoate, barely born social memory complex. Do you think a social memory complex begins by all telling all what all think? No, my children. A social memory complex begins by each loving each unconditionally—unconditionally, no matter what the cost, and so you have done with exquisite care, not even knowing why.

We do not say this to make you proud. We say this to make you see the process that you undergo spiritually, as a group that moves in service to the one infinite Creator, by offering information to others that is practical. We of the Confederation of Planets in the Service of the Infinite Creator do not rely upon inspiration only, although indeed we hope, oh, how we hope, to inspire! We know that people need resources, they need tools, they need practical things, things that they may think about and use as they work to move along the path of service to others in the evolution of their own spirits and the spirit of all, which, in the end, is one and the same thing.

And we say to each who may wish to walk with others in the service of the one infinite Creator, love each other unconditionally; bide your words, bate your tongue, hold and release your judgments. Is not each attempting the very most it can attempt already? Have you not faith in each other to this extent, that you have faith each is attempting the impossible? You know it is impossible to act ideally in this illusion. The illusion is what you see. The illusion is what will form your actions, and they will be relative, not absolute. Again and again you yourselves shall perceive yourselves in error. Is it so strange you should perceive error in others also? But if you wish to work for love, if you wish to serve in love and light, love each other, care for each other, be for each other, advocate each other, burn with love and passion for the portion of each that wishes to serve. Is this not beautiful? Is this not beyond the understanding?

Each of you has that which you may call the ego. You are aware of it in more sophisticated words, but for this message we shall use the easy term, and ask you to realize that we mean by it all those blockages of the self with the self, with each other and with a society, because you wish to be known as this and that, and do not wish to be known as the other. You wish to have a certain selfhood in others' opinions, and you do not wish to see that mirrored back to you as a sullied or distorted or criticized selfhood, for your feelings would be hurt and you would suffer.

In service to others let each be stern with the self, and full of infinite love and advocacy for each other. You have your own lessons to learn, and only out of those lessons do you have what you may give in love and harmony to the group. Take those lessons seriously, and in your personal relationships, make full use of the mirroring effect. Listen to each other honestly, but as you come together in love and light, do not seek to be understood as such and such, but seek only to understand the beauty of each other. Dwell in praise and thanksgiving to the one infinite Creator. Rejoice in the harmony that your blind faith has given you with each other. You are not harmonious together, no people are harmonious together unless they give up that which is ego, and cease to judge. The relationship of [or through] service is forever healing, forever blessing, forever giving thanks, forever finding the most passionate love of that single-minded search which each has joined together, the search for service to that most beloved infinite One whose passion, whose love, whose Thought, has originated all of creation.

We leave you glorying and giving thanks and praise at the harmony that you so blindly are willing to attempt in such a difficult illusion for the purpose of service to the one infinite Creator, and we urge you to continue so, knowing that nothing is as it appears but love, and that is all that it appears, and more.

We would close this meditation through the one known as Jim. We thank this instrument for opening itself without a query, for it has been some time since this instrument has done so and it did not feel comfortable. We thank this instrument, that it is flexible and trustful enough to do this, and so we leave this instrument in thanksgiving, and move to the one known as Jim. I am that principle known to you as Q'uo.

(Jim channeling)

I am Q'uo, and greet each again in love and light. At this time we would offer ourselves in the attempt to answer any further queries that may be on those minds present. Is there a query at this time?

K: I don't have a question right now, but I want to thank you for the comfort of your words and the validation of our work together. It meant a lot to me, thank you.

Carla: Me too, me too, thanks.

I am Q'uo, and we are most grateful to each as well for allowing us to speak upon this topic by your desires and your intentions as well as your actions. We thank each. Is there any query at this time?

Carla: Is this true universally of those who attempt to be of service, that which you have said about us? Is this a tool for everyone to use?

I am Q'uo, and though the tool we have given is that which will find application in most groups' experiences, it is not one which is without individual tailoring, shall we say, but that which we have given may serve as a firm foundation for any group that desires to be of service to others through the harmonizing of those individual energies which comprise the whole of the group. The individual idiosyncrasies, shall we say, are paradoxically those qualities which give the group wider capabilities, on the one hand, and when left in an unchecked state, shall we say, that which does not bend to compromise can also be those qualities which serve to fracture the crystallized harmony of a group. Therefore, it is a delicate balance that must be maintained when the individual personalities put themselves forth in the place of a group which desires to serve. Thus, we recommend that the ideal of service be held high for each and that each pursue that ideal through the harmonizing of characteristics as is necessary for the furthering of this ideal of service to others.

Is there a further query, my sister?

Carla: Yes, just one, I don't know if there's an answer to it, but I feel so full of love for my friends that come to me—and especially the one known as A, today—but many friends, all my friends, and I just love them so much, and I would do anything for them, and it seems that there is so little that I can do, and it makes me want to cry. I feel this way not only for the people that ask me for help, but people with AIDS, and people that are trapped in socially unrespectable things like homosexuality, which is no sin at all but just a different mode of sexuality. I don't know what to do with all this love.

I am Q'uo, and, my sister, for one who loves greatly, as do you, it is well to give that love as the bread which is cast upon the waters, that it may go where it is needed, and do its work unseen. It is the most difficult service to allow those that are so dearly loved to learn that which is theirs to learn through their own efforts, knowing that much of that experience will contain that which you call pain, but that painful experience is that which shall guide the lesson to its home within the heart of the entity, and thus is the purpose of the painful experience, and much within your illusion explained. If lessons were easily won, would they be so valuable and carry such weight within the total beingness of the entity? One cannot learn for another or take from another the pain that shall go with the learning, for these are components of this process which must all be in place in order for the learning to occur.

Thus, we suggest that you give that which you have of love in your sharing with the others that you love and that you give freely, and that within your own heart you bless the learning that will inevitably contain the pain and let your love and your blessings be given freely.

Is there a further query, my sister?

Carla: Yes. Is my suffering for these people that I love so much, which has happened to me all my life and I don't know how to shut it down, I would take all their suffering if I could, is it part of why I have physical limitations and physical suffering?

I am Q'uo, and we weigh our response carefully, for we do not wish to step over that boundary of infringement upon your own decision making and understanding of your life pattern. Your great empathic identity with those about you, especially when the emotional experience of those about you swings into that area of discomfort, sorrow and suffering, is a central feature of your …

(Tape ends.)

(The essence of the response was that these are two separate issues, and Carla expressed relief in that confirmation.) ❧

Sunday Meditation
May 6, 1990

Group question: The question this evening has to do with why is it that throughout all of recorded history, various cultures and religions and sects of one kind or another have all attempted to alter their consciousness by one means or another, whether it's by drugs or dancing or singing or chanting or ohming or meditating. Why is it that humans have found it attractive, and even necessary, to attempt to alter their consciousness? Is there something within the human brain/mind condition that is lacking or searching, or what is the reason for this attempt to alter the consciousness that has been evident throughout all of recorded history and is evident to this day?

(Carla channeling)

I am Q'uo. It is a very great pleasure for us to greet you in the love and in the light of the one infinite Creator in whose service we all walk, and in whose hope we all live. May we welcome that entity known as K to the group, and offer this entity the blessing which the Creator pours through us and through all, thanking this entity for its interest, and for the intensity of seeking that it and each of those within this circle manifests within their thoughts and their activities.

You have asked us a question this evening which we may answer in many ways. Indeed, there is perhaps no larger topic than this, as it is an examination of the fundamental nature of those imperishable entities which you are, and their relationship to the physical vehicle which carries this consciousness about and enables it to use the catalyst of experiences, which are taken in such and such a way, further to accelerate the pace of spiritual growth, further to deepen the apparent suffering and sadness of the constant life of the pilgrim, which is that of continual change and transformation.

Now, lest you feel that we begin by identifying some, rather than all, as having the desire for deeper perceptions by what we have said, we say instead that each entity, each unique portion of consciousness with whom you come in contact, has within itself as a central spring, a central motivator of the physical manifestation and of the thinking, the fundamental desire to explore a bias which is as instinctual to it as the turning to the light is in your second-density flora. This is not a learned activity, but rather an instinct. We would ask you to put aside philosophical and metaphysical consideration at this time, that you may gaze steadily into the mirror of your memory. Is there any time, if we may use that word, within your conscious memory, that you thought to yourself, "This is all that there is. I am perfectly satisfied with what is"? Very few people could make such a statement in honesty, for it is a portion of the deepest instinctual nature of each portion of consciousness first to seek to be and realize the self; secondly, to turn towards the light, whether it be physical or metaphysical; thirdly, to explore the dynamics of all situations to find within them a transfiguration that causes one to move away from the mundane.

Within your illusion you both embrace the mundane and you push it from you. You have a full range of emotions concerning the difficulties of being the self. Part of that divine discontent is the absolute certainty within each entity which is at all conscious of itself that there is more that it does not know. There is therefore within the very first chakra or energy center that yearning to move from the relative to the absolute, from shadow to substance, from form to information. Let us say that humankind is biased towards some feeling that there is a self that does not perish. In the midst of an illusion which seems to declare precisely the opposite, the vague yearning of many is quelled, and the life energy is distracted and dispelled by your gadgetry, your mundane concerns, and your concern for your position, your rights, your strengths and your improvement.

Let us move briefly to a digression about power. This culture's entities are very eager to give their power away to other sources, rather than seeking to remember the awareness that is within. Redemption and paradise are sought by some identification with some personification of that which seems to us to transcend the illusion in which you are enjoying existence. The yielding up of this personal power is not permanent. It can at any time be taken back into the individual by the individual's conscious effort, and we urge any who have not done so, so to do.

We would compare the hunger and the thirst for what this instrument would call righteousness, and what others would call the truth, or love, running throughout all of humankind, moving as does the tide, affecting each, but at a level that is beneath the threshold of consciousness, beneath the veil of forgetting, deeply down within that portion of the self from which all truths are remembered. Therefore, we ask each to retain its own power, to act not at this moment as we speak as a discriminator, for that would hinder the flow of this discussion, but to listen with an open heart, an open mind, and an unruffled consciousness, allowing those ideas which are flowing at this time to flow forth in the natural tide of inspiration and information.

Just as the tide goes in and out so within your self you are not only peculiarly and uniquely made by your previous biases to view incoming information in a certain way, but also the influx of that information is altered by those energies within your universe which affect everything from the great sea of life within your veins to the great sea of suffering that you see again and again as entities are self-sacrificing because they love that which they cannot see.

This is your glory and your power. You are an expression of consciousness. Your consciousness is made up of two things, that which we call love, or the one original Thought, that is to say, the Creator Itself, and that primary principle of free will. Without the introduction of free will the universe would be infinite and intelligent, but it would not be conscious of itself. You have been cast forth as a sower broadcasts the seeds of a garden. Within you, without knowing articulately, you are a certain kind of seed. All begin with this basic seed-nature. During the course of incarnation upon incarnation you begin to become aware in an unique way of your own consciousness. Although this is merely a recapitulation of that realization which is the harvestability of second density into third, we emphasize it again and again to you in this context. Your turning to the light, your yearning for love and acceptance, and your more mature yearning to be loving and be compassionate are such deep portions of your mind that, shall we say, the metaprogram of your existence is based upon this nature.

It is the fundamental nature of third-density entities to reach. Thousands of incarnations go by as each entity refines that for which it reaches, until finally in one way or another the entity begins to realize that much of reaching cannot be done in any environment except the environment of the silent, seeking heart. You are creatures who have a memory which is buried deeply within you and is a portion of that which makes you alive, a creature of a Creator, an entity who has a destiny, an appointment towards which you move, quickly or slowly, to the Father. Do not be concerned about the length of time that it may take to refine this instinctual sense of something more into a practice that ultimately makes immediate contact with the mystery which lies beyond all information.

This mystery is not the answer to anything, for all of your questions lie within this illusion. All of your theories, your perceptions and your knowledge cannot bring you into a state wherein you may expect to experience the knowledge of the one infinite Creator, your Father, your Mother, and your Lover. Each of you is a soul, a portion of light, and you are most personally beloved. Yet you are inextricably entwined with that free will which gives you the opportunity to seek within an illusion whose singular purpose is to throw each entity away from the center of beingness into confusion, despair, suffering and difficulty. These are not the actions of a cruel Creator. These are the actions of a Creator which has learned that no lessons are learned in the happy, holiday atmosphere of Eden. You may visit the garden, the oasis, that place where all questions are answered, but you cannot bring back words to describe this experience.

Now, as you know that your second-density entities are already instinctually turning towards the light, and seeking to grow, so too may you see that part of your inheritance from your own evolution in spirit is that absolute certainty that turning towards the light will obtain for one results which one desires, truths for which one hungers. To be without spiritual hunger is to be somnolent, and there are many at this time among your people who, in spite of all that occurs, remain in this condition of sleepwalking through an incarnation, walking past joy and disaster, worship and suffering, thinking only about the weather, and whether one should have brought the umbrella, thinking about the dinner menu, thinking, and thinking, and thinking, and thinking.

We say to you straight out, although we are not infallible, it is our opinion that you cannot by any system of knowledge become aware of the presence of love. You cannot by any special series of learnings arrive at the gates of paradise, or find yourself in a position to aid others. You seek that which you feel is there because it is there. The unknown does beckon, and there is that which pulls you forward irresistibly so that you are not entirely at any time in charge of your own development, for your instincts towards self-development will create gradual widening and focusing and maturing of the personality. Much has been said about the culture in which you live, a culture in which the idol of the day is what is called technology. Miracles are described in hushed tones and the saints which perform those miracles are your scientists, your doctors, and so you remunerate them handsomely while paying much less of your attention and your worldly goods [to those] who seek the mystery beyond that which is known.

What drives you? Your own nature. Occasionally an entity may be so disturbed by early experience that it is completely blocked and cannot find access to the doors of feeling and yearning that each normally has. There is a drive to continue evolution that is as instinctual as any other portion of the red ray. When we speak of the fundamental reason that entities seek through any and all means to alter their consciousnesses, we are not speaking specifically of indigo-ray inner work. We are speaking, in many cases, of a simple, perhaps unvoiced or unrecognized feeling, that there is more, and humankind hungers for it because it is the next step of evolution.

When we speak to groups such as this we find that there is a certain irritation factor in that we go over basic material again and again. There is a reason for this. The reason is that you have not yet accomplished this most fundamental of tools towards becoming familiar with the nature of your own consciousness, and therefore [are not yet] comfortable and willing to work hard in pursuit of a growing feeling of the immediacy of the presence of eternity. And so we move back into that which, as this instrument, whose sense of humor sometimes eludes us, would say: "Read my lips"—meditate daily. When the telephone rings, take an instant before you answer, for you always entertain angels unawares.

You never know who or what circumstance is going to enhance your ability to grasp your situation. Your situation is simple. You know that you are more than you seem; you wish to find out what that "more" is, and you are impatient because you have a very short time in this illusion. Your use of catalyst is painfully inadequate so that lifetimes must be terminated as an entity becomes completely full of that which needs healing. It has not done the meditation, it has not squared away towards the self, it has gazed outside of itself for authority. There is information which lies within, and for which channels such as this one, and all circumstances whatsoever, can be triggers, for your memory of the truths that lie waiting for you to discover within your deep mind.

The study of the archetypical mind may seem to be irrelevant, but let us hold up to you the contrast. On the one hand there is the entity which believes that it may collect learnings, and by that collection form a staircase of light which moves that entity gnostically into higher and higher realms of wisdom until it has finally realized itself. To our understanding there is no way to improve one's grasp of one's spiritual situation or one's ability to benefit from this illusion which is summed up in wisdom literature. Wisdom is not what you are here to learn. Certainly you may use it, but what you are here to learn is the open heart, the acceptance of the unacceptable, the love of the unlovable, the meaning of the word compassion, the entry in a personal way of infinity and eternity into the supposedly mundane existence.

We suggest to you that it is our opinion that there is no situation which lies beyond the pale of learning, growing and the manifesting of the love that is the nature of the self. But one thing first must be surrendered, and that is the quest for the one answer that will allow all things to fall into place neatly, cleanly and irrevocably. You are finite creatures attempting to grasp the concept of infinity. Your minds cannot hold that concept, it can only name it, and thereby feel it has some power over it. This is an illusion. Your true power lies in your realization that this is your time of action, of choice after choice after choice in which you choose to view your environment in a way which would be made possible by mind-altering substances of one kind or another.

We suggest to you that experiences using these artificial aids do not move beyond this perishable experience for you. It is only the transfiguration and epiphany of the self, caused by the process of persistent faith and will in silent seeking, that bring your biases and distortions towards oneness, love, hope, beauty and truth, which are, indeed, imperishable. The use of technology of any kind—as this instrument would say, "Better living through chemistry"—is helpful in that it gives to the lucky experiencer a glimpse of the paradise that awaits within. However, there is no substitute for the step placed after the next, and the next, and the next, not in a grim and humorless way, but as if one were on a playful, joyful walk, perhaps even running from time to time, because of the demand of the mundane world, but working always to form the understanding within the self that eternity lies before you now, right now, this moment. Feel this resonance as we speak. Feel space and time vanish. Feel this.

We shall pause.

(Pause)

Because this suggestion is powerful, and we do not wish to create a state of deep concentration for any, we will continue speaking, but we hope that you may see that which we are talking about. You are eternal and imperishable, and there is nothing that you can do within this illusion to affect your true nature, except to determine to live a certain kind of existence which embraces as the center of this existence the love of, the praise and thanks to, and the supplication before, that portion of the self that may be spelled with a capital "S," that portion of the self which we shall never find unless we die to ourselves, and by this we mean that the smokescreen, the confusions, and the embafflement of entities which keeps them from this immediacy of oneness with the Creator is tremendously widespread, and is so challenging that it is by grace alone that one is able in any sort of constant sense to attain the desired goal.

Thus, we ask each to use the intellect by all means, but not to confuse the works of the intellect and the functions of belief with faith itself; not faith in an object, for the only object which commands your complete respect is a mystery, to us as well as to you. We know nothing but the mystery, however it has become more harmonious for us to worship and to serve that mystery that is beyond all things and all non-things, that is beyond ego and egolessness, that is beyond the mind and the imagination of humankind.

Faith is that faculty which knows that all is well, and in the face of apparent difficulty, the power of faith is all-important in shaping your experience. Take your substances, imbibe your wisdom-giving potions. There is no harm in experiencing your natural state, but know too that this will cost you, for to dwell within vibrations for which you are not yet ready is often to do damage metaphysically or physically to the entity which you are.

This instrument is asking us with some fierceness to retain that which we wish to give for another time, and so we shall, but we do ask each to meditate, as always, persistently, patiently, lovingly and without regard for any outcome. Allow your realizations to surprise you. Hunting for realization is a hunt without a prey. The realization lies within the silence of your own being.

We would at this time, with great thanks and pleasure in using this instrument, transfer the contact to the one known as Jim. We are known to you as those of Q'uo, and leave this instrument in love and in light.

(Jim channeling)

I am Q'uo, and greet each again in love and light. At this time we would offer ourselves in an attempt to speak to any further queries which remain upon the minds of those present. We would remind each that we offer that which is our experience and our opinion. We do not claim to be infallible, but desire only to share that which is ours as freely and joyfully as is possible.

Is there a query at this time?

Carla: Since the other two are pondering, I would like to ask a question which I would only wish you to answer in a general way. I do not wish a specific answer. My experience this week has been that I have been praying for some time for a sign as to my path through this period of somewhat serious ill health of the physical vehicle. I am very fond of and proud of this vehicle, and feel it has a great heart, but it has suffered much. I felt that I was given a sign, a very strong sign, because of extraordinary reaction to a simple activity wherein I was paralyzed after doing exercises I had been doing for many years. The voice seemed to be saying, with all the strength of a two-by-four between the eyes, to get on with the repair of the physical vehicle, that it was not time, at this time, to release my willingness to serve, but that it was my continuing honor and duty to continue to hold in faith that while I am instinct with life I am simply to see those things which occur to me as ways of learning to serve better. I have seen people take just such signs and interpret them in a completely opposite manner. In my case, for instance, the interpretation would have been, "You had difficulty in moving, so the answer is to stop moving." It is a feeling I have from deep within myself, not subject to the answer, that this negativity is no part of one who loves life and wishes to serve. But I would appreciate any general commentary that you may have about subjectively oriented signs which are offered to entities in order to give them information from the deep mind.

I am Q'uo, and am aware of your query, my sister. We find that you have spoken to the topic of your query with far more eloquence and persuasion than could we. However, we shall speak in a general fashion by suggesting that the deep mind does, indeed, offer those clues and hints that are appropriate for the maturing entity, by allowing certain experiences within the daily round of activities to stand out in the notice, and to be seen in a light which may shine for no other. The experiences that convey the deep messages are those which evoke this inner knowing and harmonic resonance, shall we say, within the heart of the entity. By this feeling, then, does the entity know that there is a significance beyond the mundane contained within that experience.

The readiness, shall we say, of any entity to recognize and accept this kind of a signal from the deep mind is the feature which both precipitates the experience and allows it to be interpreted in accordance with the needs of the entity and the guidance of the deeper mind.

Is there a further query, my sister?

Carla: Not from me, thank you very much.

I am Q'uo, and we thank you, my sister. Is there another query?

(Pause)

I am Q'uo, and as we perceive no further queries at this time we shall take this opportunity to thank those present once again for inviting our presence within your circle of seeking. It is the greatest of honors to share with you these moments of unity and of the expression of the desire to seek more of the mystery of life-experience, that together we may illumine that which was in shadow and move a step further upon our journeys together. We shall take our leave of this group and this instrument at this time, leaving each as always in the love and in the light of the one infinite Creator. We are known to you as those of Q'uo. Adonai, my friends, adonai.

(Carla channeling)

I Yadda. I greet you in love and light of infinite One. Request to come to this gathering of souls because of previous contact with the members which is of special meaning at this time. We say greetings and love.

We say you have too much intelligence to trust your intelligence, do you not? Hah!

We thank you, we are full of love for you, leaving each in "bressing"—blessing—we get better at this as we speak; some day no accent for Yadda. We work towards that day, yes? We wish you joy and merriment—merriment, you see! We speak well. Be happy, for you need no clothing of reputation, no mask of learning. You are perfect. May your God go with you as this foolish one insists upon her Jesus. May you have the intensity, the feeling, the feeling of wholeness which passion brings. We say to you love and light as that is all that is. There is nothing to understand. You must settle your minds and ride [by] it, casting a cold eye on those who would be wise.[1] We leave you in the One Who [is] all love and light.

I Yadda. Adonai. Adonai.

---

[1] Carla: I think this phrase in my channeling came from Yeats': "Cast a cold eye on life and death; horseman, pass by."

L/L Research

L/L Research is a subsidiary of Rock Creek Research & Development Laboratories, Inc.

P.O. Box 5195
Louisville, KY 40255-0195

www.llresearch.org

Rock Creek is a non-profit corporation dedicated to discovering and sharing information which may aid in the spiritual evolution of humankind.

ABOUT THE CONTENTS OF THIS TRANSCRIPT: This telepathic channeling has been taken from transcriptions of the weekly study and meditation meetings of the Rock Creek Research & Development Laboratories and L/L Research. It is offered in the hope that it may be useful to you. As the Confederation entities always make a point of saying, please use your discrimination and judgment in assessing this material. If something rings true to you, fine. If something does not resonate, please leave it behind, for neither we nor those of the Confederation would wish to be a stumbling block for any.

© 2009 L/L Research

Sunday Meditation
May 13, 1990

Group question: The question this evening has to do with the concept of the division of the Creator into many, many portions, each of which seems to become an entity, or a person such as we are, and we were wondering at what point in the evolutionary process does each portion of the Creator become unique, and how does this differentiation, one portion from another in order that each becomes unique, occur? Where does it occur, how does it occur, and when we're in this third density and we have this quality of uniqueness added to by the experiences that we have through each incarnation, when we die is there something of this Earth plane that we take with us that becomes part of that risen body that goes on in evolution? What do we retain, what do we leave behind? What is the core nature of our being?

(Carla channeling)

I am Q'uo. My beloved ones, I greet you in the love and in the light of the one infinite Creator. There are no words to express our joy at sharing this circle of meditation and seeking, at sharing so intimately the beauty of each consciousness, of experiencing the trust you have in each other and in the Creator. We shall do our best to speak through this instrument in such a way that no part of that trust, that love or that call to us is in any way harmed, but as always, we ask you to remember that we are your brothers and sisters, and we come to you because we sorrow at your sorrow, and we yearn to soothe the ache of unanswered questions that you have.

As to the truth of your being, you must know that we are liable to error and quite capable of being mistaken. We are not other than you, but only more experienced. Our love is the one love. Our Creator is the one Creator. But what we have we share, as it is our service to you that enables us to grow, as any teacher may tell you. In teaching, it is the teacher who learns, far more than the student. And so, we who are hoping to be of service to you, know, paradoxically, that you are already of inestimable service to us, and if there could be one light that held us all that you could see, that would be the physical manifestation of reality of the situation within your circle and its contact with us at this time. We are one with you. We love you, and all of us love and serve the Creator, and seek the truth.

Your question this evening will stretch this instrument's vocabulary, for she does not have conscious knowledge of mathematics or of physics, but in some ways this is good, because those to whom we speak do not have those languages either, and perhaps it is better that we lose some accuracy in being more understandable in that which we have to share. You ask this evening about your selves at a level deeper than most ever consider. You ask about the most fundamental uniqueness, the uniqueness that is your essence, not the uniqueness that learns, or does not learn, not the uniqueness that lives and is biased, not the uniqueness that you experience as personalities, but the imperishable uniqueness of you who were before time and space.

We ask you to consider with us an impossible-seeming concept. This is not your first creation, nor will it be your last. You are the first children of the one infinite Creator, created before time and space. You are timeless, you are spaceless, and you are each unique. We are aware that this is not an easy concept to grasp. Where is the memory of all this creation? Where is the buried treasure of this infinite beingness? Where is any awareness whatsoever of this situation? You are not aware of this situation in the same way that you are not aware of the energy fields of your body, of each atom and its paths of energy that hold it together in a field, of each combination of atoms into molecules, of all the fields that interact with each other to form the complex of your physical vehicle, of all the time/space fields of energy that create your mind in such and such a way. Have you any awareness of all this activity? No, my friends, you have not. It is not your business. It is not your purpose.

It is not necessary for you to conceive of yourself in mathematical terms, but to explain your uniqueness using this faulty instrument—and making apologies for lack of specificity of terms—we ask you to move away from all concept, all beingness, all idea, all structure, all awareness, all consciousness, and move back into the unaware, infinite intelligence of the one infinite Creator, whose nature is absolute love. This is an impossible concept to ideate, and we ask that you switch off the brain that ratiocinates, and move into your artistic, feeling being, and feel the unawareness, the everlastingness, the infinity of the utterly passive, unconscious, intelligent infinity. It is only by moving to this state that you may grasp your uniqueness.

The first distortion or change from utter passivity of love, love dwelling without thought, without beingness, is what you may call free will. As love is absolute passivity, free will is absolutely various activity. As love never changes, free will always changes. If you can conceive of free will by considering the wind, you know that you cannot predict, influence or have any impact whatsoever on whether the wind shall blow, nor does absolute love have any power, nor does it desire to have any power, over free will.

Now, absolute love may be seen in your system of physics as that which you call the speed of light. This is incorrect information, but it is as close as we can come to demonstrating the absolute constancy of love. It does not demonstrate the passion, the intensity of this love, but merely its constancy. Love cannot change. Love is what is. Love is beingness before beingness begins. This love has a small portion of its infinity, which is in itself an infinity.

Again, there are calculations we could give you—but not through this instrument—indicating that there is an apparent difference, but no true difference, betwixt love as intelligent infinity, and love which has decided to know itself. The first distortion of love is in itself an absolute equal to love, but at the same time subject to a different system of mathematics in which the energy of that which is free will being absolutely various falls away—as love does not—with distance from fields of energy which are created by the joining of love and free will. The Creator wished and wishes and will always wish in that infinitely small portion of its infinite self that is active, to manifest love, to love and feel the self of love in action.

And so it created its children, children of love and free will, one unit of absolute love that can never change and will never be unique, and [an] absolutely equal portion of infinitely various free will. That is your nature. Your uniqueness lies not in that you are children of love, but in that no two unions of love and free will are the same. To the outer, or mathematical eye, to any measuring instrumentation that could be imagined, this uniqueness could not be discerned, for free will, when bonded with love, takes upon itself the quality of love. The free will portion of it, the active portion of it, is forever, and in a way that mathematics cannot describe, various. Each of you has an absolutely equal, identical portion of love, and each of you has an equal and unique measure of free will. These differences cannot be used either in time/space as you know it or in space/time as you know it, for you are timeless beings.

You are the children of love before there was a context for you. You have been in many contexts, and each of you has shared many gross congruencies. You have been formed in time/space and in space/time in what seems to be identical fields of love/light or what you call electromagnetic fields. You have taken, not consciously, but by the very nature of this bonding, the rotations that form light, each of you being thus, first of all, light, and have gone from that first manifestation of beingness to more and more complex rotations and combinations of rotations and grades of rotation to form every field that has ever been examined by those who study such things empirically.

In the scientific world, therefore, it cannot be said in any scientifically provable way that one entity differs from another. It can be shown that some fields of some entities vary. It can also be shown that many of what you would call the cosmic fields of energy have anomalistic variations. Scientists cannot deal with anomalies, for they are not predictable. Thus, if you accept a scientific explanation of who you are, that you are this and this and this, a body, a mind, a spirit, organs working in a certain way, brain working in a certain way, and so forth, you shall never be able to describe how to know, how to feel, that of you which is unique.

There are gross uniquenesses, such as personality. You are well aware that these are a portion of the illusion in which you find yourself, but this is not your true uniqueness, my friends. Your true uniqueness is that each of you is free in a different way. You know, those of you who have had children, that no two children are alike, that each child moves into life with the personality biases strongly set. Each parent is aware that it can do nothing more than guide the arrow which has already been made. It is not the Creator which caused these unique children to be unique; it is the free will which was the creator of the children of the Creator.

Now, we have said that the difference between love and free will is based upon the fact that, though absolute in its variation, love will, in a time immeasurable to yourselves, lose energy, and gradually, as the end of a creation approaches, begin to leave—not in the sense of departure, but in the sense of strength of field energy—that which is you, so that eventually, at the end of a creation—and you know we speak of millions and billions of years— eventually [Love] calls to love in such a way that your uniqueness becomes a latent portion of love, and you are drawn wondrously, effortlessly, magnetically, and in a way which this instrument cannot describe, but which has to do with field theory, back into the great gravitation of Love. Love has taken a breath, has expelled from the Self love, and has breathed back into Itself love, but that which is free will has given to this absolute Love more and more experience of itself, because each child is unique in its core beingness, in its mathematical description, and as we say, there is no mathematics, even did this child know that language, which could express the kind of field which caused free will, or which bonded free will to love.

We shall have to ask you to accept that these things are so, that they are not mysterious to one who is capable of, not only unified field physics, but that physics which is of time/space. Thusly, we bow to the impossibility of explanation at this point, and ask that you trust that we have some little understanding of the creation physics of each field which is you. We can only say that as free will is infinitely various, so the children of love and free will are infinitely various in their expression of that which is absolutely identical in each. You are unique to the core of your being. You are mathematically unique. You are unique in ways that have nothing to do with opinion, or understanding, or any way of describing time or space.

Now, we are aware that we are taking much time, but we shall attempt to go forward with other questions having to do with uniqueness, and apologize if we speak too long. We shall attempt to be as brief as we can, knowing that all of you laugh inside at our foolish words, as does this instrument.

In all compassion, gaze upon your imperishable, infinite selves. How many, many choices, learnings, adventures, cruelties, forgivenesses and experiences of all kinds have each of you had. Not one of you will react as any other one of you to the same stimulus, and why? Because everything concerning your time/space beingness and your space/time beingnesses is based upon that which is unique in you. It may be immeasurable, it may be subtle, but you cannot be the same as another, as free will cannot be the same as itself. It is free. You are free. Yet you are free to do one thing only: to distort, to play, to experience, and to learn about love, that portion of yourself which you all do indeed have in absolute common.

Now we ask you to narrow your focus unimaginably. Let the infinity of illusions and creations and billions and billions of galaxies and stars and atoms and fields of energy fly from your mind. They are illusions which follow certain rules. We wish now to narrow your focus to that which you bring into this incarnation and that which you leave behind. You bring into this incarnation an inexorable difference from all else in the universe. When you were a rock you were an unique rock, and people who are sensitive to these things will tell you that there is a consciousness—and not the same consciousness, but various consciousnesses—in rocks. It is not strong enough yet to be obvious, but it is there. Your movement through these densities of experience until this third density of choice is the movement of the awakening of the free-will faculty.

You are now, at this moment, aware that you are children of love, and that you are children of complete freedom of choice. What many are not aware of is that all things that can be imagined, be they dark or light, are distortions of love. The only thing about which you may choose is love. It is often unrecognizable, so clever are you at distorting it, but your choices have to do with love, and in this density it has been created that this imperishable self that will go through this entire very, very long, to you, creation, make a choice within the illusion with such force, such willingness, such a surrender of absolute freedom of will, that you bond your free will in a general way, either to learning and expressing love by loving all that there is, yourself, love itself and all children of love, or choosing to deny that any but you is unique, that you are the center of the universe, that you are to be loved.

And you are loved. This is not an error, it is simple free-will choice. They say that the Creator has made it easier to follow the path of service to others, because it is a path that contains more truth, and that which is truth is that which will smooth your way. Those who deny that others are like the self are those who are depending very heavily upon free will, not depending upon love, and therefore depending on that field, or way of making a part of a field, which will in time become weaker, and finally will not be strong enough to fool the self that is aware into believing that only the self is love. It becomes apparent, in what you would call the sixth density, that all beings are love, and if you love yourself, which negative entities are excellent at doing, then so, against all previous understanding, must you love all that is as you are.

The courage that it takes, in this heavy illusion, when free will is at its strongest, to take that free will, and in the middle of the night with no light to guide you but the moon, working in shadow, working by faith, working without vocabulary or understanding, choose to discipline the free will, which is the great triumph, the great challenge, of entities who are experiencing their free will at its very strongest, to choose to discipline that will in such a way that it becomes not willfulness which is eternally various, but willingness, a will to do that which is chosen: this is the greatest and most courageous step an entity can take in this illusion, for it goes against all sense data. It is only one who trusts love, by faith alone, that asks the will to choose to will the good—if we may use that word— the radiant, the positive, the caring, to choose to emphasize those things about each which are the same, and that is love.

It takes an equal amount of courage to become so self-involved that a choice is made to ignore any truth but that which the self has chosen for itself, and thus disciplines the will to ignore all incoming data, to focus only on gaining power and an intensity of love for the self which is, by definition, a love of the Creator. That others are like itself is simply denied, and understandably so from the point of view of the negative entity. The negative entity is one whose free will is of a certain quirk, shall we say, that makes it seem obvious that the differences are greater than the similarities, and that love owes to love, the self owes to self, the aggrandizement of the self into the nature of the Creator, love itself.

This is seen by those who are neutral or working positively, as negative, because the negative entity will of course arrange, control and create its universe [in the way] which is most comfortable and advantageous to it. It does, however, have its own logic, and should never be treated with disrespect, but with the understanding that there are those whose uniqueness creates for them a free will which seems to be more paramount than the love that binds one to another. There is no less worship, there is no less sanctity in the negative than in the positive. It is simply a different distortion of the one love.

When you drop behind the tattered physical vehicle that has served you so well in this illusion, you will discover that you enter this illusion hoping and praying that you would choose, and choose with the utmost purity of which you are capable, one side or the other, because evolution calls in a way that has been spoken of by your scientists. Evolution [in the physical sense] is not incorrect, but incomplete. Spiritual evolution goes on, and on, and on, and the call to evolve is always there. Consequently, as you experience the many challenges and difficulties at this time, know that you put yourself where you are, that you may more and more passionately and purely choose the way you shall love.

We ourselves are those who have chosen the positive path, and we speak to those who have chosen the positive path. We encourage you never to be downhearted, but to pick yourselves up after every failure, knowing that this is part of the illusion, to move in rhythm with the varieties of your experience, looking for ways to learn how to love. You are not in your preincarnative state, incarnated in this density to be loved, to be understood, to be consoled, to be companioned, to be happy. These are goals within the illusion. The goal that will stay with you after your physical death, if you have chosen with purity, determination, persistence and will, is your path of service. That is not perishable, for it is a bias that is deeper than your personality with which you carry on existence within this illusion.

We believe that we have made a beginning at an understanding of the nature of your uniqueness, and are aware of the lack of specificity of some of our speech due to this instrument's lack of knowledge. We do not apologize, however, for as we said, we speak to those who need to be able to understand with their hearts, and not with their measuring devices or their scientific instruments. We thank this instrument for handling concepts that were new and foreign, and we appreciate the concentration that this instrument gave to us, which did make a fairly difficult subject somewhat clearer than it could have been. Shrugging with the knowledge that we have spoken incompletely, as was inevitable with this instrument, we would wish to move on to the instrument known as Jim. We are those of the principle, Q'uo, and we leave this instrument in the love and the light of the infinite One.

(Jim channeling)

I am Q'uo, and greet each again in love and light. At this time we would offer ourselves to any further queries that may be of service to those present. Is there a query at this time?

S: Yes, Q'uo. When one seeks spiritually, one needs to learn discipline, and in learning discipline, it sometimes seems that we learn a kind of power over our own personality. My understanding, though, of the difference between the positive and the negative path, has very much to do with power. I wonder if you can speak to the question of the different ways of seeking, some having to do with power, and being what I understand to be occult ways of seeking, others having to do with powerlessness, and being of a more mystical variety. Does discipline involve power over oneself?

I am Q'uo, and am aware of your query, my brother. *(Inaudible)* discipline of which you speak, for whatever purpose used, is a discipline over that focus of energy which you call love, much as a hose with the nozzle focuses water that it moves in a specific and particular fashion, able to do work of a physical [nature]. The discipline that you exercise when you focus your desire and the energy of love that is yours may be used for whatever purpose, be that purpose to master the personality, to control events or entities, to seek more knowledge of the mystery of creation, or simply to seek union with the One, that whatever may flow from that union may flow through you, as you are a hollowed vessel that has given itself in service to the One, that each of its portions with which you come in contact might be blessed and benefited. Thus, discipline is a tool as any other that may be used for whatever purpose is chosen.

Is there a further query, my brother?

S: Yes, my understanding is that in our seeking we reach plateaus, where we dwell sometimes, and then push ahead, and this constitutes a kind of stage, a procedure in stages. Are these stages marked off by what is called initiation—can you tell me something about the nature of initiation?

I am Q'uo, and we shall speak but briefly upon this topic, for it is one which deserves a far greater amount of time and effort than we feel is left within this group this evening. It is true that there are cycles or stages in the journey of union that are likened unto transformations of the entity from quality to quality as that which is heavier and more grossly constructed within the personality is refined and burned away, shall we say, by the fires of experience, so that that which remains is burnished and bright and serves as an honestation for the Creator.

There are various stages that an entity will be available to pass through during an incarnation that are determined before the incarnation as general categories in which lessons shall be attempted. As an entity assesses the upcoming, shall we say, incarnation and the potentials for growth that it wishes to include it will survey the kind of transformations, or initiations, as they are often called, that will be necessary to undergo as a portion of the learning process, much as a student within your colleges would determine what courses of mathematics would be necessary in order to master that particular field of study.

There are also times during the incarnational experience that what you may call a plateau of another nature is reached, this being determined by the entity's overall needs for some respite from the arduous journey. All journeys at some time tend to fatigue the pilgrim, for there are those times during which the steps are taken in directions that were not planned, that necessitate more expenditure of energy in order to learn the lessons of those steps than is readily available on a constant basis to the seeker. These plateaus are more obvious than are those initiations or transformations of which we had spoken previously. These, the initiations and transformations, more frequently occur in an unseen or unrecognized manner where the entity is totally immersed in some quality or distorted quality of its being as balance is attempted and attempted again and again until the transformation is complete.

Looking back upon the incarnation one may see times of difficulty and intensity as more likely having been the experience of such a time of transformation, during which time the entity may well have felt that there was no progress being made, and that indeed it would seem to the entity that it even moved backwards. The testing, as it were, however, transforms, and a new being moves forward.

Is there a further query, my brother?

S: Yes. It seems to me that these transformations are less than unique to each individual, having to do with the course in evolution that individual has been upon. Still, when it comes to the very difficult business of balancing, one looks for help where one can find it. Is there something that you can say about this help that is available to those of us who are seeking these transformations, and balancing and *(inaudible)*?

I am Q'uo, and am aware of your query, my brother. No one walks alone. This is important to recognize. As alone as one may feel in the most difficult experiences, there is always aid that is available, especially to the entity who seeks in a fervent manner using those rituals that you may call prayer or invocation, or in the sincere and heartfelt pleading that comes from that place deep within where the personality retreats when it has been stretched to and beyond, it would seem, its limits.

Each entity has at its beck and call, as it were, teachers, friends, guides and the force of light imbued with love, that move to support and inspire the entity through dreams, meditation and the presenting of the appropriate person, book, program or experience at the appropriate time within this process of learning. Thus, the entity that perseveres beyond all hope of success and who seeks ardently that assistance from within, shall move most efficaciously through whatever difficulty surrounds the process of learning which carries the entity on to a new plateau of beingness.

Is there a further query, my brother?

S: No, thank you very much.

I am Q'uo, and we thank you, my brother. Is there another query?

Carla: I'd like to follow up personally on what S said at the beginning. It has been my perhaps mistaken presumption that whether you seek positively or negatively you gain the same amount of power over yourself, it's just that you use it differently. I didn't exactly hear that, and S was talking about powerlessness. I realize that it feels like powerlessness to surrender to a self that you only know that you are by faith, because you can't feel it, but it seems to me that you are still very powerful, but it's only that you are dedicating your power to the will of the self that you carry within a deeper part of yourself. So, the apparent powerlessness is instead, by faith and will, a force with greater power than you could by yourself consciously ever have. This is my understanding. Could you correct it?

I am Q'uo, and am aware of your query, my sister. It is well stated that the greater power is that which comes through the entity rather than that which comes from the entity, for one is infinite, and the other finite. To surrender one's will to a greater power is to open a door through which the power of the universe may move in a more or less undistorted fashion.

Each entity, during the daily round of activities and the manner in which it expends its energy through various rituals and dedications, is given a certain amount of energy that powers the activity. The entity that attempts to harness this energy, for whatever purpose, harnesses that which, in effect, has a limit. To use this energy to surrender, as you have spoken, in faith to the greater power of the One is to offer an energy in service that far exceeds that which is the daily gift, shall we say.

Is there a further query, my sister?

Carla: Yes, but you don't have to answer it, it just may be too much. A friend of mine is going through an extremely painful period because she is full of faith, but she is going to the Southern Baptist Theological Seminary and the board, which is so conservative, is saying you must believe this and this and this or you do not have faith. It is something that I've told her, and I've told many people, that belief is antithetical to faith, that you can't give up your power of discernment to anything that is personalized, not even something that is called God, if you have to believe this and this, and everything else is wrong, because faith is faith without an object such as *(inaudible)* and love and things being all right.

Have I served my friend well by speaking to her in this way, or could I speak with her better?

I am Q'uo, and am aware of your query, my sister. We feel that your words have wisdom in them, and would not alter them, for the tendency towards beliefs is a tendency towards narrowing the opening of the door that we have spoken of before, and thus is also that which tends to reduce the ability to apprehend and to receive the blessings of love.

Is there a further query, my sister?

Carla: No Q'uo, you have given me a tremendous sense of relief with that answer, thank you very much.

I am Q'uo, and again we thank you, my sister. Is there another query at this time?

(Pause)

I am Q'uo, and we are most grateful to have been invited this evening to this circle of seeking, for it is one in which we have had the opportunity of greeting many old and dear friends, and we thank each for the love that has been offered to us, and for the opportunity of returning that love to each. We bless each upon the journey which we all share. We shall take our leave of this instrument and this circle at this time. We are known to you as those of Q'uo. We leave each in the love and in the light of the one infinite Creator. Adonai, my friends. Adonai. ✣

L/L Research

L/L Research is a subsidiary of Rock Creek Research & Development Laboratories, Inc.

P.O. Box 5195
Louisville, KY 40255-0195

www.llresearch.org

Rock Creek is a non-profit corporation dedicated to discovering and sharing information which may aid in the spiritual evolution of humankind.

ABOUT THE CONTENTS OF THIS TRANSCRIPT: This telepathic channeling has been taken from transcriptions of the weekly study and meditation meetings of the Rock Creek Research & Development Laboratories and L/L Research. It is offered in the hope that it may be useful to you. As the Confederation entities always make a point of saying, please use your discrimination and judgment in assessing this material. If something rings true to you, fine. If something does not resonate, please leave it behind, for neither we nor those of the Confederation would wish to be a stumbling block for any.

© 2009 L/L Research

Sunday Meditation
May 20, 1990

Group question: The question this evening has to do with man's ability to ask questions that are quite beyond his ability to answer. This is especially true in the field of mathematics, where there is an endless array of questions that can logically be asked, but which seem to require an intellect far beyond man's ability to answer. What kind of intellect would be necessary to answer questions of this nature, and of what value to the evolution of humankind is it to be able both to ask and to answer these kinds of question?

(Carla channeling)

I am known to you as the principle Q'uo, and I greet each and bless each in the love and in the light of the one infinite Creator. May it be with you always as it is at this moment. May blessings abide, may peace continue, and may your search for the truth burn ever brighter in your souls and in your hearts. We are extremely grateful for the opportunity to share in this circle of seeking. We too seek the truth, and we come not to give you that which is infallible, but to share with you that which we have learned during a journey which has gone farther than yours, giving us the perspective that we may offer you. We ask you to listen to these thoughts, not with a mind to accept, but after all is said and done, remove the gullibility, the openness, and the clear listening that is so much a part of our being able to speak with you, and discern carefully that which has spoken to you, resonated to you, and seems to be to you a truth that is not known for the first time, but remembered. If such does not occur, we ask you humbly to leave this information, for it belongs away from your path of seeking, for we would not be a stumbling block to any. It is our purpose here only to be of service, and we thank you with open and loving hearts for allowing us this privilege, for this privilege allows us too to grow, as teachers always grow more than their students.

You ask a question this evening that is not at all what it seems. We shall, as we have before, have difficulty in language, for this instrument is completely without scientific awareness of any formal educative kind, and therefore her vocabulary—which we use always, as this is conscious, concept communication—must bridge the gap between our concepts and the clothing of those concepts in appropriate wording. However, this instrument's very lack of expertise is in some way that which opens our ability to make connections that may not have been made before.

The question seems to concern mathematics. It asks the simple yet profound question which is interesting, and which may be followed for some of your time. We will attempt not to use all of that time, as this instrument scolds us so fiercely for speaking too long, but the concepts which we wish to get across to you are not what you would expect, and therefore we must go carefully ahead with each step in our logical disquisition.

You note that mathematical questions are asked that cannot be answered. And you wonder if they simply cannot be answered, or if there has simply not yet been born a mathematician able to answer these questions. Now, we shall begin with an observation of the type of function that mathematics plays. By the use of mathematics in its pure form, a structural concept web or field has been generated which may be compared to the naming of various techniques, kinds of food, and in certain combinations, the means to prepare this food, which can then be observed to be able to create an empirically based and internally cogent system of observations which form the basis for those disciplines of the scientist which enjoy the creation of machinery, of those gadgets which work because of electricity or magnetism, and of a very large field of more sophisticated topographies or models of the universe, in which events may be seen to fall in some logical order, thus giving to the classical, rational thinker the joy of the manipulation of this self-consistent web of cogent bits or elements.

This may seem to be a less than elegant rendering of the processes of mathematics, of [the] scientific method and its extremely baroque system of corollary sciences, all developed by the empirical method of observation, hypothesis, experimentation, the hypothesis proven or disproven, and this being done in a repetitive manner, which indicates that the pieces or bits which this web offers have been useful in producing that which may move from the theoretical to the useful in the mundane sense.

It is interesting to note in this regard that the greatest intellects in this, as in any field, sometimes tend to become mystics which focus upon the mystery of those questions that have not been answered, and indeed have oftimes spoken strongly to the effect that any scientist who is not also profoundly a believer of faith and mystery has not seen the true scope of the particular discipline which has been studied.

Now let us go back to the view of mathematics. We ask that each consider its nature. It is a language. A mathematician may speak nonsensically, it may speak clumsily, it may speak with elegant exactitude. The variations in the schools of mathematicians are the variations of ability to use the language of mathematics. Just as there are those which find one truth in life, and speak in the native tongue about this truth to the absolute boredom of all around it, so there are some mathematicians which become excited about one portion of this language, and move far along this particular path of thinking, and become extremely adept at using this particular part of the language without feeling the need to move further in exploring the possibilities of this language.

If there is any residual doubt that mathematics is a functioning language, one has only to go to one of your libraries and extract from it a treatise which is written in two languages. Indeed, there are sentences in which English and mathematics are both used. The scientist will say "this and this and this" in mathematical terms, and then will say "from this it is evident that" and then there will come another series of mathematical terms. Like German, Turkish, Romanian or English, mathematics is a language, and the mathematician who is most truly suited to the pure seeking within this field is the artist who follows a muse, for it is possible in mathematics to speak badly or well, to speak stodgily or lyrically, and to form the poor sentence or the exquisite, eloquent sentence.

Those who would be most likely to be able to express simple expressions of complex, impossible questions, are those who have abilities in more than one language. If one is a writer, the study of mathematics will make that entity a better writer, because there are accuracies and nuances in mathematics that inform the writer in the use of the English language, or any language in which the writer chooses to pen his words. Similarly, the mathematician who has studied music, especially harmony, is in perhaps the most helpful situation, as these two systems of notation have a great deal in common, and therefore may flow one to the other and back again with more ease. The architecture of the music is, like that of mathematics, made up of ineluctable ratios. The creating of tone is mathematical in nature, and the creation of a musical or artistic mathematics is therefore the cross-inspiration.

Let us say that the nature of all language within third density is such that it cannot describe anything but that which is an illusion, mathematics being a language which describes the local, shall we say, environment of fields, groups of fields, rotations and quantized rotations of light which create all that there is and all that may be observed. Just as instrumentation in the study of the atom moves the scientist ever deeper into what seems to be a recreation of outer space, until finally all that may be seen of the atom is the path of its energy, and so is mystery born within the mind of that scientist, just so, in the language of mathematics and in a purer and intellectual sense, a man may seek a kind of holiness or sanctity as a mathematical mystic who is aware of that which lies beyond the limit of language, that which is beyond the limit of the notes and the arrangement of notes in music, [that which] touches and moves the soul and the heart and the emotions into a state of purified emotion which cannot be explained by the language used.

So it is in mathematics for one whose muse is truly that of the mathematics. One may see and delight in the many oddities that make the architecture of this language so rich and beautiful. This entity may then gaze upon that marvelous, euphonious amalgamation of mathematical words, shall we say, or pieces of notation, which brings one to a thrilling discovery, a purified emotion, and a wonder, a passion and an adoration of that which lies beyond the language.

Into each type of notation or language is placed two ultimate resolutions: paradox and mystery. One who follows the muse and becomes the artist, able to play the scales, able to play all that is created, and able to feel also with purified emotion the paradoxes and the mysteries which lie between the lines in the noumenal area, [so] that the mind retains each of these parts of music, of mathematics, may we say, even of computer programming, of any language, is privy to a wisdom of learning that concept [that] moves beyond words, that is wonder, that is mystery. The artist sees the beauty; the artist sees the elegance of the beautiful written language. But the artist is also aware of the most marvelous portion of the language, that language which will forever escape the tongue, or the pen, that language which is not local, and cannot describe anything, for there is nothing to describe that lies within the ken of the observer.

Now, when all this has been processed and grasped in some wise by the student of a particular language, it is possible for that student to become aware of its relationship to the noumenal, to that which is mysterious and paradoxical and beyond the ken of the intellectual mind. There shall be two children of this attitude. The first is merriment, for the deep humor of the universe lies in all languages for the entity opening up to its nuances. Secondly, and perhaps more profoundly, such an entity may realize that there is a portion of itself which is also of the mystery, noumenal, beyond human concept, beyond this density of illusion which may be described mathematically in such and such a way, musically in such and such a way, poetically in such and such a way.

Where words end, there a new and larger and non-local frame of reference begins. This frame of reference lies within one, and it is possible that one which seeks in this deep mind, through meditation, requests in the dreaming, and other means of communicating with one's own unconscious self, may begin to intuit a non-local and fully articulated concept-language which shall have to remain naked of words, because within this illusion the natural laws of the infinite One must needs be kept. However, it is entities such as this which enter into experiments as a part of the experiment, and change the results.

It is forever frustrating to entities who are not in this frame of reference that such results seem only paradoxical and cannot be useful within the illusion. There is, however, the great peace of beginning to grasp timelessness, spacelessness, true simultaneity of all that there is, the nature of infinity, and those many, many mysteries that leave the intellect stuck in paradox after paradox after paradox. To some that shift shall always be an irritation, to others, a challenge, and to others, a wonderful and beguiling poem, a hint that there is more to come, and that each seeker of truth shall one day be more than it is at this point.

This is a dense illusion, and it is well for all of those with the muse to keep themselves grounded in the local rules of whatever language they are using. To communicate with others it is well to use the language well. There is a pride in excellence that one must needs encourage, for all you have, just as all we have, are the concepts that we give this instrument. Now this instrument struggles to clothe each naked concept in shabby, poor and patched clothing. Such it is for each language, that each of you may be a poet, each of you may inspire, each of you may develop a passion, a love of this naked, conceptual mystery.

All paths lead to the love of this mystery which we call love, the great original Thought that created all that there is. Thus, each may become far more wise than he may articulate, and that wisdom, beauty and imperishability shall be his alone, his to treasure, his to place with respect and love, where it belongs, within the heart and in the soul, within that portion of the self that always has been and always will be. There is wisdom to be found in the picking up of a grain of sand, or a piece of straw. There is love in a dusty window, or the croaking of a frog. All things are sacramental to those who have acquired that language of concept which lies beyond words. Approach it from any study whatsoever, and the same results shall be yielded.

May your language be one of beauty, and may your passion for the truth build a fire within you that warms your heart and fuels your desire and your will to live as imperishable and eternal beings, not caught in the net of what must be, in this local habitation that you call planet Earth. You shall not always exist in this island of intelligence. You shall move forward, and all languages pay due respect to those things which make one's service to one's fellow man the greatest. And then, through meditation, contemplation, vision, prayer and dream, cherish that deep part of yourself which is one with all that there is, and is at bottom part of the Creator.

Look to yourself to the alleluia of love for all that you see, and all that you can learn, and with humor and excellence use the words that are your vocabulary, letting them shine, playing with them, showing their wonder as well as their use, to those who wish to see that which you know. You are both here and not here. You are infinite, and you are in an illusion. Love both of these, love the paradox, and most of all, love the Creator, yourself and each other, in whatever language you know.

We would at this time apologize, for once again we have heard the signal that says we have spoken too long. We are sorry, and we will attempt to speak more briefly when you call us next, as we do hope that you will. It has been a struggle speaking through this instrument, for it does not have the words even to describe the words of other languages, but it has put our ability to make concepts clear to a test, and therefore it has helped us to learn to communicate also. We would at this time close the meeting through the one known as Jim. We leave this instrument in love and light. We are of the principle of those of Q'uo.

(Jim channeling)

I am Q'uo, and greet each again in love and light through this instrument. At this time we would offer ourselves in the attempt to answer any further queries which may remain upon the minds of those present. Is there a query at this time?

S: I am S, and am grateful for your answers, and would like to think of them.

I am Q'uo, and we are most grateful to have been asked to join this circle of seeking. It has been our great honor and privilege to have been able to blend our vibrations with yours and to speak upon those topics which are of importance to you at this time.

If there are no further queries, then we shall, with great gratitude, take our leave of this instrument and this group, leaving each as always in the love and in the light of the one infinite Creator. We are known to you as those of Q'uo. Adonai, my friends. Adonai. ♣

Sunday Meditation
May 27, 1990

Group question: The question this evening has to do with how preincarnative choices are put into motion in the incarnation. It seems very likely that the childhood experiences at an early age—at the age of seven, or ten, or somewhere around there—have the effect of influencing the child in the direction of the preincarnative choice, so that the child may be imbued with self-confidence, or a lack of self-confidence, with anger, or with compassion, with the ability to work with other people in groups, or the lack of that ability. It seems that there is a series of experiences, usually with the parents, or with brothers or sisters, or neighbors, at that age that imprints so strongly upon the child that the child then carries that imprint throughout the life, and uses that effect to work on himself either consciously or unconsciously, so that the desires and choices before the incarnation are focused on because they're set in motion during childhood. Is this a correct assumption, and if it is, could you elaborate on how this works?

(Carla channeling)

I am Latwii, and I greet you in the love and the light of the one infinite Creator. We are most happy to be with you this evening, and are wishing to extend the greetings of those known as Ra whose company is normally blended with our own. However, this instrument prays for the highest contact it may receive in a stable and healthful manner, and it is very weak. This contact is possible almost completely because of the great love and mutual respect of this circle, each for the other. When we have this sort of harmony, we may use the energy of the instrument with far more safety.

You ask this evening about the preincarnatively chosen structures, limitations, biases and thinking processes which affect the young child until the age of seven or so. This is an interesting topic. The entity which is the young spirit is the designer of these experiences and has chosen the catalyst knowing the behaviors and catalysts that would create the lifetime pattern of learning. Make no mistake, there is no villain but your own wiser self, which wishes you to experience that which seems unbearable so that you may learn to empty yourself of insignificant expectation. This is an act of desire to learn, and may be directly attributed to yourself. This is not easy to remember, and impossible to appreciate when you are suffering, either mentally, emotionally, physically or spiritually. But each of you is not the limited entity whose ears hear our words. Each of you is a very powerful being; a being, in fact, of infinite power. It is the wish of the growing spirit so to use this power that the positivity, light and good of eternity may be apprehended by the self.

It would seem that in choosing the early childhood abandonment, invalidation of reality and scorn, that the higher self wishes to set up a no-win situation, and there are many who remain at this place or condition of consciousness for the life experience, moving around the difficulties of feeling unworthy, abandoned, lonely and sorrowful and allowing this to be, not catalyst, but a continuing picture of reality as you know it in this illusion. But within each of you there is a quality peculiarly your own, and that is your free will. The seeking entity chooses to examine not the surface of the feelings only, not the suffering only, but the reason for them.

The third-density question is "Why?" You know, more and more, what you are as you pursue your own personal truth. A curious person, a person who wants to know why it has been abandoned, and why it must feel abandoned for a whole lifetime, is ripe for a maturation, a blooming, which will involve releasing the identity of "the abandoned one." There is a fear of releasing one's identity, no matter what it is. The feeling of unworthiness is often crushing and, indeed, is encouraged and nurtured mercilessly by early childhood catalyst. This sense of unworthiness, poor as it is, is an identity and, to change, one must surrender this identity. Again you gaze at suffering and change.

Thus we link early childhood to preincarnative, eternal beingness, and state that there is a purpose for the incredible suffering that is so often the lot of the sensitive being. The sensitive being tends to build a fort, or a fortification, so that it may not be so hurt by circumstance. This fortification must be consciously torn down to effect a change in self-image. Before you came to this experience, you knew that you were loved, that you were whole, perfect, unblemished, loving and beloved by the Creator Self, a child of the Father of all that there is, of the Mother of all that there is. But this knowledge does little good if it is not challenged.

This instrument has low energy into the heart chakra because it is blocked in red ray as it questions its right to be alive. It is blocked in orange ray by its reluctance to accept freely given love. That is why we must speak carefully and slowly. This instrument is, at this moment, typical of the nature of energy blockages among your people. It is experiencing that which comes to all, or very nearly all, spirits. It has itself noted one mystery: try as it might, swear and kick and rage, it cannot give up hope. This hope, which may be called faith, is that which holds the entity in a safe energy web as it is dismantled, as programs in the consciousness are changed, and new possibilities are opened for data input and new programming, to use the terms of the computer, which so resembles the choices of the consciousness that we find them useful.

You are warriors. Let this sink deep into your heart. You are not people of peace, as your language intends this word. You have come here to disrupt, destroy and remake yourself according to free will choices having to do with why you are here. When all the reasons of the illusion are cast aside, finally the intelligence gazes upon those things which are changeless. There are two: light is not changed by any relation it might have to any other energy field or movement; love is a constant within each entity's aching and anguished heart. It may not feel loved, but, against all reason, it loves. Therefore, those who ask, "Why?" are given two considerations which speak of eternity: love and light. Such abstractness does not help the conscious mind or lift the suffering spirit. But the pilgrim soul keeps asking, "Why?" and finding that in terms of ideal or unchangeable things, this question deals with love and light. The question cannot be answered, and so each entity chooses to align itself with love and light without anything but hope or faith to guide the choice.

We shall not, this evening, attempt inspiration, for each entity is aware that first the great power of the self that lies beyond abandonment, unworthiness and loneliness is that mystery of self which does not reveal itself except in darkest shadow. You are creatures starving, and you have only faith and hope, because you see that there is light and there is love and no one can deny either, and you see yourself as one whose quest for the truth cannot be denied. Does this then ally you with infinite and imperishable things? The intuitive answer is, "Yes," and this is the rock-bottom of despair, the thirst and blankness and emptiness of the desert, the time of no hope, except that there is always hope, because you cannot help but ask, "Why?" and seek "Why?" yet find the infinite values in substance to remain. Who among you or we can expect to remain in hopeful, cheerful and joyful conditions always? This we do not promise you, but rather promise you despair, darkness, loneliness and hopelessness. But never is that condition complete, because of that within you which hopes and lives by faith. "If you go to Sheol, I AM there. There is nowhere you can go that I AM not present," declares love.

Suffer as you must in order to grow. Gaze with careful and open eyes at your choices of early childhood conditioning. You have chosen your own hell. You have also chosen your own heaven. Focus your power and ask why. Find your undeniable hope and acknowledge it without understanding it. Persevere. We shall not ask you, this evening, to be merry, for you ask, "What of despair?" There is little merriment in this condition. Yet know that this condition was created as an important and cyclical phase of your development, as a beacon of love and light to the Creator, to yourself, and to the world. Let all fail, let hopelessness reign, this condition cannot be sustained. You are irrepressible. Watch yourself grow, and remember, as you rejoice in those times of blooming, how great was the pain of birth.

We would at this time close this meeting by asking the one known as Jim if it would accept our contact. We are those of Latwii.

(Jim channeling)

I am Latwii, and greet each again in love and light. At this time we would ask if we may speak to any further queries within this group, as it is our privilege to do so.

Carla: I know you can't answer this specifically, but I just can't imagine why I put myself at bed rest for the rest of my life. I just don't understand.

I am Latwii. We are aware of your query, and your suffering, my sister, and we wish that we could speak words that would relieve the pain and the limitation, but we find that there are not only few words that speak centrally to your suffering, but that we have a great desire that you should find your way through this maze of misery, for there is no challenge given that is this great that does not have equally great rewards that await the patient and long-suffering seeker.

Your illusion is one which is unique in all of the creation, for it is in your illusion that the face of the Creator is so well hidden that oftentimes it seems that one is alone, one is abandoned, and one has nothing but one's own misery to experience. This darkness of being in some degree visits each, for this is what your illusion presents to those who enter its door, the opportunity to seek the Creator in the darkest reaches of the creation, those places where it seems no light has ever shone, those corners and closets of the self which is heavily burdened with sickness, sorrow and suffering, those qualities that are so readily available within your illusion and which so toughly test the able spirit to see if there is any place within the illusion that love cannot be found, to see if there is any wound that love cannot heal.

Thus, each of you moves into this illusion knowing that you shall move in the valley of the shadow of death, as you have had it called, that you shall call upon those inner resources that are your birthright in a way in which they have never been invoked before. In this way you imbue every cell of your soul with the strength of your seeking, with the faith that is only found in those who are already strengthened by overcoming previous suffering that is great.

My sister, you rest upon the bed of nails, as it were, for that body which you inhabit is one which is pierced by pain. It is a body which carries you now, but carefully, that you may ride further into those reaches of the self which remain to be explored, and which few ever dream of exploring, for though the rewards are great, the cost is equally great, for each endeavor that promises further advancement upon the spiritual journey has its cost. Eventually each of you shall give all that you have at the door of death, as you call it, that you might once again enter into the realm of unity and love. The price is high for those who seek purely. This is a truth which each viewed before the incarnation began, and which each undertook solemnly, knowing that there would be difficulty, yet welcoming that difficulty, for by enduring and overcoming there is the victory of the spirit and its purification that it might become …

(Side one of tape ends.)

Carla: The few which are present have all gone through suffering the illness *(inaudible)*, gone through, [having to] watch a perfectly well, living person sicken and die over many months or years. Each of us has come to *(inaudible)* and gone over them. I know in E's dying, if I hadn't been there to be as good a friend as I could to T he would perhaps have had some kind of mental breakdown. I know that if either Jim or I had not had each other when dealing with Don's mental illness I would definitely have not survived, and it is possible that neither of us would have. Is there some special reason we have been drawn together, as our paths seem to be unusually similar in this? It seems to me to be perhaps the worst burden of an ill person, that other people must suffer for the self. It seems grossly unfair, and *(inaudible)* and there isn't a thing that the ill person can do about it.

I am Latwii, and am aware of your query, my sister. When entities such as yourselves enter the incarnation with the purpose of providing as much light, shall we say, as is possible, then there are those patterns, or techniques, of livingness that are invoked. These have to do with providing the setting that will allow the service that has been desired. Oftentimes the service requires a certain kind of personal advancement that is not possible without great testing. The testing may take many forms. Within certain groups of entities it is known that the experience of the loss of the loved one is a kind of testing that will prepare the person not only for those inner initiations of a personal level, but, through the passing through of these initiations, will allow that entity to provide a service to others that would not be possible without the initiation.

Thus, you find in may cases where groupings of entities have incarnated many times together, that there is a pattern of learning and serving that is utilized within these groups, which when viewed from within the limited confines of the illusion will seem to be greatly distorted towards personal suffering, with little hint of the purpose or reason. It is only when the illusion is seen from outside of the illusion and the incarnation that one may see the purpose of the pattern, the opportunity that is presented.

As often as it is said within the illusion, it seems trite to say that there is no suffering without purpose. To one who has long suffered and long sought the purpose and yet has not found that purpose, it is not the greatest of consolations to know that there is yet a purpose. However, we tell you that this is so. That one may suffer long and deeply within your illusion is an experience that carries weight within the total beingness of the entity. There is no suffering that is unrewarded. All has a purpose; all purposes serve the One; the One is in each and every entity that one touches in the daily round of activities. As much as is possible within the painful confines of your illusion, your bodies and your situations, rest in the knowledge that you do nothing in vain. All is divinely inspired. There is a purpose.

Is there another query, my sister?

Carla: A final question is this, a general one. The one known as S feels that you are her personal comforter. She has been suffering greatly lately, and I am sure would appreciate anything that you would say, as she feels so alone at this time.

I am Latwii, and am aware of your query, my sister. Each word that we have spoken this evening may be heard by the one known as S as if that word were spoken for her, for indeed this is so. This one is close to us, indeed, we comfort her, yet many are the times when this one has been comforted and has not felt that comfort, for its isolation has been great, its perception of that isolation has been so great as to insulate it on occasion from that aid which is available.

We would say to this one, that we do indeed love you with all of our being. We are never far from you. We seek to aid you in those ways which you open to us. Find a ray of light and hope within your being and follow that ray to its source. There, on that journey which is inward only, you will find many friends, and among them we shall be rejoicing to greet you, for we know that which you endure. There are many upon the surface of this planet which feel this solitude, this abandonment, and yet we say that there is no darkness and no abandonment that does not have a purpose within the overall plan of each entity that experiences these qualities.

In order for any seed to be grown within your illusion it must be put within the dark earth. There must be a time of resting there, away from light, in order that what is within the seed might burst the shell, the limitation, the confines of that experience and break forth toward the light in order that there might be a new being born from the old. The experience of transformation for any entity within your illusion, when seen from our vantage point, takes place in but the blinking of an eye, yet we know that within your illusion this same transformation seems to last far, far into the dark and lonely night, and we feel our compassion for you growing as we become one with you and experience that loneliness, the pain of separation.

Yet, we encourage each to persevere, for each is a good seed with much yet to offer in the blooming. The cycles move, the seasons change, the soul once again will enliven the personality that lives within the illusion, and there will again be the joy of the heart that springs forth into summer and into the full fruiting that is possible for each seeker of truth.

We are with you. We endure with you, we seek with you, we await with you the light and the love of the Creator that does always nourish each, and which each in its own time will bring forth into new fruit and joyful experience.

Is there a further query, my sister?

Carla: No, I thank you on S's behalf and on my own.

I am Latwii, and we thank you once again, my sister. Is there another query at this time?

Carla: Not from me, thank you.

I am Latwii, and it has been our unusual and great pleasure to speak to this group this evening. We hope that our words might have some use for each, that each may find support and nourishment in the times that are difficult. We are with each at all times, and we leave each in that love and light of the one infinite Creator which does not fail. We are known to you as those of Latwii. Adonai, my friends. Adonai.

L/L Research

L/L Research is a subsidiary of Rock Creek Research & Development Laboratories, Inc.

P.O. Box 5195
Louisville, KY 40255-0195

www.llresearch.org

Rock Creek is a non-profit corporation dedicated to discovering and sharing information which may aid in the spiritual evolution of humankind.

ABOUT THE CONTENTS OF THIS TRANSCRIPT: This telepathic channeling has been taken from transcriptions of the weekly study and meditation meetings of the Rock Creek Research & Development Laboratories and L/L Research. It is offered in the hope that it may be useful to you. As the Confederation entities always make a point of saying, please use your discrimination and judgment in assessing this material. If something rings true to you, fine. If something does not resonate, please leave it behind, for neither we nor those of the Confederation would wish to be a stumbling block for any.

© 2009 L/L RESEARCH

Sunday Meditation
June 3, 1990

Group question: The question this evening has to do with an experience of Carla's that is generally applicable to anybody who's in a situation which has a great deal of difficulty and stress in it. When one finds oneself, shall we say, up against the wall, with a lot of pain and suffering of whatever kind, and has very little ability to change the situation, no control over it, is totally at the mercy of it, how is it that it is possible for some people to maintain a faith that all is well, a faith in the Creator, and still be totally angry at the Creator and totally angry at the situation? Is this a helpful configuration for spiritual growth, and is there an explanation for such a situation, and how can the most helpful mental attitude be adopted in the situation?

(Carla channeling)

I am Q'uo, and I greet you in joy, in the love and in the light of the one infinite Creator. Also greeting this group is the one known as Hatonn, who has come merely to give greeting to one dear to them. We offer from Hatonn greetings to the one known as H. We of the principle of Q'uo are extremely grateful to have received your call for information on a subject of the paradoxes that are apparent in stressful situations within your third-density illusion.

Let us begin by gazing at the one great original Thought that is Love, the Creator of all things. This entity created a certain kind of creation. Many have been your attempts to understand meanings, and the nuances and the subtleties of that mind which is not the conscious mind, nor the unconscious mind, nor the deep mind, nor the racial mind, but the archetypical mind. You have wondered how to use information concerning the archetypical mind. It has always been quite difficult to express the means of use of this deep resource of your infinite mind which in its totality is a part of the creation and the Creator. The archetypical mind is not a mind to be, shall we say, studied for harvesting of understanding, but rather looked to in situations which contain apparent paradox within one's own mind.

One of the principles of the archetypical mind is that archetype called Hope, or Faith. Now, these archetypes are in place as a portion of the birthright of each individual which is the son or daughter of the infinite Creator. However, it is the result of much experience involving a final and absolute strengthening of a particular pillar of the archetypical structure of the mind which makes it possible for one consciously to be aware of this unmovable archetype, part of the architecture or structure of the deep mind. It exists without regard to the third-density illusory experience which the conscious mind perceives as catalyst and reacts to as it chooses. The archetype of Faith or Hope, therefore, is much like the deep and solid earth which lies beneath the fissures, honeycombed caves, and many irregularities of the land and sea masses and their tectonic plates which make up the moveable, or malleable, or reactive body of the living creature which you call the Earth.

In each person, these archetypes may or may not, in previous experiences of incarnation, have become apparent and recognized as a portion of the birthright and very nature of the unchangeable solidity of your imperishable and infinite self. Thus, not all will experience, in a situation in which faith and hope are tested, an inability to deny faith, for the reason that each entity in its free will has in its many experiences made millions of choices concerning that of which it wishes to become aware in a whole sense.

Let us spend a moment upon this word, "whole," or "entire." The closest link which each of you has to the deeper portions of the self involves the full opening of the heart to its own nature, which is love. It has often been described to you as the seat of unconditional love. However, this suggests that it is an activity. Indeed, the fully opened heart is unconditional love, and love, therefore, is not a love for another with condition, but a love with another as the self.

Many are the confusions that have assailed each when seemingly ill, and certainly this instrument, as many have attempted to heal this instrument of the bodily difficulties it experiences; nor would we deny the obvious nature of this instrument's lack of what you would call health. However, in the sense of being whole, to the extent that one has allowed the pain, the blockage, the limitation, the self-loathing, or whatever is the deeper expression of this illness, to be accepted and loved within the heart, the entity is becoming whole, and it is this state of wholeness, aided greatly by the indigo chakra work of daily meditation, self-forgiveness and other inner work, which will most reliably and quickly make possible the resonance of daily catalyst so that the catalyst may sink into the area of the archetypical mind and the archetype which is being expressed, recognized. Once this archetype is recognized by the whole or open self, it then becomes a deep portion of the mind, a portion of the biases which survive the forgetting process which opens each incarnation.

Each of your experiences with infants shows you there are no two infants which are entering third-density incarnation with the same biases. Each is unique from the first and has been unique, wholly blessed and sanctified, as are you, by the love of the infinite One, since before time and space and that grand celestial illusion of all of the energy fields of body, gravitation and all of the mechanisms of the infinite cosmos. Therefore, this instrument was not able to deny faith or hope, because it had been recognized as a birthright, as a part of the structure of being, which would be as difficult not to accept as it would be for a person with eyes upon a brick wall to deny the existence of that wall.

In the conscious use of catalyst in third density, however, any entity will be creating, or attempting to create, a more positive action, in an unpredictable number of ways depending upon that person's momentary degree of self-forgiveness, of grasping of the nature of catalyst and of the temporal and mundane personality of the illusory self. As this instrument was paralyzed and informed that, even though paralysis left, it must remain bedfast for this incarnation, it was not surprising that a deep rage against this limitation would fill the heart and cause massive blockage and a very weakened vitality of spirit in the conscious mind. And although many other blows which have come to those within this circle may not be so serious or lengthy in their prognostication, they are, nevertheless, of an equivalent painfulness at the moment they are felt.

Some entities in this circle have become aware of the archetype of Faith, and therefore cannot deny it. Others have not made this connection with the birthright of the self. Thus, not to each person shall this particular seeming schizophrenia occur.

There are, however, many archetypes. Perhaps the most commonly discovered is the archetype of the new mind, empty of experience. This archetype is one which each in this circle is aware exists, and each could not find a way to state unequivocally that one can never make a new and fresh beginning to a life experience. Indeed, this archetype was first learned through the fires of many lifetimes of self-condemnation and the discovery that forgiveness does occur, regardless of one's opinion of oneself, at some unpredictable point because forgiveness, the redemption from error, is part of the basic truth of each entity's makeup.

Thus, each of you fails and has the subjective [self-]criticism which can be the cruelest and harshest criticism leveled by any, harsher than any other would give to you. Yet, at the same time there is the undeniable awareness of the absolute possibility of beginning anew with a new mind, a new heart, and a clean and unblemished conscience. Each of you has done the work necessary to learn this basic archetype, this basic part of the architecture of the self, and in many cases it is a part of why many do not feel it appropriate to seek forgiveness from an outer source when the Creator has placed within the self, in a sanctified and permanent structure, the very heart of self-forgiveness which must always precede new beginnings.

Each of you who has studied the archetypes of mind, body and spirit may examine each archetype to discover more and more of its basic nature. Those archetypes which one is unable to deny, no matter how outer circumstances seem to be in a paradoxical relationship to it, is a portion of the self now known as part of the whole, or healed, or open being.

We would speak of only two things more, for this instrument is asking us, as always, to be more brief. Your planet has also its evolution in consciousness. The surety of various archetypes that you feel are helpful to its growth, and above all the love of the open heart blesses and raises the vibrations and consciousness of the fragile island home which you call Earth. It is appropriate for each of you to share each learning with the native soil which has been the earthly mother and father of the physical vehicle which has made these catalytic experiences possible. Love your planet as you would love your parents, for the Earth upon which you stand loves and heals and cares for each of you without any question, for you are its children too.

Lastly, we would speak to each of the basic nature of paradox. The mundane illusion of everyday works well to instill in one a sense of less than full self-worth. It often seems to bring out in each personality the less attractive portions of each entity's surface being. This is why you are here; this is your classroom. You are here to penetrate the illusion of catalyst, to see deeper and deeper into the present moment until the basic nature of the self is more and more apparent. Meanwhile, the surface personality rages, and whines, and cries, and grieves, and laughs, and plays its many roles upon the stage of the illusion.

You must feel free to express to yourself to the fullest all emotion, no matter how hateful or seemingly harmful or subjectively not approved, for it is in expressing the self fully and then taking the self in its own arms, into its own heart, and loving, and being loved by this child that you are, consciously, that your spiritual evolution depends. Never, ever, try to repress or deny negative feelings, but open your heart to them. They are yours to love and comfort, for you are children of the illusion, and only imperishable and immature beings as metaphysical beings. You are not upon this planet at this time because you have achieved maturity. Had you achieved such a thing you would have no need to choose to love and to heal.

May you love the Creator who first loved you, and whose nature is your nature. May you honor the free will which sends you to a million emotional states, for this is your catalyst; this is how you learn to love. May you learn to love yourself wholly and entirely, accepting all of yourself. That is the healed person, not the person without physical blemish. And may you love each other, for you are all one self.

We would leave this instrument and you in the heart that is the one great original Thought of Love, which is the Creator, and would transfer this contact to the entity known as Jim, if this instrument is willing to serve. We thank this instrument and would now transfer. We are those of Q'uo and Hatonn.

(Jim channeling)

I am Q'uo, and greet each again in love and light through this instrument. At this time it is our privilege to ask if we may speak to any further query. We remind each present that we are happy to speak to the best of our ability that which is our experience and that which is our opinion, and we would wish that each realize that we are not infallible, that it is well to take those words and thoughts which have the ring of truth to the self, and leave all others behind. Is there a query at this time?

S: Yes, Q'uo. Sometimes, when one looks very starkly at one's condition, one sees a kind of rejection of perfection, very deeply rooted, which is a repulsion of self, and also directed at the Creator, for as we know we are of the Creator. It's a repulsion of the Creator as the Creator. I'm trying to understand how it comes about that the Creator, in order to know the Creator, needs this deep feeling. Can you speak to the question of why healing seems so primordial?

I am Q'uo, and am aware of your query, my brother. We give the instrument the image of the broken bone. That which was whole becomes broken by experience. The broken bone within your body, when healed, is stronger than it was before it was broken. Thus it is with the body of the Creator, the mind of the Creator, and the spirit of the Creator that indwells in each entity, that moves through the creation …

(Side one of tape ends.)

(Jim channeling)

I am Q'uo, and am again with this instrument. We shall continue.

Experiences are designed to test the limits of the entity that seeks truth, as each entity does indeed seek truth with each fiber of its being, thought of the mind, and action of the body. Experience moves the boundaries of perception and knowledge and faith beyond what are normal, shall we say, for the entity. That which is normal is that which is stably experienced and has been gained by previous experience, which in its turn broke previous boundaries. The breaking of boundaries, the breaking of rigid perception, has the function of increasing boundaries, perception and possibility. Thus, it is imperative that each entity who seeks the one Creator experience this breaking in order that that which is new, stronger, deeper, larger, richer and more varied may be contained in a vessel which is now larger, richer, deeper and more varied in its capacity, as each of you are vessels which are hollowed out by the experience which is the means by which you seek the One. Thus are you strengthened; thus do you go on in your journey.

Is there a further query, my brother?

S: Yes, one more. I understand there are certain paths of spiritual growth, ones that I have taken to be negatively oriented, that take the breaking of boundaries as a value in itself. It seems they can hardly wait to break boundaries. My understanding is that a more integrated approach to this process is more efficient. Does this involve processing catalyst through the open heart? Can you speak to that?

I am Q'uo, and we shall attempt to speak to this query. We ask that you re-question if we are not successful. Each entity, whether of the positive or the negative nature, will increase its ability to further its evolutionary process as it breaks those boundaries by which it has defined itself, for as the circle of knowledge enlarges, it touches upon more which is unknown concerning the self. Thus, there is the constant need to enlarge the boundaries. Within limited illusions this is done by applying the breaking force of experience.

Is there a further query, my brother?

S: No, I'm fine, thank you.

I am Q'uo, and we thank you, my brother. Is there another query at this time?

Carla: I'd sort of like to follow up on S's question, because I think that there was something there that he had hold of and that is that if [one] attains the learning, and growing is held in the open heart [and allowed to] flow, [through it], and [out], then instead of becoming bitter and negative, you [might] become sweeter and more loving without attempting to accept [the learning], by attempting to keep the heart open. Would this [be] a question [on which you can] comment?

I am Q'uo, and am aware of your query, my sister. The open heart which accepts the pain of change will find the means of healing that which is broken within more easily accomplished if the attitude attending the painful change is one of acceptance rather than containing any of that which you would call resistance. However, it is not easily accomplished, for that which has carried one to any present point is that with which one is familiar upon a stable basis. When changes are great enough, it often feels as if the foundation beneath one's feet is cracking and separating to the degree that one shall be torn asunder as well. The ability to move with such changes in the acceptance of the new configuration of self is an ability which is developed through great effort, and is one which most entities never master upon your plane of illusion, but are forced by circumstance to accept, and only in retrospect are they able to see the beneficial aspects of those experiences which have been greatly traumatic previously.

Is there a further query, my sister?

Carla: Just one. Would it be then impossible for a negative entity, which is not working with the green energy of the heart energy, to have this healing occur?

I am Q'uo, and aware of your query, my sister. The negatively oriented entity has the need, in order to maintain and further its negative polarization, to control those situations which bring about change, so that that which may be painful is stored, and the energy of that change then is released in a controlled fashion at the appropriate time, so that changes are not accepted as much as they are directed.

Is there a further query, my sister?

Carla: No, thank you.

I am Q'uo, and we thank you, my sister. Is there another query?

(Pause)

I am Q'uo, and we are greatly thrilled to have had this opportunity to speak to this group this evening, greeting old and new friends, and we would thank each for allowing us to speak our humble opinions, reminding each again to take those words which ring of truth, and to use them as you will, leaving all others behind. At this time we shall take our leave of this group, leaving each as always in the love and in the light of the one infinite Creator. We are known to you as those of Q'uo. Adonai, my friends. Adonai.

Intensive Meditation
June 4, 1990

(Carla channeling)

I am of the principle of Jesus the Christ, and I greet you in the full consciousness of the *(inaudible)*. We find that that to which we wish to speak this day is of shifting and uncertain energies of confusions in being and loving, and manifesting that being and that loving.

The spirit of love is one and we speak as this instrument calls us, as the living spirit of Christ in the world, and soon we shall yield this instrument to others who speak in a different vocabulary. But do not be confused by vocabulary or entity or name. There is one Father, there is one Love, there is one Kingdom, which is the creation of all there is.

We seek to reassure each of you that confusion is acceptable, if your yearning is kept right and your desire [shining] to know love. Find peace beyond the naming. We leave you in the love and the peace of Jesus the Christ, now and forever. Amen.

(Long pause.)

I am Laitos, and greet each of you in the love and the light of the infinite Creator. We are pleased to be called to this group to work with each entity in improving those abilities to rest the conscious mind and accept those thoughts which may come from an impersonal source, which has a certain amount of advantage in its longer point of view. We thank each for wishing to be of service as vocal channels for our humble thoughts and we ask each to remember that in the channeling the greatest skill is in the completion of surrender once the contact has been challenged and has passed. In this surrender comes calm and in this calm comes the clear hearing of our thoughts and ease of speaking them into language.

We would use this time as a training session for each channel speaking in a parable which may have some meaning for each. We shall not identify ourselves at each beginning and ending as we intend for this group of channels to speak in fairly short amounts of channel, telling a part of the story that all three weave together. For this is a great lesson in channeling *(inaudible)* the harmony of the group whether all are channels or only one is a channel creates the unique communication that is brought forth. We remind each channel to relax, to suspend all common sense analysis and self-criticism, and simply flow, once the source of the channeling has been accepted, with the rhythm and the energy that flows so freely betwixt we of the Confederation—we correct this instrument—betwixt those of the Confederation and you.

The sun arose upon a most warm day in a poor desert land. The chatter of the small Spanish village began. The laughter of the small children, the crying of infants, and the calling of the cockerels announced the beginning of another summer day—another day of dust and hunger and stillness.

We transfer to the one known as Jim.

(Jim channeling)

One particular family greeted this day as it had greeted many before with slow, sleeping sighs of recognition that there was little that could be done in this day that would significantly improve its state of living, for this small village was populated by peasants for the most part, who labored long for small return, that put but the meagerest food upon the table and clothes upon the body. The family was of a relatively young mother and father with two children that were of young school years in age—a boy and a girl—who were learning what it was to live in this village and to help at their young age with the chores of the family.

We shall transfer to the one known as S …

(Carla channeling)

We are those of Laitos, and would gently interrupt this small tale to admit to the one known as S that this method of teaching the channeling is usually reserved for students who have had several experiences simply in receiving contact. However, we assure the one known as S that this method will, in our opinion, best relax and open the channeling gift which this instrument does indeed have. For in telling the story which no one knows the middle or the end, it is simply a matter of placing one sentence in front of another, as one would walk one foot in front of another. There is no right story. There is no right ending. But only the creation of truth by the surrender of small considerations to the acceptance of a mystery which may or may not uncover more interesting subject matter for thought.

We would again transfer this contact to the one known as S, advising him to release fear, apprehension and analysis, and simply tell his story, as it occurs within the mind. I am Laitos.

(S channeling)

(Inaudible) is indeed *(inaudible)* in which *(inaudible)* a point beyond the *(inaudible)* of this long *(inaudible)* to ideals, hopes that could be found *(inaudible)* in this way, the children *(inaudible)* serve as beacon to all *(inaudible)* transfer to the one known as Jim.

(Jim channeling)

For it was their innocence and naive optimism that they imbued their activities and conversations with on a daily basis. These young souls were new in this world of the dust, drudgery and poverty, and yet were amidst the difficulty, filled with the excitement of being alive and enjoying that which was before them as the play toy that would amuse any young child. This enthusiasm was seen by the mother and the father as that which was remembered from their own youth and from which they wished to preserve in the life experience of their children, for they knew well that there was much in years ahead that would work to dampen and even to destroy this kind of vitality which knew no true suffering, for that which brought tears was easily forgotten with the next experience and the joy-filled laughter easily followed the trail of tears.

We shall transfer to the one known as Carla.

(Carla channeling)

These two children gazed at the sun bewildered and amazed at its gem-like beauty, brilliance and fire and saw each small desert creature as studded with gems. There was, between these two children, an unusually strong bond and they seldom were apart. One observation of beauty shared by one gave an observation of beauty to be shared back by the other and so in converse did the somewhat harsh Christian teachings of the Spanish padre take on a form and substance which was far beyond those feelings of sorrow, guilt and deadness of *(inaudible)* which were the emotions of the remainder of the village's peoples to the stark teachings of the cross and the sacred blood. Yet to these children there came to be a special place, a small depression in the desert land, which seemed to them in their innocence and imagination to be the place where they could speak to the Mother Mary, and so there they spent many hours until their parents began to wonder at their frequent absence.

We transfer to the one known as S.

(S channeling)

(Inaudible) as the years went by until it finally came to pass that as the children grew into adolescence they found they began to have less time to spend in their sacred spot and … with each other. And as is the way of the world they found they began to *(inaudible)* circumstances forced them apart and the

girl was taken by her new husband for it was the way of the land that girls were married at a young and tender age to a remote area from which it was not consistently possible for her to make contact with her beloved brother. The boy grew to a young man and remained in the town. He frequently visited their sacred spot which increasingly came to mean to him his lost sister, and he never failed to feel her presence there, but it was a feeling mixed with great sorrow for the memory of a … lovely smile is but a pale thing compared to the … experience.

We transfer to Jim.

(Jim channeling)

The separation between the girl and boy began to weigh heavily upon each mind and heart for the joy that had been known and shared between these two seemed now greatly diminished and the life that was unfolding before each, though full of its own rewards and pleasures, was quite empty in comparison to that life that was enjoyed by each when together with the other. This deepening concern caused each to reflect in those moments of quietness and solitude as to what the purpose of each life might be for was it not proper to grow in years and experience to become as the parents to others and to bring forth the fruit of life that would nourish all concerned? This pondering in the quiet silence within became for each a solace and a replacement for those times when both had gone to the sacred place in the desert to converse with that spirit that each revered.

We shall now transfer to the one known as Carla

(Carla channeling)

As the young man dwelled in mind upon the meanings of the brilliance and beauty he had remembered and seen, the beauty and holiness of his remembered open heart in the presence of the Mother Mary, he turned to the old padre and as the old priest became ill and died, so he became the priest of this place. And because of his ponderings all the harshness and pain of the Christian story became imbued with the poignant love of the Mother Mary and all sorrow was softened by his remembrance of the beloved presence of his sister, and so it came to be that though the cockerels still crowed in the dust and the heat and poverty was the daily bread, the sorrow of life began to be taught to this village in a way which spoke of compassion and love.

We transfer to the one known as S.

(S channeling)

(Inaudible) …. In his sister's life things *(inaudible)* the husband *(inaudible)* his business *(inaudible)* And her children *(inaudible)* the usual difficulty in growing crops *(inaudible)* in the constant *(inaudible)* the *(inaudible)* which were so *(inaudible)* and years passed by and finally the husband, worn down by years of labor and care, died, [and] she was left with children who had no *(inaudible)* prospects in life and she herself *(inaudible)* barely *(inaudible)* destitute. Still something deep within her heart would not be squelched *(inaudible)* her urge *(inaudible)* she decided to take her family back to the village in which she had been born and in which her brother was now an important person, for who is more important to a *(inaudible)* than its priest.

We transfer now to the one known as Jim.

(Jim channeling)

Upon telling her sorrow-filled tale to her brother who had by this time in his life heard many such tales, she discovered that the excitement for life that they had once shared in youth now seemed transformed into a quiet, yet sturdy strength that spoke in word and deed of the purpose of sorrow as being that which prepares the way for a peace and a joy which was not as their naive joy had been, yet which drew its strength from that same mysterious source that had given to them so freely in their youth the fullness of the experience of life, for her brother spoke to her of the long vigils that he had kept within himself as he had sought to penetrate the mystery of the daily life that each within this small village experienced with a mixture heavily laden with sorrow and sweat and the little leavened with the joy and inspiration that youth brought to each new child and which the grinding poverty of this area …

(Side one of tape ends.)

(Carla channeling)

This is a simple tale of simple people. Each so among all your densities are such. To each has been given poverty of mind and soul and heart. The enthusiasm and vitality and recognition of beauty that comes from young hearts and eyes, the love of one for another, and all these together make up each of you. Yes, you dwell in sorrow and yes, the cockerel always crows in dusty poverty of some kind. Seldom to those of you who are learning to love is there given a free and unasked for unadulterated joy, vitality and lightness of feeling, yet each of you has been a child. You need not let that beauty die.

Each of you has felt sanctified by whatever name you call it—you need not let that die. Your environment has almost nothing to teach you that cannot also be taught as its opposite. As you poor and hungry in a difficult world awaken yourselves remember the joy, the freshness, the love, the worship, and the presence of the nurturing mother of all things. You choose your inner reality. May you each choose wisely and lovingly and steadfastly the way of love.

We thank each of these channels and are most humbly grateful for this opportunity to work. We realize it has been very difficult and energy consuming for the new instrument and we wish to say to the one known as S that we plunged this instrument into more advanced work simply so as to use the time which we and you are given to its utmost. There is a gift within the instrument known as S which recognizes and has [been] previously used without full awareness of its nature. Thus, we do not begin at the beginning but begin at the level of skill which the instrument has.

We thank especially this new instrument for being willing to open to its best effort and to be willing to skip that which would have, for this instrument, been recreation and not the learning of a discipline and a practice which is also a gift and an art. May this instrument see the power of each word, each nuance with which it clothes the concept given to it. May it see, indeed, its particular and unique abilities that make it an excellent candidate for creating inspiration, information, tools and resources that may aid those who wish to avail themselves of such with the gift of this instrument's service.

With blessings to all, we leave you at this time in the love and the light of the infinite Creator, encouraging each in daily meditation and contemplation and analysis of those things which have caused the entity distress or great enthusiasm during each day. So that each may know itself deeper and deeper and may come to realize a more profound version of itself and may then have more and more to offer as a channel of love and light. In that love and light, we of Laitos leave you. Adonai, my friends. Adonai. Adonai. ✣

Intensive Meditation
June 7, 1990

(Carla channeling)

I am [Meta]. I thank each for calling those of [Laitos] to this circle of intensive seeking and greet each in the love and in the light of the infinite Creator. Because this circle is seeking the perfect in every way, it has yet varying levels of experience, for we shall move back through systems of protection. And as we speak them we ask each instrument to visualize each in his own light that [of] which we speak.

We suggest this not to be complex, quite simply to protect your bodies, minds, and your spirits as you undertake the opening of the conscious self to impersonal entities. We ask each to relax, quickly moving from head to foot, starting with the eyes, as the eyes are, indeed, the windows of the soul. So [pay] attention there. Keep the level of concentration necessary for good adjustment from being able to occur. *(Inaudible)* over the head and down the shoulders, the arms, the torso, the legs, the feet. Letting all the tired, tired energy from the day move from you.

Now, in whatever way you visualize, see as it really is, to the best of your ability. The workings of the red energy center in your own body. If it is muddy, ask it to clear. If it is dull, ask it to sparkle, and if it is not rotating, ask it to become active, clear-functioning. Move upwards to the middle of the belly. Gaze at the orange energy ray center, clear it right now, spin it. If one resists this, simply wait. You are capable for a certain time of clearing energy centers reliably. It is a matter of the will being serious and persistent. Gaze then at the solar plexus, yellow. When that is satisfactory, gaze in the middle of your chest, the heart chakra. Within those who wish to serve, many times you may see an overactive *(inaudible)* chakra as the attempt to love, love and love again is so earnestly meant and so intensely felt. Let that chakra be vibrant and alive and clear and harmonious. Now gaze at the throat chakra. You shall be using this chakra. Allow it to clear and spin and even, perhaps, sparkle.

For your words *(inaudible)* transform *(inaudible)* and we would that they would sparkle with a glistening gift that each of you have. Move to the [brow] chakra, that deep blue and purple [of indigo]. This is a very vulnerable chakra, yet you are using it quite actively to do this work. Be patient with yourself if it seems to remain dark and merely keep asking it to spin and shine and give off a clear radiance. Reviewing the chakras now very quickly: red, orange, yellow, green, blue, indigo. Violet appears at the head. It is as it is, you cannot manipulate it, but it does represent the balance that you have just created. Take this color and, in your mind, visualize it, swirl it around to meet the red ray, mixing to become a red violet color, the very essence and vitality that is your identity as a body. Take that color and seal your body completely with this color. Now visualize dunking it into a cup of something, painting it on, or asking it to form an armor, missing no part of you.

You are now a protected body which is working with spirit. It is therefore time to invoke what this instrument would call the armor of light. Ask the white light of infinite love to cover you completely, and in love ask that it extend around the circle, covering each of your beloved brothers and sisters, growing and eventually becoming bright enough that you almost disappear because [of] the light within, around and about the circle as well as upon the surface of your own physical body. You are now in a protected globe of white light, in a position of sacred trust with those within the circle.

This instrument does that which is optional but which may be of help to each. It asks for the Archangels, which will be described by [a] quality, to guard the place of working. It says, "Before me, Rafael." This Archangel is a principle of light. It is somewhat cold, it is full of wisdom. It has a love that is impartial and relentless and will stand your friend without judgment, and shall not be moved.

The instrument then says, "Behind me, Gabriel." This principle is a principle of the [polarity] and the generosity of love in its manifestation. It offers from a never-failing jar the waters of life, the waters of love. It has a great and gentle humor and shall never leave the thirsty seeker without spiritual drink.

The instruments then asks, "On my right hand, Michael." This is an instrument, an example, an exemplar and a principle of divine fire. It is not only the divine fire of creation but that which will dispatch any that is not complete, whole and positive. It is a warrior figure. As you become able to visualize this energy you may perhaps see an entity in various configurations of stance, which will let you know as you become more experienced what the general milieu about the group may be. Is it at attention, the sword drawn, then be doubly *(inaudible)* careful with the tuning and the challenging. Is it kneeling, sword down and looking alertly about, then all is well. Nothing can move this principle from its [vigil].

The instrument then asks, "On my left hand, Ariel." This is the absolute principle of free will. It is that which suggests that that which is born will also die; that that which is planted is also to be harvested. It suggests many subtle rhythms and it guards the freedom of each to draw within its own rhythms as it speaks the concepts of those who you have asked to share information.

The protection now being complete, we would ask that each of you *(inaudible)* at this time declare yourself in whatever way you have discovered to be acceptable to you. Declare yourself against the backdrop of ten millennia, twenty or thirty, against the backdrop of imperishable ideals that could never be denied by the instrument. Ideals by which one lives. Ideals for which one would gladly, if necessary, die in order to protect and give vivid clarity to these imperishable things, to this ideal. For the metaphysical world is a world of absolute things. There is no relativity and there is no room in the world for the metaphysical of those spirits with which you wish to make contact for relative thinking. We shall pause while each chooses, imagines, and brings into being that personification or that symbol of its absolute ideal.

Now we ask each to step into this ideal. If it is personified, grasp it by the hand. If it is symbolized, grasp, stand by, or incorporate the symbol into your being in some way. Allow it to become your metaphysical identity. Your only identity in the world of spirit is this absolute identity you have now fashioned. With this identity now, pray, speak within yourself in any way that you feel will bring you more and more into tune with this ideal, more and more into unity with it. Again, we shall pause.

Ask now, before you begin to challenge for entities only [for that] which you may channel in a stable manner without harm to your health or welfare. The highest and best that you can carry, but not too high for the balanced personality as it decides within this absolute ideal.

The circle is now at a place at which it is ready to work. We of [Laitos] ask each simply to relax, realizing that in a world where a few have the actual gift of channeling, the actual gift of speaking loud and clearly those thoughts which move from the subconscious. This circle has this gift. Thus, avoid analysis, trust in your gift and let us begin to refine this gift.

We transfer this contact now to the one known as Jim. I am [Laitos].

(The instructions on the tape said to stop the transcript after Carla finished speaking.) ✣

L/L Research

Intensive Meditation
June 8, 1990

(Carla channeling)

… You are a newly forming group and the opportunity within the entities present and absent from within this group are excellent and could indeed prove to be most helpful. [In terms of a *(inaudible)* which may come to those who seek it.]

We ask each channel to speak that which it hears and nothing else, but to trust, once the work of tuning and challenging is done, that all will be well. For when the work is done correctly, when the challenge has been met and the baton taken, then it is that those who channel may release the integrated personality and surrender to that part of the personality that is not yet integrated, that is the deep mind. And it is from that deep mind and its analogous portion amongst your stars that we speak to you.

We ourselves are a group, dwelling in harmony. For us it is very simple to live in harmony, for we require nothing, we acquire nothing, we need nothing. Each gladly does a portion of those things which ought to be done to support the maintenance of our physical vehicles. And so we would say, that the first and greatest requirement of harmony within a group is that the group is truly a group of deep love and trust and a lack of fear about loving intensely those who may not be of your family in earthly sense.

It takes courage on the part of all concerned to transcend the many all too human emotions of opening couples up to a spiritual life in common. If this experiment is well begun, communication has taken the place of that which we can see without speaking, that is, each is able to articulate within a certain degree of accuracy its nature, its troubles, its strengths, and its idiosyncrasies. This gives each entity the opportunity to realize that it is, indeed, a teacher as well as a student. Or in case of the one channeling, indeed, the student as well as a teacher. To join a social memory complex is to be unafraid to expose not only all the good things about the self but all those things which are subjectively disliked about the self, so that the group may support each other instrument in its learning to love itself, for only those who love the self may proceed far along the spiritual path.

We shall transfer to the one known as *(name)*. I am Latwii.

(Name channeling)

I am Latwii, and greet each through this instrument. There are many times when the path of service to those who you love is cloudy and obscured *(The rest of this paragraph is mostly inaudible.)* Though life is full of difficulties and … and such times as these it is best to draw back and allow things … For each has its own guiding light.

It is a process of trust in the light of others as in one's own light that allows one to come together as these lights slowly tend to converge. When such a convergence comes about one feels a sense of releasement into a greater beingness which is a higher part of being than one is accustomed to. It is a sense of purpose and of service that transcends the ordinary concerns of a life torn with anguish, filled with sorrow and perhaps with the joys and fulfillment incident to one's daily activities.

One finds, then, in this process, the give and the take between the purposes that beckon and the concerns which oblige us to keep our nose to the grindstone, as it were. The path is long and seems, from the point of view of your illusion, to be very arduous. However, this work is already begun. You all have a foot securely upon the path. And what remains is to find a way to take each additional step, one at a time, slowly, as you begin to find the heart of the center where you all are already come together.

It is time to transfer to the one known as Jim.

(Jim channeling)

I am Latwii, and we speak now through this instrument. The group consciousness that develops from the combination of individual entities is a kind of mind which entities of your vibration first become familiar with in the family situation, then within the early school years, then within the neighborhood. And it is extended therefrom to all of those groups and activities which the social creatures that you are can construct for the various purposes that satisfy curious and diligent minds. The beginning of this formation is, of course, with the individual as it is nurtured by the parents. It is most helpful to receive the kind of support in one's early development that gives one the confidence, that the entity one is, is valued by those about one. This confidence is the foundation stone for the future character structure, shall we say. This confidence provides a safety for the entity in that it may venture forth as far as it feels able in discovering new aspects of its environment, especially those concerning other selves, and then the turn again to the safety of that self-confidence. These voyages outward from the secure self are those beginning ties that open pathways of sharing of the self with others throughout the life experience.

When one finds a difficulty in any group environment, in remaining harmonious within that environment, it is well to investigate first that concept of self which may be providing difficulty when observed within another self. For it is usually the case that the qualities with which one has had personal difficulty are those qualities first noticed as difficult qualities within another. As one reassesses the seeking of certain qualities and concepts, tendencies and beliefs within the personal philosophy of life, shall we say, one may travel back along the line of formation of this quality or belief and determine to the best of one's ability the origination of this quality.

Oftentimes one will find that there is a distorted experience that has lent its distortion to the formation of a certain portion of an entity's life pattern that will then have repercussions throughout the life pattern as the entity engages in relationships with other selves. These qualities will reappear according to the entity's personal program, shall we say. The more intensive distortions, the more unbalanced belief systems, will tend to surface more frequently than those that are more balanced, in order that the, shall we say, squeaky wheel shall get the oil of the attention, and, hopefully, of the balancing action of the entity.

Thus, one very primary action that one may take in assuring deep harmony is to work intensively upon the personal program of learning so that one enters into a group situation [with] as balanced a system of energy expenditure as is possible to achieve, while recognizing that no entity in any group will have a perfectly balanced system of expending the energy that is the daily gift from the Logos through the system of energy centers of every entity.

We also would recommend that there is the possibility of increasing group harmony by reassessing the quality of desire for the group formation within each individual. It is well that there be a principle by which each within the group seeks to work in order that there might be the basic agreement as to the reason for the formation of the group.

I am Latwii. We are aware that there is one within the circle that has become quite fatigued, and we feel that we have achieved in the basic amount of transmission of the concept for this session that we had hoped to give. We would at this time thank each for again inviting our presence, and we would remind each that we are with each in the personal meditations for the purpose of helping to deepen these meditations. We look, as you say, forward to those times where we shall again be asked to join your circle of seeking, and we shall gladly do so at those times. We shall leave this group at this time, as always, in the love and the light of the one infinite Creator. We are known to you as those of Latwii. Adonai, my friends. Adonai. ☙

L/L Research

L/L Research is a subsidiary of Rock Creek Research & Development Laboratories, Inc.

P.O. Box 5195
Louisville, KY 40255-0195

www.llresearch.org

Rock Creek is a non-profit corporation dedicated to discovering and sharing information which may aid in the spiritual evolution of humankind.

ABOUT THE CONTENTS OF THIS TRANSCRIPT: This telepathic channeling has been taken from transcriptions of the weekly study and meditation meetings of the Rock Creek Research & Development Laboratories and L/L Research. It is offered in the hope that it may be useful to you. As the Confederation entities always make a point of saying, please use your discrimination and judgment in assessing this material. If something rings true to you, fine. If something does not resonate, please leave it behind, for neither we nor those of the Confederation would wish to be a stumbling block for any.

CAVEAT: This transcript is being published by L/L Research in a not yet final form. It has, however, been edited and any obvious errors have been corrected. When it is in a final form, this caveat will be removed.

© 2009 L/L Research

Intensive Meditation
June 15, 1990

(Carla channeling)

I am Latwii. Greetings to you in the love and in the light of the one infinite Creator. There was a significant pause before we began this contact because the instrument, somehow uncharacteristically, had inner work to do before it could enter the metaphysical world of spirits, and because this is a detail of some importance we shall speak of it before we begin our message.

When one wishes to be of a metaphysical nature, clear and sure and lucid in being, one cannot bring to that stance metaphysical work on a personal plane that is undone, else all protection will be faulty, and the storms of the ever-going illusion of duality, which extends into fourth density, will affect the contact unreliably, but generally in somewhat of a negative fashion. In the case of this instrument it had received messages from a negative entity which it fastidiously and carefully answered. But the final communication from this entity was a psychic assault which the instrument felt but did not accept as being a portion of itself.

When one realizes that one is being greeted psychically by negative entities, thoughts or impulses, one must do the work of accepting and loving this negativity, cradling it close to the heart, seeing in it the fear that is the antithesis of truth, and cradling this falsity and loving it and absorbing it into the self until it has rebalanced itself within the self as an accepted and loved portion of the self, which one does not choose to manifest. If a channel has fear and has not balanced this, then the entire procedure of tuning and challenging becomes unreliable to the extent that the instrument has fear. In this instance, the instrument was accurate in its reading of the degree of negativity of this particular entity, but did not do the metaphysical work required to become one with this entity in love and in light and in service.

It is written in your holy works that you shall love your enemies and those that spitefully use you, for it is not difficult to love those who love you, but all-important to love those who do not love you. We ask each to ponder these simple words, as the heart may mature and become a strong and reliable energy center, capable of being open and full of energy, with no blockage of fear.

The full and open heart. Let us gaze upon it as it touches upon the various energies and activities of the illusion, in what you call your red-ray energy center. What is the full and open heart but one who accepts all energies of life as beautiful. This heart sees the beauty of form as it is designed in this illusion and is able to comprehend the energies that move through each form, each manifestation. The heart embraces its own physical vehicle, sending light to each and every cell. Where there is any darkness, light is visualized, oceans and oceans of bubbles of light moving to each and every portion of the physical vehicle that may be in discomfort. Refreshing, easing, comforting, cleansing, renewing each cell.

In the full acceptance of this body that is yours within the illusion, is the full healing of this body. Find the way in your heart to love all aspects of this body, never to begrudge it, *(inaudible)*. Always to understand that same energy in others and to love and accept each vibration as lovely.

We will transfer this contact to the one known as Jim. I am Latwii.

(Jim channeling)

I am Latwii, and we continue through this instrument. As you move to the orange-ray energy center and consider it for its clarity, you must look to those relationships that are of an intensive nature, where you share that which is your unique nature with one other entity upon a basis where this pairing of energies draws from you all of your attention in your caring and your efforts to communicate that which is yours to communicate. This type of relationship is the first movement outward from the individualized self and the first movement which establishes a bridge or a bond with another self, which then allows a commerce, a trading, shall we say, of energies betwixt you and one other entity.

This other entity's identity may change from time to time. The significant part of this kind of relationship is that there is only one entity at the time which comes within your focus and with whom you then respond and move in a kind of dance, as it were, as energies are exchanged. Wherever there is any kind of obstruction or blockage of this energy exchange due to imperfect communication or imperfect processing of catalyst there needs to be the balancing of these distorted efforts, so that this center of energy may play its part in the channeling process and be opened to the degree necessary for minimum functioning—that is, to allow a certain amount of energy to move freely through the center without it being distorted or biased in a significant way. When this procedure has been accomplished, then the entity is ready to move to that yellow-ray center which begins the further expansion of the expression of the individual energies.

We shall transfer at this time to the one known as S.

(S channeling)

I am Latwii, and we greet each through this instrument. The yellow-ray energy center conditions those experiences which have to do with other selves, numbering more than two. In the yellow ray there is the capacity to take in those configurations of energy which express complex arrangements of interactions. We will find these arrangements embodied in institutions and in practices and more intimately in attitudes that come out of these institutions and practices. So that it is with respect to the attitudes that the more immediate work is accomplished, when working in yellow ray.

The attitudes involve a give and take of energies and an acceptance of patterns and behavior and a feeling which comes upon one as from a source which is larger than one, and which seems to be other than one. To deal effectively with the balancing of the yellow ray one must accept that the illusion in which one deals is as it should be, and one must accept the gift that the illusion offers in the form of the particular experience which is one's own. When this experience has been assimilated and accepted, the possibility of moving into relation to the energies of the green-ray center becomes established.

The green ray is a more universal image. It has to do with the beingness of the self and the illusion and the entire system of energies which from beyond both gives itself to expression *(inaudible)* keynote to the experience of green-ray energies is love and it is compassion. The compassion which one experiences at this level is a summation of the work one has done upon the other three levels of energy expression. And it involves to some extent a balancing of these energies which can be accomplished only by seeing that these energies are of the Creator and not one's own. They are not to be held but are rather to be expressed and allowed to flow. In this way, one finds within the heart a humility within which a sense of purpose may be born. The sense of purpose, born in the heart center, is the most important endowment that an aspirant to truth may find. It is the birthright of each to have this firmly instilled in the center of his being. To discover this center is to find within one the yearning which is the springboard to work in the higher chakras.

It could be said that the yearning of the open heart is the rectifying factor, the factor of purity, which gives to blue ray an assurance of having to deal with truths and not merely the concerns of the illusion. Blue ray contains within itself the power of expression. In the expressiveness of blue ray there exists the joy of creation in its occurrence. Blue ray is the first center of energy within the mind/body/spirit complex which may act creatively. With this creative power comes a responsibility. If the blue ray has been energized by the open heart, it is responsive to the energies that have come up from the lower centers, as it finds these energies balanced by love and then compassion.

There is another source of energy available for expression in blue ray, however, and this is the source known as the Christ within. This energy, to be expressed, must first be apprehended in a form sufficient for the activation of blue ray. This involves, then, already the activity of that energy center which is located between the brows and is indigo in its true coloration.

The indigo-ray center is the center of insight. It is the center capable of discerning a concept, which for its more and more discursive expression requires contact with the blue ray. Within the indigo ray the concept remains merely the concept. And experience of it is more direct, less refractory than one finds in the blue ray. It is for this reason that the more particular work of the adept is focused in the indigo-ray center when the adept has reached the point of being capable of reliably discerning the concepts and principles that are in so many various ways expressed within the illusion, but always in such a way as to transcend the illusion in favor of a metaphysical significance, which may be quite different from the appearance it takes on within the illusion.

In the indigo-ray center one finds that concepts do not stand alone, each discreet from the others, but, rather, that the situation is somewhat like a series of small streams or rivulets which empty into larger streams and then to larger ones still, until finally they join in a great torrent and seem to travel towards a single source. We say travel towards because this is the direction indicated by the adept who seeks, that is, the adept feels himself to be traveling towards that which is sought.

But in reality, there is not a single direction to this movement. It is, rather, a movement which goes simultaneously backwards and forwards, as it were. The adept, thus, finds that the movement in the direction of what is sought, a movement which, indeed, is initiated by the adept, does not terminate either at a point within the line of sight of the adept or one outside of this line of sight, but, rather, opens a [hallway] of love and light that returns again unto the adept. It is a stream which flows outward and inward simultaneously. It is this situation which is described in your scriptures when they advise the student that, "if you ask, you will indeed receive," for, indeed, in truth the asking is the receiving, the seeking is finding. This is perhaps the most basic secret known and knowable in indigo ray. That is the foundation for the platform upon which all further work may be done.

Once one has activated all the energy centers—red, orange, yellow, green, blue and indigo—the issue of first importance is one of balancing. For a mind/body/spirit complex which is so …

(Side one of tape ends.)

(S channeling)

… activated in any particular energy center that this center overbalances the entity in the direction of processing or expressing a certain kind of energy at the expense of other manners or laws of processing or expressing energy, will find that blockages occur which are due—not so much to the specific, distorting effects of individual chakras—but rather due to the fact that the entity as a whole is out of balance. It is vital to keep in mind that a sense of proportion should be everywhere maintained. For it is out of this sense of proportion that the finer points, or the fine-tuning, shall we say, may take place.

The effect of consistent daily work in meditation is not perhaps felt suddenly, is not perhaps experienced quickly or obviously in the terms of the illusion, but it is the surest and only safe approach to spiritual growth that one may take within your third density. We would suggest to each that you take heart, and in a quiet joy go about your daily routine, knowing that nothing that you do, no distortion in which you may become involved, will put you so far from the love and the light of the one Creator that you are beyond redemption. All is acceptable. You are of the Creator. Find, then, within yourself the joy and the peace that is that of the Creator. We leave you in the love and in the light of the infinite Creator. Adonai, my friends. Adonai.

(Carla channeling)

And so we open again through this instrument in love and light. We would instruct each to examine its portion of the message. For in each portion of the message was intended and is always intended a poetry, a beauty and inspiration, a surrounding of the subject with open nuances that excite the curiosity and show the way for growth in each and every subject or situation covered.

We are those who would have the fun, the playing with the subject, and we find, as we intended to, that the sense of lightness of that which is lifted from the shoulders by awareness is somewhat lacking. Each may examine its own contributions. To the instrument known as S, especially, we would [note] that this instrument's love of the teaching moves at times to limit the nuances or open-endedness of each portion of the subject covered.

There is a joyful surrender, so that to a channel there is no concern to teach, no concern to be [thorough], no concern to be complete, no concern for content, but only the concern to remain completely one with the tuning one has achieved. In this surrender, each thought opens like a flower, and bloom and beauty and lightness enhance the communication. In this case, although the instrument known as S did an excellent job in expressing our basic message, there was the nearly subconscious intention "to teach" that goes with the habits of an entire career of teaching. Channeling is a different kind of teaching. It is a teaching in which one surrenders all desires to teach, to make sense, or to do anything except to listen, to feel, to be, to float in that highest tuning which may be held in a stable manner. Then all else is a mechanical procedure of reporting upon the concepts one has received.

The teaching then unfolds in a way impossible to the conscious teacher, and the results please that same teacher in a way he could never be pleased with his own thoroughness. We say this while we say also that there was excellence in this contact. Yet, we are aware that this instrument strives for more, for inspiration, for freedom from linear thinking. And so we would look back at the full and open heart and revalue briefly that which we have covered.

In the lower energies, each has weaknesses due to the harsh illusion each experiences. This instrument with the difficulties of red-ray physical pain. The one known as Jim with difficulties of a relationship held in freedom and trust. The one known as S with the difficulties allowing interactions with groups, to be that which is inspired rather than intended. Each then, in the discussion of these lower energy centers, expresses its own unimportant but substantial enough limitations. Examine and consider, for all things point to the heart from each direction, and to give maximum energy to the heart, to throw into the heart all that one receives, is dearly to be desired. The heart is a thing in itself, a power, a resource, that which in its full and open presence heals those about it by its very being,

The higher energy centers receive their ability to do their work because of a full and loving open heart. And each who chooses to communicate or to work in consciousness is working with the green-ray energy, that is its resource. The greatest mistake that seekers make is to attempt to do the higher work in consciousness, without in due patience doing the thorough work in the lower energy centers. For each is as important as the other. All together make the body of energies that creates the energy complex of each spirit.

Value yourself, then, not for one or two manifestations of the open heart but for the fastidiousness with which in your private self you know you have worked in each energy center in each day to keep open the royal road, the pathway to the kingdom. Find joy, be merry, staying in fond companionship along the way and think not that information is the goal of channeling. Information is one portion of an axis, call it "x." The other portion of channeling is perpendicular to it at all points and in all directions, and may be called the nonlinear or inspirational or noetic or noumenal portion of that which we have to offer, by our humble opinions.

Thus, we ask each to let go in joy, to surrender to the unknown. When covering familiar material release the mind, release the heart, release the strictures of that which is already known. For there is always within each unique channel a new nuance which may be brought forward from the material which is unique to the mind, the heart, the experience, and the spirit of each channel.

Let yourself be a channel of wonder and mystery and astonishment to self. Allow this. It cannot be wanted. It cannot be desired and therefore gotten. It must be desired and then released. The true courage lies in that sweet surrender to the unknown which guides you and all, in infinite love, in the full and open heart that is the great original Thought of all that there is, the Creator Itself.

Again we say to you, adonai, through this instrument, and we wish to close this contact through the one known as Jim. I am Latwii.

(Jim channeling)

I am Latwii, and greet each again in love and light. We wish only to offer ourselves to any queries which those present may have before we close this contact. Is there a query?

S: Yes, Latwii. In my learning channeling, it seemed to me that in order to keep myself abreast of the contact I needed to kind of look ahead—would I understand that you are telling me that this looking ahead baffles the more, ah, magical and interesting parts of the channeling, so that while it may bring back intact the information, it fails to capture the nuance and inspiration? Do I need to slow down? How might I go about improving this particular aspect?

I am Latwii, and I am aware of your query, my brother. In this regard we would suggest that the practice of looking ahead, as you have called it, is that which gives a confidence to your contact, and in the beginning of your channeling it is helpful to use whatever crutch works, shall we say. In the long run of the channeling process, it would be well if you would look not so much to the approach of information as to remaining in a more free floating state, shall we say, in which you are subjecting yourself to the movement of the contact as it will, this is to say as you progress in your experience of the vocal channeling, it would be well and would be easier for you to accept information about which you know nothing in advance. All of this practice has as its purpose forming the completely hollowed channel which has neither the preconceived idea nor the desire to know that which is next, but simply offers itself as an open instrument. There are many steps along the way to achieving this particular kind of contact and we would not wish to rush you in your progress but simply to suggest, as we have, that you are at a certain stage of the practice of channeling at this time, and the succeeding steps in this never-ending process, will concern themselves in a large degree with removing the crutches which are helpful in the beginning. For these crutches are, though sturdy in their offering of their support, also limiting in that which can be seen or received.

Is there a further query, my brother?

S: Yes, thank you, that was very helpful. This goes into a little different direction. There is a subjective side to the experience of the channel in which one feels an energy, very strong, energy welling up within one, that once one gets used to it, has a certain tractability to it, if one can work with it. Now, there is an ebb and a flow to this energy, at least as I experienced it, rather than a steady stream of it. Is the process of learning to channel a process of learning to work with this energy when one feels that it is dissipated for the moment? Does one do well to pause long enough for it to gather in? Can you give me some indication of this problem?

I am Latwii, and believe that we have your query. Before any performance, the performer has the flow of the adrenaline, as you might call it, the excitation of the anticipation. This kind of energy is that which the new instrument would experience far more than the instrument which has long practiced its art. This energy can be helpful to the new instrument, much as the crutch of looking forward, shall we say, into the contents of the information which has yet to be received. As the new instrument perceives this welling of energy, the effect is to help the concentration and the focus of the concentration. This is most helpful to any instrument. However, as you become more practiced in your art of vocal channeling, you will also discover that this energy tends to be reduced, for the practice no longer elicits this, as this instrument would call it, rush of energy. It is at that time that your ability to focus your concentration will take over this function, shall we say. Thus, there are many attributes and characteristics of the channeling process that are found at the beginning of the process which may be utilized by the new instrument. But after a period of time, the new instrument, becoming a more experienced instrument, will discover that it is working more on its own resources and abilities rather than the *accoutrements*, shall we say, of the contact in its initial phases.

Is there a further query, my brother?

S: Yes, I think this is well taken, and I certainly do feel that rush. The energy that I had in mind, really, though, was one which I only began to experience later on, when I felt more calm and it is one which I have sometimes experienced in the meditative situation. I find it to be of a different order. Is—am I dealing only with a subjective modification, is that what you are describing as the adrenaline energy, or is there another dimension going on here?

I am Latwii, and I am aware of your query, my brother. There are deeper levels of the mind which each entity within the meditative state may contact, as the meditation is more successful in achieving the one pointed focus, shall we say, and in removing those distractions to the meditative state simply by failing to attend to them. As one is successful in moving the conscious focus from the upper reaches of the conscious mind to the lower reaches of the conscious mind, and, indeed, into areas of the subconscious mind, one will feel a certain power or energy, as you have called it, which is the, shall we say, the energy of potential use.

This is a relatively unformed energy and is that which responds to the reaching, shall we say, the reaching of the conscious mind as it moves its focus into deeper realms of the subconscious mind. This reaching begins to potentiate those qualities which may be associated with the more feminine aspects of any entity, those of the intuition, those of the non-rational, those creative powers which have, as you would describe it, the magical or metaphysical ability to form consciousness in such and such a fashion according to the design of the working. Therefore, the energies which you have described are those within your own subconscious mind which are available to you as you are able to stably move your conscious focus into the subconscious mind.

Is there another query, my brother?

S: No, thank you very much.

I am Latwii, and we thank you once again, my brother. Is there another query at this time?

(Pause)

I am Latwii, and we have been most filled with joy and light to have been able to be with this group this morning. We feel that the progress made with the one known as S is exceptional and we hope that this entity will take our comments and small criticisms as those areas of improvement which are expected of the more advanced instrument. We are very happy to have been able to work with this instrument and look forward, as you would say, to further opportunities to do so.

At this time, we shall take our leave of this instrument and of this group, leaving each, as always, in the love and in the light of the one infinite Creator. We are known to you as those of Latwii. Adonai, my friends. Adonai. ☙

L/L Research

Sunday Meditation
June 17, 1990

Group question: The question this evening has to do with how a person is able to deal with a situation in which another person is a psychological drain to be around. This might be a person in the home, at work, it might be a situation where you find yourself having to deal with so much of yourself just to survive in the situation that it feels like you have nothing more to give, and that you're being sucked dry, almost like a parasite or a leech is sucking the blood or the life energy out of you. How can a person find the inner strength, or the will, and the resources to continue dealing with a person or a situation that seems to take everything out of you that you've got?

(Carla channeling)

I am Hatonn, and I greet each of you in the love and the light of the infinite Creator. It is a great privilege to be with you this evening, and we thank and bless and send love to each of you, assuring that we will be with you at any time you mentally request our presence. We do not speak, but we are there as comforter for those who seek that comfort we have to give. We ask each to remember that we are limited by those things which we know and those things which our teachers have taught us. We are capable of error, and so we ask each of you to discriminate and judge those things which we say so that you may use those things which are helpful, but leave behind those things which are not, for within you is the power of all knowledge and wisdom, in a very deep memory which the truth resonates to, as occasionally this house resonates in its very walls to the sound of the train in passing, and hums; so does your being hum at the resonance of a truth that is yours personally. You do not learn from us but merely recognize the truth that you have known but could not say for yourself until we said it first, for much of what you know is buried deeply within your unconscious mind and can come to the surface only under carefully protected and loving circumstances where seekers of truth may gather together in love and grace abounding.

You ask how to protect yourself from the psychic verbal and physical attacks of one who is incarnate, that is in a body and in direct relationship with you. We may answer you in several ways, but we are sorry to say that one entity does not have charge over another, and though we may teach methods which you may practice whereby the effects of such abuse are limited or even nullified, you in your turn cannot help or rescue that unhappy and tormented person whose love is so distorted and twisted that that entity must show it in such a painful way.

First of all, let us examine the nature of one entity's hold over another. It is normally that of long habit or magnetic attraction. In other words, this entity has been accepted by you as one who has the right to enter into your own private space, within your being and your energies, due to your own love of this entity. This entity then has the control it would not otherwise have. Thus, the first step in removing abuse from yourselves is to know that you always have free will, that you are safe, but that you must put upon yourselves the whole armor of light, and remove from that entity which is abusing the privilege of intimacy, the right to that intimacy. It is as though you take in your mind's eye the scissors and you cut the bond.

Perhaps you may take your fingers and move them across the area of the navel. It is just above the navel that this entity generally has its power attachment into your energy web. Cut it, seal it, and believe and have faith that you are protected as a free will entity by the full armor of the love and of the light of the infinite Creator whom you serve. This is that which is done within, and this is the heart of protection, for you must believe in yourself, you must believe in your rightness and completeness and individual freedom. These things cannot be taken away from you, not by fire, not by water, not by threat and not by death. When you know who you are, you are free inside.

The next step in dealing with those who abuse the privilege of intimacy by causing hurt and pain and by draining your energy is to refrain from listening to the sense of what that entity is saying. Allow it to be a bubbling brook, a news show coming from a television in the house next door. Surround yourself with a silence. You may hear but you do not have to attend, you do not have to react. An entity which is vampiric in nature feeds off of fear and demands control. If there is no fear and there is no control the entity cannot feed its vampiric nature as it wishes.

The third level of protection is the walking away, the physical removal of the self from the source of the vampiric and abusive entity. Move to that room which has the lock upon the door, and lock it. If necessary, leave that dwelling place in which the entity lays, and find peace and silence in a place known only to yourself.

If the physical leaving is impossible, then the non-hearing and the non-acceptance, though passive, is extremely productive of results. There may be phrases of seeming agreement when they say "Yes, yes, of course," "Yes, my dear, that could be true," but these things could be programmed to fit impersonally, without emotion, without fear, and without interest.

Now, these are those things which may be done very quickly. There is an undercurrent which is to be done much more slowly, and we urge that each gaze deeply at the lesson of love held herein. It is said in one of your holy works to pray for those who despitefully use you, to pray for your enemies, for what good is it to pray for those whom you love? Is that not easy? Would that not be simple for you? Rather, pray for those who are not your friends, but your enemies, who wish you ill, through unhappinesses and agonies and distortions of their own. Pray for them with all your heart, pray to forgive, and as you become strong inside, pray to forgive the you that was weak enough to attain to such nonsense as that of a vampire who wished to make you a prey. Pray and love and nurture that vulnerable, small self that could not defend itself against an overpowering vampiric presence. In praying you will find forgiveness, and forgiveness stops that karmic tie that binds you to this person. In forgiveness is personal freedom. When you are in a state of fearlessness and forgiveness then you may see with clearer eyes that which you wish to do that shows the most compassion for all concerned.

Sometimes there is a spiritual principle involved, a spiritual principle such as that of the vows of marriage, or any promise that should be kept, that you as a person will die before breaking. We applaud such passion, such commitment, and such dedication to an ideal, and if that is truly the way each entity feels, let it face death gladly and joyfully, for indeed much suffering may lead to the physical death of the body, for the vampiric entity is not satisfied until all life has been taken away. If this is your ideal, we assure you, you lose nothing, and you gain much, for those who keep their promises, and who stand by their ideals in a world of relativity and illusion are the heroes and heroines of a passion play such as that of your Christ, Jesus the Christ, who kept his promise, though he truly wished not to.

If upon the other hand, forgiveness has brought insight that indicates there is a more compassionate way within the illusion of separating oneself from the vampiric entity, then in all compassion it is well to do so, *(inaudible)* do nothing in service to self, but only in compassion to all concerned, in a state of centeredness and calm, in a state of inner knowing.

You see, you have choices. You may choose several ways to be of service. In order to do this you must know yourself well. Know that of which you are capable and that which you truly desire. It may well take some time to remove the habitual reactions of fear and helplessness against such an overpowering entity, yet in truth you are, as all are, equal spirits. Because one entity is of service to self, and wishes to control others, does not mean that that entity may do that with *(inaudible)*, for each entity is of equal strength. Each of you is the warrior self, completely calm at the center, completely relaxed and able to respond in compassion and courage and in effectiveness to those attacks which are perceived.

So you see, it is the self that must be fully realized by the self. It is no interaction with another that gives one personal strength; it is the sure and certain knowledge of the self. The habits of a lifetime may have taught each that the self is not equal to the vampiric entity. But habits are only habits, you may think of them as addictions, you may think of ridding yourselves of them as you would think of a friend attempting to cease smoking a cigarette, or drinking the whiskey. You need not be an addict. You may prefer to choose another way to be. In this effort you are never alone, for as you pray, unseen entities of love and light are about you on every side, and as you in all humility declare yourself to be a person of faith, and align yourself with the best that you know, defining yourself by the best that you know, becoming your true spiritual self by this process, you do indeed become quite as strong as any entity incarnate or discarnate.

The other entity may still have, for some reason connected with your learning process, the ability to cause changes in your geographical location, and in your circumstances in general, but in no case is such an entity able, except by your own permission and acceptance, able to affect you yourself. You may be imprisoned, you may be tortured, you may be in any manner of situations, but as you recall who you are, an imperishable spirit of light that lives by faith, you become untouchable, for you have about you what this instrument would call the whole armor of light, and the Creator Itself is your protection, for you are as much children of the Creator as any other, as much to be loved and protected as any other, and in no way deficient.

Claim your birthright as loving children of a loving Creator. Do the work of forgiveness, no matter how long it takes. Pray the prayers that cut the bonds that tie you to this vampiric entity, and to all who would seek in any way to bend you to their will or to control you against your will.

We are aware that we sound as if all were very simple, when in reality we may not understand the complexity of such situations as your illusion is able to provide. This is correct, my children; we do not even wish to concern ourselves with the details of a specific instance of that of which you ask, for though the situation be knotted tightly as the Gordian knot, yet the untying is as simple and difficult as utter and complete humility and forgiveness, forgiveness of other, forgiveness of self. This is very important, that you forgive yourself for ever being the victim, and forgive the entire situation. This we do not suggest to be simple work, or work done quickly, but it is the key to all the rest, and we suggest that you pray for the soul of the vampire, for in this way you shall learn to love this entity.

As you pray, the love of the Creator surges through you, and you see this entity in its original form— beautiful, whole and perfect, just as all entities are. What caused this entity to become a creature of such agony, such pain, that it must turn and hurt others? How very sad is all that that entity has experienced that has so soured, embittered and caused this entity to become negative and controlling of others because it cannot control the self, unloving of others because it cannot love the self, unforgiving of others because it cannot forgive the self. There is much to pray for in this entity's despair, and as you pray you will find strength and compassion flowing through you, as you deliberately strengthen yourself inwardly, with a knowledge of your own birthright, by loving yourself, forgiving yourself, and girding yourself about with light. So shall you become strong enough to love.

We go no further in suggesting what might be done, but simply urge compassion. Compassion tempered with wisdom leads one within an illusion such as you are in into sometimes strange solutions. Be open to the flow and the energy of compassion and love within. In full discrimination of those thoughts which may come to you, move gently, humbly and confidently to follow the will of love itself, and do that in your life and in your actions which best expresses your best awareness of the implications of that knowledge and that love which is yours. It has been said it is impossible not to make mistakes. That is the nature of this illusion, yet each mistake is a blessed one, one which holds a lesson of love.

When you are discouraged and at your weakest, picture yourself in the arms of the Creator, nurtured and cradled and loved, infinitely, infinitely loved. Thus shall you nurture yourself until your pain is quieted and your faith is reawakened. No matter how many times this occurs, nurture yourself again, that is, allow the nurturing Creator within, that female, divine principle, to love and cradle and hold you, and rock you, and care for you, until you may rest in bliss and quietness, and renew your strength of the spirit.

Then shall you awaken to the difficult manifestations of this illusion, and move into those patterns that are so painful with a stout heart and a full armor of light and love, and you shall do very simple things, and shall love, and shall not hear, and shall not be affected, and if necessary and possible, you shall walk away. One who seeks to control others deals with indifference quite poorly, and indeed becomes helpless before a persistent and continued indifference. As the storm rages about you, we urge you to gather to yourself your birthright, and to be who you really are, children of love, children of the one infinite Creator of all things. Love one another, my children. This is the greatest wisdom that we know.

Because that which we have said contains several distinct lines of thinking, we suggest that this group of words be heard several times, that it may more completely be grasped and become a part of your deeper mind. As always, we urge you not to accept anything that does not make sense to you, but only follow the advice that seems to resonate within you, a re-echo of a bell.

My children, how we love you, and how grateful we are to have been with you this evening, speaking through this instrument. It too had need of these words, for it too faces the vampire, that impersonal one which is called pain. Too often does this instrument forget that it too is a child of love, and does not need to fear the illusion of pain. Your pain has eyes, a face, a form, and a seeming reality. This instrument can in no way seize hold of a vampire that attacks it, yet pain, of heart, or soul, or mind, or body, is of one and the same nature. It is the vampire which must be faced, loved, forgiven, realized as part of the self, taken into the self, and made so much a part of the self that is not chosen, but there is no longer any fear, there is no longer any adversity, there is no longer any struggle. Such is the power of your own faith in love.

We would at this time close this communication through the one known as Jim. We are those of Hatonn.

(Jim channeling)

I am Hatonn, and greet each again in love and light through this instrument. At this time we would ask if there might be any questions to which we may speak further.

Carla: How do you go about removing your attention from pain long enough to begin building a part of yourself that is apart from it?

I am Hatonn, and am again with this instrument. My sister, this is a query to which there is no easy answer. The steady, acute pain takes one's attention to the degree that there is little left to spend in any other endeavor. Of this you are well aware. The prayer without ceasing that is so much of your life pattern is the only avenue of which we are aware that offers any respite from the pain that would be sufficient to build a concept of oneself that did not include persistent pain, for when the prayer is offered, not only in an unceasing manner, but with a power of sincerity and devotion that is sufficient for that entity, there is, during that praying, the beginning of the removing of the consciousness from that place of pain within the physical body to that room within the heart where the prayer is offered, and where there is the possibility of grace that may work within the physical body complex to begin to calm the raging sea of pain.

However, we cannot say that this is what you would call a surefire remedy, for we are aware that there is not only the pain that you feel within your physical vehicle, within your mental vehicle, and within the emotional vehicle of your being, but that what is felt there has the eye of those who would increase your burden and take every opportunity to do so. Thus, your challenge is far greater than our words in response to your query, and we can only give you but poor words at this time with our intense admiration for the effort you put forth in enduring and in attempting to overcome the pain that is with you as a constant companion.

Is there any further query, my sister?

Carla: No, thank you.

I am Hatonn. We thank you, my sister. Is there another query?

(Pause)

I am Hatonn. We are aware that those present this evening have traveled far and are weary, and we thank each for the effort that was put forth in order that this circle of seeking might be formed this evening. We are most grateful to be able to share our vibrations with yours. We cannot thank you enough for the opportunity to speak our humble words. We hope that in some way they may be of service to you as you continue in your daily lives to seek and to share the love and the light of the one infinite Creator under all manner of circumstance, many of which seem most burdensome at this time. We are known to you as those of Hatonn, and we shall leave you at this time, glorying in the love and in the light of the one infinite Creator. Adonai, my friends. Adonai. ✴

Special Meditation
June 20, 1990

Group question: The question this afternoon has to do with the differences between the one who pursues the martyr's path, and the one who pursues the path of the mystic. What are the similarities, what are the differences?

(Carla channeling)

I am of the principle of Q'uo. Greetings to you in the love and in the light of the one infinite Creator. We greatly appreciate the opportunity to speak to you, and to be called to your group this day. It is a privilege and an honor, and a chance to be of service, and we are most humbly thankful to each of you. Because we speak to an old and beloved friend, we would have the one known as S know of who we are. We of the principle of Q'uo are those of Latwii. We are also students of the teacher known as Ra. Their social memory complex and ours have blended together for communications with this instrument, as it can no longer bear the cost of physical trance. Nevertheless, it is of an acceptable vibration to receive many of the concepts of our teachers, and of course we also contribute those things which fill out the situation as down plumps out the pillow. We are not as excellent are those of Ra at speaking tersely and to the point, yet in our rambling we find that people are able to find more to grasp onto and find more ability to grasp what is being said. And so, all of us are grateful to be with you, and those of Ra and those of Latwii send you their love, and are with you always.

Briefly we speak upon this, that is to say we are with you always, you are never alone. There are times when, in your illusion which you now enjoy, the stimulation from that illusion becomes so overwhelming that the senses are shut down and one is no longer able to be aware, or to express any reaction, to stimulus. This has no bearing on our presence or the faithfulness of the seeking soul. It is simply the symptom of dealing with the illusion, having chosen a difficult, but hopefully very fruitful, existence in service to others. Thus, we speak to the mystic in you as we say, by faith, know, where you cannot feel it, that help is near, and that the Creator is closer to you than your own breath.

Martyrs and mystics have often been one and the same, that is, it is often the entity with the ability for the abstract and extra-physical or other than physical use of senses to be a mystic, to see ideals that this illusion does not in any way confirm but may only suggest from time to time. It is these mystics that often will make an heroic gesture which ends in the killing of the self by others because of the insistence upon their ideals. Thus, the two words are intermixed often, as one follows the line of those lives are built on faith and not by words as it stretches back in glory across time and space.

However, by no means are all mystical entities martyrs, nor are all martyrs mystics.

A mystic is not a word which means one thing. It may mean any number of things, that is, it may refer to one who chooses a non-literal interpretation of life in any non-literal interpretation that entity may choose. Thus, there are no two mystics whose paths are the same, for the golden glow of sanctity is shone to one person in one way, to another in another. There is no set pattern for mysticism. It is indeed rather a process of growth or evolution which may be chosen by the seeker as the most comfortable or the most efficient way though uncomfortable, of living the most consciously accelerated spiritually evolutionary life possible while living in the illusion of third density. The mystic is one who says, "I do not need an objective referent to believe that something is there." Thus, some mystics never leave those things founded upon what other mystics would call sheer superstition. There are as many non-literal ways of looking at the world as there are entities.

So mystic is better understood as an adjective, mystical, meaning non-literal, or freed from vigorously philosophical and scientific processes of deduction. Therefore, being a mystic brings out a different point of view in each person who is, by gift or by choice, living life mystically. A mystic is not particularly liable to become a martyr, anymore than is the scientist, the ethical man, or any manner of humankind which you may choose to describe. A mystic simply believes that which it does not see, and has faith in that which cannot be touched, or felt, or measured by the instrumentation now available to your peoples. It does not suggest a creed, and it does not suggest an agenda. One's personal myth and the way one manifests one's personal myth are chosen uniquely by each unique entity.

The word martyr, on the other hand, is a very specific word, meaning that entity which chooses to allow itself to be used, even unto death. Death is not necessarily the end of the martyr, one may live a life of martyrdom, but in essence the attitude is that the self is unimportant, and that the will of a greater self is that by which the martyr seeks self-immolation, and gladly hopes for the destruction of anything that stands in the way of service to that more important self. Many are those entities among your people who are martyrs to idols. Many would call blasphemous the martyr's love of the mother for the family to the point that this nurturing entity abandons all personal hope, dreams, originality of existence and authenticity of opinion, in order to best serve in any way that is requested the demands of this greater self.

In other words, to many martyrs, the greater self is very much alive, and is living in bodily form as an human being, and often in family relationships. It may be noted that when this occurs it is a poor choice if one wishes to balance one's karma and remove oneself from the dense influences of this particular classroom, for just as negative over-activity bond one karmically to another, so does excessive and self-sacrificing love that is unnecessary and an infringement upon the free will bind the same entity, karmically, to the one idolized.

There are many within the Eastern cultures which operate upon the hierarchy of student/teacher and the Creator, who neglect to remember that the teacher is transparent, and that the Creator is to be seen in the [teacher], and not the teacher in the Creator, which is the same kind of karmic tie, the same kind of martyr's worship, which is in bad judgment, not because a great deal is not learned, for one cannot help but learn, but in the event one is wishing to prepare oneself for freedom from these lessons, it is well to recognize that karma needs to be balanced, and all entities need to be seen as one's peers and equals, neither higher nor lower, neither greater nor smaller, no teachers and no students, but colleagues.

Yes, there are teach/learners and learn/teachers, because one entity has more experience than another, or more ability to articulate than another. But the transaction is between equals in the deepest truth of human transactions. If this once and for all can be seen, then it can be seen that there is no possibility of being a martyr as long as one remembers that one is always dealing with one's colleagues, each entity being an imperishable and perfect light being.

If we speak to the unwisdom of martyring oneself for idols, do we then suggest that it is wise to martyr oneself for ideals? This is a matter of the free will of the entity who contemplates such an act. We may suggest simple this: that if the situation of martyrdom is not placed in front of one it is never necessary to create a martyr's path. For if one has in one's life pattern the lessons involved in martyrdom, they will appear of their own accord, and as Jesus the Christ prayed the day before he accepted his martyrdom, "I know my time has come, I see the cup I am to drink in front of me, I am afraid of the pain. If it is possible, move this cup away from my lips that I will not have to drink it." But the cup stayed where it was, and in humility, Jesus the Christ said "not my will, but Thine be done". At that point, in anyone's experience, when the entity is sure that it is receiving clear and positive information, and that there is a clear and positive way of redefining unconditional love for those about one, the martyr's path overcomes wisdom, for yours is a density in which you are attempting to learn to love without condition, and when at last there is a choice between wisdom and dying well for an ideal, wisdom must needs wait its turn and be learned in its proper density.

The great error with those who have a tendency, because of their mystical experiences, to see opportunities for self-sacrifice, is that they will choose self-sacrifice when it is not at all necessary, and when in fact it may well prevent or cause to make longer another entity's road towards understanding of the nature of love. For instead of seeing itself as responsible, it simply turns to a service-to-others self who loves so deeply, and that service-to-others self again and again plays the martyr's role. It is well to remember that this type of martyrdom is a kind of idolatry. There is but one Creator, and although the Creator is in each person, unless by self-sacrifice you are expressing that ideal to others in a clear communication on whatever level you wish, then that martyrdom has a karmic element, which then must be balanced.

It will never cause anyone karmic problems to be a mystic, for the mystical view is merely that of one looking through the bars of the prison of third density and seeing that there is more. Whether these entities are called philosophers, or fools, or poets, or men of god, they have a vision of the way the world is, to which those who hear it resonate, and by which those who live with it are enriched, and indeed the planet itself is enriched by the mystical view, by the love of mystery and the withholding of judgment that accompanies the mystic grasp that we do not, nor can we, know anything for certain, but by faith we see the world in this way and that, and we do not need the tape measure, and the calibrations, and the figuring, and the equations, for we see life at first as mystics in the abstract, and then watch as those abstract principles of love, affirmation and service to others find their way into manifestation as each mystic lives its life of eternity in the world which lives in time and space.

Some mystics will find it far easier to be what they feel is the best they can be, in the life of silence and contemplation that the monastery offers. Thus, by their very existence such entities raise the consciousness of the planet, certainly not by any deeds done, nor words said. Others speak a great many words, and are therefore honored, but are not the least bit more helpful than those whose service is silent, for it is the viewpoint which causes radiance to be possible, radiance through the self, radiance that lights the planet, and fills the Earth with the possibility of loving kindness.

To study the psychology of the martyr is a large subject which we cannot fully tackle within the time limitations of this working. In part, it is that which the subjectively perceived reality of humankind demands because it is aware that it is often in error, often immoral and unjust, and no matter how secret are these errors, and how unknown these mistakes, yet each entity understands quite well that it is in many ways most unworthy to be lifted up, whole and perfect, to claim birthright as the child of the one infinite Creator. You live in a pattern of duality. You speak in terms of duality, your very mind functions by duality, that is, making choices, yes or no, yes or no, over and over. And in this light and dark that is the third-density experience there is a deep need for someone to erase the night, the darkness, the error, the mistake, the need [for there] to be a way to perceive oneself as being forgiven, redeemed to fullness of self and wholeness of life and transformation of personality, so that one may more and more serve the infinite Creator, and each day start anew and fresh, without the vast burden of one's past errors causing the shoulders to sag.

Thus, the martyr is logically an inescapable part of a dualistic system such as yours. The psychology of duality demands it, for each of you was not born neutrally moral, but was born with a moral imperative, with an inner moral bias. Thus, there is no *(inaudible)* judging, and now *(inaudible)* need for there to be a martyr. The need for a martyr is the need to sacrifice part of that which humankind is, so that, somehow, the remainder of humankind might be forgiven its errors. Those who gaze at this part of myth may see that in no way could it be considered literally or objectively acceptable. But myths are not intended to be literal. If you are all that there is, you are also the martyr that expends its life that the rest of you may live, forgiven.

And so, a small part of you, the stale, the unhealthy, the self-perceived sicknesses of self, mind, body and spirit, are offered up on the cross of change and transformation, and in these special descriptions of subjective martyrdom lives the true wisdom of martyrdom.

We do not intend to indicate the bias against the historical truth of the one known as Jesus, the one known as Buddha, the one known as Zoroaster, or any of the world's crucified Christs. We wish only to indicate that those entities showed a pathway, not for you to walk through, but for you to imitate, for there is no way one in one's consciousness of duality may approach the Creator, for the Creator is one, and you are one, and one with the Creator. Thus, your own dualism is that cross that you bear; your own humanity, your own mistakes, your own errors, your own times of self-perceived wrongness, and these things you do well to drag to Golgatha and to crucify, that the rest of you may live and be renewed and be more and more who you truly are, whether that be mystic or empirical thinker. The mystic is more aware of the true nature of the illusion. However, there are many who are able to pass into that beautiful light that is the light of the density to come without ever being a mystic, but merely doing those things that seemed there to do, being there to help, however practically or matter-of-factly.

We would transfer to the one known as Jim at this time, that this instrument may close the session. May we thank each for calling us once again. We are those who dwell in realms of glory, where music of praise and thanksgiving is never still, yet we do not know all that there is to know, nor do our teachers, so, as always, we encourage each to take that which is valuable, and leave the rest as interesting but unnecessary thoughts. We are those of Q'uo.

(Jim channeling)

I am Q'uo, and greet each again in love and light through this instrument. At this time we would offer ourselves for any remaining queries to which we may speak further. Is there a query at this time?

S: *(Inaudible).*

I am Q'uo, and we believe that we have the gist of your query, my sister. It is the martyr's choice before the incarnation begins that this path shall be the overriding path which is followed, and that this path shall be followed in order that it might be that which most fully glorifies the Creator, and serves the Creator in what you know as the positive polarity. When one considers this path within an incarnation and places it among many as that which may or may not be chosen as the service that will be provided when it is unsure what that service should be, then it is that the intellect does the work within the incarnation that the entity at the level of the soul has done before the incarnation. It is not so much that the intellect shall move one in a negative path if it attempts to rock the martyr's path, as it is that when …

(Side one of tape ends.)

(Jim channeling)

I am Q'uo, and am again with this instrument. It is more the case that when one chooses a path using the intellect, laying one choice against the other, analyzing the benefits and the detriments, that one tends to move away from what is true for the self, for the path that is most appropriate for each entity is the path which has been carefully laid out before the incarnation with the aid of many friends and teachers that have the purpose of serving as what you may call a guide or a guardian of one kind or another.

Many times during an incarnation an entity will feel that it has moved its feet from that path which was more clearly felt at a previous time, will feel the confusion of the present moment, and with the great desire yet remaining to be of service in whatever way is possible, will attempt to construct by the analytical and intellectual means the path which it might once again feel at home within. Seldom is such a choice that which would move one into negative polarization or service to self. More is the case that one would simply conduct the life pattern in a place which was somewhat in a limbo [field], as you may call it, where one is not yet at the heart of the self of the path chosen before the incarnation, but one instead moves as best as one can.

Now, this is a situation in which many, many of your peoples find themselves at this time. Those who are awakening to a larger perspective of the meaning and purpose of the life pattern oftentimes at the awakening to this realization of greater purpose will attempt to emulate others that are appreciated in order that their journey might continue rapidly as they have felt the awakening energy to move in a burst through the awareness. We recommend to each entity that ponders upon this point of how the feet shall be placed as the journey is continued that there be no steps taken that do not have with them the feeling of wholeness and of rightness, that feeling of assurance that each has had experience with at some previous time within the incarnation where it has been known without doubt that the next step was such and such.

Is there a further query, my sister?

S: Not about that. *(Inaudible).*

I am Q'uo. We scan your memory. You have asked a query that is most interesting and highly symbolic in your particular case, one which the deeper portions of your subconscious mind have constructed, shall we say, in order to provide the symbol, and in some degree the riddle. The forest is most important to you at this time, for reasons which we feel you have begun to ascertain with increasing clarity, though there yet remains much which is unclear.

Consider the nature of any tree that grows within any forest. It draws what is needed for nourishment from depths that are great [and] hidden within the earth as well as being nourished by the life-giving rays of the sun which is a great distance from it, nourishment for the tree that is old, strong and wise, and therefore available even when there are dry winds and harsh conditions that move from season to season about the forest. There is little effect upon the great oak when the variations of seasons become extreme in heat and cold and dry and with rain.

The snakes of your experience have been well perceived, we feel, in that the symbolism of the action and reaction of wisdom is that which is currently playing out, shall we say, within your life pattern. To [sum,] we could suggest that you have well perceived the symbols that have been given to you, not only in your life pattern, but by deeper portions of your own mind, so that the path might always be available to you, and nourish you in the way which is necessary at this time.

Is there a further query, my sister?

S: Is there a connection between my forest and my thoughts on *(inaudible)* and the tree of life *(inaudible)*, or are they two separate arenas?

I am Q'uo, and am aware of your query, my sister. You may look at that information that we have just given as being the arena, or the parameters, within which great refinement of thought, feeling, imagination, intuition and action may take place. When one looks at the tree of life, for instance, one may see many centers of energy expression that may be investigated with the archetypical relationship of the subconscious potentiator working to inspire or inform the conscious mind in order that there may be a deeper understanding of the seemingly mundane experiences that one encounters in the daily round of activities. This is true in each case where one wishes to apply the principles of the archetypical mind. That you have discovered various of these principles and have decided to arrange your further study around these areas of study is well for you at this time, for you have both the need and the ability to penetrate areas of the self and the life pattern which correspond to the stations and the archetypes.

Is there a further query, my sister?

S: This is real, kind of strange, but it's something that has always been in the back of my mind, but why, why have I *(inaudible)* to be here?

I am Q'uo, and, my sister, as you serve others as the teacher, this is a question which often comes to the mind of the teacher, why are some students more inspired, or as you have called it, driven, to excel, than are others? Why is anything as it is? You are one who has chosen for yourself a certain kind of service that remains in most cases hidden within the unmanifest self at this time. However, as many are awakening to those inner urges according to the season and the cycle of the time upon this planetary sphere, so will there be many that bloom and break forth from those previous boundaries, shooting forth from the dark earth the vibrant shoots and stems that together will form the new forested population of this particular planetary sphere. Thus, you move with a rhythm that is coarsely tied to this cycle, this planet, and your own choices before entering into this incarnation.

Is there a further query, my sister?

S: No, thank you *(inaudible)*.

I am Q'uo, and we thank you, my sister. Is there a final query at this time?

(No further queries.)

I am Q'uo, and it is with great joy that we have been able to join this circle this day. We cannot speak our gratitude with words that are sufficient to express it, but we wish each to know that we cherish these times, and feel most especially blessed to have been able to speak to the one known as S. We hope that our humble words may provide some illumination and inspiration as the life pattern continues to unfold, step upon step. At this time we shall take our leave of this group, rejoicing, leaving each, as always, in love and light. We are known to you as those of Q'uo. Adonai, my friends. Adonai. ✤

Special Meditation
June 23, 1990

Group question: The question today has to do with the concept of forgiveness. What is the purpose of forgiveness, what is the method of forgiveness, and who needs the forgiveness in any situation?

(Carla channeling)

Our greetings, love and blessings to you, my dear brother and sister. We are known to you as Latwii, and are called to this group at this time. For this great honor we are most humbly thankful. Our hearts are full of soft spots, but the softest spot of all is, perhaps, this group, who has continued in a steady and one-pointed path, though the way is crooked, and though you are all weary. Yet we know that grace and your own forgiveness give you the strength to be that source of light that lights the darkness of indifference and negativity.

You ask us today about forgiveness, with a special emphasis upon self-forgiveness. This is an appropriate question, central to the understanding of spiritual evolution. It is not only in your own culture that it is thought that mistakes cannot be corrected, that some errors are so heinous that they can never be atoned for, and that many fall permanently outside the reach of the love of the infinite One. How cruel your people are, and how cruel all of those in all ways are! Following a life of [fate] is that which is in the East called karma.

Karma is that energy held in dynamic tension with another entity where lives the intransigent desires of the self. As you know, that which you seek you will receive. We have often urged you to be careful what you seek, for you will receive it; be certain that you wish it. Your planet is full of unused and unusable energy due to this basic misunderstanding about the making of mistakes. The erroneous and faulty behavior is subjectively seen by the one who acts or by another as karma springs to life between one who is wronged and one who has done the wrong, and because of the pain engendered by this trauma, and because it does not make any worldly sense to forget those things which have caused you to stumble, the inertia of karma goes merrily along singing a repetitive song of, "I got you, I got you," and the other person, if admitting guilt says, "He's got me, he's got me."

Other karmic relationships are even more complex. Both feel righteously wronged, and both want each other to apologize, to wipe the slate clean. But will they apologize for their own lack of compassion? Never, for they have been wronged. Thus, there is precious little forgiveness among your people, and those few who truly do forgive are often those who are able to deal with a great mass of often misguided information and misinformation which makes up the burden of a theology of that distortion of the Law of One called Christianity.

Now, let us back up for a moment and gaze at the true nature of what occurs when a lifetime has gone by and there has been no forgiveness. The hardened heart, with the rest of the physical complex of this entity, leaves its worn out physical vehicle and enters a plane of existence in which it is quite obviously clear that there was no need to hold the grudge, to hold the pain, to wrap oneself in fear, disgust or loathing. Moreover, it is seen by such an entity that this entity could just as well have played the other role. You dwell upon a stage, and you are actors in a very real sense. You may choose the lines that you will say. You are not bound by other peoples' understandings, you are not bound by the moribund morality of hard-heartedness and unforgiveness.

You see that you have all possible mental, emotional, spiritual and physical states within you in potentiation—not potentiated, but able to be potentiated should circumstances have caused your patterns of distortion and confusion to move into the difficult times of discontent and anger and hard-heartedness that precipitate a lack of forgiveness. But since you are between incarnations at that point, nothing can be done at that point in terms of correcting the situation and balancing, by forgiveness, that intransigent and inevitable movement on the wheel of karma. Only one thing stops the wheel of karma, and that is total forgiveness.

Forgiveness is based upon the knowledge of who you are. Two things are important to remember here. Firstly, you are the least of all, as are all who serve. You do not have rights, you do not have privileges, you do not mount defenses that armor you from others, for you are stronger than that, you have upon you the entire armor of white light, as your knowledge of the one infinite Creator and your experience with this wonderful and peaceful and joyful presence increases. You must also remember that you are a portion of the Creator, and that which is forgiven by you will be forgiven, and that which is retained by you will be retained. You are beings of immense metaphysical power, and you squander your inheritance with petty grudges and hardness of heart.

As the one known as S so prudently requested, forgiveness begins with the self, and we shall explain why. The one known as Jesus of Nazareth erased what you call the Ten Commandments, those negatives that put so many unfortunate ideas in so many heads. This entity said, "You have two jobs to do, love the Lord your God, with all your heart, and all your mind, and all your strength; and your neighbor as yourself. On these two commandments hang all the law and the prophets." In this simple sentence a huge body of material, which you call the Old Testament, was relegated to a dusty back shelf, and forgiveness and redemption had come into focus at last.

Now, to love the Creator is relatively easy. The Creator gives so many gifts, is so very generous He supplied us with all that we need, in whatever level of learning we are. You need oxygen, the trees give you oxygen. The trees need carbon dioxide, your very being puts out this substance. The creation of the Father is a thing of great beauty and balance, that may be seen to have a dark side—the floods, the hurricanes, the tornadoes, the ghastly and horrifying aftermaths of natural events. But this little life of yours, that will move so fast and be over so quickly, is not an opportunity for you to make yourself more comfortable. It is an opportunity to learn better how to love, and it is difficult situations that bring that knowledge forward. When one may love the Creator who has caused the whirlwind, and the fire, and the terrible destruction of great earthquakes, then you will begin to understand that the lessons of love are often difficult, and always need inevitably end in the death of the physical body.

Each entity's job is to gaze at those situations which confront one, to find love, praise and the giving of thanks. In the face of great tragedies this makes no sense to those who are fair weather friends of the Creator, and believe that the Creator is the giver-out of the spiritual lollipop, the happiness pill, the serenity pill, the wisdom pill. No, my friends, the Creator in His great and terrible wisdom and compassion has given you free will to face all that you must face, including the most difficult and negatively perceived situations, in order that you may do that which is not easy, for how easy is it to forgive the small thing, the slight error of a friend?

Forgiveness is first the turning to a power greater than yourself, and a giving to that power of an entire situation, that you may be given the consolation and the healing that you require in order to forgive yourself, whether you are the wronged one or the self-perceived wrong doer. There is always a lack of forgiveness of the self that seems to be held more tightly than the forgiveness of others. You gaze too close into the mirror of this illusion and your manifestation within it. Your birthright is to be forgiven, to realize each self-perceived error and to forgive oneself for it, and move on.

Thus, you come to a respect, and an honoring, and a loving, and a nurturing of yourself. The key to forgiveness of others is the forgiveness of the self. Release, release, release, give back to the forces of the universe those energies which are easily absorbed in infinity, and leave them not to pollute your own feelings, your mind, or your heart, but rather let forgiveness flow as a sweet river under the surface of all that you do and say.

Whatever your conceptions of yourself, if they be negative, release them. If you say to yourself, as this instrument does, "I am not pretty," there is a hardness of heart that will spill over into karmic situations with others, into a lack of ability to forgive others. If one says, "I am not worthy," there is a lack of awareness of one's birthright. Moving from the temporary to the eternal, and gazing at yourself as would a most loving mother, forgive yourself, accept yourself, allow yourself to be yourself, and lead the concern for the self away from center stage, for it is as dangerous as the blinders upon the horse to those who can see but will not. Soften, allow, forgive and turn, and ask to be in a tabernacle in the immediate presence of the infinite Creator. Ask, though you feel unworthy, to be that person who experiences unconditional love. Let love fill you, which you naturally wish to return, and as you more and more perceive yourselves as children of the great Father and Mother of the universe, you can come to treasure yourself, for you are all treasures.

When the work of forgiveness of self has been done to the point where you feel that maintenance is that which is necessary rather than complete concentration, then and only then turn to the attempt to forgive others. It is not selfish to do the work upon the self first, it is necessary, it is mandatory. You must bring your own personality and biases into balance, else how can you be the house of the Father, how can that light shine through you if you are lurching about wasting the energy of love in the distortions of self-immolation?

Let us say we have done this work, and it does come to an end, not that you do not slip from time to time back into those negative programs which have caused you to be armored against the rest of the world and survive, but that you recognize that you do not need this armor, that you are meant to be vulnerable to circumstance, that you are meant to be an actor upon the social scene. This is the density where you learn to deal with entities in more and more gentle compassion and love. Now you have forgiven yourself, you then can see that although those other entities may not have done this work, at the end of that work which they will do at some point, they will find their birthright as children of a forgiven nature, children of the one Creator, children of love in which there is no judgment.

But paradoxically, it is well to judge carefully, to the best of your ability, that which seems subjectively helpful and appropriate, and that which does not—in your relationship with yourself, with the Creator, and with your neighbor. Compassionate love includes being of service by speaking of difficult things. If you have not forgiven those difficult things, you will be speaking with a hard heart, and your judgment will be unfair. Only self-forgiven can you enter into the forgiveness of others.

Let it not wash away the intense colors of your emotions, your feelings, and your learnings, by saying that all things are well. You yourself have within you biases which have been dearly won, and to which you should listen. Why then, in all compassion, you are judge, but you are a judge of compassion, and if words that are less than easy must be said, yet they are said with love and compassion, carefully and courteously, and honestly, and fearlessly. And in such communication lies the beginning of forgiveness, of those you feel may have wronged you, or those whom you feel you have wronged. There is no difference between those two in terms of forgiveness. They are two sides of the same coin. Forgiveness is a universal currency, a kind of money, shall we say, since your people are so interested in the power that money has. Spend that currency with a whole heart.

In order to forgive the unforgivable, which is part of the lesson of learning to love without condition, it is extremely helpful to take that person within yourself and earnestly and humbly to pray for that person, for as you pray and intercede for such a person, you will grow to love that person, you will have compassion upon that person, and these changes in consciousness are wonderful catalyst for that person to be *(inaudible)*, that person may also begin the long cycle of learning to forgive. Your biases are not incorrect. You have earned them. Do not abandon them and simply say that all things are acceptable. You are miles and miles away from this elevation. First you must learn to love, and you must learn to have wisdom, and you must learn to have compassionate wisdom. Right at this moment in your development, you are simply attempting to love. Of yourself you cannot do this, but the great original Thought of Love is with you. You may block it out, you may deafen yourself against its call, but it lies just beyond the door that you can open at any time, waiting to comfort, to ease, and to offer grace.

Forgiving entities does not mean that it is necessary for the forgiving entity to continue to accept acts upon the part of the other self which are subjectively seen to be abusive and destructive enough that the self—or those young selves for whom you are responsible—[is] in danger of any kind, be it mental, or physical, but as you do those things that you must, as you decide upon the separation because you see that union is impossible, as the other entity cannot do the work that you are doing in forgiveness, you simply do that which you have to do, with love and compassion and peace, staying within the forgiveness, accepting the unacceptable that may occur, loving the unlovable that has brought about the current situation by its catalyst.

You cannot adjust other entity's states of self-forgiveness or forgiveness of others. You may drop the seeds, and see yourself as the Johnny Appleseed of forgiveness, for forgiveness is the essence of what this instrument would call the Kingdom of Heaven, and the seeds of forgiveness are like leaven, that lighten and lift and make delicious the whole loaf of life, and love, and relationships. But you cannot do others' work for them.

Consequently, realize that you must stop the wheel of karma for yourself by completing a very thorough and earnest process of forgiveness of the self, forgiveness of the other self or situation, and forgiveness of the process that has taken place, on steps that seem to have been made clumsily or wrongly. You are perceiving yourself within an illusion. You can judge to the point of your own instinct, but you cannot judge finally. You simply judge, and forgive, to increase your own positive polarity.

What we are talking about, when we talk about forgiveness, is healing. The hope of each entity is to become healed, and healing may be defined as that state wherein the karma is balanced with each soul with whom you come into contact, and your realization of yourself is a realization of yourself as whole, perfect, beautiful, and a child of the infinite One. Does this make you special and important? May it never be. This makes you the servant of all. With compassion comes humility, and you would gladly serve, as did the one known as Jesus, by washing the feet, by doing the unattractive things that make up the daily run of existence, because, since you are forgiven, you dwell in a state of redemptive joy, so that every dish you wash, every window that you clean, every flower that you touch, is alive to the light within you, and responds in love.

The creation of second density dwells in love, except in those places—and there are so many—where the lack of love of your humankind has damaged second density. Touch into perfect love. Keep your feet in that fine river of forgiveness, and your light shall shine, as it will, and that which it is given to you to do will come before you with no effort whatsoever on your part, and whatever it is, the sweeping of a floor, the saving of a nation, all is equal if it is done in utter and complete love for the Creator, the self, the situation, and any other entities that may be involved.

Always remember how short is this experience, and how important is this choice of polarity in which forgiveness plays such an important part. Love always forgives, but it does not rush in to forgive. Remember that upon the cross, in that great story of the teacher known as Jesus, there were not one but two entities, one of which did not ask for forgiveness, one of which did not turn from his self-confessed errors. That entity remained in a state of karma and imbalance. There was another entity who perceived itself as equally without virtue, the self-confessed maker of serious and grave errors, but this entity had the faith and the wisdom and the vision to turn to the face of the infinite One as it shone through the one known as Jesus upon the cross, physically turning the head, gazing at the broken body that still shone so brightly. "Will you remember me, please, when you come into your kingdom?" asked the thief, the felon, the murderer. "This day you shall be with me in paradise," replied the broken and dying lover and servant of mankind.

May you turn from error when it is perceived, without being discouraged that you have made an error, and ask forgiveness. Deep within yourself, there is the Creator self, the redemptive and forgiving self, the source of forgiveness. Allow it to flood you, allow it to make you thankful, allow the feeling of healing to take place, and know that you are self-forgiven. Then turn to the world, and by power of Christ consciousness within, you shall be constantly renewed. And as more and more of you do this, the face of the Earth shall be transformed. That is how powerful forgiveness is.

We have spoken overlong, and we apologize, but we wished so much to be with the one known as S especially, as we so seldom are able to speak with this soul in the voice that has words, but may we say to this beautiful and beloved child, that we are the clouds overhead, that we are the stars at night, that we are the familiar things that you touch day by day, that we are in the smiles of strangers, we are always with you. We wish for the one known as S to be aware of this, in a deep, and abiding, and trusting way, for we are of the vibration which causes us to be with this instrument of light as comforter, or what this instrument would call the Holy Spirit.

Let us nurture you, be aware of our love at all times, let it flood you, and overwhelm you, and heal you, when you are too weak to do these things for yourself, for we are that part of you which is a bit closer to the divine consciousness you call Christ consciousness. We are with you always, yet our usual strong request that those things which we say be regarded as the opinions that they are, the fallible and possibly erroneous opinions of those who also are students of the one infinite Creator, and companions with you on that infinite path. We will at this time transfer this contact to the one known as Jim. We are those of Latwii.

(Jim channeling)

I am Latwii, and greet each again in love and light through this instrument. At this time we would offer ourselves to speak to any queries which may yet remain upon the minds of those present. Is there a query at this time?

Carla: Yes, I have one. A couple of times in recent days I have been faced with giving advice in situations where there was an enormous amount of abuse within the *(inaudible)*, abuse which included children, and in which there was obvious agony going on in the abuser, in the *(inaudible)* the person writing to me, or speaking to me. In both cases upon reflection I felt that the best advice that I could give was to go through the process of forgiveness so that one *(inaudible)* be free from karma, and *(inaudible)* and then to engage in a conversation and communication which would open up to the abusing entity the agony which caused the abuse, in order that he may too, though he could or did not wish to be in the situation in which he was.

Especially because in both cases the situation involved children, and also physical abuse, I recommended the dissolution of the sacred bond of matrimony, because the spiritual principles by which I live seemed to point in that direction. I wonder if you could speak to the metaphysical correctness or incorrectness of my thought processes and my understandings, as I believe these people will both listen to me, and I do not want to be responsible for an incorrect application of spiritual principles.

I am Latwii, and am aware of your query, my sister. We find that you have spoken according to those highest principles with which you are familiar, and we applaud your effort, for you have given the best of your own experience in compassion towards, not just those who write you, but those who were responsible for creating a great deal of disharmony within the relationship that included the young child, and we would suggest to you that the information which you have shared may be considered, in light of the entire experience, by each entity to whom you spoke.

This is to say, that though your information and your suggestions may have been crafted with the finest of intentions and according to the highest spiritual principles with which you are familiar, there are far more factors that enter into each entity's situation than the best advice possible, and each entity will be moved by that which is most powerful and pressing within the life pattern, as, indeed, each entity has moved at all times. If your suggestions ring in harmony with the heart of each entity's current life pattern and desires, then you will have aided the entity in moving in the most appropriate direction.

If, however, either entity decides that, though the information and inspiration is helpful and hopeful, but there is still within either or each entity a desire to continue in the relationship for whatever reason, then this shall also be the appropriate path for that entity.

In short, we suggest that when you give your suggestions to another, that you give, as you have, the best of what you have to give, and then allow the entity to use this information as it will, without feeling either responsibility for moving the entity where you think perhaps it could not have moved, or by failing to move the entity in a direction which you feel is more appropriate, for each entity is complex, and will, in many places, move in a pattern which is incomprehensible to any entity other than itself, and it must be realized that even those puzzling steps upon the path play their part as certainly as do those which are clear and strong in their forward movement. Thus, we applaud your efforts, my sister.

Is there another query?

Carla: No, I really thank you for that answer, that's all I wanted to know and hear. Thank you.

I am Latwii, and we thank you, my sister. Is there another query at this time?

(Pause)

I am Latwii, and we are filled with joy at the opportunity to speak to this group. It is, indeed, our favorite, shall we say, for we have long been with each in this group, even before those times of the first contact of a vocal nature, and we look forward to each blending of vibrations with our own. We walk with you, we see with you, we experience with you, we rejoice with you, and we breathe with you at each moment in which you experience the colors of the emotions of your density of illusion.

At this time we shall take our leave of this group, rejoicing in love and in light, and praising the one Creator in all things. We are known to you as those of Latwii. Adonai, my friends. Adonai.

L/L Research

L/L Research is a subsidiary of Rock Creek Research & Development Laboratories, Inc.

P.O. Box 5195
Louisville, KY 40255-0195

www.llresearch.org

Rock Creek is a non-profit corporation dedicated to discovering and sharing information which may aid in the spiritual evolution of humankind.

ABOUT THE CONTENTS OF THIS TRANSCRIPT: This telepathic channeling has been taken from transcriptions of the weekly study and meditation meetings of the Rock Creek Research & Development Laboratories and L/L Research. It is offered in the hope that it may be useful to you. As the Confederation entities always make a point of saying, please use your discrimination and judgment in assessing this material. If something rings true to you, fine. If something does not resonate, please leave it behind, for neither we nor those of the Confederation would wish to be a stumbling block for any.

CAVEAT: This transcript is being published by L/L Research in a not yet final form. It has, however, been edited and any obvious errors have been corrected. When it is in a final form, this caveat will be removed.

© 2009 L/L Research

Sunday Meditation
June 24, 1990

Group question: The question this evening has to do with how we make our way through the illusion, working with the catalyst that we have planned for ourselves. We are assuming that we put the catalyst in place before the incarnation in the form of various experiences that make an impression upon us so that we have a basic personality with which to operate, and as we go through the incarnation this basic personality that is formed early in our lives then has a series of lessons that come in the form of various kinds of catalyst, difficulties, problems, confusions, challenges. How do we use the basic personality that we have put in place, and how do we face the catalyst when it is, as many people feel more and more, overwhelming, and seems to have no end, there seems to be little rest? Is this a function of growing older, or a part of the cycle that we're going through now since it is so close to the end?

(Carla channeling)

Greetings to all of you in the love and in the light of the one infinite Creator. We are known to you as Q'uo. We are humbly grateful to have been called to this place of desire for knowledge and truth, and we shall do our very best to share what truth we personally feel to be so with you. As always, we wish to remind each of you that we are not infallible, but rather those who have teachers just as you do, those who walk the seemingly restive trail, without time and space, but standing always upon holy ground.

We, like you, are finite in our own manifestation at this time. We are all dust that lives in the presence of the infinite One.

Your question this evening has to do with how one may find a point of balance within your illusion where one feels relatively safe, where one cannot be overwhelmed by circumstance or difficulties. So as you picture yourself walking upon this infinite trail, the first tool, or resource, that you have in order to work with the illusion which so often attempts to bring you from your center, is to remember that, as this instrument would say, wherever you go, there you are. You cannot cope with life, for life is an illusion. The only thing within this particular illusion, or any illusion that we know of in the kingdoms of the Father, is each imperishable spirit to whom we speak. You must make it through yourself. It is not circumstances which overwhelm one, but rather the self's choice of reaction to circumstance.

Now, let us look at one's handling of one's self. Do you handle yourself as if you were a precious Chinese vase? May we say that no, you do not, in that how much more precious are you than such a manmade artifact? How little you value yourselves, how much difficulty and grief do you cause yourselves by asking to be perfect in every way, according to your own personal definitions of this behavior, in an illusion which was created specifically not to be ideal. The Creator gave you consciousness. This same Creator did not give you happiness, nor should you expect that this quality will come to one who is wise, or compassionate, as a reward for living well. As in any schoolroom, you are here to learn, and there is never a comfortably given test in the history of education, according to most students. But being within the illusion, you focus upon the material which you are receiving, rather that upon the consciousness that receives it, that is, yourself.

The experiences are transitory. The choices that you make in reacting to these circumstances slowly build up a non-transitory resource. If you have had courage once in choosing what was subjectively perceived as the ethically correct thing to do in a situation, you have made a difference in yourself, you have chosen, and with each choice your polarity, your positivity, your service to others, becomes intensified, until there begins to be within each who continuously seeks persistently, the fire, the passion, to do and to be that which is love. There is no activity that can give you this attitude, and the test that you will take at the end of this life experience has everything to do with attitude.

You may find within the illusion that circumstances are overwhelmingly difficult. Often one is stretched to one's limits or beyond them, and one may consider that one has misbehaved and done wrongly, and regrets and rues each seeming *(inaudible)* and wishes with all its heart that it might return to that moment and do it again, only this time with love. That is why time is so vastly important within your illusion, the stream runs one way. You have a shot at creating a conscious light-filled moment, fresh and new and joyful, every instant of your life, and once that instant is gone it is gone. This is true, not of a few people, or of most people, but of all persons in whatever path of service has been their destiny, their burden, and their honor.

So when you look at situations and hear the difficulties coming into your ears and feel them growing in your heart, know that you are experiencing yourself, and that that which has happened to cause these feelings is within you. You cannot escape yourself. You cannot escape every other thing in the illusion including the illusion, but in each escape there is the wasted opportunity for learning the lessons of love. Thus we hold up to you a picture of yourself, as beloved, created as beloved children, rocked and comforted and held by the mother nature of the infinite Creator, and strong in heart to wish to do that which is of service.

When as an adult, so-called, you are hurt, mentally, or physically, or emotionally, or especially if you suffer that most painful of all sufferings, the spiritual suffering, you know that you do not have anyone to run to. You are no longer a toddler that can run to the all-embracing mother and hide your head upon her lap and cry until you are released from sadness. You must be that nurturing mother self to yourself. You must treat yourselves well. This is not service to self, for if you cannot treat yourself well, out of a pure and unconditional love for yourself, with all of your imperfections and errors, then how can you love and serve those about you?

Thus, the first resource revolves around your own self-concept. You need to know yourself more and more deeply. As always, the daily meditation is a great aid in this search for the universal and unique self that you really, deeply are.

Secondly, we would talk about the resource of *(inaudible)*. When one is not aiding, caring for, and loving the selves about it, family, friends, strangers and humankind, one may do all manner of things and yet not *(inaudible)* oneself at all engaged in the joyful possibility of living. There is tremendous spiritual help in having an attitude of servanthood to all those about you. Let your thoughts run towards what you might do to be of service to all those who cross your path. How twisted and convoluted are so many entities' feelings towards those whom they meet. How very often in judging and biased opinion the content of one's thoughts instead of the realization of each person as precisely as important as you, and every other being within your density that you now enjoy. We do not mean that you should doff all other priorities and simply follow other people's instructions. That is not the kind of servanthood that we mean. As a matter of fact, we may suggest that often you will find yourself in a position, as you attempt to be of service, in which you are being unpleasing to the entity whom you wish to serve. Now, as you can see that another is addicted to some strain of thought or action that is unhelpful and self-destructive, and you are then asked to aid in this addiction, the one who wishes to be of true service is the one who will refuse, but never without compassion, never without clear communication, and never without forgiveness.

The service-to-others path seems simple. One pictures oneself as being a kind of celestial waitress, bussing the tables of humanity, easing other peoples' passage through the difficult times, splitting the great Red Sea so that your friends may pass dry shod. We do not see this as service to others, for each entity needs to be given room to learn for itself. Therefore, sometimes the greatest service is to allow a being that depends upon you to make it safe to live, to make mistakes, to make errors, for those whom you wish to serve will not learn if you do the learning for them. Rather, in relation to others you create an atmosphere in which learning is safe.

If your heart is full, and energized, and open to the love about you, you will feel those times when love bubbles forth from within you as a spring into a fountain, and you will see yourselves used as beautiful, as inspirational witnesses to the light that you are within. Many of your people are afraid of this light, and will indeed shutter it from your sight, because in order to become aware of oneself as light one must square with oneself one's true nature, and although each entity is unique, each contains all emotions, potentials and possibilities of which one may think. Thus, you do not get to know yourself by behaving, or doing well. You get to know yourself by observing yourself being precisely what you want to be, and what you feel to be. And then, when the day is done, asking yourself where the stress points are, where *(inaudible)* or the delightfulness of the day has occurred. So you begin to find out your own nature. And as you learn your own nature it becomes transparent.

One does not need to act out one's own nature with anger and trauma, for one is quite aware, having done the work, of what is actualizing, or causing the entity, yourself, to be thus and so. So you not only nurture yourself, in, of yourself, and by yourself, but you nurture yourself in relation to others, by offering, through your simple attitude, a sort of atmosphere of helpfulness, a relaxed and welcoming aura which invites entities to feel safety and peace when they are around you. In that atmosphere, then perhaps you may be of further service by the talking, the speaking together, they enjoyment of laughing, friendship and love. For to be of service to others you must needs have some sort of idea as to who you are, and you need to have given up and surrendered that childhood need to protect oneself by behaving. *(Inaudible)* not behavior. Your actions are spontaneous moment by moment. *(Inaudible)* invulnerable, *(inaudible)* as has been said this evening, or as *(inaudible)*, are girdled, so that we may include women, to be of service in whatever way you can. No service should ever be put down by the self, or *(inaudible)* anything that is done for the love of the one infinite Creator is equal to anything else that is done in that love.

The last resource that we shall cover, because we realize that this instrument is telling us we are speaking too long, [is] what you call among your peoples the sense of humor. People who are extremely serious about accelerating the path of spiritual evolution have a tendency to sound like the Volga boatmen, putting their poles in the deep rivers of the Volga, and pushing slowly, and with difficulty, to make the *(inaudible)* barge move. This is not the true nature of spiritual evolution. The laughter quotient, shall we say, of your days should be gradually moving upward. Many things should be transparent to you who have been upon the trail for awhile, and therefore deeply humorous, in the humor that goes beyond the smile and warms the heart. For this life that you experience is the joke without the punch line. You *(inaudible)* yourself. As you gain perspective and see yourself as soap opera characters, cartoon characters, creatures that would be ridiculous and still be *(inaudible)*, secure and undaunted, so will you lose the many, many layers of fear which cause you to armor against the delightfulness of life.

We are aware that this is a world in which young children get run over in the roadway, in which young men die fighting for something that they do not understand. We are aware that there are many, many injustices, that life is not fair. This is an illusion designed to cause you to act, to cause you to think, to assist you in making choices. Shall you be the cynic, the one who is usually correct for the moment? Or shall you be that idealist, who always suffers for the ideal in the present, but who, in a millennium or so, will find that that ideal still holds truth, and is something to which it has been worthwhile to be loyal. Idealists, in your extremely relativistic society, are most often seen as fools. Can you accept that, or do you need to behave in such a way that people will never see you as fools, but as one who knows the score, one who is in the know, one who is a player in the game of *(inaudible)*, and *(inaudible)*, and *(inaudible)*? If you choose to retain your ideals in the face of life as you experience it, you are both accelerating your path to consciousness, and becoming more vulnerable to appearing strange to those about you. If you care about your reputation more than you care about your ideals, you will most truly be more successful during this short *(inaudible)* of a lifetime. But what shall you have done for yourself as a being of light?

We ask that sometime in the next few days you do two things. Firstly, sit, quietly, and watch your grass grow. You will be delighted by the life that you see teeming all around you, the glory of the sky, the beauty of the foliage, the music of the laughter of children, and the human dark comedy, with anguish over misbehaving children and friends. How funny and beautiful is your illusion, if you can but slow down and look at it. The other thing we would ask you to do is to laugh. Not a giggle, not a chuckle, we ask you to lose yourself, to find that one thing that for you takes you out of yourself. All of you are in need of healing and laughter *(inaudible)*. You patch together melancholy, and *(inaudible)* lists of what to do, and naturopathic remedies. Simple laughter.

Thus, we would leave you with those two thoughts. Love and nurture and honor yourselves. Love and nurture and honor others, who are all yourselves. And be merry in your love. Give to your life the light touch. Let the world come to you, for you are not *(inaudible)*, you are *(inaudible)* upon yourself. We know that you love the Creator, *(inaudible)* whatever way you choose to think of this higher power. You love the mystery. You love the dream. Please know that it loves you back …

(Side one of tape ends.)

(Carla channeling)

… that it loved you before you loved it, and that it and you are love. You may now [take] two steps backwards, and take the long sigh of relief. And we urge you always, when you are feeling harassed, to take those two steps backwards, and take a long, deep breath, just a moment to praise the Creator, to thank the Creator for all the blessings of life. It need only take a moment that you would *(inaudible)* turn *(inaudible)* situation *(inaudible)* eternity.

We would speak to the one known as S, in explaining who we are, for there is a portion of our principle that is Latwii, and this portion of ourself wishes to extend our assurance to this being of light that it is never absent, though it never speaks, it is always there as a battery, as a carrier wave, to strengthen and smooth and comfort the path of this entity. We are a principle made up of two social memory complexes, that of Ra and that of Latwii. Ra is unwilling to risk this instrument by further speaking in the sleeping state. Those of Latwii are also students of those of Ra, and are most happy indeed to be able to blend our vibrations to offer to this instrument all such thoughts as she may be prepared *(inaudible)* to offer.

We thank and bless each through this instrument, and thank this instrument for offering itself to our service, now and in each day. We will close the meeting through the one known as Jim. I am Q'uo.

(Jim channeling)

I am Q'uo, and greet each again in love and light through this instrument. We are pleased at this time to offer ourself in the attempt to speak to any queries which may have arisen in the minds of those present. Is there any query at this time?

R: Yes, Q'uo, I'd like to ask one.

(Rest of tape is inaudible.) ☙

Intensive Meditation
June 29, 1990

(Carla channeling)

I greet you in the love and in the light of the one Creator. I am known to you as Latwii, and I have the great honor of speaking to those within this circle who vibrate very closely with us, so that we are always with you. We speak of the one known as Jim and the one known as K.

We are what this instrument would call the Holy Spirit or the Comforter. There are many, many, many facets of the immediate presence of the Father, but because of the many lifetimes each of these two entities has spent in vibrations very similar to our own, it is we who have the privilege of abiding with you in fair weather and foul, not to speak with you, but to be with you, as Comforter. When you are weary, allow the Comforter to hold you, to nurture you, to bring you to your true home within.

But as teacher of this group of channels, we have a different role, one which is far less easy for us for we must use words.

We would like to work this evening upon the harmony of the group. We shall, therefore, be speaking of several subjects and moving quite often from one contact to another. We ask that each contact be scrupulous in checking our contact as it comes, and opening each contact in love and light, and naming who we are as it comes to you, and doing the same as you leave, for whatever we have to say can be summed up in two words and you know what they are: love and light. That is the thought and the material that is all that there is in this creation.

In order to continue tuning automatically the greetings—specifying your name and moving through the words of love and light—act as a centering device or lodestone, so that incoming energy patterns which move into conceptualization in the group mind are regularized and made easy in passage through each mind/body/spirit complex. Each entity is using the throat charka—the entities known as Carla and K have a naturally open throat charka when their instruments are tuned. Consequently, in these two instruments especially, attention should be paid in the tuning during another entity's speaking, to [the] rotating and effulgence of that known to you as the indigo ray center.

Each of these two instruments have a tendency to recognize that work in consciousness is necessary but also very hard. Consequently, as you center and center and center again, see yourself constantly as worthy, perfect, beautiful and unique; a gift from God, as it were, and in perfect reciprocity, a gift to the Creator.

For the one known as Jim, difficulties that this instrument is having stem largely from the wavering of the green ray energy center. This energy center needs not to be overly stimulated or artificially stimulated, but allowed to be what it will be.

In this incarnation this instrument is working with this center and may well not be completely satisfied with the full opening of the green ray energy center. Remember that the key here is balance. Unlike the other two channels, this entity has very little difficulty in keeping the brow or indigo ray center totally open, working consciousness is a natural process or gift that this instrument has been given. It is well to know where your weak link is.

In the case of those who have the extremely dominate blue ray energy centers very full, very light, and very beautiful, there is a tendency to think that perhaps it is not necessary to do as much work in consciousness as would create the optimal balance for these entities as channels. In the case of the one known as Jim, it is well for this instrument to remember that the green ray energy center is the all-important center for spiritual work, and that the overworking of the indigo ray center, when work has not been fully completed in open heart green ray, the resultant vibrations are to some extent strained.

Consequently, we suggest that this instrument be very gentle in its channeling, accepting the perceived amount of energy which may not be full and lush, as is the very open heart centers of the other two channels, but rather respect that place where the one known as Jim is, for it is the perfect place for that instrument at that time. Be sure, therefore, that the channeling that comes forth is channeling that uses well, but not overuses the energies of the instrument. For such can be deleterious to the instrument and can certainly cause the instrument to feel that it has not done its best.

We are, of course, most grateful to each of these instruments for offering themselves, their ideals, and their lives to be servants of humankind, as humankind moves through difficult times in which it will be increasingly appropriate for entities to be able to see your radiance, that which flows through you because of your spiritual life, so that you may more and more speak of that which you have learned, and in the meantime there is always the sowing of little seeds of spiritual thought that in no way threaten, proselytize or evangelize, but merely cause someone to take a second look, to think and to notice the paradoxes and mysteries that surround this illusion.

We will transfer at this time to the one known as K. We are those of Latwii, and leave this instrument in love and light.

(K channeling)

I am Latwii.

And in my challenge I ask do you come in love and light and service to others?

I am Latwii, and we do indeed come in the love and the light of the infinite Creator and we serve together with you, and we seek with you to be of service to others. We will continue to speak this evening of an aspect of this service that is evidenced by the harmony within this group which works together in service, to each other and to us when we are called to *(inaudible)* and to those who may hear, our humble opinions be helped in some measure on their own paths of service.

As you prepare yourselves for service as vocal channels you may be aware of many different thoughts that come to you *(inaudible)* to this instrument in love and light. We are extremely pleased for we have found it possible with this new instrument to achieve a very high ratio of our thoughts to this instrument. The effort made when such an instrument is near is great and each time that such a contact is given the mechanics of the process of channeling will become more familiar and more trusted, for you will find again and again that they do not let the instrument down; they do not leave the instrument without the finishing thoughts. And the various energy rushes and experiences of being overwhelmed will, as experience adds to experience, become those things which fade into the background and disappear.

We continue briefly through this instrument.

(Carla channeling)

Many thoughts go through the minds of those who channel. This is inevitable and part of even the best tuned channel. Its environment is never completely pure, it is simply the best it can do. Therefore, it should be emphasized to each instrument that a perfect instrument is a concept which is useful in goal-making, but not at all necessary in expectation.

We expect each instrument to work imperfectly, as we would describe the content of the message, as opposed to the content of our concepts, as always being less than 100%. Indeed, we encourage that there be some input, some sharing, of the experiences, the special verbal skills, the way with words, the knowledge, the experience, the reading vocabulary of the instrument. All of these things are perfectly acceptable tools for creating the verbal channeling.

We do not wish or expect that our concepts will be offered 100% in any conscious channeling, however. Having experimented with trance channeling, the Confederation has found that in using the trance, the vernacular of your people has to be forsaken, which means that that which comes through is conceptually perfect, but very difficult to grasp in many cases.

There are those that appreciate the more pure, accurate and lucid communications, for instance, of our brothers and sisters of Ra through this instrument, but it is also true that we find that we are to speak to a much larger group of entities which call for help at this time, by using conscious light trance channeling, so do not be a judge of the self because the occasional thoughts [move through the light.]

We would now transfer this contact to the one known as Jim. We are those of Latwii, and leave this instrument in love and light.

Jim: Whenever it is necessary for me to open my eyes to flip a tape or a microphone movement, I repeat the creation of the pentagram of light, surrounding clockwise by the circle, again surrounding the room as the umbrella of the cone, to redo the tuning.

I feel the conditioning in the jaws and movement of the lips at which time I ask who comes in the name of the Christ Consciousness and the service-to-others polarity.

(Jim channeling)

I am Latwii.

Do you come in the name of the Christ Consciousness and the service-to-others polarity?

We do.

You are most welcome to stay and to speak; if not, you must leave immediately. Do you come in the name of the Christ consciousness and the service-to-others polarity?

I am Latwii, and I come in the name of the Christ consciousness and service-to-others polarity, my brother.

You may speak as you will.

When one feels the presence of the thought concepts within the mind as the contact has been made and as it has been ongoing, it is well to speak these thoughts as freely as is possible without undue concern as to the immediate content or the direction of the information that is towards any particular aim that the information seems to be headed, for this is the beginning of the perception of parallel thoughts, shall we say, that tend to interfere in any instrument's mind with the clear perception of those thoughts which are being transmitted by whatever contact is utilizing the instrument.

However, as we spoke previously, we are aware that the depth and complexity of the human mind is such that it is almost impossible to completely remove stray thoughts, side thoughts, thoughts that spring from an immediate apprehension of the perception of that which is being tuned. Therefore, it is well for the instrument to regard the stray thoughts with as little significance or importance as one would regard the wind rustling through the branches of your trees as you converse with a friend or neighbor below.

If one places one's attention overly much upon either the wind in the trees or the stray thoughts that blow through the mind as one is serving as a local instrument, the focus of the attention may become diffused to the point where the contact becomes first polluted with more personally oriented thoughts and if these thoughts continue then the contact shall surely be lost, so we recognize that each instrument, being in the possession of that great tool of the mind in all its depth and complexity, will often become aware of a background of static, shall we say.

When an instrument has been successful in keeping the attention focused upon the thoughts as they are being received, then the instrument will find that there is a lengthening of the contact which is much like taking two magnets and putting them in an alignment so that each strengthens the effect of the other, rather than misaligning the poles so that they seem, and indeed are, slightly at variance with each other.

The ability to cast oneself freely off the cliff, shall we say, and to remain confident that there shall be support for each step that is taken into what seems to be thin air, is the quality of foolishness that we have described many times previously that is well for each instrument to cultivate, for as the one known as Carla spoke earlier to the one known as Jim in the purifying of the tuning so that there is no dedication or desire of the self that is confused upon the tuning, so it is well to purify the desire to serve while channeling so that there will be no unnecessary infusion of personal material within the contact.

It is difficult, we know, for any entity within your illusion so carefully bounded by that which is solid in either manifestation or expectation to remove such boundaries from the mind so that the mind might become the hollow vessel that shall transmit thought communication. We sympathize with each of you as you attempt to move against the grain of your illusion, shall we say. However, it is becoming more widely known among many of those of your peoples who are becoming conscious of the evolutionary process at this time that the brain which you have in your illusion has the division of lobe that corresponds to both the intellectual and to the mode of perception that is active or male, shall we say, and there is the lobe of the brain which is more concerned with the female qualities, that which awaits the reaching and that which partakes of non-logical or intuitional inspiration.

It is this latter mode of perception and of being that is utilized within the channeling process so that the mind becomes in as relaxed a state as possible, shutting down for the moment the analytical procedure—that which is active and that which inspects—so that the more receptive portions of the mind complex might become activated and utilize the receptive qualities to a great degree during the channeling process.

At this time we would wish to open this particular session to any queries which may have arisen during the practices that have been utilized this evening. We will, before entertaining any query, like to speak our appreciation and congratulations to the one known as Carla for her implementing of the framework for this particular evening. We find that chopping wood is very helpful for each instrument for it is well to review that which has been set in place by conscious design in order that one might more fully and freely exercise the instrument in service to others.

At this time we would ask if there are any queries to which we may speak.

Carla: I would just like, if it is possible without infringing on free will to confirm my impression that the one known as K *(inaudible)*.

I am Latwii, and I am aware of the query, my sister. You are quite correct in your assessment of the progress that has been made this evening by the one known as K. We are aware that this new instrument has cause to feel, in her own mind, that is, that she had difficulty in maintaining a clear contact. We would like to state that the contact which was maintained was indeed quite clear and we chose the general format of proceeding with fewer thoughts at the normal pace and then exercising the instrument by giving silence so that there might be the opportunity for this instrument to look again, shall we say, for our signal or our contact, as it is quite easy for any instrument to become concerned during prolonged pauses. It is at this time of concern that most instruments, in a small panic shall we say, tend to pad the contact with a bit of patter that is recognized as normal channeling procedure. This is well for any instrument which needs to utilize this as a crutch. There are many ways to begin contacts and this is one.

(Pause)

I am Latwii, and am again with this instrument, and we greet again in love and light.

[To continue.] However, after some point within the new instrument's development, it is well that the instrument, in the desire to purify the channel and to purify the contact as it is pursued in the mind, to allow whatever pauses may occur, whether they be those inserted for emphasis or consideration on the part of the Confederation entity, or whether they be the result of the instrument having difficulty in perceiving the next grouping of sound vibration complexes, it is well for the instrument to rest within the pause, confident that there shall be a continuation of the contact and of the message and it was in this area this evening that the one known as K excelled and we are greatly pleased that this entity has been able to perceive both our words clearly and our pauses clearly.

Is there another query?

K: *(Inaudible)* … confusion that I was feeling and was wondering if you could help me sort it out so that I need to grow comfortable with pauses. I was feeling overwhelmed, both by numerous thoughts that I was having and I was quite unsure as to what was being transmitted to me and what I was maybe trying to come up with to make sense of it to myself. I found myself judging it and wondering how the others present were going to judge it and at the same time I was trying to dispel those thoughts so that I could just concentrate on what I was doing and as I found myself feeling more and more unable to dispel the judgmental types of thoughts then I started panicking more, and what I'd like from you are some suggestions about what to do in those situations in trying to sort those things out. What I could do to sort of stop and try to start over and catch a clear thread, and it seemed to me that that never really happened. Do you have any other suggestions?

I am Latwii, and I am aware of the query, my sister. We give this instrument a vision of the feline known as Chocolate Bar. This entity frequently frightens itself so that it jumps at its own movement and perhaps shall jump again at the jump. This is a rough analogy that may describe the activity within your mind as the contact was occurring. The suggestion is one we find we give frequently to all new instruments, so simply stated yet much practice is needed, to simply relax the mind, the worry, the analysis, the panic, as the surface of the pond is moved by the wind of concern one must move below the surface activity and sink more and more deeply to the bottom of the pond, to the bottom of the mind, so that one may perceive that which is given.

We have a word of encouragement in this regard and that is that with practice this ability to relax shall be enhanced simply by the repetition of this process time and again. There is much of that which is like unto muscle memory, as you call it. When any new procedure is learned there will be the time of dropping the ball, shall we say, of making the mistake and misperceiving; of catching the self in the error of berating the self for the error; of finally relaxing enough to allow the reestablishment of the contact. As you stated, we are also aware that it was more difficult than was comfortable to you this evening to again find that thread of logic or of contact with us, and again we can only recommend practice. The relaxation shall develop as a result of practice.

Is there a further query, my sister?

K: Yes, I believe I was attempting to do what you are suggesting *(inaudible)*. I was also aware of a fear that if I waited too long *(inaudible)* that the contact would be lost and would I *(inaudible)* and I was a little frustrated by that also. Would it be helpful for me if I needed to take the time—I assume you are aware of this process going on within me—but would it be helpful also for me to state that, "I need to take a minute here, don't go away. Let me…*(inaudible)*."?

I am Latwii, and we would agree with your suggestion that this would be a useful format in that it is one with which you feel comfortable. When we are aware, as we were this evening, that a new instrument is becoming increasingly frustrated with the self-defined difficulty in reestablishing contact, then it is that we move to the more experienced instrument to give whatever information is pertinent and helpful to the new instrument through the experienced instrument. However, we feel that you have moved to the point in your practice at this time that if you are comfortable with the prolonged pause and with the stated need that you would like to take as much time as is necessary to reestablish the contact, then we are quite happy to work within this format. We look upon this type of work as very helpful to the new instrument or any instrument which has difficulty in maintaining the contact and which would wish to have the contact reestablished through it in order that it might, shall we say, mount again the horse which has thrown it. We applaud this dedication and perseverance.

Is there a further query, my sister?

K: *(Inaudible)*

I am Latwii. We thank you my sister. Is there another query at this time?

Carla: *(Inaudible)*

I am Latwii, and we are aware of your query, my sister. We suggest that the most efficacious manner of availing oneself of the feeling of the comfort which is ever available, that times of meditation might be set aside on a regular basis, whether at the beginning, the middle, or the end of the day, or at any pattern of sequence. That this is the means by which the concerns of the day are for the moment set aside, that the comfort which they call for might be perceived. We are aware that it is difficult for many entities to find time for meditation within the busier portions of the day which are most likely to bring the self to the point of feeling the great need for this comfort.

However, if it is possible for the entity to devise times during the day which lend themselves easily to such meditative periods, there might be constructed within these meditative periods [the] symbol which holds the feeling of comfort, whether it be a cup that is full, a certain scene that is meaningful to one, a landscape, a vista, a fragrance, a feeling, a touch, a work of art, sculpture, a piece of music or whatever symbol might be able to be filled with the comfort that one obtains from a regular period of meditation. Then this symbol might be utilized for a brief periods of time during the busier portions of the day when there is a chance for a small breather, shall we say. Whether this be for seconds or minutes, there can be the transfer of this all-pervading peace by the use of the symbol that is energized or filled with the peace and comfort during the regular meditation time.

Is there a further query, my sister?

Questioner: *(Inaudible)*

I am Latwii, and we thank you once again, my sister. Is there a final query at this time?

(Pause)

I am Latwii, and as we have exhausted the queries for this session of working, we would take this opportunity to again congratulate this instrument for the progress that each has made this evening. Indeed, each has done so. It is our privilege to utilize each instrument and we thank you for your dedication to service in this manner. We especially appreciate the dedication to detail, the care in the chopping of wood. We are known to you as those of Latwii. We leave you at this time, as always, in the love and the light of the one infinite Creator. Adonai, my friends. Adonai.

Sunday Meditation
July 1, 1990

Group question: The question this evening concerns UFO abductions. UFO abductions are occurring at an increasing rate in this country, and much is written about these "gray" entities who seem to do most of the abducting. Not only do the people who experience these abductions report profound feelings of fear as a result, but much is now being written about agreements between these gray UFOnauts and world leaders that suggest that these grays are seeking to enslave the population of this planet. As a result, many people who are consciously seeking the truth report a feeling of helplessness and hopelessness. What would you say to such people who feel that their free will is soon to be taken from them? In what perspective can we put this and any other phenomenon that seems to remove the ability to act as a free entity?

(Carla channeling)

I am that principle known to you as Q'uo. Greetings to each of you in the love and in the light of the one infinite Creator. Our pausing was in order to encourage this instrument to relax, as during the challenging process it had become most fierce in protecting the purity of the contact, and was consequently clenched as for battle. We do wish those who are vocal channels for the Confederation of Planets in the Service of the Infinite Creator to be alert, however clenched is somewhat beyond our needs.

The subject of which we are to speak this evening is a subject that is indeed on the minds and in the hearts of many who have had experiences with so-called extraterrestrial entities. Since we who come in the name of love and light and service to others are also alleged UFO entities, it is what we would call our loyal opposition of which we would speak this evening.

Let us move backwards from the heart of the question to describe methods whereby entities external to your planet and its web of energies are given access to the attention of those who are incarnate upon your planet at this time.

We who come in the name of unconditional love and limitless light, we who are of the one infinite Creator, the one original Thought that is Love, must go before a group of entities, which is chosen from among our Confederation, and which changes from time to time, and offer to them our intentions, our plan if you will, for aiding entities upon your planet. These requests for service are taken most seriously, and it is an honor indeed to be allowed through quarantine to be able to share our thoughts with those who ask for them.

You may ask why the planet is quarantined. It is quarantined because it has been put, shall we say, in an unbalanced state by those from the Confederation who have, in your far past, erred in decision making. To avoid this occurring again, the planet was quarantined some of your years ago. Why do we wait for the calling and not speak to any who would listen? As a curiosity we could speak to many. However, we have found, by careful experiment, that attempts to speak to those who are not specifically calling for information which we are able to offer will be misused, misunderstood and ineffectual regarding the goals which we have, which is to offer information to those of your peoples who request it, and who will use it.

Just as there are those whose path is service to others, there are those whose path is service to self, and control over others. This is not a strangeness to your thinking. Each who sits in this circle of seeking together knows those whose delight is in controlling, sometimes not even for the benefit of the self. Those who have truly moved along the path of negativity—or, as it is sometimes called, the path of that which is not, or again, that which is sometimes called the path of separation—control strictly for their own benefit.

Because of the fact that positive information—that is, information of love and light and service to others, information concerning the path of unity and peace and love—is available to those who ask, it was considered right or just that an opportunity be given to those whose call was for information of a negative type, who desired information on the path of service to self and control over others. Consequently, in your web of space and time there were built in, with the impossibility of prediction of where or when, these windows of opportunity that occur, openings in the web of time and space, in space/time, that, if the negative entities were able to be there at the correct time, would place them in a position to offer the information to those who requested it.

There are various densities of learning, both in the service to others path and in the service to self path. Those entities in the service to others path always obey free will and will not abridge it, because if they do so they cannot sustain the contact with the vocal channel that has been able to receive the information they have come to offer. Those who are, shall we say, of a more sophisticated nature along the path of service to self, having wisdom as well as love—that is, the love of the self—await the free will contact of those who seek negative information, for such contacts are likely to be fruitful, in the negative sense, and satisfactory in the transferring of information which is helpful to those who are upon the path of service to self in your density, and who are preparing for harvest.

Those entities who are less sophisticated and closer to your density—that is, who are of the density of love—feel that they have come in simple conquest. Therefore, they do not feel that there is any need whatsoever to avoid the abridgment of free will, for their thoughts are those of warriors who attempt to battle what they see as a light which must be put out, a strength which must fail, a faith which must be vanquished, a foolish group of people who are not aware of the relativity of the illusion as they understand it. Speaking ethically, we gaze at the battle of situational ethics versus ideals.

In your third density illusion, it has been clear from the first ophidian representative of negativity in your Garden of Eden to the great dragon that now thrashes its tail among your people in its death throes, that the illusion seems to be weighted heavily, sometimes, on the side of the negative or service-to-self path. This is a necessary and salutary virtue of your illusion. It is the background or the drama against which each of you shall make a choice that is so important that the remainder of millions of your years of life, a significant portion of the life of yourself within this creation, will depend upon it. You may choose to be foolish, unworldly and idealistic, and find yourself constantly at odds with situational ethics, which is the way the world wags. Or you may choose to be those who serve the self, what this instrument would call "numero uno." The negative path is a path that leads to the Creator. It is simply a difficult and long path.

In this density, in which one attempts to learn the lessons of love and is perfecting lessons of social intercourse and movement towards the light, the negativity revolves about learning to do those things which one considers to serve the self more of the time. Those upon the positive path will be attempting the exact opposite of this, that is, they will be attempting to think in terms of service to others, or simply service of any kind, because of the love of the infinite Creator which is in their hearts. They are attempting more and more to spend their precious few moments of this small time of choice choosing again and again to help, to attempt to be of service. In both cases, positive and negative, it is the attempt, the sincerity of the desire, which registers as the polarizing factor of the entity.

Thus, those who are indifferent in your density are those most to be mourned, for as they eat and drink and be merry without regard to serving others or the self, they simply continue in this density of experience, finding upon graduation that they have not graduated, they have not learned to love, they have not learned to turn towards the light, or to use the light. And so they shall be given—not hell, any more than third density is hell—but simply another third density experience lasting approximately 75,000 of your years.

Positive entities who have polarized adequately move into fourth density, become closer and closer, and begin to form themselves into societies so harmonious, because of all thoughts being open one to another, that they become social memory complexes, each entity within this society able to know and to feel whatever has been known and felt by all other entities within that particular group. In this setting, which is far more harmonious, and far less given to strife, the lessons of love, and service, and compassion, and understanding, are perfected to a minimal point. It does not have to be perfect, but it must be such that the next density, with its greater density of light, may be accepted with great comfort and enjoyment, and therefore be the native light which that entity has earned.

In negative fourth density there is a similar attempt to polarize ever more strongly, to perfect the lessons of love. In the negative case it is always the love of the self and control over others which is a constant drain upon those who are in fourth-density negative, for they form uneasy alliances, and are always ready to challenge someone they think they know best in order to gain their power and to control them. Thus, although thoughts may be known by all, thoughts are attempted to be hidden, armored and guarded in as many ways as possible. Then the entities must gain enough of a strength of love of self and the ability to use that love in what they think is honest service to the Creator, whom they love, to be able to use light of the next density, which is that of wisdom.

In fifth density positive and negative, one finds a good deal of isolation of entities, both positive and negative seeking the path that is its unique path, holding finally the wisdom of knowing itself totally.

However, in fifth density positive, there is the constant flowing back towards community and communion, the communal meals, the communal services of worship and adoration to the one infinite Creator, and the happy blending of mates and friendship. In fifth density negative, there is nothing for the fifth density entity but the cave, the rock, the solitude and the seeking.

Graduation to sixth density is very difficult for the negative polarity, for sixth density is the density of unity. When negative entities reach the point in sixth density at which they fully understand the lessons of sixth density, that is, that all things are One, they find that their negative path is at an end, they are at a standstill, unable to evolve one iota more. Using every bit of determination, will and faith that they have, they cause themselves to switch polarity in order that they may go on evolving. This seems at the time to be a service-to-self choice, for one thing that may be said of all densities is that there is an undeniable drive towards evolution. However, when the negative entity has switched polarity, it quickly discovers the sweetness of its choice. It must review a great deal of material it has missed, but it is the convert that is more fervent, if anything, than the one who has always been positive. It is the most positive of positive entities, the most loving, the most desirous of service, for it knows that it has finally discovered the truth that will continue its evolution.

Therefore, you see that of which we shall speak in a moment must be seen against a backdrop of a great length of time, and, indeed, in sixth density is not the end of learning, for those in sixth density study and perfect the combining of compassion and wisdom, until compassionate wisdom has been grasped to an acceptable point, and the final lessons of egolessness and foreverness begin to be yearned for, to be learned, and so there is another graduation into the density of foreverness.

Now, in mid-sixth density your future self turns towards you in what seems to be the past, and gives you a gift, the gift of your self in a state of compassionate wisdom. This is your truth within. It is yourself.

In mid-seventh density, as spiritual gravity begins to move the ego into a lack of desire for form, for self, that creature turns back and in turn gives a gift to the mid-sixth density entity, so that in actuality each entity in third density has two levels of its own guidance to depend upon which are gifts from your future, as you would call it in your illusion. This mid-seventh density gift is, quite simply, the total data of all possible choices and all possible tracks at all decision points that have been registered along the way. It is a very subtle and complex gift, holding within its memory all those dreams that were not followed, all those paths that were not taken, and the results that would have happened had these paths been taken. It is your deepest intuition, and it is your gift to yourself.

As the seventh density entity loses all need to feel selfhood, the power of love which has infinite intelligence and no awareness of self at all calls it home, and it rejoins the Creator, which is intelligent infinity. At that point, so we understand from those few who have come to us from future creations, loss of self is in itself an illusion, for that which the Creator has created is never lost. There is no beginning over. The knowledge of this entire octave of creation is simply a gift to love itself, and love learns about love, and the heart of the universe beats once more, and a new creation, based upon the learnings of the previous, begins.

As far as we know this is an infinite process, but we urge you to be always aware that all things of which we speak are our opinions only, they are not infallible, and we only give you that which we believe to be true. You must hold each thing which we say to you to the mirror of your own discrimination, and if it is not your personal truth, [if] it does not seem to spring from your memory with a recognition and a resonance to you, then it is not your truth, and we ask you humbly to let it lie, for we would not be a stumbling block before you.

Now let us return to the drama of third density, as both positive and negative entities are attempting consciously to achieve harvestability, to positive fourth density or to negative fourth density. Many are the stories of contacts and arrangements betwixt governments, or individuals within governments, and those who are not from your world. Because there is no way we could speak of these things that would not interfere with the free will of those who hear these words or read them, we shall simply say that were such things possible they would be part of an illusion which is soon to end, part of the fifth act of a play. You may make it a comedy or a tragedy. It is not anyone's choice but your own.

There have indeed been many, many landings, abductions, and that which seems to be abduction but is in reality work upon the computer within you which you call your brain, placing within it programs which seen as much the truth to the one experiencing such, upon awakening, as any other memory. The basic intention here is to create fear. There are other designs which we cannot speak of because of that same Law of Free Will, but we can say that they are inconsequential to those who choose to live a life of faith. Yes, these things are occurring, and yes, many, many positive contacts are also occurring for those who seek in love and light and the purity of intention. Of course, both experiences will be far more active towards the end of a cycle.

Your density is quickly moving towards its end, and you shall, each of you, walk the steps of light, and when you find the light that comforts you the most you shall be either in third density or fourth. The polarizing that you do now is that which you came to do. The judgment that so many fear among your people is a simple and objective matter of how much density of light you have learned to use. There is no fire and brimstone, objectively speaking, for those who must repeat third density, but only the matter of fact reincarnation upon a third-density planet, and another very short period of time, 75,000 years or so in your measure, to make the choice to love and serve the one infinite Creator by serving others, and by serving the Creator, or by serving the self, which is serving the Creator, which is of course understood to be the self.

Now, there is fire and brimstone, there are angels and harps, there is anything that an entity has desired by way of healing and expressing that which it wishes, after the incarnation, and it may rest in this heaven or this hell until it is ready to release the third density experience in which these things were necessary archetypal images, to undergo the healing of the previous incarnation, to view it, to see that which was learned and that which was half learned, and with the aid of the Higher Self, and many other angelic presences, you may call them, or extraterrestrial entities, to determine those lessons which each shall focus upon in its first fourth-density incarnation.

Always are you in the classroom, always are you learning, and yet always do you have the choice to make the learning merry or solemn, to find the vacations and the play time, or the weariness, and the tiredness, and the hopelessness.

Those who do not polarize do not control what occurs to them with any particular preferred reaction—reaction is random. Those who wish to polarize in service to others choose by faith to feel that all situations are situations in which service is possible, that simply to be and to love the Creator, to worship and adore that love which created each of them, is a service worth performing, and, indeed, may we say that as many upon your planet awaken to this choice the consciousness of the planet has grown lighter and lighter in the past few years, as this instrument would measure what you call time.

You are never without the ability to choose that which occurs to you, because if you have no fear you may have negative experiences which you will see only as environments in which to learn challenging lessons of love. Positive entities can gaze at one, shall we say, of the loyal opposition, and find in this contact the opportunity to realize that this entity too is a part of the self, and is to be loved, and blessed, and prayed for, and cared for, and taken into the heart.

It has been said in your holy works that it is easy to love those who love you. Better is it then to love those who revile you and wrongfully use you, without fear. These entities who are called the "grays," or any other entity or situation whatsoever which is attempting to make one feel helpless and out of control, are completely malleable and transformable by love, love unhindered by any fear, for, indeed, there is nothing to fear.

You yourself are not either a good person or a bad person. You are, if you can consider good and bad as the full circle of being, a 360 degree being. It is by your choices that you define who you are and where your loyalties, where your choices and your faith will lie. And as you move further and further, building choice upon choice and polarizing toward service to others in the name of the one infinite Creator, as you become more and more a transparent channel for the love and the light of the infinite One, you create your life, you do not react to it, for the reactions are automatically those of one who seeks to help.

We realize that we have spoken too long, and we are apologetic, but there was much information to put into perspective these seemingly terrifying events.

They are local third-density phenomena. They are controllable by love, faith and honest realization of one's union with all that there is, whether it be called good or bad. The duality is an illusion. You are all things. It is your choices which create the you that is unique and will be refined from this point through density after density after density. This is your choice. These are your precious moments. Know in your heart how passionately you wish to move on and evolve as a spirit, an imperishable metaphysical being of light. Your physical evolution in this density is over. Your spiritual evolution is beginning. Make your choices fervently, carefully and persistently.

In order to aid you in these choices, and in your point of view, we ask two things of you. Firstly, we ask that you find a path that includes love of the infinite One shown as worship, adoration or simple attention, on a daily basis. We do not ask for any particular path to be followed. We are not those who ask for one religion or another. You choose the path that works for you and brings you into awareness of your true self and your true relationship with the infinite One. Daily time spent in silence, listening for the voice that is silent but speaks so loudly, is recommended as an aid to this process of choice.

Our other request of you is that you be light hearted and merry, and find every chance to be joyful, and to love one another, not as a solemn duty, not as a reason to polarize, that negates the polarization, but find joy in the service that gives you the true freedom and peace of doing that which you have now found that which you wish to do with all your heart, all your mind, all your soul, and all your strength. Be merry in your service, be merry in your worship, for the most serious choices of millions of years are being made by you now, and you would be crushed by your own solemnity, and your own realization of your importance of this choice, did you not have the saving grace of a sense of humor. See the illusion and the choices that you make, not only as the life and death choices that they are, but also as part of the unimaginably funny human comedy of the soap opera that is called third-density experience.

Oh, how high your emotions run, and how important everything seems. Step back whenever you feel too intensely disturbed, or saddened, or despairing, or inconsolable. Step back, and see the thousands of years that lie before and after this moment. See the true situation. If you are upset with someone, be ridiculous with him mentally. Undress that person. Cause that person to act in a ridiculous manner in your mind. Tell him off. Take the clown's bat and harmlessly bat him about with it, while the circus audience laughs. Do whatever is necessary for you to break the spell of the illusion, and then gaze up at the stars, which are part of the love of the infinite Creator, and know that you are a player upon a stage, and you do choose the comedies, and the happy endings, and have no wish to be stabbed through, in great Shakespearean agony, in the fifth act. The critic that is you, you can be assured, will give you a better review for the comedy.

We are thankful to this instrument for allowing us to use it to speak upon a subject which its long history of study of the particular subject at hand had rendered it somewhat less than agog with interest concerning. However, we hear the call of many who wish this information, and we thank this instrument, and leave it in love and light. At this time we would move to the one known as Jim. I am Q'uo.

(Jim channeling)

I am Q'uo, and greet each again in love and light through this instrument. At this time we would offer ourselves in the attempt to speak to any queries which are upon the minds of those present, again reminding you that we give that which is but our opinion, but we give it happily and honestly. We ask that those words that ring of truth be the only ones that are retained, leaving all others behind. Is there a query at this time?

Carla: I have one question. Is it true that the free will that was being not abridged by the refusal to give certain information was mine? I do not wish to give any information that would cause any involvement with government forces of any kind, I don't wish that kind of attention, I don't want that kind of knowledge, and I don't want to channel that kind of information. Was it my free will, or was it the free will of all that was being observed?

I am Q'uo, and am aware of your query, my sister. The free will of which we spoke was your free will in the manner you have described, and also included the free will of those who would have received this information. Thus, we chose not to give that particular information, for we do not wish to become a stumbling block to any.

Is there a further query, my sister?

Carla: Do you consider that the information I requested not to discuss is of any value to the spiritual seeking of those on planet Earth at this time?

I am Q'uo, and am aware of your query. We see little apparent or actual value in such information in that it partakes of that which is as the sparkling toy, lasting in the total beingness but for a moment until another toy replaces it. We wish to give that information which endures and do not wish to distract entities from their journeys by giving that which is of but the moment's interest.

Carla: Then you're speaking of all phenomena that point towards the fact that there is a mystery Creator behind this illusion, not just the information that was discussed this evening, that is, not just UFOs, but Bigfoot, and glass skulls, and that kind of thing. Is that correct?

I am Q'uo, and again we agree basically with your summation of the kind of phenomenology that we speak of. There is at this time much of distraction within the daily round of activities for most of the peoples of your culture, and there is much information in the areas that are primarily focusing upon the external appearance of phenomena that hold the potential for even greater distraction. Therefore, it is to the heart of things and entities that we wish to speak.

Is there a further query, my sister?

Carla: Then was it part of the plan of the Creator that these things and many others, in all sorts of walks of life, be plaints, and questions which have no answers, but which point to a mystery and are therefore of value in that way? In other words, do phenomena have the value of pointing towards the mystery, or the noumenal, or the imperishable?

I am Q'uo, and this is correct, my sister. Is there a further query?

Carla: No, I'm satisfied, thank you.

I am Q'uo, and we thank you once again, my sister. Is there another query?

Carla: I have one last question for you. Are you still pointed towards a mystery?

I am Q'uo, and we are indeed pointed towards great mystery of being, looking beyond what little we know into the great distances, depths, heights and vistas of seeking and knowing, being and becoming, so that we discover more and more how our choices are the essence of the Creator knowing Itself.

Is there another query, my sister?

Carla: No, and thank you, as a fellow walker on the path. Thank you, Q'uo.

I am Q'uo. Again we thank you, my sister. Is there another query?

(Pause)

I am Q'uo, and as it appears we have exhausted the queries, we would take our leave of this instrument and this group, thanking each for inviting our presence, and leaving each in the love and light of the one infinite Creator. We are known to you as those of Q'uo. Adonai, my friends. Adonai. ✧

L/L Research

Sunday Meditation
July 8, 1990

Group question: Potluck.

(K channeling)

I am Hatonn, and I greet this group in the love and in the light of the infinite Creator. We spoke with our own sense of humor to this instrument describing ourselves as *(inaudible)* and because this instrument was asking for a low energy compound we discovered after we said this word that, to this instrument, this word is [a name] for a disease. We wish to apologize for our joke.

Our message today is quite simple. It is so simple as to be unbelievable by most of your people. You are made of love because love wished to know itself. The Creator loves you as a mother and a father and as a student of itself.

All conversations that you have are conversations of gripping interest you created, for It is listening with gripping interest of the self speaking about the self. The Creator was courageous in this creation by giving each of its children free will. Each may chose to love or not to love the true Creator of its spirit.

What is on the mind of each today and this instrument? It is the question of identity. Much has been asked of this instrument in the way of initiation and to a different behavior and different way of living, a different way of feeling. What is the essence of an entity? Moving this [point] to be pondered, we await the realignments of the one known as K to receive the information. I am Hatonn.

(Pause)

I am Hatonn, and greetings to those again in love and light through this instrument. We were waiting for final preparation for this instrument as it prepared to challenge those entities that might come and we are pleased at the fastidiousness at which this was undertaken. We wish now to offer such information that may be of some help to you in your journey upon your path of service which continues, as does ours, toward the light of the Creator, toward the mystery which draws us ever onward. My children, it is of this mystery that we will speak to you this evening. One that is always before us no matter how deeply we seem to be able to penetrate the finer layers, but is [receding] infinitely before our grasp, ever beckoning, ever urging us onward in our journey lest we become complacent and satisfied with the progress we have made. For as soon as we have reached the crest of the highest mountain that we can see before us we discover yet another range and yet another beyond that.

There's a long view of the meadows available to us. Most of the time we only notice the mountain in front of our faces. We are faced with a journey upward and ever upward. That, my children, is your choice as to what you will give your attention to in this journey, in this climb, in the focus on the top of the mountain that seems to ever recede before you, and the tiredness of your muscles, soreness of your lungs, the tediousness of the journey, the pain of stepping on rocks, the weariness, the frustration, however you focus on the sky and the clouds above you, the trees, the wild flowers, the small creatures that join you along your journey for small distances and the whole of second-density creation that is there to aid you in your journey. You have also sometimes time spent with third-density companions upon your climb. Some may travel with you for a short distance before their path leads off in another direction, at another slant than yours. There are others who may go with you all the way to the top. Again it is your choice upon that on which to focus. Shall you focus upon the irritations produced or the constant contact with your traveling companions? Shall you focus on the differences or shall you look for what joy and merriment may be made together, how the climb may be regarded, not as fight but as a gain in which one may have as much fun as one is able. You may notice as you climb defects you may have upon your fellow travelers in your own choices of focus, whether they are beyond the difficulties of the journey or its joys. And no matter how your choices affect the mood of those around you, you have [alternatives that can go] back to you. The choice is yours as to what type of journey you will experience. We urge you, my children, to make it a merry one and to focus on the delight of summertime and smiling faces. For these indeed make the climb much less arduous and greatly aid in serving the tired muscles and lightening the weariness of each one.

You are studying your journey as you gaze at the faces of those *(inaudible)* companions about you. But you attempt to see the Creator in each of those who [seek]. These are, as we have said, simple facts, my friends, events of which each is quite aware. Yet we find as we attempt to communicate these simple truths which are always and ever the same [that] there are infinite number of ways to state these truths yet with each a slightly different presentation. Perhaps some new thought will occur to those who see them as helpful to aid them in their journey. Perhaps some new way of looking at situations with which you have to do on a daily basis and with which you have grown weary will appear.

(Carla channeling)

I am Hatonn, and thus speak to you through the instrument known as Carla. This instrument is much nurtured by listening to inspirational thoughts and we are always in a state of enjoyment as we find this instrument soaking up like a sponge the words of comfort, truth and beauty which we offer in the hope that it may be of help. We find this instrument to see how its question of identity is only a question within its own mind. But to the other-self the identity of the one known as Carla is completely known and accepted. So often we have heard this instrument cry, "How can I love others so much and yet be so upset with myself?"

This is the mark of a service-to-others entity who has left out but one very important step, the realization that before one can love one's neighbor as oneself one must love oneself.

This instrument has yearned for nurturing from others and nurturing lies within the self. The gentle rocking in the cradle is the rocking in the arms of the Creator. As this instrument finds it incredibly easy to forgive and forget, why is it that this instrument does not forgive the self? This is a lifetime process but is a lesson of love. It is an almost universal lesson. Each seeking entity finds everyone easier to love than the self, because the entity known as Carla knows itself, it knows each thought, it knows each self-perceived error. It sees itself in each moment but is judged to be foolish or unkind. Where it would forgive instantly such behavior in others, it begrudges itself its own humanity.

Do any of you who think you came to this planet and entered into its illusion to be untouched by it? Spend time each day to fall in love with yourself and you are a child of God. The Creator loves you with a love so passionate no words could express it. The Creator loves just precisely who and what you are and the Creator sends to each person who is blind His companions along the way, who reach out the hand of the Creator to you and call out, "I love you." These are the words of the Creator. That is why we ask each of you to love each other because each of you need someone's help in loving yourself.

Oh, how we wish we could emphasize to you greatly enough the enormous difference you can make in your life experience to truly love the self as the self is, with its biases towards excellence and biases towards what the self perceives as faults. Does not each entity have many faults? As you forgive your comrades along the way realize that you are forgiven yourself and each time to sit in meditation spend a moment within the deepest part of yourself to say to yourself, "I love you with my whole heart," the love, the thought which is the lesson of this density.

We feel the energy growing most [perceptibly] weaker and we pass the *(inaudible)* to the one known as K. I leave this instrument, with thanks. I am Hatonn.

(K channeling)

I am Hatonn and greet each again with love and light through this instrument. This time we would ask if there are any queries from those who are present.

Carla: Yes, Hatonn. I would like to know if the experience that I have had … gazing into the eyes of a companion for a long enough time to forget all sense of self, that is, first the feeling of noticing the color of the eyes and the other physical attributes of them. Then finding myself at the level of being able to see through the eyes into the, I guess you'd say, surface of the inner being where lies the emotional pain that I was feeling sometimes and then my sense of being changed in a kind of electromagnetic wave is the only way I can describe it, I felt that somehow we were operating as one energy field instead of two. I wondered if you could comment on those ways I felt during this meditation and tell me where the truth lies and where I have not seen things clearly.

I am Hatonn, and, my sister, we find that usually your perceptions of the situation are both insightful and articulate.

Carla: Would it be a good idea to tune that light *(inaudible)* and have a larger group of *(inaudible)* people better as any one member instead of *(inaudible)*?

I am Hatonn, and we find that we will leave this up to your assessment of the various personalities present at such a meeting, where those whose experiences of this very intimate type of contact and all of those present that at any one time may not be, shall we say, up to such an exercise. But given the assessment of the appropriateness of such or whether or not those present *(inaudible)* we would say that the effort would be an excellent form of tuning to use.

Is there another query?

Carla: No, thank you for your opinions and comments.

I am Hatonn, and we thank you, my sister. It is time to leave this instrument and this group in the love and in the light of the one infinite Creator. We may also *(inaudible)* our path of seeking because this instrument and the one known as Carla were the cause of our being with your group tonight. As always, it has been a great privilege for us to join you and we look forward, as you would say, to being with you again in the future. We are known to you as Hatonn. Adonai.

(Carla channeling)

I am Nona. It is our specialty to feel by *(inaudible)* and we have not been called to this group for a long time. Forgive our causing this instrument to move at a quicker speed than it normally would but it is much more comfortable to work the contact as we *(inaudible)* our love and light and feeling from the one infinite Creator to all of those who need it. We would, since the instrument known as K, has not had a previous contact *(inaudible)*.

(K channeling)

I am Nona, and greet you again in the love and light of the infinite Creator …

(Tape ends.)

Intensive Meditation
July 12, 1990

(Carla channeling)

I am Q'uo. Greetings, blessings and love, light and peace and rest to each of you gathered here this evening. It is a great pleasure to be with you and to be called to this work. Technically this is still called the training of a new channel and technically the one known as K is a new channel, but only within this incarnation. The experience this new channel has just had is the experience of being contacted. Normally, we would not do this with a beginning channel nor would a beginning channel be able to distinguish a first and opening greeting. However, this particular instrument has deeper gifts that are remembered in that portion of the mind that is reached in meditation, and so we thought we would give it a whirl, as this instrument would say.

We are glad that this instrument has had the experience of being contacted and the fact that it was not acted upon [it] is quite to be expected of one who has had so little experience in this incarnation. This instrument will surprise itself, although not us. The key is the gaining of that inner peace that comes with meditation.

We would like to speak in terms of those things that are on the mind of those present this evening. Perhaps the most common of those concerns present here this evening is the difference between the daily state of mind that has been achieved by each as it has gone through its day, and the state of mind that it is experiencing at this time, having done the necessary work to bring into harmony the deeper desires of each, the desires to serve, to love, to share.

All have had their excellent and uplifting moments during the day, but we ask each of you if you are happy and satisfied with the basic level of consciousness, or to put it another way, the degree of conscious living that was achieved during the precious moments of this day.

How little is the span of your incarnation and how high are your spirits' ambitions for you during this tiny piece of what you call time. As you rest and bask in the love and the light of the infinite One, you yourself wonder how could I have moved from my center—how could my life not reflect this peace, this gentleness, this loveliness, this caring, this worship of the mystery. And yet we say to you that your days were more light filled than the majority of those upon your planet by a great deal; so you see, there is much to do.

To paraphrase a cliché within this instrument's mind, love is long and time is fleeting.

We transfer at this time to the one known as K, leaving this instrument in love and light. We are know to you as Q'uo.

(K channeling)

I am Q'uo, and greet you again in love and light through this instrument. We are pleased to have established contact so readily with this instrument, and we see that the paths to the deep memories are beginning to be opened little by little and would encourage this instrument to deepen and strengthen this process through the daily practice of meditation.

As we have stated, the ease of this contact comes as no surprise to us and we await the ease of the instrument with the contact through the process of repeated practice.

We would speak to you this evening on the subject of meditation. It is, as you know, a process by which access is gained to the deeper portions of the mind, the deep memories that lie therein which nibble at the edges of consciousness, the small thoughts and feelings experienced during the day that one may wonder at. Those things that seem to be half remembered, those things and entities that seem to be so familiar, yet with no conscious link in experience of this incarnation.

The process of meditation will begin to expand your awareness of these half-buried memories and recognitions. You will increasingly become aware of thoughts not running through your mind as in a daydream to which only scant attention is given, but as being those with which you are deeply familiar to which you turn your conscious attention and intention to the further pondering of such and the further integration of these old memories brought to light as part of the current experience.

Each of you here this evening is aware of the existence of the deeper self, of the metaphysical entity, of the imperishable light being, and of the network on this level, the connection on this level of all the entities of this planet. And the dichotomy existing between that connection and the apparent separation that exists in your day-to-day illusion. Each of you is also aware of times when that illusion is penetrated to some extent and the connection with some other self is made. The awareness of the other self as Creator brings about a momentary dispelling of the illusory bonds of flesh and societal structure.

What comfort there is in such connections. Such experiences may be realized on a more or less conscious basis, ranging from the barely conscious hint of feeling of familiarity to the relatively full conscious awareness of the deeper levels of existence of the self and the other self. We realize this may add a great perspective to life in the illusion as each realizes each is playing a part of sort upon the stage of Earth that each chooses, what part shall be played, and how each character shall interact with each other character and situation.

It is our hope that you may find enjoyment in playing these roles as you realize the necessity of the illusion for the purpose of growth in spiritual evolution, and the polarization process, as well as in the opportunities presented to be of service to your fellow inhabitants of planet Earth.

As each experiences from time to time memories of deeper connections with other entities as echoed in current experiences, whether slight or strong, the response is often one of joy, of remembered community. We experience peace and love and ease of being—yet that joy may be often tempered by the realization of the difficulty of maintaining contacts within this illusion.

Each of you has very difficult tasks before you and in that each present this evening is what we call a wanderer. The tasks may be experienced as being even more arduous in that the heaviness of the illusion is even more weighty to those accustomed to greater degrees of light. We laud your efforts, my friends and urge you to continue one step at a time. Allow yourselves to be encouraged by the glimpses of the deeper reality behind the illusion. Know that you exist in truth in that deeper reality; that you may contact it at any time in meditation and as your choices and interactions allow in those connections with others who are of like mind, know that you are beings of light. That within the shell of third-density flesh that surrounds you your beingness shines with a radiance so bright that were you to be fully aware of it, your joy could not be contained.

We urge you to make enough contact with that light to encourage you in your endeavors, painful though they may be, difficult though each of your struggles is in varying degrees at varying times, and you are here to encourage each other as well.

Do not underestimate the value of each to each in this journey and in your working together, for each is of inestimable value to each other and to us and to the Creator.

We urge you also as you encounter the pain and difficulty that each day *(inaudible)* brings, as you gaze at each entity and circumstance that you encounter, to attempt to be aware of the Creator in all things. In each difficult situation, in each difficult entity, the Creator is there as teacher, as guide, as friend, as love and light.

We know you are aware of these things, but we also know the difficulty in maintaining this awareness when in the mindset of mundane experience. We urge you to look for the joy in all things, to savor it, to choose the light touch, the merry twinkle in the eye, the smile when none was expected. These things mean more than you think, for your society tends to weigh the value of things in terms of what has been accomplished. But on the metaphysical level, those things that are of the greatest value lie in the areas of intention and in the state of being. So be who you are, my friends. Be light, be love, be joy.

We thank this instrument and this group for this opportunity to be of service in speaking to you. I look forward to the continued training of this new channel in what you call your future and the ongoing work of this group as it resonates most harmoniously with our own vibration.

We would at this time transfer to the one known as Jim and close the meeting through that entity. We are known to you as the ones of Q'uo.

(Jim channeling)

I am Q'uo, and greet you again in love and light through this instrument. At this time we would simply offer ourselves to any queries which may hold importance for those present. May we speak to any concern at this time?

Carla: I've got a concern about *(inaudible)* make your own decision as to whether you want to answer it or rather it should be a subject in itself. When I invoked the archangel this evening, Raphael—who is usually very prompt and very much in tune with me, and who is the archangel of the air, the land, the spirit—was reluctant to appear and when it did appear, it was not with the usual fellowship that I feel, and I asked myself why this could be. And the obvious answer was that I was not flowing with the wind of spirit, that I was stuck, that I had a subjective feeling that this was a very bad day for me. And the truth of it is that this was a day off. I kept myself from doing work by sheer discipline. Work would have been easier for me than taking the day of by myself. I was alone with my pain. And I know it sounds dramatic, but I've never had this much pain before and I don't know how to flow with it and make it transparent and be the *(inaudible)* that I am when I'm doing things for people.

When I'm doing things for people, I always feel full of love and full of light and as if there were nothing that was impossible. But when I'm not helping anybody but myself I feel really stuck and I don't seem to be able to get past my aches and pains, and I don't need to go into all that, you know. But it is a new level of pain for me and I am not able at all to deal with it gracefully. I know that this is my hardest lesson—I don't care how long it takes me to learn it—I want to learn it, but could you give me some comments on how to make my sister, my pain, into a true heart sister; to love it and to allow it to be transparent so that I can feel the self-esteem and the worthwhileness in being that I do when I'm doing something for someone else. I am on my knees with this one.

I am Q'uo, and we feel the sincerity and intensity of your query, my sister, and we extend to you our heartfelt sympathy that the pain has presented to you. We know that entities within your illusion feel much distress at this time as each attempts to use those dwindling opportunities for polarization and service to others that are presenting themselves within each incarnation as your cycle moves quickly to a close.

This is much likened to the last minutes of cramming for your final examinations within your learning institutions as we scan the memories of each present here for analogies. Those lessons which belong to each, those services which are possible for each, now are offered in a most vivid manner. In your terms this means the intensity of experience is increasing. The illusion which you inhabit may provide all that it is constructed to provide; that is, the veil that hides the truth of unity and the fundamental purpose of experience. That [purpose] is to move beyond the limitation of the confines of the illusion that exists without the senses and within the mind and the attitude which perceives the illusion. To surpass limitation is a painful process, my sister.

In this regard, you have set for yourself, as you are well aware, lessons which have the purpose of focusing you inward. You have found in your own estimation before this incarnation began, that the experience of limitation and the concomitant experience of pain with its limitation would be most effect in focusing your attention in an inward manner that would make more likely the choices of living the conscious life. For that which is full of the experience which you call pain tends to grab the attention in a way in which there is no ignoring the opportunity. Much catalyst for many people may be ignored until it presents itself in another form at another time, perhaps within another incarnation. This is not so for your catalyst, my sister. You have desired to be of service in a manner which requires an intense degree of what you would call purity or single mindedness—total dedication to service. It was your wish to so hollow yourself out that you would become a clear reflection or channel for those energies of love, which you identify so closely with the one known as Jesus, the Christ, as this entity experienced the final portion of its incarnation nailed to that which you call the cross—and in that crucifixion of the physical vehicle achieved a transmutation from that which was human and moving towards the divine, to that which was truly divine, that which transcended this illusion, that which pointed the way which could be traced by others with similar desire.

This is your path, my sister; to so transmute the daily experience of your life that it becomes a purely formed manifestation to the one Creator. This is not an easy program or series of lessons to undertake. However, with the increasing price of the pain, you may comfort yourself by knowing that you attain that pearl which has no price within the metaphysical levels of your own being. If this could be easily seen within your own illusion, few entities would pay such a price, for it is indeed a great price to pay. The veils of forgetting shroud this process and all progress from your earthly eyes of perception. You seek and seek and seek and seek; you endure and endure and endure for that final moment of knowing that comes when you move through the doors of this life, that you call death, and realize that there has been a purpose known at the deepest levels.

(Side one of tape ends.)

(Jim channeling)

We shall pause briefly that this instrument might retune …

(Singing)

I am Q'uo, and greet each again through the love and light of this instrument. This instrument wishes to apologize for the delay. [This challenging process is lengthy.] We shall continue.

Thus you shall find that the purpose and the pattern of the incarnation will make sense only upon looking back and seeing it in the full perspective. The short answer, my sister, to your query is that though the price is great, the reward is greater.

We cannot express to you the nature of our gratitude for each instrument such as yourself which endures the increased levels of difficulty that go with those who wish to be of greater and purer service to others. With such desires move responsibilities of equal proportion. The responsibilities that form themselves as testings, temperings, tunings and purifications in your daily round of activities are merely the means by which you shall accomplish these goals. That your experiences become more intense and more difficult is an indication that you are ever moving forward upon the paths which you have chosen. This is not to say that your portion of contentment, pleasure and joy shall always be small, but that added to these joys will also be those difficult moments that are the times during which the food of a metaphysical nature is being eaten, being processed, and being transformed into a kind of manna that will nourish those portions *(inaudible)*.

Thus we offer to you, my sister, the larger picture which recedes when pain pulls the attention inward and dissolves the ability to see beyond the pain. Fear not that you wander from your trail, your feet are ever planted there, and although the steps are painful, the progress is steady. The service is offered and the purpose is fulfilled.

May we speak to any other query, my sister?

Carla: Yes, a very short one. First of all, I made a tentative decision, based on how I feel during the rest of this month, to allow myself to use marijuana to eliminate the pain when I really needed to, knowing that I would lose a great deal of my ability to function, but feeling that it was a kind of vacation for me, and I would not have another kind of vacation. I wondered if this was self-indulgent?

The other question is this general topic of such a nature that there is more material that you would wish to offer and [would] you would wish to take it up in a full-length [kind] of session?

I am Q'uo, and I am aware of your queries, my sister. To the first query, we may not speak for this is a subject at this moment being debated within your own mind and we feel it would be an infringement to offer an opinion before you have made your decision.

To the second query, we may say that we have no desire other than to be of service in which we are asked, if it is within our ability to do so without infringing upon any entity's freewill choices. If you would wish to ask us further upon this topic we would be happy to share that which is ours to share. We have no other desire than to serve.

Is there a further query, my sister?

Carla: Let me ask that last question in a different way. Is there further material that is possible for you to give as your opinion, which is, of course, [valuable.] If asked the same question again, is there more material? More of your thoughts and opinions which you would give us?

I am Q'uo. There is a great deal of material that may be shared in the area of which you speak—that is, the experience of pain and the tendency to utilize the pain-filled experience as a means to focus the attention towards one purpose or another—for there are many avenues that offer themselves as an entity undertakes that experience generally known as pain.

Is there a further query, my sister?

Carla: No, Q'uo, thank you *(inaudible)*.

I am Q'uo, and we thank you my sister, for your perseverance and your dedication. Is there another query at this time?

K: Yes, At this point in my channeling, I have no sense whatsoever what might be coming from me and what might be coming from whatever entity I'm channeling, and I don't know if it's possible to have *(inaudible)*. I did feel that the contact was very comfortable and very easy but I would like some feedback from you Q'uo *(inaudible)* myself, as to how *(inaudible)*.

I am Q'uo, and am aware of your query, my sister. We are very happy with the proportion of information that has been able to be transmitted from us through your instrument and blended with experiences, concepts and thoughts that are your own. We feel that we are approaching the level which we attempt in the training of each instrument that is, approximately two portions, or a 70% from our source, and one portion, or approximately 30% of that of the instrument. We feel there has been great progress in your ability to perceive that which is given within the last two sessions of work and we applaud your willingness to open your instrument to the degree that is necessary to achieve this ratio, for this opening requires that one be willing to move out from the safety of the trunk of the tree further upon the limb where one is unsure of the next concept, the next word, that she make sense, as you say, within the overall pattern of the message. We are very happy with this ratio at this time and commend you in your efforts.

Is there another query, my sister?

(No further queries.)

I am Q'uo, and we thank you my sister. As we have exhausted the queries for this evening, we would close with our expression of great gratitude to each instrument for allowing us to exercise each instrument. It is a rare privilege to speak to a group which has this level of dedication in offering the self as an open channel for concepts which seem quite insubstantial when compared with the heaviness of the daily round of activities. We find that it is a great paradox within your illusion that the weightiness of your experience can be cradled, but so carefully, by such seemingly insubstantial concepts which at their heart contain the most solid centers of integrity and in truth can support such burdensome experiences with ease, when such experiences are seen as the catalyst and most mysterious of opportunities to learn.

The weightiness of your experience seen in this perspective gives way in its seeming solidity and dissolves in the light of truth. Only when the inner eye remains steadily fixed upon these concepts and there is a regular returning to these metaphysical principles through your meditation, your contemplation, and your times of prayer as you move through your daily experience, only by applying, moment by moment, these principles to the life experience can one lift the burden from one's shoulders and then, but for the moment, however, even these small moments of realization and centering of the self may sustain one through any life experience.

We know your tasks are difficult and the moments of such relief too few. We are honored to be a part of the renewing of the dedication and the refining of the center of one's being. We too walk this trail with you. We offer ourselves as comforters to you, and we rejoice with all of creation as you move ever more in harmony with the center of the self, which has never left the unity with all that this.

We are known to you as those of Q'uo. At this time we shall take our leave of this instrument and this group, leaving each, as always, in the love and in the light of the one infinite Creator. Adonai, my friends. Adonai. ✸

Sunday Meditation
July 15, 1990

Group question: The question this evening has to do with following our path and learning lessons, dropping old patterns and developing new patterns of behavior, in the overall pursuit of the choices that were made before the incarnation by the soul and Higher Self. How do we accomplish the dropping of old patterns that we have known for so long, that have provided us with a great measure of support, and adopt new patterns of behavior when we feel that there is change that is necessary to acknowledge and to reflect in a new pattern of behavior? How do we find the assurance that the new pattern is truly our path that has congruency with the soul's choices, and how do we release the old patterns of behavior?

(Carla channeling)

I am Q'uo. Greetings to all of you in the love and the light of the one Creator, infinite, invisible, intelligent, creative and full of glory. Under the influence of these purified emotions, and with the understanding that love and light compose all that there is, we are with you this evening, thanking you for calling us to you. As always, we ask you to listen to that which we give as you would to any friend's opinion, giving it neither less weight nor more than you would any friend who is a friend in spirit of unconditional love. We always mean well, but truth is subjective and personal, and if what we have to say is not a portion of your truth at this time, we ask you the great favor of allowing us and our thoughts to be moved aside, that we may not become a stumbling block before any, for we are fallible and prone to error, as are all who seek mystery and are not yet the mystery.

We are experimenting with the mixture of the two social memory complexes involved in this contact, and if there are pauses that seem to move to more length than usual we would ask the one known as Jim to squeeze the instrument's hand. We do not want this instrument to go into trance. But the instrument asks, as it always does, to be better than before, and in this particular case that involves going deeper into the subconscious and allowing more of that which is impersonal and that which is finely tuned to match the fine tuning of this instrument. Therefore, we ask that the one known as Jim be vigilant.

We do not come to you as those who have not changed. We have been where you are. We have been where you were. We have had our choices to make, and we remember the density in which you now dance your dance and make your choices. Stage left, stage right, lights up, lights down, how shall you be? That is perhaps the first thing we would ask of each of you. When you relax, so that you are with yourself in a loving and nurturing way, who and what do you wish to be? This is the density of choice. Not to define one's choices is to remove from oneself the opportunity of making them. Not to know who you are at this moment is to keep from yourself the ability to choose a specific other way to be. This is not seen to be a large subject, a large challenge, yet it is the beginning of all spiritual work.

We see each of you in part as precisely the same as each other person in third density consciousness upon the surface of your planet. All of you have a God self within. Within each of you is the inestimable, imperishable jewel of the Infinite One. You are children of love, and you are love. In order for you to have been flung out from the heart of the Creator, to pass through so many dimensions and energies, and to choose this particular experience, there needed to be added the first alteration, or means of changing, that love, which is the Creator, and which is precisely the same from before you can ever conceive, now, and forever to come.

Yet, each of you is unique, for each of you is also bound in that love to a portion of free will. Free will is as absolutely various as love is absolutely the same, and free will is expressed in all of the emotions and ways of being possible to imagine, possible to be thought, possible to be attempted. You are the man inebriated and lying in the gutter, you are the thief, you are the murderer. All that is possible is within you, as it is within all. This is not due to any shade or nuance of love. Love is fiery, creative, and absolutely stable. Your choices are made as your free will begins to recognize of its own choice that role which it wishes to play in your own spiritual evolution.

And so we ask each of you to begin to know, truly know, the self. Do not judge the self which you know so well. Say no judgmental or negative thing to yourself about yourself. Recognize your patterns. Discover those things which you wish to encourage and those things which you do not. You yourself are the basic tool, the basic resource with which you have to work. Elements of your free will, which this instrument calls will, and faith, create for you a place—not a geographical place, not a place in space or in time, or in your imagination—let us say, a room, which you answer and close the door behind you, and all alone with the Infinite One, drenched in love, marinated in life, dissolved in light, you are upon holy ground. If this place is within your mind you may take it with you, and wherever you stand is holy ground.

To develop the tools of will and faith, several things are helpful. Firstly, a daily meditation, be it long or short, momentary or part of an intentional praying and fasting, this way you use to listen to the still, small voice, as it has been called in your holy works, within. This intention, this will to seek the truth of the Creator, is your strength and your heart and the motivating factor of that which will occur to you.

Faith is a word which we use, not perhaps as others would use it, for we wish to distinguish between faith and belief. It has seemed to us as observers of your people that rigid belief systems kill faith and destroy being, giving the person instead the choice of behaving instead of being, and holding on dependently to a set of rules in order that from the outside to the inside the redemption and forgiveness and healing of the self may take place. We suggest that all belief systems be examined, and none taken up before it is understood that in each orthodox belief system, some distortions of love are unraveled and made clear, while other distortions or ways of learning about love are confused and difficult to accept for you.

We are not those who preach. We are not those who evangelize. But this we will say: if you wish to increase, or accelerate the intensity of your spiritual path of evolution, living a life in faith, day by day by day, and using its tools of discipline, and service, and conceptualizations is all important. We speak to you of the way that we believe that the universe works. We can only tell you that you are at the crux of what is often called the density of choice, the choice between loving the Creator by serving others, and loving the Creator by serving the self, these paths often being called the path of service to others and the path of service to self.

Many times it is indeed a stumbling block in the way of those who wish to be of service to others that they must needs spend so much time working upon themselves. Yet, we say to you, that if you do not have your roots deeply spread, if you do not know what those roots are, if you do not live as you have faith to live, if you do not express and manifest that which you know, you shall be, this instrument would say, stuck in the gravitational well, spiritually speaking, of basic indifference.

Until you have found your passion, and we mean this on all levels, not ignoring the lower energy centers, sexual passion, the passions of friendship, the love of the work that you do, the love of your society and your world and all its people, you shall be holding back from the center of spiritual love the energy that that center needs. We speak of the heart energy center. This is not a job that you can do for yourself once and have it done. Again and again you shall turn from the truth, and do those things which you would not wish to do, or regret, or do not do, something you wish you had done. Should you chastise yourself? Please, my friends, if you wish to attain the goal of which you spoke this evening, never chastise the self, but form all internal dialogue positively. Instead of saying, "Oh, 2 plus 2 does not equal 5," say "Oh, I have learned something, 2 plus 2 equals 4." That is the nature of mistakes, all errors, all of what this instrument would call sin. It is like an error in arithmetical calculation, simply seen, and slowly and carefully replaced by the truth, by the correct summing, by the correct grasp of the situation.

Most entities have a great deal of difficulty doing this, because their opinion of themselves, though they love other people, is harsh. The voices of childhood parents and authority figures still ring in the heart's ear with negative expressions and warning and judgments. Many of the most difficult portions of your lives are difficult because you are still listening to these voices. When you hear them, say instead the positive affirmation of that criticism which has for so long been unfair. When you were small, when you were a child, you could not defend yourself, but you can defend yourself now. You can live a life of faith in which old voices need have no power over you, indeed, in which no voice on the Earth, over or under the Earth, no discarnate voice, none whatsoever, need have power over you.

You are made of precisely the same infinite intelligence and free will as every spirit in the infinite universe, and, speaking metaphysically, you are a portion of utter, complete and final democracy of spirits. There is none better than you, and there is none worse. You are a portion of the Creator, which is everything. Thus, the choices are yours. They do not have to be handed to you by society, by friends, or parents, or spouses, or the ubiquitous "they." "They" say you should do so and so. "They" are not a pleasant breed with which to deal. Remove "them" from those voices you wish to grow with, to attend to, to identify yourself with in terms of ambition.

Your life in faith is a life without words, for there are no words to express faith. Faith is a basic attitude that one finds, because one wills it or wishes it to be so, but because as a result of willing to know the truth it comes to you, and the prodigal son and daughter have come home. Faith is simply faith that the Creator that made all that there is, including you, is a Creator of infinite and intelligent love, that it loved you as part of Itself, as a child to nurture, as a personality from which to learn about itself, as all parents learned from their children. Aiming toward living a life in faith is nothing more than releasing fear, and allowing that which is to be, to be.

Oftentimes, that help which you have with you personally at all times, whether you call it spirit, or guidance, or the Higher Self, will give you hints and warnings. Do not ignore them. Ask for help in visions and dreams, and listen to them. Go into meditation, not simply to listen, but with a question asked, expecting not to awaken with one answer, but expecting and knowing that you will eventually know the answer for yourself to your own satisfaction. A great deal of faith is patience. A great deal of will is persistence. We are well aware that these are not the same as the mountain top experiences offered to you by those so-called seers or prophets which make the choosing of a live lived in love seem so very, very easy.

Were it easy, there would be no reason to work through so much of pain and limitation and change, for choice is change, make no mistake. Each choice that you make will change you, and you will feel pain and discomfort, because it is painful to change, and as you meditate, and seek, and live a life in faith, you will change, and change, and change again. Some truths will remain the same forever for you. Some truths will be outgrown, and must be let go.

Against this backdrop which we have attempted to paint, let us look at the way of encouraging ourselves to release from ourselves old, and undoubtedly unneeded, and certainly negative, habits. Again, most of what we have to offer you is a tool called forgiveness. We do not prefer one method of achieving redemption over another. All myths contain within them redemption and forgiveness, no matter how great the error. You may choose your path of faith, or you may create your own personal myth, but be sure it contains a rock solid foundation of redemption and self-forgiveness.

Oh, it is easy to forgive others, is it not? For you love them anyway, and you are sure that whatever they said amiss was not said meanly. But to love the enemy in yourself, or outside of yourself, ah, my friends, that is more difficult, and we assure you that each of you sees some part of yourself as your own enemy. This is the attitude we would suggest that you tackle first, for you are not your own enemy, you are simply being offered choices. Each time that you choose to be of service to another you recreate the strength of your polarity.

But let us remind you of a particularly apt teaching from the known as Jesus. In two sentences, he tossed the ten commandments, with all of the damage that they have done, away, and gave a new covenant, or promise, as he would use the language. "Love the Lord your God," he said, "and your neighbor as yourself." This is why you must begin by forgiving yourself. How can you love your neighbor in utter and open forgiveness if you have not forgiven yourself? We do not deny that you are imperfect in a personally valid way. We only remind you that this is an illusion, and that all things, including your body, your intellect, and the artifacts which you make, a part of an illusion, a local habitation for the spirit within you.

This illusion was created not to promote happiness, although the writer of your Constitution seems to think so, much to the confusion of those who seek spiritually, for you do not seek happiness, you seek the truth, you seek to be mature, and ripe, and ready for harvest, and this involves a great deal of choice. Firstly the choice to forgive yourself, first, for all those things of which you may think you have done wrong in the past. Sometimes it is helpful, as a tool, to take one person with whom you have a high level of trust, high enough for confidentiality to be no question, and state, simply and directly and thoroughly, each and every mistake you feel you have made. Speak this to another entity, for this entity is also the Creator, and this entity's forgiveness is as true, and real, and honest, as that entity is true, and real, and honest.

We are trying to move the mind from behavior to being. It is not behavior which you wish to correct, for behavior is the manifestation of your being. It is that which is held inside as a portion of yourself and of your identity upon which you wish to work. There are teachers everywhere. The creation of the Father teaches a thousand lessons in a minute, if you can but stay in talking to them. Each of your comrades is a Christed being, to some extent or another unaware of its true nature. But as it holds its hand out to you, the Creator is holding its hand out to you. As it expresses friendship and love, so does the Creator. Look beneath behavior for your healing of those things which have harmed you in the past, and which you now see as useless.

The physics of this process is easily comparable to that called the physics of inertia. Many, many years before now you set into motion, by choice, patterns of behavior and thinking that were not helpful to you, and that you now see as not only unnecessary, or unproductive, but hurtful and harming, and you wish to heal. Forgiveness is that which stops what this instrument calls the wheel of karma. Karma may in this sense be defined as inertia, an action put into effect and never forgiven.

Now, can you forgive another and have that power to cease the inertia of karma for another? Not at all. When you forgive another, you do not affect the other, unless he chooses to observe the difference in your attitude. You are working upon the only thing in this universe which you can work on: yourself. Part of forgiveness is forgiving others. The further part is forgiving all the situations which created this pattern. Some of you are more aware of past lives than others, and for those of you who trace the pattern that is unhelpful to what you would call the karma of a past life, know that there is no karma or inertia which is not braked completely and stopped forever by unconditional forgiveness, of the other, of the situations, and of yourself.

You cannot make yourself change. You can only put yourself in tabernacle of the most high, and tune yourself in silence to the most loving and peaceful and light-filled state which you are able to hold upon a steady basis. You do not want to do these things without being extremely careful that you have opened your lower energy centers, thereby allowing that prana, or love/light which strengthens each and gives life to each, to move into the heart chakra where it can be called on by those doing work in consciousness, which is largely at the brow chakra, although instruments such as this one will use the energy center of the throat, often called the blue chakra, in order that it may communicate. Others may choose to stay with the green, open heart, that it may heal others in that way.

But to do work upon yourself, you must move through the green, and blue, into the brow chakra, the indigo center in which all work in consciousness is done. In your sessions, prepare yourself for them, and when they are over, release the power which you have gained by this working, for you deal, in dealing with your metaphysical self, with a magic, if we may use that over-used word, that is very dangerous to attempt to hold in a steady state.

Thus, we urge you to recognize and respect the changes you have wrought in yourself during each meditation, and in some way give that glory, that energy, that peace, that love, or that irritation of the self because the meditation seemed subjectively not good, back to the Creator. During the rest of the day, touch in to the consciousness of eternity. Live in eternity. Then the illusion becomes more and more transparent.

If you have those with whom you are constantly in contact—spouses, mates, friends—inform them of that which you wish to accomplish, and ask them to be mirrors for you. If they are good friends to you, they will not please you by ignoring those things which you have asked them to help you with. They will instead choose to seem harsh, because you have asked this, you have asked for a mirror which you can count on, which is as objective as the other entity can be, and this mirror gives to you its point of view on what it considers you to be doing, to encourage or to discourage unwanted ways of being.

You are a wonderful resource for yourself, but so are those with whom you walk this path. Rich indeed is the pilgrim who has many companions along the way. You come together in love and in service, not to be sweet and dear and darling to each other, but to serve. Sometimes the most difficult thing for a friend to do is to choose service over pleasing a friend. See yourself, therefore, as a resource for others, and be careful in your spiritual communications with them, respecting them as equals. There are no teachers, there are no pupils. There are points of view, there are those who have more experience than others, but we are no more enlightened than you, for in our deepest selves we are one with you.

We have spoken to you now, as much as we can within this time period, of the healing of the self by forgiveness and by the choosing of the path of service. In short, the path of service consists of doing that which is before your vision at this time with as much love as you can. Most paths of service are anything but dramatic, and all paths of service are equal. The quieting of a crying child, the smile to a stranger upon the street, the sharing of the self, of food, of shelter, of listening, the doing of a job which seems to lack an opportunity for service, with faith that indeed it is of service that you have not yet penetrated, these attitudes will keep you in a positive and loving relationship to yourself. Each needs a path of service. Each needs a high self-esteem. These are gifts you give to yourself in will, in faith, and in constant self-forgiveness.

May you love yourself infinitely, for you are a child of God. Your mother, your father, is the universe, love itself. Rest, and have peace and confidence in who you really are. See the illusion for what it is, as much as you can. And when you fail and fail and fail again, as you will inevitably think that you do, never chide yourself, but with patience and care and love grasp once again your desire, your hope, your dreams and your ideals, and go forward on this path of mystery.

We would at this time transfer this contact to the one known as Jim. We are pleased with the newer adjustments we have made in our combining of energies to this channel, and we thank this channel for being open to the adjustments we have made. We are known to you as Q'uo, and in love and light we transfer to the one known as Jim.

(Jim channeling)

I am Q'uo, and greet each again in love and light through this instrument. We realize that we have spoken overly long once again this evening, and we apologize for our lengthy speaking, but those queries and concerns which you posed for us are of such a deep level of meaning to each that we felt it was appropriate to speak at some length. At this time we would offer ourself to any further queries which may remain within any mind present. Is there a query at this time?

Carla: Well, before *(inaudible)* I have one question that's been on my mind for *(inaudible)* also, as we deal with the cost of a new publication, a new publisher that seems to be much more *(inaudible)* of us. We will, however, be making a quality product and charging for it, such an expense that we ourselves have to change our policy. The change that we have come up with seems to preserve the freedom of people to purchase our work with any cost that is comfortable to them. The addition is only information, that is, the cost to us of each item. In no way do we wish to suggest that people pay that, that is simply information. Is there a flaw in such an attitude toward invoking the spiritual Law of Plenty?

I am Q'uo, and am aware of your query, my sister. We would suggest that the course of action which you have set for yourselves is one which you have invested with your desire to be of service in a manner which allows you to continue that service within the framework of trade and exchange that is utilized by almost all of the entities within your culture. That you have found it important in your previous experience to deviate in a significant fashion from this stated means of exchange, that is, the setting of prices upon one's goods and services that is fixed for all, illustrates your desire to offer that which is of your service in as free a manner as is possible within this framework. Your current decision and refinement of this decision is also within the boundaries that you have set previously, that is, to offer information in a free manner while seeking to preserve the continuity of this service.

We would suggest that the intention that propels any decision upon this policy is the governing factor, shall we say, that determines the purity of the principle that one honors. We are aware that your desires are within the proper degree of purity, and would not recommend any addition to this decision at this time.

Is there a further query, my sister?

Carla: No, thank you.

I am Q'uo, and we thank you, my sister. Is there another query?

(Pause)

I am Q'uo, and we feel that we have, at this time, spoken at sufficient length for this particular gathering, and we would thank each most heartily for inviting us to do so and to share that which is our opinion upon this topic which is of such great interest to each, as each pursues in a diligent manner the path of the pilgrim, the seeking, the learning, the serving. We commend each upon this path, and we thank you for making a place upon your journey that we may walk with you. We are greatly honored that you would invite our presence.

At this time we shall take our leave of this group, leaving each as always in the love and in the light of the infinite Creator. We are know to you as those of Q'uo. Adonai, my friends. Adonai. ☙

Intensive Meditation
July 19, 1990

(Carla channeling)

I am Q'uo, and I greet you in the love and the light of the infinite One. If you will pardon us, before we begin, we will chastise this instrument, realizing that this runs close to the Law of Confusion, but we shall have a much more difficult time using this instrument because it has allowed a level of pain to exist over many hours, which is a natural and survival-oriented blockage of energy in the red-ray center to deal with pain the physical vehicle is not intended to sustain.

We ask this instrument and all instruments to be aware of their bodily preparation, and if there must be some medication taken, anything that might be lost because of the side effect of the medication may be gained in the strength of the contact. We realize this instrument dislikes pain medication, but we ask all instruments to be responsible and to come to channeling as comfortable and rested as possible, that in rest and peace and confidence you may stride forth as your magical imperishable self, your metaphysical self, and so speak with spirits having sorted them out by the time honored method of challenging.

We would like to ask each that hears our voice what it has done in the last few days that it could have put off or done in an easier fashion, so as to maximize the strength and minimize the weaknesses of your particular situation. You are stewards of a treasure. The treasure is yourself. How shall you spend yourself? We say there is no virtue in pain, no virtue in guiltiness, no virtue in judgment, no virtue in any negative or separating condition, thought or awareness. Thus, as you prepare for a meeting, let your mind be lifted, allow it to let go enough to realize the true state of the body that moves you about. Tend to it, care for it, show it the love as you show all others [with]. We do not advise taking the martyr's path unless there is no alternative and the martyr's path is clearly marked by an unanswerable destiny.

It is time to speak of a subject that all who channel deal with, and that is that there is only one truth, though there are many ways to say it and many approaches to take to it. Thus, you will not find yourself offering something brand new and exciting to those who seek. If you are in an advanced group, where entities are attempting to live as they are learning, you will indeed receive exciting results if you find metaphysics exciting. You will find yourself more able to be a conscious being. You find yourself ready to hear things on a level that is deeper than you heard things before, so that your mind does not block you from the wonderful experiences and discoveries of the deep mind. But, in effect, you who serve as vocal channels will be offering information of a certain type, in an endless series of ways, but always with the same basic thrust. We are concerned with building in your mind's eye a theoretical model of the universe which most closely approaches the Creator's. But you may see the universe and its purposes as does the Creator insofar as we have learned this vision. Thus, we do not teach you to love. We explain to you why choosing to love and how to love is so very important in this particular experience. We transfer to the one known as Jim. I am Q'uo.

(Jim channeling)

I am Q'uo, and we greet you again in love and light through this instrument. We speak to you of the benefits and the necessity in your own spiritual life of learning to love. My friends, it would seem that this would be a most pleasing task, to love …

(Blowing sound in microphone).

We shall pause.

(Pause)

I am Q'uo. I greet each again through this instrument. As we were speaking, the difficulty in learning to love is not apparent from considering this process upon the surface. For when one thinks of loving, it is easy within your culture to think of these things which are lovable, which attract your admiration, your attention, your affection and to which you would easily give all that you have. This concept of love is that with which most of your peoples are familiar. However, the love of which we speak is beyond that of mother for child, of lover for mate, of friend for friend. It is beyond any concept of love which you are familiar with and which you have experienced in a steady state.

The love of which we speak is beyond the description of words. But when we use words it is well that your word "unconditional" be foremost among words used to describe that concept. For of the previous kinds of love, the conditions of closeness of relationship, of specialness of relationship, of previous experience with an entity, are primary in this kind of love. However, the love of which we speak has no condition tied to it, so that this quality of love is given without any consideration of the entity, the situation, the time or any other consideration that might qualify the object of the love to be loved.

The love of which we speak is that feeling tone that comes from the green ray energy center in a free and open manner and has as its focus the entire creation about one. It is a quality which is developed from within the being. The only effect in the outer experience an entity will have on this quality of love is to become the focus for it. To develop the ability to love, one must experience the testing. This is a kind of testing that is similar to the tempering of your metals, that known as steel, for example, by the fire, the flame, the heat. The heat of your experience as you live your incarnation and your ability to process this heat into a light-filled consciousness will then allow one to express the product of this processing, which is that which we have called love.

The perceptions, the attitude, the manner of seeing is that which is formed and focused through this tempering process. As one works one's way through the incarnational experiences, one will have many, many different responses to situations that become the focus for work in consciousness. All situations, all entities, all thoughts and experiences become the food, the catalyst for this process; become that which is burned, the fuel for this process. As one works with the heat, the friction of the experience, there is a slow smoothing of those rough places of those distortions within the lens of one's ability to see, to see in a more and more clearly and specifically focused matter, so that one does not see that which is other than the self, other than the Creator. There is much work that is entailed, as you are well aware of, in this process. The process of smoothing the lens of your consciousness, of your attitude, of your perception, is a process which, within your incarnational experience seems to be a very, very slow working process.

However, we may assure you that from our vantage point, without your illusion and without the veils that are the natural portion of your illusion, this process occurs very rapidly. That is the great virtue and value of the illusion in which you now find yourselves. This is the work, not of just one lifetime, but of many, many experiences which you call your lifetime; is a process upon which you have been endeavoring for a great period of what you call time to accomplish. You shall continue to work on this process for another great portion of time. Yet, we assure you that within each incarnation, no matter how slowly they seem to proceed, there is much work accomplished, much of the polishing of this lens perception.

We shall now transfer to the one known as K. I am Q'uo.

(K channeling)

I am Q'uo, and greet each again in love and in light through this instrument. This process of refining the lens, through which you view reality of existence through the various illusions you experience, is then, as we have said, a process of many, many lifetimes. And, indeed, is not yet at an end with the harvest from this density, but proceeds throughout the densities until each again has become the awareness of All That Is. For this is eventually the perspective the lens of viewing becomes, the range of vision broadens to include all. The clarity of sight perceives all and penetrates through each layer of illusion that is experienced by the individual, by the social memory complex, by the higher selves, by the mind/spirit totality complexes, and all the various and progressive layers of consciousness which you shall experience.

We urge you not to be discouraged by the length of this process, but to realize, as we have said, that in each incarnation progress is indeed made, though you will be largely unaware of such within the illusion you now inhabit. We encourage you to realize that this is but a part of the process of "learnings" of your life, and it is a part of the progress towards the great mystery which again stretches out infinitely before each. But in your day-to-day life within the illusion, you may still consciously focus on and be aware of your problems and your intentions in the areas of which we speak, that is, the perfecting and the finding of the lens of perception through which you view the Creator and the universe of the Creator as expressed in the world around you and the entities who you meet each day.

As you greet each entity that you are encountering in your life's journey, whether that meeting be but for a moment or for a lifetime, you will be aware to a greater or lesser extent of the face of the Creator in the face of this entity. And you will also be aware to a greater or lesser extent of that process of the love of the Creator radiating out from the green-ray energy center to this entity, whether in the moment or throughout the lifetime. This is a process upon which you may choose to focus consciously, [may just] attempt to develop consciously. There is also one of which you may become more and more aware. For the reality is that the love of the Creator is all pervasive and your task is but to become aware of that fact. For all that you see about you, no matter how positively or negatively perceived, is but a distortion of that one great original Thought, which is the love of the Creator, and it is this love which pervades you also and radiates from you also, in whatever distorted manner it might be received by your self and those other selves around you.

Now, how shall you go about attempting to become more aware of this process and to begin to refine the distortions, so that what radiates from you is more closely aligned and not distorted? We may suggest first of all that which has been suggested to this group before in the form of simple exercises, that is, the attempt to heal the self as Creator, the attempt to view each entity about one as the Creator, the attempt to view each second-density entity about one as the Creator. As these exercises are practiced it will be noted that there is less and less necessity to make the courageous attempt because of the growing awareness of the fact that all about …

(Tape ends.)

L/L Research

L/L Research is a subsidiary of Rock Creek Research & Development Laboratories, Inc.

P.O. Box 5195
Louisville, KY 40255-0195

www.llresearch.org

Rock Creek is a non-profit corporation dedicated to discovering and sharing information which may aid in the spiritual evolution of humankind.

ABOUT THE CONTENTS OF THIS TRANSCRIPT: This telepathic channeling has been taken from transcriptions of the weekly study and meditation meetings of the Rock Creek Research & Development Laboratories and L/L Research. It is offered in the hope that it may be useful to you. As the Confederation entities always make a point of saying, please use your discrimination and judgment in assessing this material. If something rings true to you, fine. If something does not resonate, please leave it behind, for neither we nor those of the Confederation would wish to be a stumbling block for any.

CAVEAT: This transcript is being published by L/L Research in a not yet final form. It has, however, been edited and any obvious errors have been corrected. When it is in a final form, this caveat will be removed.

© 2009 L/L RESEARCH

Sunday Meditation
July 22, 1990

Group question: The question this evening has to do with personal guides or guardians, the spirits that oversee the progress of an entity. We would like to know what is the purpose of the guides, how they function, and how we can become aware of their work and work with them in our lives.

(Carla channeling)

I am known to you as Q'uo. Greetings to you all in the love and in the light of the one infinite Creator. We thank you for calling us to your group and allowing us to be of service to you, for without you we could not serve and we could not learn, for you are most appreciated for seeking the truth. We ask, as always, that you realize that we have not come to eternal truth and do not speak eternal truth. We are not authorities and we come to you as brothers and sisters along the way of seeking the truth.

Pilgrims and colleagues and warriors of peace and love. You and we will always be much misunderstood. Consider that a great compliment but do not let it keep you from the humility demanded of those who would be servants, those who would serve all others in the name of the one infinite Creator. For you are not here to learn how to be loved. You are to here to learn to love. You are not here to learn how to be happy and content and peaceful. You are here to learn and in learning is change and in change is pain. You are here to be uncomfortable a great part of the time but with the divine discomfort of one who is progressing in its evolution as a being of light in the metaphysical sense, that does not perish, that has always been and is now and will be forever. This is who you are. This is what you've come to uncover, the part of yourself that was created by love and is pure, whole, healed and perfect love. For that never varies or changes.

Of course, in this incarnation you are blessed as are all those who begin the walk of conscious speaking with an equal amount of love and free will. As love is a constant described in your mathematics as c^2, so free will is infinitely various. So you are all the same, precisely the same and paradoxically because free will is always various.

Each of you is unique. So let us begin from where you are and examine some of the questions that have occupied a creative and seeking mind.

We would note that as is often true, though the questions asked seem quite dissimilar, they are clumped in the basic quest for understanding of existence beyond this density. So we shall touch upon things other than guardians, leaving others to be more specific of about those things of which we speak more general. This instrument is telling us to be short and so we shall attempt to be.

As you know, we have a slight problem being short as your Danny Devito that is in this instrument's mind. Our heads are bigger than our bodies in the metaphysical sense and on and on we go and we do apologize. We are so eager to speak with you and to share with you.

The reason that you have guides in this incarnation is quite simply that you need guides in this incarnation. Now there are two ways of answering the question of identity of these guides and we shall answer them twice so we feel that mathematically this has significance. These guides are portions of your deep self, the self that you identify as the nurturer; the self that you identify as the provider and the self that you identify with spirit having little to do with anything but abstract thinking.

These guides are also those independent personalities which you call angels and which are in congruency with ourselves in nature. Do you think we would appeal to you as angels? Angels are passé. We learned many years ago to lose our wings and gain a planetary identity. We speak still the truth and yet not all of the truth. So we are angels and we are those who come from without your planet, adding planetary influences of our own. So it is we who most happily as a Confederation choose this path of service as guardians, as guides, as compassion, and wisdom that can be reached for and achieved by faith, by listening within.

Why does a third density entity need guides? In all of the densities except for the third density there is not a veil between conscious thinking and the memory and the thinking of all of those with whom you share a geographical propinquity. Only in this density are you purposely made unaware that you are all one. You see yourselves as separate and you see the world as very, very challenging if not indeed nearly hopeless. This is no mistake. We ask you to learn to appreciate that which is known as negativity. If you wish to think of matter and anti-matter that would be one way perhaps of thinking of free will. There is no getting at the heart of things and at the heart of your self while your will is completely free and undisciplined.

Oh, you may have your joyful moments. You may smile in the sun and be kissed by the rain and rejoice in the snow. But in and of yourself you are not one who seeks the depths. For it does not seem that it is possible to achieve joy by being serious, by being passionate and by being persistent. This is what we are here to help you to do. It is always your choice.

Your days are days spent in a classroom. Again and again you may ask yourself, "Why am I angry, why am I happy, why was I irritated by what just happened?" And as you honestly ask these questions of yourself, either at the moment or at the end of the day, doors will open to you because you have asked and what you ask you will receive.

You will find as you ask these questions that your free will is a rogue in the sense of being out of control and unpredictable. It is in its purest sense willfulness. It chooses at random that which it will do and pushes love before it. So love finds goodness in everything and will not insist on having an agenda to follow. The taming of the free will, the teaching it to understand what freedom of will really is, is the job of yourself aided by those portions of yourself that are of the deeper mind, of the comforter, of the various aspects of yourself which together make the higher self.

However, in this dualistic density it is often important for entities to feel that they can come into contact with the feminine principle or the male principle or the principle that has nothing at all of duality. And so the spirit, the comforter, divides itself for your use in case it is needed as such. You ask questions that are too deep for words and in a number of days you have your dream, your vision, your answer. And the longer that you pay attention to that which occurs to you and how you react to it the more you know about yourself and the biases that you have. You can then decide what of yourself you wish to keep. You cannot get rid of the love and you cannot change it. But free will is free and your will may discipline that free will, for you are free to do so. Yours is the freedom and yours is the will.

You will begin finding that you habitually act in a negative way concerning yourself, for instance, and you must call upon the nurturer for you do not feel that you are worthy. And the comforter is there to hold you and to keep you and to love you just the way you are. It is not the purpose of these guides to change you. It is the purpose of these guides to offer comfort and the wisdom that is part of yourself, in your deeper and hidden self. There are times when you find yourself engaged in a habit which intellectually offends you and you will probably call upon the male principle, for you wish not to be nurtured but to be kicked, to be shaken, to be taken out of yourself, that you may have a longer point of view and begin to see the damage you are doing and so cease to do it.

Usually the last portion of the guidance offered to you from within and from without is the androgynous or spirit-filled entity which has no bias and is a portion of oneness. You come to this comforter when at last you see that of yourself you cannot free yourself from your free will. The work you have done so far has given you a vision of what you wish to be. You are ready to make your choice. You are ready to surrender your willfulness to the higher self within, that self which is of love, which is of the Creator, which is connected with the heart of yourself and of all others. It is that guide which has no bias neither towards compassion or wisdom but only the consciousness of oneness that can aid you in surrendering your most precious free will in complete trust that you are only surrendering a small will to a will that you have created through many, many lifetimes, a will that you have deeply been yourself connected directly and immediately with the one infinite Creator.

Then it is that you discipline your will and you become passionate in your path of service. For you see that of your free will you may chose to serve and be a servant to all of humankind, serving the Creator in every moment, in every thought, in every hope and dream and ideal and in every humble chore in all things. Can you have the consciousness of serving the one Creator if the reason you will to do that which you do, even if it be sweeping the floor, is that you do it for the love of the one infinite Creator?

This is the illusion of separateness. You must be separate so that you can be hurt, so that you can be challenged, so that you can be taken beyond yourself and given opportunity after opportunity to chose to love Creator by serving others or love the Creator by serving yourself and forgetting the others. As always, there is the divine paradox that before you can serve others you must learn within yourself to love yourself. For the commandment reads loving your neighbor as yourself. Therefore it is not selfish to work upon the self. This must be done persistently, patiently and compassionately. You would not be here if you could do this well. You would be learning other lessons. To love is your lesson now.

It is also, as has been mentioned this evening, for that reason that the Creator placed the attraction that creates the mated situation between men and women. The thinking processes are the same in a mated pair of men and women but the woman has, physiologically speaking, a much stronger link between logic and intuition. This creates for the mated pair a mutual ability to serve each other as teachers. To honor your mate is to honor yourself, is to honor your teacher, is to honor the process of choice. Yet have few of you in this density used the opportunity to communicate with another unique entity made of love, to find the differences in thinking, to use misunderstandings as challenges, creating abilities to improve communication. Opening the mind, especially of the male, to the gentle and pleasant waters of trusting and resting and being inspired. The female also enjoys in that equal partnership during clear communication, the practicality, the effectiveness, the different way of approaching the same subject that the mate has.

Skill at communication is poor. Skill at communication between men and women is poorer. This is not, nor is it intended to be, an easy and unchallenging relationship. Due to free will in this density the oddest people mate. We find it always, especially that part of our self that is *(inaudible)* calls for humor.[2] For we look at mates that vibrate in such different ways that to pull together as yoke to oxen the cart of learning and advancing is the challenge of a lifetime. How poorly sometimes you entities do mate. It is well to find someone to whom you can speak.

In the density of love and understanding the mated relationship is there but there are two great differences. Firstly, there is no jealousy because the sexual experience is as common as the shaking of the hand. It is an electrical exchange that occurs without the need for the body or the vehicle touching. It is natural to those who are seeking together to share this energy. This energy is not remarkable, star-crossed, romantic or sentimental. This energy is the foundation of your passion. This passion the Creator had for you when He created you. This orgasmic intensity is love.

Realize that when you approach a mate you are touching the Creator and you are experiencing a communion that is holy; a sanctified, blessed Eucharist, a sharing that is part of your metaphysical being if you chose to make it so. You may chose not

---

[2] Carla: I would guess that their thought was, "especially that part of ourself that calls for humor to take things lightly."

to but what a waste. The other thing that is different about mating in fourth density is that vibratory patterns are not hidden. Consequently, there are very few masochistic enough to chose one with whom one is eternally at odds. In fourth density all problems do not go away. Much remains to be refined. But you see in third density you have made the choice. Will you be master and cause others to serve you and control them for your benefit? Very well. You are upon the negative path and are so with the blessing of the one infinite Creator. Have you decided to become a servant one who helps without asking for return or thanks or acknowledgement of any kind? Then you have opened your heart to service to others. And in fourth density positive you shall not have to marry anymore than you shall have to have a name. Vibratory patterns and the blending together of vibratory patterns to create a deep third vibratory pattern which is the Creator, the male and the female.

It is obvious to all, the need for language is lessened considerably by the ability to move in harmony with the thoughts and the feelings of others without judgment and with the desire to help. If you will look at your church congregations you will see what was intended to be a social memory complex, a community based upon absolute and unconditional love. We are afraid that the teacher known as Jesus was not able to sell that idea to third-density humans but it is held forth as the ideal. For no matter how different you seem all of you are the Creator and to serve anyone is to serve the Creator. Never argue or criticize yourself but when you feel that you have acted inappropriately begin again. Allow that female spirit to nurture you in forgiveness and redemption until you are strong again, worthy again, and able to go forth with the feeling of blessedness that is truly yours.

Mathematics, from density to density, is impossible to express. There are certain characteristics which have been mentioned of this language. Those things which are true but have no way of being proven. For instance, if you have a language …

(Side one of tape ends.)

(Carla channeling)

We shall continue. We are those of Q'uo. If you have the language, "A squared plus B squared," it would seem that the answer would be the square of the number represented by A and the square of the number represented by B *(inaudible)* and here is an indication of mathematics to come. There is a different kind of squaring which means that one must include A and B with a 2, the language being, "A squared plus 2AB plus B squared." We ask for corrections as we have difficulty giving this instrument subject matter she is unaware of as she is not in trance.

What we are attempting to say is that the squaring changes. This density has a local habitation, a local geometry and physics and mathematics, a local time and a local space. All models that you can create which seem logical within this density are those which inform one only tangentially of mathematics of the future. Just as in the married relationship, to become one in third density, in fourth density and above, two remain two but they are squared or as this instrument would call it, doubled.

The energy of such doubling is that which we meant by exponential in our last speech on this subject. It is not a concept to be understood in this density. As this instrument already knows, to examine the first inklings of fourth-density physics one may look well to the work which describes this density as movement or velocity, called the reciprocal system. It offers two equal and simple bits of language, $v=s/t$, $v=t/s$. This density is an illusion to the very last idea of this illusion. In that which will come it will be more transparent that one may move in space, one may move in time, and one may move in eternity, the third option that has no mathematics at this time.

We are being told by this instrument that it is time to move on. This instrument and the one known as Jim are both most happy to entertain further questions at this time and we shall at this time transfer to the one known as Jim. In love and light we are those of Q'uo.

(Jim channeling)

I am Q'uo, and greet each again in love and light through this instrument. May we ask at this time if there is a query to which we may respond.

Questioner: If I could, the last time we spoke you used the phrase *(inaudible)* concept language *(inaudible)*. Could you elaborate on the components of this language?

I am Q'uo, and we are aware of your query, my brother. We shall speak to the best of our ability through this instrument. This instrument has not the depth of meditation necessary to bring forth concepts with which it is not familiar. However, we feel that we may make a beginning upon this topic. The non-local nature of this language refers to a philosophical description that attempts to describe a situation in its most fundamental components. This has to do primarily with the articulation of the qualities of love and light as they are acted upon by free will. The free will being that consciousness which has evolved to a certain level of understanding or breadth of perception according to its own experiences and its efficacy in blending its vibrations with the creation about it so that it discovers the nature of the events, entities, ideas and interactions by becoming these events, ideas, entities and interactions.

This type of language is that which expresses itself by what you may call a kind of concept communication. Quite literally in your terms it is the equivalent of walking in another entity's shoes so that one approaches complete efficiency in the communication.

May we speak further upon this query, my brother?

Questioner: No, thank you very much. On another topic, could you comment on the nature and seriousness of divorce as you have already spoken of marriage.

I am Q'uo, and aware of your query, my brother. The mated relationship is one which provides the greatest amount of efficiency to those entering into the relationship and the learning of the lessons which are those chosen before the incarnation by each entity. The efficiency is achieved in a direct proportion to the intensity of the relationship, the vividness of the relationship. This intensity is enhanced by the familiarity between the two entities. As the entities become more and more aware of and informed by each other and the dynamics that grow between two entities as they share the life experience, this familiarity then describes in clearer relief the nature of the lessons that are being worked upon by the entities.

When there is a difficulty in perceiving the depth or breadth or ramifications of any lesson or set of lessons then there is the disharmony, the friction of the parts which do not fit, shall we say, into those places in the life experience that each entity has made for them. If the difficulty in fitting these pieces or portions of the life experience together persists and is not reconciled or given a place in each entity's life pattern into which it may comfortably fit then this disharmony we have found within your culture frequently results in that which you call the divorcing of the entities. That is, the removing of each entity from the relationship in order that there may be a cessation of the friction, a removing of the frustration that results from the inability to find a place for the lesson that was being attempted within each life pattern.

The seriousness, as you described it, is only that of the efficiency of the relationship and the efficiency of learning and being able to be of service as a result of utilizing that which is learned in the life pattern. The entities will find that the lesson which was being attempted shall repeat itself in whatever future relationship is attempted even if no further relationship is attempted. However, in the solitary situation the efficiency is greatly reduced for there is the lack of the mirroring effect, that which intensifies and in most cases clarifies the lesson at hand. In the beginning again with a new relationship there is the need of retracing steps that have previously been accomplished with the former partner. This, of course, in your terms takes time and there is much of the repeating these steps which means in most cases that the efficiency of the learning has been greatly reduced. However, there is always the opportunity for the realigning of the dedication and determination so that there may again be the resumption of the pattern of lessons and services and once again there may be the finding of the mirroring effect so that this process might continue the pace.

Is there a further query, my brother?

Questioner: Could you comment on the fact that is has a *(inaudible)* on marriage?

I am Q'uo, and am aware of your query, my brother. In your terms, that is, in the mundane terms of the culture in which you live …

(Tape ends.) ✣

Intensive Meditation
August 2, 1990

(K channeling)

We greet you in the love and in the light of the one infinite Creator, whom we serve together with you.

It is, as always, our great privilege to work with you and to share with this group a new seeking. When you are seeking together, you are most congruent, though it may not always seem so to you in your illusion as individuals, and we take great joy in being able to share with this congruency of seeking.

We thank you for your dedication as individuals and as a group to the spiritual work to which you have dedicated your lives. It is a great service that you perform. But again, you are not aware of what you do and when what you do may be of help to others. We thank you for the service you perform both in aiding those about you in the third density and in offering to us the opportunity to be of service also, for it is rare that we may find such a group as this through whom we may speak as directly as we are able to in the vocal channel.

This instrument desires to know when it is being of service and we are aware that each of you has also had this desire or questions. We reiterate to you that what is of importance upon a metaphysical level is the desire to be of service, and the purity of the intent in the offering of the self and the dedication of the self to the work and to the purification of the self for the work.

The services you perform are many and yet they are one. They are many in that they manifest through a variety of activities which you perform throughout your days and these activities may seem to be largely different, one from the other. Your service may vary with a smile given to a stranger you pass on the street, to a look of love exchanged with one who is close, to the more obvious form of teaching and the vocal challenge which exists.

All these seemingly various services you perform are but one and that is the radiation of the love of the Creator, which pervades you and your illusion, have you but the ability to perceive. This is your service; to aid in the perception of the love of the Creator in yourself and in those about you. Is it not simple, my friends? Why then do you spend time worrying over whether you have been able to be of service?

When a being is full of the love of the Creator, and as you radiate and manifest the essence of that being, those who come in contact with you, whether knowingly or unknowingly, will see that which you have to offer. That is who you are—that is the Creator, who is love.

Now, there is much confusion in this illusion about the concept of love. We are aware of the differences in the expression of the concept in your various languages and of the various types of love expressed as different concepts.

When we speak of the love of the Creator, the metaphor perhaps most analogous which we may use to attempt to explain to you the metaphysical nature of love is that of the radiance of your sun. The sun does not necessarily do anything. The sun is. It radiates the essences of its being. It radiates heat and light and gives life by its radiance. This is the nature of the Creator's love—giving, simply and freely as part of the nature of its being.

This is the love that you may also radiate to those about you. The nature of your being does not necessarily do, it just is. It radiates this love. So, all you have to do, my friends, in order to be of service is not to rush about finding various services to perform, but merely to look to the heart of yourselves to perceive that which your true nature is; to allow that perception and realization to so pervade you that your awareness of it becomes also clear to those about you.

This is why we speak of the importance of knowing yourself. The true nature of the self is known. A certain transparency of the self is achieved; the penetration of the walls of third density illusion which surround you in the form of the bodies and the various societal conceptions and misconceptions of the nature of the individual and the illusion. When the true nature of the self radiates through the self that has become transparent, penetrating through the illusion, it shines out as a beacon into the thick darkness of the illusion that covers your planet.

We are aware of many groups such as yours that are attempting to do this work on an individual and on a group level. And it is this dedication on an individual and a group basis that is lightening the consciousness of your planet.

There are those that say that the small lights surely will not make any difference in the vast darkness. We know great beacons of light in the history of your illusion—the teaching of the one known as Jesus and other masters of the various religions and spiritual paths.

The individual may become discouraged in comparing oneself to ones such as these, feeling oneself to have but a small light to offer. We say to you that no light is so small it makes no difference. No matter the size of the light, it still shines and as you band together in your efforts, the effects of the light that you project are multiplied.

We will at this time transfer to the one known as Jim, thanking this sister for the willingness to receive our contact. We are known to you as those of Q'uo.

(Jim channeling)

I am Q'uo, and reach you again in the love and light through this instrument. We are very pleased with the progress that was made this evening by the one known as K. We are aware of the difficulty with which the contact was initiated but we felt that it was worth the effort to remain with this instrument and to give encouragement that it was indeed ready to make the initial contact.

At this time we would offer ourselves in the attempt to speak to any queries which remain. May we begin with a query at this time?

Carla: I know that everything you've said about life being worthwhile no matter what is true, but how can you tell that to yourself when you're feeling really down?

I am Q'uo, and am aware of your query, my sister. Indeed this is a question that few entities have the opportunity to ask upon a prolonged basis such as you have had, my sister.

The very asking of the question is an event within the consciousness of the entity that asks it. That offers to the self the opportunity for the gradual transformation of the point of view. The feeling of great pain and discomfort which limits one's potential or activity are qualities which cause the attention to be focused in a manner unlike most experiences which you will have in your lifetime.

The intensive effort necessary to maintain the consciousness and the attitude and the desire to continue is an effort which, along with the asking of the question, causes a kind of tempering of the will while at the same time providing the will a further testing that will in the mundane sense seem to be discouraging, for as the will is tested and stretched to the limits for that entity in its exercise, it will seem to the entity that there is little that is left for the generation of further desire.

This is a most intensive testing. It is one which you have set before yourself as a means by which you shall further purify your desires regarding service to others and in a personal sense, regarding your acceptance of yourself for your ability to endure. The product of such a test is ultimately quite simple in that the entity has persevered long enough to give itself the opportunity to do so once again.

There seems to be no end to this kind of work upon the self. For the pain-filled situation tends to gather a kind of momentum and has the overall effect on the physical vehicle of wearing it down so that its energy reserves are low. This is the work of those few who wish to so purify their own vehicles that the sense of self and the security of the self are seen as those things which are fleeting, and the tension then is driven further inward in order that the focus might continue to seek the truer heart of that which sustains all that is.

This in its purest sense, or essence, is that indefinable quality which we frequently call love. Because of your love for the Creator and the son of the Creator whom you revere as your savior, the one known as Jesus, the Christ, you continue day by day, moment by moment to make the choice to serve in ways that are unknown to you, ways that are provided simply by your existence, moment to moment, you choose, moment by moment to continue and to continue and to continue, though there is little in the way of good reasons that the intellect may provide, that analysis may uncover. Yet there is that unquenchable thirst for the waters of love and by seeking the cup of such you radiate that which is not apparent to your eyes, but on the physical plane is obviously quite apparent as a desire which has been tested, tempered and found to be true.

Is there a further query, my sister?

Carla: No.

I am Q'uo, and we thank you, my sister.

Carla: Do you have any suggestions for me to teach channeling in a better way or [on] improving my technique?

I am Q'uo, and am aware of your query, my sister. We are very pleased with the openness with which this group approaches the learning and teaching of vocal channeling. There is the perception on the part of each instrument that a variety of techniques is most helpful in this process so that the training of new instruments might always contain some element of that which is familiar to serve as assurance for the new instrument and some element of that which is unfamiliar or new in order that there might be the opportunity at each working for the new instrument and indeed for each instrument to expand the abilities in this area.

Thus, we would not offer at this time any specific suggestion for the improving of this process for we are well pleased that the process is one which is firmly underway and we really are exceedingly happy with the progress that has been shown by each instrument and especially by the new instrument.

Is there a further query, my sister?

(No further questions.)

I am Q'uo, and again we thank you, my sister. Again, is there a further query at this time?

(No further questions.)

I am Q'uo, we thank again each entity for taking part in this process this evening and for generating a desire to come together for a working which removes the consciousness for a short time from those areas of the mundane activity in which you find yourselves ever more dutifully and intensively immersed. As your world about you tends to move you as though you were a pawn, it is a joyful sight for us to observe that there are those such as yourselves that are willing to move themselves from the dizzying round of activities to find a quiet place within that there might be the opportunity for the settling of much catalyst; the processing of it into experience; the giving of thanks to the one Creator and the generation of the desire to serve that one Creator in whatever manner is appropriate.

It is easy in your illusion to lose yourself in detail for much requires the attention within your illusion in order to accomplish what you call your daily round of activities and within such detail focusing of the consciousness it is easy to forget that there is a wholeness, a rhythm, and a pattern to the life which gives it stability and to which one may retreat in silence and in solitude in order to enjoy the nourishment there.

Again we thank you for inviting our presence again this evening. We look forward, as you say, to these gatherings and we are eager to join you each time that we are called.

At this time, we shall take our leave from this group. We leave you, as always, in the love and the light of the one infinite Creator. We are known to you as the ones of Q'uo. Adonai, my friends. Adonai. ✣

L/L Research

L/L Research is a subsidiary of Rock Creek Research & Development Laboratories, Inc.

P.O. Box 5195
Louisville, KY 40255-0195

www.llresearch.org

Rock Creek is a non-profit corporation dedicated to discovering and sharing information which may aid in the spiritual evolution of humankind.

ABOUT THE CONTENTS OF THIS TRANSCRIPT: This telepathic channeling has been taken from transcriptions of the weekly study and meditation meetings of the Rock Creek Research & Development Laboratories and L/L Research. It is offered in the hope that it may be useful to you. As the Confederation entities always make a point of saying, please use your discrimination and judgment in assessing this material. If something rings true to you, fine. If something does not resonate, please leave it behind, for neither we nor those of the Confederation would wish to be a stumbling block for any.

CAVEAT: This transcript is being published by L/L Research in a not yet final form. It has, however, been edited and any obvious errors have been corrected. When it is in a final form, this caveat will be removed.

© 2009 L/L Research

Sunday Meditation
August 5, 1990

Group question: The question this evening has to do with what Jesus meant when he was quoted as saying, "I am the Way, the Truth and the Life; no one comes unto the Father lest he comes by Me." We need to try to balance that with the fact that when people pursue any particular spiritual path that person will construct for him or herself a unique path that may or may not—does it?—partake of this position or concept of which Jesus spoke, "The Way, the Truth and the Life."

(Carla channeling)

Greetings to you in the love and in the light of the one Creator. I am Q'uo, and it is indeed a privilege to share your meditation at this time. We bless you for your generosity, and your desire to know the truth. To listen to our humble opinions is indeed kind of you, and we are most grateful and honored to be asked to come among you at this time. As always, please remember that those things which we offer to you are our thoughts, not an infallible truth, but the truth that we have been able to call our own, at the place where we are now in our own learning.

The question you ask this evening needs answers in two different ways. We shall move to the first way as the lesser of the two understandings that may aid in diffusing the tremendous damage the phrase, "I am the Way, the Truth and the Life; no one comes to the Father but by Me", has caused. This instrument is not familiar with the day-to-day living, the means of worship, and the sociological description of the times of the teacher known as Jesus. Suffice it to say that as now, then also, the more learned was the teacher, the more complex and sophistic his rationalizations might be. The teacher known as Jesus wished a return to simplicity, and a turn to the realization of the unity of all things, a calling to all of the children of the Creator.

This entity did not agree, nor accept, the pluralistic ways, the negatively oriented hints which characterized the theology and the teachings of the teachers of his own religion, which was Judaism. The entity never asked to be elite; he asked only to be a servant, and he related to others as teacher and servant, not being authoritative, except by the authority that was heard and could not be ignored within this entity's tone of voice, mode of expression, and knowledge of those prophetic writings, holy works and sophistic, argumentative commentary which at his time pervaded his religion.

As is almost always the case, it was through intense examination of his own religion, through active, day-by-day immersion in the belief systems of that religion, with all of its faults, its idiosyncrasies, and all of those things which he considered to be wrong, that he became aware that he had been born in order to express a channeling, in order to learn how to be of service in the deepest way open to him personally.

He was given insight and vision through his contact with his Father. This humble servant called himself the son of man, not the son of God. He repeatedly said, "When you hear me, you hear not me, but the Father within." He said this many, many more times than is repeated in your holy works. He said this every time he spoke, just as we say to you we are your servants, we are your teachers, any truth which comes, comes through us, and through this instrument. We are not wise, we are students of the great mystery. So too, was the teacher known as Jesus.

The name of the Creator, within his religion, bore a great deal of resemblance to the word we use so often, that is, consciousness. The Creator's name, never spoken aloud, simply meant, "I AM I AM," or, "I AM because I AM," or, "I AM that I AM." I AM. This is the Old Testament Creator. This is a concept of great promise, great authority, full of nuances and mystery, and there was indeed a large body of Jewish mystics, which line exists to this very day. As a mystic, Jesus attempted to express the nature of redemption as being a surety of consciousness, a bonding with that Creator which could withstand the threat of death, for eternity was more important to the teacher known as Jesus than this little life, but he knew what it took to embrace eternity, and as teachers do, he attempted to use that which he had, the name of the one infinite Creator most familiar to those whom he was teaching. I AM, I AM. I AM the Way. Identification with the Creator, the Way. I AM, the Creator, the Truth. I AM, the Creator, the Life. Stand up and be counted, for until you know I AM, you shall not come to I AM. Faith comes first. To think that this teacher meant that it considered itself a human doorway is a potentially wholly destructive distortion of that which was meant by the teacher known as Jesus.

You will note that we do not deny that Jesus was the Son of the Infinite One. We do not deny Jesus the Christ. We meet the challenge that this instrument offers. To her, Jesus is Lord, and by Jesus she means that which cannot be spoken, that is beyond our words, but that is the one infinite Creator. Let us call it love. Let us say love is the Way, the Truth and the Life. No one comes to the Father but by love. This is a New Testament change, which would have been acceptable to the one known as Jesus, for to Jesus his experience of his beloved Father was love given and love received. Difficult things were asked of this man, but this man was a channel with great determination and greater faith. He was speaking to entities who were very simple people. He spoke to them in words that left nuances, aromas, questions to ponder, but simple ones. Those of his own time knew the name that could not be spoken. Jesus *(inaudible)* spoke half of it.

That is the first way of understanding this phrase. It was a simple teaching. It was the preaching of faith, which leads us to the second portion of the meaning of these words, and why they are not the only words that lead to eternity, but merely words which show the intensity, the devotion, the worship, the surrender; the love, and the desire to serve the Creator by serving each other.

All paths of service, if they be positive, full of love and light, harmless to all, are helpful to those who are comfortable with that particular story or way of bridging the gap between present and infinite. This entity indicated the intensity necessary for a life in faith successfully to move from the mundane world into an arching bridge connected with eternity. Those who call themselves Christians, and go to church once a week, are as little likely to be able to graduate into the next density as those who have no path at all, but simply are looking, and testing and trying, and thinking, and mulling, and refusing to make a commitment that leads to surrender of the smaller self, in order to make room in the earthen vessel that is your body for the expansive and loving self that you truly are, the self that is Christed.

That which is called religion works as a tool to polarize, purify, and discipline the seeker, not only one day a week, but every day. Better is the path which is alive in faith and service and worship that has been created by the entity itself, but that includes the forgiveness of self, the forgiveness of all others, an adoration and worship of the Creator, and a surrender to the Creator-self within, the self that is you but is a deeper and unknown part of you, to your conscious mind.

How do you get from your conscious mind to this extremely deep realization that allows a safe and peaceful surrender of the self, a trusting surrender, a safe surrender? It is the faith that comes from persistent, daily attempts at meditation, no judgment of the meditations, no taking the spiritual temperature, but looking always for ways to see the Creator, for ways to recognize the hunger and the thirst for that which the Creator can give only to those who have surrendered to their Higher Selves.

Any path, be it orthodox or personal, must consist of several things. A complete and unutterable faith that the Creator loves you, that the Creator made you because He loved you, and that it is only appropriate that you love this Creator in return. It is necessary that you deal in some way successfully with the understanding of your own eternal redemption. How could such imperfect entities as we be eternally forgiven and eternally given another chance, over and over and over, so that we would never lose courage, but simply pick ourselves up and try again? There is a requirement that we stand so four square, so honestly, earnestly, eagerly and completely in the light of this love and belief, this faith, that we realize it is our identity, something that we cannot possibly deny, that we would refuse to deny upon pain, even of death, for we have found out who we are, and we will not deny that.

This attitude, once digested, shall we say, makes us realize the enormous preciousness of each moment that we are conscious in this milieu which you call third density. Here, and only here, can you demonstrate your faith, for you have forgotten and do not see the reality of your light being, the illusion of your mundane self, and the great beauty that you may make of a life in faith, a beautiful gift, a substantial, marvelous gift, a rich and honeyed gift, for the Infinite One.

We speak to a group of cultural Christians. Each of you knows it is not necessary to find the Creator in one place or another. The Creator did not need houses built for it, for the house of the Creator is your heart, that room into which you may go and shut the door behind you. The most personal and intimate part of yourself is the part that has faith. If you do not have faith, you do not have a way, you do not know a truth, and you do not know how to live your life. Nor do you know why you are living, nor can you rejoice at the moment of your death, whether it be natural or placed upon you because of your beliefs, so that you are a martyr. Most unusual happening—seldom will anyone have to die for what he or she believes—but that concept must be seated deeply within yourself, because it is part of knowing for sure, in no uncertain terms, who you are metaphysically.

We accept a kind of vibration, which you may call Christ consciousness, or any other name which you may wish to use, as a description of one who is committed, and (our) hope when speaking to those of third density, is largely to help people remember who they are, that they are as tall, and as deep as eternity itself, that they have being, that they are and that they will be, but that this is the moment—and in cosmic time, 75,000 years is a moment—of decision. It is a decision that must be made without reservation or evasion. You cannot say, "I know I am supposed to believe in something, so I choose this path, and I will believe it." Rather, you must become what you believe, insofar as you are capable of it. You must begin to realize that the life you channel is a life of love.

You yourself upon the surface of life are in tempest after tempest, and your small boat often loses its rudder, but in faith that frail barque will ever be afloat, and ever be moving toward the destination of paradise, for you who live a life of faith, you who grasp the need to become committed to a daily recognition of the Creator, will find yourself in a well-watered and most beautiful place upon release from the clumsy, chemical shell which you now use to carry your spirit. If you do not know, if you do not live as a light being, or, and this is in the end the same thing, attempt each day, give time each day to the attempt to became aware of being a light being, then you will feel uncomfortable with the need of the metaphysical world to be absolutely who you are.

The paradise of which we speak is that portion set aside after an incarnation in which each soul is healed, each pain eased, each tear wiped away. It is not necessary to be successful, happy, wealthy, or any other of the values so shallow in your culture. It is necessary to seek, to ask, to turn, to forgive. How difficult to trust in the Creator, and how much easier to trust in that Creator when you are aware of who you really are, and that things which may seem unkind that happen within your life experience are those offered in true kindness that one may learn more and more to be authentic, real, healed of all lack of self-forgiveness and forgiveness of others, so that all is forgiven, all is accepted, and there is no thing which can separate you from your faith, no tragedy, no horror that can remove from you the knowledge of who you are, an absolute and explicit part of the Creator, a being of love.

We do not hesitate to answer this entity's challenge that Jesus is Lord. This instrument has invested a great deal of passion and intensity in coming to know, to feel, to think, to act with an awareness of how the teacher known as Jesus might so react. The entity is active in faith. Each of you may be active in faith, but it cannot be done once a week, or when one needs comfort. It needs to become a part of each of you, to ponder, to revel, to rejoice and to allow your own absolute nature to be made known to yourself. You are an imperishable light being. You have chosen to be of service to the Creator by attempting to love those about you as if they were yourself. Are you a channel yet in your life, a way, a living truth, a silent witness, an example of life that reaches beyond the physical, the dropping of dust, and the disappearance from this illusion? One decision to move along the path of service is good, but you must keep making this decision, for your life experience was designed to allow you honest doubt, clear evidence that the Creator is not kind.

It is not easy to life a life in faith. Indeed, the more intense one's faith becomes, the more central and important, the more it is tested in the fire of experience, for faith is not rigid, it is flexible, adaptable, accepting. It allows people their own paths. It allows people not to find a way to eternity. It allows people to be where they are without regrets for them, because of the sure knowledge that one day they will awaken to their true self, to the I AM, and they will turn to seek the Way, and the Truth, and the Life that is yours in eternity.

Nor need you wait for this experience, for eternity lies in each present moment, and as your path of service moves onward, we pray you the grace, the alertness, and the ability to flow and adapt that will bring you to your own I AM, your own surrender, and your own experience of yourself as an absolute and ideal being, the greatest blockage to this way of thinking, being and manifesting, of the lack of self-forgiveness, the low opinion of oneself, a tendency to characterize the self as unworthy.

How long shall we accept the appearances of an illusion? Work as you will with those things which keep you from your awareness of who you are. Do not be discouraged if the rest of your life is taken up in the first step, self-forgiveness and forgiveness of others. You have all the time in the world to become your own I AM. Courage, my children.

(Jim channeling)

I am Q'uo, and I greet each again in love and light through this instrument. We realize that we have spoken for a lengthy portion of your time this evening, and once again we apologize for the wordiness which we find necessary in expressing those concepts which are our response to your most thoughtful query. We would ask if there might be any further queries at this time?

C: I have one, but on a slightly different subject. I study karate. There is a concept called the "chi," which *(inaudible)* that the power dwells in the area *(inaudible)* down about three inches below the navel. I was wondering if you could tell me anything about this concept of chi, and its relationship to the *(inaudible)* energy chakras, as far as location goes?

I am Q'uo, and am aware of your query, my brother. We will do our best to speak to this query, though it is one which leads into a subject which is interesting and intricate. The center, physically, of the physical vehicle for most entities, is that location of which you speak, and for any entity which wishes to move its physical vehicle in a graceful, power-filled and controlled fashion, will do well to move from this center, with this center fixed in its consciousness, for from this center, or any center that may be measured by gravity, there is a leverage which is possible that is not possible at any other point within the physical vehicle. This is a function of what you would call your mechanical physics. Because an entity is well grounded or in a firm foundation at this point, it may exert force in any direction in a more efficient manner by remembering this point, and by moving in harmony with this point. It is also true that from this point flows a kind of power which is also, shall we say, multi-dimensional in its nature.

This is a point which is very close to that physical location which you call the navel in which each entity upon birth is connected to its mother by the umbilical cord. Though this cord be severed, as is the case with each entity within your illusion, there remains a connection that is not visibly seen and is seldom felt, but is quite powerful, for each entity. This connection is with what you may call the prana, or creative energy of the universe. It is as though this energy were funneled into the physical and metaphysical vehicle of the entity through this connection.

When an entity is aware of this centering point in both the physical and metaphysical aspects then the entity has at its command a great deal of energy that may be expended in a manner of efficiency that is in direct proportion to the entity's discipline of the mind. The practice of the karate, as you are aware, is a practice which trains not only the physical vehicle, but the mind as well. Indeed, the physical vehicle is but a tool of the mind and has but little use without the mind to direct it. In the practice of the art of which you speak this is most apparent to those who seek to master the ways of this art.

Is there a further query, my brother?

C: Which energy center would *(inaudible)*, what color would *(inaudible)* be in that area?

I am Q'uo, and am aware of your query, my brother. The center of energy most closely aligned with this particular area is that of the yellow ray, and in many drawings of your Egyptian culture you may notice that the entity that seeks power in this world and in the mundane sense will be depicted as having a center of energy flowing out from this area. However, the entity that seeks to blend this more mundane type of power with its own spiritual learnings will begin to transform the metaphysical nature of this power into that which proceeds from the brow chakra, or that which is the indigo ray. Thus, in its simple and unadorned state the energy is of the yellow ray, however, it may be refined until it is of the indigo ray as well.

Is there a further query, my brother?

C: *(Inaudible)* function well, I feel more a flush over *(inaudible)* much like the initial flushes that I had when I was *(inaudible)* a channel, it involves a *(inaudible)* that I *(inaudible)* tonight *(inaudible)*.

I am Q'uo, and we are unsure as to whether we find a focus for query, but we shall comment, for we feel we have a grasp of your statement. The feeling of wellness, of being flushed, as you have described it, throughout your energy centers, in both the channeling, the conditioning for channeling, and in the practice of the art of karate which you now experience, are means by which you have been able to bring your energy centers into a temporary alignment and balance that allows each to express in an unified manner the energy which is unique to each.

Thus, the feeling of well-being that occurs at these times. It is at these times that you are able to move your focus of consciousness from the more linear type of activity to that which, though it may be physically active, is more of the receptive mode, taking in the pranic energy, or that which in your art is called the chi, and moving that energy in a balanced fashion in order to accomplish a certain set of goals, whether these goals are simply to feel the energy in its movement and radiation to move the physical vehicle in a certain prescribed series of patterns or to serve as an instrument for contact such as of the Confederation of Planets in the Service of the One Creator.

Is there a further query, my brother?

C: *(Inaudible)* for the first time in a long time I really felt intense conditioning. I know *(inaudible)* try to, I find that what I need to do *(inaudible)* choosing not to channel, but the conditioning tonight was very intense. I felt, *(inaudible)*?

I am Q'uo, and am aware of your query, my brother. We must apologize for being overly enthusiastic in our greeting of you, my brother, for we were wishing only to aid in the deepening of your meditative state. There is also the consideration which we had hoped that we had accounted for, and that is that there were two instruments in proximity to you which you were able to feel the conditioning as a result of the closeness to these instruments and the sensitivity of your own instrument. Thus, there was the doubling effect of the intensity of the conditioning which you felt. We do apologize if there was any discomfort. This was not our intention.

Is there a further query, my brother?

C: No, thank you.

I am Q'uo, and we thank you, my brother. Is there another query?

Carla: Thank you, Q'uo.

I am Q'uo, and we thank each most heartily for we have enjoyed this evening once again …

(Tape ends.) ☙

Sunday Meditation
August 12, 1990

Group question: The question this evening has to do with the general topic of the energies that are in motion in the Middle East, why there seems to have been such turmoil and confrontation within this particular area of our planet for so many thousands of years and what exactly is the pattern of the playing out of these energies that is now continuing in the Middle East.

(Carla channeling)

I am Q'uo. Greetings to each of you, my friends, in the love and in the light of the one infinite Creator. What a blessing it is to join in your meditation this evening, to thread our energies through yours and feel our oneness with you as we both seek the mystery of the Creator of all that there is. We are especially glad to greet and welcome those who are coming to this meeting for the first time. We hope that we do not *(inaudible)* make your mind going on as well in speaking too long. This instrument speaks to us often in her mind of our wordiness. We shall therefore surge through this evening's question with only one thought. We do ask each of you to be responsible for listening, understanding and taking in that which we say, but only as an opinion. We are not without error. We are not infallible. We are simply entities such as yourself who have been working to walk that path which leads home a bit longer, as you would estimate it in time. And so we reach a hand back to you hoping that we may be of service to you in our opinions and our thoughts. But please listen and if anything seems to be incorrect to you drop it and forget [it] without a second thought. For we would not mislead you nor be a stumbling block in your path of seeking.

That area of your Earth's surface known as the Holy Land is and has been for millennia a trigger point, as this instrument would call it. A place where whatever an entity has done in working upon its own consciousness will be magnified. It is a powerful place. A place of beginnings. A place lost in the roots of time upon the surface of your planet. And to this place more attention has been given, more love extended. It is as though there were upon the surface of your planet certain places which have their own power. There is none so potentially great as that which you call the Holy Land.

The energy has been placed into that earth, that sky, and on beyond by the prayers, the cries of terror, the joy of learning, and the passionate yearning for understanding of many, many of your peoples through many, many of your generations. Were all of these people moved by some magical means to Cleveland they would not be doing that which they are doing. Rather, they would be responding to the portion of the Earth's surface upon which they stand, this particular location not having any intrinsic spiritual power except that power that is understood to be in all things. That power is enhanced to some degree by those who lived there before you and your people and to some extent all of your land is blessed because those who lived before you, whom you call Indians, are greatly aware of the Law of One and the way of life which may be called conscious, magical or faithful.

Those who live in the Holy Land are in a place which magnifies that which is upon an entity's heart. Now let us move away from this particular situation long enough to express the nature of your metaphysical makeup in terms of being a person of power, what some would call magic, what others would call wholeness. The Creator is best known to us as love. Love in its [classic meaning,] that which may be called intelligent infinity, contains most of that which is the Creator. But the Creator, by the power of free will, has the desire to know Itself. And so creations begin in those parts of the Creator created of love which is the Creator and an equal amount of free will, which is infinitely different for each person, have created each unique being, including yourself. Each experience that you have, each decision that you make is of vital interest to the Creator of all things. For as One gazes upon consciousness that is Its own consciousness becoming an actor upon the stage of the world, It learns about that infinite entity which has been made finite by this illusion in which you now enjoy yourself.

The Creator planned lessons based upon what It had learned from each of you and all beings that have been created and the last creation before this one. Its lessons were simple and you are at the heart of them. You first learn of consciousness itself and in that learning you may be anything, a rock, a sea, the wind, fire, earth. Everything is conscious that you may think of or touch. Everything is the Creator and [when] this has been seated firmly, you as an imperishable entity moving through these illusions learn the lesson of the light, of turning, of motion towards that which brings you warmth, blessing and help.

And so you experienced being part of the creation of the Father that you see about you—clouds, trees, animals. Eventually you are not just an animal but rather through loving some entity such as a pet who loves its master and being loved in return, your metaphysical self meets for the first [time] itself in a self-conscious manner. That is, as a person conscious of self.

This is your arena, your stage. Here you made a choice. You chose to express all those things that have gone before. All the lessons of consciousness and turning to the light with an innate love of that infinite One which made you. But there are two basic ways to express this love. You may attempt to serve others and thus are serving the Creator or you may attempt to realize that you indeed are the Creator and thus manipulate people so that you have control over them and have power in yourself. These are short explanations of that split, that choice which you must make as to how to express that love which you have for the infinite One which loves and created you.

There are lessons which await you: love, wisdom, the unification of love and wisdom so that for the first time love does not end in martyrdom nor wisdom in solitude. Once you have learned all these lessons you begin to turn back towards the Creator, your learning for this creation nearly done. The cosmos has experienced in terms of the time which is part of your illusion many millions of years. But as you are imperishable and will live eternally, whatever illusion of time you experience does not mean that there is a deadline or a [threat]. It is indeed true, as far as we know, that the time draws near for the close of this density of learning on this particular sphere. Consequently, many entities are here desperate to learn enough of the lessons of love to be able to graduate into the next density where there is much more harmony and where the lessons are those of one who has already chosen to love and be of service to others. It is indeed a different atmosphere than you are now experiencing and certainly different to that of your Holy Land.

We feel that you needed this background to understand that those who live in a place of power are like the crystals that you dig in your mines. Different crystals contain different properties and there are those healers that are able to use these properties to effect changes, to make entities feel more whole or healed. But often what does not occur to people is that the healer itself must be at least as crystallized within as the crystal it is holding or else healing will not occur in any significant amount.

So we have in the Holy Land those who are all potentially crystallized beings, even literally and physically speaking, that is, speaking of your physical vehicle that carries your consciousness around. You are potentially a crystallized being. So the greater portion of yourself by far is a kind of crystal. It is, however, not charged most of the time. That is the water that is a portion of all your fluids. They are all capable of crystallization. Great portions of your consciousness reside in a portion of your physical vehicle that is almost completely unused that is the frontal lobe. And there is great chance of crystallization there also which carries with it the inner centering consciousness of the energy center of the brow in what some people have called the indigo ray chakra.

More than this there are crystallized beings which you recognize as pyramids, the Sphinx, and other artifacts put there for the balance of this complex and troubled Earth. This crystallization has great power yet it is out of the frame. It is not placed correctly because of the passage of time and because of its misuse in the past. It was intended to heal and seldom has it been given the chance to be used in that way. It was intended to be a place of initiation and at this point it cannot be what it wishes, what it was made to be, for it is no longer properly aligned.

Consequently, [there is] this great energy in this place of so many people's thoughts and deepest feelings and prayers and that attention from the infinite One; and there are those of faith who are discarnate, who are there in hopes of helping to stabilize that place and the globe upon which it sits, [but who] are increasingly unable to be effective. The people have taken the power of crystallization and have chosen the path of separation, the path of controlling others for their own benefit. Called holy by so many, it experiences now a complex jungle of many, many entities whose lives dwell upon negative thoughts of holy wars and brave soldierly deaths.

It is at this time critical upon your planet that those entities of good faith and good will realize the importance that they have and the ability that they have to be responsible for lifting this heavy and powerful state of mind so that the entire planet is not engulfed in this dark tide of anger and grief.

As you meditate know that your consciousness is the most important thing about you. Your consciousness is light if your thoughts are joyful, if you find a cause for giving thanks and offering praise to the one infinite Creator. You can by your smiles and the lessening, unjudgemental ear share with people that light. They do not need to know how you came to be able to offer this. Never volunteer this information. Speak of these things only to those who ask of it of you. The world will change not because you are persuasive but because you are sincere, passionate and persistent in opening yourself, aligning yourself to become crystallized. We say the crystalline shape offers space, a spaciousness in which any sort of light which you wish may arrive. Each time as you decide to do that which indicates love for someone else and unselfishness of yourself, you are crystallizing your own being and lightening the consciousness of your planet.

It is not money that people need to solve this problem for man has his toys and always will. It is the realization that all people are powerful and they will be crystallized and opened up to depend on those repositories and carriers of love infinite and unending compassion.

We must stay away from the specific things that are occurring in this region but never not to lose contact. We can only say the time now is critical. That that which is called the holy city is indeed a holy city not because the Creator considers it a holy city but because it is old, because self-conscious entities lived in society there for a longer time than almost any other place upon your sphere. Millions and millions of souls have placed heart and soul and mind towards the protection of, the pilgrimage to, the deep respect for the Holy Land. Those who are between incarnations or who have chosen to remain discarnate also are very sensitive to those such as Galilee, as Jerusalem.

The loves of the Creator have not always been the same but they have inspired the same faith. Unfortunately, the more crystallized of many of the entities who are most devout have chosen to place the power of their crystallization in attaining more and more power, wealth and importance, not truly realizing that they are a trigger point, so that that particular area becomes truly hostile and warlike; the will of necessity to be that which no one wishes; the war which takes all of your peoples and polarizes them in separation from each other. It is not a desired outcome from the standpoint that we have of service to others that this should occur. We would encourage each of you to allow yourself more and more to be a crystallized being, a planet healer, one who is love made manifest.

We will always fall down. We will always make mistakes. We will forget to meditate. We will not think upon our own personal power, your own deepest ideals. Do not by any means scold yourself or feel that you have in any way failed because of these things. Were you able to do all that we say you would be running out of lessons, not learning. Simply begin again. Persist, endure and love.

There is more that could be said upon this subject concerning the nature of the crystallization of entities and of how the crystallization of the pyramids and other such structures have caused changes. But we wish to not infringe upon free will. Therefore we satisfy ourselves with giving you the spiritual principles that make this particular area a sensitive area of this particular planet, more sensitive than many, many other somewhat sensitive areas, and to give some idea that the entities there have chosen to act in the way that they have.

Can you alter them? No, you cannot, [not immediately]. For all through the planetary consciousness, that the power that has become negatively oriented is short-circuited to some degree. Yet, my friends, you can [in that] you are part of the solution. If you do not pray, simply sit and think. Contemplate that which you are praying. Or visualize the love and the joy and the peace that you feel when you know that you are centered and in touch with the creative self within. Allow yourself to radiate like a beacon, a lighthouse and know that you are one of millions who attempt at this time to cause this planet to lighten this consciousness to feel it quite crystallized, now fuller and fuller of love. Many entities ask what is my service, what is my path, what must I do, what did I come here for? And we say to any and all the first and foremost thing of which you came here [to do] was to be loving in the face of a cold and unloving environment.

(Side one of tape ends.)

(Carla channeling)

We are known to you as those of Q'uo, and we shall continue, realizing that this instrument tells us that we must end quickly.

The illusion tends to give one the feeling that one is helpless and at the mercy of one's environment. You are not helpless. You have always the power of choice. Chose to seek that mystery which is beyond our telling or understanding as well as beyond your own. Seek the mystery and the paradox of spiritual truth. Steep yourself in love knowing that you are loved, loving in return and experiencing with an authenticity which touches your very soul the forgiveness of yourself in every and all circumstances. Then may you forgive all about you. That too will diffuse this potential difficulty as harvest approaches upon your planet.

We thank you for listening. We urge you to take your own self and your consciousness quite seriously. For you are indeed children of love and there you are by yourself seemingly little, yet together you have the power to become transformed into that crystallized being which has no sense of smallness or largeness but only of being love. That love can transform the face of this Earth which you love so dearly. We hope that you shall take yourself seriously, not denying yourself laughter or fun or joy. Be *(inaudible)* when you meet sullen seekers who have not yet learned of the joy. That is the concomitant of love.

Our thanks to you. We must leave this instrument for it is giving us a boot. Therefore we thank this instrument for its willingness to work with us and if the one known as Jim is willing to close the working through this instrument and leave the one known as Carla. We leave this instrument in love and in light. We are known to you as those of Q'uo.

(Jim channeling)

I am Q'uo, and greet you again in love and in light through this instrument. At this time it is our privilege to offer ourselves in the attempt to speak to any questions which those may find value in asking. Is there a query at this time?

Carla: In our family tree there is a myth or story …

I am Q'uo, and am again with this instrument. Do you have a query at this time?

Carla: There is the story about the Garden of Eden. I've never known whether it was a literal Garden of Eden or whether it was just the symbol of the beings living then in third density. Is there a Garden of Eden and if so is that just an old part of the world or is that the general [impression]?

I am Q'uo, and am aware of your query, my sister. This story, that of the creation of humankind upon your sphere in a Garden of Eden is one which has used semantic images and entities as a means of transmitting information that is primarily metaphysical in nature. Thus, there is no physical location that may be associated with this particular story other than the recapitulation of this creation within each entity as the entity becomes a conscious seeking entity.

Is there another query?

Questioner: This is a question for B, and we realize that you may not be able to answer but she would be grateful for any information. She has been in contact with an entity known as Kega and her experiences with this entity have been very positive. Would you have any information for her about this entity that you could offer, perhaps about its origin, about any connection that exists between this entity and herself or any information at all?

I am Q'uo, and am aware of your query and that of your sister known as B. We scan this entity and find that its great desire to know more of the entity Kega is that [barrier] against which we may not pass for we do not wish to infringe upon this entity's free will as it seeks those portions of its experience that are yet mysterious and which play an important role in its current path of seeking and of being of service to others. It is important for entities such as the one known as B to learn their way through the many mysteries, puzzles, confusions, doubts, disappointments and so forth which are a natural portion of each seeker's path.

When an entity has offered itself as a vocal instrument as the one known as B has done, the need to protect this entity's free will searching is doubled. For the entity has placed itself in a more obvious position of influence, not only the ability to influence its own journey and expansion of the point of view, but also the ability to influence others through the service that it has chosen. We can only say to this entity that as it seeks the solutions and answers to the many queries which are natural to a seeker in this position that it utilize those tools which are already well known to it. That is, that it seek with the purest desire available to it *(inaudible)* through its contact that may be illuminating in the process of the evolution of the mind, body and spirit. That it might share this information with those interested in such, that it might give as freely as it has been given to it. And that when there are doubts and puzzles that it repair to that inner being within the self and meditate and pray until it finds that there is peace and resolution when before there was turmoil and doubt. This entity has utilized these practices for a great portion of its incarnation and we are aware that it continues upon this path with diligence. We send our blessings to this entity in its chosen service and we send also our desire that this entity continue in faith and in will upon that path that it has chosen.

Is there a further query, my sister?

Questioner: The group of people that *(inaudible)* has been working with here today is very positively oriented [compared to] the contacts that she has worked with, that are [known as] innocent contacts, and she's noticed a great difference between those and what she's used to in a Confederation contact. The parameters seem to be quite different and she's noticed a great difference in the entity's place on considerations of free will by the Confederation whereas with the innocent contact that doesn't seem to be a consideration at all. Can you comment on those different kinds of contacts?

I am Q'uo, and am aware of your query, my sister. Those entities of this planetary sphere who have during some portion of their experience here have been incarnate and have walked upon your planet's surface are natural citizens, shall we say, of this planetary influence and when they have retired themselves to the discarnate experience, that of the inner planes on this planet, carry yet with them this naturalized citizenship that allows them to speak in a more broad-ranging fashion concerning others of this planet, energies of this planet, and the potentials or possibilities within both the future and that which you know of as the past of this planet and of its inhabitants. This is a natural working out of the energies that are of this particular planetary sphere.

When we or others of an exterior origin to this planet answer a call that originates upon this planetary sphere and seek to be of service in our own way we find that there is what you have come to know as the Law of Confusion or that Law of Free Will which is necessary to consider before any service is offered. For our frame of reference and place of origin, as you would say, is not only other than this particular planet but is different enough in its parameters that we must remain within those concepts or principles which are general enough to unite all entities in our attempts to be of service to those which have called for our service. Thus we are far more restricted in those areas of which we may speak freely. For in many ways we [are] able to see those energies and entities which have, shall we say, gathered about a certain area or entity and have influenced this area or entity. We are able to see these in a way which is both more intricate and in some ways more misleading if we were able to comment upon them than are entities who are native to this planet in their ability to see and to comment upon such inter-relationships. Thus we find our service is more effective if we remain in those principles which unite rather than focus upon those principles which upon the surface appearance and examination would seem to separate entities, one from another, by the simple description of one as being more or less of this or that quality, location, determination or nature.

Is there a further query, my sister?

Questioner: No, thank you.

I am Q'uo, and thank you, my sister. Is there another query?

Carla: I have a final one and then I promise that I'll leave you alone. *(Inaudible)* asked a good deal about the mysteries within those *(inaudible)* and wanted to know if he could ask specific questions in that line and also has requests from a colleague from the university who wished for you to tell him his social security number so that you could prove to him that you are real. The professor was aware that these questions were not [useful] as far as any spiritual or metaphysical meaning, and his question was why was he curious about things that have no metaphysical interest.

I am Q'uo, and am aware of your query, my sister. The entity of which you speak has found that there has been given through our contact information that is intriguing enough within his field of study that his curiosity about further information has moved in a fashion which you may describe as that of the shotgun. That is, he wonders if this contact is indeed legitimate, wonders if this contact can give further intriguing information, wonders if this contact can prove in an objective fashion to a colleague if it does indeed exist and can do tricks, shall we say.

We do not feel that this is at all unusual for many upon your planet to involve themselves in the seeking for information to enlighten and inspire the spiritual journey [and] also wonder about more mundane matters concerning the reality of this search for so much upon this path seems ephemeral, seems of the mind, seems to be slightly unreal. The setting is as the fool who walks off of the cliff without the slightest care as to where the foot shall be placed upon the next step. That is the nature of the journey for those who seek within the realm of the metaphysical, that which stands beside, indeed, that which undergirds your physical reality. However, we remind each seeker that those qualities and concepts and principles which are of most importance to each fail to be proven to any. For has any entity ever proven love, has any entity ever proven that there is such a thing as wisdom or peace which passeth understanding? Yet there are qualities such as these and others which each entity holds as a portion of its ideal and would give its very life for in the searching upon the spiritual journey. We are happy to speak upon the philosophical and metaphysical nature of any query, be it of mathematics or in any other field. However, we shall leave all proofs to those who write with pens and measure with rulers.

(Tape ends.)

L/L Research

L/L Research is a subsidiary of Rock Creek Research & Development Laboratories, Inc.

P.O. Box 5195
Louisville, KY 40255-0195

www.llresearch.org

Rock Creek is a non-profit corporation dedicated to discovering and sharing information which may aid in the spiritual evolution of humankind.

ABOUT THE CONTENTS OF THIS TRANSCRIPT: This telepathic channeling has been taken from transcriptions of the weekly study and meditation meetings of the Rock Creek Research & Development Laboratories and L/L Research. It is offered in the hope that it may be useful to you. As the Confederation entities always make a point of saying, please use your discrimination and judgment in assessing this material. If something rings true to you, fine. If something does not resonate, please leave it behind, for neither we nor those of the Confederation would wish to be a stumbling block for any.

CAVEAT: This transcript is being published by L/L Research in a not yet final form. It has, however, been edited and any obvious errors have been corrected. When it is in a final form, this caveat will be removed.

© 2009 L/L Research

Sunday Meditation
September 9, 1990

Group question: The question this evening has to do with acceptance, and the ability to balance the responsibility one has in a situation that one sees as a problem. We have the ability to act, to react, to think, to analyze, to respond in different ways, and eventually, if one discovers that there is nothing that one can really do, it seems you are faced with the need to accept. How do we balance the need to accept what is in a situation with the need to have an effect upon a situation and to form the situation in a way that we think would be most helpful to ourselves or another person?

(Carla channeling)

I am Q'uo. Greetings to each of you in the love and the light of the infinite Creator. We are most glad to be with you once again to share our thoughts with you and to accept the sharing of your meditation with us. We use terms like honor and privilege and gratitude when we speak of the opportunity of sharing our thoughts with you, sharing just a few steps of your path as we sit with you in meditation, and it seems like perhaps the overdoing of courtesy or politeness. Indeed, we are neither courteous nor polite; we are truthful. We are with your people at this time for this purpose. Our work with color is for this time period finished. We have, as you know, become a principle with Latwii's agreement to move from the study of your color complexes in the various densities as you approach harvest in order to be able to aid the brothers and sisters of sorrow that you know as Ra.

Thus, at this particular space/time we have only one hope, and that is to serve. This is our means, not all of it, but a large part of it, of polarizing further towards service to others as our method of accelerating the pace of our spiritual development. So there is no one-sidedness; we do not stoop to speak to you, for you are our equals, indeed, you are ourselves, and we, you. The rest is illusion, for all is love.

The question that you pose this evening is one which seems, upon the face of it, to be a question regarding challenges that are impossible to achieve a satisfactory outcome with. When things are unacceptable to an entity, the unacceptability is usually not shallow, not having to do with the petty and the mundane. Usually, those relationships which one finds unacceptable for one reason or another are a substantial portion of the catalyst for learning that you yourself have set into motion before the incarnation. You are not faced with these unacceptable relationships because of some failure on your part to understand, or some failure on the offending entity's part.

Rather, you are gazing at a situation and you may assume, in most cases, that this is not unacceptable in the deepest sense, but rather a condition of relationship that you yourself chose because you felt that there were, in your loving and compassionate nature, those difficulties within yourself which made the limits of your love and compassion, and the very power of your metaphysical or magical being, less. These you wished to bring into perspective. These are lessons with which you wished to work. You have in unveiled knowledge before incarnation done this to yourself, for there is almost no one upon your planet that has not come far enough along the path of choice that he cannot work actively in the arrangement of catalyst for an upcoming incarnation. Therefore, those things that you find unacceptable were intended by you for your own spiritual work.

When you gaze about you, you gaze about you with unique eyes. No one else sees what you see. No one else hears what you hear. No one else interprets things as you interpret them. There are times when the strongly inbred, inherent, deep personalities of two entities are unacceptable, either one to the other, or one-sidedly. It is because this problem has been worked on in this relationship in past incarnations.

However, that which is known among your peoples at this time as karma is only one reason of several that one may have had when one chose such relationships. One very substantial reason is the desire to graduate from this density, and seeing a lack of one particular way of loving within the self, the larger self and the God self choose to make agreements with those with whom there is no previous karma, but rather it is an agreement based upon one's own desire to work upon one's ability to love so that one may graduate and move onward to learn more harmonious and different lessons in the next density.

We would, in fact, give as our opinion that it is by no means the majority of entities who find each other unacceptable in some way, shape or form, that have had karma to be balanced. It is just as possible that the entities that you truly are—they being far more pure than you can imagine—have made agreements, one with another, for the mutual benefit of each. Each need usually in these relationships to learn the same kind of lesson about love, and we believe that the word in the question was "acceptance."

We would suggest, to begin to get an idea of things one may do in this situation, that you think of the pure and beautiful spirit that you are and that the other entity is, who fearlessly and boldly and courageously made these agreements to come into a path which involved the ordeal of not being understood, and in many cases, not being loved. It is even more intense an experience within your illusion for those who are wanderers, for their sensitivity registers at all times a state of some discomfort with the planetary energies of your particular sphere. It is as though you faintly remembered a beautiful tune, a wonderful song, a lovely poem, but you cannot find it. That is because the veil has been dropped, and those things are not within this illusion.

Thus, we suggest that you immediately, when faced with a recognizable situation of finding another unacceptable, move back and contemplate the process of spiritual evolution. It is, in each case, a drama, of whatever kind you wish.

The natural wish among your people at this time is to be loved and accepted and cherished. Very few entities are able to experience this state of mind in a steady state, for it does not fit the parameters of the illusion you now enjoy. Largely, there will be some misunderstanding at all times between all peoples, for the veil has been dropped, and instead of gazing at the perfect beauty of the true being encased in such heavy chemicals and water and all of those things which are held in the complex energy field of your body, it is necessary to look at that which is not visible, that which is not even thinkable within the illusion.

So, it is well to put the intellect to one side, and to realize that this acceptance of entities which you find unacceptable is for you important, not to find the solution, for when these agreements have been made before incarnation they normally have been made because the entities have very, very deep biases which will give each other catalyst; thus, it is unlikely that the outward situation changes. Although it is always possible, it is not probable.

Now, when it is karmic, as you would say, it is simply a matter of forgiving, and the lesson is over. Most people this close to graduation are somewhat beyond these lessons, or at least have very little karmic difficulties which have been bred within this illusion. What, then, can you do? "Where," as this instrument likes to quote, "is the love in such a situation?"

The answer, though simple, is difficult to enunciate. Those upon your planet have, because of their sightlessness, metaphysically speaking, the tendency to wish to control situations so that they are not so agonizingly difficult. It is a natural inclination for those sensitive souls who are already dealing with discomfort from the vibrations of third density. When you add to that intense and unacceptable relationships, you have given yourself a great deal to learn. May we assure you, nevertheless, no matter how unglamorous it seems or how sorrowful, that you have a good deal at stake in taking on these substantial challenges.

You as a spirit are honored and thrilled to be able to be incarnate at this time. Yes, you incarnated here, each of those in this circle, as wanderers, with a wish to help others. But because of the opportunities of third density, it is quite typical for those who wish to serve also to wish to become even more transparent to the love and the light of the infinite Creator. This, of course, does mean the ability to accept the unacceptable, to love the unlovable. You did not come here to learn how to be loved. You came to this particular sphere to love. If the unacceptability of someone close to you is not recognized as cold-bloodedly as possible as the opportunity you have given yourself to accept the unacceptable portion both of yourself and the other person, then you shall at least know the direction in which to move.

Let us back up and review just a bit of information about the way entities think within your illusion. In your illusion things are finite. The highest form of communication among your peoples is word by word communication, a most difficult way of gaining understanding, because even the most intelligent and dedicated communicator uses words which have more or less power for the self, but not the same power for the other self. Consequently, communication on a logical, conscious level is almost bound to be often extremely difficult, never impossible. Does this sound like a challenge you would give yourself?

We have spoken before of mirrors. When there is an unacceptable relationship, part of the love in the lesson is to realize that this unacceptable entity is yourself, not because of something unique between you two, but because we all are one. When both entities who have placed themselves in situations where they are in relationship with a difficult personality for them, the natural human attempt is to communicate, or to avoid. To avoid dealing with the relationship is to turn your back on a challenge you have given yourself.

We may note that taking this challenge too seriously will cloud your heart so that it cannot operate properly. If one of the entities does not yet remember why it chose this relationship, then it is that the love lies in seeing into the physical vehicle, seeing and comprehending in trust and faith and without fear. Thus, each time that you see the unacceptable entity, it is very well for you to say to yourself, "I came here to love and serve. I do not have to be loved. I do not have to be understood. I do not have to be consoled. For all of these resources are within me." This is the thought process, as you clear out the attic of mistaken ideas, that brings you closer and closer to high polarization and service to others.

When one says "unacceptable," one is judging the self and the other self. The thought itself is damaging. If there is a possibility of keeping the mind centered long enough to say, to yourself, "I am here to serve, I am here to love, I am here to forgive, to heal,"—and all of these things are possible through surrender to the self in its higher forms, which in the end becomes the God self—if you can take the few seconds to remember who you are, what sort of being that you are, and if you correct yourself every time that you say "This is unacceptable" within your mind, you are most likely to make great progress. Progress on your part is not dependent on progress upon the other person's part. Your part is simply to learn better how to love unconditionally.

There are many, many, many distortions of being, and all of you are fooled. You have suspended your disbelief by a radical move of moving into service in third density where there is a veil of forgetting. Now, you know that that veil is there, and you know that beyond that veil lies a truth that is a higher illusion, that is, one closer to that which is the mystery of creation than the one you now experience. Thus, it is well to tread lightly upon your own thoughts, to avoid any sort of blame of yourself or the other person, to recognize that neither of you has learned exactly who you are, exactly where you are going. Third density is a density in which learning is done in very dim light, in which choices must be made by blind faith against a backdrop of often quite negative circumstances. Are you your circumstances? Are you your relationships? Or are you a co-Creator?

Now, we would answer in two ways the practical, down to earth—please forgive our pun—tools of dealing with this situation. First of all, it is necessary to see that the responsibility for this reaction is not the fault of the catalyst that you have been given, but the fact, which is not a fault but merely a condition, that you are not yet able to see that other self as whole and perfect. This is an attitude, a bias, that you came here to shift and change. To one who has no fear, to one who wishes only to serve and love, nothing is unacceptable, for each entity is the Creator, or as this instrument would say in its distortion of belief, each entity is the Christ. All of you are potentially Christed beings. It is up to you as to how you go about moving along the path towards unconditional love.

The second way that we would suggest that you think about this situation is to gaze within the self, and to try to communicate, not with another person, but with the self, for the root of the seeming difficulty in all of its enormity, often, is that there is that within yourself which still retains some desire for control and for protecting the self from the realization that the faults that you see in others are only a mirror image of yourself. If you did not have work in consciousness to do in an area, you would not react by having difficulty. Those things you have already learned become part of the human comedy. Your goal, to put it whimsically, is to see more and more of life, not only as the opportunity to serve and love and move forward in your own development, but to appreciate and find, in the end, merriment in all facets of the human experience.

You are within your body human, that is, a term connected with incarnation itself. Humans are those who breathe in the limitless love and light of the infinite Creator, without realizing by any outward knowledge or any proof that they are doing so. So turn this mirror clearly towards yourself, and release the other who is unacceptable in your thoughts when you are working with your own contemplations, prayers and meditation, for the only entity that you may effect changes within is yourself.

It is the gift of grace, of simple faith, that enables one to pull away from the seduction of confrontation and unwise communication. It is better to remember that one is a servant, a humble and loving servant to humankind. Those who are closest to you are usually those one finds unacceptable. Thus, you receive the catalyst that you asked for and that you need according to your own opinion so that you may erase from yourself those last vestiges of desire to control, desire to make things happen your way. What you wish to do in your heart of hearts is to move deeper, and to open the heart past those last conditions, those last expectations, remembering always that those expectations and feelings will encourage the use in your daily life of what you may call affirmations of the deeper truths and of your true desire, for what you desire will come about.

Thus, when you begin to think poorly of another, find a way to break into the pattern that you are attempting to change within yourself, that will allow you to judge another simply because you yourself have work to do in the same area, and therefore are uncomfortable.

This was not intended to be a comfortable life; this was intended to be an incarnation of very hard work, for the surrendering of the desire to control, and the acceptance of the need to be loving, whether there is love returned or not, to be understanding, whether there is understanding returned or not, is paramount in your path of service. This is what you are doing for yourself. This is the gift you gave yourself. Cherish it. Be honest with it. Be thankful for it. And use the tools of stepping back, making affirmations, and, if necessary, walking away from the situation in which you have to some degree become unable to do these things, long enough to be able to regain your perspective of infinity.

It is not that you have enemies and friends, that is the illusion. In truth, you do love all beings, as you love yourself, and if you do not love another, you must look within yourself to find why you are upset, why you cannot accept. With entities who are very close to you, and who are in this situation of mutual antagonism, the patterns have repeated themselves so many times in communications, each with the other, that they seem to become set in stone, and it seems impossible to change the situation. And that is true—you cannot change the appearance of anything. What you can do is realize, through the work that you do with your own consciousness, that you do love yourself, and you do love all others, for all of you are one being, and how could you hate, or find unacceptable, your own consciousness? To do so is to place the brake upon the advent of your spiritual evolution.

Now, we are not suggesting that you become prim and proper. Perhaps the most effective tool to use in situations where you must move more quickly than you would prefer is a sense of humor. If you have a genuinely deep sense of humor about the human condition, the more outrageous the temptation to find another unacceptable, the more of the sometimes bleak, but always unimaginably funny, human comedy can be seen, if you are able to find the perspective to do so.

You are not your bodies. You are not your intellect. You working to open your heart. We do not suggest that you embrace servanthood to the point of your own self-destruction unless you feel that it is your path to do so. What you wish to do, in truth, is to recognize what is your situation, and to keep recognizing that situation as it changes, accepting that the goal of this incarnation is neither happiness nor contentment, but service to others, and the learning, for yourself, of how to love without condition.

We ask you not to be discouraged as you strive and strive to do so, but seem somehow unable to accomplish that which you attempt. Long term relationships which have suffered from unacceptability in one way or another take an equally long period of time usually to untangle. Instead of wishing for the entity to do things your way, it is well to feel what you are feeling, but also, at a later time, to realize the dynamics of those things which give you catalyst. They are wonderful resources for your own work in your own consciousness.

We realize that as usual we have talked too long. We were about to launch into further considerations, but we feel that our time is up and this instrument wishes for us to say farewell through this instrument, and so we shall. We thank this instrument for speaking upon a subject which in truth she was loathe to attempt, as the instrument is indeed one of those who asked this question. We hope that the tools that we have made available are part of what you may use to move into harmony with love, acceptance and the allowing of all entities to be as they are, and that includes yourself. You cannot push a flower out of the ground. You must wait, nourish it, feed it, water it, let the sun shine upon it, and give all credit, all glory and praise and thanksgiving for the bloom to the Creator of that bloom. You all are stewards of an immeasurable bounty of riches. Your birthmark is joy unrestrained, and overwhelming love for all.

We pray and hope and have faith that each may find this occurring as each works with his own catalyst. However, if our words have not aided, and do not speak as your personal and subjective truth, then as always we ask you to disregard them.

At this time we would transfer to the one known as Jim. I am Q'uo.

(Jim channeling)

I am Q'uo, and greet each again in love and light through this instrument. At this time it is our privilege to offer ourselves in the attempt to speak to any further queries which those present may have for us this evening. We realize that we have spoken long this evening, but we are quite happy to speak to any query at this time. Is there a query at this time?

Carla: Yes, I have one. Two other channels, whose contacts are quite a bit different than my contact with you, would like to get together with me and work with *(inaudible)* get together that you may speak *(inaudible)*. Is that a *(inaudible)* so often attempt to find the differences between one path and other.

My question is this. First of all, is it acceptable to you that we do this project? Secondly, *(inaudible)* while my eyes are open and I am attending to what the other contacts are saying? *(Inaudible)*.

I am Q'uo, and am aware of your query, my sister. First of all we are happy to serve in any way that it is made possible for us to serve. We go where we are asked, shall we say. Secondly, speaking to your concern that you be able to keep your eyes open in order to determine what is being channeled by the other instruments, we might suggest that this is acceptable, and it is then easily possible for you to close the eyes when it is necessary for you to speak our words through your instrument. There is a contact that will remain lightly present while your eyes are open that may be reaffirmed and strengthened when you close the eyes in preparation for speaking our words.

Is there a further query, my sister?

Carla: Yes. Usually when my eyes are open and I am focusing on *(inaudible)* channel is deaf, and consequently her speech is a bit muddled, *(inaudible)* with my eyes open, but *(inaudible)* or shall I just *(inaudible)*?

I am Q'uo, and am aware of your query, my sister. We would suggest that you proceed by allowing each instrument to voice the words of her contact in a "round robin" fashion, so that each has the opportunity to speak in turn, continuing the cycle of speaking for as along as you predetermine the sessions shall continue at a sitting. It may take you some time longer to prepare for your contact since you go through a more lengthy process of tuning and challenging than do most instruments. However, each instrument is unique and there is space and time available for each entity to be comfortable within the framework that it has developed for itself.

Is there a further query, my sister?

Carla: Are you comfortable with Emanuel and Aaron and are they comfortable with you?

I am Q'uo, and we speak only for ourselves in responding that we are quite comfortable with these entities.

Is there a further query, my sister?

Carla: No. No, thank you.

I am Q'uo, and we thank you, my sister. Is there another query at this time?

(Pause)

I am Q'uo, and we observe the lull in the questioning that corresponds with the waning of the energy of this group and we do appreciate the attentiveness of each within this circle of seeking, for it is quite helpful to have the concentrated efforts of each entity in order that the energies available to the one serving as instrument be constant, and we are always glad to be able to work with this group, for the level of concentration and interest and desire is quite high, and stably so.

At this time we shall take our leave of this group, looking forward, as you would say, to those times in your future when we shall be able to gather with you again. We leave each, as always, in the love and in the light of the one infinite Creator. We are known to you as those of Q'uo. Adonai, my friends. Adonai. ✲

L/L Research

L/L Research is a subsidiary of Rock Creek Research & Development Laboratories, Inc.

P.O. Box 5195
Louisville, KY 40255-0195

www.llresearch.org

Rock Creek is a non-profit corporation dedicated to discovering and sharing information which may aid in the spiritual evolution of humankind.

ABOUT THE CONTENTS OF THIS TRANSCRIPT: This telepathic channeling has been taken from transcriptions of the weekly study and meditation meetings of the Rock Creek Research & Development Laboratories and L/L Research. It is offered in the hope that it may be useful to you. As the Confederation entities always make a point of saying, please use your discrimination and judgment in assessing this material. If something rings true to you, fine. If something does not resonate, please leave it behind, for neither we nor those of the Confederation would wish to be a stumbling block for any.

CAVEAT: This transcript is being published by L/L Research in a not yet final form. It has, however, been edited and any obvious errors have been corrected. When it is in a final form, this caveat will be removed.

© 2009 L/L Research

Sunday Meditation
September 16, 1990

Group question: The question this evening is a continuation of last week's question, which was on the general topic of how one deals with a totally unacceptable person or situation when you have attempted to do everything that you know how to do. How does one balance the doing what is possible with the accepting of the situation? There seemed to be more information from Q'uo last time; we would like that information this time. Then at the end, if you have time, you might give us a little information about how Latwii and Ra have blended together to become Q'uo, just how do you do such a thing—equal parts of one, stir, bake at 350 and serve chilled, or what?

(Carla channeling)

I am Q'uo, and greet you in the love and light of the one infinite Creator. To Her service we are dedicated. It is our great privilege and honor to be asked to join your own seeking as you sit in meditation this evening. We are pleased that you asked us to continue speaking upon some of the more telling ramifications of the concept of unacceptability. We ask, of course, as always, that all remember that we are not infallible, and discrimination is requested. Each will know his own truth, what seems not appropriate to be left behind, for we would not be a stumbling block before any path that leads to the presence and the awareness of the One Who is All.

We are continuing to speak upon the subject of accepting of the unacceptable, forgiving the unforgivable. We have noted much upon this subject in general, and so we would like to speak about an aspect of this question that we are happy to be able to have more time to discuss. Each of you is well aware of the way those things in the distance appear very small, whereas those things just before one loom large. Many call this a sense of proportion. It is the key to observations of any kind which may be helpful when they are of an intellectual or reasoning nature. In situations in which the intellect is not used, the sense of distance, or proportion, continues to be an excellent tool for achieving a state of mind in which the heart, the true and deep mind, may learn the lessons presented by the unacceptable and unforgivable entity, relationship or condition.

We have spoken already about love. We would speak now about the free will that is beyond understanding, and is the first distortion of intelligent infinity. Without it matter could not have been illusorily created. Without it there would not be dimension, or the illusion of time. Without free will there would be only love unknown and unknowing, that is, the essence, the Logos of Love, which is the Creator. As this love is unconditional, whole and pure, just so is free will absolutely unpredictable.

Thus, as each sub-sub-logos—each of you—chooses to enter upon the path of accelerating your spiritual growth, you are dealing with a sensibility of mind which is all too firmly connected and concerned with the bodily, mental and emotional needs which have been acquired within the illusion that you now enjoy. Many, many choices that you make are not based upon spiritual principles, for your experience of life is that it moves too quickly sometimes in its actions for an entity to have a sense of proportion about what is occurring. The reasons for this are bound up in the principle of free will. No two entities are alike, and no one entity shall remain as it is throughout an incarnation.

The incarnate state is one of constant flux, learning, loss and opportunity. The loss is artificial in that it consists of the empty places made by those persons once loved, now discarnate; by truths, once loved, but now seemingly necessarily discarded; by ideals which the world you live in has provided enough catalyst to undermine in your own experience. And so, because free will, like the wind, blows hither and yon in all entities, it is inevitable that those who plan to learn as much as possible in one lifetime will arrange to have serious and fundamental challenges to its understanding or grasp of the principle of unconditional love.

In order for an entity to be able to find the self that can do this, it was necessary to find that which is woven with free will in order to make a physical illusion, and work with it in such a way that you are at least temporarily able to untangle the strands of love and free will. When you see, and know, and trust the absoluteness of love, the mind may rest much easier, the heart may become aware of its truer intelligence, and the responsibilities of meeting the challenges of difficult relationships and impossible situations begins to change and transform in shape.

We of the Confederation of Planets in the Service of the Infinite One have often spoken of the need to discipline the personality. By this we do not intend to mean the controlling, the suppression or the repression of any feeling that you truly feel, any thought which you truly think, any action which you do feeling that it is appropriate. These are each entity's choices, choices which one is unable to make while remaining concerned primarily with that which is mundane and of no spiritual consequence as far as you subjectively can see.

In fact, all things are fraught with spiritual teaching. All of the creation sings its song of love to you. But it is the disciplined personality who has gained the perspective on the value of mentation and the far greater value of the infinite wisdom of the heart. Thus, when challenging situations occur, one who has the firm foundation of a life in faith will not fear the unforgivable, will not fear the unacceptable, will not need, in fact, to react unless as an entity of the heart there are those things which you feel may aid in a spiritual way that one which is unacceptable.

Thus, your only responsibility is to love. You do not have a free will responsibility at this point, for free will does not forgive, it is love that forgives. Thus, as you step aside, disciplining your own freedom in order to serve and learn, you experience a love you could never experience within your humanity, a love which is in infinite supply. And to that difficult or impossible situation or entity you simply send love, and use your mental capacities to reason with yourself as to the cause of unacceptability, gazing at the situation, not with an eye to solving it, but with an eye to understanding the unacceptable entity or condition, and when that is done, to forgive it, to forgive yourself, and be clear and ready to gaze without any fear whatsoever at the situation or entity, for there is love and service in this opportunity.

This is a simple and seemingly rather glib summary. It does not take into account the enormous difficulty of doing these things within your illusion. And so we would speak of an aspect of your illusion that is absolutely necessary to the illusion, but is that which baffles almost all entities. You know free will if you know the wind. The winds move here, the winds move there. The winds bring rain and are a boon to your Earth. The winds bring storm and destroy life upon your Earth. The winds are zephyr soft, touching the cheeks of lovers on a summer night. The wind carries raging snow that blinds those who challenge it. In short, the wind is an influence not to be influenced.

In metaphysical sense, the wind that blows for you and moves you about on a level of which you are unaware is free will. It cannot be predicted. It cannot be wholly understood, and yet it is the same experience for all entities. If the wind is blowing within your illusion, no matter how many entities experience the same wind, they all will acknowledge that it has passed them, for they have felt its effect.

The world of metaphysical things is more subtle. The effects of free will are just as subtle, but set up situations within your energy web where you are open and vulnerable to the challenge of a distortion of love brought about by another's free will.

So it is not you that finds another unacceptable, nor is it another which is unacceptable. You have the same nature, but you do not have the free will you had yesterday, and tomorrow it will shift again. So it is with the other entity. It is that free will portion of yourself, not your deepest self, that generates judgment such as "unacceptable," "unforgivable." Within the heart which is freed by a discipline of personality, and given a path of service by freely made choice of the entity, love abides, and your instinct is to send love to that entity which is in enough agony to act inappropriately and to act as painful catalyst for you.

In this painful catalyst you may see in the other's free will choices, free will choices of the self, made with distorted understanding. Consequently, all statements of judgment of others are made not with the heart, but with the mind and undisciplined free will, for the heart will not judge. The heart will accept and allow the self to be the self, and other selves to be their selves. The heart of one who is positively oriented does not control an unacceptable situation to cause it to be acceptable. It controls the often destructively illusory free will portion of itself that it may move into a deeper self, into the wisdom of the heart, and from that standpoint all conditions of entities are seen as part of a blueprint of evolution which it is up to you to learn to grasp at least in essence.

Now, the wind is often used also as a simile for that which in the spiritual distortions called Christianity is named the Holy Spirit. As all things are holy, if it is acceptable to each we shall use the term, "Comforter." That which is carried upon the wind of spirit is alive. The spirit of the consciousness of Christ is alive and speaks to the world today saying, "Peace, peace, forgive, console, pardon, and start with yourself."

Now, this Comforter does not give comfort any more than the teacher Jesus the Christ gave comfort. Healing this entity gave, and freely, strength to the weak, sight to the inwardly blind as well as outwardly blind, strength of limb to the lame. But did this entity ask to be understood? In your experience, has any entity whom you have considered great or wise asked that you understand him or her? It is unlikely, for it is unimportant to those who live in the heart. They do not need to be understood, and consequently they do not attempt to be understood. Spirit does not attempt to be understood. The comfort is in its understanding, and your comfort also is in understanding.

Step back, back and back to the beginning, before the beginning of time to the very beginning of creation. You were created before your environment. You are the light, the active principle of the Creator, and we use that term apropos, for we wish you to understand the term "principle" as we use it. You are, in the deepest sense, the Creator, and in distortion upon distortion, because of your illusion and your own biases within that illusion, you are more or less a distortion of the Creator. Thus, you too begin to take within yourself the unpredictability and the divine guidance of the wind of spirit. Without fear you are capable of moving as you feel to move, capable of learning that which you feel you need to learn. Little by little, the disciplining of that free will, which is your very nature, yields to meditation, contemplation and experience, and you take the wind within yourself, the disciplined wind of the most perfect free will, that will to seek, know and be a transparent exhibit of the love that flows through all.

The process of opening one door while closing another is again difficult because of perception problems in this illusion. Free will in its raw and untamed state is almost precisely the opposite of true freedom of will, which is the will of one who is disciplined and freely chooses. Thus, not being blown about by the wind of the self, you may then internalize the wind and become aware of the spirit. And as you become aware of this spirit you shall find yourself moved in mind, in emotion, and sometimes even geographically, in order to do those things which you have not after all forgotten you came to do.

The wisdom of the heart is full of this blueprint. The conscious mind, governed by logic and free will, can never accomplish this. To move from head to heart, while retaining the concept of mind, is not anatomically sensible, but it is the best vocabulary we have to describe the deep love and security which you may find when you have accepted the wind within you, for you are spirit. It is the body which is weighty and full of chemical reactions that are part of this illusion.

As you offer your free will to the blueprint you have planned for yourself, you become free and enabled in your actions. In this awareness there is nothing unacceptable, nothing unforgivable, but only that which may be seen as this or that distortion of love brought about by untamed free will. Free will holds up the mirror to free will. If you gaze at another and find unacceptability, realize that that is a mirror. Now you may do your inner work, for you have been aided by that entity which has been disparaged and judged. What is there within you that must be forgiven? For if you judge others you have not forgiven yourself. If you are completely self-forgiven you have absolutely no need to judge, for you have no fear and nothing to defend. You can see through the free will, having seen through your own. You can tame the wind for yourself, and you can be of service to others by mirroring to them as honestly as possible that these are actions that you choose to make, and you choose them because they are of spiritual aid in the service of the Creator to this beloved self, that is you, in other-self form.

You picture yourselves, most naturally, as entities with a head and a backbone, two arms, two legs, the requisite number of organs and digits. You are a kind of entity you cannot understand as you gaze upon your physical vehicle. The difference between you attempting to move through …

(Side one of tape ends.)

(Carla channeling)

… the difference in your consciousness between seeing yourself as this physical vehicle, and seeing yourself as spirit, is the difference between being blown by the wind and being the good and kindly wind that blows love always, that is open and fearless and is vulnerable, unafraid. Once you have found your own essence you shall never fear again. It is the catalyst caused by facing the unacceptable, and finding ways to offer love and to glean and harvest love in the situation as well, is the wisdom gained through this shift in identity from chemical plant which moves you about to the essential self which is humble, nonjudgmental, completely unafraid, completely free, and completely able and willing to listen, to understand and to love the tormented hearts of those caught in this illusion which you now enjoy, caught painfully, caught unbearably.

If someone is unacceptable to you, that entity is deafened by the wind of his own free will, and has an extraordinarily distorted expression of love to offer. You cannot heal or help the other self, but only make your own choices. The entity that is unacceptable does not impinge upon you. It is merely catalyst if you still have work of your own to do in forgiving yourself for being all things, including many, many things which you consider unacceptable. You are carving out for yourself the right to ride the wind of spirit. Judgment, which is behind unacceptability, and fear, which is behind judgment, anchor your feet to the ground. You cannot fly, you cannot soar, you can only be injured and injure as you seek through judgment and the putting on of mental and spiritual protection to attempt to make yourself more comfortable in the prison of your bones and sinew.

When you find the love within in its pure state you are not confined, you are not finite. You have found your own eternity. In this eternity the wind of the present moment offers all lessons, whether it is necessary for the illusion which causes judgment to seem appropriate to be very hard to penetrate, so that you, that beautiful and wondrous unique spark of love and free will, will make your choices to judge or to appreciate, to ask for service or to be an agent of infinite service. If you are able to let your love free to ride the wind of spirit, you are always following the blueprint you have laid out for your own growth.

This is the density wherein you decide the nature of all entities about you as well as yourself, and with this understanding choose how you shall serve that mystery that created you and all that there is. Do you wish your feet anchored to the earth by judgment and the need to get points across, or do you choose to soar in the wind of spirit, judging neither yourself nor others, but asking, and asking, and seeking and hoping to be love, to be a channel for truth, to share in the infinite that your light may be a catalyst that frees others from their own bondage.

We are sorry for having spoken so long, but we believe this may deepen the understanding of that which was offered in the previous session upon this subject. If there are other questions we are always glad to entertain them.

We have had one question concerning ourselves, which is fairly quickly answered, we feel, and so we shall end this instrument's contact by speaking briefly upon this.

We are a social memory complex whose teacher of choice of the sixth density is the Ra social memory complex. We, as you, hold this complex in esteem. We were already in very harmonious contact with this group. That which occurred, though always possible, is rare, usually because a channeling entity will not be capable of receiving information of one type or density and another as well which it then relinquishes. Our teachers, those of Ra, were pleased when this group refrained from continuing to attempt to contact an entity whose ability to communicate was severely limited by a need for harmony not often seen in your density. These of Ra were, and are, grateful for the total willingness of this channel and this group to be of service in a way which was within the blueprint of the existence of each, even though this meant sacrifice on each entity's part.

As the entities which survived the most serious of psychic greetings continued in the same dedication, undeterred even by the apparent cessation of life of a beloved one, those of Ra felt it was still appropriate to communicate with this group insofar as this entity could carry a message in a stable manner. And so those who are known to you as Ra suggested to us a signal honor, that of sharing at the level of social memory complex sharing, with the wisdom and the compassion of our teachers.

This was a project which was apart and separate from the Law of One channelings. It is we of Latwii who speak with this instrument, following the general way of conscious contact, gauging by feedback the stability of the group, the purity and stability of the instrument, so that we know that which is possible to be shared without damage to the instrument, and that which the instrument would sacrifice too much of itself in bringing through.

So we are both Latwii and Ra; or you may think of us as Latwii taught constantly and in a much closer configuration than most teachers and students; or you may see us as a melded principle, as we both serve the one Creator, and are both upon the same path, and are more and more of the nature of Ra, the lower awareness being blessed always by close association with higher truths and spiritual principles. So, too, has this instrument had the experience of becoming in part one with those of Ra, as it spent many hours in the company of those of Ra, who looked over it as others of our social memory complex spoke for Ra. Only to the Creator can thanks be given for this occurrence, for its approval, and for our carrying out this attempt at service. We thank you for this opportunity with our whole heart.

We would at this time close the meeting through the one known as Jim.

(Jim channeling)

I am Q'uo, and greet each again in love and light through this instrument. We realize that we have spoken long once again in your terms, but we would wish to offer ourselves at this time in the attempt to speak to any queries which may yet remain upon the minds of those present. Is there a query at this time?

K: What were you referring to when you mentioned the approval of the occurrence which I took to be the joint project between those of Latwii and those of Ra—what approval was this?

I am Q'uo. The approval is that, not only of each social memory complex, but of that council which sits and serves as what you would call the Guardians of this particular planet, those entities which oversee Confederation attempts to be of service to entities upon this planetary sphere. This council, the session council, is known to you as the Nine, or the Council of Saturn.

Is there another query, my sister?

K: I assumed that's what you were talking about. Then the Law of One channelings also had to be brought before this Council for approval, and do these social memory complexes, when they are considering offering themselves for service, in service as contacts through vocal channels, do all those projects need to be approved *(inaudible)* before the council as *(inaudible)*?

I am Q'uo, and this is correct, my sister, for there is, as you know, that which is called a quarantine of this particular planet because of previous efforts to be of service to various groups of entities upon this planet by members of our Confederation who were, though very well intentioned in their desire to be of service, mistaken in various aspects of the means by which the service was carried out, thereby infringing upon the free will of some entities and groups of entities upon this planet. Therefore, it is now quite carefully guarded as to contact between Confederation entities and the peoples of this planet.

Is there a further query, my sister?

K: Not on that, thank you.

I am Q'uo, and we thank you. Is there another query?

K: I do have another one. I presume also that Wanderers have to present themselves individually before the Council for approval as well?

I am Q'uo, and this too is correct, my sister, for each effort of service to this planet from those from elsewhere, shall we say, has the possibility of affecting the entities of this planet in a pronounced manner. The effect of each Wanderer's service must be carefully gauged in order that the service is offered in a way which will serve as catalyst to the point of information without infringement.

Is there a further query, my sister?

K: Do Wanderers who offer themselves for service have specific projects in mind, or do they just come hoping to help in some generalized manner with the harvest of raising of consciousness or things of that general nature, or is that specific enough in itself?

I am Q'uo, and each Wanderer has a variety of services to offer, the first being the presence which is of a lighter vibrational quality, and which shines without any action being necessary and lightens the planetary vibration by its very presence and radiance.

The second level of service is that which you would call more specific, in that the entity will have brought with it into the Earthly incarnation those talents and skills which may be utilized in a more specific or focused fashion in order to operate, shall we say, more as would the surgeon's scalpel.

The third level of service is that which is more personalized in nature, in that the entity will also take the opportunity to provide a service not only to others, but will seek to balance or harmonize some portion of its being that is in need of such balancing or harmonization. As all interaction with other entities provides a catalyst which is a service this is also a level of service to others that is valuable, though it also has a personal component as well.

Is there a further query, my sister?

K: No, thanks very much.

I am Q'uo, and again we thank you, my sister. Is there another query?

Carla: Earlier today, Jim and I were talking about the project that Aaron and Barbara and Emanuel and Pat and yourself and me, and together we realized that we hadn't asked a question of preferences of you, and for the life of me I cannot remember what it was we didn't ask. If it is possible to look into either my mind or Jim's, I wonder if you could comment on the question that I can't remember, if that makes any sense *(inaudible)*?

I am Q'uo, and we feel that we have a grasp upon your query that is as firm, we hope, as the grasp upon this entity's mind at this moment, however, perhaps that which we have to say will jog your memory as well.

We have no preference as to whether the project is focused in a chapter by chapter fashion upon a series of topics, or whether there is the opening of each instrument to what you have called in your past meetings the "pot luck" agenda, that is determined more on the unconscious or subconscious level of the mind than the conscious level. We are happy to offer ourselves in whatever way is asked of us. We do not feel that it is our place or proper purpose to choose an agenda of topics arbitrarily, for we feel there is great benefit to be realized by each entity partaking in this process of choosing of topics and agenda.

We do not feel that two session per day would be too great a burden for any of the entities involved, as long as those sessions have a reasonable length to them. We realize that that which we call reasonable may be in question concerning our previous speaking to this group, that is, somewhat overly long in duration. We would recommend a flexibility with the first day's worth of work in order that each contributing instrument might be allowed to assess that which is possible for it and that no one be asked to partake in any longer or more strenuous sessions than she can comfortably partake in.

May we speak to any further facet upon this topic, my sister?

Carla: No thank you, Q'uo. I remember now that those were the questions that we had discussed, and you've answered them very well. I will share them with Barbara, who will share them with Pat. Thank you.

I am Q'uo, and we thank you, my sister. Is there another query at this time.

Carla: Is there any need to cleanse the house especially for this project?

I am Q'uo, and we find that this domicile is well tuned in its basic vibrational quality. We believe that this location will provide an harmonious setting for this undertaking.

Carla: Is there an exaggerated problem with my electromagnetic field anomalies because of the intensity of these sessions, and, if so, should we attempt to *(inaudible)* the microphones and recording systems as we have done before?

I am Q'uo, and as we examine that which has been discussed concerning this project, we are aware that there shall be a redundancy of recording devices, if each instrument brings her own recording devices. We would continue the recommendation that you have as little direct contact with any recording device as is possible, touching only those portions of the device that is necessary for having the microphone resting upon your physical vehicle. Other than this precaution, we do not feel that there is any need for further concern in this area.

Carla: I am aware already that Jim and K are part of the circle for this project. Others known to you of our group would probably enjoy coming and sitting in some of the sessions. I speak of the one known as R, the one known as S, the [other] one known as S, the one known as L, the one known as T, the one known as B, the one known as J. These are those entities which come to mind quickly. Is it helpful, neutral, or unhelpful for more entities than Jim and K, Pat and Barbara and me to sit in session?

I am Q'uo. We would suggest that you consider two factors in this regard. One is the preference of the other instruments that will be taking part in these sessions. The second being the ease of scheduling and carrying out any session when there are fewer entities to be considered.

Is there a further query, my sister?

Carla: So it's neutral, as far as helpful or harmful, as far as you're concerned, and merely a question of logistics?

I am Q'uo. For most of these entities, that would be correct. However, we do not wish to place ourselves in the position of one who judges. In some cases it would not be helpful to include additional entities.

Carla: We shall inquire separately of anyone who wishes to join us before *(inaudible)*, and we will most certainly take into full account the wishes of all three of us. Thank you.

I am Q'uo, and again we thank you, my sister. Is there a final query at this time?

K: Not from me, thanks.

I am Q'uo, and we thank each again for this opportunity to blend our vibrations with yours and to speak to the heart of each entity in its desire to know more of that which you call the truth. We share that which is ours to give and share it with the hope that there will be some benefit to those present and to others that may eventually come in contact with this information. However, we share most centrally with a freedom and joy that we are able to walk a step or two with you upon your paths of learning and of service. This is a blessed and precious time for us. We cannot thank you enough for sharing it with us.

We are known to you as those of Q'uo and we shall take our leave of this group at this time, leaving each, as always, in the love and in the light of the one infinite Creator. Adonai, my friends. Adonai. ✼

Intensive Meditation
September 20, 1990

(Jim channeling)

I am Q'uo, and I greet each in the love and the light of the one infinite Creator. It is our privilege to join this group this evening in the work of the development of the instrument, each instrument always needing the exercise in order to develop those abilities to become aware of information and the continued refining of the perception of that which is available to be transmitted. Each instrument works with a certain set of parameters that are entirely personal in nature, being composed of those qualities which comprise the active personality, the means of perception which allow the interpretation of that which lies outside of the personality structure, and the unique way that each entity has of relating the self to the external environment.

These are basic components of any entity, and the one wishing to serve as an instrument will find that the nature of the personality, the means by which the external environment is perceived, and the bridge of relationship that is built between these inner and outer components are also those qualities which are utilized in the broadest fashion in the beginning work as an instrument and continue to be refined for as long as the entity desires to serve as an instrument. These are basic tools and this evening we would exercise this instrument and the one known as K as each attempts to broaden the ability to perceive that which we have to offer and to express it in a manner which is both clear and concise

At this time we would make our first attempt to speak this evening to the one known as K and would ask that this instrument continue in those practices which it has used previously in the tuning and in the challenging, paying special attention to the ability to sense our presence and to perceive a somewhat more in detail or complex set of vibrational patterns which we shall attempt to transmit as concepts through this instrument this evening. At this time we would transfer this contact to the one known as K. I am Q'uo.

(K channeling)

(K's channeling is mostly inaudible.)

I am Q'uo, and greet you once again in love and in light through this instrument. It is our privilege this evening to continue to exercise more than one instrument, and we are grateful for this opportunity to be of service. It is also a joy to us to be able to walk for a time with you among that path on which we all continue at all times towards the great mystery. Though at times it may seem to you that you travel alone, we share … on this path at all times … same path as you. And if at times it may seem that we are far ahead of you, out of sight, out of reach, be sure that the separation is part of the illusion … For we are with you at all times … and you may … exciting time … focusing … path … This evening we wish to encourage you on … difficulties along the path … And at times it seems to each that the obstacles … and you find yourself being stuck not knowing if the journey or yourself … Feeling … because … We would like to assure you that this … And as you gaze on the obstacles that seem urge you to be … at such time … Available to you … may take various forms. There may be those such as ourselves who walk with you and are available for comfort and support … Those companions with whom you walk day to day … Other teachers and guides … are aware …

(The rest of K's channeling was not transcribed.)

(Jim channeling)

I am Q'uo, and greet each again in love and light through this instrument. At this time we would offer ourselves for any queries which those present may have for us. May we speak to a query at this time?

K: Do you have any suggestions for anything I can do improve the contact?

I am Q'uo, and I am aware of your query, my sister. As far as the actual practice of the vocal channeling is concerned, we are most pleased with your efforts. You have been able to perceive an increasingly more intricate series of thought concepts than previously, and we see this as a definite step forward in your practice of channeling. It is always well for any instrument to continue with the daily self examination that may take place in your meditative or quiet and thoughtful moments, so that those centers of energy upon which these contacts are based may offer to the contact the most purified and clarified balance of energies possible for each instrument. The balance for each instrument will, of course, be unique, for each instrument works upon the same centers but from a different perspective or point of view. Each instrument therefore has a certain set of balances of an internal nature which are necessary in order for the instrument to be able to release those cares and concerns of the day, as you call them, knowing that that which can be done, has been done to balance them and that they are being, shall we say, balanced in a steady and persistent manner. Other than this reminder, which we would offer to any instrument at any time, we feel that your work and your progress are most rapid, and we appreciate the dedication which you bring to this endeavor. It is quite obvious to us that this is an effort for which no effort will be spared.

Is there a further query?

K: No, that's all, we thank you.

I am Q'uo, and we thank you, my sister. Is there another query?

(Pause)

I am Q'uo, and as it appears that we have accomplished the task set before us this evening, we again thank each for offering this opportunity to us and look forward for each such gathering. We shall take our leave of this group at this time, leaving each, as always, in the love and in the light of the infinite Creator. We are known to you as those of Q'uo. Adonai, my friends. Adonai. ✣

Sunday Meditation
September 23, 1990

Group question: The question this evening has to do with the situation that many people find themselves in when they have either a disease that does not yield to any kind of healing, or, perhaps, they find themselves in a situation of poverty, where they seldom have enough money to meet their expenses and are always wondering where the next meal is coming from. Oftentimes, people will say to such a person, "If you only would remove certain blockages, allow yourself to be in a certain way, then you would have plenty of money, and you would have good health." The question this evening has to do with the possibility—is there a deeper meaning and purpose to some diseases and to some situations of poverty where the person might have another opportunity opened by that situation rather than looking to heal or cure that particular situation of poverty or ill health?

(Carla channeling)

I am Q'uo. Greetings to this group in the love and the light of the one infinite Creator. Greetings and blessings and an infinity of love be with you. Let us pause for a moment with the sheer joy of sharing in your meditation and your company.

(Pause)

I am Q'uo. You are most kind to have allowed us this privilege. We are most happy to be asked to share our opinions and give what insight we have found to be so on the subject of the spiritual, or metaphysically correct, life necessarily being reflected in perfect physical health of the physical body complex, which is the vehicle for such a mentally, emotionally and spiritually whole and healthy individual. You notice that we segregated the body, that is, your physical vehicle, your personal animal, which has sacrificed its instinctual life in order that it may house the self-conscious spirit that each of you is. It is not that there is not, within the illusion, a tie there that cannot be broken and have the physical vehicle sustain life. It is simply that who you are is not that which you see in the mirror. Who you are is not that which loved ones, friends and enemies recognize as you.

Your animal, having done its very best on your behalf, will surely die, and this is part of the necessary function of this vehicle, for your spirit has a great deal further to go than your physical vehicle can take you. You are beings finishing the evolution of your physical being, continuing your mental and emotional evolution, and either continuing, or just recognizing and just beginning your evolution in spirit. Paradoxically, this does not make you as you are less than one unique entity. However, it is well to gaze at the mechanical arrangement of body and spirit.

Much has already been said concerning the difference between mind and brain, and we will not belabor that point, but say only that in addition to the brain of a body, and the mind of the mental complex, there is a wisdom of the spiritual complex. Like the spiritual complex itself, it is not relative, it is absolute. It is that which is most deeply hidden within each of you, the true wisdom of spirit, the true compassion of spirit. A great deal of patience, purity and persistence is required that that spirit may awaken within you and become what it always has been without the knowledge of the conscious mind, that being your true, absolute and perfect self. As all things are one, so do all things in spirit occur perfectly, simultaneously and with joy. This includes any condition whatsoever.

Now, let us take these three parts of the unity of your being, and artificially separate them that we may gaze upon them separately, for there is no one answer to the question of healings occurring in body because they have occurred in mind or spirit. The body is an entity of instinct and reason. In the early stages it was called the tool-making animal. It, in and of itself, has a body wisdom. If, in the opinion of the wisdom of your own body, you have done harm to it, it will react to protect itself.

Thusly, those who abuse their bodies in one way or another—and this is usually done because of an underactivation or overactivation of some point of energy entrance—the body will react by causing a necessity for the body to heal. Thus, you may see those who press themselves against the limits of substances which are harmful to the body becoming ill, because they need, in a simply bodily way, a rest. If there is that in the nature which is somewhat sensitive, the body can be put in many situations, one of which occurs to this instrument as malaria, during the building of the Panama canal. These illnesses are examples of illnesses which have to do with the bodily complex, for the most part, although it is always true that the mind can control the body to the point of which the mind is capable. Thus, the first kind of illness has absolutely nothing to do with anything but circumstance.

As you gaze at the mental/emotional complex, we see that portion of the belief you have mentioned, that is, that the body is acting out the illness which is emotional or mental. Your people, and we speak of those who are technologically advanced, have used the technology, not to free themselves from labor, but to become ever more enslaved by it. Light, which was to give leisure to the people of your planet, has been used to extend, artificially, daylight. Your particular physical vehicle is not designed to be a night hunter. Its diurnal rhythm is to wake with the sun and sleep with the darkness. When asked, this remarkably adaptable body will do its very, very best to support alternative diurnal cycles, but it is at its weakest when the schedule is not steady, that is, when there is no set time of being awake or of being asleep. This is very confusing to an animal which turns to the sun instinctively, and which controls its environment for its survival. Consequently, unless an entity has thought deeply about such a simple thing as attempting to remain upon a schedule of sleeping and awaking, an entity can induce a high degree of stress while seemingly not overworking, nor giving oneself enough time to rest.

There are many other stresses through which one may put the body because of concern of an overactive imagination of a personality that swings in its attitudes and needs to a greater extent than is comfortably handled by the physical vehicle. Thusly, it is quite obvious that in many cases the mind is the parent of the illness, and the illness is the acting out of that which was refused as catalyst by the mental/emotional complex of the self. There is the cancer of anger that grows upon itself. There are the lung diseases of those who have not said the words that they must say to be healthy, have not told the truths that must be told to be free of misunderstanding at a deep level in relationship. There is the acidic condition brought about by sheer overwork, which ruins your gastrointestinal tracts. Many are the illnesses that are the outworking of mental imbalance or emotional imbalance. We do not use the word unhappiness, because we, in our experience, have not found that concept helpful. Joy, not happiness, is a spiritual concept.

Because the mind and body are so closely linked in many diseases, they are indeed responsive to love. You may name any emotional or mental complex distortion that has caused illness that you wish, and we say to you that that is love, poorly expressed. But the mind is not closed, and consciousness is as creative as you allow it to be. Consequently, those who undertake, in healing, the will to health, and a faith that that which has been caused by their own minds' concerns can certainly be turned around, will indeed respond to positive suggestions. Indeed, the habit of saying anything whatsoever about the self or others that is judgmental is a harmful and unhealthful thing to do, both metaphysically, and physically.

This is a large category. Many, many entities can, and are, healed because of a change in attitude, of a renewed passion for life, of the solving of the anguish which brought about the illness, the forgiving of the self and the proper attention to those things which this animal that has been so good to you may need that you are not giving it. You make sure that your pets have food that will give them what they need. Each entity is unique in that respect also, and it is only common sense to eat those things you feel are either good to eat, or in the case of those who have so many allergies they cannot find foods to which they are not allergic, those to which they are least sensitive.

The third category is the one of spirit, and the cause of so many entities neglecting this portion of the characteristics of healing [is that they] think of the spirit as that which is in the same relativistic configuration with regard to this illusion as the mind/emotional complex, and the body complex. Such entities, though spiritual, have not grasped that each entity is absolute. What you see, and hear, and taste and touch will die. What you are, if you think of yourself as your body, will die. All illness is healed by the entrance into larger life, if it be done in a natural manner, that is, if one lets nature use its wisdom, and spirit, its decision making ability.

It is not only those who have come to this planet to help with the harvest that have, with the aid of the greater Self, which is Love, the one great original Thought, planned the difficulties and limitations, as subjectively perceived by the entity within the incarnation. These have been set forth for a reason. Most of the entities upon this planet are capable of graduation from this density to the next—are capable, if they wish to make difficult choices of learning the last lessons of unconditional love that they can learn while in this illusion. They have had their part, you have had your part in planning just those things you may bewail the most, because if you consider it carefully you will see that your intense periods of learning have so often coincided with intense periods of discomfort, anguish and pain. It is not altogether false that an artist suffers, and from his suffering makes beauty, for that is the way of spirit.

The goal of spirit is not happiness, for that suggests a static, unmoving self, comfortable, and unchanging. Evolution suggests continual change, continual new learning, and continual dropping off of that which is no longer helpful in the process of spiritual evolution. Thus, in order to distract them, or in some way focus them away from the mundane and everyday world, many entities choose to incarnate with illnesses, diseases and unhealthful situations of mind also, that are deemed necessary by the self and the greater Self, in order to give to the pilgrim the best possible chance of learning the lessons, of having the realizations and the transformations occur, that you yourself felt were needed.

Consequently, if repeated and earnest attempts are made in a single-minded and careful manner, and poverty does not open to riches, or ill health to heartiness, it is then that one must look at one's situation. The first realization is that this is a relativistic illusion. For instance, each in this circle is unwealthy; one, extremely unwealthy, others closer to being comfortable and without worry, but not close enough to avoid difficulty when unexpected expenses occur. Why would we, and you, sometimes choose such situations? What have they to teach us? In a relativistic world, a simple geographical move to any of your civilizations that contains a large majority of people who do not have enough to eat, or a place to sleep, will indicate that even those in this culture that consider themselves the poorest are seen as rich by those who have even less. To one who is dying, an illness that does not kill does not seem serious. To one who has a non-killing disease, but one which limits, those who are able to move around without limitation seem healthy.

When preincarnative choice has given to you a difficulty, have faith that you are a spirit advanced enough to participate in your own destiny, that occurrences do not happen simply by chance, that the seeming poverty, the seeming limitation, the seeming difficulty, the seeming illness, is also a forthright aid in setting up a circumstance in which a lesson of love can be learned under adverse conditions. Yours is the last density with truly adverse conditions for the positive, or service-to-others oriented person. Only in this density, the density of choice, does this occur. Know then, that that which is in front of you is not more than you can work with, is not that which defeats; you would not program that for yourself. But you are stretching yourself, because you wish to change, you wish to become even more polarized in love and service to the Creator and others than you are now. There may be a lesson to learn, there may be a part of service that you chose that could not be achieved in any other way, given the uniqueness of your person, the uniqueness of your character. Consequently, there are illnesses, limitations and what seems to be a grinding and degrading poverty, that may be seen, only in a spiritual sense, as challenges, rather than difficulties; as chances to learn, rather than sentences of condemnation.

It is well, when one is gazing within at one's situation, to consider all three possibilities. First, give the body what it is asking for. If you are still ill, if you have worked hard and are still poor, offer to the mind the opportunity of thinking carefully about the possible healing of this sorrow of self by a change in attitude, a change in the way you treat the body that has been so good to you. And if these things are tried, in all sincerity, persistently, and yield nothing, try the assumption that this situation, though seemingly negative within the illusion, is the very cornerstone of your evolution in spirit. The lesson there will be learned during the suffering, the pain, the anguish of learning, and change, and the transformation of the self.

Can it possibly feel good for the felled tree trunk to be hollowed out? Yet, if it is not hollowed out, it cannot be the canoe, it cannot carry anyone anywhere. So, too, are lessons unique. You seek in yourself a hollowing out of those petty concerns that you cannot afford if you wish to be open to spiritual evolution.

Certainly, do all that you can to maximize the use of the vehicle that you have. But gaze beyond that. If you are a player of a violin, and you begin to get fingers that are numb, a doctor will say to you that you are holding the instrument incorrectly, and are causing some nerve condition. Pills and treatments will ensue. If that does not cure the difficulties of the hand, gaze within and see if the mind enjoys what it is doing. If it does, and affirms so in a persistent manner, and there is still the pain when playing the instrument, the situation may well be preincarnatively chosen in order that your path of service may be changed to another direction, another impetus, perhaps one better served to the deeper gifts of your unique self.

In any case whatsoever, release all fear, fear of the illness or the limitation; fear of the stigma this may bring upon you; fear of what others may say as they misunderstand you. All of these things are as nothing to one who is paying attention to that source of information that is by far the most reliable, that is, the self. As always, daily, persistent meditation, acting upon those new points of view that this meditation inevitably brings, and praising and thanking the infinite One for this opportunity to break the walls of previous misunderstandings within yourself, no matter how small. Here is your opportunity to gaze steadily at the illusion until it blinks. Do not accept any negative explanation or condemnation. Take it not in.

You are engaged in walking a path of spirit, the mind and body in complete cooperation, from before the beginning of this incarnation. You chose the physical vehicle you now have. You chose preexisting, usually genetically caused, in the eyes of the world, physical vehicles that may seem, in the case of preincarnative choices which are challenging, that your body has betrayed you. This is never so. The body that you have is second density. It will do anything it can for you. It loves you. It accepted you. It wishes to do what you wish it to do. Sometimes it cannot, because you chose this situation at this time.

You will move from these words to the many other situations that are criticized as being those of failure of some kind. Take them to heart and have courage and faith, and the will to learn that which you came here to learn; the will to love ever more purely; the will to allow the pettiness of humanity gradually to depart from you as water from a pitcher, that you are an empty vessel at last for the love and the light of the one infinite Creator as expressed through the gifts manifested by you in greater and greater understanding of the true goals of this life of choice.

At this time, we would, with some embarrassment, apologize for speaking longer than the thirty minutes this instrument requested of us. Unfortunately, neither this instrument nor us understands time very well. We leave this instrument in love and light, and transfer to the one known as Jim. I am Q'uo.

(Jim channeling)

I am Q'uo, and I greet each again in love and light through this instrument. At this time it is our privilege to offer ourselves in potential response to queries. We take great pleasure in being able to speak directly to your concerns if there are any questions at this time. May we begin with the first one?

Carla: Q'uo, I find myself in a situation where physically I am completely disabled; mentally, I'm adequate; spiritually, I'm an emotional slob. I was having a conversation with the instrument this afternoon in which I was discussing being, rather than doing. This, I feel, is one *(inaudible)* I was sidelined completely, because it is *(inaudible)* for me *(inaudible)* to be, and that means I have to channel *(inaudible)*. Yet, at this exact moment in time, as *(inaudible)* in the illusion, I am feeling more and more to do, and I like doing things, in fact, it thrills me *(inaudible)*, to do useful things, although I am an invalid. Even the instrument, who has a *(inaudible)* viewpoint, felt I would *(inaudible)*, if there was one person left who asked me for help. I would never be able to ignore a request for help.

This means, and I do accept this entity's *(inaudible)*. I am confused. Can one be, and do? Or need there be set aside a time for experientially feeling the nakedness of being with no props, no one moving, nothing to distract the self from *(inaudible)* meditation, but *(inaudible)*. Which of these two options is more appropriate? Any comments that you can make at this point would be helpful. I don't think I can be more confused than I am.

I am Q'uo, and we feel that we have a grasp of your query, my sister. You have two desires: to be, without adornment; and to be helpful, to others. One concerns, it would seem, only the self. The other concerns, it would seem, only others. It is true that your nature is of that kind which seeks to give where there is need, and seeks little in return, if anything is sought, for such actions. On one level of understanding, it could be said that a choice must be made, for one desire to be fulfilled and the other to be dropped.

However, rather than dwell upon this more shallow interpretation of your question, we would suggest that what you seek in the heart of your being is how to be in the presence of the one Creator in all your life experience. This, of course, is a product of the attitude, the motivation, the initial impulse for all that occurs in your life pattern.

Thus, we do not see the query as one which needs to make a choice between being and doing, but that which seeks an attitude of being filled with the presence of the one Creator, so that the moment is sufficient unto itself, and that as you exist in that moment that is ever-present, that which is appropriate for you to be or do will present itself to you without question. This attitude is that gift of grace which all seekers seek and revere, yet achieve not so much by ritual, by action, by prayer, or by any activity. It is rather that which is born in its own time through the persistent exercise of desire to know the truth.

This path of the pilgrim is the path which all walk. There is much effort expended physically, mentally, emotionally and spiritually as the table is prepared for the guest of great honor. No one knows when that guest shall walk through one's door. Thus, it is well to be prepared at all times as best as one can be.

We have no clear cut answer for you, my sister, but offer these words in the hope that they will show a small light upon your journey upon which you may focus your attention in the hope that that light shall grow in brightness and in strength to illuminate ever more clearly and carefully the placement of the next step upon this path.

Is there a further query, my sister?

Carla: No, my brother, that answer was as light as the sun, and I have no more questions.

I am Q'uo, and we thank you for the opportunity to serve. Is there another query?

Carla: I have a question, that I'm curious about, because it hasn't happened to me exactly, I always *(inaudible)* somehow had half a jar of peanut butter to eat. Why do people choose the experience *(inaudible)*?

I am Q'uo, and am aware of your query, my sister. The choices that lead an entity into that situation which you call the deprivation, the poverty …

Carla: The starving.

… and yes, indeed, that which is disease and starving among your peoples of your planet, is a placing, if we may use a phrase, of the nose to the grindstone in a fashion which cannot help but gain the attention. It is a situation in which many entities find themselves at this time. When life is tenuous, and of such difficulty that one is always forced to attend to basic needs, then there is also the opportunity to discover basic principles, of either that which you call service to others, or service to self. Deprivation upon all levels on which it occurs is that catalyst which forces the attention and the decision-making process to choose, each moment of your existence, how one will be, how one shall respond. The nature of the entity is signed with each choice. Thus, this looking into the mirror is as basic in its brutal honesty as is possible to achieve within your third density illusion, that illusion which is already so full of catalyst for all that inhabit it. Trauma teaches, oh, so well, for it does not allow the attention to waver.

Is there a further query, my sister?

Carla: Just one. If I took an AIDS patient into my home and my heart, and gave that patient the love which I have in such abundance, could that love heal?

I am Q'uo, and am aware of your query, my sister. Love, freely given, always helps to heal any wound. However, that entity which is in need of the healing is the one which must accept, seek and accept, love into its own life pattern, and that love which it seeks is the love given from self to self. We speak of the entity that has put itself in a situation from which it may only escape when it unlocks its door. Efforts of others await as resources, but may be allowed through that door when that entity opens that door.

The riddle of the key is the riddle that each must answer. Each entity has doors and walls built by its own hands. The life is given as the opportunity to open doors, to open windows, to move through these doors, to see light through windows. Thus, though one may wish to give all one has to another, the success of the giving will depend upon the other.

Is there a further query, my sister.

Carla: No, I truly am done, and I want to thank you for *(inaudible)*.

I am Q'uo, and we thank you once again, my sister. Is there another query at this time?

K: I have none this evening.

In that case it seems that we have found that for which we have been not so diligently seeking, the end of our speaking. We enjoy greatly this opportunity to speak with you, if you had not guessed as much, and we thank you for being patient with our many words, and with our growing sense of humor, we hope, through this instrument. At this time we shall take our leave of this instrument and this group, leaving each, as always, in the love and in the light of the one infinite Creator. We are known to you as those of Q'uo. Adonai, my friends. Adonai. ☙

Sunday Meditation
September 30, 1990

Group question: The question this evening has to do with why is it so difficult when we have ideals that we believe in: that God is love, that all are One, and different interpretations of how we would treat people using these ideals. Why is it so difficult to keep that ideal foremost in our mind? Why do we find ourselves slipping and having negatively oriented thoughts, talking to ourselves and others in negative terms, rather than living up to those ideals which we cherish?

(Carla channeling)

I am Q'uo. Greetings to each of you in the love and the light of the one infinite Creator. It is such a pleasure to share this meditation with you. We cannot express the joy it gives us to welcome those who are not new to this group and those who are new, especially the one known as S, the one known as B. We bless each, send love to each, and thank each for calling us to share our fallible opinions with you. We do not, in any way, shape or form, declare ourselves to be infallible, and ask you please to use your discrimination in listening not only to our words, but to all words, for the truth you shall recognize as though you remembered it, and it shall resonate within your being. That is your truth. Other truths may be other people's truths, but they are not yours. So let them not be a stumbling block in your life, but be straightforward, and to the best of your best ability work upon your own path, and your own truth.

And that is what we shall speak of this evening, for you ask us to speak about how it is that a pilgrim may know to a nicety the various names appropriate to a situation, yet be quite unable to halt the self from speaking amiss or acting inappropriately according to subjectively perceived rules of conduct. We shall have to do some groundwork first, so please excuse us if we seem to be a bit off the subject; we simply must move into it from a larger viewpoint than one life, one will or one circumstance.

Each of you is quite familiar with the fact that the Creator was generous and brave and foolhardy enough to give to His own creation free will. Each of you, and each of us, are the creations and the children of the Father, and as the Creator has its nurturing side, the Father/Mother perhaps would be a way more appropriate, to your species, to speak of infinite intelligence. In truth, the Creator is Love Itself, which is father, and mother, and all.

Now, each of you is created of this love. Consequently, there has never been an unworthy spirit incarnate upon this planet which you now enjoy, for through all behaviors the birthright of your creation remains, as it must, precisely the same. That which is of love does not change, go away, or run out. You were love when you were created, before all that you see of the cosmos. You are love now, in the midst of this heavy illusion, and you always shall be love, until at last you return to Love Itself, and become truly one once more with the source, the alpha and the omega of all that there is.

There is, however, another portion to your being. It was impossible to create a manifestation out of love, for there is no motivation, ambition or curiosity in love. There is, however, in the first distortion of love, which is free will. By the use of free will the Creator chose to allow a small portion of its infinity, if this non-concept may suffice, to fly apart in sparks of love. Free will was bonded to each spark, free will being as absolute as love, and its antithesis; that is, free will is never the same, while love is always the same.

So, that creature which you are is quite often confused with being a single being, but is actually made up of all that your consciousness is plus all that the physical vehicle is (which you think of as yourself but which is in actuality a highly developed second-density animal). This instinctually perfect entity agreed, before it was given this life, to be the physical vehicle which carries you about, which gathers data from all of its senses, and which makes available to your consciousness the bio-computer which is your mind. To that animal, that body, that vehicle, all thanks and praise should be given always, for its sacrifice has been complete, its instinctual behavior bowing always to the will that has learned, and that accepts, allows and loves each characteristic of that physical vehicle.

Thus, perhaps the first way of gazing at your conscious behavior that so often is not what you wish it would or could be, [is to realize that] you well may be gazing at instinctual reactions which occur faster than your mind is able to respond. In no way, when this occurs, should the physical vehicle be blamed. In no way should the mind and the spirit governing this vehicle be dismayed or discouraged. There are times in this extremely dense illusion when the survival instinct of your physical vehicle will take over, simply because the computer of your mind keeps the entity alive as a first priority. It is not your spirit that wishes your life to linger, it is your body.

The second and very common reason, or cluster of reasons, which keep the spirit from moving only from its center, is the emotional, mental and spiritual distortion of self-worth that you may call low self-worth or low self-esteem. Blessed and well planned are the lives of those entities whose childhoods did not leave one with an inner conviction of low self-worth. All the more blessed they because they are rare among your peoples. All of you have baggage of which you must let go. Why is this so? Why should you let these things go? Why is your opinion not respected by yourself? Even if it is negative, after all, is it not what you think? The answer to that is much too complex to receive either a yes or a no. The voices which echo in the mind may echo from many, many decades ago, from early childhood, from early traumatic time in which many, many negative signals were given to your spirit, either by yourself or others. Those who are seeking in the service-to-self path do not have the problem which you have, for they of course would refuse any guilt, or any judgment of the self as being less than perfectly worthy. It is the entity who desires to be the humble servant of all mankind that most finds itself trapped by its own feelings of inadequacy.

There are several things one may do to work upon this challenge. First of all is the daily meditative period. We suggest at least a few minutes of meditation each day. We do not advise long meditations, except for those who meditate all the time, and are aware of how much power there is in the silent, listening meditation. Rather, we recommend approximately fifteen minutes. We also recommend that mated couples attempt to do this together, as meditation brings change, and it is well that each understand the other's discomfort as the change occurs. Change is always painful. Thus, to the pilgrim we offer love, it is true, but discomfort, dustiness, feelings of aloneness, and all that goes with doing that which is seldom attempted within your society, and almost never understood. That is your first great resource.

The second great resource is your own observational powers; this instrument would call it paying attention. We do not mean to say that you should pay attention to other people's foibles, or to the right and wrong of argument, but rather we ask you to pay attention to your own consciousness. We encourage you to be truly self-conscious, to know the exact thing that was the catalyst for your moving away from the center of love and light. It can be an excess of happiness, or an excess or despair, doubt, disbelief, dislike, the feeling that darkness lies all about you and you do not know where to turn. These dark nights of the soul, as they have been called, are very much a part of the path of the pilgrim, and it is difficult at those times to see that one has ever made one iota of progress. Never, ever judge yourself or others.

At the end, however, of each day, as you have been paying attention, without judgment, to those things which move you, especially to those things which have made you uncomfortable and might be a stumbling block in your ability to deal as you wish with others, we suggest, at the end of each day, the consideration, either intellectual, for those who have strong analytical powers, or by feeling them again, for those of you who depend mostly upon your hearts for decisions. As those are by far the majority among those who seek spiritually, we will simply say that which this instrument is already aware of from the Law of One material, that is, that the emotion which was deemed inappropriately off center and negative by the pilgrim be allowed to exist again, to be affirmed by you as being completely acceptable. Let it, in fact, become as sharp and dramatic as it will be, allowing the energy within that to express itself. As you are forgiving yourself, then, as you sit in meditation, allowing this feeling to wash over you, gradually notice that that feeling is receding as a wave, and in its place comes its opposite, the other side of its coin, the antithesis or its thesis.

So, if you have experienced anger, and intensified it, and forgiven yourself for that feeling, you spontaneously begin to feel forgiveness, and caring. Prayers may be said for the one who has acted in a way you would describe as hateful, and all is forgiven, the other self, your self, and the transaction between the two of you.

You have often called these times failures, and berated yourself because of them. But do you not see that you must make the mistakes, you must err, and be bold about it, be yourself, in order to learn who you are, to find where those soft and sensitive areas are that cause you to move away from your center? You must go through the process of knowing yourself, truly, truly knowing yourself, for in your life lies the universe, the creation and the Creator, in a part of you so deep that it is not within this illusion for you to penetrate that portion of your informational store with any ease whatsoever. The veil hides it completely, and that is why meditation is so helpful, as it makes that veil between conscious and subconscious more and more semi-permeable.

When you have done these two things for a while you will discover that you have tucked away in a corner of your heart a brown paper bag, unmarked, crumpled up and shoved as far back as possible, out of sight, but never out of mind, for the true mind as you know lies in the heart. Within this paper bag lives all the things that you have said about yourself. How do you come to be able to say about yourself such negative, negative things? Do you not know that thoughts are objects in the world very close to your own? Do you not know the weakening effect that these negative sentences told to the self by the self have upon you, upon your self image?

When you hear yourself saying that about yourself which could be construed by yourself as negative, simply speak again, and place yourself in some positive perspective, for this illusion is not a place where perceptions are objective. You may perceive your universe as you wish. All things are your choice. You are never imprisoned in your mind unless you take yourself into slavery. No one can do it to you. No one.

So we ask that you think of yourself—this entity has a bit of difficulty with this concept, but we shall move ahead—to think of yourself as an employee to which you are the boss. Evaluate your behavior towards yourself. Have you been a good boss today? Have you been kind to yourself? Have you loved yourself? As you worship the Creator, have you loved yourself enough to give the gift of yourself in complete surrender to the will of the infinite One, knowing that it is truly your will also? Perhaps you have not, and if you have not, it is undoubtedly due to the fact that a state of forgiveness does not exist between your self and your self.

The reason that we are being so insistent in talking about being able to do that which you wish to do, in speaking of loving and forgiving yourself, is laid out very simply by the teacher known to you as Jesus the Christ, who said that the new covenant was to love the Creator with all one's faculties, with the uttermost passion possible, and to love the neighbor as the self. Loving the Creator is often difficult not to do, in our opinion. On a sunny day, can anyone decry the Maker of such beauty?

When one is familiar at last with the concept that the Creator loved us first, is it any wonder that our instinct is to love back and to wish to serve, as children always would their parent? But in order to love others, which is the service-to-others path, one must first love the self, for one can love others only insofar as one has learned to love the self. We are not speaking of a narcissistic love which demands an echo, a pat on the back, a recognition, a thank you, or a noticing of any kind for any other entity which walks your sphere.

If you love others as you love yourself, and you love yourself, then your point of view shall be enough changed that you will surprise yourself, because you will find that you have, in the difficult times of hollowing the self out to be a channel of this love, become able to shine with an infinite love that reaches and touches people. They do not need to know the rationales of love, they only need to know that they are loved. It is the greatest feeling in the universe.

And as for each of you, you did not come here to be loved; you came here to love. Much blockage and distortion of communication betwixt peoples, especially mated people or people intimate in their friendship, is that each has expectations of the other. We strongly suggest that love be conceived of as that which supports, that which puts the other before the self, that which is loyal, that which does its very best. And if that very best fails, then it fails, with the love intact. And if compassion is learned in the failing, were you never to make the pushing of the envelope turn into the breaking of the envelope, were you never to suffer from having done your best and failed, in other words, you would never have the kind of compassion for others that you do after such an experience, for you know you have tried your best, and you know that when you reach your limits and go beyond them, it will seem a failure, and in an outer sense, of course it is. But in the inner sense, if you intended with love to do all that you could, absolutely all, holding nothing back, then metaphysically speaking you have acted as one who runs the straight race.

Again we say to you, never condemn or judge yourself, for you know that you have been redeemed, you know that you are in a state of grace. You do not need to keep telling yourself of your poor habits. You do not need to be hag-ridden by a conscience that looks for ways to criticize you. What you are looking for is not that entity who ruthlessly shoves below the level of consciousness all that is not positive. We do not even suggest that you attempt to control your moods. We suggest going through the process, the painful learning process, and discovering how you are programmed, in other words, who you are in this illusion.

Your consciousness is not programmed, but your mind is. Your mind is a machine, biochemical in nature, and much like a computer in that, through a series of yes/no decisions, a very, very small percentage of all that you see, and hear, and feel, and taste and touch, is filtered, ruthlessly, so that you may gain the picture that your biocomputer has chosen to show you, which gives you the greatest amount of information concerning the survival of the entity's physical vehicle, and the safe storage of one's habitual thinking processes. This is for the mind what comfort is, that is, stasis, or lack of change. It is just as though in meditation you opened up to yourself a large body of data which you may begin to allow to be programmed into your biocomputer. It is what we may call a metaprogram, a program which will change, and sometimes dump whole programs as it realigns those yes/no choices concerning that about which it shall prioritize its report to consciousness.

The longer that you have had a mental habit, the harder it is to remove that program, and the more painful the removal. However, it is inevitably successful when the seeker is persistent. You see many who speak of results. We speak of work. We speak of learning to become willing servants of humankind. By nature you are programmed to think of the self as master of the Earth, and perhaps master of the cosmos. You may see the amount of the programming that is necessary when you consider attitudes such as this, plus negative attitudes towards the self that have been picked up so long ago that their origin is almost forgotten. Yet, there is no need for these half forgotten melodies to crowd the mind, if they are not attractive, if they do not sound sweet, for is not your life the gift you wish to give to the Creator as you enter larger life? Then make of it that which is beautiful.

Perhaps this is what this instrument would call a cliché. Yet it is well to gaze objectively at the self, as one attempts to weave the tapestry of a genuinely impassioned and intensely lived life, for there is no lukewarmness about the creation; it is only a distraction from the creation that causes people to consider the nature of things as being everyday or mundane. Indeed, if one has found within the self, love, then one is full of love, love of God, love of others, and love of self.

It is time for us to come to an end. If more questions are considered appropriate about this subject or any other, we shall have the opportunity for the asking, and may we also say that if there seems to be a query which may benefit from a longer discussion, there is much material in this area which we have not covered this evening.

Come with us, yokefellows. Bend your shoulders and follow, for carry we burdens, carry them we must, but we may carry them with joy, for we know they are only the disbursions given to us as catalyst, that we may die to petty things and be born to imperishable things. Much of the basic second-density mind does need reexamination as a conscious spirit. May you do this without discouragement, without self-criticism, and with much merriment, for to laugh is to worship. Love each other. This is the answer to so many questions, and remember to love yourself, to forgive yourself, and to live in the resonant, infinite presence whose love you wish to practice and be.

We would at this time wish to transfer this contact to the one know as Jim. We are those of Q'uo, and leave this instrument with thanks.

(Jim channeling)

I am Q'uo, and greet each again in love and light through this instrument. At this time it is our privilege to offer ourselves in the attempt to speak to any queries which those present may have yet remaining upon their minds. If there is a query, we shall be happy to speak to it at this time.

Carla: If you are really upset with someone, is it better to go ahead and communicate, or is it better to go into meditation *(inaudible)* forgiving *(inaudible)* without having communicated your feelings?

I am Q'uo, and am aware of your query, my sister. As a general rule, for most effective use of catalyst in the life experience, it is well to allow one's spontaneous feelings and thoughts to be spoken if they are not of such a severe nature as to be damaging to another entity. In most cases, the thoughts and feelings are well to speak, as well as one is willing to take the responsibility of continuing the communication until there is a resolution of difficulty, realizing that all difficulty is but a means toward an harmonious end. It is not well to remain within the condition of anger, and oftentimes it is only through the communication of such anger that one is able to allow its movement through one's being in a manner that will allow resolution in an harmonious fashion to result.

Is there a further query, my sister?

Carla: There is, but it's on another subject, and I think I'll give *(inaudible)* an opportunity first.

(Pause)

Carla: I guess all the questions are mine tonight. I am equally puzzled as to why we can't stop some tapes from running to their end. I've tried the Jesus prayer, I've tried *(inaudible)* to help me, or for the *(inaudible)* to help me, although I much *(inaudible)*, I've tried spontaneous prayer, I've tried sticking my head in a book or turning on the TV or going to sleep. Actually, none of these things truly works except going to sleep and waking up again. Why is it that a person who is genuinely living a life in faith cannot use that faith to place the bar against unwanted behavior? Because it seems impossible not to err, it happens no matter how strongly you try not to.

I am Q'uo, and am aware of your query, my sister. That quality that you have called faith is a quality which is, shall we say, recently developed within most entities who recognize its value. Those qualities which seem to propel one's actions and thoughts in what you have called erroneous or sinful manners are those qualities that run much deeper within the creature that is human, and are there for the purpose of moving one in a manner which will place one in the position that will allow the learning of that which is appropriate for each entity, for only by experimentation within your illusion are you able to discover what are your potentials, what are your limits, and what are your lessons.

It is not meant that all should be harmonious within your life pattern, for the life of contentment is that life which does not change, does not grow, does not expand the point of view beyond that which is comfortable. Thus, you move beyond the boundaries of comfort, the boundaries of self, the boundaries of that which is known, in order that you shall grow through the exercise of free will, and grow in a manner which is most auspicious for you. That you may call some portions of this growing, trial and error, success and failure, is a definition which is not always helpful when viewing the overall process. Thus, we urge each not to judge, the self or any other, for none within your illusion have eyes which see far enough to accumulate wisdom and understanding. It is that newly developed quality of faith, propelled by the will to continue, that will allow you to continue in a manner which is helpful to your overall growth and the growth of those about.

Is there a further query, my sister?

Carla: Yes, it's on another subject. I've been completely sidelined recently, and I'm having a great deal of trouble sitting up. It doesn't seem to be at this point possible for me to recover from the waist up, and consequently there are some indications of nature along the lines of a two by four applied to the forehead in my case, that I will probably *(inaudible)*. I've been *(inaudible)* a long time anyway.

My question is, when you look at that situation which I have, you think of it as you wish. You can think of it as something against which to work, to enable yourself to get in as much use as possible for as long as possible, which is what I've been doing anyway, trying to find physical therapy which would just exercise my legs and things like that. There's another way to look at it, at least one more, that being, why not cut the *(inaudible)*, why not accept the fact that there is a disability, that there is a discomfort and *(inaudible)*. Why not become one who is able to *(inaudible)* the beautiful things, but perhaps not be *(inaudible)*, or who is content with going to church, but not being *(inaudible)*. The poorest person may be wonderful *(inaudible)* exception, and instead being *(inaudible)*.

This could be done fairly easily by me, at this time, or at any time in the future, as we have other land that is extremely cheap to live on. I do not know which path *(inaudible)* to working against *(inaudible)* what seems to be *(inaudible)*, and cooperating with it, to go ahead and be *(inaudible)* for a contemplative life, which would be further out than this and with less people around. Do you have any comment at all that you can make? I know you can't answer specific questions.

I am Q'uo, and am aware of your query, my sister, and you are correct in your assumption that we may not speak with great specificity upon this particular topic, which is one which strikes quite close to the heart of your incarnational pattern, and it is well for each pilgrim to make those kind of choices for the self. One cannot delegate such to another. However, we shall comment by suggesting that you have learned well a part of your personality structure is that which moves against limitation and exercises the will and the faith mightily in this effort.

As you are aware, there is great virtue in this kind of pattern of behavior, for it continually stretches the limitations and strengthens the will in so doing. There is also, as you have mentioned, great virtue in being able to accept one's limitations, accept that which cannot be changed, and look for the door that is opened when another is closed. It is well that one in your position develop the ability for such acceptance, for the limitations, as it is well known to you, are relatively set.

The balance between these two modes of being is that balance which, when finally struck, will allow the greatest amount and quality of growth within your life pattern. It is the nature of this balance which is best discovered through your own efforts. However, we shall say that you have done well in your diligent pursuit of this balance, and we would counsel a quieting of concerns to a large degree in this area.

Is there a further query, my sister?

Carla: Thank you, Q'uo, but I don't think so, not at this time. As the energy is pretty low, perhaps the instrument is even *(inaudible)*.

I am Q'uo, and again we thank you for your queries, my sister. May we ask if there is a final query at this time?

Questioner: *(Inaudible)*.

I am Q'uo, and we thank you, my sister, for offering to us the query upon which we may offer our service, for without such queries and such calls for our service we would have no beingness within your experience, and it is a great joy to walk with each of you as you seek more and more of that which you call the truth.

At this time we shall take our leave of this group, leaving each as always in the love and in the light of the one infinite Creator. We are known to you as those of Q'uo. Adonai, my friends. Adonai. ❧

Sunday Meditation
October 7, 1990

Group question: The question this evening has to do with Reiki energy. Some within the Reiki movement would say that the energy that is used in healing in the Reiki technique is a specific kind of energy that is different from the universal energy that anybody might be able to tap into at any time and use for healing. What we would like to know is, is the Reiki energy any different than this general type of energy that people use for healing, and if it is, what exactly is the difference, and how is it used? May anyone tap into that kind of energy, or must one have the specific Reiki training?

(Carla channeling)

It is with great pleasure that we bless and greet each of you in the love and in the light of the infinite One. We are those of Q'uo, and feel greatly honored to be asked to join in your meditation, and to take a few steps with you upon your path at this time. We are sorry to repeat the same caveat each time that we speak, but each time that we speak it is necessary in order for free will to hold full sway. Beware of listening to these words or any others with an eye to a rigid belief. We could be wrong, indeed, all could be wrong in terms relative to the illusion in which you live, or in terms of your personal needs and truths; perhaps not wrong for us, perhaps not useful to you. Therefore, discriminate carefully in what you take in of what we say, discarding that which does not seem to be half remembered, so that your responses are, "Yes, I recognize that truth."

This evening the question concerns healing, specifically the Reiki healing, also any form of the laying on of hands. To approach this subject, we must state a few premises upon which we base our opinions. We consider it as an easement rather than doing metaphysical healing work when one self attempts to heal, and perhaps does heal another by the force of his own will and gift. Neither the healer nor the supplicant gains for very long. Often those who heal because of a gift do it simply to make their life more comfortable because, as people value their health, so they value one who makes a poor condition feel much eased. Unless the one to be healed allows the healer of this type to remain within himself, and not take in the implicit demands of such a link betwixt two entities, there can be much deleterious effect upon the healer, for to the healer's mind there are two selves, one self serving the other self. There is no focus and concentration upon the Creator, the giver of all gifts, the source of all things.

It is a kind of power which is much appreciated, but one who has such power has an extraordinarily difficult task in disciplining himself to refrain from taking upon himself any credit for that which has been given. This is seldom the case. Consequently, the form of healing by natural gift—without the temperament to see the Creator at work in the world through the manifestations of such as he—will always be limited, unable to advance because of a blockage of his own perceptions concerning the separation of himself and the person considered to be ill.

The other difficulty with this type of healing process is that it does not last. An effect is felt by the will of another upon the will of the self. The body of the ill person may respond to the help, but permanence is not something human. Consequently, it is folly to expect a human believing that the power is his can do even as much as we have described; nevertheless, this is so.

The healing gift which is most prized is a self-healing that is the prerequisite for any type of work in consciousness. It is not necessary that one be perfect, which is fortunate in your density, for you are not designed to look or feel perfect at any time. It is sufficient that you see yourself as a channel through which an infinite amount of energy, power, grace and healing may be offered. You may even see the channeling of that gift as a manifestation of that gift, but not a gift given by the channeler, for the channeler has given itself to the contact. Thus, many healing modes, such as Reiki, do indeed create a catalytic environment in which, through love alone, the protective field of the body is opened, and an opportunity given for the entity to allow itself to heal. Thus, those who train to become healers may work in consciousness much as do those who learn to channel, or simply to do the will of the Creator.

The Reiki healing is of the second kind. Because it is not of this culture that you enjoy, it is difficult for most people of your culture either to practice it or to benefit from it, for it takes a kind of sensibility which is not distracted, but is at peace. Your people are normally greatly overstimulated. There are many people, things, chores and considerations, some of them literally beating the ears, some of them beating the heart that has not forgiven itself. Reiki is designed for those who are able to become quiet and allow themselves, as a hollow pipe, to be used as a catalyst for opening the body's opportunity for self-healing.

There is no mode of healing that does not benefit many, but those which are desirable are those including Reiki which realize that there is no separation betwixt he who puts hands on the body of the patient, and the patient, for at that time, and with the protection of spiritual guides, the entity drops all barriers, defenses and armor, and makes itself vulnerable, empty and asking, and in humility, it receives the gift it has been given and passes it on, knowing that it is no more responsible for the healing than the water faucet is for the water which comes through it.

The type of healing used in Reiki is especially effective for those whose illnesses are not transitory, but result instead from a chronic mind/body disconnection, blockage or overage of energy at one point or another. It is not specifically so that a Reiki student does not need a living, present teacher. It is, however, the only careful way to learn that which has personal power, or could have personal power distortions, for those who wish to heal must first heal themselves, and by this we do not mean healing of the physical vehicle, but rather a healing which may have the connotation of balance and poise.

The links between mind and body, the psycho and the soma, are well known among your people. Reiki is especially effective when the distress has first been emotional and mental and then has moved into the body complex, because there was no decision to resolve the discomfort by analysis, meditation and self-forgiveness. Because of the length of time that Reiki takes, it is able, through the system of the faith of the students in the teacher, to produce effective healing. Its energy, like all healing energies, is unique. It works most specifically upon emotionally related illnesses and conditions. If a person has a physical difficulty that is within, self-forgiven, whole and healed, the Reiki will simply be comfortable and pleasant. There is, however, the psychosomatic element in so much of disease, that in the majority of cases this particular vibration of energy is an excellent healing catalyst.

Again, we suggest to you that it is our opinion that the healer does not heal. The healer loves, and in the crystallized purity of its love it creates the opportunity and the catalyst for the person to decide to release the illness, the condition, the blockage, the overstimulation, the stress, whatever it is that is the difficulty. The beauty of the Reiki technique is that it is effective across all cultures, across all languages, and in any sort of condition which has a psychosomatic element.

This vibration at first is hard to feel for most students of Reiki. Again, faith in the teacher keeps the student at the task until it has been able to learn. It is also so that at a very deep level of the mind, of which you are not aware and which you cannot alter, you will make your unique contact with the genuine gift of that teacher, feel and sense how that power moves from the head, to the heart, to the hands. Thus, the healer having a teacher in the Reiki technique is most valuable, just as the teacher is valuable in learning any skill that would be too difficult to learn without persistent effort. The company of the teacher enables the student to remain faithful.

We feel that the idea of healing has been somewhat misunderstood among your peoples, for they see a physical vehicle, an animal, and think that it is you. There are an infinite number of reasons to be ill, the three main categories being chance, intention and preincarnative choice. Preincarnative choices are not available to be healed. It is the first two categories that call for attention. Indeed, we would wish you to think of healing in a somewhat different way, perhaps, for healing is not simply of the body. You may have an extraordinarily healthy body, but the rest of the complexes which make up your uniqueness are quiddities, idiosyncrasies of each person. The healing work has as its base a faith. In those who give others a jump start from their own energy, faith is not necessary. In those who are open-minded, kindhearted, though skeptical, healing is possible. It is seldom possible in the presence of cynicism and negative feelings.

So we move from the healing to that which underlies it. All are one. The healing of the self that has taken place in the healer before his ministry is public is that crystallization which enables the other self to receive the catalyst that makes it possible to choose physical wellness, emotional wellness, spiritual wellness, mental wellness, whatever it is that is required, or desired. It may well not seem to the practitioner that the entity is becoming healed, for the body complex may have been intended for some good reasons to have its limitations. Healing is rather a feeling of wholeness, a feeling that one is free to love and be passionate, to care intensely, and to follow the heart. The open heart is the key to manifestations of all kinds that are spiritual.

We feel that this is as far as we wish to go with this question without receiving more specific questions. We have laid the groundwork for them.

We would speak briefly upon the question also asked this evening concerning the second density animals and how much of consciousness of their own destiny they may have. You know the nature of second density, and you know that you are, by your love of your pet, investing an instinctual animal with an awareness of itself. The vast majority of all pets and all wild animals, stem in their species from a gene pool.

Let us use the word, which is not a word, "catness." There is that thought form that contains living material, and it produces, in love and joy and rhythm, its young, its life, its death, without ever being self-conscious, that being the nature of second density. Therefore, for the most part, if an animal is hit by a car, or finds another untimely end to its existence, it is chance, not destiny.

If the pet is deeply devoted to its human, and its human is deeply devoted to the pet, there may well have been enough investment of love and consciousness within that second density entity that it becomes, through this investment, harvestable to become a person, as you call yourselves, a human, a spirit, with breath. In that case, there may be the opportunity to graduate which is taken, or suggestions from those who enjoy doing mischief, that are obeyed by a mind not yet awake to reasoning processes to a great extent.

There are those pets with which an entity may have some of what you call karma, because each entity is responsible for what it knows, or believes it knows. Thusly, if you believe that by love you can aid a cat, a dog or any pet in its journey to third density, and you offer that catalyst, you may indeed find that you have woven into your own tapestry the stark thread of a beloved pet's demise at the hands of the metal machines that move along your roadways. The comfort that you may take in this case is that only those harvestable to third density are capable of this type of connection. If a pet dies thusly, it is to become a third density entity, and though the loss of that dear pet is great, you have given that pet the opportunity to feel love and to give it to such an extent that self-consciousness has taken place, and yours has been the catalyst which encouraged that graduation.

We would at this time transfer the contact. We thank this instrument, and move in love and light. We are those of Q'uo.

(Jim channeling)

I am Q'uo, and greet each again in love and light. At this time we would ask if we may speak to any queries which may yet remain unresolved within the circle of seeking.

K: What comfort may be taken when an animal, either companion or wild, dies an untimely death through chance?

I am Q'uo, and am aware of your query, my sister. One may see the return of the second density spirit to that great pool of consciousness from which it came. As like unto the return of water from your oceans to the skies that may form there into the clouds to fall again upon your land masses causing growth in second-density plants, the return of a spirit from incarnated state is a portion of the rhythm of life as you know it within your third-density illusion.

One may take joy in knowing that the animal entity has lived its life fully, for it knows no other way to live. It does not hinder and restrict itself in ways that are created by mental activity that is distorted in one fashion or another, more or less helpful to an entity's progress, for the second density entity is free of such machinations, and has instead the instinctual activity of a being which is as it is without compromise.

When one sees that such an entity has passed from the incarnation, one may give praise and thanksgiving that it has returned this energy to the Creator to again be formed at another time and at another opportunity into yet another creature that is somehow enabled by all previous creatures' experience and their contributions to those energy patterns that you call the life, so that further life may generate from this energy and move forward in the great expression of the one Creator through the infinite variety of the one creation.

May we speak in any further fashion, my sister?

K: Not right now, thank you.

Carla: Does the unself-conscious second density entity suffer when *(inaudible)*?

I am Q'uo. We may say that any creature which feels pain suffers that pain, for pain is not a state which is easy to accept for any entity with flesh, blood and breath. Yet the kind of suffering which those second density entities upon your planetary experience is a purer suffering, one which does not have mental connotations or distortions placed upon it. There is no grieving for the self, there is no grieving for another, there is no blame for the self or for another. There are none of those emotional attachments that many of your third-density entities place with the experience of pain. Rather, it is as pure an experience of pain as the life pattern is a pure expression of the energy of the animal as it is.

Is there another query, my sister?

Carla: I have one that I would like to ask, but I want to make sure that all the other questions are asked first.

K: If an animal is suffering due to illness, due to terminal illness, is it interfering with its working out of its own life patterns to put an end to its suffering by ending its incarnation?

(Side one of tape ends.)

(Jim channeling)

I am Q'uo, and am again with this instrument. We speak now to the query of the shortening of the time of suffering for the second density creature which experiences the illness which is in all probability that final illness for the life of the creature. We may suggest that this is an area in which one's own philosophy of life plays the greatest portion, for to the entity that suffers the terminal illness, there is the limiting of the ability to live the normal life of its kind. This it recognizes in only a very simple manner, much as you would feel the addition of greater and greater weights upon your shoulders if you were asked to carry such about with you and could not remove them but had to endure the added weight as you moved about your daily activities.

The animal, therefore, does not in most cases bemoan its fate, but does what is possible within the new set of circumstances, and expresses itself and uses this opportunity to the fullest extent. However, that quality of compassion that is the hallmark of the beginning third-density lessons oftentimes will, for the third-density entity which loves the pet that is dying, express itself within the third-density entity in a desire to relieve that which is seen as suffering, that which is pain to the creature, and because of the great desire to aid the pet, then the action is taken to terminate the life within your illusion so that there might be a cessation of the pain for the second-density creature.

We can suggest that this can be seen in a number of ways, depending upon one's sensitivities, and that there is good argument, as you would state it in your illusion, for proceeding along the path of terminating the life as well as proceeding along the path of spending time in shared love with the creature that begins its slow departure from the life experience. In either instance, the overriding principle is the intention to share love in as great a facility as possible.

Is there a further query, my sister?

K: Are second-density creatures capable of any type of karmic connection in and among themselves or originating from themselves, connecting to third-density entities rather than the other way?

I am Q'uo, and am aware of your query, my sister. In the most successful cases of investment by a third-density entity of a second-density pet, this is indeed so, for the bond of love which has been awakened between the two entities, and oftentimes awakened for the first time within the second-density creature, is that bond which will often tie these entities together until the second-density entity has been invested to the degree necessary for graduation into the third density.

Thus, you see many times the reappearance within the life pattern of the pets that have been in association with the third-density entity previously in this incarnation and in previous lifetimes. Thus, the bond of love brings these entities together time and again in the same way that the bond of love will bring together third-density entities many times in order that the overall karmic patterns may run their full course, that is, allow biases of one kind to be developed and then balanced over a period of many lifetimes.

Is there a further query, my sister?

K: Is there ever continuing contact between the second-density entity that is harvested into third density? Is there any contact after the harvesting into third density with its previous third-density owner/companion/protector?

I am Q'uo, and though this is possible and occasionally occurs within the third-density space/time continuum, more often the continuing connection occurs as the third-density entity which has invested the entity that is newly third-density will take the form of the guide or teacher that operates from time/space as the new third-density entity enters the space/time incarnational nexus.

Is there a further query, my sister?

K: No, I think I'm done for now. Thank you.

Is there another query at this time?

Carla: I have one which you may not be able to answer except generally, but I will accept any comment which you wish to give. I have sensed that I have had, recently, for the last few months, when challenging you, it seemed that at first I hear—I don't actually hear it, but I perceive a rather fuzzy, not-quite-right identification. I've done a lot of thinking about this, and I've finally come up with a thought about it, which is, that since you are a principle made up of Latwii and of Ra, and because I know that in the past Latwii was able to aid me in averting psychic greeting by the fifth-density negative entity which is observing this group, and has been for many years, I felt that it is possible that the fifth-density negative entity—which is not quite as powerful as Latwii, but close—might be attempting to piggyback, having come through the quarantine and being able to work in thought as it will.

This evening I quite fervently stated that, in my mind, as my opinion, when I heard the muffled first, "I am Q'uo," and specifically suggested to the negative entity that I was upon a cross, that my hands were nailed, and that I was dying to save mankind. This is the most heartfelt and firm mode of challenging that I know at this point. The result seemed instantaneous, and the contact has seemed quite clear and quite crisp since. Can you confirm my supposition as to what has been occurring *(inaudible)*, and the appropriateness of my dealing with it?

I am Q'uo. In a word, yes. We are pleased that you have perceived this situation with great clarity. It is one which is unusual in that there are few groups that have had access built into them by such entities and had this access available so often, and which have been able to avoid the influence of such an entity and its minions for a significant portion of your space/time experience. We also commend your response to such greetings, for this is the heart of your self and your purpose, and is well-stated in the manner which you have chosen. We feel you are accomplishing the necessary tuning and challenging to a great degree, and we thank you for your conscientiousness and recommend it for all future workings.

Is there a further query, my sister?

Carla: Just a theoretical one. I know that my nature is that of a martyr. I approve of that. I have consciously decided not to change that. One of the things that comes very easily to me is that I would gladly die to save others. Could anyone do what Christ did, who had a pure enough path of service and felt strongly and utterly faithful about the possibilities of such a path?

I am Q'uo, and am aware of your query, my sister. The willingness to give of the self to the degree that one gives all, one gives one's life, is a willingness which, though rarely expressed within your illusion, is a possibility to all who inhabit your illusion, given the appropriate circumstances. Oftentimes, within that condition which you call war, there are such acts of bravery and selflessness that one entity shall take the grenade that was meant for comrades, and give its life in so doing.

In lesser expressions of this kind of selfless giving, those called the parents will often sacrifice to a great degree in order that the children of the mating may benefit in some fashion. However, the giving of the life is that which is most often reserved for but few within a life pattern. At some point within each entity's evolution there will come the opportunity and the willingness to give of the self to that degree, though the giving may not be done in an instant, but may be the giving of the entire life pattern, which may be lengthy, in order that others may benefit, and that which is given to the self is only enough to continue the life pattern. Each third density entity will find a spectrum of possibility available to it in this regard, and the harvestability of the entity draws nigh when the amount willing to be given to others exceeds the amount desired for the self.

Is there a further query, my sister?

Carla: One last one, which ties the two together. It is my supposition that the reason my challenge from the cross has an effect which is the strongest that I know, is due to the fact that I am telling the truth metaphysically, that I would do that. Can you confirm this?

I am Q'uo, and we can indeed confirm this assumption.

Carla: OK, then I continue, as I teach those few who really wish to learn, to be that *(inaudible)* about their highest ideal. This is an excellent way to develop the personality which can channel and challenge successfully. Can you confirm that?

I am Q'uo, and again we confirm that which is a correct supposition. This is the ideal towards which each instrument moves at its own pace and according to its own internal rhythms. There will be for each instrument the uncovering of deeper and deeper commitment to that which is the essence of its self. Thus, all need not be the same to be equal in will and faith.

Is there a further query, my sister?

Carla: No. Thank you very much, Q'uo.

I am Q'uo, and we are greatly honored to be able to join this group as we are asked once again. We cannot thank you enough for this honor. We take great pleasure in these moments that we spend with you, for, indeed, to us they are but the blinking of the eye.

At this time we shall take our leave of this group, leaving each, as always, in love and in light, in the power and in the peace of the one infinite Creator. We are known to you as those of Q'uo. Adonai, my friends. Adonai. ♣

L/L Research

L/L Research is a subsidiary of Rock Creek Research & Development Laboratories, Inc.

P.O. Box 5195
Louisville, KY 40255-0195

www.llresearch.org

Rock Creek is a non-profit corporation dedicated to discovering and sharing information which may aid in the spiritual evolution of humankind.

ABOUT THE CONTENTS OF THIS TRANSCRIPT: This telepathic channeling has been taken from transcriptions of the weekly study and meditation meetings of the Rock Creek Research & Development Laboratories and L/L Research. It is offered in the hope that it may be useful to you. As the Confederation entities always make a point of saying, please use your discrimination and judgment in assessing this material. If something rings true to you, fine. If something does not resonate, please leave it behind, for neither we nor those of the Confederation would wish to be a stumbling block for any.

CAVEAT: This transcript is being published by L/L Research in a not yet final form. It has, however, been edited and any obvious errors have been corrected. When it is in a final form, this caveat will be removed.

© 2009 L/L Research

Sunday Meditation
October 14, 1990

Group question: Tonight we're taking potluck.

(Unknown channeling)

I am Hatonn. Greetings to you in the love and the light of the one infinite Creator. It has been so long since we have spoken through this instrument on your regular meeting. We had to undergo a most rigorous challenge *(inaudible)* as the instrument had its doubts and we thank the instrument for its doubts for it is indeed *(inaudible)*.

We are with you this evening because you have asked and we had our freedom of what to say to you. With the permission of *(inaudible)* we shall be speaking concerning spiritual principles not in parable as we are talking to those who need no parables. But as is somewhat unusual for us solely concerning spiritual principles and to use … to use in this walk that you take that is called the spiritual path, or the path of the prodigal, or the path from the source to the source. Within your American Indian lore it is simply returning to the Great Wheel. We will be moving between these two instruments to give both an experience which is new to the one not as *(inaudible)* lack of use, in working to use the best of each person's unique experience, vocabulary and knowledge to tell the simple story that we have come to share.

It is well to remember that the greatest function of philosophy and religion or mythology is to tell stories that have archetypical resonance. That is, if the story does not seem to be relevant to the acceleration of spiritual growth, then it has not been fully examined, for there is that in seeking the truth which is not usually and cannot ever be discouraged by the fact that there are no answers. It is the job of this particular entity not to have answers. Those who have answers are the very ones who are perhaps soon to be repeating third density. Those who are humble before the mystery of their own creation and see the dust on the path and the blazing sun and the cold desert night in the times of no stimulation, when all is calm in the dark night of the soul. The times of overstimulation, when you can't be uplifted one more notch, accept what you are.

In all of these cases, the most important thing about them is your opportunity. In truth, the Creator thinks not as many would have the Creator seem to think, of vengeance, of protecting of one against the other side. That the Creator would be of one side and not the other … this is not our understanding *(inaudible)* and I hope that it is not an understanding of your own function as a seeker to stand in judgment. To use discrimination is necessary; to judge and to close the mind is not necessary, nor is it preferable to one who wishes to *(inaudible)* when the object of division *(inaudible)* self the damage to the self is incalculable.

It is a spiritual journey and we are on it. Those who know they are on it and those who do not know. Yet how … how can the ideas and ideals which are the deep truths that enable humankind to *(inaudible)* and to have faith in the infinity and eternity of the spirit. How can these things be true of every situation? How can that be? Each of you has asked this at different times. Two entities here have asked themselves that question during this week. Varying by guilt or disappointment in the self inappropriate by the self as is not *(inaudible)*. We encourage people not to do that but it is very difficult for entities to avoid judging themselves and yet that one mistake … that one simple error is at the heart of so much *(inaudible)* on your sphere.

We would now transfer to the one known as K.

(K channeling)

I am Hatonn, and greet each again in love and light through this instrument. It is a widespread concept among your peoples to view the self as being less than worthy in many situations in which you find yourself in your present illusion. Each of you have been taught this from your earliest childhood. The crying baby, the spilled glass of milk, the simple and myriad things that each child experiences from day to day with which each parent gets exasperated and may, in moments of not thinking clearly, berate the child *(inaudible)*. In each of these situations, the message comes very clearly to the child that indeed it is not worthy. Not worthy of the love of the parent, not worthy perhaps of the love of itself, for from whom shall it learn of this love if not from a parent? The child as it grows older continues to receive these messages from parents, from teachers, from siblings, from playmates. And it also observes those same parents, and others with whom it comes in contact berating themselves when they fall short of *(inaudible)*. Thus these behaviors and attitudes are learned early and are well reinforced until they become, not second nature, but first nature, with most *(inaudible)*.

Is it any wonder then that you have difficulty in attempting to unravel the tangled threads of these tapes of messages and messages that have been given to you and woven into the very fabric of your being? We suggest to you that it is unrealistic in the extreme to expect yourselves to be able to do so merely by trying. You cannot change the pattern of a lifetime in an instant by decision, but you can start to do so. And when you fail, as you inevitably will, we can but urge you to look kindly on yourselves—to choose not to reinforce the messages which you have received from those exasperated, overtired and overworked parents from your infancy, to choose not to repeat the messages you heard from all those others from your early life, and continue to hear in your present existence. For when you berate yourself for your failures, you are doing just that, thus negating the very work you are attempting to do on yourself.

It will be most difficult for many of you to begin to be able to accept, to truly accept, not in the sense of merely acknowledging, but in the sense of taking into the self with the sure knowledge that it is indeed truly alright to fail, according to your present perceptions. For we see that many of you, in your attempts to change your attitudes about yourselves, about the way you view yourselves, in your attempts to accept yourselves as you are, what you are really attempting to do is to change yourselves, to make yourselves alright, and therefore acceptable to yourselves. This is not where you must begin my children. This is, as the saying goes, placing the cart before the horse. That is, as we have suggested, only reinforcing those very patterns you are attempting to change. So we would suggest to you that your goal is not to not stray from your ideals, but to truly accept that you do so because it is your nature. And as you are able to fully accept those qualities in yourself, then and only then will you realize that they are beginning to change. Because only then will you truly have begun to unravel those messages at a deep enough level to effect change in yourselves.

This process, as you know when you view it clearly, is the task for most not only of a lifetime, but of many lifetimes. And as is the case with all monumental tasks, the tendency for those of you who desire perfection in yourselves at least, if not in your environment as well, would be to want to give up in despair, because the goal seems unattainable. This is the nature of the spiritual journey, my friends, for the mystery recedes ever before us. Were we to look only at the ultimate goal, we would never take that first step for it would seem pointless. This is no less true for us than for you.

We urge you therefore to view that which is before you to do. It may seem small. It may appear to have no relevance to the grand scheme of things, with your desire to be congruent with your ideals, and yet in whatever is before you to do, you have an opportunity to continue the process of learning about yourself, observing the self, learning your true nature, and accepting whatever it is that you find there. Whether you personally at that moment approve or disapprove of that, your approval or disapproval is not relevant to your spiritual growth at this time. What is relevant is your accepting of yourself. Judgment of yourself is never productive for positive growth, but only a reinforcing of those old, undesired patterns.

It is a challenge indeed to approach this task from outside the framework with which you have been taught to *(inaudible)*. For the tendency is to use the same old tools that were given you by your parents and those other early teachers. It is indeed difficult to discard those tools, feeling then that you have none with which to work and to discover totally different approaches to working with yourself. We urge you, my brothers and sisters, to throw away those old tools of judgment and condemnation for they have never been of any value to you. To drop them by the wayside and continue on your way, unarmed perhaps and ill-prepared for any work you would like to do, but continuing on with new faith that new tools will be given you, or that you will find new ways to work.

At this time we would transfer again to the one known as Carla.

(Carla channeling)

And what are these tools *(inaudible)* would suggest? Faith is one of the resources that may be developed from a continually closer look at the nature of self. Let us look at *(inaudible)*. Each of you have the *(inaudible)* you have the entire human range of human emotions, which are tempered only by biases hard won through many incarnations *(inaudible)* listen*(inaudible)* but the leap of faith with no net, no doctrine, no dogma, is an act of spiritual courage. It is a statement of the self to the self *(inaudible)* blessed holy nature of the Creator, the universe and yourself. Or to put it in a simpler way, Creator and all of His parts. The infinity of the Creator is not active. It has not been directed *(inaudible)* yet remains the Logos, the thought, the created thought of divine love.

The tool with which this faith is *(inaudible)* may be summed up in three words: praise, prayer, and thanksgiving. It is well to live life in these modes as we just listed. As if life itself in this illusion are complex and ever changing—a kaleidoscope of images *(inaudible)* becoming emotionally involved perhaps *(inaudible)* but if you seek with a full will to do the will of that Creator, which is *(inaudible)* self *(inaudible)* all burdens will be dropped and you have only to *(inaudible)*.

Now all of this can be accomplished without recourse to a story of redemption, and this is why we encourage each, if the world religions or philosophies do not fit the path that you are on, this is why we ask you to make up a path, for the important thing is not recognizing the path, but persistent praise of all that you see and hear. Along with that, prayer mostly in the form of silent prayer as you listen within to the silence that moves deep inside the unconscious mind as you live bringing forth fruit in its *(inaudible)*. All of these things you cannot do without that faithful leap into the abyss of the unknown, into the void, the mystery.

Many choose to turn towards the miraculous things that indicate that there is a mystery. We suggest to those interested in spiritual principles that the attention fundamentally be kept upon spiritual principles, for it is by those that you gradually do change the programming of your life.

We realize that some this week in this group have had difficulty and we ask, did you see each difficulty as a difficulty or as an opportunity? Had you faith that the Creator had placed this particular situation in front of you so that you might find the love in the unlovable and acceptance in the unacceptable and hence polarize in compassion and purity of emotions as is your heart's wish on the path? You cannot help but be upon the path of the pilgrim when you decide to know what the culture believes is good and *(inaudible)* you have chosen the long way back to the Creator. Not everyone at the end of second-density harvest wishes to *(inaudible)*. Content to rejoice in the moon and the sun and nourished by rain *(inaudible)* in your wild state, untamed, that you may be in touch with that you too are a second-density creature. Your consciousness lives in one. This consciousness that lives for you and houses your consciousness has far more wisdom than you are privy to in the half-remembered vista of all that there is, for it is a *(inaudible)* memory and there is no path.

That mind of which we speak is indeed deep inside the subconscious and becomes semi-permeable, more or less, depending upon the ability of the entity channeling to feel the love that is being transmitted *(inaudible)* by voice. Language transmits that love that is between one. The beginning of moving from one place to another is to know where you are and where you are is defined well by whether you have given praise or whether you have spent time tabernacling with the One on holy ground and how you have seen catalyst within *(inaudible)*.

It is not good to take your spiritual temperature even if you may feel that you have completely lost contact with that self which was transcendent to life as you know it now. Even those who dwell comfortably and peacefully in a faith which they do not feel pressured to explain, knowing it is a mystery, have many times when they cannot *(inaudible)* and are instead caught in these old programs of the mind given in childhood which convince so many that they are not worthy nor shall they ever be. Let us shake off the dull *(inaudible)* of unforgiving memory. You have no need of that baggage. Your arms and shoulders and back ache from carrying it. Lay it down beside the peaceful waters of your own self. For are you not Christ within, Christ without, Christ *(inaudible)* and Christ *(inaudible)*? Are you really a second-density animal that makes people recognize? It hardly seems likely.

To love one another, just to love, is an enormous gift, one which lightens the consciousness *(inaudible)*. Not to love the self is to reduce by far the amount that you can love others. You can only love others insofar as you love and have compassion and forgiveness for yourself.

The path, once it has been taken—and it was taken long before this incarnation—to incarnate, to experience and to polarize in service to the Creator, either to others or to the self, is a monumentally great choice, *(inaudible)*. The gift people find it easiest to give is the activity: volunteering for the homeless, the *(inaudible)* soup kitchen, arranging *(inaudible)* clothes people who need it. And all of this is indeed an integral part of worship. Yet you are steward over your very soul for it is not you, only your freedom as you *(inaudible)* your freewill that is so often impulsive and so often *(inaudible)* there is a time for all when the decision is made to step forward into a new realization and this decision allows you not only to do things that seem helpful. This decision to find the love and the opportunity in every challenge creates a consciousness capable of *(inaudible)* spirit on which you live *(inaudible)* and in aiding the human race, for the human race is as sick as the planet that it has *(inaudible)* the plunderer the second *(inaudible)*.

(Side one of tape ends.)

(Carla channeling)

I am Hatonn, and we *(inaudible)* continue. The doing of the active service, whether it be parenthood, being the peacemaker and "cheerer-upper" of those with whom you work, whatever may be your condition in life, you will find it easier to do nice things for people than to attempt to do sufficient inner work to dwell in eternity while you are *(inaudible)* the mundane. A portion of your mind that is the artistic or intuitive portion is underused in many in your culture's age of fact and *(inaudible)*. You are here to offer other options to entities who did not know they had other options. What are you to yourself? Are you love? What relation do you feel you have with the One? What relation could you have, if love created all there is? And why then, from all these choices, free will is indeed a distortion but is necessary for manifestation. For in this choice lies the very clear objective in reprogramming that within yourself which may resist commitment, worship, practicing the presence of the one Creator, and so forth. So many actions, so many opportunities. Let the meditation be only a touchstone for each day that is spent whenever a sharp sound is heard remembering the encapsulated form, that state of mind that held you enthralled in the light during those fifteen precious minutes that you give to the Creator each day. This is your basic gift. This is your basic method of being of service to others as catalyst. So often it is not what you say, but the person that you are that makes the words that you say substantive.

We find the one known as C has given into complete exhaustion and feel that there may well be few if any questions. However, questions or no, we would like to ask if *(inaudible)* speaking through the one known as K. With thanks to this instrument and to the one known as K for making themselves available to us and offering their uniqueness for us to find new ways to say these simple truths. We thank each and at this time *(inaudible)*. We are those known to you as Hatonn.

(K channeling)

I am Hatonn, and am again with this instrument. This time we would ask if there are any questions upon the minds of those still present here?

Carla: I just have one that I ask over and over again because occasionally I learn something new. In what way could I improve my teaching of not just your thoughts but of how to hear them? If you have any comment, I'd be glad to hear it.

I am Hatonn, and, my sister, may we say first of all that we are most pleased with the methods you presently employ both in your own rigorous tuning challenges, processes and the continued focus of attention upon our contact with you as well as your communication of these concepts as you understand them to those who *(inaudible)* of learning these concepts *(inaudible)*.

Carla: OK.

It is, as you know, our privilege to be able to work with those such as you, and we would suggest at this time on the continued focusing of attention upon that which you already know. We are aware of your desire ever to seek that which is new and would encourage you not to be tired, shall we say, of these same old methods for in our opinion these same old methods are most effective, if only they had more continued attention, as it were.

Carla: Thank you.

May we ask if there are any further questions?

Carla: No, thank you *(inaudible)*.

I am Hatonn, and we thank you, my sister.

Questioner: *(Inaudible)* questions *(inaudible)*.

I am Hatonn. We have been saving … savoring the correct *(inaudible)* the last few moments of being able to share your journey with you for we, as always, have enjoyed our contact with this group but are most appreciative of *(inaudible)*. At this time we take our leave of this group, leaving with you our blessings and encouragements upon your journeys which at times *(inaudible)* difficult to you. We look forward to being with you in the future whenever you should desire to call us and are, as you know, with you in all other times. We are known to you as those of Hatonn, and leave you in the love and the light of the infinite Creator. Adonai, my friends. Adonai.

L/L Research

L/L Research is a subsidiary of Rock Creek Research & Development Laboratories, Inc.

P.O. Box 5195
Louisville, KY 40255-0195

www.llresearch.org

Rock Creek is a non-profit corporation dedicated to discovering and sharing information which may aid in the spiritual evolution of humankind.

ABOUT THE CONTENTS OF THIS TRANSCRIPT: This telepathic channeling has been taken from transcriptions of the weekly study and meditation meetings of the Rock Creek Research & Development Laboratories and L/L Research. It is offered in the hope that it may be useful to you. As the Confederation entities always make a point of saying, please use your discrimination and judgment in assessing this material. If something rings true to you, fine. If something does not resonate, please leave it behind, for neither we nor those of the Confederation would wish to be a stumbling block for any.

CAVEAT: This transcript is being published by L/L Research in a not yet final form. It has, however, been edited and any obvious errors have been corrected. When it is in a final form, this caveat will be removed.

© 2009 L/L Research

Sunday Meditation
October 21, 1990

Group question: The question this evening has to do with free will. We know from the experience of others and from our own experience that the power of our will, when focused, is great, perhaps the greatest power in the universe. Considering the extreme power of the will, why is it that we do not automatically and always polarize towards service to each other and the seeking of the Creator and the serving of the Creator? Why is it that we have to work our way through so many, it seems to be, difficult choices, choices off the path of service, choices that seem to be other than service to others, realization of the self and realization of the Creator in all?

(Carla channeling)

I am Q'uo. It gives me great pleasure to greet each of you in the love and in the light of the one infinite Creator. We are so grateful to you for allowing us to share your meditation and your thoughts, and for calling us to speak upon this question. We will attempt to keep this instrument speaking loudly enough for all to hear, and would ask that any unheard words be questioned for repetition, as this instrument's voice is not naturally very loud. We also ask a favor of you. We ask you to take our words lightly, for we are not authorities, but pilgrims as you are. The mystery that fascinates all seekers recedes infinitely ahead of us and you. We have been upon your path, and perhaps we are more experienced that you, but we are completely equal, and completely full of knowledge, each equal to each, for all are one, and only one, creative thing, love, created into manifestation by the use of light. This is why we greet you in love and light, for that is all that there is; the rest is illusion.

We come to these questions wishing to step with careful feet, for it is a central question, a guiding question, and we could expend more time upon it by far than this instrument prefers. We will, however, attempt to heed this instrument's request for brevity.

Let us begin by laying the foundation for our response to your query, always remembering, please, that each person has a personal truth. Some truths are ageless, and some have their age and then fall away to a greater point of view. Thus, take all that we say, and toss away without a thought that which does not strike within you recognition, for you do not learn wisdom and love, you only encounter the catalyst to remember it. It is all within yourself.

It is our understanding that each spirit, or soul, or entity, according to the vocabulary, is created prior to any stage for manifestation. It is created by the action of free will upon an infinite but tiny portion of the vast infinity of intelligence. This intelligence, were it to have a name besides Creator, indicating One Original Thought, would be Love. However, a love of such a fiery, creative, disturbing and magnificent nature can never be confined by language, so we must make do with the pale shadow of the reality of this Logos, this Creator.

The method of this creation was to place finity within the infinite. Thus, a spark of love was given an infinite and equal spark of free will. We realize that these are paradoxes, and have no choice but to say them anyway. Again, your language has its limitations. Just as love is infinitely and ever the same, so is free will infinitely and ever various. Thusly, although each of you is as a snowflake, unique in pattern and color, so are each of you snowfall, and part of the whole cycle of the year that you experience as your island home circles about your sun.

Equipped with free will, you set forth on a journey through illusions. These illusions, in our understanding, make use of the illusion of time, so that lessons may be taken in order, and all possible aid given to each density of light, or classroom. The first density is that of being—the earth, the air, the fire and the water. Consciousness first rests there, and awakens to its surroundings, is warmed by the sun, is blown by the wind, and gradually each spark becomes aware that there is a darkness and a light, and it conceives of the idea of movement because it is attracted to the light.

And so comes the second density, as the elements grow in consciousness and become capable of expressing the Creator. As they express the Creator they express perfect service, a beautiful and complex dance of bird and butterfly, leaf, flower, the breathing out of that which you breathe in, the breathing in of that which you breathe out. More and more in second density do entities begin to become more than instinctual, more than creatures of love and service and instinct, to begin to be aware of themselves, usually, because third density entities have ministered unto them and loved them.

And when they have learned the instinct of turning to the light, their graduation is at hand and they become self-conscious sparks of the infinite One. But in this grade, and only in this grade or density, is there a brevity of the time allowed for learning, and a great veil drawn across most of the mind. It is intended that this illusion be so heavy, so earthy, so entrancing and distracting, that it would be completely obvious to the casual observer that we are brief incandescent beings, alive so little and dead so soon.

At this point the entity is asleep to the choice that is the business of this density, the making of the choice. For you see, there are two paths to the Creator; they are both valid. We do not teach the path of negativity, often called the path of the left hand, or by us the path which is not. It is, however, a valid path, though very difficult compared to the service-to-others, or positive, or radiant path. This choice must be made blindly. Thus, there will never be, has never been, and is never any objective proof, that is, objective enough to be objective to a scientist, of the possibility of anything but that which can be felt by the senses by a living entity using the senses that limit it. It is in this darkness, by blind faith alone, that a leap is taken from the safety of sleep to the risk of being awake.

Now, each of you knows the sacrifices that he has made to be listening, or reading, these words, not that we are the prize, but that only those who truly are seeking would be interested in what we have to say. Most entities are not highly oriented toward thinking, feeling or dreaming the ideal within your culture. Your culture is highly situational in its ethics. It is a culture in which the end always justifies the means, and within the illusion there is little observable justice or truth.

This is not the Creator's idea of either a dirty trick or the way things should be, but rather a carefully planned schoolroom. You may leave your rulers, your protractors, your pencils and paper at home, for this is the lesson of abundant life, and homework is written in the heart, sometimes in true blood. Each of you has painfully come awake, and made the choice to search. You have not stayed in the garden. You have chosen to come forth and experience, and out of this experience you begin to see what is obvious to you now, that was at first perhaps a shadow compared to that which is the star of your life now. You have encouraged yourself and others.

Now, the lesson of this density and the choice you are to make is all about loving. One may love in one of two paths: loving the Creator by serving others, or loving the Creator by serving the self, and manipulating and controlling others that the self may be aggrandized, and as the self is aggrandized, so all glory is given to the Creator. We teach the positive, or service-to-others, path. We believe that this choice of service to others offers the swiftest road of spiritual evolution, spiritual evolution being evolution itself, from this time forward, as you have completed the evolution of the particular physical vehicle in which you move about at this time.

Let us glance ahead, for this too begins to explain why relatively few entities seem hungry for the food that satisfies each of you so, so well. Looking forward, we see in the next grade, or density of light, a density called the love or understanding density, in which the lessons of love are perfected, and there is study of the lessons of wisdom.

At the end of this density, graduation moves into a density in which the ways of wisdom are perfected, and the ways of learning compassionate wisdom begun. And when an entity has graduated from this density, the next classroom is the classroom of unity, where the lessons of compassionate wisdom are perfected, and the return to the Creator begun.

Graduation out of this density moves into the seventh density or grade, which is the grade during which the entity makes its final preparations as social individuals, or social memory complexes, offers its best back to the Higher Self of its third-density self, and gains enough spiritual gravity to be pulled into the unmanifest, where you are no longer the snowflake, but part of the snow; no longer the bubble, but part of the sea.

And creation beats its heart, and rests in timelessness until the next creation. And what the next creation will be, we do not know, though we have had brief acquaintance with those few who move from creation to creation. Of those we cannot speak except to say they exist.

This, you see, is the path of spiritual evolution. Thusly, in your grade or density of light, your interest as a spiritual seeker is in tuning into love. Love, that much misunderstood word, in our definition, is unconditional. It does not judge; it only supports and appreciates, listens and has patience, consoles and pardons. Does love do this because of what it has given the entity in third density? No. If this were so, then all would be saints, and free will would not be to be reckoned with as it is, for free will begins as willfulness—it is completely various, unpredictable. It is an absolute, just as love is an absolute; they are given to you equally.

As long as the entity is willing to get along, to be asleep, it may be very comfortable. It has not polarized, of course, because it does not value sacrifice, and to polarize by serving others seems, to those who have not yet done it, a very hard task compared to pleasing the self one way or another. But for everyone there comes a moment, and one must wait for that moment in all cases, when the soul must awaken for that individual, in the rhythm of that individual's destiny and story. And in that moment the choice becomes clear—to serve the self, or to serve others; to be put simplistically, as so many of your society would, good, or bad. Except that there is no good or bad. Realizations such as this continually rock the foundations of the seeker's cultural conditioning.

Think about this for a moment or two. What is your cultural conditioning? Were you taught the value of love by those who were your first teachers? Were you face to face daily with worship and joy and peace? Is there aught in this society that seems to be worshipped but vain idols: money, power, position, genius? Who are the healers? Were the carefullest health lovers correct, the highest and most advanced beings would all be splendidly athletic. Somehow, that is not often the manifestation of love, for love is of the heart, and those who have learned to offer not their love, which is finite, and which is in short supply in any third density entity, but the love of the Father that flows through the seeker who is open and has emptied itself out, then that love becomes the love that is available for the seeker to manifest.

Then has that seeker begun its life's work, lightening the consciousness of this planet at this time. No matter what dramatic talents and gifts he may possess, no matter how well one may do anything that is manifest, the greatest service in this density of the search for the lessons of love is being itself. Your essence—to put it another way, your magical personality, or to put it another way, your metaphysical reality as a light and imperishable being—is completely at the mercy of illusion here.

So, you see it is intended that this choice be difficult, and that the rewards of service to others, the rewards of a servant of all, never be guessed at until after the fact. For you, and almost all entities, are born into the world in a state of utter and complete forgetting of who they are, whence they came, whither they go. The nature of the Creator or their relationship to the Creator, or even of their own nature—all of these things are unknown. And it is against this backdrop of unknowing, of scenes occurring which begin to test the individual's ability to love, that the drama, which stars, you, which has as its chief critic, you, which has as designer of sets and costumes and props, you, which has as its author, you, begins its act upon the stage, which is this illusion. You have free will, but that does not necessarily mean that you understand the free will.

It is not easy to understand that you are not this being or that being, not this self that has so many idiosyncrasies, but under different circumstances would be anywhere within the 360 degrees of third-density activity and manifestation. Who is the killer, who is the rapist, who is the forgetful parent, who is the man of war, but you, and you, and I, and all of us? The essence of the reason that you are not given an instinct for purity is in this understanding of free will. The discipline of the personality is the greatest tool for coming to understand and to forgive the 360 degree self, to acknowledge and love that self, that self that must be loved. This is a key that many miss. You must love yourself; you must forgive yourself for the thoughts that you have thought, the errors that you have made, those things you wish you had done but did not. Subjectively, you feel that these make you unworthy. You could be anything about you that you choose not to like about yourself, and to that extent you fail to love the Creator, the creation, in all of its love, all of its Christ, all of its holiness.

Now, how does one discipline the personality? Our brother spoke most beautifully upon the subject. It is most difficult to live with complete freedom and always to make what you would subjectively feel to be the correct decision. One of the great traits of the seeker is its persistence, for gathered persistence is absolutely necessary, for the failures self-perceived, not perceived by anyone but you, seem so many, and if you do not forgive yourself, how can you expect to forgive others, and how can you bless others if you do not forgive, if you do not feel healing love pouring from you? Whether this entity is known to you or unknown, whether this entity may be subjectively described as friend or enemy, the same love is needed by all. For the needs and the behavior caused by the variousness of free will, and the variousness of man's understanding of it, there is love, and only love, and it is always and ever the same creative Original Thought.

Thus, in a dark time and in the shadow of death that you call life, you seek to forgive, and pardon, and love, and turn darkness into light wherever you see the way, and to serve, if not to please. You may all be judged because you do not please, but those who wish to serve often do not please, and if you are reviled for your love of the Creator, then you have done something right, and you are beginning to create the catalyst for fear among people that are already fearful, because they do not wish to change, because change is uncomfortable.

Pilgrims upon the path of seeking are always uncomfortable, always changing, always seeking. One cannot say to another, "Come with me on this journey, it will be all rose petals and ambrosia, there will be nothing but good times, for the Creator is love." The best that you can say is, "Come suffer with me until we learn that there is no such thing as suffering, but only pain, and not my pain and not your pain. Come die with me, that we all may live. Come, let us empty ourselves of self, that we may be earthen vessels filled with treasure, dust in the presence of the Creator."

You are on holy ground at this moment. Let us pause, that we may share this ecstasy.

(Pause)

I am Q'uo. I am Q'uo, and we thank you for that incandescent experience. It is a joy to be with you.

The first choice that one makes may be seen to be the fulcrum, or the crux upon which the remainder, not only of this incarnation, but of many, will depend, and each pilgrim knows that that first choice is the hard one, for it must be made with no prior experience. It is not until some time has been spent, on faith alone, attempting to live in faith, and by that we do not mean a belief, but simple faith, faith that the Creator is love, that we were created out of love and because we are loved, and because we were loved first it is natural to love in return, faith that anything that occurs is part of the lesson of love, and offers us opportunity.

When you are stymied, and your free will wishes to circumnavigate a situation, allow the choices you have made to polarize toward service to others to make you strong in your will. Allow yourself to remember your previous choices, and how, although they seemed hard, they were one hundred and one thousandfold rewarding. For it is not until there has been some time spent in sheer persistence of effort to listen to the will of the Creator that there comes a hunger for that silence that speaks louder than any words.

In a lifetime of choices you forged in yourself a life of faith, a gift for your Father, the gift of a poem, of a tapestry, rich, lovely, filled with high ideals and high hopes, against all odds, filled not with happiness, for only those things that turn to dust are happy things, but filled instead with joy, joy within sorrow, sorrow within joy, until you are blissful, and gentle, and willfulness had become willingness to love and serve the Creator and the Creator in every person.

Subjectively then, you begin to be rewarded only after you have made your choice; that is the cause of the illusion's being this heavy, this thick, this opaque. The Creator, in giving free will, gave it without stint.

There are hints in one's own deepest inward thoughts, in the very nature of this very polarized environment in which you live with hot and cold, winter and summer, light and dark. But they do not speak unless you wish to listen. And as you listen, and as you change, you must change so much of yourself, that which seems to be your self, that is, in reality, the programs that your own brain/computer has set in place for your survival, shaped by the culture which has almost no impulse towards holy things of the Creator, but only towards beautiful things of man. The spirit within must sense its own reality, and choose freely what seems to be the great sacrifice of taking up the cross, the carrying on of the endless journey that ends by the water, the water of life, crystalline love.

We realize that we have spoken longer than this instrument requested. We hope, not too much longer, and we ask all of your forgiveness. We have a poor concept of your time. We would, however, cease speaking through this instrument with thanks to it, and, if the one known as Jim is available, we would like to transfer to this instrument in order to close the meeting. In love and in light I leave this instrument. I am known to you as Q'uo.

(Jim channeling)

I am Q'uo, and greet each again in love and light through this instrument. It is our privilege at this time to offer ourselves in the attempt to speak to any queries which those present may find value in the asking. Again, we remind each that that which we share we share with great joy, but do not consider ourselves to be in any way infallible. Therefore, we ask that you take our words lightly, and use them in the way that feels most helpful for your own journey of seeking and of service. Is there a query at this time?

Questioner: *(Inaudible)* love, light, Infinite Creator, Hare Krishna. My query pertains to faith, the actual definition of faith in relation to hope, and when an entity after some time travels *(inaudible)* on that leap of blind faith, *(inaudible)* hope come in to awaken the soul so that that faith becomes "solid ground."

I am Q'uo, and we are aware of your query, my brother, and we greet you in that same joyous love and light that you so willingly share. Concerning your query of the maturation of hope into that which is faith, we would suggest that each entity begins with that spiritual food, as you may call it, that it can digest with comfort. For many this beginning is in that term or concept that is known as hope. The entity with hope is aware that there is more to the earthly existence than those things which seem to comprise the earthly life, that there is more to the purpose of one's existence than completing a daily round of activities after another daily round of activities, and completing an infinite number of such days, and accomplishing the tasks that come with them, that there is a Self which is greater than the self, that there is a binding force within all of the creation, that there is indeed a purpose which gives the life a nobility and a shining quality, a strength to continue and to find a more fully realized conception of that which is life, that which is direction, and that which is service.

This entity, however, being somewhat young in the spiritual childhood, as it may be called, is tested by the passage of days and the catalyst that is contained within each day that will, as the fire tempers the metal to strengthen it, will also temper the spirit of this entity as it is manifest in the personality. And as the entity continues on in the hope that there is a purpose behind all of its actions and all of its desires, the entity grows in this inner knowing that it has first called hope.

As it continues in growth and grows in strength, the entity begins to enter that concept or area of the metaphysical or spiritual self which is called faith.

The quality here which differentiates the faith from the hope is that when the faith becomes developed within the entity it has a sureness that comes not only from the experience that the entity has gained in its own growth, but in a feeling deep within the self that is like unto the iron filing as it approaches the strength of the magnet. The entity begins to feel that it is drawing close to a power that is far greater than any power it has found within itself or its own experience before.

Thus, the entity begins to feel and experience this quality of faith and finds that its feet are placed upon a firmer ground with each step that it takes, each testing that it passes, shall we say, for all of the experience within this illusion serves as a kind of catalyst that will allow the entity to become a crystallized being so that there is a strength and clarity to the purpose for such an entity's life pattern.

Thus, we would say it is the experience of the entity that moves it closer and closer to a realization of its oneness with all of creation that eventually changes the entity's philosophy, shall we say, of the life, from that which is guided by hope to that which is stayed by faith.

Is there a further query, my brother?

Questioner: *(Inaudible)* project *(inaudible)* city of God, and if so *(inaudible)* may be a part in helping very many people in polarizing towards service to others and love and at this time/space, space/time *(inaudible)* now.

I am Q'uo, and am aware of your query, my brother. We scan the minds of those present and can confirm that, indeed, this project of which you speak is most helpful to all those which are a part of it and all those which may come within its influence, for there is an openness in the seeking and in the sharing of that which is the purpose for the life, the learning and the seeking in that location which shines as the candle in the darkness, the beacon upon the shore for those which are cast upon the sea and who seek a clear and safe harbor in which to find a place to seek in their own way and to share in their own way that which is theirs to give.

We cannot speak highly enough of the effort that you partake in, and we would suggest that there are those within our density of experience who take great joy in observing this experiment in creating the new human being upon your planet. We bless and send our joy to each that the efforts may be doubled and redoubled, for it is as each light upon the planet shines more brightly and makes a web of light around the planetary surface that this planetary sphere shall eventually be moved into its rightful place within the evolution of the population that seeks so earnestly for that which has always rested within each heart awaiting the earnest pilgrim.

Is there a further query, my brother?

Questioner: We thank you for your blessing.

Carla: I would like to ask if there is a need for *(inaudible)* Q'uo?

I am Q'uo, and we feel that though the energy of the group begins to wane that there is enough energy and harmony for the remaining queries.

Carla: OK.

Is there another query at this time?

Questioner: Is it much easier living in amongst a community of like minded souls, *(inaudible)* energy for polarization of *(inaudible)* takes place much easier?

I am Q'uo, and as you are aware from your own experience, my brother, and the experience of so many others within your community, such a community is a great aid to each seeker that is part of it, for those who of like mind together seek shall far more surely find.

Is there a further query, my brother?

Questioner: From scriptures, various scriptures, *(inaudible)* particularly those scriptures revealed to *(inaudible)*, that in different ages a different process of self-realization is recommended, and that in this particular age, creative *(inaudible)*, the recommended process is to attempt the calling [upon] the name of God. How do you perceive this, how could we *(inaudible)* enlighten others, *(inaudible)* of thanksgiving *(inaudible)* culture, and possibly within other traditions in the world?

I am Q'uo, and am aware of your query, my brother. Each entity, as it enters the incarnation, has placed before it a pattern of experience that will allow it to learn those lessons which have not been well learned in previous experiences, and will then allow it to take these learnings and share with others as one who teaches. Thus, learning and service lies before each entity as it enters the incarnational pattern.

However, there is the necessity, in order for the learning to occur in the most efficacious manner, for the entity to pass through that which you may call the veil of forgetting, so that only the most basic remembering occurs within the incarnation. The incarnation then becomes a process of discovery of seeking that which is mysterious, that which is hidden, that which has a price and that which, when discovered, also has the reward, the broadening of the perspective, the point of view, the ability to accept, to love.

However, each entity has the incarnational personality which is, relative to the soul, undisciplined and within the Earthly illusion subject to distraction, temptations and, shall we say, some degree of laziness. Thus, it is necessary for each entity in some manner to discipline the personality.

There are various ways of doing this disciplining of the personality. There are traditions within each culture, and within each religious heritage, that have called upon those practices which you have mentioned as being most helpful for the primary, or foundation discipline, for each entity that seeks to learn those lessons that are appropriate to it and to share them then with others as a service to others and to the one Creator within all. The chanting, the use of various devotional songs, dances and other rituals are most helpful in beginning this process of disciplining so that the expenditure of the inpouring prana, or cosmic energy, may be most efficiently accomplished, for this energy is much like the power of the water that moves through the hose. If the nozzle of the hose is turned in such a fashion as to cause the diffusion of the water to move through in a spray there is little power achieved. However, if the nozzle or the attention is turned in such a fashion as to cause the water to move in a small, boring, forceful fashion, then there is far greater power possible to achieve with such a focus.

Thus it is with the focus of consciousness. If the entity is able to discipline the personality to such a degree, then it is able to move in greater harmony with the cosmic energies that are available to it and to utilize these energies in the accomplishing of those lessons and the giving of those services which are the entity's incarnational pattern.

Is there a further query, my brother?

Questioner: I have a query. The names of God which we repeat *(inaudible)*, we tend to focus on to align and balance our being in harmony with divine will, are spoken of as being absolute in nature, they are non-different from the Creator Himself. Are you able, from your density, can you perceive that absolute nature in the sound vibration? For example, Krishna, or Allah, or Adonai?

I am Q'uo, and am aware of your query, my brother. The one Creator is described by various sound vibration complexes in order to cause a certain facet of the one Creator to vibrate in resonance with the entity calling the Creator's name. It is our humble experience to partake in this seeking process, and it has been our experience that, though many names reflect many different facets of that one jewel that is the Creator, that there is no one name which can capture all of the essence of the one Creator which is mysterious and beyond capture, shall we say. Each name, however, allows a certain sacred quality to be awakened within the seeker which vibrates the name. This harmonic resonance, then, begins its work in the appropriate energy center or chakra within the seeker and calls forth from the seeker that quality which is embodied in the name of the Creator which it vibrates. Thus, when properly vibrated within the seeker it is as though the creation sings. This vibrational quality is that which each seeks as it vibrates whatever name of the Creator is sacred to it, or is utilized by it at a certain time in order to enhance that quality within the seeker.

Is there a further query, my brother?

Carla: I have one. I *(inaudible)*, and other people have to suffer so hard, *(inaudible)* confused, *(inaudible)*, and live so long *(inaudible)*?

I am Q'uo, and am aware of your query, my sister. There are many qualities for each entity which are either well expressed or poorly expressed depending upon the incarnational pattern that has been chosen and the incarnational patterns that have been utilized previous to this incarnation. Thus, some entities bring into succeeding incarnations those talents which have been well developed, those which have been reasonably well developed and those which yet await development. Each entity will have an unique pattern to pursue during each incarnation. The hallmark of an infinite Creator is variety; therefore, one may expect to find an unique pattern of experience, of lessons and of services within each seeker of truth. Thus, each need not be the same to be equal in will and in faith.

Is there another query, my sister?

Carla: No, no really, I just *(inaudible)* why some people have *(inaudible)* because they can't deny their faith, while other people, *(inaudible)* hope *(inaudible)*. Perhaps could it be that some types of faith *(inaudible)*, just different types of faith?

I am Q'uo, and am aware of your query, my sister. In some cases this is so. However, it is more generally the case that as each school will have the beginning, the middle and the higher grades within it, there are students for each grade, and each student will pursue a different course of study, in many cases while being within the same school. There are those who have learned some lessons well, and have not learned others as well. These are their challenges; these are their path; these become their service. Each learns at his or her own pace. Thus, each may serve as teacher to another that travels the same path.

Is there another query, my sister?

Carla: No, thank you very much, Q'uo.

I am Q'uo, and we thank you once again, my sister. Is there another query at this time?

Questioner: Can we engage in some chanting together?

I am Q'uo, and we would recommend that this would be well. We would suggest, however, that the channeling portion of this meditation be completed.

Questioner: *(Inaudible)*?

I am Q'uo. We have chosen this vibration for this particular group. It is spelled in your English language with a "Q," then your apostrophe, followed by a "U" and an "O." This group was curious as to the meaning of this vibration and after some period of time asked us about it, and we responded that we have chosen this vibration for this particular group in order to cause it to ask "Who was Q'uo", for within your Latin language it was discovered by this group that "quo" was "who." We are an amalgamation of two social memory complexes or races of beings which have answered the call of this group and which takes great delight in being able to speak through the instruments in this group and be of whatever aid is possible for us within your illusion.

At this time we shall take our leave of this group while watching, shall we say, and partaking in our own way with your chanting. We leave each in the love and in the light of the one infinite Creator. We are known to you as those of Q'uo. Adonai, my friends. Adonai. ☙

Intensive Meditation
October 25, 1990

(Carla channeling)

We are known to you as those of Q'uo. We greet you in joy and offer you blessings in the name of the love and the light of the one infinite Creator. As you well know, it is deemed by us an enormous privilege to be able to share with you in your concerns. As one becomes more and more refined in one's awareness of what a family truly is, perhaps of what remains of one's unwisdom one is most concerned. We have been concerned about your people for some time, as you know. And when we feel a call go forth, that enables us to try to be of service, it is as so someone from our family would be calling us, someone we love and would want nothing in the world more to do than to go to them to share their sorrow, ease their pain and strengthen their walk upon the path of the search for truth.

We are the privileged ones. We were able to be perceived by an instrument who was able somehow to receive concepts and to speak words which we find almost entirely appropriate. We would speak to you at this time about this as each of you is attempting to channel ever better. It is well not to regard words with an idea to their having one effect upon people. It is not hypocrisy to speak in a language of those whom you come to serve. It is not hypocrisy but kindness to use no more of emotion in your expression than the circle is able to accept without invoking either fear or guilt, which is actually a kind of fear. The silence itself will teach you better than that.

So we wish to be very careful to speak always in terms that have relatively little power within your illusion, insofar as they are emotionally charged. We do not say, for instance, the word "God." From time to time, because we are allowing the instrument freedom, it will speak that word. And it is acceptable to us. Of our own self we would prefer a less emotionally charged term. One that moves cosmology out of superstition and into a simple knowledge of how eternity creates itself. So we ask each channel, always, to hear and remember words and phrases that are particularly delightful; we may be able to use them. Remember, we came to light as experiences that gave you joy, that fired your passions and that created the purest you that you have yet been. Move always back into these things that are your strength, your gifts. And one of the gifts of a channel needs to be that of grasping the nuances of vocabulary. This is not a group to which we must lecture, for each is already quite aware, for the most part, of this helpful information that it is well to be reminded again and again, that as servants of men and as sons of the one infinite Creator it was given to you to be the humblest, to be the least, to be strong enough in self that such things are irrelevant to your state of mind. The path asks a great deal for one who begins it. Little by little, untruth must be slugged off as if it were dead skin. Those blockages which could always be blamed on a childhood are suddenly those blockages for which you are responsible. Because you know how to clear them. You also know the kind of work and time that this effort will take. But we exhort you to continue. Those who seek the path of spirit must also seek the path of discipline. For the time to do spiritual work is always now, not tomorrow, not last week but right now.

[And I spoke with channels], each of you has begun that process of realizing the responsibility of policing yourself, of gauging for yourself, not the quality of the message, but only the quality of the preparation. This instrument, for instance, has never been satisfied with its preparation. We shall not give our opinion of this, as this instrument does not want to channel it. However, it is well not to assume that you now have become good of channeling, ever, anymore then you can reach your limits as an artist in any work of art, in any work of creativity, in any work where imagination and craftsmanship work hand in hand. It is only necessary to remember all that comes through you, because you have tuned yourself to your innermost self, the self that loves [without sin]. Often against its own will, but loves and loves and loves.

We are ready at this time to transfer the contact to the one known as K. I am [*(sounds like)* Mantuk], and I am one of those of Q'uo.

(K channeling)

I am Q'uo, and greet each of you once again in the love and the light of the Creator and this instrument. We are aware of this instrument's weariness and shall therefore speak more briefly than usual, but wish to continue upon a subject of the concerns that each of you have: in your performance, in your integrity and in your desires to communicate as clearly and accurately as possible the concepts you receive as you [serve as vocal channels].

There is concern in this group, especially among those less experienced, such as this instrument, with regard to concepts that they are either not translating, shall we say, as accurately as may be desired, or that are missed all together. We know this is not an altogether unknown occurrence for those with more experience also. We wish to encourage you in your efforts in this regard to seek to grasp those concepts which seem the most clear to you. And if there is a concept that you have difficulty in grasping, we urge you simply to let it go, not consider it lost, for if it is part of the message that we wish to bring to you, we will bring those thoughts back again.

We urge you each to be diligent in the continued scrutiny of your own lives as you continue what we consider to be the most important work of those serving as vocal channels; that is, the work upon yourself, the process of becoming ever more transparent, where you become more and more transparent in yourselves. The concepts that are communicated to you will flow through more clearly, more easily and naturally and there will be less blockages within yourselves to help with the progress. Everything that you experience in your life you experience as an end result, that which is passed through many and various filter systems which you have set up for yourselves. You are aware of this process.

As you continue in your efforts to know yourself, you'll become more and more conscious from the way this process operates and will become more and more able to consciously choose that information which you wish to receive from all that is available to you. Processes will become less automatic, shall we say. And you will find yourselves able to incorporate more and more of life as the experiences and energy of the entire universe that is around you enter yourselves. All of this will aid you in your work as vocal channel, as this work is, indeed, that part of your journey along the path.

We would at this time transfer to the one known as Jim, and thank this instrument for the efforts she has made in sustaining this contact this evening. We are known to you as those of Q'uo.

(Jim channeling)

I am Q'uo, and greet each in love and light once again. It is a privilege to work with each instrument this evening. We feel that we have made progress with the one known as K, and the ability to generate concepts which are complex in nature and which continue a logical thread of thinking, developing it with further information and illustration as the contact continues. We are very grateful to be able to enlarge that which we offer in this instrument and we would commend her perseverance. At this time it is our privilege to ask if we may speak to any queries which are upon the minds of those listening.

(Only portions of Carla's questions have been transcribed.)

Carla: I have one. Actually, are you aware personally *(inaudible)* who was able *(inaudible)* are you not happy *(inaudible)*. This is the feeling I have got all along.

I am Q'uo, and am aware of your query, my sister. We scan ourselves for permissiveness. We are, shall we say, most happy to be able to make any kind of contact whatsoever with an entity who wishes to serve as an instrument. If we are able to make ourselves known and are able to speak the simplest of concepts through a new instruments, we feel as do those of your planetary sphere who become parents, shall we say, in that we have a new opportunity through which to offer concepts which, though they are, as it has often been said, ever and always the same, yet are a means by which at least one entity shall experience the possibility of being in service in a way which we find most helpful. The concepts which we offer are, as you have surmised, of a layered nature, as are all concepts within the creation, for all evolves from the one great original Thought of love. This one simple thought of a creation made of love, generated by love, formed in that fashion is that from which all multiplicity [depends]. Thus, when we speak through any instrument we offer that which is the instrument's comfortable level of ability to perceive and to transmit in a fashion which corresponds in clarity and precision to the crystallized nature of the instrument through whom we speak.

You ask if we have had any opportunities to utilize instruments who were able to perceive each nuance which we have to offer. We are sure that you shall not be surprised to discover that the answer to this query is no, for that which we have to offer is beyond the ability of any entity which depends upon words for communication to express. Language itself is a barrier. However, we accept the limitations, both of language and of the understanding, if you will pardon the misnomer, of each entity in its previous knowledge and experience in the areas in which we speak. It is not our intent to give information that is minutely illustrated with each possible nuance. In certain instances and at certain times it is helpful to be able to describe the concept in finer and more precise terminology, using terminologies which are especially apt. However, what we wish most in these communications is to repeat, in whatever manner is helpful to a student, the simple nature of the creation and the strong and simple relationship that each has to each other and to the one Creator, to the creation, to all things, that this relationship is one which endures, that there will always be mystery, that there is always loving support for those who venture into the dark and mysterious night of the soul. Thus, in short, our answer to your query, my sister, is that though we seek to refine each instrument's ability to perceive that which we have to offer, we rejoice at every word and concept which we are able to transmit through any instrument.

Is there another query, my sister?

Carla: Just a comment … The reason that I felt that this was true is that one of the best channels I know …

The other question is … I really would not know how to speak to this … And I wonder if I have …

I am Q'uo, and I am aware of your query, my sister. This is a query which would be interesting to investigate at any time in which there was the proper energy, shall we say, to move deeply into the nature of the creation, and its relationship to each entity in your third-density illusion. We may recommend that this might be one topic that could be explored during the workshop for contact, shall we say. For there would be at that time the interest and the opportunity to exchange points of view that may be illuminating to all concerned.

I am Q'uo, we are grateful to you once again, my sister. Is there another query at this time?

Carla: The other question is about free will …

I am Q'uo, and am aware of your query, my sister. If it would be helpful to you in your preparation for one of these sessions of working to make a conscious dedication to open the instruments and the self freely, then this would be well. In our way of perceiving your desire to serve as instruments, we see that this commitment has been made when the commitment to serve as an instrument has been undertaken. Because the first work of the instrument is upon the self and the clearing of and balancing of those energy centers in need of such is undertaken, this, of necessity, means that each wishing to serve as an instrument presents itself, and its course of study, which is the self, freely. Thus, we see no problem with the concept that you have called "pot luck," though it is oftentimes more helpful to each within the circle of seeking here [that] there has been an agreement upon a general area of investigation for the evening. We are happy to work with each instrument, even when there has been no specific designation for a topic agreed upon.

Is there another query, my sister?

Carla: No, thank you.

I am Q'uo, and we thank you, my sister. Is there another query?

Carla: I would just like to know …

I am Q'uo, and we are grateful, my sister, for your dedication to this work as well. At this time, we feel that we have both exhausted the queries and the participants in this circle of seeking. We thank each for offering the self as instrument for our humble words and thoughts. We send you our greetings and our blessings upon your journeys which move each of you in ways which are not always easily understood nor easy to assimilate. We commend you upon the dedication with which you undertake each of your days within this illusion. At this time we shall take our leave of this instrument and this group. We are known to you as those of Q'uo. Adonai, my friends. We leave you in the love and the light of the one infinite Creator. ✷

L/L Research

L/L Research is a subsidiary of Rock Creek Research & Development Laboratories, Inc.

P.O. Box 5195
Louisville, KY 40255-0195

www.llresearch.org

Rock Creek is a non-profit corporation dedicated to discovering and sharing information which may aid in the spiritual evolution of humankind.

ABOUT THE CONTENTS OF THIS TRANSCRIPT: This telepathic channeling has been taken from transcriptions of the weekly study and meditation meetings of the Rock Creek Research & Development Laboratories and L/L Research. It is offered in the hope that it may be useful to you. As the Confederation entities always make a point of saying, please use your discrimination and judgment in assessing this material. If something rings true to you, fine. If something does not resonate, please leave it behind, for neither we nor those of the Confederation would wish to be a stumbling block for any.

CAVEAT: This transcript is being published by L/L Research in a not yet final form. It has, however, been edited and any obvious errors have been corrected. When it is in a final form, this caveat will be removed.

© 2009 L/L Research

Sunday Meditation
October 28, 1990

Group question: We need a sharp definition of the universe.

(Carla channeling)

I am Hatonn. Greetings to all of you in the love and the light of the infinite Creator. We cannot tell you how much we appreciate and are grateful for this opportunity to attempt to serve you, asking you always to remember that we are fallible and prone to error, as anyone with opinions must be, and acknowledge himself to be.

We would speak to a subject which is closer to our area of interest than most, as we have been, in our years of service with the Brothers and Sisters of Sorrow, attempting to grasp the distortions, solutions and thoughts that entities have had in this area. Perhaps we would phrase our definition of creation or the universe by speaking firstly of the entire universe, and then only secondly of the local phenomena and locally observed phenomena.

The Creator, in a very literal sense, is the creation, as it is in its pure state single and containing all that there is. The most gratifying way to look at the mathematics of the eternal is to gaze at one's own feelings about that which is eternal. One may make certain logical assumptions: the creation is all one place; the creation is all one time. The creation is the active portion, itself infinite, of the intelligent infinity which is called Love, or the Creator, or Christ consciousness, or whatever term most aptly describes each entity's own vision of the Creator. To put it another way, the creation, seen without distortion, is completely unified, from the sinew and bone, all the way through evolutionary patterns. To put it another way, the creation is that infinite space that the Creator has called into manifestation. It has in a cosmic or galactic way created a Oneness through diversity. This is a third-density vision of the Creator. Each density pictures the Creator less anthropomorphically and more realistically, because as the truth recedes before you, you find yourself more aware of the creation of the Kingdom, both without and within.

Consequently, a sharp definition in third-density vocabulary would be that creation is that limitless and ever-expanding area of light that surrounds infinite intelligence in its passive state. The Creator in its passive state, though the originator of love, and having created by love, should also be seen to be love—love creating love—and in this great love, offering to each entity the freedom of opportunity to choose that which we wish to do.

Those who have studied, meditated and worshipped long upon the Creator of humankind have, more often than any other way, apprehended the Creator as light. This is, in fact, neither Creator nor creation, but rather love bonding with free will and deciding to build, create or manifest a series of illusions helpful to those sparks of the Creator which were before all worlds were, and which shall be after all worlds are not anymore. Thusly, the mathematics of the eternal must reckon with only one number, and that is the number one, for the creation is infinite, full of creative power, and continually expressing itself in spiritual ways to those who open the door requesting that information.

The free will of each entity is called the first distortion. In actuality, it is the first distortion in the human drama. That is, each of us decides and chooses to eat of the apple, the symbol of good and evil. Once entities are aware of the duality of each day as opposed to the unity of the truth, it becomes more difficult to imagine, ideate or allow such a simple concept as the Creator being that area of light, infinite in nature, which contains all manifestations of consciousness which the Creator has offered. It is a changing set of illusions, each of which is biased toward that which has been called spiritual evolution or consciousness. These lessons are not easy, and they are extremely time-consuming, taking many, many lifetimes.

So, the paradox here is that each of you has two clocks within. One kind is humankind's time. The other clock is a face with no numbers and no hands, no digital readout, simply a blank, that is the eternal now under which all things fall. This is our witness to the Creator and its love in building this universe that its active sparks then kindle in their hearts the power to choose again and again to love where hate would be more normal, to console when you felt least like consoling, to remain forgiven, and especially self-forgiven. If we do aught else, we are criticizing our Creator, as well as ourselves; if we argue or are in contention with another, this not only expresses our views, it also separates us from love, and thereby, from the Creator.

The largest problem that we have in speaking to you about the universe is that we see that universe as a live organism, whereas you tend to see the universe as that which is static, as an inert entity. This circle of light, if we may call it that, about the Creator, is anything but careless. As the Creator brooded over the sea and caused a living environment for learning, so the Creator in each entity may be found by that entity as it reviews that which has increased the light and radiance flowing through them, and that which has decreased the light and radiance flowing through them.

It would be extremely difficult, at the level of instrumentation and discourse as well as philosophy that your science now offers, to give a particularly specific view of eternity, as the only so-called number that is reckoned with is one. Because the creation is an infinity, it can only be one thing, for there are no numbers in infinity except one to build a mathematics upon one, or one over one, that being love over light creating manifestation, and light moving towards love, creating humankind's experience. There is more upon this subject, but we realize the time is not as short as we think it is when we speak.

The way of looking at the universe from a standpoint of humankind is interesting, inarguably so. However, it does not have the advantage of realizing the absoluteness of the Creator of eternity and of the self. It attempts, each day, to make some kind of difference, moving along what this instrument would call an inherent talent or gift, that is, the yearning and the pulling towards this unity. All pilgrims are on a road bound for home. They have been spendthrifts; each of you has in some symbolic or literal way created much confusion. It is also possible to create non-confusion, contentment and hospitable feelings towards all.

When one stays within the illusion that is available for measure by instrumentation by your scientific instruments, one sees not that which is, that is, varying energy forms within which the light of self-consciousness has moved forward.

At this time, we would wish to transfer this contact, and in order that each entity may practice the experience of receiving contact, we shall simply say, "We are now transferring this contact." We wish you love and light through this instrument. We are those of Hatonn.

(Unknown channeling)

I am Hatonn, and I am again with this instrument. We have been asked to finish these thoughts through this instrument, and then move the auditory instrument to another.

The goal of each pilgrim is, of course, to arrive at home. That is the prodigal's dream. Now, entities are not brought to this place, or moved from second density in this place to third density in this place, in order that they might play in the garden, although many do so, remain innocent, and are always ready for graduation. But it is a portion necessary to this illusion that it make logical sense. The logic of the universe, though it cannot be explained, is visible. The atoms that form compounds of atoms which form cells, and gradually the manifestation of the entire being, are those forces irresistible to the entity which seeks.

However, if one seeks within the plane or density which you call third density upon your planet Earth, one will learn that which humanity has to teach you, which is no inconsiderable thing. However, contemplation, reading, writing, is the way of a person that finds spiritual food in these activities *(inaudible)*. However, within this illusion the natural laws do distort eternal truths into observed truths; that is the key to that which is most difficult for scientists and mathematicians. When dealing with this illusion from whatever perspective, one discovers at the end of the inquiry a remaining mystery which is an inherent part of an universe which is noumenal, where things not making sense and becoming paradoxes is simply a sign that the pilgrim has an awareness of its own growth processes.

Mathematics itself is extremely precise within this local illusion. However, just as one measures extremely low temperatures by using Kelvin numbers, so can we describe the universe using a different kind of measurement, having, however, to do with the concept of heat. It is doubtful, though possible, that there is an entity with enough of a vision to create social change by invention. This has occurred many times among your peoples, and will occur again. And so we continue in a multitude of questions, experiences and emotions. These are local distortions. They are of interest to the Creator, but often the use of the gifts of the spirit create the beautiful bond of love and love itself, or love divine.

Just as entities cannot channel our thoughts without words, just so can we not avoid distortion using terms that are not only of this density or local illusion, but are also not informed by the central spiritual core of faith. So a choice is left for each pilgrim to make. Although you cannot prove it, do you feel that your path of service brings you onto holy ground? This is part of the definition of the universe in its active phase; that is, that entities will be drawn by spiritual gravity at a variable speed depending upon the resistance, conscious or unconscious, of the entity. Experience hones and clears and forgives many things for which it has held itself responsible. This is moving from the life and death nature of third density to a more enlightened point of view, in our opinion.

One final note: the creation is quite simply a mystery. We do not know, truly, of the first things, any more than any baby in any crib can know of the of affairs of the day. They hear only one thing; each of us hears the sorrow of your people. And so we come to give you not only hope, and not simple homilies, but also workable and efficient exercises for moving the consciousness back to that place where it was in meditation when you were living in eternity. As you love one another more and more, your own subjective universe becomes more and more lovely and spacious.

Thusly, speaking as to a mathematician, who asks this query, we may say that much of mathematics is quite capable of manipulation of various minerals, gasses and liquids, of creating environments which the Great Self or the Creator and the individual co-creator have decided that which it wishes to do as a path of service. In some there are two definitions of the universe. One definition is absolute, without any space or any time, being as all one thing. The creation is intelligent and infinite and kindly towards those who seek the spiritual path which leads to radiance and servanthood. Self-aggrandizement, fear of losing one's reputation, and other such concerns, are for those who do not feel that the Creator speaks to them in the silence of their hearts.

In the creation of the Father all things are truly one. This instrument clasps another's hand; that apparently is as close as two entities can be. However, it is in the deep mind, not in the second-density body that you use, that information regarding you as an imperishable individual is stored, and this deep mind cannot be uncovered except by meditation, spending some time daily doing inner spiritual work.

For us to know intelligent infinity and to experience what this instrument would call holiness, one must gaze from a viewpoint of informed compassion. In this particular density you are learning more and more how to love each other, an absolute necessity preceding the day when there shall be a new Heaven and a new Earth. However, its only newness will be that it is entering third-density space/time at the particular time during which another third density should begin. So, like truth, part of the Creator is truth itself, absolute and unified, without space, without time and without polarity. From a human perspective, a local environment is quite various, and not a possessor of large truths, but only of creating a vast array of confusions.

We ask each to allow oneself to feel this light, this living creative light as it moves through your body to the heart chakra. As you breathe in, visualize and begin to feel this. As you breathe out, breathe out fatigue, worry, illness. It is always being requested by your people to realize many phenomena—past life experiences, karma that is still owed, and so forth. However, neither in metaphysical or godly time, nor in group consensus time, is this possible. Thus, we always suggest meditation, but more than that we suggest the singing for joy, and the becoming aware—when there is a sharp sound, a knock at the door, a telephone call, the ringing of a bell that you can hear, a honk, any sudden sound through the day that can be used as a reminder—of the state of mind you have had during and shortly after meditation, as compared with the last several minutes or hours of daily attitude.

So, the mathematics of infinity are done all with one. The mathematics of local areas of space/time are set up by the Creator and each spirit as it is tossed as a spark from a great hearth, the great transfigurational furnace of faith. There is a saying upon this instrument's wall, "All is in the All, and the All is All." We are all one being; the rest is illusion.

We are impressed by this entity's query, for it shows that the entity is familiar, instinctually, with new thoughts and new ideas upon the nature of metaphysical mathematics. It would, of course, be metamathematics, but it has its possibilities, although we find it doubtful that any could carry them forward. But you do live, moment by moment, in eternity, in infinity, in any Kingdom of Heaven, if so you wish it to be. That is an absolute. Resist or refuse faith, unconditionally, and you are left in believing those artifacts of which mankind has been the author. Of the two sources, the former is by far the more trustworthy and accurate.

Again, there is still more upon this subject, but we realize that we have worked quite a bit overtime, as we heard your machine ending some time ago, so we shall say that which is not yet said, that is the remainder, shall we say, of the paragraphs, the theme of which was offered in one sentence, a more complete discussion and a fuller grasping of the entire notion of there being a universe as opposed to there being that which seems to be. Both of those things happen to be true of the creation.

One thing is for sure, all things are made of love, and free will acting on love to produce light which can create and manifest matter. May you love each other; then you shall learn more and more about the Creator, and you will prefer the mystery of the mathematics of one over the finity of ideas which humankind creates and the artifacts it produces, for like the clay of your physical vehicles, they also will become obsolete, not for any specific reason of age, but simply because it is the nature of things.

We would like at this time to transfer the contact, if we may do so, for the ending of the session. We have attempted a sharp and precise definition and found ourselves in a great deal of trouble with vocabulary, for that which is eternal has concepts for which in your density you have no way of describing. The best we can do is to point you in the general direction of the truth you seek, and then build a wall that you can climb over easily. You can climb over that wall and rest at any time. But those who wish to work for the Creator are zealous, and loving and sharing. When we see this, we become humble before each of you who has achieved true harmony, for you have moved from truths to truth, and you have begun to operate in your everyday life according to spiritual principles, moving from the many to the One.

We will now transfer. We are known unto you as Hatonn, and we thank you again, and greet each in the greatest love. I am Hatonn. We now transfer.

(Unknown channeling)

I am Hatonn, and am once again with this instrument. We *(inaudible)* that a precise definition of infinity *(inaudible)* been possible for *(inaudible)* itself, the use of an inexplicable, mathematical *(inaudible)* may well be those due to the nearness of this particular planet's negative vibration until the fourth-density light is here. That light hurts those who are not ready to be able to enjoy it. Consequently, we who wish to share with you the joy and the strength of faith, and the life of service, wish each to know that it is no shame or burden unique to yourself, that there are many seeming difficulties in the life. It seems as though one goes through truth after truth after truth, until one becomes fearful that there is no truth. My friends, there is truth, but within your culture there is very little truth. Consequently, if you are always honest, you are being as rebellious and as courageous as any warrior, making yourself however to a *(inaudible)* that may well come to you for living a life motivated by faith. Do not let this disturb you, for you are prodigal sons and daughters, and you are being called home, *(inaudible)* sparks of the great Creator. Eventually you shall add your spark to the infinite and illimitable light, that creative light which many call prana, that moves through your spiritual body, and has good symbols for allowing one to begin to assess one's own behavior.

We encourage the use of discernment and the use of truths. We encourage that you not be dismayed when you discover that a truth is no longer valid. This simply means that you have gone through the uncomfortable process of spiritual growth. But always remember, in order to express the universe's high density you must attempt to live consciously and mindfully in the present moment, which is eternal. This is why we ask that you say a very, very short prayer whenever you are reminded by any loud noise that you are indeed more than glued to the desk that you are sitting at, or the place where you are standing or reclining. Each of you is a spiritual warrior.

We wish to take the world of materialistic thought and implant within the hearts of those present the love and the sharing of bounty. This is not wrong, it is simply that it does not work within a life that the most helpful life is that of cheerfulness and happiness, but rather one of suffering that great change of attitude which creates the choice of the loss of innocence by the desiring of the fruit of the tree of good and evil. You each have that choice; you could have remained a part of the unselfconscious, latent or inactive portion of the Creator. Instead, you set off upon a great adventure, a prodigal adventure, with a fortune to spend and time and energy and talent, the time for polarizing by praying, loving, giving, sharing.

We truly hope that this had aided each of you, and if there is more information requested, we shall be glad to comply, but we are conscious of this entity's informing us that we have talked too long. Consequently, we leave now to move to any questions that you may have. Have you any questions?

(Pause)

Since there are no questions that have been vocalized in this meeting, we shall be glad to await any questioning that you may have at a later date. It is such a great privilege to be with each of you we are sorry to leave, yet joyful in that you have called us to you. We thank you, and offer thanksgiving for entities such as yourselves who are aware of the dreamlike quality of so-called consensus reality, and are therefore forced to consider the mysteries that surround us.

In that mystery lies no thing that makes intellectual sense. In that mystery which is both Creator and creation, things simply are, and each of you, recapitulating the state of the universe, are. Everything is an I AM, a Yahweh, that so seldom is one able to minister to oneself. Listen to those about you struggling with truth that have had an end, or will soon, and help them to see that there is no punishment involved, but only the giving of a greater opportunity. That is all, for now.

Once again we thank you, and leave you in the love and the light of the infinite Creator. May you know that you are in that circle of light. May you know that you stand upon holy ground. May you always feel free to ask for help, for all those who love you, incarnate and discarnate, truly enjoy being of service, for by this they become freer and freer to roam the creation within one's head at will. May the truths lead you to the truth.

We are known to you as Hatonn, and leave you in love and light. Adonai vasu borragus. ☥

L/L Research

L/L Research is a subsidiary of Rock Creek Research & Development Laboratories, Inc.

P.O. Box 5195
Louisville, KY 40255-0195

www.llresearch.org

Rock Creek is a non-profit corporation dedicated to discovering and sharing information which may aid in the spiritual evolution of humankind.

ABOUT THE CONTENTS OF THIS TRANSCRIPT: This telepathic channeling has been taken from transcriptions of the weekly study and meditation meetings of the Rock Creek Research & Development Laboratories and L/L Research. It is offered in the hope that it may be useful to you. As the Confederation entities always make a point of saying, please use your discrimination and judgment in assessing this material. If something rings true to you, fine. If something does not resonate, please leave it behind, for neither we nor those of the Confederation would wish to be a stumbling block for any.

CAVEAT: This transcript is being published by L/L Research in a not yet final form. It has, however, been edited and any obvious errors have been corrected. When it is in a final form, this caveat will be removed.

© 2009 L/L Research

Sunday Meditation
November 4, 1990

Group question: The question this evening has to do with the concept of worship. What is worship, especially in regards to the one Creator? What kinds of worship are there, besides the kind that we're familiar with in church? How does worship affect us, and how we can enhance this effect?

(Carla channeling)

Greetings and blessings to each from the Brothers and Sisters of Sorrow of the principle known to you as Q'uo. The joy that we feel when we are called to your meeting to attempt to begin to examine the question that is at the heart of that which we come to share is a great privilege for us, in addition to the privilege of sharing in your selfhood, your meditation, your seeking, your tolerance of the illusion that is about you, your desire for harmony, and your single-minded desire to serve in love and faith and praise, thanksgiving and prayer.

The one known as Hatonn has been requested by the instrument because of that which the instrument does not itself understand, and it is part of that which we would speak of this evening, that when this ideation moved into the floor of this instrument's conscious thinking, it did not doubt its own instincts. There are reasons for the one known as Hatonn to be with this instrument as the energy, once again, is quite low in the group. The placing of the meditation in low energy timing is a choice that you have made because of the schedules among your people, the appointments, the details, the needs to be here and yonder. We hope this is subject for some thought.

We would turn now to the question at hand this evening, the question of worship, in what it consists, what its various subgroupings may be as to type, what function it plays, and how it can be encouraged as well as begun. We would like to begin with a seemingly shallow linguistic point, yet we feel that this damaging translation of the holy work most familiar to your culture is in the present instance, and in regard to the present question, misleading and even damaging. There are many urgent requests from those whom you call, since in any and all religious paths, but especially within your Judeo-Christian culture, the basic emotion laden word that is almost always misunderstood when read, as it has been misunderstood when translated, is the word "fear." In worship, there is not fear; in worship, there is a surrender, without fear, and without knowledge of that which is to come.

Having chosen the path of service to the infinite Creator by means of service to others, why would any entity make such a choice? There are humane and humanitarian reasons to care for one's fellow man, but not to feel that it is necessary to surrender the heart, the mind, the soul, the strength and the life to a voice which cannot often be heard, but which must be taken upon faith by its outer garments of manifestation. The fear of the Creator is simply awe and wonder, and fortunate is the entity who has released itself from all fear, for only within this illusion which you experience is there this fear of the Creator. This is simply a distortion of that love which is so great that the desire to serve this Creator fills one with awe.

Fear, of any one, any thing, any circumstance or any idea indicates that there is preparatory work still to do within the boundaries of the illusion which you now enjoy. The illusion is placed before you not only in a day-to-day manner, but in subtle and myriad ways. Your very consciousness, that is, that consciousness of which you are aware, is or can be constantly informed as to what means of service lie before you. In order to reach this consciousness of awe and wonder, there must be a variable amount of your time spent in whatever kind of contemplation reveals and manifests to you personally the most information about the state of your mind, your emotions, your physical vehicle and your consciousness.

Within that which is called the negative path, the consciousness more and more begins to conclude that all power, all glory, indeed, all of the creation resides within the consciousness of the self. Insofar as this conclusion is reached, it is identical to the conclusion reached by those who serve others. The negative path, however, chooses to worship not that which created this universe experienced, but the self for containing all that there is. Those who can handle this concept in a positive manner are few. There is no true surrender, no true desire to do the will of the Creator, but rather the Creator and the self, so co-mingled, become a non-thing, a non-thought, and in the end, an unworkable path of service.

Let us move to another way of gazing at this question. Within your social intercourse, one finds many, many ways of perceiving others, perceiving one's own thoughts, perceiving meanings which may be given to various manifestations, either mundane or highly spiritual, and your choice of accepting the reality of the self seems to include accepting the reality of the illusion. However, this is not, in our opinion, an accurate, logical conclusion. Can you control the wind of spirit, or must you allow the spirit, that living principle of the Creator, to move you? Many, many desires are those things which are natural to the natural entity, that is, the entity in an unawakened state. To people such as this, worship may well be important, but they see themselves as those who take advantage of the sacrifice of another without whose sacrifice there would not be a life or consciousness continued beyond this one.

So, you may see that which worship is not. Worship is not the pressing forward to one's goals, the satisfaction of one's desire to accumulate and amass those things which encourage happiness. Many have called devout love of many finite things various kinds of incorrect worship, that is, worship of those things which do not endure, and are therefore only able to be worshipped within this local and provincial illusion, so soon over. And if the entity who wishes to worship does so for any motive other than love, awe, amazement, joy and a seeking after truth, one has chosen that to worship which shall surely not last as long as the consciousness which at present inhabits your physical vehicle will last. Thus, if one worships a religion, a person, a goal within the illusion, one is worshipping in a negative manner, blocking the natural flow which the spirit intends to be available to you at all times, that is, the spirit of Love Itself.

Worship is that which underlies whatever complex or simple structure of personality and desire one has which manifests as an incarnation. Worship begins with the awareness that is known, but much may be inferred. Clues within the illusion that hint at one single Original Thought, which we call Love, or Christ, Christ consciousness, or the Creator, is a kind of firm ground upon which the self may stand as it gazes at, evaluates, discriminates and analyzes its own thoughts, feelings and emotions, until the self has concluded much about the nature of the self, the illusion and the program of lessons which was intended. Worship is that surrender to imperishable and perfect light and love which is the Creator. Worship is a blind thing, a shot felt to be in the dark, having an unknown target. Worship is that gathering of purified emotions which moves the entity from considerations of the milieu of the physical vehicle to considerations of the milieu of the imperishable light being which you have found within yourself as the deepest portion of yourself.

There is a great difference between love and worship. Those who seek to love will in the end find all that they desire because of a great steadiness and firmness of desire. But neither the leap of faith nor the intensification of desire can move that true self within one to that which is basically a protection, for the Creator is within you, yet within you cannot be seen by you. Thus, for all except the most non-literal and lyrical of mystics, worship generally consists in an attitude of surrender in purified emotion to that which is considered the source of the being, and of all that there is.

There is a necessity in most to objectify worship so that there is an identifiable object, idea or person onto which one may reflect one's deepest desires to serve. And as no one within an illusion can know adequately how to serve any entity in the best way for that entity, the worshipful or faithful entity watches and waits and prays and does all that it does for the love of the object of that worship, the infinite One.

In sum, worship is that gathering of purified emotion which kneels in surrender to the purity itself, the beauty itself, the truth itself, the love itself, that is the Creator. The outgrowths of worshipful, faithful living, moment by moment, are those things which many may perceive to be most beautiful and hard won contests against the temptation to make sense within the narrow definitions of your mind, of that which is infinite as the object of worship is infinite.

There are identifiable types of worship. There are three main categories of worship. The first is worship without an object. When one moves into the frame of mind that says that all that there is is the Creator, and all is to be worshipped, one has failed to identify any object of worship beyond the phenomena experienced by the self. The closest name that you have to this type of worship is pantheism, that is, the thoroughgoing worshipful attitude towards all that one beholds, but with the unspoken inference that when one comes to the end of all that there is, that is the limit of the Creator. Thusly, with those who worship without an object, many see difficulties connected with the inability to move beyond a certain point in evolution of spirit without either a subjective or reflective object of worship upon which one may focus again and again and again, infinitely, in each present moment.

The worship of an object, or symbol, which indicates to the entity a living and participating Creator, is most, most helpful in the simplification and clarification and lucidity of what one is aware of about one's self, for worship must be the worship of an entity for nothing or something. The unexamined thoughts and feelings and actions of many of your peoples create distortions which indicate that worship is a kind of hysteria within which one is able to release all the negative portions perceived subjectively within the self. This is not particularly helpful to the evolution of the individual's spirit. However, we mention both worship without an object, and worship of an object, as being somewhat helpful, for these are stages which may be traversed as the incarnate entity slowly begins to open the door to the possibility that the object of its worship is an utter and complete mystery.

True worshipful living is a high risk occupation. It is not a loop into the light, but rather a loop into darkness. The illusion creates an emotional, mental and spiritual twilight in which ideals, the purification of emotions from attachments, and the mindfulness of continuing awareness of the worship bloom in the darkness of blind faith. That is, the true worship is worship of a mystery; awe, wonder, a greater and greater subjective feeling of being held firmly by that which is not illusion, although one cannot understand it, so that the entity rests at last in a completely subjective and subjectively truthful journey. In this regard, worship may be seen as motion, motion of a metaphysical kind rather than a physical kind.

We would once again advise this instrument to peruse these thoughts upon worship, for in her nature, in order that she may be what she wished to be and do what she wished to do before incarnation, she has gifts of faith and will. This instrument, therefore, has little idea of what may form worship, what may begin a craving for impossible virtue, for it experiences these things as a portion of its nature, and in this it is not incorrect. However, most are aware neither of the surety of faith nor a complete surety of desire.

Knowing that one will receive what one desires, one attempts to desire the most whole, beautiful and truthful expression of the Creator that may by made available to it. The entire panoply of a culturally gutted civilization …

(Side one of tape ends.)

(Carla channeling)

… the choice of the intellectual to worship nothing or everything, both of which contain a weak strength of acceleration, although the vector is promising. Those who worship an object, but do not go beyond the literal object in itself, are those who do not yet desire to surrender to that which is, in the end, the unknown. Such entities have the need for structure, for certainty, surety, a firmness of intent which is the blossom of that structure, and many are those who have found the gateway to eternity in this way. But they are few, in that they have not become universal in their thinking, feeling and acting process.

It is to those who acknowledge that nothing is known, and yet who choose to be certain of those things which they feel as they consciously purify their emotions, that the sight of what this instrument would call the Kingdom, comes. There is no visualization of objects, such as being seated at the right hand of the Creator, or ruling, or judging, or being in some way a master of the creation. The one who wishes to develop the ability to worship must first square off against two illimitable concepts; that is, that nothing can be known, objectively; and that the self can be known by the self more and more through meditation, contemplation, analysis, prayer, and the observation of one's personality as it shows itself in any present moment.

Worship, then, is worship not only of the Creator, but of the mysterious and largely unknown Creator. The choice is then made, with no evidence whatsoever, to surrender to that unknown, for as one is aware one did not make oneself, one is aware that whatever the nature of the unknown, that unknown is responsible for one's being, one's continuance, one's imperishability and one's opportunities to express and manifest the glory of this mystery.

We realize we have only begun upon this subject. It is a large one, and because of this instrument's request to us, as it perceives the very large amount of material on this subject, we shall be satisfied to have begun. We would at this time transfer this contact. We are known to you as Q'uo, and for those of Hatonn, we bid you fond farewell as we leave this instrument. We are those known to you as Q'uo, and we would at this time transfer this contact.

(Jim channeling)

I am Q'uo, and greet each again in love and light. We would offer ourselves at this time in an attempt to speak to queries if there are any queries that we may address. May we begin with the first one at this time?

Carla: Yes, I have a question. In my teaching, I request that those who are working with me choose a symbol or an object to specify who they are in order that they may do work in metaphysical realms, but you suggest that true worship is worship of a mystery. Am I misguiding anyone by my method of teaching?

I am Q'uo, and am aware of your query, my sister. When an entity wishes to offer itself in the service which those present seek to offer, as the vocal channels, it is well to have a central concept or representation of this great mystery which is the Creator and the creation available to it to offer as the means by which unseen spirits may be challenged or hailed, shall we say. It is recognized that there is no concept or quality that can adequately summarize the infinite mystery of the Creator, yet the vocal channel does well to find a facet of this mysterious Creator by which it may approach the Creator, and through which it may offer the challenge to those contacts which would wish to speak through it. Though a concept may be fashioned, and an approach may be made, it is always known in the heart of each seeker that mystery is at the heart of each concept and each approach.

Is there a further query, my sister?

Carla: Just one, and I was asking this of Jim this morning. It is difficult for me to grasp that people honestly don't open their eyes, look around, take it in, and immediately feel the instinct of faith. Nor it is it understandable to me personally why people lack the intensity of desire to attempt to learn and serve at the very limit of their ability with a complete passion, because of this instinctive identification with the Creator, which is faith, and love and surrender, and willingness to serve, all sort of mixed into one. How can I brook this chasm in my own understanding, in my own failure to understand, in such a way that I can better serve? Because it's my blind spot.

I am Q'uo, and we are aware of your query, my sister. The central mystery of which we have been speaking is reflected in each entity that seeks the one Creator. Each approaches this path from an unique position. There is much learning within the life pattern of any entity that is quite incomprehensible to most other entities that may be acquainted with a specific entity and may wish to know more of that entity in order to draw closer to it in companionship, compassion and in common seeking.

That each of you contains mystery may be seen as a benefit or detriment depending upon one's point of view. Many feel more justified, shall we say, for lack of a better word, in their own idiosyncrasies, when they realize that others contain such as well, variety thus becoming an enhancement when looking at the qualities of the human species. If an entity is not comfortable with the mystery within itself, perhaps it will have more difficulty in adjusting to that which is mysterious within others, for there is much of what seems to be of—we allow this instrument to search—undependable nature that mystery represents to some entities.

However, when that which is known of others is explored, oftentimes it is seen that along with the differences between entities there is much that unites those of your population. Entities will pursue their paths of seeking in a conscious or in an unconscious fashion with the character of the seeking determined by forces which are unique to each entity. When it is realized that each entity is unique, relationships between entities and the attempt at understanding between entities will then be seen as doubly unique.

Is there a further query, my sister?

Carla: I just want to clarify what I think you said. I think that you basically implied that what I see as an instinct, as a part of the self that could not be denied, is that, but that is for the most part in other people covered. And further, you are intimating that a teacher for the most part teaches by being, not by what it says. Are these conclusions acceptable?

I am Q'uo, and though we have not specifically iterated our reply in such a manner, we find that the interpretation which you have made of our words is an interpretation which stands on its own as valid, in our humble opinion.

Though entities are most mysterious, each in his or her own way, much of this mystery, though remaining in a covered, as you have called it, condition, due to perhaps the lack of conscious seeking, would, even with active conscious seeking remain mysterious, not only to others observing such an entity, but to the conscious seeker as well, for this illusion which you inhabit is one which guarantees a great deal of mystery, since the unifying qualities and the fundamental concepts of the Creator, of the creation, and of each entity within the creation, are covered over, much as the earth beneath your feet covers the gems and jewels that may be found within your geological strata.

It is also well said that a teacher will provide the most effective instruction to those who learn from it, not so much by what it says, but by, as you have said, its very being, for it is the being that informs the working.

Is there another query, my sister?

Carla: I do have a trivial query, and then I'll shut up. I was struck throughout this contact by a change in your focus which prohibited me from using pretty words. I assume, as I did surrender, and I believe I was getting an accurate flow, that this had a purpose. Is it within the bounds of free will at this time for you to express the purpose of speaking in such a clinical manner of that which is at the heart of all passion, all life and all eternity?

I am Q'uo, and we are aware of your query, my sister. Before beginning this session we were aware that you felt some concern for your ability to channel in an undistorted fashion upon a topic which is quite dear to your own way of thinking and being, shall we say. Thus, we wished to facilitate the transmission of concepts by forming those concepts in a manner which would not continue to trigger this concern within your mind complex as you observed familiar phrases being utilized in the fashioning of this concept.

Thus, we attempted to speak in a manner which was not only somewhat foreign to you, but which would seek to describe this core concept in a manner which would be more acceptable to many entities upon the intellectual or analytical level that may come in contact with this information, and to the conveying of more objectively oriented concepts, that find an easier entry into the more emotional or, shall we say, heart-filled areas of the personal life pattern.

Is there a further query, my sister?

Carla: No, my brother, I suspect since you said that there is more, that we will be hearing more, and I will wait. Thank you.

I am Q'uo, and we again thank you, my sister. Is there another query at this time?

(Pause)

I am Q'uo, and we are most grateful for this opportunity of speaking to this group. Indeed, there is a good deal more information upon this topic, which we shall be happy to share with you at your request in your future gatherings. We are always happy to join this group, for we find that the queries from this group are fashioned from the desires of the heart and not just those of the mind or of the curiosity.

We shall at this time take our leave of this group. We are known to you as those of Q'uo. We would leave you in the love and in the light of the one infinite Creator. Adonai, my friends. Adonai. ✤

L/L Research

Intensive Meditation
November 8, 1990

Group question: The question is about faith.

(Carla channeling)

[I am Q'uo.] Greetings and blessings to you in the love and in the light of the one infinite Creator. As we work with each channel this evening, we wish each to know that there are those of the Confederation of Planets, which many prefer to call the angelic hosts, [who] will be with each. Those of the principle of Q'uo, which are of Latwii, shall be with the one known as Jim. That entity known as Laitos and that entity known as Oxal shall be meditating with the one known as K. And we find this instrument to be well guided by its own comforter.

How blessed it is to be in the company of those who seek to have that which the world can give them not, that which the world promises not, that which the world can never promise. It is a joy to us to experience your questing hearts. In each moment of anguish in the life experience, there has always been, sooner or later, that turning towards a quest for the truth of the spirit, a sincere desire to know the spirits well—in that dogged persistence of an absolute being in highly, worldly, mundane illusion, which is entirely relative. We would share some thoughts about that which we call faith, and we shall be doing so to each channel, in order that each may give its own special gifts to this very large subject which may well, if interest continues, be ongoing within this group for some time.

That which one calls faith has been, within your holy works, called, "Hope in things unseen." How difficult it is for you within your culture to hope in things unseen. The illusion all by itself, without the many distortions which have occurred in difficult and ambivalent polarizations among your peoples, is such that the contemplation of claiming an absolute, living by it, being willing to die for it as witness to the truth, is ludicrous. This is the outer environment in which you are attempting to become aware of your metaphysical, imperishable consciousness, that spark of the Creator which expresses its unity and hope, and all that may be expressed within your illusion.

Though you may be of little faith in your own estimation, the search itself is a search begun only in the blindness of faith. This is one of the elements of faith itself which creates a kind of meniscus or layer of resistance for those who wish to have faith. For if one claims faith, the world that is seen, the illusion that is perceived, is forever changed and not in ways which exemplify the search for happiness or the contentment of resting in a comfortable space. There are comfortable belief systems, systems which enable one to know all the truths all the time according to the subjective path of literal, dogmatic belief systems. However, that which each Christ that has come into your environment has offered is not a comfortable or happy journey. It is a journey begun on courage alone. It is a journey in which one persists by will alone. It is a journey which claims that which it does not feel with its whole heart, but which instead is felt as a hunch, an instinct, a bias. On these slender threads hang the beginning of a life in faith.

We would at this time transfer. We are known to you as Q'uo.

(K channeling)

I am Q'uo, and greet you in the love and light of the one infinite Creator. We return again to the same that is given in your homework. Faith is the substance of things hoped for, the evidence of things unseen. Now, you know that the essence of faith is that surety that each entity has without objective, tangible proof of same. This inner surety is the substance and evidence I have spoken of. There are many among your peoples who have not developed a conscious awareness of their own inner sense of that surety and choose to believe that they will accept and act on nothing unless they have objective, tangible proof of such—what man would call "scientific proof." What these entities are unaware of is that they accept many, many things on faith but do not realize it, for these beliefs have never been called into question. They pride themselves in not accepting ideas which seem foolish to them or to others, merely on the basis of a feeling of congruity within themselves.

The spiritual journey with each begins at that point when an entity feels this sense of congruity and acts on it for the first time. It may not be an obvious action but may be simply the acknowledgment of the feeling itself, the acknowledgment and the validity of a feeling. And it is at this point that faith becomes part of conscious action on the personal path. As each seeker continues to grow and develop, this capacity for faith, the ability to deny on the inner sense of congruence with an idea, is developed further and further, until each entity has created for itself its own personal collection of truths, that are based not on objective proof but on subjective assurance. The part of this process that each of you is aware of is the realization from time to time, the causes of obsolescence of some of these truths, when this first occurs. The faith of the seeker is often shaken, sometimes to a very great degree; especially, if this process occurs with truth that has been known long and deeply.

Sometimes, balance is never restored within the seeker, who then, as it is said, loses faith and never consciously returns to a path of seeking. For the undaunted, however, those who continue on the path despite their feelings of disillusionment, discouragement, despair, anger, pain and confusion, balance is eventually restored and the seeker begins to realize that truths, like faith, are not objective but subjective. As this concept is assimilated more and more, the seeker continues on its journey, developing more and more surely the ability to discern those truths which have the greatest degree of congruency for itself at that particular time. The capacity of faith is also further developed as a part of the same process, so that the seeker rests comfortably with the truth it finds, and grows with, and grows beyond, and finds others which it grows into.

Observing the ebb and flow of this process is part of the ebb and flow of All That Is. Throughout this process, the capacity of faith, although it grows stronger, unlike the truth which varies from time to time, remains the same. Now there are some, as you are aware, to whom this capacity comes most naturally, such as the instrument known as Carla. There are many among your peoples who possess this gift and have no awareness of the fact, but live their lives in a most simple, natural and harmonious manner.

These people may often be considered, by those among your peoples who have been taught by your societies to have a bias towards the strength of intellectual functioning, to be simple and perhaps of less value than their intellectual counterparts. There are many such peoples on your planet living an unconscious life within, in harmony with the natural rhythms, a very second-density life force in the planet itself. And as each here is aware, these beings have often made far greater spiritual progress than those others who pride themselves in demanding their [proofs].

Those entities, however, who have been the most strident in demanding objective, tangible verifications for their various beliefs, once having grabbed the door just a little, having dared to act in however small way on that first intuition that is acknowledged, once these doubters make their way, at first timidly along the path, and then more boldly, will also be those whose faith is strongest, because it has been so rigorously questioned at the start. These may also be ones who understand the process of faith to a much greater extent than those to whom it comes naturally, because, again they have questioned the process so deeply and may find opportunities to help those they find in situations such as they themselves once where.

At this time, we would transfer once again. We are known to you as those of Q'uo.

(Jim channeling)

I am Q'uo, and greet each again in love and in light through this instrument. We offer to those, whose path is well traveled or only just begun in the conscious sense, the concept of faith as that which shall be the rod and staff to steady the pilgrim on his journey. The faith with which an entity begins is a faith which is pure in its intention, is as yet innocent in its exercise, and which is full of the potential for engaging an entity's resources. And through this expression developing much of quality of character and of personality, primarily in the ways of the disciplining of the personality. For the seeker, no matter what place it may imagine itself to be, or may actually be upon its own journey of evolution, we have spoken this evening of that call of your faith which is recognized from within an entity as a kind of inner confidence that propels and sustains movement and exploration.

Faith is as truth, that which is subjectively experienced, that which an entity can affect by its own perceptions, [judgments] and beliefs. For the truest quality of faith that we can express in your words is an inner confidence that all is indeed well, that all entities and activities and interrelationships are proceeding with the same surety, rightfulness, purpose and completeness of expression. As the winds that blow upon the planetary surface in all seasons, as the sun which shines its warming and life-giving rays upon your planetary sphere, as sure as the earth which receives the [molding] effects of the wind and the fire, and as able to reproduce itself in any situation as is your waters that give a place of birthing to many forms of your second-density creatures.

This quality of faith is as sure as the procession of cycles of all kinds that are an expression of the evolution, not only of individuals but of planets, solar systems, galaxies and the one Creator as well.

Faith is, and this instrument discovers that that was our complete thought—faith is! We can give analogy after analogy, likening faith to those things which exist within your illusion seemingly without doubt, and yet faith is far more. It underlies all Creation, all activity. Oftentimes, it is ignored as one ignores the ground upon which one walks, the air which one breathes, yet it is. For those who would wish to study the concept of faith, he shall find that it permeates all of your existence as you know it.

Each entity exercises a faith in various things, various concepts, various entities, associations, relationships and exercises. Without the concept of faith, indeed, there would be little activity upon your planetary surface or within any life pattern. For there must be this basic quality that concerns the sense of self, the sense of the environment, the movement of the self through this environment in such and such a pattern. All of these things at the very, very basic level are taken as articles of faith.

"Faith in" is one of the primary concepts with which each entity begins each incarnation and each activity within the incarnation. What we would wish each entity to realize through the speaking that we have offered this evening is that this quality of faith, though everywhere expressing and mysterious at the same time, is that which may be affected and directed by the consciously seeking entity. That which is at one's disposal may be utilized evermore effectively with conscious attention, with the refining of one's disciplines of the personality of discrimination and perception. Thus, we do not introduce a new topic to any entity but only seek to make each entity aware that this quality is always in affirmation in some form or another within the life pattern. To take this quality and utilize it in a conscious fashion is much the same as refining the general characteristics of the bonfire, so that that which could be likened to the laser beam is then utilized in a far more precise and powerful fashion.

At this time we would wish to close this particular topic through the one known as Carla. We are those of Q'uo. We shall transfer at this time. I am Q'uo, and we thank this instrument, as always, for its scrupulous attention to request [certain] contacts whenever contacts are moved. The desire of an instrument to be the best it can is a self-fulfilling desire, as are all desires.

We would like to leave you with a thought that has many ramifications, and like most thoughts within the spiritual realm, it is not a logically acceptable thought. For within spiritual seeking, one of the great hallmarks is that of the inherent illogic according to the logical systems of humankind at this time. For we present you with a circular thought, a tautology, one which has nothing of logic in it, but, perhaps, may be more helpful as it contains a carefully observed situation. Faith is not possible in most cases without the profound and persistent …

(Side one of tape ends.)

(Jim channeling)

I am Q'uo, and continue. There is the tautology for circular argument concerning faith and will. It is the persistent and thoroughgoing will which leads each to wherever it truly desires within this illusion or outside of it. And so it is the will that enables faith. Be persistent, determined and ever hopeful in vocation of the will, no matter in what circumstance of mind, body or spirit. Will is impossible without the faith to persist in that will. Thus, faith and will are enabled by each other!

How does one move into a willing determination to see not the letter but the spirit of all that occurs and offers one catalyst? Your culture is so literal minded, that the very language which you use is being altered by the ruthless logic and limitation of a computer. This is informative, however, in that as one understands the methods whereby computers calculate their choices of the truth, thusly, it is that the mind complex has its mechanical functioning.

The mind complex is more than a computer, but that portion of the mind which entities most often use in the evaluation of catalyst is that of a computer. In a sense that computers operate according to a series of swiftly made choices, the analogy is most informative when gazing at the excellent qualities and the addictive qualities, which are one characteristic, seen from two different points of view of consciousness.

Within this illusion it is helpful to be able to reason and to make choices in a conscious manner. It is many times extremely helpful, and sometimes the only helpful suggestion that we may offer due to a momentary emotional or spiritual confusion, in attacking or analyzing the challenges and opportunities which catalyst presents. Thusly, it is well to grasp the nature of the mechanical workings of a mind. Just as you are in the illusion of choice, so is the mind created as a living computer which estimates the relative importance of all incoming catalyst.

It, and it alone, chooses the types of perception and the choice of those things to be perceived. For instance, you sit upon furniture. Yet, have you in any conscious manner considered the feelings of your integument? Each tiny portion and cell of your physical vehicle is, at this present moment, reporting pain, pleasure, coldness, warmth and a myriad of other details, along every single inch of the physical vehicle. Almost all of this catalyst tends to be ignored completely, gaining attention only if the program which you have accepted as your consciousness discovers within all the sensations that which may in some way fail to promote the continued health and welfare of the physical vehicle and its survival.

You are in a less illusory and imperishable way the choice-maker. It is not your intellect but you that chooses each perception of experience. Consequently, if there are those things which the mind has targeted for notice and prioritized heavily, and if those things do not redound to the strength, the love, the faith, the will in the path of seeking and service of the one infinite Creator, it is not the behavior which needs to change.

Were that so, you would be slaves. Slaves to computer programs within yourselves that cannot be changed. But you are not slaves, but free men. You have the will towards faith. You have the faith to use that will. If you wish to change, know that before any change can manifest, the actuality of the desires of the deep mind must first change in actuality and in practice. Those things, seen by any seeker to be those things which actively delimit and confuse spiritual search, have been noticed because they have been given priority as being relevant to the survival of an entity. There is a [thoroughgoing] process of realization of one's identity as apart from that of the physical vehicle that enables a much accelerated development of spiritual faculties and the disciplines of the personality.

The intellect is not a dictator, unless you accept that nothing can change the pain, the sorrow, and the various anguishes that have previously programmed the computer of your mind towards safety, security, self defense and caution. It takes a great deal of courage, given only by will and grace, to be able, consciously, to work at the reprogramming of the mode of perception used by the conscious mind; the reprioritizing of concerns from those things which seem vital at the mundane level; to value given to those things which, within your culture, would be dismissed as the musings of the [sophomore wise] school must be grasped and in actuality surrendered. The surrender of long held convictions, as to that which is of priority in life, will cause a kind of mental pain that is a result of the energy involved in delving into the conscious prioritizing portion of the self, and the specific reprogramming of the self towards the affirmative, positive, self-respecting, self-forgiving consciousness that has no part of the illusion in which you live.

My beloved, the journey that you take seldom requires a physical step, seldom necessitates a physical pilgrimage. For the impact of geography and novelty of experience is in and of itself trapped by the ruthless decisions of the programming of your mental capacity to notice this but not that, and that but not this.

Before we depart, although we did not feel within this group at this time the pressure of queries, we would, as always, open the meeting to any query which any might have. Ask us at this point anything that you wish, and we shall be most humbly grateful to share our most fallible opinion with you. Is there a question at this time?

(Pause)

Peace reigns within each of you. That is good. We appreciate the self-confidence that it takes to know when one must ponder and listen rather than forever thinking and questioning. For that which is of importance is that which will take much of your time to process from realizations to manifestations. And in that process, we of the Confederation of the Planets in the Service of the One Infinite Creator, or, if you prefer, we of the Angelic Host in Service to the Infinite Creator, are always with you.

You merely need mentally to request the strength of our vibration, and we shall join you in silence and faith and in determination. Yours are the choices, and they need not be made by an unquestioned intellect. Indeed, they must not be made by such. As you think within yourself in meditation daily, have no attachment to this process, for this process is not that which makes sense to the computer of your conscious mind. In meditation, those deep knowledges hidden beneath the veil, those sparks of the infinite One, which you all are slowly and gently given the opportunity[to receive], rise within the deep mind and cross the threshold in many ways, informing most deeply and most purely the faith, the will, and the journey without words and without steps.

We leave you to the excitement, the challenge, and the pain of the learnings you seek—the learnings of love, service to others, and the secrets of true manifestation of the consciousness of light. You may feel alone—you are not. Have you the faith to know that? You will feel often in error, bewildered, uncertain. These are often times of great growth. Reassess these times of seeming sorrow and despair. And as you begin to know the self that is love, much of what is now programmed within you will change and you will seem to die a little at a time. You are not dying, you are being born. Be persistent and judge yourself not. For the moods and the weather of your conscious being are inevitable, acceptable and necessary to the process of growth.

Cease the present moment, make it your own and seek evermore a purer priority of concerns. For you are a treasure. You must learn to cherish that treasure that is you, and to cherish and deeply adore the Creator who gave you its own being and then allowed each to make all of its own choices, to follow its own destiny, to move to its own rhythm and to experience its own truth. The Creator is love. And love alone would take this risk. Put yourself at the same risk. For you, too, create your experience.

We shall speak as long as you wish upon this multifaceted subject. You have only to inquire, either mentally or more formally. May we say, that though we do not mind the speaking to those concerns which you have, we do ask that if a group question is not vibrated that each of you mentally offer us permission to gaze within each, to find the most common and deep concern shared by the group. We would not infringe on free will. This permission, however, heals that infringement. And we ask each to take a moment at this time, retroactively to offer us that healing, for we would not wish to mislead you as to the ways this contact could be abridged. We must not infringe upon free will. Our concern is based upon the very stringent free will requirements of a contact such as ours.

We thank you for this acknowledgment of that [meaning] and the giving of permission. We thank you. We celebrate our unity, and together we turn towards the rising sun of an ever new day, the day of the spirit, in which that which has been dim comes to light, freeing the preceptor, to learn that which has been learned, and to hear for the first time new refinements that are possible in the [conduct] and the characteristics of blind programming, that were not available until summary [reprioritizing] has been accomplished. This is a multi-syllabic way of saying a very simple thing: "The road goes on forever." The road of seeking, the road of promise, the road that leads finally to self-knowledge of congruency with love itself, the great original Thought and Creator of all that there is.

We would leave you now in peace. A peace that you may begin to understand more and more. It is not the peace of your culture. It is neither sleep nor contentment. It is the peace of one who has chosen completely the dedication of self to the journey of seeking, the desire to become evermore aware of the true nature of the self, the growing hunger for the kingdom within.

May you be light hearted and merry as you suffer, and may you never forget your suffering when the gift of happy days is given to you. In this way, you may find much greater use of your catalyst and much quicker rate of acceleration of your spiritual evolution.

Oh, eternal beings, oh, blessed children of life, we leave you now in the love and the light of the one infinite Creator. Adonai. Adonai vasu. We are known to you as the principle of Q'uo. ❦

Sunday Meditation
November 11, 1990

Group question: We continue on this evening with information on the concept of worship.

(Carla channeling)

I am the principle known to you as Q'uo. We greet you in the love and the light of the one infinite Creator. It is a blessing to be among you and to be asked to serve in our humble way. We are, as always, eager to express our desire that we be considered as fallible, and not infallible, for we tend to catch the spirit of that which forms not in words, and our own spirit is still limited. Within the boundaries of these limitations, we believe our opinion to be fair, but subject at all times to the personal considerations of each, for each has a personal path to truth, to love and to service.

We are most pleased to be able to continue upon the subject of worship. The instrument known as Carla has the underlying alarm which expresses the emotion-laden thought that it has no concept of that which we wish to speak upon. However, we ask the instrument to steady itself, and to allow us to speak.

We spoke earlier of the three basic approaches to worship: worship of nothing, that is, worship without an object; worship of an object; and worship of mystery. The worship without an object runs contrary to the genetic structure of many of your races which in glad array make up the population of your sphere. To those within a highly technological culture and society, worship without an object is much like loving without an object. This creates confusion within entities such as yourselves who have been exposed to many, many objects. Thusly, although this path is useful to some, it is not easily conformed to the character of what you would call the Western or Occidental racial natures.

The worship of mystery cuts to the heart and spirit of worship, and without this instrument's being aware of it, its underlying nature is that of worship of the mystery, although it has successfully created an object in order that it may participate in refining the gifts of emotional intensity and unstinting compassion. Without the grouping or societal nature which is so deeply a portion of the character of your density—we must begin again with that sentence, we would correct the instrument. Without the gifts of faith offered to all people, but available only to a few, it once again is difficult to conceive of a passionate and active devotion. This is, however, an excellent type of worship for those who have a predisposition to mysticism, or love of mystery.

Thusly, what we would speak about at this working is the second of the three choices, or, as this instrument would say, the middle part: the worship of an object. The situation within manifestation—and we all dwell in various illusions and manifestations …

We must pause, for this instrument is moving in consciousness into sleep. We are sorry, and will encourage this instrument to move away from the unconscious state.

The situation within all the densities of manifestation is that of illusion. When we encourage each to worship, although we are aware that the true, infinite Creator is without manifestation, the possibility exists for the Creator with Its free will to send forth messengers which speak of worship in homely and simple ways, ways which are adapted to the culture in which the messenger abides. Various cultures and atmospheres within those cultures have produced various Christs which are willing to pour out their own personality upon whatever earth there may be, in order to be filled with that which may be called the Christ, or mind of Christ, or the consciousness of Christ. This Christ is one. Its various manifestations are called for when a culture reaches the stage of yearning for an object of worship that is able to express the deep truths that when pondered over and over begin to create biases within the mind which are spiritual in nature. An entity without this influence is in chaos, and no amount of rigid structuring of the entity or its environment shall be able to induce an entity to emotion.

To better center the focus of worship of an object, it is a fortunate consideration that faith may be explored by those who do not have faith. For instance, one who honestly questions may find it impossible to claim the love of an object as a pathway to the worship of mystery. Many there are among your peoples who do not move from the love of an object to the love of the mystery that sent the object as messenger. Consequently, we suggest that those of little faith, and that includes the great majority of those among your people, choose a common household object that is seen each day, perhaps something like a chair, or any other mundane, and seemingly un-spirit-filled thing.

That which is deified must first be reified, that is, first made a thing, so that attention can more easily be paid to it. This is the working of your cultural mind. Each time, then, that you wish to pray, pray to your chair. When you are in despair, throw yourself on the mercy of the chair. Praise the chair as you rise, in the heat of the day, at dusk, and as you move toward rest again, eager that the night watches may pass so that again praise may be given by your refreshed spirit, to the chair, which is the Creator, or more accurately, is the messenger of the Creator.

You must realize that within subjective experience of any entity there are what may be called mixed signals. It is difficult for most entities to yield to the wishes of that which is perceived as another, whether it be one's superior in work, one's mate in life, one's friends, one's teachers; it is difficult to yield to any thing. However, one of the seed thoughts which produces the fruit of worship is the realization that the illusion is truly thoroughgoing, and it will count for nothing within an entity if it does not choose to attempt to grasp the nature which lies beyond illusion.

When one attempts to open to the deeper and more purified emotions, the first thought vortices which appear are those daily beneath the threshold of consciousness, a milieu given over in large part to fear. Thus, again and again, when entities begin to attempt to learn from the electric silence of spirit, they are opened to messages reflecting the simple mental fears of all peoples—the fear of the dark, and the fear of the unknown, the fear of death. It is at this stage that many spiritualized entities capable of much more become quite stuck, for they have conceived a desire to seek, a desire to love and a desire to serve, but they defeat themselves by gaining access only to information within the deeper mind which is an artifact of the conscious mind. This is not the direction in which we suggest entities experience the learning and searching out of a personal life in faith.

In order to move past one's fear, one needs to be aware without need of self-reproach or defensiveness that one is oneself not able to gain access to authentic experiential data concerning worship. Thusly, there is that impossibly difficult first step, that being the decision to suspend disbelief long enough to experience the illusions which are involved in belief systems. As there is no direct way to apprehend that which occupies no area or period of time, those within the illusions or manifestation of the creation are placed in an untenable position, where that which they seek involves fearlessness of the dark, of the unknown, and the apparent death. One at this point, most likely, does not have sufficient faith to leap into an abyss that is extremely dimly lit, an interior landscape whose first requirement of an observer is utter patience.

To move into worshipful and adoring qualities, one must redefine oneself without reference to that which takes up space, or that which takes up time. The physical vehicle itself, which carries you about, is that which produces the deepest fears, for it is a second-density entity in all but consciousness, the consciousness being without time or space, the manifestation being quite necessary in order to gain appropriate experience. When it is clearly seen that there is nothing to fear, that there is only the unknown, that there is only the dark, and that there is only death, in terms of the physical entity, one may then proceed to grasp the vaunted nature of the physical vehicle. Although the spirit creates its mark upon the lined visages of those who have had experience within an incarnation, and who are what you call old, it itself is without age. There is that within you of glory. However, to this you do not normally have access. Consequently, without any knowing the seeker first makes its decision to love, to worship, to serve others in the name of the one infinite Creator, having no idea how to do this. It is as if the seeker fell off a bottomless cliff.

However, due to the effect upon the connections between conscious and subconscious, when this decision is made and this action taken with an whole heart, the entity may find itself certainly without a floor, certainly without walls or ceiling, and certainly alone within itself, but it will not be without experience, for the will and faith to begin with has been created.

Thus, it is most often a conscious decision to begin to see the self as a steward of the property called consciousness, which is one not with time or space, but with the plenum of infinity, the place of the object of worship within this path. To this pilgrimage, which begins with the deliberate rejection of fear and the determination of a fool or a madman to worship that which is unknown, comes the beginning of a blooming that starts because of the message you have given your deep mind. You are now far more suited to be able to gain access to that within the deep mind which informs, nurtures, uplifts one. One may in visualization grasp the object which denotes the mystery to oneself, and with that security within, one may begin to explore the almost unbelievable choice that has been made. You choose to have no fear; you choose to love. This is a deeper way of stating the same fact.

The you that worships is already worshipping. You, as an incarnate entity, are not aware of this. But as you distance yourself from your physical vehicle, and become more aware of the alien nature of manifestation to the deepest self, you begin the process of shedding the garbage of total responsibility. It is not possible for an entity to be entirely responsible within manifestation. It is not possible for an entity to be truly wise, or truly compassionate, for as the entity is limited by its physical vehicle, so the mind limits consciousness. When one realizes that one needs not buffalo oneself with one's mind, or any other manifestation of the illusion, it begins to seem hopeful that access may be had to the deeper, worshipful awareness that that place whereon you stand is holy ground.

Within your culture it is encouraged that each take complete and full responsibility for the self. If you will examine this concept carefully you may see that within each day there are a multitude of things said or done that you would gladly unsay or undo, and upon the other hand, there are hiatuses which you have not filled, places you did not go, within the heart, in listening to another, in cherishing, in listening to and cherishing the self. Does this mean then that you are poor at being responsible? We suggest that it means only that you are incarnate, and within that which is by nature flawed by polarity and crazed by indifference, that it is impossible not to make errors. Yet you know within yourself the divine, and you hunger, or you would not have taken that first step.

Thusly, you proceed to deepen and solidify the daily awareness of being a spirit of eternal gifts, a messenger of eternal life. In short, to be that which you so adore, to identify more and more, and to be open and vulnerable to the wishes and the guidance of that entity which symbolizes the infinite Creator. Thusly, if one gives oneself the message, "I want to believe, I seek to understand," and so forth, it is well to realize that the yearning and the hungering of itself will bring you just so far.

There is this generous thing of which you need to be aware within yourself, that being that the Creator's will is in no wise different from one's own; it simply sees from a vastly improved point of view. To this point of view ten thousand years mean little, for the values which create the absolute you that you are, are also absolute. Thusly, it serves one better to affirm to oneself, as well as to express the seeking. This may be done by changing questions into declarations. We speak in an area difficult to express, however, one of your ministers of grace whose works are recorded in your holy works, the one known as Paul, in the body of work which he left indicated with a good deal of clarity the identification of the self will to the will of the source. The entity saw clearly that within what you may call the human condition, or third density incarnation, the leap was impossible. Thus, the entity prayed honestly that he did not believe, but that he believed. He chose to make the declaration even while expressing doubt and many remnants of fear.

In this way, worship is a self-generating process wherein one realizes one's identification with an object, a messenger or a symbol which denotes the infinite Creator in manifestation. When that choice has been made it is affirmed and reaffirmed, not in a dogmatic or doctrinal way, but in the spirit of the teachings of the one Christ to which you give the honor of devotion in the *(inaudible)*, for you are not truly worshipful of the object, but rather that source to which the object inevitably points, that which is shrouded in mystery, and until we become without manifestation or the need for it …

(Side one of tape ends.)

(Carla channeling)

I am Q'uo. I greet each once again in love and light as a principle of members of the Confederation of Angels and Planets in the Service of the Infinite Creator. You will notice that we included in our identification, "angels." That is because of the biases which this entity has. The force or spirit is such that the yearning for it will create a manifestation which betokens mystery. Within your culture, the manifestation of angel, or being of light, holds little attractiveness as a messenger of mystery, whereas that which is, and we use this term in quotes, "scientific," is of a seeming authority, a seeming and obvious advancement beyond the human condition. The phenomena associated with unidentified flying objects is in large part the objectification of that which comforts an entity, that which speaks to the entity of the noumenal, the unknown.

You see, we are attempting in this portion of speaking about worship to reposition one's own intelligence with regard to the image of the self as seen by the self. If you see the self as caretaker of the body, then you shall take care of the body and refrain from allowing yourself to be remade. That each of you has chosen this darkness in which to seek, that each of you has chosen the catalyst that does in fact occur, is difficult to grasp or to believe in any logical way. However, the further one moves in mind from the identification of the self with that which seems to be living within manifestation, the greater the rate of acceleration of that which may be grasped of evolution in spirit can occur.

The troublesome question that remains is that simple question, "How can we know? Are we being duped? Are we being fooled? Are we giving our will over to the forces that we neither understand nor trust?" This may be addressed at another time. And for now, with many thanks to this quite exhausted entity for allowing us to use it for a conduit, we would at this time transfer to another instrument within the group. I am Q'uo.

(Carla channeling)

I am Q'uo, and I am again with this instrument. It is to be noted that we did greet the one known as K, but found the entity to be concerned, overly, and greeted the one known as Jim, who was also found to be in a state of concern.

The only reason one would choose a life of devotion and worship is because one might apprehend the unseen hand of the true source of self within the *(inaudible)* and thusly yield, while becoming open and vulnerable to the spirit of love. The accepting of a channel is simply *(inaudible)* to the accepting of the self, as an assistant or servant to and for the source, the source that cannot mix with any free will of the world that you experience. Thusly, we suggest that as we again transfer to end the meeting, that the one known as K allow herself to be vulnerable to the spirit of love. That which can never be understood can at last be trusted, and with each entity that accepts the servant role of the manifestation that reflects the unmanifest, so does unmanifest light illimitable begin to move through such an entity building light not only in a metaphysical sense, but also in a very visible sense in which the difficulties of a situation are seen, not as implacable, but as that which creates opportunity for learning and growth.

This openness and fearlessness is the chief necessity of creating for oneself the point of view which becomes truly and absolutely worshipful. And in so doing, there is created within you the potential of altering the face of your sphere. This is the power of faith. It is a program that is beyond the capabilities of the computer which you use to think. It is indeed, literally, an higher authority. And the life lived in praise and thanksgiving to the source lives in whatever object you choose, lives in total surrender, that moment of the most freedom, the freedom to do that which you truly wished to do before you entered the miasma, the phantasmagoria, of illusion.

We would move now to the one known as K. I am Q'uo.

(K channeling)

I am Q'uo, and greet each again in love and light through this instrument. This instrument is feeling considerable concern over the attempting to be a channel for the answering of queries which may be *(inaudible)*, and it wishes for us to convey the request that if any answers received are not acceptable to those entities asking, the queries be asked upon another occasion. This is acceptable to us. Is there a query at this time?

Carla: The only question I have is to concern over the instrument. *(Inaudible)* if the entity is uncomfortable, then I don't understand why the one known as Q'uo wished to *(inaudible)*. What is the principle involved *(inaudible)* this instrument *(inaudible)*?

I am Q'uo, and we find that this instrument is experiencing various physical and emotional concerns at this time which *(inaudible)* feelings of imbalance and discomfort, as well as its trepidation at attempting to answer queries. These other feelings, however, are exacerbating this natural trepidation at this time on the part of this instrument. We find, however, that the instrument, despite its degree of discomfort, does have a strong desire to be of service, and has offered itself to us at this time for that purpose. Therefore, we are willing to work with this instrument to whatever degree it is able to work with us at this point.

Is there a further query, my sister?

Carla: Yes. *(The question is almost completely inaudible, but has to do with concern over infringement of free will in using the instrument despite its degree of discomfort, principles and/or purposes involved.)* *(Inaudible)* is it to challenge and *(inaudible)*?

I am Q'uo, and this instrument is requesting that we transfer to the one known as Jim for the purpose of the answering of this particular query.

(Jim channeling)

I am Q'uo, and greet each again in love and light through this instrument. We look at this query in respect to the kind of exercise that is offered new instruments. Each instrument as it begins the work of familiarizing itself with the nature of the contact will feel from time to time the trepidation concerning some facet or other of the contact that it is now focusing upon, having mastered to its own satisfaction those previous concepts. We have offered ourselves to this instrument, the one known as K, this evening, in the attempt to expand her abilities, and to begin to familiarize her with the opportunity to exercise her instrument in those areas which may be more challenging, for this instrument has willingly offered itself, though it is not comfortable in this capacity.

It is not necessary that the entity be comfortable with a new level of learning, indeed, that lack of comfort is oftentimes a quite efficient means of focusing the attention, building that which you call the adrenaline, and calling from within the self those resources which will aid the entity in accomplishing that task which is set before it.

Thus, what we have offered this evening is much like that which we have offered many instruments at many times in your past. That is, the opportunity to expand the level of channeling work. We do not wish to make any instrument unduly uncomfortable, but as you are aware, the process of learning in general is one which takes place within a certain degree of discomfort, for it is when the attention is caught by that which causes discomfort that an entity may first begin to notice an aspect of the self or the pattern of learning that has heretofore been ignored. This is true in each area of learning in which any entity shall engage. We wish only to offer ourselves in the attempt to meet with the instrument this challenge. We shall not, if at all within our ability, challenge an instrument overly much.

Is there a further query, my sister?

Carla: I'll have to think that over. Thank you.

I am Q'uo, and we thank you, my sister. Is there another query at this time?

Carla: Yes, I just want to make sure that it was not an error on my part in channeling when I received the concept of handing off to K.

I am Q'uo, and you are quite correct in that we were attempting to speak through the one known as K with the first, as you call it, hand off. This is correct, my sister.

Is there another query?

Carla: Well I have concerns about infringement on free will, but I feel that I am unaware enough at this point *(inaudible)*. Indeed, I am almost not aware of what was channeled *(inaudible)* possible to finish *(inaudible)*?

I am Q'uo, and we are happy to accommodate you, my sister, for you have offered yourself as instrument in quite an openhearted manner this evening when your resources have been at a low level. Thus, we thank each entity in this group for inviting our presence. We take great joy and pleasure in being able to blend our vibrations with each of those in this circle of seeking, and we shall take our leave of this group at this time, leaving each as always in the love and in the light of the one infinite Creator. We are known to you as those of Q'uo. Adonai, my friends. Adonai vasu borragus.

Intensive Meditation
November 15, 1990

Group question: The subject is "joy."

(K channeling)

(K's channeling is nearly inaudible.)

I am Laitos, and I greet each of you in the love and the light of the infinite Creator. We are most pleased to be called to your group and most grateful to each of those present for offering themselves in the work of the vocal channeling.

We use the term "work" in a sense of the working of a ritual of power. For such is this ritual of the disciplining of your spirits and the quieting of your mind, that you may hear that still, small voice, that Creator which is not far away by a *(inaudible)* that spirit of love that speaks to the world this day and always.

We thrill in the love and the light which greets us as we greet you in love and light, and we thank each for the sacrificial and effortful study that has brought you to this point. Now, each of you is wet-footed and ready to move at your own speed, into your own voice, your own channel, your unique gift to those who may be interested in that which you may have to offer, to yourself as you polarize by giving freely, and to the one Creator for all things are done for the love of the one Creator or not done well.

We grasp that you wish to enjoy the freedom to take "pot luck," that is this instrument's phrase. So we shall speak in short segments and move circularly in a clockwise fashion about the circle. We would speak with you this evening upon the subject of joy.

We would now transfer to the one known as Jim. I am Laitos.

(Jim channeling)

I am Laitos, and we greet each again in love and in light through this instrument. The subject of joy is one of which you heard us speak upon many times before, as it is the outgrowth of the life which is lived in a balanced fashion and which has successfully weathered many metaphysical storms, shall we say. It is that natural state of being for the uncreated universe in that portion of yourself, that maintains contact with the Creator, that has yet to be moved into action and separation of any kind. Thus, at the foundation of each entity's being there is this quality which undergirds all which does move and seek within creation. This kind of joy is that which is, shall we say, virgin, pure and undiluted. It has as its motivating factor, shall we say, the thrill of being, the exaltation that each tiny portion of the creation exudes as a matter of the fact of its existence—the entire creation sings.

However, each entity, such as yourself, has for a great portion of time moved from this state of unity and undifferentiated existence and has sought to discover the nature of the self and its relationship to other portions of the same Creator. This movement has brought the temporary shielding of the self from this joy in the daily round of activities.

We shall now transfer to the one known as S. I am Laitos.

(S channeling)

I am Laitos, and we greet you again through this instrument whose decision to serve in this manner causes us great joy.

(Inaudible) we have found mostly *(inaudible)* the joy of which you speak is a *(inaudible)* and part of the very experience of the *(inaudible)* for all to live have the joy of the Creator *(inaudible)* live in the boundless and bountiful joy of the Creator.

Why, then, do those who discover themselves in the heavy illusion find they are upon occasion bereft of all joy and must seek through great difficulty and with great effort to reunite themselves to that joy which is their birthright? The Creator has gone forth in each seeking to fathom the fullest extent of the love which it is and finds that the effort to fathom this love entails a pathway through the greatest separation that is possible.

The greatest separation from the Creator known to you is the first density being, where the Creator is as yet only a vague longing and a dim recollection of a time when the separation has not yet taken place. The evolution of spirit is already afoot, however, upon a pathway of suffering, as the entity, who has thus been separated from out of the Creator, seeks to reunify with the Creator and the story of the further development through the densities of second, third, fourth, fifth, sixth and beyond is well enough known to you.

The point to be taken is that within the spirals of growth, with the spirit finding its way back to the Creator, there are endless opportunities for experiencing anything else but the Creator. And anything else but the Creator is experienced by the Creator as pain. The pain and the suffering, however, serves as a motif for returning to the Creator, that which is of the Creator and returning it, so that the joy may be experienced manyfold. The joy of the one who has returned to the fold, is manyfold what the joy of the one who remains within that [primalness] would be. And so we say that the aim in the end of all seeking through the suffering of the dense illusion is the joy of reunion with the joy itself, the joy of being yourself. And there can be joy in the very seeking. The seeking does not need to have the heavy character or the character of being a great burden; in fact, the seeking comes more into its own as it becomes lighter in barrier, so that it comes more clearly to express the character of joy which it seeks.

At this time we would transfer to the one known as K.

(K channeling)

I am Laitos, and greet each of you again in the love and the light of the Creator. This joy of which we speak is so central a concept to the process of spiritual illusion and the fact of being itself, but as you progress upon your journey, you will find *(inaudible)* Begin to discover this quality more and more as a central portion of your [being] is that which results from the fire of the contact between yourself and the Creator. This takes place upon many levels *(inaudible)* densities *(inaudible)* The appearance of the type of contact between entities and Creator changes from density to density, but the core nature *(inaudible)* is the same.

(The rest of K's channeling is inaudible.)

(Carla channeling)

I am Laitos, and speak now through this instrument in love and light. We would know those things which hamper the subjective awareness, or that which we call joy. Perhaps the single greatest confusion concerning joy is its often perceived interchangeability with your word, happiness. Your culture so values happiness, or at least its pursuit, that it was declared, by those who created your governing instrument, as one of the chief foundations upon which style and method of government was to be modeled. For it was seen as a social activity of a government that was desirable to give to its citizens the opportunity to seek happiness.

We use the term happiness not in its etiological sense which, indeed, means "lesson" as well as "happy," but in the much lessened impact as it is used at this time among the peoples. Is happiness a goal? Is the pursuit of happiness successful? The difficulty with happiness [is] that it can be as easily taken from you as given to you. Happiness is seen, not as an inherent characteristic of yourself, but as that state created by certain arrangements of objects and entities within the life experience of the one which seeks that goal. Is it any wonder that happiness is, therefore, such an ephemeral experience? Real enough, enjoyed most heartily, but a state as difficult to maintain as constant good weather. Rains will come, sleet and snow will fall, and no happiness may withstand the metaphysical weather of sorrow, need and suffering.

Joy, upon the other hand, is that which each entity must create. For as love abides absolutely, so does the experience and joy at the touch of love's presence. Like the deeper loves, it is remembered rather than met for the first time, being each entity's birthright. There is no thing which may remove or rob from you the joy which is perceived by the immediacy of the presence of that which is holy, that which is blessed, that which is true and beautiful. These experiences of joy are your own gifts of grace from love itself and nothing can rob you, either of the memory or of the confident expectation of these immediate experiences.

We would at this time transfer to the one known as Jim. I am Laitos.

(Jim channeling)

I am Laitos, and we speak through this instrument once again. The immediacy of the joy which one may feel as a portion of the birthright is a feeling which inspires any to share what can be shared of the enriched life experience with others, with far more attention paid to that which can be given as opposed to that which can be [gotten]. For joy is a quality which not only radiates from the entity experiencing it, but so transforms a life pattern that the eyes of such an entity look upon a world which appears far more harmonious and unified than before the experience of joy.

The transformative nature of joy begins, as we have said, with the very foundation of each entity. And as it becomes established within an entity due to the balancing of distortions, the clearing of perception, and the continued exercise of faith, the joy-filled experience tends to reorganize the patterns of perception and expression in such a way that the life experience moves in harmony, now, with what may be called a higher pitch of light. This would seem to be a mixed metaphor, shall we say, for that which vibrates is most frequently described or detected by the ear, whereas light is usually detected by the eye.

However, the inner vision of an entity experiencing joy perceives a greater illumination that is a result of an increase in vibration, so that the song or music of the spheres, as it has been called, becomes available to the entity in the most basic of fashions, so that each cell of the mind/body/spirit complex begins to resonate and vibrate in harmony with the new way of perceiving. Thus, joy has little to do with the mundane definition of happiness, for it is that which partakes of the widest possible view of the life experience that an entity may hold.

At this time we would transfer to the one known as S. I am Laitos.

(S channeling)

I am Laitos. We would now address ourselves to the question of how one might hold steadily, therefore, the gaze [upon] a pearl of great price, which is the joy all by nature seek. It is true that occasionally life in its daily patterns affords a glimpse or a vision of higher purpose, and in this higher purpose there truly does reside the joy which one has all along been seeking.

(Side one of tape ends.)

(S channeling)

I am Laitos. Again we are with this instrument. So often it is the case that once one has experienced such a glimpse of joy, one attempts to recreate this feeling, and one's attempt fastens rather upon the husk for the shell of the joy, that is to say, the circumstances in which one found it embedded in. By attempting to recreate the experience of joy in this fashion, one finds only failure.

For the experience of joy, itself, was never to be equated with those circumstances in which it was discovered, in which it quite gratuitously appeared. And so we find that no set of circumstances and no actions which the seeking self may undertake are up to the task of providing a glimpse of joy at will. The experience of joy is so ephemeral that the confusion with other moods and experiences, such as those you call happiness or glee or fun, is rather the rule than the exception. And it is a matter of some experience to be able to [find] out exactly the true [calling] from the false; the true joy from those experiences with which it is so easily confused, even when joy itself is somehow genuinely present.

And so the question arises concerning how one might hold steady the course, that it may be the joy of one's existence that is sought, rather than that which would so readily masquerade as the joy. We find that there is no formula for this seeking, but that one may say that the holding before the gaze of the seeker are the joy, cannot be accomplished by means of an enforced discipline which is superimposed upon the one who seeks, perchance even by the one who seeks. It is rather the case that the joy that is sought and that may be held out as the prize for the seeker is rather like a dancing pearl that refuses to hold still and must be caught on the wing, if there is a result to see this joy as a matter of experience. There is a deeper access to the joy, however. And it is one which holds still that which would dance, although it does so by continually sacrificing the effort that would hold it still and simply allowing it to be; allowing it to be in the part and to expand from within the seeker as the very heart of the seeking the self. This is, in fact, what we mean by saying that the joy is not something that one bumps into, as one could bump into something new. It is not something which one discovers, but is something which one recollects out of oneself.

With this thought, we would pass to the one known as K. I am Laitos.

(K channeling)

I am Laitos …

(K's channeling is inaudible.)

(Carla channeling)

I am Laitos, and greet you once again through this instrument. To conclude our thoughts, we would leave you with this one in which all the others subside. The pursuit of happiness is possible due to the freedom to seek after the object of one's earthly desire, to arrange situations that promote the inclusion of the preferences which you hold. The freedom to do this is uncertain, for circumstances and conditions are often beyond your control. Consequently, the one may feel that happiness is de rigueur. Indeed, [it] is not, but is rather a gift, a kind of teaching, so often missed among your peoples and taken for granted until it is ended. There is true freedom whose bloom is joy, and in this freedom there are those things which those who are not alert, mindful and aware might easily miss.

There is a tremendous and life changing realization which of necessity precedes true freedom. For all freedom is shallow and insignificant compared to the freedom to serve, to serve the Creator, to serve your other selves in the name of the Creator, and to see yourself as loved and forgiven—a blessed and beloved child, no matter in what condition or stage you may be, of the one infinite Creator. This infinity is part of that of which you are made. You are infinite and absolute. Within this illusion, you have accepted finity, you have accepted the necessity of dealing with relative values, ethics and choices, the hunger for the absolute as reflection of the hunger within, for its own home country—eternity. It is so deep within the self, the deep self of the home country is through meditation, contemplation, observation and a million paths realized, and that which does not serve the uncovering of that deeper self, the seeker chooses through a process of realizations to choose to slip away as unneeded armor against a universe in which there is no need to have fear.

For you may suffer and you will surely die, but you shall only leave this illusion to enter a larger and wider one. This realization lifts one from the bonds of the existential [sphere], lifts one from the open and illogical and logical processes and removes the point of view, distantly enough from this journey *(inaudible)* of that which passes for life within your illusion, that it may see that as one chooses to be one's deepest self and to serve—for love alone answering love alone, speaking to love alone.

This joy is now available. How brave each entity is to make the sacrifice of a seemingly solid self, that it may sort and *(inaudible)* the self and open the self to the vulnerability of learning. And further open itself to the vulnerability of seeming loss. It is not that any loses that which is his own, but, rather, that all who wish to evolve choose eventually the forum of their spiritual evolution, that is to say, the choice of a path of service and worship and learning. These are surely yours for the asking. These seekings shall surely be answered in the joy of service, in the name of the One, none can take from him.

As the only queries that we sense are those concerns of the newer channels as to their progress, we may simply say to each that each is now within that area of the learning of the vocal channeling, where the voice has been found and the song is dimly heard. The fidelity to our concepts is excellent for those of small experience, and even the most gifted could not do any better. For we wish you to understand clearly, that in this process of learning the vocal channeling, as in any learned art or skill, it is experience alone that eases and opens the mind, that releases the fear of error, that suits the fear of plagiarism or of speaking too much of one's own thoughts. Each is now beyond the stage where criticism is helpful. Each has passed the minimum competency for work. Now, the time of faithfulness to the task, to the honor and the duty of a chosen path of service must carry you, for our words, judgments and opinions would only burden you. May you continue channels for light, young and old in experience, ever growing, ever mindful of love.

We would close through the one known as Jim. We are those of Laitos.

(Jim channeling)

I am Laitos, and we wish only to speak briefly through this instrument, to give our feelings of delight at this opportunity of speaking through two new instruments who work with diligence and two more experienced instruments who work with perseverance. We cannot tell you in words how very filled with joy are we at this opportunity. For to most we must satisfy ourselves by making our presence known in the form of undifferentiated love which is sent into the energy web of those calling for inspiration and nurturing. This also gives us a great deal of joy and satisfaction. Yet, when one is able to refine one's sending of love and support to the degree we have been able to do—by utilizing concepts and words through these instruments, there is the indescribable satisfaction that comes from knowing that one has moved in step with those who call. We shall be with you in your future.

At this time, we shall take our leave from this group. We are known to you as those of Laitos. We leave each in the love and in the light of the one infinite Creator. Adonai, my friends. Adonai vasu.

Intensive Meditation
November 16, 1990

(Carla channeling)

I am Hatonn. I greet each of you in the love and the light of the one infinite Creator. We are sorry for the delay. However, this instrument spent only the requisite, appropriate time removing itself from the world of delusion and reorienting itself to the world of love. There was work to be done in the yellow ray. There was the greeting of the instrument in a new way which the instrument took the time to decipher and finish. And there was then the calming of the mind once again.

We apologize, yet all of this was appropriate, and we suggest that each instrument be likewise careful, cautious and trusting of its deeper hunches and instincts. Far better would it be to speak not a word than to speak [when] in doubt of the source of that word. For where we speak, words have no power. Our thoughts do not need such inadequate clothing and are clear in their fuller conceptual form. However, upon your sphere there is third-density illusion and words have a great deal of power. That is what created the opening for the greeting.

This entity was preoccupied with the movements of power, forgetting, momentarily that there is only faith. It is not faith in an outcome, whether it be preferred or not, but faith in and of itself, absolute and whole. It is appropriate to do those things which are given for you to do within the illusion, it is, however, inappropriate to find your trust invested in people or institutions. For people shall die and institutions shall crumble. But all will be as it is and as it has always been, quite perfect. How the illusion pulls at you and how easily you yield to it. Is this a necessary portion of experience? Yes, it is necessary that each err and be mistaken as often as it takes in any present moment to affect a change in consciousness for those who polarize as we do towards service to others as an expression of their love for the infinite One. This renders appropriate concern and prayer for all involved. For in creation there is no separation. All that seems separate is illusory and temporary; all are held in utter safety and may rest in [the] Creator if they have faith.

We do not mean to suggest that if one has faith outcomes will always seem favorable. We only speak of larger truths because the larger truths overshadows and renders inoperative lesser truths. This one truth is, overall, the truth of the one great original Thought. In the I AM there is only love. To suspect otherwise is to move away from serving and towards fear, separation and a path of that which is not. For upon a path of that which is not you may experience a universe created of fear. And in so far as you accept fear, you shall be victimized from one incarnation to another. In love there is no room for fear. Although you identify yourselves with a house of flesh, yet you may dissect all portions of this clothing of flesh and find no consciousness, no evidence of life, or love, or passion, or thought.

All beloved and unbeloved, through error, entities are in the end one. One is a victim and a thief. One is both things. As your mind strays from this certitude, so shall your polarity decrease. Thusly, in time of trouble or woe equally as in time of [weal] or gladness call to the same faith, encourage within yourself the same compassion. For in you is both victim and criminal. And each, this equal for each, is one, with all the barriers. When the illusion seems to cage you in, realize forthwith and firmly that the cage is transparent, that you may slip in consciousness through the bars and render them needless as you lift up your gaze to the one infinite Creator in praise and in thanksgiving. For you have been created, you have been given life and consciousness, you are now in an arena. It is to be taken lightly, as all things and never with other [than serenity] yet it is to be taken passionately and seriously. For in this arena, you may use the allegory of life and death. You do the battle within your incarnations. Each of you has the scars to verify this and if you are successful, you shall not kill by thought, by impulse, or by idea. That to you is life. That which is one is [precious ambition] and pride of self is loss to your imperishable self.

So rouse the self from its daze with a shout of joy and stand in glad acceptance that you shall do all for love and in that giving you may perhaps have one outcome or the other. But whether the little life of flesh is ended or is preserved, then you shall be with the Creator. Take these opportunities to polarize, to experience unconditional love, to experience a deep forgiveness of all concerned, and most of all of yourself for being dazed by the illusion once again.

We will now move on to the exercising of each instrument. The message given was given primarily for the further tuning and inner ear of the one known as Carla. We thank you greatly for giving us this opportunity to work with each of you. We humbly accept this request. For it is not only a pleasure to be with you, but it is also our method of learning more. For as we serve you, so you [will bless] immediately ten and a hundred and a thousandfold, infinitely, and we are much blessed. We shall be moving about and will not stay very long this evening, for there is a low energy level within this instrument, and we do not wish to outstay the instrument's stability and, indeed, by this instrument's request we are not able by the instrument's free will request to stay longer than the instrument is completely stable. We shall not be predictable, for we wish each instrument to gain independence and sensitive contact, thusly, we shall simply say at this time we would transfer this contact. I leave this instrument with thanks in love and light, I am Hatonn.

(Pause)

I am Hatonn, and greet each again in love and light through this instrument. We have spoken at some length this evening about the ability to remain centered within the heart and faith as the world about oneself moves in unpredictable ways. So it is as one wishes to serve as a vocal instrument. It is necessary to find that quiet room within, where one may remain quietly alert as the contact is awaited. The first perception of contact is noticed and allowed to speak the feeling to the instrument as the instrument listens carefully. There is the temptation to feel at one's own thoughts or at the door. However, if one is careful to remain centered in the certainty of the self and one's ability to sense stimuli, one will then develop the patience to allow a contact to be established in a careful and secure pattern. We shall transfer this contact. I am Hatonn.

(Unknown channeling)

I am Hatonn, and we have …

(Microphone difficulties. Telephone rings.)

… as this instrument was most scrupulous in its challenging procedures. This is all to the good. For it is one of the great dangers of the beginning instrument to leave oneself open to those energies which have not been examined and scrutinized as to their origin and their polarity. We find in this instrument a willing student and rejoice that this is the case. For the creation abounds plentifully with those who would take pleasure in the tuning instruments, such as this one, who have earnestly dedicated themselves to the fight of the positive path. The practice of channeling is like any art, in so far as a certain skill is obtained in maintaining a dutiful and watchful state of attention which is sustained by a confidence that one's activities are adequate to the task at hand. No channel who channels truly is ever fully familiar with the contents of that which is to be channeled. And it is a mark of a channel that begins to make some progress that a willingness to allow what is unexpected to come within the area of the mind to be spoken out, plays a greater and greater role in the process of the vocal channeling. The practice of channeling is a constant succession of re-centering and re-tuning, as a myriad of distractions are available for those within your density. [And] every cell of the body, it sometimes seems, rebels at being put through the task which is not well understood by that second-density vehicle which carries you about. The increasing dedication to the art of channeling is at the same time a commitment to spiritual growth in all of its facets as, indeed, the process of tuning is a process which is analogous to the disciplines of the personality which are essential to spiritual growth in all of its energies.

The experience of tuning is an experience of finding a calm and stable car behind and beyond that which is tremulous and that which is variable with the shifting currents within the illusion. More and more this stable car becomes the living reality of one whose experience is assimilated to a higher spiritual vibration. And the higher the spiritual vibration the instrument is able to bring to the practice of the vocal channeling the clearer and the more direct may be the message that comes through. It is a process which may never be forced, and there are times when the information given to be channeled does not agree with what the channeler expects or wants from the session to which he has committed itself. And in this situation the channeler does well to understand that the will of the channeler is temporarily suspended in favor of that message which is brought forth.

We say that the will is suspended in favor of the message, but never is it the case that the instrument is without the power of discernment concerning whether or not it wishes to continue with the message which is at hand. There is a "yes" or "no" proposition at hand. That is, if for any reason the channel begins to suspect the nature of the source which is being channeled, it's quite appropriate to end the session and to turn to a process of silent meditation wherein a calm center may be obtained. There is much that this new instrument, [as in the] old instruments, has to learn upon the subject of the vocal channeling. We do feel that a good beginning has been made and that an earnest commitment has been taken, and this is a cause for rejoicing for us. For it is a happy occasion, indeed, when we find that the horizons of those we may serve have been broadened, as they are always broadened, with the addition of the new talents and abilities of new channels. At this time we would return to the one known as Carla.

(Carla channeling)

I am Hatonn, and greet each one again through this instrument in love and light. We would thank each for the integrity of honest and single-hearted effort. We bathe ourselves in your desire for the truth, whatever the highest truth is that may be seen. We are most happy to have been able to share in your vibrations and meditations and the love for love itself that we have shared this time.

How noble is the aspiration of the treasure that is held in the prison of flesh. May you always, each, look through the [bars] of this temporary confinement, to behold infinity, dropping millennia like pros, scattering by the thousands. We would at this time close the contact without the question and answer period, for we do feel this instrument nears the end of its stability and tuning. We leave you as we found you, and yet, leave you not at all, in the love and in the light and the source and mystery and the wonder of the infinite Creator. Take heart and go your way, in peace and compassion. We are known to you as Hatonn. And with thanks we leave you, Adonai. Adonai vasu. Adonai. ✦

Intensive Meditation
November 17, 1990

(Unknown channeling)

I am Oxal. I greet you in the love and in the light of the infinite Creator. We are most pleased that this entity has perceived our vibration, which is not as readily received by this instrument, because of a strong bias towards wisdom upon our hearts, and a strong sense of compassion and wisdom in configurations that are not within our grasp at this time.

However, we are most thankful to be called by this instrument, because we find our ability to communicate with the instrument known as S, and the instrument known as Jim, to be far nearer congruency, especially in the case of the instrument known as S. We would, therefore, greet you through this instrument and transfer the contact to the one known as S, expressing as helpful the information that we are a strong but somewhat more narrowband vibration than some others. And, therefore, this instrument subjectively perceives our contact as moving into the energy web of the physical vehicle farther back upon the crown of the head. We leave this instrument at this time and are most willing to be patient if the one known as S must adjust and acclimate its instrument for comfort in our contact.

I am of Oxal, and I now transfer to the instrument known as S.

(Pause)

(S channeling)

I am Oxal, and I greet you in the love and in the light of the infinite One through this new instrument. It is with a great feeling of warmth that we find that we are able to have our thoughts expressed by this instrument. For, indeed, as this instrument has already come to suspect, it is as a homecoming for us. We feel very much at home within this energy web. And the opportunity to find a voice within this web of energy gives us a life within your density that we have not known for some time. We find that there are many things that could be spoken today, but none perhaps so appropriate as the words of joy and of welcome that we feel through our depth, as we seek the resonance within the body complex and the mind complex and the spirit complex, who is beginning to open now to the more subtle reaches of our particular kind of greeting.

We are Oxal of the wisdom density, seeking to find our way to the density in which wisdom is blended with compassion. And we are among those fifth-density social memory complexes who have undertaken to study with those magnificent golden beings you know as Ra. We work cooperatively with others known to you, of our own density, those being the ones of Latwii, with whom this instrument has begun its experience of becoming acquainted with the art of opening to receive the channeled messages. We have found that, since our energy tends to be rather heavy, and in this sense is a somewhat challenging energy to carry for the new instrument, that there was appropriateness in the beginning with the gentler Latwii, whose turn towards compassion has already well begun. And who, therefore, has been shown to be preeminently fit for the role of comforter to those beginning the process of opening to become an instrument for the expression of the love which may pour forth from the realms that to your realm seem higher

It may be subject, as always, to the free will self-determination of this entity, that we would be called in the future to the sessions which have begun upon a regular basis. For the energy match with this instrument is great. And even now, we feel this instrument rejoicing at this match as we rejoice ourselves. The way of the path towards excellence in channeling, as all here have already surmised, is perfectly analogous and, in fact, of a relationship of identity with the thought of general spiritual development, and excellence in becoming an instrument depends almost entirely beyond that certain point at which the elements and the skill have been acquired. Depends almost entirely, as we say, upon the achievement of those disciplines of the personality which mark the growth of the spirit, so that it may find increasing expression in the illusion which is uniquely characteristic of third density.

We feel that we bring no new information to those of this group in announcing that all here are native to densities that are other and therefore are related to this one in an unique fashion. For in addition to those lessons which are learned in a manner native to those who work through the third density for the first time, those who are, what you call, wanderers bring a certain task and a certain responsibility, which may be viewed as operating so as to put into an unique light, a particular slant or bias, those precise lessons which within third density all must learn. And so, in a sense, the task is compounded proportionate to the unique gifts which have been brought from other densities, so that they may be laid down in service to the souls which seek, so hungrily, to reach beyond the limits which are those of third density, a density of choice.

We wish to be clear upon one point, absolutely and always, and that is that we ask that all of our thoughts and our words be understood solely in the light of the need to make and to constantly reiterate the choice, which is the choice of polarity. We feel that all within this group have made this choice, some exquisitely so, and are in the process of discovering that the choice made seeps down to the roots of [mind] and triggers a process of recollection of who you are. Had this process not been well begun, we would not be able to make contact with any of this group. We rejoice in this, and we encourage you to be ever watchful and ever scrupulous, for the pitfalls are many and sudden. And no vigilance is ever too much vigilance when addressing the issue of how the spiritual path shall be preserved. We find great wisdom tempered with great compassion already available as a resource within the thinking of this group. And we commend you to drink of this delicate and fragrant brew whenever the opportunity affords.

As we find, this instrument is suggesting to us that enough is enough, we shall proceed, if we may, to transfer this contact to the one known as Jim. I am Oxal.

(Jim channeling)

I am Oxal, and greet each in love and light once again through this instrument. It has been some time since we have been with this group, this instrument, and with this opportunity to speak our thoughts. For this we are very grateful and would offer ourselves in addition, at this time, to any queries which may be upon the minds of those here gathered. Is there a query to which we may speak?

Carla: I have a question, but it might involve the law of free will. I have concepts which I could suggest to a girlfriend of mine who is handicapped and her abilities are limited *(inaudible)* multiple sclerosis *(inaudible)*.

I am Oxal. We scan your mind. Though you exist in some degree as a teacher to this entity, you are as one with her, as you are with all third-density entities upon your planetary surface at this time. Therefore, we see no difficulty in any suggestions that you might make to this or any other entity. For each is free to accept or to reject any such suggestions.

Is there a further query, my sister?

Carla: Not on that point. I am extremely pleased to hear this *(inaudible)*.

I am Oxal. We thank you as well, my sister. Is there another query?

S: Yes, Oxal. I wonder if you could tell us a little bit about yourself, whatever you think is appropriate on this occasion.

I am Oxal. And as are all contacts which this group has experienced within its past, we are a social memory complex. Thus the "I" and the "we" are one. We have for a great portion of time traveled through the density of wisdom, seeking as a group to perfect our understanding of the nature of the creation and of our place and purpose within it. We evolved upon the third-density level in a far more harmonious fashion than we observe the evolution upon your planetary surface to be expressed. It was our experience in the density of choice to move through each of the major cycles of experience in an increasingly efficient manner so that at the end of the third cycle we were seeking as one.

Thus, we moved into the compassion of fourth density with relative ease, and were blessed with success upon the expression of unconditional love—both the offering and the receiving. During our experience within the density of light, we have studied carefully other third-density experiences and have found that, though most proceed in a similar fashion to our own, there are those which have difficulty due to many reasons. The experience which your planet now passes through is one which has interested us for some time, for we seldom have the opportunity of partaking in such a direct manner as we do now with you, with third-density planets that are what you may call the repository of those who have found the need to repeat this cycle of experience. Thus, your planet has been influenced by many other planetary entities of third-density vibration which have completed their own cycle upon, what you would call, their home planet and who have found your current planet, that location and vibration which is most helpful to their own repetition of this experience, with the desire for achieving fourth density graduation. Thus, we work in a light-filled environment looking at the nature of your experience with regards to the introduction of significant amounts of disharmony within individuals, groups, races, nations and, indeed, within the planetary entity itself that you now evolve with.

We seldom have the opportunity of speaking our thoughts in this manner, for though we are within the evident reach of many of those of your peoples who choose the career, as you may call it, of service as a vocal channel, we are narrowband enough that our signal is usually perceived only upon the subconscious levels by the deeper portions of individual minds, and this most often within the sleep or meditative states. Thus, our service most frequently takes the form of our sendings of undifferentiated light and love to those who call for such.

Is there a further query, my brother?

S: Yes, one more. You've said on the onset that you have spent a lot of time seeking the nature of the Creator and your place within the creation. Is it the case that the place within the creation—of individual mind/body/spirit complexes and of social memory complexes—is unique, each to each, so that the conditions of the search and of the character expressed in the search are unique, each to each, and in such a way that individual mind/body/spirit complexes would naturally gravitate towards others that show similar characteristics, as they come to the point of joining themselves into one social memory complex?

I am Oxal. It has been our experience, through both observation and our own evolutionary process, that as entities become more aware of that which they value and that which they seek, that there is a natural drawing together of interest, which is not necessarily bounded by either what you call time or …

(Side one of tape ends.)

S: Yes, would it be possible to characterize those differences which exist, such that it makes sense to say that some are "like unto like," while others are "like unto other likes." In a general way, what comes to my mind at this point is "earth, air, fire, water." Do individual social memory complexes work within principles or lines of energy oriented or distorted in some fashion or another?

I am Oxal, and am again with this instrument. If we have correctly perceived your query, we may say that there are deeper and deeper or more and more harmonious affiliations between entities according to the accumulated experience of each entity which then becomes the primary motivator for the further gathering of the experience and the balancing of all experience. Thus, as entities find certain lines of inquiry of interest and pursue them to the point where there is mastery of a field or body of knowledge, then there is also a natural brotherhood, shall we say, which develops around the focus or points of interest.

Is there a further query, my brother?

S: No, I don't think so. That's enough for now. Thank you very much.

I am Oxal and we thank you my brother, once again. Is there a final query, at this time?

Carla: *(Inaudible)*.

I am Oxal. We are most honored to have such a happy and open reception from this group, and again express our great joy at having made contact with the one known as S in a manner which will allow a further exploration of this contact on both our parts. We cannot express our gratitude in words sufficient to describe its depth and richness for this opportunity. We thank each for voicing our words during this gathering and we shall leave this group now. We are known to you as those of Oxal, and we leave you in the boundless love and the limitless light of the one infinite Creator. Adonai vasu borragus.

L/L Research

L/L Research is a subsidiary of Rock Creek Research & Development Laboratories, Inc.

P.O. Box 5195
Louisville, KY 40255-0195

www.llresearch.org

Rock Creek is a non-profit corporation dedicated to discovering and sharing information which may aid in the spiritual evolution of humankind.

ABOUT THE CONTENTS OF THIS TRANSCRIPT: This telepathic channeling has been taken from transcriptions of the weekly study and meditation meetings of the Rock Creek Research & Development Laboratories and L/L Research. It is offered in the hope that it may be useful to you. As the Confederation entities always make a point of saying, please use your discrimination and judgment in assessing this material. If something rings true to you, fine. If something does not resonate, please leave it behind, for neither we nor those of the Confederation would wish to be a stumbling block for any.

CAVEAT: This transcript is being published by L/L Research in a not yet final form. It has, however, been edited and any obvious errors have been corrected. When it is in a final form, this caveat will be removed.

© 2009 L/L Research

Sunday Meditation
November 18, 1990

Group question: The question this evening has to do with how individuals and groups, or any people that are in relationship with others, can work through the blockages that seem to get in the way of sharing as fully as possible the feeling of love, with ourselves, with each other, and with the group. How can we remove those patterns of thinking and behaving that tend to drain away, or even keep us from seeing the feeling of love and compassion for others?

(Carla channeling)

I am Q'uo. Greetings to each of you in the love and in the light of the one infinite Creator. We thank you most humbly for allowing us to share in your meditation and for calling upon our people to offer what information it is within our grasp to offer. By this we mean to imply that we are not without error ourselves, for we are brothers and sisters along the infinite path.

We have had your experience, and you do not think that you have had ours. That is an artifact of your perceptions of time. Time, space and all that dwells in those areas are illusions. Not relative illusions, but absolute illusions. Were one to be able to see with the eyes that pierce flesh and see spirit, we would see beings of light surrounded in a matrix of energy vortices. Each of you is an unique being, yet one with all that there is. It is when one finds paradoxes such as this one that one realizes most clearly that one is treading on fruitful metaphysical ground, for paradox and mystery are the signs of the infinite One.

You wish this evening to know more about the alteration of behaviors in order to operate affirmatively and positively. We would ask you to move one step backward with us, for it is not your behavior, but your being, your consciousness, your inner choices, that dictate with a ruthless certainty that which you shall perceive and notice, as you are not within the density you enjoy aware that the illusion is so complete it is easy to identify consciousness with behaviors, and gaze at the behaviors instead of finding the root of those behaviors. Now we have said to you before that the bio-computer which is your conscious mind is designed to make choices. In reality, your consciousness has the very basis of the illusion, that is, thesis and antithesis. So let us turn our gaze inward, and realize that our bio-computers have been programmed for this incarnation on a continuing basis; however, as it is popularly suspected …

(Pause)

I am Q'uo, and greet you once again in love and light. This instrument was much distracted because it required a liquid. We shall proceed. Those decisions made early in the incarnation when one was quite behind hand in grasping the larger truths concerning the great difficulties those you know as parents experienced. You were therefore victimized by whatever patterns of their negative influence were at that time present or at any other previous place in your flow of time present; further, much of the popular culture of your people given as the absolute understanding of "they," as in "they say," "they think," you have purchased, without reading the ingredients, metaphysical food that you may find giving you a metaphysical stomachache.

The most common legacy of the childhood in your culture is low levels of admiration and love, nurturing and forgiveness of the self. The entire world of personalities you may well be willing to forgive; but you yourself are often dazed by such excellent [conditioning] that there is no way to please the self, each having internalized in its own way the negatives of parental disapproval and lack of understanding, verbal and physical abuse, often in subtle ways, that you have experienced. Once these patterns have been set up, and this occurs quite early in life, usually, the rest of the incarnation is spent upon an arena which has been constructed to challenge you with these seeming self-destructive and limiting programs within the bio-computer. After these biases are in place, more and more the entity will notice and be aware of those things which are relevant to its self-destructive concerns. We ask you to allow the inner feeling of self to become crystallized at this time, and we shall pause.

(Pause)

Do you see the treasure that lies within you? Which do you think is reality? Which do you think is illusion?

The first step towards altering one's state of consciousness is the honest and actual realization that you are not that which begins and ends in this incarnation or within this illusion. This begins to distance the self, that is, the consciousness, from that beloved animal of second density which sacrifices a great deal to carry you about. It is well to be a careful and generous steward to your own physical vehicle; however, it is your ally and your friend, rather than yourself. When you have clearly made that distinction, you may begin to see the absolute subjectivity of perception, which is your own.

The environment gives you a thousand messages, a hundred thousand, a million, so quickly, so very quickly, and the computer chooses that which it will notice, that which it will perceive. However, most are not aware that they have, at some point in the past, chosen to program the computer in such a way as to offer detuning, depolarizing and the heaviness of blocked lower energies. Instead of feeling helpless, instead of watching your behavior that you may behave correctly, take thought of your spirit and realize that all choices that have been instrumental in creating existing programs are your own.

Listen. Can you hear the sounds of the household? Were you aware of them before we asked? Feel the slight breeze that drifts languidly in warm air currents across your skin. How many millions of receptors there are. Think of all that you have seen as you came into this environment, this domicile, and met those in the circle of one, some for the first time. How much of that which you saw did you perceive? Perhaps two or three percent at the most, for the computer cannot carry the full sensory stimulation and create aught but chaos. Thus, choices are made which enhance, or seemed at one time to enhance, one's ability to survive, to cope, and to behave. That which has been programmed can be reprogrammed.

Now we do not speak as if the Creator has nothing to do with this process. However, we believe that it is the will, passionate and joyful and complete, of the seeker to become an authentic being, that allows one to reach a state of mind in which the seeker may gently, sweetly and lovingly move into the deeper mind to find the seeds of the low self-esteem, the tendency to repeat patterns of addiction or abuse of various kinds given by parents which seemed godlike. Inevitably, either imitation or refusal to imitate figures of seeming authority in childhood forms the essence of your programming. One, having discovered to the best of one's ability the nature of the trigger of self-destructive behaviors, can then, with enough passion, will and grace, reprogram the bio-computer.

Let us give an example well known to this instrument. This instrument has a physical vehicle which has been created by its own choice in such a way that it shall do inner work. These seeming limitations, on the other hand, have been seen by this entity as opportunities. This leaves that artifact known among your peoples as pain. The instrument, therefore, realizing the distracting nature of pain, spent some time recently in reprogramming in order to fail to notice pain. In this way, when there is enough need, when there is a perceived suffering within the self, then one is motivated to do the very disciplined work necessary to reprogram.

Remember that each of you is a co-creator. You have been created, but you have not been created imperfect. You have chosen to leave the house of the Father, to travel the circle path from source to source, from mystery to mystery. There is a program which can only be reached by one who is willing to do meditation and persevere, for in most cases this does take time. As one sits in meditation, day after day, year after year, one slowly becomes aware that one is more able than previously to discern intuitions and deep hunches. Thus, not only are you programmed for the tangible things, but, perhaps more importantly, for the intangible.

Quite often, entities within your culture have a native programming of working hard, creating a safe amount of your money, and seeking that which is known as happiness. Happiness is entirely a portion of your illusion. For if the Creator is absolute, then so are you, [joy] is absolute. Have you found it today? Have you looked for it? You may encourage each other, exhort each other, comfort and console each other, and so minister to each other, that each mirrors a more and more accurate reflection of the other self and the self, so that there is constant opportunity to learn, to consider, and, when a behavior has been identified as not being congruent to the being, to move into that behavior and remove it from your programming, with the help of the deep portions of the mind, where dwell what we might call a metaprogram of divine inspiration, and a deep awareness of all that there is, then one may work in consciousness.

One may have come to this point from different agendas. One entity may wish to be of more service, another may wish to avoid suffering. The reasons are as many as entities are. But truths do remain simple, and that which you seek, you shall find. Thusly, if you but persevere in the reprogramming, and request the aid of that vast metaprogram of enhanced knowledge not available to you as a personality, you become more and more able effectively to create your experience.

The old question of the tree in the forest that we find in this instrument's mind is quite apt here. That which you do not choose to perceive does not exist for you. Thus, it is quite important for the seeker of truth to identify those things which separate it from others, which cause distress to the self, and which limit love, and so speak to that necessity that effectual transformation results, more real, again and again, on ever deeper levels of bias, that may well be self-destructive in your own opinion, for you in your free will are anything but simple.

When the programming, however, is to be tackled, it is well to become simple, single-minded and wholehearted, because you are asking yourself, in a subjective sense, partially to die, and to be no more. Thus, your faith that all will be well, and your will to continue spiritual evolution are the strengths and resources that bring you to holy ground, whereon the Creator, that lies so deeply within, in the metaprogram of love and infinite peace, is made available. Again and again you must seemingly retrace your steps. However, it is our opinion that this seeming repetition is in fact the peeling of the onion, layer by layer by layer. Many things which are self-destructive have only been kept because the programming is so deep. There are so many layers with which one must work, and one cannot fully reprogram one's bio-computer unless one actually and in truth is ready to allow that portion of the personality to die. However, it is in that death that you find larger life, in this incarnation, or in any illusion.

We would at this time transfer this contact, offering it first to the one known as K. It is perfectly acceptable if this instrument does not wish to speak, in which case we shall transfer to the one known as Jim. I leave you through this instrument in love and light, and with great joy. I am Q'uo.

(Pause)

(Carla channeling)

I am again with this instrument and we find that neither of the other channels within this particular group wish *(inaudible)* this instrument wishes to complete the main message. This is acceptable to us and we shall continue through this instrument in love and light.

(Pause)

Greetings again from those of Q'uo. We have said that the most difficult thing one can do is to forgive oneself utterly. Most entities require some kind of structure, which seems to dispense understanding, enlightenment or redemption from without. These forces are without and within and as you are the only inhabitant of your creation and everything else is perceived through the ruthless economy of your biocomputer there is little or no hope of discovering truth using only an object which symbolizes worship. This is quite appropriate and acceptable as a path of inspiration, as a guide.

However, you yourself are indeed in dominion over that which you wish to have in you. That which this instrument calls the Holy Spirit—which many call guidance, or guides or inner masters—is able at all times to allow one to rest and to be comforted. When one allows oneself, finally, to love the self very deeply and passionately, one is then ready to serve. For the one known as Jesus spoke—we must pause. I am Q'uo. This instrument is having some difficulty.

(Pause)

I am Q'uo, and we are again with this instrument. The master known to you as Jesus said that it was not he but the Father that strengthened him. So it is with you, eventually. You are more informed and more powerful in a personal sense than you realize quite often. You have by the grace of the one infinite Creator enlightenment, redemption and love of self alone, for the two requests that the one known as Jesus made to replace entirely the Ten Commandments were to love the Creator and to love other selves as the self. Consequently, it is essentially important to work with the self in consciousness until one realizes that regardless of the illusions in one's own spiritual temperature-taking, it is not selfish or service to self but indeed necessary first to find charity towards the self. For you contain all within and if you do not feel self-forgiven how then can you feel in truth the joy of all being self-forgiven? How can you feel joy for the truth that is someone else's and not your own?

The hardest work that you can do within this incarnation is work in consciousness. Yet this work in consciousness is by far the most effectual means of accelerating in any spiritual evolution, innovating, enlightening the consciousness of your sphere, when you have no solemnity, no love, that many enjoy and so shall you, each of you, as you find you truly are a person to be esteemed, a person who has gifts and whose only desire is to offer them to the one Creator. Is this not a beautiful thing? Can you not step back and see the courage involved in having faith where there is no evidence to support it? Nor can there ever be, for this is the density of choice, blind choice. You work in the dark, you suffer, then discover the suffering, accept it, grasp its nature and eventually reprogram it over and over and over again, moving away from suffering and towards mindfulness not because you have behaved differently but because you have told your mind to register different portions of catalyst. Have you ever, for instance, purchased an object which you had not seen before but thought well of and then found in every nook and cranny someone else who had found the same thing. They had, of course, been finding that all along but you had not. So the information was not relevant to you and was simply [deleted] from conscious thought.

(Side one of tape ends.)

(Carla channeling)

We find that as this instrument's fatigue is great, it is well, in addition to each entity's sore derrière, [that] we leave this instrument. We would like to attempt to crystallize the material we have offered you. Your universe is completely subjective and consists only of energy and magnetic fields. Within those vortices of magnetic fields rests by a slender thread an infinite consciousness. Your power cannot be seen by you, for you dwell in clothes of flesh and bone. Yet this power is within you. The mind is a kind of computer. It may be analyzed as to what choices it has made that are disruptive, unpleasant or inappropriate. Yet, one cannot change oneself from the outside in. One must first find the truth of oneself and then the truth of consciousness. Moving from that point, more and more aware of love being all that there is, the courage slowly becomes gained to allow self-destructive portions of the self to die that a new and more harmonious state of mind may be the response when one is faced with the choices of what to perceive.

Never judge your behavior or your thoughts but rather be compassionate, openhearted and above all, persistent. And as you discover your beautiful self so will all others become beautiful. As you discover that you are all things possible, including all the negative things—the thief, the rapist, the killer—you then become aware of that great importance of choosing again and again for you cannot only perceive good so-called, you perceive in a full circle and have a full complement of abilities to act negatively and positively in the normally understood sense of those words. Take the leap of faith when you are ready, not before, and certainly not after for the adventure in this arena becomes much more interesting, we feel, for those who create rather than accept their own universe—we correct this instrument—universes. May you create yours and recreate yours gradually, persistently and with great love for the self as a spark of the infinite One until at last you are hollow through and through with no blockage to keep infinite light and infinite compassion from flowing through you.

You are not a victim, but it is your choice which determines your perception. Choose well that which you desire, my friends. For as the cliché goes, yet it is true, "seek and ye shall find." Be therefore careful of that which you seek.

We are those of Q'uo, and would at this time transfer the contact to the one known as Jim in case there are any questions upon the mind of any present.

Again we leave this instrument in love and light and service. I am Q'uo.

(Jim channeling)

I am Q'uo. I greet each again in love and light through this instrument. At this time it is our privilege to offer ourselves in the attempt to speak to those queries which may be upon the minds of those present. Again, we remind each that we do not wish to be considered in any degree infallible but wish to offer our thoughts and opinions freely, asking that you take those which ring of truth to you and use them as you will, leaving behind all others. Is there a query at this time?

Questioner: This is one that we use. We were taught and it has been very effective in my experience to use the holy name of God to concentrate our minds at all times. It seems that from this type of doing I've been very much able to get rid of a lot of bad programming as we've been speaking of. How do you all view this?

I am Q'uo, and am aware of your query, my brother. When one uses the sound vibration complex that you call name for the one Creator and give to that name your own acceptance and adoration then you provide for yourself a channel or a gateway into that portion of your being where this is true. For within each has the one Creator hidden Itself that through the expression of the individualized self the one Creator might know more of Itself and each portion of Itself might then partake in this discovery, one for the other, as the yearning for union grows.

Is there another query, my brother?

Questioner: Also, you spoke earlier of acknowledging the negativities or the positivity of one's being in the programming of the bio-computer. This is not very clear. Could you restate it in another way so I might be able to understand it more easily?

I am Q'uo, and I am aware of your query, my brother. It is often the case for many of your peoples as they look consciously and carefully at themselves that they will see those portions of behavior that they do not appreciate and consider to be less than worthy of study, those portions which may be seen as inability to love, the ability to give insult and injury, the less than honest expression of truth, and so forth. Oftentimes these characteristics are ignored or discarded, hoping in the ignoring of them that they will disappear.

We suggest instead that they also be honored as portions of the self which have a role within the larger scope of the incarnational process and that such character traits or behaviors or beliefs might be followed to their source in order that the entity might discover a more complete picture of the nature of the self and the specific kind of balancing that is in process in the entity, for it is oftentimes true that the negative expression of a character trait is merely one end of a pole or a range where a more positive expression may be found if first the roots of both are uncovered.

Is there a further query, my brother?

Questioner: Thank you for that.

I am Q'uo, and we thank you, my brother. Is there another query?

Questioner: I'm not sure but I think my brother may have been asking about the idea of the—each person can have all various personality traits *(inaudible)* the full range *(inaudible)*. Correct me if I am wrong.

Questioner: The answer that was given was very good. I understand it to be that we have to follow those negative aspects of ourselves to find out from where they arise and in doing so we gain that greater knowledge of each of ourselves. I assume that's what's meant by exhibiting negative characteristics [and] outward demonstration.

I am Q'uo, and this is correct, my brother. Is there another query?

Questioner: My query is what density are you operating on and do you have access or perception of all other densities either through travel or exploration?

I am Q'uo, and am aware of your query, my brother. We of Q'uo are what you might call a group mind or more correctly the blending of two such group minds for the purpose of making an entry into this particular group for the purpose of being able to communicate our thoughts in response to this group's queries. This is the reason for the blending of two such groups in our case. We seek at that level of vibration which you would equate with the fifth density of experience or that which is of light where the limitless light of the one Creator shines in such a fashion that the truth of unity is without doubt and the relationships between various portions of the one Creator might be more clearly seen.

We of Q'uo seek the lessons of unity, those lessons which are found within that density numbering six where those we call teachers reside. We may travel in thought to such locations and experience a portion of what is available there and as our point of viewing or ability to perceive is expanded by our own learning and experience then more of that which lies ahead on our path becomes available to our perception. Thus, we can speak from experience only through the density numbering five and must rely upon that which has been told to us by our teachers and those bits of our own perception where we have traveled in thought in relation to densities beyond our own.

Is there another query my brother?

Questioner: I was wondering, I have a teacher in this density also [that] I hold with great reverence and adoration. I call him by the name of *(inaudible)*. In what density is he vibrating now on this planet? Or what density has he come from or descended into this incarnation, if you have that information? I am curious about that.

I am Q'uo, and am aware of your query, my brother. We find a difficulty in giving a direct answer to this query for we do not wish to infringe upon the free will of any who revere this most positively-oriented entity. To describe such an entity by the density to those who honor this entity would be perhaps in some cases to skew this appreciation in an undue manner, which would obscure perhaps the message this entity had to offer. Each entity of this nature comes to serve those of this planetary vibration by hollowing the self in such a fashion that it becomes a pure and clear channel for the one Creator in order that information and inspiration of a certain nature may be offered. This is the message and the purpose of the incarnation for such an entity and each such entity wishes that the message might be delivered as clearly as possible with as little tendency towards distortion as possible. We humbly beg your forgiveness for being unable to give the density of this entity for we wish this entity's message to remain as clear as possible.

Is there another query, my brother?

Questioner: No, I appreciate that answer. Thank you very much.

I am Q'uo, and we thank you once again, my brother. Is there another query at this time?

Questioner: Just on the off chance that you might give suggestion—when I do a reprogramming *(inaudible)* out what I wish to change and the reason involved and a kind of object that makes it, I suppose, more real psychologically and as I write it I vow and I request my mind to accept the new program and to dump the old one. Is there a number of different ways to do this or is there one that you would recommend? Have you any suggestions upon it?

I am Q'uo, and I am aware of your query, my sister. There are as many ways of reprogramming one's bio-computer as there are entities wishing to do so. The most potent program for any entity is that one which has been constructed from the pure desire found within the heart. The expression of this desire is that which gives form as a channel to that desire. This, however, is secondary to the successful reprogramming. The generation of this desire so that it is complete and fills the entity and overflows the cup, shall we say, is that which is of primary importance in the root—we correct this instrument—in the reprogramming of any thought or behavior pattern.

If, as in your case, an entity finds it is helpful to form this desire by writing it upon the paper, by speaking it as a vow, by dancing it as a dance, praying it as a prayer, or meditating it as a mantram then this is the form that is appropriate for that entity. It is well to use those tools which one has been given in which one has found a certain degree of mastery in previous use in order that a form which is most effective might be utilized in giving the clear voice to this heart-generated desire for a closer approximation of love within the life pattern.

Is there a further query, my sister?

Questioner: No, I'm done. Thank you.

I am Q'uo, and again we thank you, my sister. Is there another query?

Questioner: You mentioned the deep mind and I was wondering what are the symptoms of reaching the megamind or the infinite intelligence and whether one can actually be in that awareness or consciousness all the time within this density, third-dimensional density? And the symptoms, of course, you can elaborate on and can maybe give a clue to the path to tapping into that gateway that we can manifest greater love and light of the infinite Creator which I call Krishna. That is my question. Thank you.

I am Q'uo, and we are most appreciative of this question which ranges quite broadly within the field of the evolution of consciousness. To give a full answer would be the work of many sessions such as this one but we may give a, shall we say, a crystallized response and ask that further queries be given if there is more information desired.

The ability of any entity to reach deeper levels of the subconscious mind and move therefrom to other levels of mind which would include the racial, the planetary, the archetypical, and the universal mind depends upon the ability of the entity to still the conscious mind to such a degree that silence is able to prevail and open a door that is more clearly seen, or shall we say, felt, due to the lack of interference in the activity of the mind. This ability to move through this doorway to deeper levels of the mind is a, shall we say, product of work done upon the personality.

This includes work at each level of existence that corresponds with each chakra or energy center as you know them within the physical vehicle, each center allowing the entity the opportunity of more fully expressing the intelligent energy or prana of the one Creator. It is within each center or chakra that various blockages have been programmed before each incarnation to bias the learning of the entity in such and such a fashion.

As this learning proceeds apace the entity is able to see the self, all other selves, and the creation and experiences about it as those expressions of love which have for some time been disguised as other than love. Therefore, the greatest indication or symptom of an entity able to move through deeper levels of mind is the ability of the entity to see love in all portions of the creation. This is a product of a great deal of work over many periods or incarnations for the seeker of truth.

We feel that this is a great deal of information which if added to at this time might be somewhat confusing, therefore we shall allow any further query that you would have at this time.

Questioner: I have one more query. The bias towards learning or the biases that are created within the consciousness for learning I'm being taught more is, even though [it] sometimes creates in our experience pain—what we experience is pain or the illusion of suffering is also perfect in the eyes of the Creator and the consciousness of the higher self …

(Pause)

I am Q'uo, and we feel that we have the gist of your query and would agree that though much learning partakes in that which appears to be great suffering, disease, poverty, pain and separation one from another that these are often the most effective means of directing the attention which has not focused clearly upon the lessons at hand. The catalyst of pain, for example, is that which grabs your attention and points towards an area which contains the opportunity for uncovering a portion of the self which waits to be born. With each birth there is the pain of the delivery. That which is old and has been replaced by that which grows anew oftentimes must be allowed to be removed in a painful fashion.

Since the illusion in which you move has many veils across the far-seeing ability of any entity, it is necessary oftentimes that the eyes which see only dimly be given the assistance or the reminder that trauma and suffering provide. However, when the pearl has been won, no price or pain is too great.

At this time we feel that we have extended the energies of this group far enough that it would be well to give rest. Therefore, we shall once again thank each for inviting our presence and shall leave this group as we have found it in the love and in the light of the one infinite Creator. We are known to you as those of Q'uo. Adonai, my friends. Adonai. ❧

Sunday Meditation
November 25, 1990

Group question: The question this evening has to do with how one can find the way of being of service that is the most appropriate for that person at that time. Are there any techniques or procedures or ways that a person could make this information more available or discover this information in any way whatsoever?

(Carla channeling)

I am Q'uo. I greet each of you with great joy and gratitude in the love and in the light of the one infinite Creator. It is most delightful to us to be able to have the chance to attempt to share our thoughts with you, but we must ask, as we always make a point of asking, that our words not be taken as unexamined truth, for personal truth is different for each person, and that which may help another may be a stumbling block to you. Consequently, take that which is recognized by your own discrimination and discard any other words which did not make personal sense. Trust not any source but yourself, for within yourself lies a far better discernment than you know. It is within the grasp of each to imagine, but what you know is not that of which third density is greatly privileged to know, and although our illusion is more transparent, yet still we also seek to learn, as we are still aware of our own consciousness, and we have a long process ahead of us. So we feel not in any way different from you, for all consciousness is one.

How pleasant it is to listen to the soft household sounds through this instrument's ears. The melodies of your planet are beautiful, and we do appreciate them—the melody of your environment, the melody of your elements, the melody of the tone poem which is your incarnation. These are sweet, and sometimes sorrowed songs, yet they have called us to you, for there has been more and more a call among your people for information, resources and tools to use in the path of spiritual growth. We thank this instrument and all instruments for making themselves available to serve in this capacity.

However, we would, and not for the first time, point out that all services are dependent, not upon your assessment of your importance, but on the wholeheartedness with which you pursue that which is in your eye's shot. At any particular moment your path of service is with you. It is in many ways very difficult, we realize, to grasp the nature of service. And it is appealing and interesting to wonder if one could become a healer, or a channel, or some other dramatic path of service that would consume the life. However, service is not graded, except insofar as it is sincere in the attempt and genuine in refusing to do work in consciousness until you have examined, satisfactorily, any blockages that might be caused by misunderstood, misused or misperceived catalyst.

The Creator's thought was part and parcel of Its very nature. This thought is what we call love, because we cannot find any more appropriate word in your vocabulary. But it is a love of charity, of positivity, of creativity and of transformation. The main offering that you give in your incarnation to the world about you—and make no mistake, this is the density wherein one reckons with society, and all that it implies, for weal or woe—the first thing that you offer to the Father is yourself, your consciousness. The Creator, as described in older holy works, wished sacrifice. We ask only for the sacrifice of praise and thanksgiving, regardless of circumstance. In this lies the main and fundamental service each entity has to offer to the planet and to the Creator, which is Love Itself.

It is difficult for an entity within the illusion in which you dance to believe that something as simple as consciousness could be your greatest service. Yet consciousness is only simple to those who have not begun to search for the truth, and above all, we do not wish you to stand by in opportune polarizing situations, and say, as Pontius Pilate did, "What is truth?" and then walk away. This is not an incarnation in which you shall walk away from the catalyst, the lessons, the personal service to yourself, and the service to others that stems therefrom.

Let us gaze upon this concept from a slightly different point of view. The love that you have within you is finite due to the limitations of the heavy chemical illusion and your physical body whose sensing equipment is designed more to make choices than to understand. So, what is necessary for you to grasp if you wish to be of primary service in this incarnation and at this time, is to, as frequently as possible when you find yourself drifting into a nonpolarized or negative emotional state, to think back to that meditation with which you began your morning. Remember that then you did stand upon holy ground, no matter what your conscious experience, for it is your intent, it is your thought, that is real in the metaphysical universe.

We realize that this is a bitter pill to swallow for those who wish to have a path of service, for in working to find your own definitive self, in the effort to polarize, is often implicit the suggestion that one must somehow radically alter one's set of experiences and choose a path of service. This is not necessary, for you cannot leave the path once you are on it. You may sit by the roadside, you may walk, you may sing or you may cry. But once the mystery is perceived clearly for the first time, and once the nature of that mystery is gazed at clearly, one must see that, indeed, consciousness itself is chaos from which the mind, working like a computer, chooses this and that, this and that, to notice, but for most of the rest, not to notice. This is the physical and mental body complex's way of protecting itself.

The most strengthening gift that you can cultivate in the regard of this most important and central service is the gift of persistence and unflagging acceptance of any and all circumstances, because it is only an illusion that lies between you and that which is the truth. To extend across the chasm between doubt and faith some entities need great structures to guide them. Other entities find their chapel in the woods, or in the mountain, however it is that you are most comforted by meditation. Therefore, a basic step, if you wish truly to accelerate the pace of spiritual evolution, is first of all to learn to honor, love and value yourself as an absolute whole and perfect being. All else is illusion. You within are imperishable. You will one day discard this physical vehicle in order to grasp by review those things which you have done in this life, so that you may, with guidance, whether you call it the Holy Spirit, inner planes aid, or contacts such as this one, [form a new life plan]. This inner guidance is most transparent when the meditation is daily, without necessarily being as long as this instrument informs us our messages are.

The next point that we would like to discuss is that of the seeming disparity of potential for service that various entities have. Some seem to have many gifts, and as each gazes at itself it realizes it is lacking somewhat. That thinking needs to stop right there. In order to follow the law, which this instrument calls the Law of One, it is quite necessary to be vulnerable and open to circumstance, guided always from within, and if that guidance is not seemingly forthcoming, patience is your next, greatest, resource as a spiritual seeker.

There are many whose voices have been heard who speak of prophecy and doom and planetary catastrophe. We do not cavil at these people's messages, but only make note that where there is love there is not fear. If there is to be an opportunity for you to share that which you now are aware of as difficulties happen to cause those about you to remember that you are a spiritual seeker, then that is a beautiful service to offer—to answer the questions asked, to bear witness to the truth that you can have faith in, blind and unreasoning faith.

Now, we do not speak here of doctrine, of dogma. We would express our bias that these theologies are to be realized as structures available to people who find that particular structure to be the appropriate way to increase polarity, to drink of the water that shall never make you thirsty again, to eat the bread of eternal life. We use these images because this instrument is a Christian. However, these thoughts may be expressed in many variations of vocabulary, and perhaps the one that we would choose might be different. In each case where we speak we gauge the needs of the group, or gaze at the universal need that the group expresses by being more than two.

(Pause)

I am Q'uo, and greet you again in love and light. The instrument was experiencing catalyst which it could not continue channeling with, and we believe this is now back to an acceptable level. We shall continue.

In the event of what you call your catastrophes, the service-to-others entity will be given great opportunities for service, and bear in mind that service is action, is doing, as well as being, but the doing is not important, it is the frame of reference from which you approach each moment. We are not being mysterious on purpose, but the truth does not lie within our ability to offer to anyone without one's free will being abridged. However, if one relaxes, finds merriment to be freely bubbling forth, finds a place where the joy of loving and being loved is immediately experienced, then each may gaze at whatever one does as being done for the love of the infinite One. And as the emotions of devotion are turned towards the environment of the existing life and gazed at with an eye to being one who offers the positive point of view, then you may see that in any circumstance an entity with a positive, affirmative and hopeful point of view may well be foolish, which is acceptable in third density, indeed, almost necessary, for who but a fool would take the leap of faith that would say "I do not need to be concerned about my path of service, for I see in front of me a dish to wash, a compost heap to turn, a child or a friend to hug and share love with."

Develop the listening ear, for you have nothing to sell. We ask that it be considered whether or not evangelism is not an infringement upon free will. No matter how excited you may be over that which makes complete sense to you, it is not well to offer this to others without first dropping a few seeds, measuring things and seeing if the area in which you are interested is the area in which another is. If the two paths are mutually exclusive it is a kindness not to attempt to change others' paths because you feel that you have found more truth. You have found it because you were able to hear it. Those who are not ready for this material, or any material, simply will not take it in, or will have a mistaken opinion of that which was said.

It is very difficult to face the great key that unlocks the path of service. Meditation is a matter of discipline, and is very important. Reading inspirational things is helpful; many things are helpful. But where the Christ consciousness is allowed to seek opportunities to serve, the self finds that it never has enough hours in the day, but that the work is worth it. It all begins with the journey from temporality to infinity, and you are most open to infinity when you stay in the immediate present moment, for that is eternity. When the resonance of each moment can be felt, instead of simply a river of time moving from birth to death and robbing you of all that you have and eventually your body entirely, gaze at this entire experience with a calmer eye. You are here not to be happy, but to serve. This was your choice, else you would not be here, for the number of souls wishing to incarnate at this particular time is large, and [incarnation is offered only to] those who, by what this instrument would call seniority of vibration, that is, souls old enough to take an active part in designing the life experience so that they may learn.

It is difficult to believe that it all begins with forgiving yourself. Everyone has a different perception of himself than entities do of that entity. In other words, it is our observation from the limited experience we have had with your people that your culture is such as to greatly discourage precisely that which you are doing. But if you can— and you can—move back always to the memory of that holy ground, then you will be open to murmurings of spirit. This entity experiences the will that is greater than its own as a kind of two-by-four hitting one between the eyes so that there is no question about what the choice of service should be. This is a sensitive instrument, consequently it does experience the touch of spirit strongly. Others have less success in discerning guidance.

Perhaps the second greatest service an entity can provide is the giving of self in relationship, for by this means each can mirror to each the perceived personality, thus enabling both entities, if both entities are honest and clear, to proceed much more rapidly than if they did not have a mirror, if they were not held accountable for self-deceit. Especially of service is the sacrificial care and tending of young ones, for if you are able to offer support, confidence in the small entity, and charity, the charity of the greatly opened heart, then you shall have done a service for this soul that redounds through many lifetimes.

In all cases, if the presence of mind is yours at a time, ask yourself, if it is your catalyst, "Where is the lesson, where is the love in this catalyst?" If you have an analytical mind, it is helpful to think about it. If you are one who moves directly from the heart, it is well, rather, to ask for clear dreaming, and to keep the dream notebook at hand. We realize that that which we have to say may seem to deny each entity the choice of service paths. Indeed, although the decision has been made, it was your own. What is remaining is for you to discover by whatever means native to your gifts are most excellent, how to perceive the urgings of the guidance of the Christ-self or the love within.

The journey of service is the journey of the servant. This is not an easy mentality for your culture, but in truth, having loved yourself completely, you are then free to love others with the same unconditional flowing of love. First yourself, then others. We do not say this to make you be selfish. Quite the opposite; we say this to make you effective. For if you embark upon work in consciousness in an unworthy manner, soon you shall be exhausted, and sit at the side of the road you shall, until you regain that blind faith that keeps you stepping out constantly into thin air.

We have circled back to the key concept that creates the possibility for entities to take courage and move forward. It is when the self has been learned to the best of one's ability that one may be able to carry a more and more impersonal and all compassionate consciousness, trusting that although you did not make this up within your lifetime, as the arena upon which you would play your part, you did choose it, but there is no proof that you did chose this program. There will never be spiritual proof, for you are a being of free will. That is, there will not be truth itself, but you can be in the immediate presence of the most high, the most infinite, Creator.

Firstly, to love the Creator and to share it forth in your very consciousness in whatever condition, this is the first and greatest service. Secondly, in order to prepare yourself for service to others, the self who is going to be a servant needs to be well enough grasping of its own nature that it does not transfer the biases that it has towards the self to another. Thusly, we urge each always to give the first thought to clearing the self, polishing up the brass, washing the windows of the soul, becoming able to be a conduit for an infinite love, a resonant and creative love.

We feel that this is a beginning, and would now transfer this contact, due to the instrument's fatigue, to the one known as Jim. We thank this instrument for serving, and all instruments who serve, and we would thank all entities who may discover their paths of service by looking in front of their face, and seeing for the first time that in a universe created of love, no matter what the illusion, all is alive, all will return the love you give, tenfold, a hundredfold, and a thousandfold.

At this time we would leave this instrument. I am the principle known to you as Q'uo. I am at this time transferring to the one known as Jim. We leave you in love and light through this instrument. I am the principle known to you as Q'uo.

(Jim channeling)

I am Q'uo, and greet each again in love and light through this instrument. At this time we would open this session of working to those queries which may be upon the minds of those present. Again we would remind each that we offer that which is but our opinions, and though we offer them gladly and freely we would not wish any word that does not ring of truth to the listener to be kept within that listener's mind. Take only those words which seem useful to you and leave all others behind. May we ask if there is a query at this time to which we may speak?

D: I have a question. Is the planet healed by third-density attempts to heal it?

I am Q'uo, and am aware of your query, my brother. We find that there have been for many, many years attempts by various individuals and groups upon your planetary surface to bring about the healing within this planetary vibration, a healing which would seek to mend that which has been broken and distorted by the careless and violent upheavals within so many of your cultures for so much of your history. Those angers and acts of disrespect for self, for other selves, and for your planetary entity itself, have the accumulated effect of causing these disharmonious vibrations to be accepted by the planet itself, and these vibrations then build up a kind of karma, if you will, that which is the wound within the planet. This is also added to by the carelessness of the manner with which the planet and its resources are utilized within the human process of evolution, industrialization, standardization and the large scale manufacture of items for convenience.

Though there are many efforts that have had marked success in attempting the rebalancing and healing of your planet's ruptures, we find that there shall be for some period of time that is significant in your measure of time, a remaining evidence of this disharmony that will necessitate a continuation of this healing process into the fourth-density experience that has begun upon this sphere at this time. We encourage all such efforts at not only healing that which has been broken, but in ceasing to cause further damage by the conscious application of those principles of stewardship which each entity and culture creates and undertakes as a way of life and realizes as a standard of living, or of relationship, each with the other and with the planet itself.

Is there a further query, my brother?

D: Is the planetary entity being formed more by the passive sending of love and light than *(inaudible)*?

I am Q'uo, and am aware of your query, my brother. It is quite correct that the planetary entity is greatly benefited by that which you call the passive sending of love, light and healing energy, which may be done in any number of ways, including the meditation, the imagination, contemplation, prayer and the simple attitude of right use which each entity vibrates as a tone of the being, shall we say, as it accomplishes its daily round of activities. These sendings, or thoughts, in the metaphysical sense, are things which are felt and which find their place within this planet's web of energies and which work in an harmonious fashion with the planetary energies.

Is there a further query, my brother?

D: Is it better to accept someone who *(inaudible)* as they are even though it may be self-destructive, or to encourage change?

I am Q'uo, and am aware of your query, my brother. We find that it is helpful both to accept every entity that one meets as being whole and complete in the basic sense of being a portion of the one Creator which seeks to know Itself. That there may be apparent disharmonies within an entity's thinking or behavior may become a means by which a relationship is established with this entity in order that both entities may learn of a balanced path. It is such relationships that allow entities to work upon that catalyst which is the life's pattern and purpose, for as each partakes in the mirroring process it is as though each helps the other much as would the sculptor, in chiseling away that which is not desired, so that that which is the ideal becomes more clearly formed in each entity's life pattern.

However, we must add that the most important ingredient in this relationship and process of mirroring is the acceptance each of the other so that there is no need for change to occur for the entity to be accepted. When this level of trust has been established the foundation work has been accomplished and the structure of the relationship then may be built upon this firm foundation, and when there are difficulties that arise within the relationship, as most assuredly they will as a part of the playing out of catalyst, it is well for each to remind the other that the foundation of the relationship is acceptance, that is, not conditional, and which is all-embracing.

Is there a further query, my brother?

D: Is the form of energy work that I've come across out here in Oregon beneficial for spiritual growth, and how?

I am Q'uo, and am aware of your query, my brother. In this work, as any work which focuses upon the contacting of that shuttle known as the spiritual complex, is work which is beneficial to the evolution of any entity which partakes in it, for the most *(inaudible)* ingredient in any such work is not necessarily the apparent efficiency of the philosophy, the ritual or the practice, but is instead the intention of the entity which undertakes the philosophy, the ritual or the practice.

When the intent is strong and when the intent persists, then there is constructed within the entity a channel to those energies which are being expressed in whatever manner the practice sets up as a means of expressing these more subtle energies. Working as you are with the subtler energies that enliven and undergird the physical expression of spirit, you may notice that there is within the life pattern added a certain vitality which is as a resource or reservoir of energy which may be utilized according to one's desires and will. This choice of use of subtle energy vitality is a choice which is crucial in the polarization of any entity, for the choice to utilize such energies in service to others will continue to enhance the evolutionary process.

Thus, the energies with which you work are powerful according to your intention, your perseverance and your choice of usage.

Is there a further query, my brother?

D: No, thank you.

I am Q'uo, and we thank you, my brother. Is there another query at this time?

Carla: I have one, which you may or may not be able to answer, because it's specific, but it's something that I've been experiencing for awhile and I felt that I should question you for any comments you might have. I keep waking up in the middle of a sentence. It's very distracting, and has thrown me off a couple of times this evening because I must have sort of, without leaving my body, just gone very deep. And the question is, is this an artifact of my low vitality, or is it a sensitivity of some kind to something that you have in mind, for instance, *(inaudible)* the best state that I can be in without being in trance?

I am Q'uo, and am aware of your query, my sister. Your latter assumption is more nearly correct. We are working with your instrument and your vital energy, especially the physical energy level, in a way which we hope may stabilize the contact at a level which is both efficient in the transfer of concept and relatively comfortable to you as you partake in this process. We would recommend that you not be overly concerned with the phenomenon of awakening, as you have put it, in the middle of a sentence or a concept, but continue as you have for lo these many years to step off the cliff without knowing where the foot will land. It is this willingness to offer the self wholeheartedly as an instrument which will aid any instrument's progress as it seeks to improve its function as an instrument.

Thus, we congratulate you on your continued perseverance and practicing of your art and would comfort your concern with these words.

Is there a further query, my sister?

Carla: Just what is happening? I mean, am I going out of time, because to tell you the truth, tonight it was—I thought I'd been talking for maybe five minutes, and the recorder clicked, it was supposedly 45 minutes. I guess it's the truth, but I wasn't aware of most of it. What was I doing if I didn't leave my body? I mean, was I actually going to sleep? I'm not overly concerned about it, I just want to understand it, in case it happens to somebody else that I have been teaching.

I am Q'uo, and am aware of your query, my sister. The process that is ongoing as you continue in your channeling is one which takes you deeper into the subconscious levels of your mind complex and which approaches that which you call the trance level without actually entering into this level of mind, for we do not wish to work with your instrument in that kind of experience, for reasons which you are well aware. However, that which we have noted within your conscious mind more nearly approaches what you would call the sleep state, or more correctly, the hypnogogic state that is associated with the rapid eye movement or dream state that is within the sleep state. This …

(Tape ends.)

L/L Research

Intensive Meditation
November 29, 1990

(Jim channeling)

I am Q'uo, and greet each in love and light this evening. It is our great privilege to be called to your group once again. It is gatherings such as these for which we are most thankful in our attempt to give voice to those concepts which are answers to your heart's seeking.

We have been observing your group this evening and have noted the sense of fatigue and discomfort that is present within the circle and we shall be mindful of these distortions as we utilize the instruments this evening. We would not wish to tax or overtire each instrument. We realize that your daily round of activities, as you call it, provides each of you with as much food for metaphysical use as is possible for you to process at this time.

Each of you works with a personal system of processing that utilizes both similar and dissimilar means of interpreting catalyst. Each is able to make a certain kind of sense, shall we say, out of those activities that occur as part of the day's natural rhythm, that many entities, less aware of the evolutionary process, fail to notice or would notice in ways which would not be to the heart of the meaning and purpose of the catalyst. This is not unusual, for most entities will satisfy themselves with penetrating but the outer shell of experience and in this way will remain somewhat at a distance from the transformative effects of catalyst that has been well used.

This distance, however, though it may provide a certain amount of shielding from the intensities of the well-perceived catalyst, does not offer the opportunity for the entity to immerse itself within the sea of experience. So it is for those who choose to look more deeply and more carefully, with respect, looking again [many] times at those moments of imprinting, where catalyst moves through the perceptive film or net, and is seen in a certain way, according to this net of perceptions, this grouping of ways in which certain events, certain entities and relationships are formed and have an effect upon an entity's senses, both those of the outer or normal way of sensing and those senses which are more of an interior nature and which take a more active part in providing an interpretation of outer stimuli.

These inner sensing devices are those qualities which have been developed during the early part of the incarnation, according to the experiences at that point within the incarnation which came before the entity [was] able to recognize certain configurations to be significant and to be worthy of consideration when perceived.

An entity will notice those portions of its environment which in its past [were] proven to play an active part. Now, this active part is determined by the entity itself and not by the structure of the stimuli. However, there is the necessary interaction between the entity and its outer environment that there is the establishment of correspondences between certain stimuli and the welfare of the entity.

We would at this time seek to transfer this contact so that we may continue this topic with the one known as K. We transfer this contact to the one known as K. I am Q'uo.

(K channeling)

I am Q'uo, and greet each of you once again, in love and light, through this instrument.

We were speaking about catalyst on a day-to-day basis by those aware, to various degrees, of the process of evolution. The procedures used by various entities in processing this catalyst vary greatly. Many, as you are aware, simply go through their lives, day by day, taking part in their various activities with no clear concepts or even much thought given to the purpose of their lives, the nature of the spiritual dimension, of the personality, or the process of spiritual evolution itself.

There are those who give some thought to this process, but what realizations they may come to do not impact their lives. There are those others which we may call the serious seekers which give much thought to the process, attempting each day as much as possible to utilize those awarenesses they may have come to in their lives. This is a very frustrating process for many, for, as each of you are aware, it may seem that one is making no progress. Much thought may be given, much may be studied, much may be realized, and yet their life seems unchanged. This is part of the nature of the illusion which you inhabit at this time. And we salute your continued efforts for you are, as we have said before, largely groping around in the dark.

As you continue upon your metaphysical journey you know you are pointed in the direction of mystery and in that direction you ever proceed. But you are constantly entangled in the day-to-day-ness of your daily round of activities. How busy your peoples are! How intensely focused on the many, many details of the life. We realize the extreme difficulty of transcending this nature of your culture.

The encouragement we can offer you is that the progress you make is largely invisible to yourselves. It may go unseen, unfelt, and yet it is taking place, for on the metaphysical planes, the intention is all. The desire and the will are what carry you on toward your goal. We would urge you not to judge yourself in these matters, not to be constantly taking stock of your estimation of your progress or lack thereof, for this serves only to inject criticism and blame, which is never helpful. Your powers of observation are valuable to you, and we do encourage you to observe yourselves, your reactions, your thoughts, and feelings. And, whatever they may be, to continue your journey in the dark with the companions you have to comfort you in this process.

We would speak to you now of the one thing we would have you keep uppermost in your minds upon this journey, and that is faith. The faith that there is, indeed, a mystery beyond the illusion. That there is just cause to warrant your great and often painful efforts and sacrifices as you continue your activities upon your goal, as you continue the disciplines of the personality, the integrity in upholding the spiritual principles which are truth for you at this time. The faith to continue when all the illusion about you seems to be calling you the fool—for such you are, in the eyes of the illusion.

The journey of the seeker, with regard to the illusion, may be a very lonely one. You have your companions but they do not always walk with you, for each has his own truth to follow, which does lead to the same mystery. The will of each in this group is strong, yet we would offer what encouragement we may, for we see your weariness, and would seek to encourage you where possible. We know you are aware of the nature of the illusion, and from our point of view, outside of your particular illusion, we are aware of many things. Yet, faith and will must remain strong with us as well, for the mystery recedes ever before us, and we, as you, must continue on our path.

The catalyst that comes to you day by day may seem to you to be often of an overwhelming nature. You are aware that you have programmed for yourself large amounts of catalyst to maximize the experience available to you in this incarnation. We are aware that there is much inefficient use of catalyst. Yet, the encouragement we would offer you on this point is that, once again, much progress [is] made on levels not perceptible to your conscious mind. The conscious focusing upon spiritual principles you wish to incorporate into your lives, the disciplines of daily meditation, the examination of the life, are types of work that you do on a conscious level, but they do not stop there. They begin patterns that continue, carried on by levels in your sub-conscious mind to process the catalyst that comes to you.

Thus, changes may begin in your life of which you are not aware. This is the nature of the change which you would call "from the inside out." Only much later, if at all, will you see the changes manifested, and yet they begin to take place at the core of your being.

We would at this time transfer once again to the one known as Jim. I am Q'uo, and transfer now.

(Jim channeling)

I am Q'uo, and we greet each again in love and light through this instrument. At this time we would offer ourselves for the answering of any queries which may be helpful to those here gathered. Is there a query to which we may speak?

Carla: I would like to ask a question, which you may or may not be able to answer, and that is simply that I am not aware because I haven't been in this situation before, where a sustained period of intense pain has made me feel that perhaps I could not tune properly. I went through the tuning *(inaudible)* and I felt surprisingly secure even in the midst of the physical illusion of pain. It is now my perception that neither pain nor lack of pain has anything to do with the clearing of the energy centers or the tuning process, if the heart and the mind and intent are purely positive, which surprises me. I would have thought that there would be some point at which I would be unable to carry a strong positive signal. If this is, in fact, an illusion, incorrect information which I am perceiving incorrectly became I am in pain, I would enjoy knowing that. However, I totally accept your need to maintain free will and release you from any obligation to answer this question in any way if it is not important *(inaudible)*.

I am Q'uo, and am aware of your query, my sister. We thank you for your great care in providing the easiest environment in which we may speak to your query. However, we find that there is no infringement in reminding you of that which you know. You have discovered that there are certain activities that are a central portion of your being, which you may engage in and have the release from the physical pain. You have been able to put aside, through a process of long experience of dealing with this pain, great amounts of this catalyst. It has been your experience that singing sacred music will bring your perceptions to the door of beauty and devotion, without the feeling of the great discomfort which pain brings while you are engaged in the singing of sacred music.

You are also aware of this effect as it is related to the transfer and sharing of the sexual energy exchanges. This is due to the fact that there is a certain enjoyment and expression of this enjoyment of the life experience which you find closely connected to the worshipful attitude, and this phenomenon of the ability to move aside the pain during these experiences is also noticed within the offering the self as vocal instrument. These experiences are those which you place a great amount of faith, devotion and praise in the doing and experiencing. It is your ability to set aside the concerns of the mundane level, and also of the physical pain, which serves you now in the vocal channeling process. However, this is not a phenomenon that has no limitations, shall we say, it is only that you have not currently exceeded the amount [of] the pain that you may experience without affecting your ability to serve as a vocal instrument.

Thus, we commend your willingness, your dedication, your preparation, your perseverance. However, we would take this opportunity to remind you of that which you are perhaps becoming more familiar, and that is that the increase in pain past a certain point can have the debilitating effect of removing one's ability to carry out the desires of will and faith. However, at this time you have found yourself yet within that area where the ability to experience pain does not yet overcome your ability to worship and serve in a manner which is central to your life path.

Is there another query, my sister?

Carla: Well, I am extraordinarily thankful for that answer. I have a little follow-up, and then I have one more question based on what you said. When I get to the threshold where I cannot make safe contact, will I know it ahead of time, that is, will I be so involved in dealing with the pain that it would not occur to me even to try? Or need I be watchful past any particularly overtly evident signs?

I am Q'uo, and am aware of your query, my sister. We have found that you are sensitive enough to all stimuli that you will be able to discover this configuration in which contact would not be possible by your own experience. For you it would be as though a door had not been opened that you were used to having open almost without effort.

Is there another query, my sister?

Carla: Yes, there was something that you said that I've always meant ask you. It has been my feeling for as long as I can remember that the physical act of making love is kind of a thanksgiving or Eucharist, a sacrament, and is as holy as the passion of the spirit and the passion of the open heart or service-oriented passions are. Does this idea show some distortion, and if so, in what way? What is the clear perception?

I am Q'uo, and am aware of your query, my sister. It is, to our best knowledge, true that the sexual energy exchanges offer the potential for the most sacred of worship as the two entities become one in seeking, one in experience, and one in expression of that which is sought and that which is experienced. However, for most entities, as is the case for most opportunities for such worship and serving, there is only the beginning movement into that which is truly sacred and that which gives the heartfelt praise and thanksgiving that is possible to give within [this] type of energy exchange, and expression of this exchange. Thus, again, we have the intention, the purity of intention, being the primary factor in determining whether such an experience, or any experience, shall provide the sincere and sacred joy and praise to the one Creator.

Is there another query, my sister?

Carla: No, thank you very much for all, and just thank you in general.

I am Q'uo, and again we thank you, my sister, for your queries, for your presence and your perseverance. Is there another query at this time?

K: I have a question. I am usually unable to distinguish between my own thoughts and what I consider to be those given to me by you. Can you let me know whether I was adhering relatively well to *(inaudible)* approximate *(inaudible)* what you communicated to me, and, if so, when I felt there was time to transmit a thought, were you done at that time?

I am Q'uo, and am aware of your query, my sister. We find that this evening you were able to perceive and transmit our thoughts in quite an accurate manner and to a degree which is quite acceptable. We are very happy to be able to make and maintain a secure contact through your instrument. We were satisfied with the amount of information we were able to transmit through your instrument, and though were not completely ended with that which we could have offered through the instrument, we found that the degree of fatigue was such that in order to maintain your instrument at a more efficient level of functioning, shall we say, it was well to end when we did, rather than to attempt to extend the exercise period with what one may call diminishing returns, due to the degree of fatigue.

Thus, in the case of every instrument there is the limit that is reached where it is well for the contact to consider termination of the contact, in order that the information transmitted might be of the highest quality or the most accurate transmission.

Is there another query, my sister?

K: Do you have any suggestions as to how I might focus more clearly on the contact, or improve the contact in general?

I am Q'uo, and *(inaudible)* working with this instrument. The degree of concern you have shown for the practice of vocal channeling is commendable and we thank you for your care and for the increasing desire that we have noticed within you for wishing to improve the service which you offer. For most instruments that are new to this practice it is almost always correct to suggest that the relaxation during the channeling process is most helpful, continuing the honing of the inner perceptive skills. This is to say that allowing undue worry to wash away from one's consciousness and to relax as much as is physically, mentally and emotionally possible provides the framework in which work may be done most successfully. Thus, we have for you no suggestion beyond that which you already do, and have done well for some period of time, and that is to be as meticulous as is possible in the tuning, in the challenging, and then to give away the cares and concerns so that one may relax into that inward posture which will allow one to perceive and transmit those thoughts which we give to you.

Is there further query, my sister?

K: *(Inaudible)* practice. Thank you very much.

I am Q'uo, and again I thank you, my sister. We find that we have spoken for a relatively short period of time, for us, this evening, and we take this opportunity to—this instrument has some difficulty with this concept—to congratulate ourselves for curtailing that which we have to offer. We, however, cannot take full credit, for, as we have noted before, this group has some significant degree of fatigue this evening. Thus, our credit-taking is offered as our form of humor, which this instrument has some difficulty in penetrating.

We thank you, my friends. We enjoy your presence, your determination, and your good-humored laughter. We shall leave this group at this time, in the love and the light of the One infinite Creator. We are known to you as those of Q'uo. Adonai, my friends. Adonai. ☙

L/L Research

Sunday Meditation
December 2, 1990

Group question: The question this evening: what happens, from the metaphysical view, as a channel and supporting group begin to receive a positive contact? What happens in the way of attracting negative temptations and attention, and why do so many groups end up with such a strange mix of information?

(Carla channeling)

I am Q'uo, and I greet you in the love and in the light of the one infinite Creator, whose name, though ever unspoken, and unrevealed [in] its nature, [is] the source and ending of all that is, all that has been, all that will be, all illusion, and all of that which we know not, yet hope [for], that lies beyond the mystery, unknowable by personality, words, consciousness or activity. We speak in the name of the unnamable, we speak in adoration and worship of a mystery we cannot plumb. We are humble, and we are also humble before you, that all of you are to us the beloved self that holds that mystery, as do we for you. Yet we cannot give it to ourselves, we must give it to others, and you give it a hundredfold and more to us. We are your brothers and sisters.

We have made a major concession to this instrument, for it has requested repeatedly that we assign ourselves more than the name we have given, and, indeed, less, for this instrument is not gazing and searching for new models. This instrument is provincial and archaic, and requests that we use the term "angels" as we greet you. It increases her ability to channel, and aids each of us in the other's polarization. We have found in this instrument no taint of personal bias in the worship of the Creator, but only in its usage of myth to focus upon the mystery. Consequently, we may say to you that we are those of the Confederation of Angels and Planets in the Service of the One Infinite Creator, and so we shall attempt to address ourselves to this instrument, but we do not ask you to accept either our angel status, or our extraterrestrial status. We care not. Think that we are of this instrument's mind alone, that would satisfy us, and it would satisfy this instrument.

And so we move, hopefully without breaking the seamless thought, into the question you have asked this evening. The first temptation to a channel is the temptation to channel before the creation of a mythical pathway that one holds personally sacred, that one holds to with passion, with dedication, and if necessary, with life effort, for all of you strive and age and die in your senses and your physical vehicle. Yet only those who know why they are living, and for whom, or for what undying principle they would stand firm, [can endure] against every temptation, every deceit, every anger, every grudge, every human emotion that rips the positive polarity from the soul of the minister of the word. It is essential to the achieving and the continuation of a contact which has a lifelong integrity, or any duration whatsoever on a stable basis, that the instrument be an instrument who is an advocate of the mystery, and is no longer struggling terribly with "why."

Those who must sail are sailors, and others would do well to stay upon land. Those who wish to use spiritual contacts such as this one with purity over a period of time must continually practice that which they focus upon as their mythical path, from the past and present and future to the timeless infinite, the spaceless everness of the One. The centrality of this cannot be overstated. We mind not by what end you choose to make your stand. We care only that you have chosen, and that your choice is made in utter blindness. Never, ever, make a choice because of someone else's path or someone else's truth, for all paths lead to but one place if they are efficacious. And one which you create knowing yourself will accomplish, if there is worship, adoration and the purification of emotion, the same end as this instrument's quite prolific, many-peopled, greatly-historied myth. Indeed, this instrument does not carry what many Christians would call the Christian myth, for many Christians do not realize that myths are created by those who know their importance, that Jesus the Christ intended ever, from the beginning of this entity's ministry, not to create understanding, but to create confusion and challenge and mystery.

And does any true spiritual path, proven efficacious to many, ever offer proof, or specificity, or any claim to know what lies beyond the veil of deity? Who claims to know the Creator in any but experience? That one you will watch carefully, for there is a personal bias, there is a limit, there is an intolerance. How great the difference between those who have the religion of fear and those who have the religion called love. That is not religion, but life itself.

Given that the instrument is prepared, has dedicated itself to a ministry in which it knows ahead of time that it shall be stripped of much of its humanity as it gains experience in joy and forsakes the glamour of happiness, then that instrument may listen further. But we imagine many would stop just now, and say, "Perhaps I have some work to do, perhaps I have a self to examine, a life choice to make, and perhaps there is too much at stake for me to choose now, for I do not know whither I go. I must be moving on for I have not found my path home." Let those who seek and yet feel a dedication to ministry move on blind faith, but not for any other reason but the feeling of vocation, the love of people one at a time, never humankind, but individuals such as yourself. That is who listens to you, not humankind.

That is the first and greatest temptation, to think that you can save the planet. My beloveds, there are many of us here, numbers you would not understand. They have not been able to do anything except talk to people who are all ready to awaken, and this is the season of the year in which, although all that grows in second density has buckled down into the earth to gain sustenance over a long sleep, you humans, yearning for the light and warmth that seems so reminiscent of the Creator, seek the hardest and look the hardest for the truth. This season of darkness is the perfect beginning place for faith. It is not possible to see, but then, since one cannot see or sense in any way the truth of the mystery, one needs one's heart, one's strength and one's life, and a dedication to serving in the name of love.

The first temptation is to be more than a servant, more than a foolish—we find this phrase in the instrument's use greatly—religiously preoccupied person, more than any hysteria could account for. Those who are not able to withstand being foolish shall never be able to offer others any description of Holy Ground that is provocative enough to create an area of thought in which people may begin to feel the concepts we cannot speak in words. Concepts are helpful, but they themselves give no understanding in this density.

Thus, anyone who comes to you with specific information that has been channeled may be carefully studied as to the source of this information and the history of the group, for it is not of the Confederation to move from the role of aide and helper, comforter and succorer of the lost and wandering, to speak of specific events. Would that not be to infringe upon the free will of many for nothing? Is there some reason that we should interrupt the Creator's harmony? Yes, it looks to those who live within the flesh. But there is a time of terrible trouble already in motion, and within your illusion this is so. But is it not clearly seen that it is in the dark ages, the dark times, the perilous situations, that one is minded of mortality and likelier to think upon the possibilities that their candle shall not be blown out when the flesh ceases viability? So then the channel must be ready, not to predict safety for the body, but safety to the soul.

Now why do instruments choose to ignore our simple refusal to answer from a Confederation channel? You who are not as precise in your terminology would call this an ego problem, but since that is only a jargon term used by a most biased healer, we would not choose that. We choose simply to offer what we can to those words, "ego problem," which are further made specific with our terminology as difficulties in the various energy centers of the lower body. That is ego, the blocked, overactive or otherwise imbalanced or obstructed lower energies. For only they can stop the full flow of love, energy, power, illumination, transformation and vitality to the heart, for the heart must bear the greater part of this incarnation for each of you. Each of you seeks to learn lessons concerned with love. There is an intellectual love, but it is a folly of the mind. The wisdom of the deep mind is an open heart, and love has never made any sense, nor can you make it make sense.

Consequently, any ego blockage will cause a new instrument, or even one who has much experience, to wish that it had an answer for this question or that, or perhaps the channel itself wishes to speak a concept, and when it perceives a refusal from us, decides that it would do no harm, since it is such good advice, to offer it, while not in the flow, not being the servant of love.

Those who do the best channeling make their requirements known as they make the connection, with fastidiousness and dedication, only to that which they call master, to that love of which they are the servant, and can be proud of being the servant. There is no energy except faith, call it hope, or love, or faith, or charity. The open heart is the protection against this single most telling detuning mechanism, and that is the interference of the channel itself.

Look at as suspect any prophesying, and as very suspect any prophesying which has to do with your numbering system, for we have always confessed to you each social memory complex that has moved through this instrument has expressed the difficulty, which approaches impossibility, of dealing with your local geometry, arithmetic and numbering system. It is, indeed, an artifact of human observation, quite relative and quite local, as you shall undoubtedly discover when, and if, you are able to plumb the deeper riches of space as you see it.

Think of it. How many among your peoples are not in some way bound by fear, or attachment, to this physical incarnation. It is understandable that people would come to you, the channel, with many, many questions, for they do not know where to begin. Each culture has chosen in its religious practice so to divide and multiply that unity is so far from being within even any one religious system, that each belief oddity vies with each other artifact of humanity and logic, and all fall by the wayside, with endless wrangling and division. Nothing could please what this instrument would call the loyal opposition more, for any leaving of the unity of nonjudgment in persons not immaterial leads to division in thinking processes more basic that a simple error caused by bias.

Examine the way you look at people. How do you judge them? For the terrible cultural penalty of being poor? Your culture seems to have abandoned most of the Ten Commandments, but that is the one commandment it does not seem to be able to do without, "Thou shalt not be poor." But those who are not poor in heart, as the one known as Jesus said, among you will find yourselves all too entranced by the human condition, all too full of desires, whimsies, fancies, needs, supposed or real. We judge not, but only note the incredible shortness of the time you have here, the incredible amount of work there is to do within, and as witness to love in whatever way each person feels is appropriate.

Where is love and service if all is wasted and spent upon vainglory, the feel-goods, position, power, ambition—what are these things but uses of ego, as you would call it, those to unbalance the self and to live through one's relationships and one's position. My friends, each of you is better than that, stronger than that, more single than that, less needy than that. Each of you has every basic qualification to be a living saint, as this instrument would put it, to be a servant of love that is not swayed. But, oh, the work that lies ahead of one that stands at that choice. Yet we say to you in each moment that is the choice: to do very hard work for eternity, or to be ambitious within this school. If things come to you, their value may be the richest person in gold or power or position, whatever there was. But if you have an attachment to it, insofar as that attachment lies, that deeply shall you be tested.

The testing is the second area. In testing, you are not yet tempted, you are simply offered ways that are difficult and ways that seem easy. Look out for the easy way, for the way that is glib, and simple, and short, and painless. Look out for the weekend that will change your life, or the seminar that will awaken your consciousness forever, for what you seek you shall get, and you must be ready to deal with that responsibility, for with each honor does come responsibility, with each learning does come the doing.

One who channels in dedication and quietness of heart is itself one who has abandoned much. Let those who are positive channels tell you individually their stories. We assure you they will not feel that they have given anything up. It has flowed into their lives and away from them, and the less they have resisted it the easier it is.

Pain is always there for one who follows what this instrument calls the Christ, and what we feel comfortable in calling Christ consciousness, for we would not be a stumbling block before any, nor seem to blaspheme, for we are lovers of the mystery, and honor Jesus, this master who opened the doors of perception to eternity for any who choose to take up the cross of life and live it as if it were the last three hours of your life. Burn that hot each day, and you will see various ways in which the humanity within has been burned away, not to be replaced by indifference, or a lack of perception, or care, or compassion, but rather purified somewhat, and able from that stance to have at least an idea of what it takes to tune the self to the highest that it can be tuned. It is this dedication and this realization that may keep you who wish to channel purely from testing. But each new realization, each new piece that is found in the strife within of humanity versus eternity, will be tested.

We do not deny humanity. It is precious, every moment of every life, precious beyond telling, for the Creator chooses here the nature of Its experience, and you are the spokesperson for that consciousness within you. You, light itself, love itself, carried about by an animal, a greatly sacrificial animal that has offered its pure, excellent, instinctual life of non-suffering and non-self-awareness and bliss, that it may serve that which it sees to be that which is closer to the infinite One. Love your body, bless your body, care for it, cherish it, but do not be attached to it one way or the other.

If an entity is hesitant, or troubled, or moves into negative emotion when it has polarized to the point at which it has attracted the loyal opposition, then it may experience the next level of detuning influence which is personal, and although clumsy, not unclever, and ever ready to use existing biases that separate, that destroy—either the self or others within the mind as perfectly acceptable—the temptation comes. These opportunities in a polarized being are precious to those who wish to offer a different view of the New Age that shall be and is now becoming so. They wish to focus the mind upon those things which people fear, because they identify themselves as those who look such and such a way, talk such and such a way, think such and such a way. If all this has not been considered, the temptations will be very easy. You will be tempted in weak moments to give opinions to those who are new to the path, opinions too strong for their fragile faith.

Any judgmental opinion of any spiritual work offered to a new soul, one newly aware of the choice and of the path, is creating a disservice to the one infinite Creator, for all information is placed there because someone desired it. The great preponderance of negative information is a cultural artifact of a lack of passion, a lack of belief, faith, dedication, hope or sense of destiny, that involves anything to do with eternity. *(Inaudible)*. Many seek wisdoms which would make one feel special, elite, different. Well, each of you is different, each of you is unique, there is only one you in the entire creation. And when you say to the Creator, "Listen to me. I am—" and you name yourself, it does not matter what name you use; it is the way in which you use it.

If there is a desire within any to appear a better channel than another, to appear a cleverer or more advanced studier than another, to have a more advanced level of understanding, ah, those things make one ripe for the picking, for there is no message that has come before your people that has not been requested; even those of negativity cannot sell their wares where there are no buyers. Those who do not fear will not buy fear. Those who do not buy love will buy fear. Let those who fear pay attention to channels that have been taken over by fear and are causing fear.

We do not say that this or that channel is true or false in terms of this illusion. We say only that this illusion is very short, and that you are not attached, except by choice, to it. You came here by choice. You do not leave here by choice, but by destiny. You do not move from one moment to the next, from one heartbeat to the next, from one breath to the next. You cooperate with destiny, or you do not. And as you resist, so the forces of separation test and then tempt the faith that you have begun with. So make sure that you are standing upon a faith you can live with, and if necessary die for, because, and we do not say this lightly, there is the tendency of those who are fools for love to find their manner of living and their manner of dying unusual, so that it may be remarked that so and so gave one's life for love, for divine and sacred love. We do not speak only of martyrs, but of all those who have lived and died in faith and never remained, always to be forgotten by history, but always at home in their path that has opened to them the gate of eternity.

There is a chasm which cannot be crossed except by faith, and the stirring up of faith is that with which all ministers, lay or clerical, are concerned. Any other business is that of emptying the self to be an appropriate servant, for we must use the purest pipe we can, to …

(Side one of tape ends.)

(Carla channeling)

I am Q'uo, and I speak again through this instrument in love and in light. We continue.

For we must use the purest instrument in order to offer the purest contact, and thus be of the service that we most humbly came to offer you, and for which we are so grateful.

We see by the clicking of your tape recording machine that we have once again spoken what this instrument has explained carefully is the limit this evening, for this instrument. We have been so, so glad, so blessed by your call and your beautiful company. We offer you the joy of communion in love, and in oneness, and we hope that you may go forth in joy, shining like the sun, ready to gaze with humor and a light touch, and always invoking merriment upon any occasion, as you wend your way through what would otherwise be rather jagged territory. This is third density, the density of choice. Have you made your choice, and having made it, are you a witness of your own truth? We do not just ask this of vocal channels, to whom this message has been dedicated, but to all, for all channel something, as this instrument has often said.

We now leave this instrument, and transfer to the one known as Jim, to close the meeting, for which we greatly thank you again. We are known to you as those of Q'uo.

(Jim channeling)

I am Q'uo, and greet each of you again in love and light through this instrument. We would close the meeting this evening by, as always, offering ourselves to any queries which those present may find helpful in their own seeking. May we ask if there is a query at this time?

Carla: Did you really let me say "angels," Q'uo? I want to make sure I didn't *(inaudible)*.

I am Q'uo, and we did indeed, my sister.

Carla: That's the nicest Christmas present anybody ever gave me, Q'uo, thank you, *(inaudible)*.

We are happy to offer a gift which is wrapped in a paper that is more joyful, and we thank you for your service. Is there another query at this time?

Questioner: *(Inaudible)*.

I am Q'uo. We are also very grateful for this opportunity to welcome one who has been in your terms long absent from this circle of seeking, and we greet her in love and in light. We find that her journey has been one that has taken her a great distance from her normal surroundings, and we look upon her with joy and send our blessings as her journey continues, to move her both in the outward and in the inward sense to those places where light is needed and light grows ever more brightly. We thank each for offering us a means to which to speak thoughts which we offer freely.

At this time we shall leave this instrument and this group, leaving each, as always, in the love and in the light of the one infinite Creator. We are known to you as those of Q'uo. Adonai, my friends. Adonai. ✤

L/L Research

Sunday Meditation
December 16, 1990

Group question: The question this evening has to do with what Q'uo would say to a person who is just beginning the search into the area of metaphysics. What are the salient, most important concerns? What should you focus on, and are there any things that we should not consider, should avoid? What should be the most important considerations of a person who is just beginning the conscious seeking into the area of metaphysics and the so-called New Age phenomena?

(Carla channeling)

Greetings in the love and in the light of the one infinite Creator. I am known to this group as the principle Q'uo. We have been called to a great blessing upon this day, and we wish to bless each of you and thank you with great humility for considering our opinions worthwhile. We have indeed perhaps been upon this road of which you ask for a longer period of time in your way of measuring. However, we are not at all infallible, and wish to ask each to listen with great discrimination, and to accept only those thoughts that seem helpful and truthful and loving to each individual entity. Anything that is other than that we ask that you do us the favor of putting aside without any second thought, for when information is yours, you will know this, and when it is not, you will know this, for deep within each of you is excellent discrimination based upon the knowledge of all that is that is locked securely and deeply within the very heart of your being.

We may say that it is to the benefit of any seeker to approach the path as if it were its first day upon this path. Consequently, when we speak to those who are beginning the path, we speak also to those who take another step upon the path; to those who are sitting, weary and tired by the side of the path; to those who have seemingly been treed in the rocky terrain of this path by fierce wild beasts; to those who are enjoying gifts of the path, and who may perhaps be less than pleased when the path becomes difficult, and it shall become difficult, and infinitely easy, by sudden turns. Meanwhile, the truth that you seek, that we seek, and that the Creator seeks of Itself, recedes in mystery forever beyond the seeker.

Yet, the endless path is indeed ended at last, as in cosmically large amounts of what you call time, all of the universe, all consciousness, coalesces once again in the unaware, intelligent infinity that is the closest that we have been able to come in your language to describing that which we would call the Creator, and that which we perceive to be a nurturing Creator which has infinite regard for that which It has created. It was noted that the prayer to the Father[3] was perhaps a limiting factor. Indeed, the nature of one's relationship to the Creator may be any

---

[3] The Lord's Prayer, with which the sessions are begun.

relationship which nurtures the entity. It may be considered as father, as mother, as father and mother, or as any unknown, mysterious, but somehow kindly, spirit, that is Consciousness Itself, just as you are, in essence, consciousness.

The difference between the consciousness of all that is and the consciousness which you experience is that in order to experience Itself, the Creator created entities which are self-aware and which made free choices so that there was nothing slavish about the possibility of loving the Creator—in the Creator's mind—but rather an infinite curiosity. Each of you is experiencing, and in your experience, the Creator Itself is enriched and learns, and as that giant heart beats from creation to creation, each creation builds on the last, and each of you, beings of light, infinite and eternal, move also, from illusion to illusion, and then into non-self-awareness, and then once again moving outward into individuation, learning and experiencing. Is this not a pleasant infinity? Always learning, always moving, and always resting.

Now we have laid a groundwork upon which we would like to build. Let us talk for a moment or two about what you may call your mind or your brain, or as this instrument does, your biocomputer. The nature of your mind is such that it is geared, as a computer is, to make a large number of choices very quickly in order to tend to the survival of the physical vehicle of which it is the intelligence. The programming of this computer is most usually not done by the entity within the incarnation in any conscious manner, but is a reflection of those needs for survival—physical, mental, emotional and spiritual—that were being experienced at the survival level when you as an entity were powerless and unable to defend yourself.

Consequently, there is strong programming toward self-protection, and much of that which is programmed to be noticed is that which has to do not only with physical needs for survival, such as the breathing the air, but more subtle needs which are discovered as the entity grows in years and experience. Usually there is much more programming concerning the behavior requested of those who wish to enjoy the privileges of being considered normal and aware of consensus reality.

Because so much of the program is concerned with behavior, the mind finds itself programmed in sometimes quite extensive defense mechanisms for slowing, stopping and being able to control uncomfortable environments. All of this programming was undoubtedly offered to each entity before it had an opportunity to consider whether or not it wished its programs to run thusly. This is an important point, because only, perhaps, two or three or four percent of the available space, shall we say, for the retention of data within your biocomputer is accepted as worthy of notice. The rest is ruthlessly ignored.

Think to yourself: what have you noticed this day that was not useful in some way to your survival or your enjoyment? We suggest to you that it is within your ability to reprogram this computerized choice-making in order that you may notice more of those things which you feel have spiritual significance and less of those things which you feel have become undesirable things to notice. Those things may be any portion of yourself which is judgmental towards yourself especially, which is not accepting of the self, which defends opinions instead of listening to those who speak.

In other words, much of that which is programmed is programmed not in order to learn but in order to survive, so that the entity who wishes to learn along a spiritual path has a considerable amount of reprogramming to do, that you will be able to notice the present moment, and be able to release from the necessity of notice those things which you cannot change, those being the past.

Once all attempts at asking are done, what is there to do with the past except accept it, learn from it, and move on? Yet, among your peoples there are often many, many bits of program involved in defending any past action because the sense of not being worthy is crushing, and it is not known how one can become worthy.

May we say this is indeed true. Each entity is both worthy and unworthy, both hot and cold, positive and negative, honorable and dishonorable. You have available to you as an entity all manner of behavior and, more importantly, of thinking and being. It is within your ability to choose, in the first place, that which you wish to perceive, and in the second place, the reaction that you wish to create within yourself, a reaction that is loving and compassionate and does not fear being foolish.

Once one realizes that being foolish is not a killing disease, one is far more able to accept the seeming vagaries of the spiritual path, for those upon the path often live life more intensely than those who are not attempting depth in their lives. It is easier to grab gusto than to become aware of the true nature of the self, and what the self's hunger is for.

The most direct and efficient way to reprogram the self is to ask the self to sit and listen within on a daily basis. We do not encourage entities to do this for long periods of time. The practice is powerful. It is within this entity's mind that it has never been a good meditator. This entity is not capable of judging its ability to meditate. This entity is not capable of assessing the intensity of its desire. It is the intensity of desire to know the truth in order to serve others that creates the excellence of the meditation, not the subjective experience of the conscious mind, which within your culture is, from your childhood, a consciousness so overstimulated that it knows not how to rest and perhaps will never have the experience, in a normal state of consciousness, of peace.

Yet, do you not seek peace? Do you not seek a Comforter? Do you not seek guidance, that you may make choices that have authenticity, that speak of you as a truly real entity, not a collection of chemicals, not that which sprang out of the primeval ooze, but consciousness which is unique to yourself? You are your own creation, and the more you accept responsibility for the creation of your life, the more lovely may that life seem as you find each delicious part to be a gift, and each difficult patch to be a challenge and an opportunity.

We speak here about something that within your culture is called attitude. We ask that those who wish to seek spiritually refrain from any attitude except hope—hope that they may know more, hope that they may serve, hope that there is in fact a deep and heartfelt truth that cannot be expressed except by living lives faithfully. To what shall you be faithful? Yourself, that which is treasure within you, that of which you shall only become aware as you listen and open the gateway betwixt the conscious mind and the infinite resources of consciousness which lie within the subconscious mind, and, more specifically, within the frontal lobes.

We are here to serve, and in our serving do we learn. Consequently, we would point out to each that there is no way to be unselfish to the point of being without reward. It is never expected. It is never that motive for which the actions of a spiritual person are performed, for spirituality is not behavior. There is nothing more hypocritical than behavior. Spirituality is being authentic, whoever you are, and finding that power within you, using whatever story, or thought, or inspiration may move you to move deeper and deeper and with more and more respect into that portion of you which contains infinite treasure, as though you were indeed an earthen vessel filled with gems. This is your true nature. Not the vessel, but the gems. Your physical body is that which carries you about and enables you to be so blind that you must live by faith, and not by proof of words of any kind.

The spiritual path begins with trusting yourself. Resources that are useful to the beginning mind—and as we say, all need the beginner's mind in order to continue to learn and not to become self-satisfied—include various ways of communicating with the self. The most efficient of these, after meditation in silence, is the keeping of a journal, whether it be the dream journal, or the essay journal, or any kind of remembering journal where various difficulties are examined and ruminated about. All of these journals are helpful in opening a voice to you. In truth, this is the reason that each Christ has come into your illusion. At various times, as you call them, there have been great needs for the creation of a way, a gate, a bridge, betwixt the daily, limited, little life of the body and the infinite life of the soul. As you are both, it is greatly worthwhile to proceed with this investigation with all enthusiasm and intensity and passion.

We ask several things of one who wishes to seek the truth and is willing to change, to reprogram, and to evolve. We ask that discouragement be accepted, be felt, but never be considered to be anything but an artifact of the illusion. Perceived errors are simply mistakes. Sin is an emotion-laden word which means only that someone added two and two and got five. There is no more emotion in correcting an error than there is in using an eraser and writing down the appropriate answer. When you have realized that two plus two is four, have erased the five and written down the four, you are not in error and there is nothing to forgive. In just such ways, in very much more complicated emotional mathematics, shall we say, again and again you perceive yourself to be a failure, unworthy to the task, or in some way at fault.

Was there any soul with a 360 degree capability to love and to not rove that did not have, in the brightness of light, a shadow to cast? Can you not accept both your light and your shadows, for as your light grows brighter the shadows will be more sharp, and you will seem always to yourself to be one very iniquitous and often in error.

This is primary to your ability to move forward: that you are able to let judgment of yourself go, for only insofar as you love, accept and refuse to judge yourself can you be compassionate in such wise to others. And only in compassion, as you see the treasure within you and within all, can you truly serve in a love that is without condition and that demands no return. We do not mean to suggest that you will not have any return, for, indeed, as you console, your life is consoling a hundred times more. It is never known where love will come from, but it is a subjective truth of those who love and attempt to love without stint that the love that is received is overwhelming. This is our experience. This may also be yours. But it is in those who finally become ready to give what they can, to multiply their talents, shall we say, as this instrument has the holy work called the Bible much in mind, it is to those that moments of enlightenment occur, because there are no truer words than "Seek, and you shall find; knock, and it shall be opened to you; ask and you shall receive." Indeed, we would warn you that this is literally true, and ask you to be very careful about what you do desire. Let it be the deep and true desires of your heart, for you are an authentic, imperishable being.

Do not let the heavy, chemical, physical vehicle, that has sacrificed itself in order to hold your consciousness, fool you. There is no knowledge in science or any other discipline that may explain to you your nature. This is unseen, is without proof, and must remain without proof. We ask you simply to meditate, to feel free to desire to know love, to know the experience of tabernacling with the infinite One, in immediate presence, for you may be dust, but you are dust in the presence of the infinite One, and nothing can take that from you. Nothing. Certainly not the cessation of viability of your physical vehicle. Release yourself from that prison in your consciousness, and the universe is yours to roam at will. Identify with that which shall decay, and so shall you, as a soul sinking to repine, cynicism, and a settled hunger that knows no food, no drink that may satisfy.

Food and drink for the physical vehicle are seen, but food and drink for the spirit are never seen. Take those delicacies with thanks and praise, and, as you ask for daily bread, know that you do not ask simply for food for the body, but for the spirit as well, for there is a spirit of love which is always with you, which is of the nature of the one infinite Creator. There is no lack, no loss, always companionship and comfort. But it must be allowed to be. There is a door within you which must be opened by your will and your faith, and comfort will come. And as you are comfortable, so shall you be able to shine a light that comforts others, not as one who is powerful, but as one who has finally reckoned with its weakness and accepted the aid of the Infinite.

Do you wish to live an infinite life? Then you may be in the New Age, so called, in the Kingdom of Love, now. You are experiencing a marine boot camp. You have loaded your plate with every difficulty that you can possible cram into one incarnation because you wish to be harvested, and you know that the harvest is upon you. This may be your last incarnation in this particular opportunity to move into a new level of lessons and learning, loving, serving and giving, and dwelling in ever increasing harmony.

But to begin is to take a step, not a great step, but a cautious, interested, open-minded step. Submit yourself to silence each day, and be persistent, through faith alone. Do not judge any experience. Do not take your spiritual temperature. Do not attempt behavior that is holy, but learn who you are. Learn what brought you to this path, to this moment. It was right; there are no mistakes. You have done precisely what you wished to do in coming to this moment, and now it is yours. Seize it. Use it. Remember that which is helpful to you. Accept and allow the love within you. Accept that you are a channel through which an infinite amount of this love may flow and that you need only move the bits of yourself that dim that light to one side, choosing not to be those petty things which staunch and constrict that energetic and creative light and love which is the Original Thought.

Yes, the Creator, as closely as we can say it, is in Its active aspect a thought, and that thought, in the weak words of your language, is Love, unlimited, unstinting and all compassionate love. It has created you and all that there is in wonderful unity. Yet you are unique; there is only one of you. You are quite,

quite without peer. No one can be you except you. As you weave the tapestry of your life, weave it truly, weave it as you are, and have the confidence to know that the Creator would not create that which was not wonderful.

We hope that we have satisfied this instrument's need to keep things limited in what she calls time. We are very poor at this, and we do apologize. But we believe that we have beaten the sound that we always hear with a sinking heart. We are those of Q'uo. We welcome you to an infinitely long path, to a path that is rocky, a path that each walks but yet a path in which there are companions along the way that make every step of the journey sweet and beautiful in their sharing. My friends, love one another. There is no greater wisdom for you than this. This is the choice that you make in every moment of your experience. It is for this that you came here, to make this choice in such a firm way that you discover that the feet upon which you stand are made of light, and the rock upon which you build is as firm as eternity. May you build to eternity.

We would transfer the contact at this time to the instrument known as Jim. We are most grateful to have been able to speak to you at this time, and to have been called to service. It is our highest pleasure, and our deepest reward, and we thank you. We would now transfer. We are known to you as those of Q'uo.

(Jim channeling)

I am Q'uo, and greet each again in love and light through this instrument. At this time it is our honor to offer ourselves in the attempt to speak to any query which may yet remain upon the minds of those present. We would remind each that that which we offer is freely given, and is that which is our opinion, harvested from many experiences, but we do not wish any word that we have to offer to be taken overly much, shall we say, if any word does not ring of truth, and we ask that you set it aside without a second thought, keeping only those that seem useful to you in your journey at this time. Is there a query with which we may begin?

Carla: I noticed that you didn't say anything about humor, and it would be something that probably *(inaudible)* person would say to *(inaudible)* person. *(Inaudible)* sense of humor is one of the most important *(inaudible)*. Could you speak to that?

I am Q'uo, and am aware of your query, my sister. That which your peoples call the sense of humor is, indeed, most helpful to any entity, no matter the position upon the path, or the placement within the life pattern. We see that which you call the sense of humor as being a sense of proportion where an entity is able to gain enough experience within the life that one may see a broader view. One stands upon a somewhat more elevated position, building experience upon experience, until that which you call wisdom is begun.

There is much in every entity's life pattern and daily round of activities which lends itself to humor, nothing so much as the entity itself as it attempts to make a sense of and to form a cohesion from many disparate parts of the life which seem not to be held together well at all. There are innumerable instances in every entity's life during which the entity will find itself playing the complete fool. This, in your mundane way of seeing things, often lends to the feeling of insecurity, doubt and wondering if there will ever be a time where the entity will have control of itself and be able to do that which it wishes, when it wishes, and in the manner it wishes. We would utilize your sense of humor at moments such as this, if we were in your position, in order that we might be reminded that each of us contains those elements which are less than ideal, but are completely acceptable as portions of a personality that one attempts to discipline as one would the wayward child, in order that the lessons set before one might be learned with more efficiency.

However, when those portions of the self, or activities of the self, seem to go awry, it is more nourishing to the small entity that always resides within, much as the child in each entity, to reinforce the concept of wholeness and acceptability, for the divisions and definitions of acceptable or unacceptable behaviors are man-made, and it is always a whole and acceptable entity that places any foot upon the path, whether that foot is solidly placed or not.

Thus, we highly recommend the utilization of your humor, that you may gain a degree of mirth from your foibles, and those of your fellow seekers as well, for in some sense each of you is always exactly where you need to be at each moment, and in another sense each of you is dancing a dance which you do not understand, and which has steps that may puzzle, trip and fell you. Yet it is all a dance of one piece, and in this dance you move as the whirling dervish, the child which is set upon the careful exploration, the kitten which tumbles with its sibling across the floor, bursts out of the room and runs smack into the radiator, this is all a part of your dance, this is all a part of your learning, and you are whole and acceptable beings that partake in it.

Is there a further query, my sister?

Carla: No, my brother, *(inaudible)*, thank you.

I am Q'uo, and we thank you, my sister. Is there another query?

L: I have a question about free will. Sometimes it seems like there are outside forces encouraging us in a certain direction, and I wondered if that's just imagination or projection of a pattern where there is none or *(inaudible)*. I mean, is that ethically really free will, or is it some kind of guidance *(inaudible)* ever happens?

I am Q'uo, and am aware of your query, my sister. We find that the answer to this particular question is one which partakes both of yes and of no. In the incarnation, there is always that which you call free will. No matter what force one may become aware of that tends to exert itself and bend your will to its, you as a free entity always have the choice as to how you will respond. In some instances it may be that you will respond in a manner that is congruent with the demand of another, however, this has been your choice. In another sense, there are patterns of experience which you yourself have placed within this incarnation that have the purpose of guiding you along a certain way, perhaps with a certain attitude, or predisposition. There are those that you call guides, or angelic presences, that are unseen, yet whose hands move within your daily pattern, guiding and protecting as is possible to do, this with your permission, and with your request before the incarnation began.

Thus, within the incarnation you see the meeting and the blending of that which you might call determinism, and that which you might call complete free will. Though you have certain biases and choices that you have made before the incarnation, though there are unseen entities, and entities perhaps more visible, that exert an influence upon you during the incarnation, yet at each point within the incarnation you are free to choose how you will respond to these movements, these guidelines, these energies of effect. You, in fact, may choose to ignore, may choose to accept in some degree, that which is offered, may choose to refuse. Yet always are you free to choose.

Is there a further query, my sister?

L: Yes, how—are these always positive guides, or if not how can we determine if they are or not?

I am Q'uo, and am aware of your query, my sister. The guides, as many have called them, or teachers, or angelic presences, that have been with you for not just this incarnation but for many, are always of a positive orientation. If you are ever aware of any influence that does not seem positive in its nature, you may offer to that influence a challenge that asks it the question that you have answered well for yourself, and it is well for each seeker to know the answer to the question of what it would live for and what it would die for, what is the essence of its being, what is it that gives it the energy, the ideas and the inspiration to continue in each day of its seeking.

When you know this you know something very important about yourself, and it is this knowledge that you may use and offer as a challenge to any entity that you doubt, asking that entity if it comes in the name of that for which you live and that for which you would die, if necessary. Thus, you may be sure that you will be able to banish from your presence any entity that seems of a negative nature, and who would influence you in a manner which you would not wish to be influenced. In this way do you exercise your free will in its most basic and profound sense.

Is there a further query, my sister?

L: What if it doesn't exactly seem like an entity but more like a sort of a trend, I mean, an influence that's not exactly an entity?

I am Q'uo, and am aware of your query, my sister. We cannot speak with certainly in a case such as this, but we may suggest that when a seeker feels that which you call a trend that seems to be of a negative nature, and that seems to bring one under its influence so that one behaves, or is guided, in manners that are deleterious to the entity's well being, that it would be helpful for the entity to evaluate choices that it itself has made at previous points within the incarnational pattern, perhaps moving back as far as the earliest remembered days of the childhood, to see if there might be some programming, some accepted belief that the child welcomed into its being, in all innocence, from a respected other self, and which has become the foundation for those later behaviors which have gathered a kind of momentum, shall we say, and which at some point within the incarnation then begin to seem as if it was of an other source, or outside of the self, and moves the self according to its own design, rather than being a seed which has been sown by the seeker at an early time and which now is full grown within the pattern of the life.

Is there a further query, my sister?

L: Thank you.

I am Q'uo, and we again thank you, my sister. Is there another question at this time?

Carla: Well, if no one else is going to ask a question I have a question that's been *(inaudible)*. Is it infringing upon any free will to ask why the archangels were *(inaudible)* in my *(inaudible)*?

I am Q'uo, and am aware of your query, my sister. We find that in this instance there has been a certain kind of rejoicing on the part of more than one entity in this group that there has been the opportunity for the seeking which has brought a kind of resolution within each entity's pattern of learning. This resolution has created a kind of light which serves as a most effective carrier wave upon which we may infuse our signal. Light created by this group at this particular session of working has provided a great deal of radiance and joy for all those who partake in this session. We may not speak directly to any of these realizations that have occurred, but to each for which this has occurred the realization shall become more and more clearly known.

Is there a further query, my sister?

Carla: No, thank you. Thank you very much.

I am Q'uo, and again we thank you, my sister. Is there another query?

(Pause)

I am Q'uo, and we would take this opportunity to thank each present for inviting our presence to your session of working and your journey of seeking on this afternoon. It is through such opportunities as this that we are able to provide a service which we cherish greatly. Few are our opportunities to give words to those sendings of love and light which we have for your planet and each entity upon it. In this particular season we find that there is a great deal more radiance that your populations are generating, and it is an honor to partake in this season with you and in this particular seeking. We thank you. We shall take our leave at this time from this instrument and from this group, leaving each, as always, in the love and in the light of the one infinite Creator. We are known to you as those of Q'uo. Adonai, my friends. Adonai. ☙

L/L RESEARCH

L/L Research is a subsidiary of Rock Creek Research & Development Laboratories, Inc.

P.O. Box 5195
Louisville, KY 40255-0195

www.llresearch.org

Rock Creek is a non-profit corporation dedicated to discovering and sharing information which may aid in the spiritual evolution of humankind.

ABOUT THE CONTENTS OF THIS TRANSCRIPT: This telepathic channeling has been taken from transcriptions of the weekly study and meditation meetings of the Rock Creek Research & Development Laboratories and L/L Research. It is offered in the hope that it may be useful to you. As the Confederation entities always make a point of saying, please use your discrimination and judgment in assessing this material. If something rings true to you, fine. If something does not resonate, please leave it behind, for neither we nor those of the Confederation would wish to be a stumbling block for any.

CAVEAT: This transcript is being published by L/L Research in a not yet final form. It has, however, been edited and any obvious errors have been corrected. When it is in a final form, this caveat will be removed.

© 2009 L/L RESEARCH

Sunday Meditation
December 30, 1990

Group question: The question this evening has to do with what may be various stages or steps in the path of seeking. When the first feeling of passion for a path occurs, it seems like the seeking is more active in a worldly sense, and then it either begins to cool or calm down, it mellows with age. Is this due to a passage through the energy centers and differing kinds of expression of this passion then coming forth, is it due to getting tired and having old age set in, or is it due to perhaps natural progression of the stages of seeking? Is there a progression of this kind, where an entity is more on fire to start with and then begins to move more inwardly as the path continues?

(Carla channeling)

I am Q'uo. I greet you in the love and in the light of the one infinite Creator. Indeed, I greet you in the love and the light of the one infinite Creation. We indeed greet you in all that there is, seen and unseen—love, the creative word, and light, all manifestation. Where can you go that is not built of love and light, that is not of the word, which is love, the thought that created all that there is? So we speak to each of you as beings of love and light, who create catalyst by misunderstanding love, because of the manifestations of light which have been biased by those co-creators which are each and every conscious entity among your peoples. And we greet each of you with absolute love and great blessing, and with gratitude for asking us to share our opinions with you. Let the listener beware; we are not perfectly authoritative, but only those with opinions, such as your own. We ask you to use your discrimination. Never attempt to accept, or believe, or have faith in any concept that is not your own. Those that are your own you shall recognize, for they have been within you, and you are merely relearning them with the conscious mind. If this deep connection is not there, however informed our opinion, it is not your truth, so leave it, and walk your own path.

This day you wish to know what it is about the spiritual path which creates at the beginning ecstasy, excitement, exaltation and a great outpouring of evangelism. That does not last. What is it that creates the situation in which the passion, the intensity and the dedication may well become more and more attenuated, less and less strong, in the face of the mundane and horizontally lived incarnational experience? May we say to you that, indeed, there is some of accuracy in the questioner's suspicion that this is in some part a natural progression. However, the questioner does not take this progression to its completion. Let us speak upon this particular vision.

When one discovers, by whatever means, information that is so inspirational and so relevant to that entity's growth that it is that which seizes the attention, then is there excitement, glory, joy, optimism and the strength of new knowledge. Were this to be treated appropriately, the passion, the intensity and the dedication which you experience at the beginning should never fade. But you, being of an illusion which uses words, and of natures which crave the companionship of spiritual communication, are often incapable of protecting your realizations with careful, cautious and deeply felt silence, thanksgiving and praise for the realizations that have been the gift at the end of long desert experiences.

We speak not, in this case, of time, but of the subjectively felt length of any experience in which the spirit starves for spiritual food. When it finds that food, its appetite is great, and it wants to feed the five thousand with its loaves and fishes immediately. However, that which has been born in you, though it feels stronger than any previous faith or enthusiasm, is yet a faith-filled and enthusiastic infant.

These are your days of what you call Christ's mass, in which you kneel, strong, supple and able as each is, before a helpless, dumb, blind infant, placed in the roughest and most animalistic of shelters, the home of the animals. Let us consider this. This story is, in our opinion, an excellent myth, as are many in your cultures. It is filled with, as are many, symbols which offer to the spiritual seeker and student lessons carefully to be considered. You may see the new transformation, the new realizations, as being like the infant in the manger, endlessly beautiful, infinitely loving, and utterly vulnerable. Because of the intensity of the birth of this infant self within— and all are nurturing this spiritual being, which is born in third density, by choice—all feel that they have no problem in expressing such strong feelings, emotions and beliefs to others. How you mistake infant faith. To cast the pearls before the swine is the teacher known as Jesus' analogy of speaking of one's own hard learned spiritual lessons to those who have no inclination or request to hear those wise and compassionate words which the spirit has offered to you in this realization, symbolized by the helpless child.

What causes the student, then, to wish so much to share that which is too delicate, too immature, too helpless to be exposed to the harsh winter of intellect and skepticism? Often it is the desire to help. However, though one may be working intensely upon opening the heart as much as possible, it is indeed true that many do this without sufficient respect and time spent in preparing the earthen vessel—that is, your physical vehicle, and the mind, which is your mental vehicle—within this illusion. For all their strength and for all their truth, these realizations must wait for witness until the entity that you are within this relativistic illusion has cleared the pathway, made the rough places plain, brought the high places low, and made straight your own pathway to your heart. The one known as John the Baptist said, "Make straight in the desert a highway for God with us." Make straight in your hearts the pathway for I AM.

How does one make this pathway straight? Largely by coming to terms with your three so-called lower, but what we would call perhaps fundamental, energies, through which all living light must pass to flow into the heart to give it the power and the strength and the stability it needs in order that it may heal, or communicate, discern wisdom, discern spirits, or any other gift of the open heart, all of which are concerned with loving the Creator and human kind. How can you do this if the heart is open, but the energy moving into it must move through far too small an opening because you have not come to terms with yourself, you have not accepted yourself, you have not accepted your relationships; you have not accepted the primacy of love, unconditional love, over any personal preference whatsoever; you have not done the work of forgiveness, perhaps, or self-forgiveness, acceptance, or more likely, self-acceptance?

In this instrument's life, for instance, this instrument struggles to like an entity close to her which she chose for the precise reason that she in no way could possibly like this entity. What was the lesson? To love. Not to like, not to prefer, not intellectually to crave, but to love, simply that. In each entity's life there are these things which cannot be liked, but which can, through the grace of an infinite Creator which is love, be loved, and in the loving of them floats a continuous prayer like a bell tone that rings throughout space and time and eternity.

So you wish, above all else, not to advertise but to protect this child, while you, to the best of your ability, amend and improve the basic energies of a physical, weak, finite vehicle with finite energies, finite amounts of time and space in which to do the work of a complete incarnation, and to do that right quickly, for in truth, a century of your time is far too short even for you to achieve the first true maturity.

So know yourselves as perpetual teenagers, perpetual rebels, perpetual prodigals, far from home, confused, poor in heart, until you are able to realize the richness that lies within this vessel of earth, which noble earthly vessel carries you through an incarnation with its greatest devotion and care.

If your quarrels are with yourself, let them not be that you are ill, or poor, or unhappy, or unfulfilled. These are situations extremely productive of spiritual growth, and cannot be judged within your illusion for their true worth. It is a matter of faith not to rebel against the stringencies that open the heart and cleanse the more basic emotions of love for the self, for life itself, for the relationships that you have with entities and with social groups. Before one word should be spoken, the dedication to the daily clearing of these energy centers needs to be complete, for it is in persistence and patience and an unflagging desire to realize the truth that we have heard, that all densities' entities may move forward in evolution in the spiritual sense.

There will come a time when you no longer are hampered by obvious encroachments of underactivation or overactivation or other sorts of blockage of letting light move into the heart. But if those obstacles which you can feel catching you as a fish is hooked, if your own temptations and self-aggrandizements [seem to be released], then you are ready to speak, but you will find that once you gain this maturity, relatively speaking, you will find to your surprise that you are no longer an evangelist, that fervid eagerness, great charismatic power of self, and all those things which go into making an entity an excellent evangelist, have been seen by the maturing spiritual youngster within to be useless of true worth, for the spiritually maturing child has begun to learn that it can only work upon itself and be a witness to the nations in and of itself.

We shall pause.

(Pause)

I am Q'uo, and am again with this instrument. This instrument wished to show courtesy by allowing entities which are not interested in this material to move through the surrounding domicile. This has been accomplished, so we shall continue, with thanks to the instrument for keeping us from any hint of infringement upon free will.

How then should an entity which has found a personal truth, a personal path from the mundane to eternity, express itself in regard to other people? Two things especially need to be kept in mind. Firstly, the most important witness an entity can offer for the one Creator in glory, in peace and in joy, is the manifestation of the self with conscious encouragement of the self in unspoken and uncontrived witness. We expect those who have achieved this much maturity to have chosen a path, and to be able to speak of that path. But the first gift that one may give is presence, simply practicing the presence of the Creator within the self, and allowing the practice of that presence to shine forth so that those of any kind may sense that peace which is not the world's, that joy which the world only knows as happiness, the palest shadow of joy, of love, indescribable, but quite clearly observable among those who would gaze at the face of one who truly loves. This is your greatest witness, it is your greatest help to your beloved people and to your planet as a whole, for the planet itself responds to self-acceptance, self-forgiveness, and unconditional love. These are metaphysical vibrations as strong in mending the Earth as the pressure of tectonic plates is strong in mending the adjustment of the Earth in catastrophic style.

Secondary witnesses are quite simply those which answer questions which have been asked. When there is a request, there is an opening, a softened spiritual ground, and into this ground it is well that you witness to the extent of your ability as a realized entity, as a user of the language, and as one sensitive to word allergies, if we may put it in that way, which the entities to whom you wish to bear witness may have.

Why, then, does a new path seem to become old? It seems obvious that novelty is a great distorter of perception. If there is love, it blossoms into passion, if there is friendship under adverse conditions, it blossoms into lifelong kinship. Yet, even the greatest of truths, even the most sublime of realizations, must deal day by day with precisely those conditions of incarnation designed to test the personal spiritual awareness of the entity which is consciously working upon gaining spiritual mass or polarity.

Do not dare to seek to have faith unless you wish to have an uncomfortable life, for as the Creator manifests Itself in the wind and fire of spirit, ever moving, ever changing, ever unpredictable, so too does the spirit manifest itself in each entity's life. If you are not always open to that which the spirit has to offer, this day only, then you shall be working with information which has grown stale, and the day that you do not attempt to act as you have learned is the correct way to act, is the day when you must stop any hope of moving further or bearing witness, that you may go into yourself and review that which you have learned, for there is nothing half-hearted about love, if we may make a poor pun.

Love does not regard circumstance. If you are regarding circumstance, it is time first to set the mundane house in order, and once you have made this plan and are sticking to it, it does not need to be complete, but merely needs to be that which is realized as the stable necessity before one can hope for a stable spiritual life. Just as you cannot draw beautifully upon a stained and dirty drawing table, for then you shall gain the unwanted and random stains of previous paintings not so well informed, so you do not want to paint the picture to the outside world, or even to yourself, if your easel is awry, your palette filled with muddy colors, and your paper stained through from water colors of the past, or your canvas stained through from paintings from the past. Take you then each day the new canvas, the new drawing paper, and begin each day as the beginner that each of us is.

To begin again, to begin again, to begin again—how the human spirit rebels. Yet within the present moment there is only beginning, and there is nothing but the present moment in any spiritual consideration. So look to the loving and acceptance of the higher power which you may call as you wish. Look to your relationship with that love that created you. Allow within yourself the birth in the manger of your heart of your own spiritual beingness, true, imperishable, consciousness. Guard it, just as the story speaks of this infant's mother and father fleeing to protect their child. Protect this child as lovingly, and with as much feeling of honor.

When you are ready, the opportunities for service, consonant with your unique gifts, shall be given. But you may retain passion and dedication such as was felt at the beginning only by creating in an artificial manner the novelty of the original experience. It is not, however, a decline that you experience, but rather a cycle. The cycle of your planet and its second-density creatures is perhaps the best analogy to this cycle within the spiritually active pilgrim.

New realizations are born in the deep darkness of what seems like a winter of discontent. They are nourished by faith and strengthened by the will to persevere, although the road ahead is blind. Move along that road as guided. When you have been faithful, and achieved a stability that expects no rewards for that faith, but only the joy and peace of living in faith, then there will be in front of your eyes the right usage of your time offered to you.

At that time it is neither an act of false humility or false pride to take upon the cross of humanity that Christ of the gifts that have been given each for each to be stewards, to multiply their gifts, and to maximize their ability to offer love to this dark planet. You may go through the summer of this marvelous experience of the realization that has been nurtured, protected, and finally has found the sun and grown to bloom. Yet still the cycle is not complete, for as flowers wither, and as the trees of deciduous nature lose their leaves, so shall the fall of each cycle of understanding or realization bring with it its own temptations, its own opportunities to move in false directions. Eventually, whether you have learned from this blossoming of the self or no, the harvest time does come, the harvest of that realization is gathered, and another winter of discontent follows.

The cycle moves around, and insofar as a life in faith has been preserved in the individual through the predictable difficulties, just so far may the next realization be more and other and even more helpful than the first, thusly creating a new spiritual self, with new realizations, which then must go through the springtime of nurturing and protection, the summertime of manifestation, beauty, peace, and the words of freedom, faith and healing, and again, the harvest will be complete, and the imperishable spirit that you are, voluntarily and gladly, in a subconscious manner, moves to the next realization, the next spiritual infant, the next learning, the next blooming.

To achieve an ability to maintain stability in good times and in bad as perceived subjectively by the self, it is necessary to gaze at the creation day by day, within the present moment, and without judgment of any kind, except insofar as you are discriminating concerning that which you may take in and that which you may offer to others as service. When this cycle is understood, if we may use that term, the seeker may indeed minimize the heights and the depths …

(Side one of tape ends.)

(Carla channeling)

I am Q'uo, we continue through this instrument in love and light. This is not necessarily the correct manner of dealing with anguish and ecstasy, for, indeed, the very sharpness and depth of these emotions offers to the spiritually growing entity the opportunity to gaze at these emotional states with an eye to their purification of those mundane concerns which may be mixed in with imperishable ideals. Do we wish to have the cute and the pretty mixed with the beautiful? Perhaps in the mundane, but certainly not in the imperishable sense, for there is nothing that is relative, in spiritual realization.

One last thing that we would say before we leave this instrument is never to demean, degrade or criticize the self for lacking the conviction, the faith or the strength to meet a situation as one would wish. For the will of the spirit and the faith of the spirit are expressed in the fruits of intention, first of all, and only as the spirit grows stronger from intending, and intending, and intending to show love in difficult circumstances, does the spirit grow strong enough, hardy enough, and full enough of faith to manifest in any nearly accurate way the infinite beauty of spiritual intention.

Let yourself continue as beginner. Let yourself remain infatuated, in love, and shield that passion from a world which has seemingly no positive passion, except in isolated instances at this time. Shield that light until it may grow through you without destroying you, for it is indeed a vibration too great for third-density consciousness. Yet, you who are harvestable potentially have also the ability to hold light and love in manifestation, [which is] not able to be offered [by those] who have not worked toward graduation from this density. Never discourage the self or others in a spiritual sense. Support all selves, and speak those pearls that so inflamed and overjoyed your open hearts, by your presence, and upon request, by witness of a verbal kind. In this way may you never lose the novelty of the present moment, for is any present moment like another, and yet, are they not all the present moment?

We thank you for this opportunity to speak through this instrument upon this most interesting question, and we thank the questioner. May all who read or hear be blessed. We are those of the principle of Q'uo. We leave this instrument in love and light, and wish to close this communication through the instrument known as Jim. We will now transfer. I am Q'uo.

(Jim channeling)

I am Q'uo, and greet each of you again in the love and the light of the one infinite Creator. At this time we are privileged to offer ourselves in the capacity of speaking to any queries which may be offered to us. Is there a query to which we may speak at this time?

Carla: Could you offer us specific techniques for the maintaining of the beginner's mind?

I am Q'uo, and we are aware of your query, my sister. The beginner's mind is one which is full of the excitation of new discovery. The beginner's mind is one which is full of the desire to share what has been discovered with others, for it is that which is bright, shining, novel and inspirational to that entity's life. It is often difficult for those who have long been upon the path to remain excited about this journey, for the nature of this journey is one of sacrifice. There is a price for each effort and learning and service commensurate with the purity and intensity of learning and service. Many such rounds of learning, of spending time within the desert, of climbing of the high peak within the inner mind, and of tripping and falling upon the path as one continues to persevere, to have faith, wear down much of this excitation within the seeker. To regain some portion of that excitation it is well for the seeker to place itself in these situations, to find within itself new thoughts on those subjects which it thought it had settled.

To read, to view, to converse with new sources of information is one means by which any entity may refresh those opinions which have settled, and the excitation which has settled with them. In such a way does one not only add information and experience and opportunity to the life pattern, but one may also find that there is the opportunity to refine, even to reconstruct, that which seems to have been settled within the being, for it is a danger, shall we say, or a temptation for each seeker who has traveled for some time upon the spiritual path, to feel that there are settled areas that need no further examination.

There are, it is certainly true, certain principles which are cornerstones for any seeker, and upon which the seeker shall place the structure of its mythology, shall we say. However, there are an infinite array of possibilities in the perceiving of these principles, and for the seeker to assume that that manner in which it has perceived is set, and in no need of examination, is the first step in the calcification of opinion, which when allowed to proceed from one assumption and lesson to another, may harden those interpretations of truth which, in order to have any hope of approximating truth must be open to further elimination, for if there is one principle that may be depended upon to have sway within your third-density illusion, that principle is the variety of possibility within an infinite creation, that any truth which may be apprehended in a certain manner may also be apprehended in many other ways as well.

It is well, therefore, for the seeker to shake itself up from time to time, to perhaps engage in a game in which all that seems to have been known, gathered through much searching in the past, be for a moment, perhaps a day, or a week, thrown out, so that the seeker must begin anew. Now, we are not saying that what has been gathered through a long process of seeking should be discarded completely. Perhaps for only a moment, it will be well for the seeker to look with new eyes for those answers to the riddles of its life. It may be that the seeker shall return to those principles and means of seeing, interpreting principles, that it has long held, but to journey from them for even a short period of your time, and to look for a new perception, a new mode of apprehending, is an exercise which shall refresh the seeker in its gathering of information, in its processing of this information and in its formation of new relationships, and the seeking of these relationships within the appropriate energy center.

By such a process of reevaluation may the seeker then discover that there is a continued thrill and excitation that comes from this seeking process. The gathering of information, the gathering of experience, and the increased variety in all of this, adds to the excitation that may propel the seeker to more closely strike to the heart of the incarnation and its purpose within this illusion.

Is there a further query, my sister?

Carla: *(Inaudible)* Jesus offered the Creator's words, "Peace I give you, my peace I leave with you, not as the world gives, give I unto you", *(inaudible)* a writer in writing of that passage, wrote "The peace of God, it is no peace, but strife closed in the sod, but brethren let us pray for but one thing, the marvelous peace of God."

It seems to me that mundane peace is a symptom of that which is no longer changeable, *(inaudible)*. Is it too large a question to ask about spiritual peace? Should it be kept for a Sunday main topic, or in it a matter fairly short to answer the question, what is the Creator's peace?

I am Q'uo, and am aware of your query, my sister. The topic of which you speak is one which would be well to reserve for a time during which it may be explored with the intensity and perseverance that it deserves, for this is a topic which has been little considered among those of your peoples, and it is one which is well to be considered by each entity who would seek the love and the light of the one Creator.

Is there a further query, my sister?

Carla: No, my brother, I would like to thank you *(inaudible)*.

I am Q'uo, and we again thank you, my sister. Is there another query at this time?

K: I have no questions at this time.

I am Q'uo, and we thank each of those present for inviting us to join you in your circle of seeking. It is a great honor for us to do so and we are filled with joy at each opportunity. At this time we shall take our leave of this instrument and this group, leaving each, as always, in the love and in the light of the one infinite Creator. We are those of Q'uo. Adonai, my friends. Adonai. ❧

Year 1991
January 6, 1991 to March 27, 1991

Sunday Meditation
January 6, 1991

Group question: The question this evening concerns the nature of the mind/body/spirit complex; in particular, what is the specific nature of the spirit complex, how does that relate to what we know of as the soul, how can that knowledge help us in our learning about ourselves and in being able to be more of service?

(Carla channeling)

I am Q'uo, and I greet you in the love and in the light of the one infinite Creator. We are most blessed to be able to share this experience with you, and blessed even further that we may possibly be of service to you in your seeking, as our seeking at this time, as you would say, is all focused upon that which we learn by attempting to be of service to you. Thus, you are offering us a great gift by your questions, for this is our means of service and learning at this time. We too are upon a path to the infinite One, and we too are yet finite and unimpeccable. We are mistake makers, we are opinion givers; we are not and can never be completely accurate, for accuracy lies not in words. We can only offer you an estimation in your language of concepts which we have come to grasp. We thank you for this opportunity, but request that each use the discrimination of its own wisdom. That which is yours you shall recognize and remember as if you had heard it before, but only now remembered it. That which is not yours, leave; perhaps you will one day return, and it will then be your truth, but under no circumstances allow a puzzle of ours to become a stumbling block to you.

We begin now with your question upon the nature of the spirit complex and its relation to the entity you have called soul. We would begin by asking each to move in consciousness from the cerebral patterns of intellectual knowledge into the open heart and the wisdom that lies therein, for that wisdom is deeper, though conceptual and illogical rather than the ideation and ratiocination of the conscious mind, for much of the question which you ask is best answered by the wisdom of the heart rather than by strictly logical means.

As we depart now and then from logic in our attempts to express concepts not within your vocabulary, we ask you to suspend notice of our illogic, and await the sum, for only in sum can substance be seen. We thank you for allowing us the freedom of this process, for the question you have asked is less than easily answered in purely cerebral terms.

Each of you is an entity. Let this be basic and imprinted. Each of you is an unique consciousness. You are unique because of the choices that you have made. It is your choices which define you, your biases which express your nature. It is not in the clarity of your Creator-self that you exist in terms of the solution, but as an unique portion of infinite consciousness which has been mated with free will in order that you may go through the choosing process again and again, creating, enhancing and altering your biases and distortions. What could we offer to any, clear and lucid enough to be a perfect and empty instrument that could all be filled with the treasure of the infinite Creator? Nothing. We offer words to you because both we and you are learning, and yet do not know, but we are persistent, as are you. This free will moves firstly by chance, and in terms of your time/space continuum, this occurs for a long period. In the density which you now enjoy comes a very critical period in which the unique and distorted entity that you are must choose blindly, in the deep of midnight, how to follow the light.

Thusly, all discussion of the entity which is you as a purely metaphysical entity must in some way be wrapped in mystery, for it is not important to know the nature of the soul, or the true entity, during an incarnation. It is, in fact, baggage, for you are not here to practice discarnate skills. Each of you is here to be affected by an environment you know to be an illusion. Yet, why would you choose to be in an illusion which is so often challenging, unless that which is truly your self is aware of the great value of not knowing, and having to choose in faith, blindly?

Therefore, seat yourselves, and your knowledge of yourselves, firstly as one who respects the incarnation, one who values the illusion, for this illusion is a tremendous opportunity for you to know more and more clearly the nature of your self. Yet, this can never be a measurable or quantitative knowledge, for you, as what you would call a soul, are incalculable, inevitable, inestimable and eternal. Yet should we speak to you as imperishable beings of light? We think not, what good would that do you? You could not hear the words of light; you could not value concepts that have no words. We would become those who spoke in tongues, not your own; perhaps an exquisite experience, but not an information-filled one.

(Pause)

We are those of Q'uo. We greet you again in love and light. This instrument must sometimes pause to take liquid, and we apologize for this delay.

Now that we have thoroughly rattled your cages, and made you see the quiddity of your selves and your incarnation, and underscored this illusion's value to you, we may be free to speak upon your question, for we feel that we have de-emphasized it appropriately.

As we said, you begin and end in mystery. However, within the illusion we may say some things about the relations between the mind, the body and the spirit. In terms of learning, within the illusion, the primary, or first learner of which most entities are aware is the mind complex. This is a portion of the self within the illusion. It is a type of computer which functions quite simply by answering "yes" or "no" to each stimulus which is received. Each entity answers "no" to the reception of perhaps 99% of all that is offered. The self chooses endlessly what it will perceive, and from those choices follow all the conscious choices. Thusly, it is firstly up to the mind to determine what it wishes to perceive, for the instrument known as the mind is programmed only for survival. And, just as the small animal which is one of your pets moves in relation to our energy in fear, so do each of you instinctually move either in fear or in the active fear called aggression against those things which are deemed a threat. Fear moves all entities until they are delivered by that leap of blind faith into an awareness of love. This is always the basic choice: to fear, or to love. Choices made in fear separate; choices made in love unite.

The mind, in and of itself, instinctually cannot move into the area of choice with any realization. It will, left to itself, continue any patterns that have been begun in the early days of the incarnation of that entity. Thusly, the unawakened life path is one of distraction, avoidance and aggression. By these means, the mind controls the environment, and considers itself safe. Fears, and lack of fear, move into the body complex, if there is no intervention either by dealing mentally with outside catalyst or invoking faith. Thusly, the body slowly sickens and dies, because the nature of the illusion is that of steady loss.

However, into this closed and incomplete consciousness moves the voice of that which may be called the spirit complex, although indeed the spirit complex itself is a gateway, or opening, or channel, which is able to transmit into the deep mind, through itself, higher principles and ideals that do not have to do with the illusion, but are, in fact, fixed. Like yourselves, certain principles are imperishable. Thusly, the simplest way, perhaps, to express the nature of the spirit complex is that used by the one known as Ra, the spirit complex as a shuttle, a means of taking the thread through woof and warp to create the tapestry of solidified beingness as experienced subjectively by each entity, each weaver, of the tapestry of an incarnation.

How can one access the spirit? One desires. All entities desire. This is the process of choosing. But what an entity desires is as various as the four winds until faith is invoked by will. We do not speak of beliefs, for beliefs limit, define and solidify into illusory distortions the imperishable truths of which they are the sons and daughters. There are many, many entities among those of your people making this choice at this time who are comfortable in not thinking, in unthinkingness. They wish the structure told to them that they may learn it by rote, and spend their time in devotion. Mistakenly, however, because of the nature of the mind complex, it is felt that one particular story about the Creator is the story about the Creator, and all others are not acceptable stories about the Creator. This is incorrect. However, each story appeals to those of a certain temperament. This entity has a temperament which finds the story of Jesus the Christ most helpful. Thus, it has become this entity's way to objectify the shuttle of spirit, and to open within the heart and within the consciousness the gateway to Intelligent Infinity.

There are other stories, many and various. We ask not that the spiritual seeker choose any particular one. We do ask that the seeker choose, and, having chosen, never look back. It may take as long as you wish in the incarnation to make that choice, but when the choice is clear, it is very well to move upon that path with the greatest intensity and devotion possible, for what you wish to do as a unique consciousness, or soul, is to become more and more powerful in the metaphysical sense. Until you have done the work of spirit involved in discovering the imperishable part of yourself, until you have made and dedicated the choice of how to love the infinite Creator, the self, and all other entities, polarization cannot begin in any settled form which may deliver one more reliably into a denser light, and a more skillful use of that light in being and in manifestation, but most importantly in being.

The mind will endlessly inform one; the body endlessly informs one; and the spirit lies fallow. To request an end to incoming data seems a simple enough thing to do. This is the nature of meditation, the nature of contemplation, to remove oneself from the stage of manifestation that one may rest and seek its own self within. Learning is done in silence, especially silence potentiated with pain. Thusly, as this instrument has said this evening, pain is to be recognized and respected for the great ally to learning that it is.

You may deliver yourself into suffering if you wish, and say that you suffer in order to learn. This is a distortion which is subjectively true to many. You may also say that you maximize your opportunities to learn in order to learn. This is another way of saying precisely the same thing. Thusly, you may have pain, greeted like the sister or brother that it truly is. Welcome it with respect into your life, treat it as an honored guest, and be free of any suffering, or you may choose first one and then the other, as you desire.

The spirit, however, will only inform the intelligence when asked. Thusly, each entity has its time of the first and fundamental realization that is appropriate for its rhythm of beingness, and when that time comes, the heart is opened, the body quiet, and the shuttle is suddenly full of an effulgent light, an all-embracing love, and the entity, struck, is never the same again. This is a natural awakening, but it is all that is natural about awakening. Through the illusion is allowed that first impulse of spirit, but all choices after that first experience, which may be repeated from time to time, are the specific free choice of the entity. No learning comes without desire and persistence.

Now let us turn from consideration of the spirit complex to the consideration of the soul. The term mind/body/spirit complex is an approximation of description of the nature of the entity without distortion, that is, distorted only in the balanced manner that lies behind illusory distortions. The entity which you are, which you may call the soul, is first, last and always to be understood as consciousness itself, and as love.

Let us consider the phrase "I am, in love, with you." Consciousness is "I am." To define it beyond that is to distort it. The nature of this consciousness, this "I am," is love, and the nature of all other entities in your density, and in any density, is love, manifesting through rotations of light. Thusly, all may say at all times, in any relationship whatsoever, "I am, in love, with you." Let us pause and experience together the "I am" of us all.

(Pause)

I am Q'uo, and am again with this instrument. May we thank you for the privilege of enjoying the beauty and the harmony of your unified vibration. To be allowed the privilege of this experience is very humbling to us, and we thank you, in deep gratitude, for your beauty.

This entity that you are is subjectively experienced by yourself through illusion, while the integrity of your beingness is always preserved in mystery. You cannot analyze a mystery that has no answer. Thus, we move in a circle, coming again to our first point. To analyze an unique entity is to do the impossible, for both that which we call love, or Logos, or the Creator, which is a portion of you, and the portion of you that is unique, are mysteries, now and forever. It is a matter of allowing that mystery to be a mystery. That is most helpful within the incarnational experience. It is acceptable to be unknown to the self in a final way if one realizes that that is the situation and will be the situation until the allowing of consciousness becomes such that one no longer desires to know about consciousness, but only to be consciousness. At that point, which we have not yet reached, there is the returning to the infinite One, and the creation moves from creation to creation, as entities are sent out and then return, that manifestation may blaze in its appropriateness within the infinity of intelligence.

You are all things. The soul is the universe, and the universe, the soul. All that is within you is in fact outside you, and all that is outside you is in fact within you. All things can be known, and all things cannot be known. You are a living incarnation of paradox and mystery. Does this challenge you? We think not, for we think that each within this group has become aware that there are infinite concepts which cannot be expressed within your illusion.

Indeed, as we speak through this instrument this instrument's main asset besides its purity is its craft, for we offer concepts to the conscious channel, which must needs then be given words. And how should we describe by words that which is the soul, except to say that the soul in manifestation is a bonding of love and free will, and process through the densities is choice, upon choice, upon choice, as free will is first paramount, and all other things but the individual will seen as threats, or potential threats, this moving on until the process of evolution of mind, body and spirit, brings each entity to the realization, hard won or won easily, depending upon the incarnation, that the will of the self, in its deepest sense, is the will of the one infinite Creator, and this will often does not make sense.

Consequently, the more realized the consciousness within the illusion, the more it may seem that one is a servant with a master; yet, you are the master as well as the servant. All is truly illusion. You experience this objectification of the master as you need solidity. Eventually you shall not need to be solid, or three dimensional, in the way that you now see dimensionality and solidity of form. You will be free of needing to solidify pain, pleasure, or any experience. And at that point, you are then free to open the heart, to do work in consciousness, and to share that work with others as the gift has been given to you.

What is the soul? The soul is you. The soul is the Creator and the created, an infinite unity, given objectification through the use of illusion. May each of you value both the self in its soul nature, its endlessness, its mystery and its paradox, and the incarnational drama which offers to you endless opportunity for learning the great lessons of compassion which may deliver you into a more realized observation of yourself.

What have you judged today? Each judgment has pulled you away from your soul. Unlike discrimination, which is a subjective matter of saying "This is mine, but this is not," a judgment is a matter of "This is correct, and this is not." To judge yourself for yourself is to do your work; to judge others for the self is to be a critic. And how shall the critic grasp the nature of the play if it is only an observer? Nay, you do not wish to be a critic; you do not wish, though you may think so, to be clever, and intelligent, and intellectual. You need simply to straighten up the household of your mind, and when it is tidy, to move into the heart. Through love, open the heart, so that without fear you may greet yourself.

Oh, beings of love, we greet each other in you, and you, in us. We are consciousness; we are soul; we are one. The rest is illusion. May you love each other, and in loving and serving each other, learn the lessons of divinity, for as you love, without judgment, without let or stint, so shall you learn your nature. We salute you, souls, all, our own selves, and we encourage you to respect, use and enjoy the opportunities that will so quickly flee before you. No one, after leaving the incarnation, is ever truly satisfied that it has chewed it all up and used it well. Therefore, may you burn with desire to do this deep work. May you learn your oddities and your gifts, and may you then maximize them through the opportunities that are given to you moment by moment by moment, remembering always that it is how you perceive the chaos about you that you begin.

We thank you for having given us this chance to speak upon this interesting subject, and would at this time ask if there are any questions that we may attempt to answer. Is there a question at this time? I am Q'uo.

M: I have a question. In the opening message you said that accuracy is not in words. Where is accuracy? Where does accuracy lie in understanding our relation to the infinite Creator and service to others?

I am Q'uo. My brother, within the bounds of your subjective experience at this time, accuracy lies in the open and loving heart.

May we speak further?

M: That is sufficient, thank you.

We thank you, my brother, and we extend our love to you. Is there another question at this time?

M: I greet you again in love and light. I was wondering, in the higher densities, is there also illusion?

I am Q'uo. There is indeed illusion in all densities before that of the density of foreverness and return. Each density has its proper and appropriate portion in your learning experience, and you shall, although you experience them all simultaneously, by the use of illusion, have the ability to experience each lesson in its own appropriate area, which you understand as space and time, but which in reality is a field without space and time.

May we answer you further, my brother?

M: Do you have a knowingness of a sense of what is forever and beyond? Can you show that at this time?

I am Q'uo. You wish to achieve an intellectual grasp of that which is not an intellectual concept. Therefore, let us pose to you that which is interesting to us, and that is that each of you is capable of asking questions that it cannot answer. From where comes this ability? It is not within the computer of your mind. Where, then, comes this hunger for that which obviously has no place in a relativistic creation? That is all that you can see. Why should you ask for more? Do you not see that the very thing that you are asking is in its very impulse its own answer? We would speak further if you do not see this. Do you see this, my brother?

M: You may elucidate more.

I am Q'uo, and we would be happy to do so. The concept of infinity is impossible. Consider this concept. You must go to the end of all finity, and then move onward. Yet, as you imagine moving onward, you are imagining a finite concept, which by definition has its own end. Consequently, the closest that the intellectual mind can come to a realization of infinity is a series of finities. This is not infinity. Each of you is forever, yet the realization of this foreverness, when complete, ends all need of any illusion whatsoever, and the individuality, which is more and more refined through the densities for many millions of your years in reckoning, increases the individuality of each, and it increases the unity of all, for each entity must make its own unique reckoning with unity, so that harmony and unity may become one, and as you are a chord, yet also you are one tone, and in that tone lies the concept and the actuality of imperishability, or eternity.

In fact, the nature of infinity is specifically the present moment realized for the first time in its many overtones, undertones, harmonics and depth. The resonant present moment is infinity, and is the home of the self. Now and always, we greet you in love and in light, because you are love, and you experience yourself in these as do we, through different arrangements of manifestations of light which express themselves as fields which solidify sufficiently to create manifestation, helpful and intelligible, through the apparatus used by those of a particular density for learning.

Thusly, we speak to you in words, our teacher speaks to us in concepts. Yet these are the illusions that we need, each at this subjectively perceived time, in order to carry on with our evolution. We believe that it is well, if one wishes, to increase the pace or degree of acceleration of one's evolution in mind, body and spirit. We believe that in the third density, the foundation of the spiritual evolution is made.

May we answer you further, my brother?

M: Thank you.

Again, my brother, we thank you. We feel that you are somewhat overwhelmed with data, and we apologize, but the questions that you ask are very mindful, and when one is truly mindful, one rapidly runs out of good ways to express truth, for as words are in manifestation, just so, they lack truth, and become relative.

The special entity that you are will take these words and perceive them subjectively. We cannot do more than attempt to map out the topography of the concept which you seek. Thusly, as you speak with entities such as we, it is well to accept the re-examination of material from time to time for various levels of information which may be of interest at one particular time or another.

Is there another question at this time?

H: I would like to ask you a question. You mentioned earlier that it's not the particular beliefs or tradition, religious tradition, that one follows, but it is important that he chooses one, and then sticks with it, with his whole heart,

Now, some traditions are—some people, some students prefer one tradition than other, and it seemed to me that after reading this Ra book, that you're offering another tradition, at least as far as the concepts of this universe go, of the creation, the densities, and I was wondering, are they all correct? Is neither correct, or does it make a difference?

I am Q'uo, and we believe that we are aware of your questions. First of all, as you surmise, there is a paradox in that all traditions are correct, in all of their many confusing ways. That is to say, that the nature of the illusion is helpful, so that, in order to transcend experience, one must enter freely into experience. The way to realization of the nature of the soul and the nature of the Creator is through the illusion, not around it in any way. It is when moving through experiences that are appropriately valued and respected that one may begin to transcend them,

and to achieve an immediate awareness of the presence of love, that is, the one infinite Creator.

Thusly, if you wish to move from shadow to light, it is well first to realize that the search shall be in shadow, and that you shall be in the shadow more and more, in pain more and more, as you continue to learn, to evolve and to grow. You are in pain because of the subjective nature of experience. It is painful to reprogram your computer, but as you go through especially traumatic experiences, or as you go through nontraumatic experiences in attentiveness, you begin to have the motivation to use each opportunity for learning amidst all the shadows.

May we elucidate further, my brother?

H: Please.

Will you direct us, please?

(Pause)

I am Q'uo. Let us rephrase that so that we may direct you to direct us. We wish to know the area of your confusion, as precisely as you may state it, that we go over ground no more than once. If we have been completely confusing, restate your question. We thank you.

H: *(Inaudible)* quite at a loss *(inaudible)* direction.

I am Q'uo, and we are one with you, my brother. Let us begin upon an intellectual state, and stay there for a brief period. An entity within the illusion is trapped and imprisoned until the entity realizes the transparency of the illusion. Each path, or way, to transcending relativity and achieving an experience of eternity, is just that, a means of ordering and discriminating amongst the choices of what to perceive and how to perceive it. The entity moves into the distortions of one particular path, and by thinking along that pathway expressed by an entity or entities, which may all be called that of Christed consciousness, the entity within the relativistic illusion, which you are experiencing, may become immediately aware of that which transcends the illusion in a final way, that is, the experience of the Creator as immediate.

When the experience of the one infinite Creator has been collected, reaped and gathered, blessed, thanked and honored, then a portion of the self is aware, in a way that it cannot express in words, of the nature of love, of the Creator, and of the self.

Then, this immediate, ineffable experience, which is not learning, but the result of learning, may be broken, opened, as infinite as it is, and offered as love within the illusion, to the illusion itself, to those one meets within the illusion, and to the self.

What the paths are for is to deliver the relativistic self over to the worshipful and open and faithful heart. When that state has been achieved, even momentarily, by the seeking entity, the experience of unity with the infinite Creator is had and stored and remembered. It is at that point that all paths become one, just as all manifestations of Christed consciousness tell different stories, but in their essence are all one.

May we answer you further, my brother?

H: I am quite satisfied. Thank you Q'uo.

We thank you very much, my brother, especially for having the patience and honesty to direct us.

Is there another question at this time?

H: May I ask if the Vedic concept of the creation of this universe, and its controlling directors, known as demigods, can fit with the system of the Logos and the different densities and the entities within those densities that are described in the Ra material?

I am Q'uo. We find this instrument not to have the energy stored to respond in full to this query, and would suggest that this query be entered at the beginning of a working, in order that it may be given due consideration, for, indeed, this is a large subject.

May we ask for a final query at this time?

M: I have one question. If this is too lengthy, perhaps later we can ask at another time. Is it always necessary to ask spirit, the spirit complex, for directions, in order for the intelligence to receive it, or can the intelligence simply be receptive or open to what the spirit has to say, or the direction that needs to come from spirit?

I am Q'uo, and we shall attempt to answer this query. The questioner comes to the question and becomes the question. The spirit is not the kind of complex that is grasped within illusion. The spirit is, indeed, imperishable. It functions not as an information-giver, but as a water pipe. Information is delivered through the spirit complex into the conceptual portion of the mind, and in the depth of the mind it is allowed to take root, because of the desire of the student to know. And insofar as the entity desires and continues to desire with the most patient and full concern the answer to each present moment, so this opening of the shuttle of spirit may be encouraged.

It is also greatly encouraged through the loss of the ego in meditation, chanting, contemplation, creativity and other manner of losing the small and relative self in experiencing those echoes of imperishabilty which lie within each entity.

May we answer you further, my brother?

M: No, that is fine, thank you.

We thank you. I am known to you as Q'uo, and we hope that we have not only confused you, but also opened a few new thoughts to your consideration. May you be blessed with help and aid. May you allow the blessing of that help and that aid, which is always available if you may allow the help. It is often help in disguise, but if you acknowledge it, it will make itself known to you. That is the nature of spiritual evolution. You will evolve as quickly and as painlessly as you allow yourself. The secret is the attention. Pay attention, each moment. Extend the meditative self until it encompasses each moment, and then in each moment that which is yours will come to you, and will make itself known clearly. We speak of that which is beyond the normal evolutionary pattern, but we speak in a way which we hope draws you onward in hunger and thirst for that which cannot perish, that which you are.

We leave you in that which you are, in the love, the light, the peace and the joy, of the one infinite Creator. We are known to you as those of the principle of Q'uo. Adonai, my friends. Adonai. ☙

Intensive Meditation
January 10, 1991

(Unknown channeling)

I am Q'uo, and greet each of you this evening through this instrument. We are pleased that this instrument has been able to receive our initial contact.

We would speak to you this evening on the subject of suffering. This is a subject which many of your peoples do not wish to pay attention to, a subject which many wish to ignore or avoid as much as possible. It is also a subject with which each serious seeker is personally quite familiar and we know that each in this group have given much thought to the nature and purpose of suffering as it has been observed in each life and the lives of your other selves.

We are aware that there are differing so-called popular views of the role of suffering in the life of a seeker. Traditionally, many groups among your peoples have held that suffering is necessary for the purification of the soul or the advancement of the seeker on the path. This concept has been "adopted," shall we say, by others in the more general society, as well as may be observed by the term that is in this instrument's mind, "No pain, no gain." There is also, as you are aware, a group or groups, especially in the so-called New Age movements among your peoples, which hold that suffering is not only not necessary to spiritual growth, but may even be a sign that individual has not taken whatever steps are necessary in order for it to be truly a seeker. We would suggest to you that both of these views are extremes and that suffering is neither a necessity for spiritual growth, nor a sign that spiritual growth is not taking place, but rather simply a byproduct of that which you call change.

Now, as you are aware, the process of spiritual growth involves much change and this takes place on many different levels. Change is at times most welcome and it may not be perceived at those times that there is any suffering taking place. However, each choice that is made involves, of necessity, a sacrifice of all other choices at that moment and suffering may be felt on many levels.

It is possible to follow the paths outlined by the more traditional viewpoints that adamantly hold to the view that suffering is essential for purification, for growth. It is possible to adopt this viewpoint in whole or in part, to use suffering in the life intentionally to accelerate one's process of spiritual evolution. As you aware, the conscious use of catalyst in this way is the means whereby one's growth is accelerated.

You are aware that there is much catalyst among your peoples that is unused, indeed, much that is little even noticed. This is to be expected as the nature of your illusion is most heavy and you are constantly bombarded with more than your senses are able to focus on.

Thus, the role of suffering in each seeker's life may, in actuality, be chosen by the seeker. It may be catalyst on which the attention is focused and therefrom much understanding and much growth may take place. It may be ignored or avoided as much as possible, but we would suggest to you that, as a seeker, this would not be the most desirable course of action if progress on the path is what is desired.

Many among your peoples have gone to great lengths to provide certain types of suffering for themselves in their life in order that attention may be brought to the life, to areas that need examination, to provide a focus that will eventually lead the conscious mind through the illusion. For this is the first thing desired by each entity as it enters this *(inaudible)* incarnation, that the illusion be pierced. The realization occurs that this indeed is illusion.

How great is the suffering among your peoples and how many there are who suffer completely within the illusion, not realizing the opportunity it brings them. The sorrow within and we hope that our humble words may perhaps be the means by which some are enabled to begin to pierce this illusion.

We are grateful for the opportunity to speak to this group and would at this time transfer to the one known as Jim. I am known to you as Q'uo.

(Jim channeling)

I am Q'uo, and greet each of you again, in love and in light with this instrument. We would at this time offer ourselves for the answering of queries if that is appropriate. *(Inaudible)*. May we ask if there is a query at this time?

Questioner: *(Inaudible)*.

I am Q'uo, and we are aware of your query, my sister. At this point in the progress of each instrument in this circle, there is but one necessity and that is to persevere. Each has a firm grasp of the process both in the mechanical sense of how the process works and also in the sense of the inner discrimination and ability to speak the words that are given and which appear within your minds. Each entity is now striving to become aware of more of the richness, shall we say, that may be found within the concepts and the words and phrases that we give each during the contact.

There are potential avenues of exploration that are open to all instruments no matter the amount of experience involved for there is indeed an interconnectedness between all things and it is possible to be finely enough tuned that ways of describing that which is given begin to open more easily as practice is accomplished. Thus the subtleties and nuances of the message for each practicing instrument can enrich the process and the content of each contact. Other than continuing to practice *(inaudible)*, we would not have any recommendations for additional tools or procedures at this time.

Is there a further query?

Questioner: *(Inaudible)*.

I am Q'uo, and am aware of what you are asking. We would agree in general terms that your estimation is correct. However, though each of you have a more finely tuned receptive ability awaiting further exercise and therefore are also in need of looking for the finest tuning within that can be found, and the most appropriate phrases for the chiseling of the concept. The entity known as Jim, through which we now speak, has this need, as you have surmised in more obvious configuration as it tends to synopsize both in thinking and in speaking as a result of the receiving in like manner.

However, we would not wish to omit that *(inaudible)* each instrument can receive both more finely and more clearly with the practice and the developing of the inner sensitivities that allow certain portions of our words to be as seeds and to speak what may spring from them, rather than speak only seeds. We attempt at this time to use this analogy to make an image appear within this instruments mind that allows concepts to permit. We shall retrace this thought, not wishing to *(inaudible)*.

These seeds are cast upon the ground. They are crystal concepts. Instead of speaking each concept discretely, these can be allowed to blossom, to grow, shall we say, so that there is a trail that is followed.

We apologize for the moodiness of this response, but we were, in this response, allowing this instrument to do that which was given as an exercise.

Is there a further query, my sister?

Carla: *(Inaudible).*

I am Q'uo, and we are of your query, my sister. We would answer in the affirmative that you have a good grasp of that which we would have many more words to express. Is there a further query?

Carla: The other question is about *(inaudible)*. Something that just came up when we were talking before *(inaudible)* and I got all of that, if I am on the right track. *(Inaudible)*.

I am Q'uo, and am aware of your query. You are quite correct in your assumption that each instrument can construct a model or inner visualization to use as a sensing device and by attending to this tool may receive an impression as to the nature of the protection that is available to each circle that is seeking such as this one. The visualization may also, for those that are more able to utilize the inner senses, be that which allows the sense, the tone of the circle, to be perceived in much the same fashion as the tuning fork when place in motion *(inaudible)* here. We take this instrument as an example whereby the feeling for the group would be internalized so that the circle was felt to be *(inaudible)* body and the, by virtue of the circle, monitored in this fashion. Others may be more comfortable with a visualization that would give a momentary image to the instrument as the means by which the protective vibration of the circle could be monitored.

Is there another query?

Carla: *(Inaudible).*

I am Q'uo. We thank you for your assistance in aiding each instrument and improving *(inaudible)*. Is there another query at this time?

Questioner: *(Inaudible).*

I am Q'uo, and am aware of your query, my sister. Indeed, there is a great opportunity each day for each instrument, we find, to refine these sensitivities. In that at any moment with there are stimuli reaching into any of the senses of an instrument a few moments may be taken to focus as carefully as possible upon each stimulus and the response that each feels within. There will be a reflex kind of response as the first response in a situation in which the instrument has paused for a moment in order to receive some of the inner workings of itself. Thus, you may find yourself in a crowded room with a number of conversations occurring and by taking five to ten of your seconds—we believe this is correct—in inner silence one may take an inventory of the vibrations that are resonating within in harmony or in disharmony and one may also note the flavor or color of harmonious or disharmonious vibrations so that there is a coding or checking, careful noting of these responses as this inner inventory is practiced more frequently. The sensing ability will energized even more acutely, much as any learned activity becomes easier with repetition. Thus you may decide to take such as needed, [an] inventory of vibrational sensing two or three or more times per your day as a regularized exercise.

Is there a further query, my sister?

Questioner: *(Inaudible).*

I am Q'uo, and we thank you, my sister. Is there another query at this time?

Questioner: *(Inaudible).*

I am Q'uo. We are most appreciative for each opportunity to speak our thoughts to this group for we find that each asks that which is both upon the mind and the heart. It is well that all faculties be brought to bear upon it, the learning process with this group for utilizing all the data tools and for expressing your dedication, your desire to be of service. My sister, we shall take our leave of this group, thanking each again for renewing the opportunity for us to join you this evening. We are know to you as those of Q'uo. We leave each in love and in light of the one infinite Creator. Adonai, my friends. ♣

Sunday Meditation
January 13, 1991

Group question: The question this evening has to do with the situation in which Carla and I are experiencing difficulty in maintaining our normal harmony in spite of our very intense efforts at trying to communicate clearly. We know we have been targets of psychic greetings in the past, but we aren't aware of making openings for these greetings at this time. What is the quality, in general, in mated relationships, that Ra described as adversary in nature, and how can people become aware enough of these factors to create a harmonious relationship?

(Carla channeling)

I am Q'uo. Greetings to each of you in the love and in the light of the one infinite Creator. It is a privilege to be called to your group at this time to speak upon the adversarial relationship between mates. First, however, we would note, for your interest and *(inaudible)*, the absolute beauty of a great portion of your planetary sphere's inhabitants' prayers as they rise from the mundane events which cause them into planes of intercession, healing, forgiveness, and enlightenment.

My brothers and sisters, we cannot stop your wars, nor would the Creator. These are energies within you which have not yet been balanced. That balancing is a portion of your learning. There is a correspondingly drastic amount of negative energy upon the Earth plane at this time which is only inevitable since the harvest grows nigh, and, indeed, has begun occurring on an individual basis, as those who are capable, upon leaving their incarnations, choose to take the walk of light and discover the density of their next abiding and learning place.

Your beauty is transcendent, your prayers heartfelt, and given every support by those of positive orientation, whatever the nature and manifestation of your consciousness and personality. So, although events look hopelessly muddled upon a mundane level, there is great polarization taking place, both for those positively oriented and those upon what many have not yet determined as the negative path. Many are moving along this path at this time who will, predictably, reverse the nature of that polarity when the difference between imagined carnage and real carnage is made clear by some personal experience.

We ask you to look at these days not with trepidation and not with fear, but with enormous compassion. There will be, regardless of future events, great grieving and suffering among all peoples. We do not know what will occur in the future. It is always in the hands of free entities to choose the destiny of a people. Some of these free entities are imprisoned within their minds by concepts neither positive nor negative. This is a great confusion upon the mundane level. We ask you to move beyond it, and to be a portion of the ceaseless cry of prayer and supplication that rises so beautifully, so deeply, so richly at this time from your planetary surface, rises to the infinite One in glory and beauty. Know that your prayers are heard. Know that you are not forgotten.

We move now to a more personal, intimate point of view with regard to that within third-density entities which contributes not only to war and the possibilities thereof, but also to what is called an adversarial relationship, whether it is between friends, family members, enemies or mates. Let us gaze for a moment at the basic truths to which we will be contrasting experience within the illusion.

The most basic truth is that all that there is is created of one Creator, and of one material. Love has chosen to move into being through the use of light. When we greet you in love and light, we greet you as all that there is in all that there is, hoping to imply the spiritual reality that all are one. The most you may experience normally within third density is harmony. You are not just harmonious entities, you are One. You are truly each other. As you love others, you love yourself.

Our second background proposition to you is our opinion that the mated relationship, indeed, any close relationship, seems especially biased against the possibility of doing great spiritual work because inevitably neither entity in such a relationship is at one with itself. Thusly, all relationships, to the extent that the disharmony in one and the disharmony in the other can be multiplied, will result in a certain strength of collision. The more discordant the vibrations of each, the greater the impact of the collision.

We speak in metaphysical terms, but the motion of emotion, and its vector, are both important concepts to consider when examining disharmony between two mates. The energy that is being experienced subjectively has a certain intensity depending upon the degree and the kind of disharmony in the entity. The vector of that energy, which is of a negative nature, is a free choice also, and may be pointed inward towards the self, or outward towards others, or it may be ignored because of guilt or other reasons, repressed, and thereby become a fixed and unmoving solidity of disharmony.

Thusly, no matter how subjectively miserable it makes a spiritually oriented entity to speak disharmoniously, it is at all times far more appropriate for service to others entities to move any expressions of emotion whatsoever into clear and honest expression than to keep it within the self that it may putrefy and sicken the self in one way or another, because the energy of that disharmony must express itself. If it is not expressed as catalyst by the mind and the emotions, it shall move into the body complex and create disharmony within the second density manifested entity which is the temple or tabernacle within which your consciousness meets the infinite Creator during this incarnational experience.

From this beginning, you may perhaps see that we shall start not with two entities, but with one, for the source of disharmony is fear, fear of one kind or another. When there is disharmony it is well first to move within the self and ask the self to look at the expression that was disharmonious, not the other's expression, but the expression of the self. Examine it not for excellence—you are not a judge—but examine it to discover the underlying fear.

We may use an example. A common negative emotion which creates disharmony between entities is jealousy. As this is specifically not the situation of the precise couple asking the question, we feel this is a better and more general concept to work with using this instrument, for the instrument must be to some degree protected against the temptation to offer the specific advice regarding the self while in this altered state of consciousness.

Why would a woman or man in third density experience jealousy? The experience of jealousy is linked to the fear of loss, which creates anger, which creates guilt, which creates a host of echoing and re-echoing discordant emotions within the self. Let us look at the entity who has attracted this negative emotion. Let us say that this entity is innocent. Why is this entity experiencing the adversarial negative emotion? Largely, the innocent entity who is experiencing jealousy is experiencing the fear of being utterly misunderstood and misjudged. It is angry because it does not like to be kept in a cage, and the emotion of jealousy in an active phase is the making of a very small prison for an entity.

If the entity is guilty of that action because of which the mate is jealous, that entity is also fearful. What is it afraid of? Perhaps it is afraid of losing that which has been comfortable, useful and kindly in its life experience, the settled home, the children, the family experience, and this fear creates anger and frustration and the feeling of being alone. Indeed, the feeling of being alone, bereft, stranded, abandoned and forgotten is at the heart of the great majority of the day-to-day fears which create in entities an adversarial inner relationship between the portion of the self that is devoted to unity, peace and concord, and the part of the self that is devoted to protecting its boundaries, enlarging its fortune, creating greater comfort or happiness, however petty or great.

Thusly, in those who are of one piece, those who have developed a personality that is seamless, they are not open to the experience of adversarial relationships, because in themselves they have no adversary. All of themselves is focused in one direction. May we say that this entity is seldom found among your people, but that it is very frequently an hoped for ideal. The unity of the self is in little [i.e. in miniature] the unity of the creation. Peace within any relationship betwixt two people involves the illusion of war because the progress of any one person in third density includes the experience of hard won wars. There is almost always a significant amount of friction in at least one substantive area of the personality in which part of the self feels one way, part another, and instead of being content to allow that balance to go forward until it has resolved itself, entities push and probe and pull at themselves emotionally and analytically, attempting a sort of Band-Aid treatment of that which is as deep as the Grand Canyon.

It is the wounded entity that is truly at war. All other expressions of disharmony come from this adversary relation of self to self. It is, therefore, never intelligent to work upon another without regard to the self, for there is no right and wrong, there is only disharmony. We do not say this to include acts of needless or unprovoked violence of a random kind. We say this to express the opinion that entities need, when faced with disharmony, to turn not outward, but inward, for within the self are the seeds of all negative as well as all positive expressions of mind, thought, emotion or action.

How does one go about this? As always, the daily meditation, perhaps at the beginning, perhaps at the end, perhaps both times, in the amount of time needed by the individual, is the daily bread that enables all of the spiritual work which you wish to do, for your energy to do this work comes not only as the gift of the infinite Creator in the very creation of the self, in the way the physical vehicle is able to internalize the infinite energy of the infinite One, it is also a matter of focusing that energy, of experiencing from intelligent infinity, by this calling for love and light, that immediate presence that is the fruit of faith.

Now that each is aware that each is responsible for the self, we would offer our opinions concerning the mated relationship, its—to us—quite obvious advantages, and its—to you—quite obvious disadvantages. The great advantage and the great opportunity for disadvantage in the mated relationship is one and the same thing. Entities without the intention of going through difficult times as well as good are excellent mirrors for a time. But insofar as honest discussion and expression of disapproval and so forth is repressed, the relationship will remain distant, and it is the very intimacy of relationship that makes it both extraordinarily worthwhile spiritually, and often extraordinarily difficult.

When an entity perceives the true kinship and potential unity of the mated relationship, especially, it seems wonderful. To some few, who either do not have the wit to be disturbed, or the wisdom not to be disturbed, there is no particular down side. This is true of perhaps a handful of entities upon your planet at this time, compared to the vast normalcy of friction and subjectively experienced pain from intimacy. However, the discussion of instruments within this circle recently produced an image which we may use to good effect. That is the image of the cocoon. When entities choose the mated relationship, they are temporarily, in a romantically oriented marriage, not quite well. They are ill, they are ill with too much giving. Because of the tremendous attraction that brings people together romantically, mates often begin with extremely unhuman concepts of the capabilities of third-density entities, including themselves. All that has been said has been delightful, company has been enjoyed, and even though it may be spoken intellectually that this has been a Sunday relationship and is now going seven days a week, the impact of this upon the psyche cannot be gauged.

Think of the image of the cocoon in winter. From the outside it looks protective, smooth and comforting. Upon the inside every available space is crammed with life and food, consciousness and catalyst. In a mated relationship two entities agree before the infinite Creator and in its presence to live as one entity serving the infinite Creator. This is a magical and profound promise, a covenant. Each of the mates has expressed its co-Creatorship, and a new entity for use within your illusion has been born. It is difficult to remember that there are not two, but either one or three entities in that cocoon. There are those who would express oneness by saying that as each portion of the creation is the Creator, there is only one entity in this womb that produces so much beauty. Just as legitimate is the opinion that there are three, the self, the mate and love itself, the one infinite Creator, Who has become the bridge between the self and the mate, enabling two singular entities to harmonize, strengthen the strong points, release the weaker points in terms of harmony, and create an entity, that together with a full heart and merry laughter, may continue long and without the burnout of being solitary which afflicts many of your peoples, in polarization of the service-to-others aspect which is so very profoundly the great mover and shaker spiritually for one who seeks the acceleration of the pace of spiritual evolution.

Now, if an entity is unable to deal with the concept of being in a cocoon, and being crowded, then there is that within the self which may not have the most rapid growth in the ability to deal with the petty disagreements which excellent and truly loving entities still always seem to offer. This is as it should be. How could you learn if you did not have catalyst? The placing of two entities this closely together is that created by the Creator as an opportunity for two to do intensive, accelerated work which neither could do by the self. It is an invitation to a series of seemingly disastrous misunderstandings and a seemingly endless chain of negative emotion and pain.

Within the illusion, this is what change and transformation feel like. It does not feel good to release the portions of the self that are not able to come into harmony with portions of the other self. This does not mean that entities need to change in order the be active and powerful co-Creators of beautiful, service-filled lives. It simply means that each entity has its lessons to learn, and although it can learn them through the random catalyst of strangers, acquaintances and the indifferent friends and family, yet the more intimacy that is in any relationship, the more the opportunities for disagreement, debate, confusion, hurt, guilt and many other seemingly negative experiences which may, by the free choice of an entity who is spiritually aware, be perceived as opportunities for service, for learning and for growth.

To become truly intimate is to release the self from its strictures, for true intimacy, within the illusion of third density, is found only by guess and by hunch. One may do work upon one's own consciousness and one's own personality to attempt to eradicate pettiness, meanness, the irritability, the friction. But just as you cannot deny any degree of the 360 degrees of the third-density personality, so you cannot get rid of any of those degrees within this illusion.

Consequently, in all but the most—we shall use this instrument's word—saintly, there are the variations in behavior which predict with great probability continuing disharmony, as normally innocent entities—that is, innocent of malice—discover themselves misunderstood, disturbed, distraught or upset by the actions not only within the self, but some action, speech or thought which the mate has had.

Now, you are in a cocoon and you are facing each other. By this cocoon of mating with commitment until death the entity agrees to accept the conditions of intimacy. How can one become nonadversarial? The first step, needless to say, lies completely within the self. Look through the life experience in any way deemed appropriate, with an eye to discovering recurring themes of discontent, recurring triggers for fear and the often extremely biased and difficult to understand actions of those who fear. As the entity known as Aaron has said, do not gaze at the situation, as it is a symptom [of fear]; gaze instead at the fear until you grasp what you fear, and with what method you wish to welcome love and allow fear to go its way.

This is an ongoing process which must be done by the self of its own free will. A mate can suggest, but it can never do the work of another. Often the more advanced within third density entities are, the more difficult the hands they deal themselves within a life experience, for they wish, knowing the value of third-density decision making, to have the opportunity to make unifying music, harmonious solutions to scratchy, discordant, relationships.

Once the self has done all the work that it can at one particular time in scratching the surface of this area of fear, do not feel that it is arranged, fixed or repaired, for the levels of emotion which come to the surface in an intimate relationship through a process of many years are those that move deeper and deeper into the self that is below the door sill or threshold of consciousness.

Now, some are within this cocoon. Most of those within this cocoon do not know its nature, or the reason for the discomfort. It is not simply the closeness to another entity. It is the mirroring effect brought to a state of honesty not possible to be offered by those who are not privy to the especially private moments, be they happy or sad, which occur between two people alone. Indeed, this is true of every relationship in which the self is committed in some degree. Close friends of whatever kind may also do work together, but they must be willing to be repeatedly uncomfortable.

After one has done all the work that is possible within the self at a particular time, it is temporarily a friendlier mirror, a kinder reflection, to the mate. However, each of you is not intended to find it easy to be of a positive polarity at all times. There are various, and often subjectively confusing cycles of energy within the mind, within the body, within the emotions and within the spirit. The combinations, in their endless variance, of the particular energies at a given moment will cause the most stable and unified entity to behave in seemingly various ways. Although there is a general tenor of character and personality in the kind of events, there is no aforeset series of actions, beliefs, thoughts and beingness upon which one may count, not for anyone, not at any of your times. Each entity is free, within that cocoon, but free. If it does not wish to become a butterfly it may leave the cocoon, and be pupa and larva and so forth once again, eating and growing and preparing.

The state you call marriage is that cocooned, protected state in which two entities vow to enhance their service to others by joining together, and to enhance each other's personal polarity, creation and creation of service to others, each for the other. It is an absolute ideal which flies in the face of the illusion. It is a claiming of eternity where before there was a passage of time betwixt physical birth and physical death.

Now, there are many who do not experience this in the marriage ceremony or in the marriage. This does not mean it is not real. It means that it has been unnoticed, unvalued and unused. Those who asked this question wish to use the cocoon in which they have placed themselves for the purpose of supporting each other, and supporting an enhanced collaboration for the service of humankind. When the relationship, because of outer or inner circumstances, may change, then there is outward as well as inward pressure placed upon the close knit intimacy that has gone before. Each entity, then, is experiencing two separate kinds of catalyst: the catalyst from within, the catalyst from without.

The catalyst from within comes as two entities discover their helplessness. It is not usual for entities which are not in a stressful position to experience helplessness. It is the nature of each entity's instinctual mind to protect the self. Thus, one goes from protecting the self from one's own negative 180 degrees, to protecting the self from the negative 180 degrees of an intimate other self. This protection is done, as always, through the fear of annihilation. Entities so close must, at last, it is thought, blow apart because they cannot breathe.

We suggest to you that this image of the cocoon is that of a cocoon without substance except for light. It is indeed a place for transformation. It is indeed a place where every ounce of humility and humbleness and peacefulness and compassion for the self and for the mate will be endlessly useful. But at heart, the only answer to fear is love itself, whether it is expressed in faith, in expressions of hope, or in a simple, inarticulate embrace, indeed, expressed in any way whatsoever that is understandable by the two within the cocoon.

This is the key to moving into harmonious mirroring once again, to remember that you are truly inharmonious not with the other, but with the self, and that the other has been a mirror to you, a painful, honest and rather irritated mirror. This does not mean it is necessary to placate the mirror. It is necessary only to give thanks for that mirror that is causing you, seemingly, such pain, for it enables you to grapple with spiritual principles and issues of which the self has not been aware.

It is very difficult for a well working spiritually oriented mated couple to be blind-sided and surprised by the difficulties of mundane life, for in that mated relationship which is sturdy, the structure has been built with love, with creative love. That cannot be defined, but we may say that romance is not a deep portion of the relationship that achieves oneness, but rather love itself, and the shared work of creating a stable and unified home of love. That is the beauty of the successful, continuingly agonizing, but continuingly hoping and thankful cocooned mated couple. Two people seeking together, trusting themselves, trusting each other, and trusting in love.

Hope, trust, charity, love; these are only words. The reality lies deep in your hearts. Move, you poor in heart, into the richness of the heart visited by infinity, and see butterflies dancing amidst a metaphysical field of infinitely beautiful flowers. This is a gift you are paying for that will not be delivered within the incarnational experience for longer than moments at a time. You see the struggle, you see living in a sardine can, living in a cocoon. We see the maturation of a thing of surpassing spiritual power, delicacy and beauty.

We thank you for this extremely interesting question, and feel that it is especially interesting as so many among your people are dealing first with the war that is outside, and perhaps only then becoming honest enough to see the planes of Megiddo within the heart of every third-density entity. Yes, you struggle, and may we encourage you to struggle, wrestle, fight or relax, and rest and observe, completely depending upon each entity's personality and needs. It is indeed greatly worth the doing, and is in fact the beginning of the learning process that creates the social memory complex. It begins with you and yourself. Come into harmony with that precocious, maddening self. Forgive it, love it, accept it, and you shall be prepared to work at your lessons of love as mates.

We wish all mates strength and courage and persistence, for love is far more than you think it, and each mated entity is the beginning of love made visible, even in third density. Lose not your interest in psychic greeting, but with these thoughts observe for yourself those opportunities created by a lack of humbleness as regards the nature of the self.

We apologize for speaking overlong once again. Indeed, we have never been more surprised to find the time pass. We feel this instrument is moving more and more away from awareness of time. It is not giving us data because it does not have it.

Although this is acceptable to us, if there is a desire for a shorter format, we might suggest some outer stimulus, for without this instrument's awareness of the passage of time, we have none. We would appreciate your aid if you wish us to speak more economically. Let us know not when the time to speak is through, but when, perhaps, there are five or ten of your minutes before the desired end, and we shall do our best to comply. We leave this matter in your hands and in your free choice, for we are always willing to speak as much as you would desire.

We would like to close this instrument through the one known as Jim. We leave this instrument in love and light and in joy that we have been able to offer our opinions to you. We do hope most humbly that some of what we say may be helpful, and, as always, ask each to take only those things which are helpful, abandoning the rest as truths not for them. I am known to you as Q'uo, and I transfer at this time.

(Jim channeling)

I am Q'uo, and greet each again in love and in light through this instrument. If we have not overworn our welcome, we would ask if we might be of further service by tending to any queries that you may have at this time. Is there a query with which we may begin?

Carla: *(Inaudible. Essentially, Carla said she would have to review and digest the material given and then would probably have questions at a later time.)*

I am Q'uo. Then we are satisfied that we have served to the fullest extent possible at this time, and we are very, very grateful to have been able to share that which we have shared with you. We find that these gatherings are delicate in their tuning and powerful in their desires to know more of that truth which shines equally upon all. We thank you for offering your queries, your desires, and your selves to these circles of seeking. We are thrilled at the light that is generated here, and we shall take our leave of this group at this time, leaving each, as always, in the love and in the light of the one infinite Creator. We are known to you as those of Q'uo. Adonai, my friends, adonai. ✤

Sunday Meditation
January 20, 1991

Group question: The question this afternoon is a continuation of last week's question concerning the harmony that is possible to be generated within a mated relationship, the problems that we have in experiencing disharmony, even though we attempt very much to be clear in communication and compassionate in communication. We are wondering this week if there is some relationship between the various portions of our characters or personalities. We find that there are different aspects of ourselves that have different ways of expressing, and that are perhaps even contradictory from time to time. Is there some way that we can gain a greater understanding about increasing the harmony in a relationship by integrating or becoming more aware of those various portions of ourselves that seem at times to be at odds with themselves?

(Carla channeling)

Greetings in the love and in the light of the one infinite Creator. I am Q'uo, of the Confederation of Planets in the Service of the One Infinite Creator, and I thank you most humbly for calling us to your circle of seeking, and for giving us the opportunity to talk upon this subject. Indeed, it would be well for all third-density peoples to examine well not only the answers to questions such as this, but the questions themselves, for the seeds of truth lie not within answers, but within questions, and it is the more skillful spiritual student who pays attention to the questions that his incarnational experience generates.

How, indeed, to live in harmony with the self or with another? That is a dilemma for those of your density, locked outside of the knowledge of others' true resonances, and seeing only that tip of the iceberg which is behavior. How can entities choose most wisely, especially when they require of themselves a choice which must be made, often before the entity is aware of its deeper desires? Consequently, many mates and many behaviors are chosen because of shallow and petty reasons, reasons which will not endure, truths that will not hold.

Let us again begin within the self. What is it that causes an entity to feel that it is self-contradictory? Indeed, it is a fact that entities are self-contradictory. This is a part of the illusion that may be taken as truth for the purposes of learning. Like all other portions of the illusion, there is no permanent or lasting truth connected with this personality that you experience as yourself. Indeed, you have simply taken on a personality, a solidity, an incarnation, in order that your consciousness may experience this very illusion of separatehood. Not only are you within your physical vehicles apparently separate from all other solidified entities, but within yourself you are apparently solidified into various portions, or voices, or personalities within the self which are responding to various stimuli.

Let us use a created example. Let us say that a seeker has a father, a mother, a brother and a sister, and perhaps one other relative which has affected interaction with the seeker at very young ages. There is within the capability of absolutely every behavior possible. That is true not of those who are seemingly evil in their behavior or negative any less than it is true of those who are seemingly very positive in their behavior. Behavior is simply a way of responding in a situation in which it is not safe to be. Consequently, the personalities that do not seem to be congruent as one integrated self are most often those voices that spoke when you were helpless in the years of your incarnation before you gained any maturity or strength. These voices were powerful; you were not.

The voices, however, were not often, in some cases, kind. The voice of the father, perhaps challenging in one way, perhaps refusing to consider any point of view but the father's own. The mother's voice, perhaps a particular mother was cowed before the authority of the mate, and did not choose to stand with a child, even if the child might be in some sense correct, if the mate, the father of the child, wished to exercise negative authority. Perhaps the brother, the sister, the aunt, put one in a bullying position, or only bullied the seeker. There are many, many hurts that to a mature and independent entity are only scratches, but before the infant has created for itself a nexus of experience full enough that it attempts to control its environment, it has been compromised into fear by the voices that it hears that have power over it, and so the seeker develops behavior.

It is a role directly at odds with being, because it mimics being, often perfectly. One can behave, although one is under great stress if one does, for all of the entire waking hours of its day. One can choose never to be simply as one is, and instead one may simply respond to each situation with the appropriate voice, the appropriate behavior. This is a life lived in primary fear. The fear is reasonable for the small child. The same fear can be employed by the self as a learning tool if the self is able to decide for itself that its choices will no longer include those drawn from the soil of fear.

Each entity to whom we speak is what you call adult. Within the adult there lies the universe, and this creates in you great treasure, but it cannot be known to you except insofar as you release fear and the behaviors that it brings into being. When, for instance, an entity who has been terrorized by a parent finds itself in a position where it must make a decision, a hard decision with which it must live, it experiences the fear of that voice saying "You, you small child, could not possibly have the wisdom to make the correct choice."

Let us reexamine this voice, this portion of the personality that you think is your own voice, but in fact is not. That voice speaks fear, but what have you to fear? Shall you be wrong? Mistakes occur. Out of that wrongness, no matter what it is, a desirable and beneficial result will take place, for in the mistakes that are seen in men's eyes are the happenstances of spiritual evolution as seen in the eyes of a living spirit of love. What is feared? Being wrong, being foolish.

Let us put this in perspective. Do you fear that the wrong decision shall cause your physical death? That is unlikely, and yet perhaps that can be taken as the worst possible outcome. Gaze at that outcome. Do you fear entering larger life? Do you fear leaving behind the pain and the heaviness of third-density illusion and entering into a creation more filled with light, feeling and knowledge? My friends, this is an interesting thing to fear, indeed. Yet, this is the worst that can happen to you.

Let us recall to your minds the basic purpose of third-density incarnation. You are here to make choices. It is imperative that you make choices. If the choices that you make are unskillful, that is acceptable to the infinite Creator. The process of making choices creates in the seeker more and more skill at the process of making choices. Like any other process, choice making improves with practice. If one is able eventually to claim and name all of the portions of the personality, one is then able simply to say, "I know not how these portions of myself fit together, and I lay that before love itself, for I know not what to do, yet love knows that which is the very best for me, and I will allow that love to lead me, and I shall follow."

We are aware that this seems in some ways very glib, because the tearing and rending of the self, as one develops in maturity, is certainly most painful, and almost impossible to understand while it is going on. It is necessary only to understand that all things within the self, though contradictory, confused, and to whatever extent unenlightened, are acceptable, beloved, and supported by the one infinite Creator, and by that spirit of love that moves with you and is your companion at all times. There is no way that you can move away from love, except by ignoring it because of fear. You see, to the Creator, you are never guilty, you are never unaccepted. To the Creator, you are always in a paradise, but each of you is in an illusion which decries the apparent inaccuracy of our previous statement, and it is only by faith that you may feel that love, that acceptance, that forgiveness, and that support. It is only by faith that you may continue standing when you feel that life has cut you off at the knees. It is only by faith that you can stay alive when you feel that your life is not worth the living.

Feelings of despair are normal portions of the experience of humankind in third density. There is no negative feeling, passive or active, of which you are not fully capable, given the appropriate circumstances. It is vitally important that you are able to see that, scattered as you may be in this illusion, there is within you a center, a core that is the very treasure of all that there is. Within you is a spark of love that whether you wish it or not, unifies you, not within the illusion, for there you must struggle to learn, but within that underlying reality of your spiritual self.

Let us gaze one last time at the struggle of the self with self. Which portions of yourself do you like? Which portions do you not like? You may write these things down about yourself, or you may trick your conscious mind by attempting to write down those things which you like and dislike about an entity whom you truly, seriously, have arguments with, or dislike. When you write down those things which you are willing to give to that entity that are of goodness, and when you write down those entity's faults with which you are so in a struggle, you will discover that you have written about yourself. This is a useful exercise for learning how each entity within the illusion of third density distorts the love and the light that moves through the universe in a way unique to itself.

It is well to trust that all the personalities within have made their own quite lucid unification. It is equally clear that an entity cannot express at the same time all of that which it feels, thinks and is concerned about in a situation. There you have a window into the process of making choices. Come to know the voices that speak within, not so that you may silence them, necessarily, but so that you may recreate a list of priorities in which those voices and the behaviors that they have caused are of a far lower priority than the self forgiven, accepted and loved in the present moment. Claim this self, for this is who you are. There is no you but you. You are unique, a child of love who has made choices. Whatever you have done to this point, know that this is a new moment, as is each moment, and that all choices are equally open to you at all times. Yes, you must bear the consequences of the choices. One of the beauties of this density in terms of its being an excellent environment for learning is that entities are indeed held responsible for their choices. This enables the spiritually growing self to be aware of the importance of making choices.

Now, let us look at the kind of choice that you wish to make, whether it is for yourself or for another. First of all, if the Creator loves and accepts and forgives, is there a significant rationale for refusing to accept to love and forgive either yourself or another entity for behaving or being in a certain way? Here is another question. Can you see in the behavior of yourself or another the consciousness that lies beyond, beneath, above and around that behavior? Have you any clue as to the nature of that entity's unique being? Remember that this is a place for positive action. Positive action in third density is not simply in the arena of the body, but in the arena of the mind. If you find yourself judging, belittling, demeaning or engaging in other negative interactions with yourself or portions of yourself, or with the behavior of others, take a breath, stop, rock back on your mental or emotional heels, and ask yourself if you are appreciating and respecting the freedom and the beingness of yourself or another, for it matters not whether you are dealing with yourself or another. Respect for consciousness suggests that you and others are equally worthy of respect, care, attention, service, and above all, love.

Another question that is fruitful to consider is whether you expect an outcome from yourself or another. To ask of yourself this and this and this outcome is, in the way of making plans, simply a sensible process. If the plans that have been made are not possible to fulfill, then it is the wise seeker who does not waste time bemoaning the undesired outcome of some action or thought. Any action or thought done in order to please or palliate or expedite or control situations is also behavior that will likely engender the harsh edges of other entities' personalities, for when one acts through fear and attempts to control the environment of one's incarnation, one is also controlling other entities. Usually, there is rationalization given to the controlling of other entities for their own happiness. However, to the one being controlled, any control whatsoever feels like interference, and consequently the fear within that entity comes alive and moves to defend the perimeter of that personality.

Relax the mind now, and see all solidity fly away. You are not solid entities; that is an illusion. You are not your behavior; that is part of the illusion. You are yourself and your choices and the deep biases that they bring. If you attempt to define yourself in permanent terms while in this illusion as anything but a student who is attempting to learn the lessons of this classroom, you have moved into an area which will be confusing and debilitating.

At this time, because of the sleepiness within the circle, we would choose to conserve this instrument's energy and simply ask if there are any questions that we might answer before we leave this group this evening. Is there a question at this time?

(Pause)

I am known to you as those of Q'uo. We are most pleased at being able to speak with you further upon this interesting subject. There is no immediate end to the number of ways to address this subject, and we are happy to speak more upon various aspects of it as you gaze upon this material and are able to ask further questions, if that is what you would desire. We are most pleased to speak further at another working.

In hopes that you may truly love yourselves and one another with confidence and faith, we leave you in the kingdom of eternity that this basic attitude delivers you into. We thank you for the beauty of your vibrations and for the peace of your seeking. In its persistence and depth there is a beauty not often seen among your people, and we are humble before third-density pilgrims such as you who struggle and weep and survive to hope and have faith and love tomorrow. Move that tomorrow, my friends, into the present moment, and never let it go, and you shall be one, and all shall be well. And when you cannot do this, forgive yourself, accept yourself, and love yourself, for these are the tools with which you learn to love all that there is.

We bid you adonai. We are known to you as those of the principle of Q'uo. We leave you in the love and the light of the one infinite Creator. ✤

Intensive Meditation
January 24, 1991

(Carla channeling)

… the satisfactory challenging process, because it had not declared itself specifically in a metaphysical manner, that is, it did not declare what symbol, story or ideal described best the metaphysical center of this entity's passion, intensity and essence. As there was no clear essence, this entity was unable to challenge in a matter—we correct this instrument—in a manner satisfactory to the instrument.

It was not until the instrument walked back over the road of its own declaration of self, that the necessary, specific declaration of Jesus the Christ as this particular instrument's center of being, that the tuning was complete.

We suggest to all instruments that their tuning be as specific and clear as is possible. That it be ultimately honest and truthful, and that if there is not the passion felt at the beginning of the tuning process, the tuning should extend until passion, intensity and essence are, once again, revealed to the self through the process of tuning.

We would at this time transfer this contact to the one known as K, with thanks to this instrument for allowing us to use it. We leave this instrument in love and light. We are those of Hatonn.

(K channeling)

I am Hatonn, and greet each of you once again in love and in light through this instrument. It is, as always, a great and esteemed pleasure to have the privilege of working [with] this group, for we see the dedication of each here and appreciate it, for few there are among your peoples who have the courage and will and faith to continue upon the path in the darkness, sometimes with the aid of the moon's light and many times without it.

We would speak to you this evening on the subject of passion, as we believe it is most central to each seeker's journey.

Your peoples are much motivated by goals, by ends to reach, and a great portion of the consciousness of each throughout the day and even throughout the lifetime is directed toward that which is sought to be attained, that is that which one does not have presently.

These goals or ends are many types. Some may be deemed to be lofty, worthy of attention and dedication, others may seem to be more shallow in nature, having to do with more temporary players and comforts.

Many seekers on the path may pride themselves with in keeping a certain goal before the eyes of the mind as an end to pursue and, indeed, we are not suggesting that this should not be thought of. However, the attention belongs not on the goal the seeker is reaching toward but on the present moment which contains the process of the seeking and, indeed, all that there is.

Each of has, as a goal, the pursuit of the mystery. This recedes ever before us and in finite terms, is quite unattainable. Nevertheless, we still strive to know of that mystery what we can and to become of it what we can. It is well for this to be a part of the awareness.

The concept of an infinite mystery, because of the almost total lack of ability to comprehend such an idea, will be for most an unlikely source of passion in the day-to-day life. This is why we recommend that each find the particular mythology or symbolism story or even cosmology that pulls at the heart of the being. We do not attach great significance to what particular mythology is chosen or even that one be chosen at all, if it is possible for the seeker to generate the intensity of passion necessary when focusing on so nebulous a concept as intelligent infinity. This is rare among your peoples.

Thus, it is advisable that study be undertaken until that which is found to resonate within the heart of the self is discovered and then that particular path be focused upon and pursued with all the intensity and passion that may be mustered from within the self. We realize that this is easier for some among your peoples than others. We also realize that passion is thought of among your people as primarily a particular emotional state. We would suggest to you that is not necessarily so. There are those among your peoples who find it easy to feel passionate about one thing or another. This will aid them in their search. However, for those to whom this kind of feeling does not come easily, we would say that intensity of passion consists in large part [as a result] of focused will and faith, that an entity whose pursuing its chosen path with its will focused and intensified, proceeding by faith in the mystery beyond the story, that this is a passionate seeker, whether or not the particular emotion you may know of as passion is subjectively felt. The opposite of passion in this sense may be seen simply to be a lack of interest or focus, the blowing with the winds of comfort and convenience. That is so typical of many of your peoples.

At this time we would transfer to the one known as Jim, thanking this instrument for its efforts in maintaining the contact. We leave this instrument now in love and in light and transfer. We are known to you as Hatonn.

(Jim channeling)

I am Hatonn, and greet each of you again in love and in light through this instrument. It is our privilege to be able to exercise each of the instruments in turn.

We are very happy with the work that has been done this evening by the one known as K. This entity was able to pick up the contact after noting its growing faintness on a couple of occasions. We see this as a maturing of the instrument in that there is not the loss of concentration that would inhibit again perceiving the contact's return. We were hoping in this exercise to strengthen the instrument's confidence in its ability, not only to perceive our contact in its initiation, but also to be able to do as it did, that is to wait patiently for its return and to begin again without undue concern. We would, at this time, offer ourselves in the attempt to speak to any queries which those present may have for us. Is there a query or concern at this time?

K: What would the cause of the contact becoming more faint at times?

I am Hatonn. The initial growing faintness was primarily due to fatigue upon your part for both the mental and physical complexes. As we noted your patient awaiting of the ability to receive our contact again, we then initiated a second experience in order to do that which we have previously described, that is, the observing of the patience, the dedication, the focus of the attention and the reestablishing of the contact. Thus, a chance occurrence was our opportunity to allow you to work upon these areas which are more and more important as an instrument matures, for the ability to maintain concentration and an open channel when the opportunity to be distracted is presented is the practice of being a more mature instrument.

Is there a further query, my sister?

K: In the end I was waiting again and I was interested in continuing, if possible, but I didn't seem to be getting anything. Was that because I was judged to be too tired at that point? Or did I just not wait long enough, or was I just not perceiving fully?

I am Hatonn, and we noted the low energy level toward the latter stages of your exercise of your instrument and decided that after a significant amount of your time had passed, and the contact was not then reestablished, that it would be well to allow the amount of work that had been accomplished to suffice for this evening. Thus it was both a case of the expression of your aforementioned fatigue and our desire not to overtax your instrument.

Is there a further query, my sister?

K: Not at this time, thank you.

I am Hatonn, and we thank you, my sister. Is there another query at this time?

Carla: I have noticed that the conflict in the Middle East has coincided with the growing consciousness, first of restlessness, then of anguish, then of actual metaphysical pain in my own field of consciousness. Is this my protection of my own personal feelings? Or is there an actual energy which is expressing this to me, which is, shall we say, audible to the inner ear *(inaudible)*.

I am Hatonn, and we are aware of your query, my sister. We are happy to speak on this topic to the limit of our ability but we must preface our response by saying that the answer is drawn from many levels of experience for you at this time. There is the growing sensitivity of your instrument due both to the increased exercising of your instrument and the conscious application of your art. There is also the press of pain which has continued for a great portion of your time which also tends to make your instrument more sensitive to any vibration or stimulus of any kind which comes within your auric field. There is also growing upon a planetary level a sensitivity that is a portion of the mass consciousness, shall we say, of your peoples due to the nature of your communication systems being so widespread and nearly instantaneous in reporting that which occurs in that area of the Middle Eastern nations at this time. This conscious sensitivity is a portion of the experience that one may expect when your peoples are eventually able to blend each consciousness into a group consciousness or the preliminary social memory complex. The disharmonious vibrations are those easiest to perceive and those therefore that are now being noticed by this beginning social memory complex. Those of your peoples that are the most finely tuned or sensitive in your terms to stimulus are those who are the first to be able to tap into this perception of the group mind of the disharmony in this portion of the planetary sphere.

As one who is not only sensitive but increasingly so, you have within your electrical bodies begun to resonate in an empathic fashion with the pain of your planet, to put this in simple terms. This can be quite distressing when there is no immediate or comprehensive manner of protecting the self from such intrusions of vibration without also causing some numbing of feelings, shall we say, in other areas of your experience as well. However, we may suggest that you may end your prayerful moments and in those of meditation as well, [creating] a simple image or short prayer that sends love and light to all those who feel pain in the Middle Eastern nations and around the world at this time, and which sees this experience of pain as being a portion of the perfectly balanced mystery of the one Creator expressing upon your planet at this time in order that those who are concerned with this kind of transmutation of energies might be alerted to the growing opportunity to burn off that which is disharmonious in a vibratory nature by attending to the vibrations of disharmony with the sending of love and of light, to be utilized in whatever manner is most appropriate. This may be a prayer, an image, a feeling or take any inward form that has meaning to you. It may in your case be given to the one known as Jesus the Christ as a prayer for intercession.

Is there a further query, my sister?

Carla: I have a feeling of what I can't get away from. That *(inaudible)* George Bush, than, man *(inaudible)* is the only affirmative thing that I can do with this realization is to let Jesus speak *(inaudible)*.

I am Hatonn, and we would suggest, perhaps, one further possibility in that as you move through your daily round of activities, you may see those activities as being those opportunities to give love, to make the choice to give love and compassion that are analogous to the movements of energy now occurring in the Middle Eastern area. This would allow you to move the energy of these feelings of identity through you in a manner which is of a service-oriented nature, in congruency with that desire to express love that is portion of your nature as well.

You would be in effect carrying out an interior psychodrama, shall we say, that you have identified with, as you begin to experience the creation as that which is contained within you and in so allowing this energy to move through your being would then begin to transmute those feelings within yourself of the identity with each of the aforementioned entities so that that which within yourself identifies with lesser qualities, those which are yet to be accepted, would then be available for the acceptance within your own being as your feeling of identity with these entities and those portions of your self which they energize might be completed.

Carla: Okay. Thank you.

I am Hatonn, and we thank you, my sister. Is there another query at this time?

Carla: No, thank you. Thank you very much.

I am Hatonn, and are also full of thanksgiving that we could be a portion this group's exercising of instruments this evening. It is not often that we are able to partake in this way with this group, for its desire to seek and to serve have called to it other entities that are equally as willing to join in your seeking and who are also as thrilled as we to be a portion of this working. Thank you, my friends. We are with you always in meditation and available for the deepening of your meditation at any time that you request such. We walk with you upon your great journey and observe with you in awe and wonder as the planetary consciousness begins to look ever more clearly into the mirror of the self and begins to work upon that giving and receiving of love that is the healing of all wounds and disagreements.

We shall take our leave at this time of this group. We are known to you as those of Hatonn, and we leave you in love and in light in the presence and in the mystery of the one infinite Creator. Adonai, my friends. Adonai.

L/L Research

L/L Research is a subsidiary of Rock Creek Research & Development Laboratories, Inc.

P.O. Box 5195
Louisville, KY 40255-0195

www.llresearch.org

Rock Creek is a non-profit corporation dedicated to discovering and sharing information which may aid in the spiritual evolution of humankind.

ABOUT THE CONTENTS OF THIS TRANSCRIPT: This telepathic channeling has been taken from transcriptions of the weekly study and meditation meetings of the Rock Creek Research & Development Laboratories and L/L Research. It is offered in the hope that it may be useful to you. As the Confederation entities always make a point of saying, please use your discrimination and judgment in assessing this material. If something rings true to you, fine. If something does not resonate, please leave it behind, for neither we nor those of the Confederation would wish to be a stumbling block for any.

CAVEAT: This transcript is being published by L/L Research in a not yet final form. It has, however, been edited and any obvious errors have been corrected. When it is in a final form, this caveat will be removed.

© 2009 L/L Research

Sunday Meditation
January 27, 1991

Group question: The question this afternoon has to do with fear and the various ways in which it expresses in our being. We have various ways of experiencing fear. Some of them have to do with relationships with others; we curtail certain thoughts, feelings or actions hoping that we won't excite the response from another person that will cause that fear in us to be realized, or we don't curtail the action and we express violently, angrily and become fearful of the emotion itself, also, fearful that it might have repercussions, causing a disease such as cancer that would be a way to point out the distortion so that we would work on it. We have, of course, the concept of love, in which we feel and believe that love can overcome fear, can heal wounds, but how does one put love to work in one's life and make the balance again come into being? How do we overcome, or is there an overcoming? How do we work with fear, and how do we bring love to bear upon the situation?

(Carla channeling)

We are those known to you as Q'uo. We greet you in the love and in the light of the one infinite Creator. We greet this instrument in the name of Jesus the Christ. We thank this instrument, as always, for the care with which it prepares for contact, for it creates the secure contact, both for us and for the channel. May we express our appreciation and gladness at this opportunity to blend with your vibrations. The beauty of your seeking is beyond telling, and the continuing growth in harmony within each in the group and within the group is also a pleasure to see growing. We are much in appreciation of this circle, and would address the question that it has put to us at this time.

Fear is an experience in which an entity perceives itself as helpless, and therefore a victim for those who are powerful. The infant is born into a fearful environment. Whereas within the womb the infant has warmth and secure cradling, a constant supply of food and liquid, and the reassuring heartbeat and enfolding maternal love of the entity which carries it, it suddenly experiences exposure, wetness, coldness, pain, stricture, and vastness, enormous, unbelievable vastness. Against the cold, the damp, the vulnerability and the lack of easily perceived love, the infant has no power or control. It is helpless. And so the life experience of an incarnate entity begins, rooted completely and solidly in fear.

To this original bias are added the many, many ways in which larger entities may create perceptions of helplessness in their dealings with smaller entities. When a larger entity disapproves, corrects or simply says no, the smaller entity has no power of appeal past its ability to use the language. Even if it does use the language it is not likely to be heard, or if heard, grasped with any degree of respect. So, the entity experiences throughout the years of being small and human, more and more reasons and occasions upon which fear has been perceived. During these same years perceptions of love have also been received. In some cases, either the young entity perceives all that the parents do as beautiful and loving, or the parents are actually creating a supportive, loving and helpful environment in which the child perceives again the heartbeat of love that moved from the mother so easily to the heartbeat of the child in the womb. However, it is most likely that entities will have chosen situations within the childhood that will specifically sharpen and make keen some of the primal fears with which the entity began the incarnation.

If fear is not a mistake, then it must have been planned. The plan of learning in third density is the plan of creating opportunities for entities to make choices. These choices need to be made freely and without duress. To cause an entity to allow fear to evaporate and to turn instead and embrace love is acceptable. But to cause an entity to do so is an infringement of free will. Consequently, it is just as incorrect for an entity to cause itself intellectually to turn to love as it is for another to evangelize, and pull the unready or unripe entity away from the fear which it needs, that it may embrace a love which it as yet is not able to embrace.

In the mature years of life, when the basic elements of physical security have been established, when there is food, clothing and protection, then it is that the entity's mind is free to consider how better to experience the incarnation than it may experience it at the present moment, and the first notions that entities tend to bring to the mind's eye as undesirable are those emotions which cluster about those things which are feared by the entity. These are perceived as personal, difficult and uncomfortable. Perhaps the key in finding a larger viewpoint of how to gaze at fear is to move backwards and see that the nature of the self being infinite, it cannot consist in finite matters. The fear is not finite. It is spiritual material, or catalyst. But the fear becomes a catalyst seriously taken when that which is its object is accepted as a real object.

In other words, if one were aware that one were viewing a three dimensional movie, and then one saw the car coming at one, one would scream, but with delight mixed with the fear, for one would be aware that this was a special effect, an illusion created by technological and advanced methods. However, if instead this same vehicle rushes towards the entity within the illusion which is called the incarnational life, this auto is perceived not as illusory, but as real and dangerous, and the illusory physical vehicle instinctively jumps out of the way. No thought need be taken, for the instinctual physical vehicle moves on fear, away from discomfort, far more than it moves toward truth or beauty, dignity or grace, in existence. It asks only that it not be hurt, and that it be fed and maintained. This is the portion of the self that fears. It fears because it does not perceive itself as an illusion.

Let us gaze at this statement. Do each of you perceive yourselves as an illusion? Or do you feel that you yourself are real, dwelling within an illusion? It is our opinion that in a very important way each in third density is, indeed, an illusion. The portion of the intellect that identifies itself and its consciousness with the continuation of the physical vehicle not only acts within the illusion but is, in its very nature, an illusion. For the goal of consciousness is not to preserve the incarnational experience beyond its natural length, and the length natural to any incarnation seems quite arbitrary to the entity which continues until it does not. There are, however, rhythms, and a natural death, no mater how violent or quick, is that which is a part of the function of the illusory vehicle within the illusion which it has been made to enjoy and from which it has learned.

So you may see all of these fears that you experience as illusion perceiving illusion. What is yourself? Is it an ounce of this, or a cup of that? Can you locate yourself? Is there a point about which your consciousness is fixed? Not within the illusion, my friends. Not within the illusion. It is part of the illusion that you perceive yourself as a fixed self about which radiates the entire universe. You are, however, not fixed. You are not fixed. You are not fixed within the body which you inhabit. You are not fixed within the choices you have made in the past. And you are not fixed in your perceptions of your own nature. Your own nature, in fact, is infinite and therefore cannot be in any way fixed. You do not have the need for mass. Your nature is that of light. Light is created by one thing only—love. Because of free will you experience various things, and because of the perceptive web of your physical vehicle, because of the way this vehicle's mind takes in data and prioritizes it, the untutored soul will pay first attention to those which it fears, but only in order to avoid them. Now, if you do not have a fixed self, you are not a target. Fear is always of some thing, and you are imperishable light. What do you have to do with things?

Turn then, in blind faith, when you fear, and look at what you fear the most, as long as you may. It is no shame to be unable to do it very well. It is, however, to be hoped that the practice would continue, and continue, and continue, for in each seed of fear that your infanthoods and childhoods have sown, there are collateral and dependent sub-fears which radiate out from the solidification given to this point of fear. When one examines the object of the fear one will find that which is of love, made of light; a situation, a creature, a concept, whatever is feared, which has been created by the infinite One, by logoi, sub-logoi, and most probably largely solidified and made fearsome by the sub-sub-logos which is yourself.

Turn and look at the object of fear. Define what it is you fear. Much of the fear of things is that they are making you feel helpless and powerless. Look at these feelings. Look at the object of these feelings. Leave the feelings completely and gaze steadily at the object. See it. Perceive it. In and of itself it does not stimulate emotion. It simply is. The fear is an entity which is a kind of quality. Only by choice can it be attached to any object. It is a modifier of objects as your adjectives are modifiers of words. As nouns are distorted by their qualifying elements, adjectives, adverbs, dependent clauses, so is your consciousness disturbed by fear, when it has been attached to an object. Detach it from the object, and you may see that it is not your fear. It is not anyone else's fear. It is a quality known as fear which modifies the opinion of an entity who chooses to perceive through the lens of fear some certain object. Remove the fear; gaze at the object. You cannot own fear. You can only borrow it from the stockpile of possible qualities. Like all negative and positive emotional sets, it is not personal. It is not yours. It is not anyone's. It is a potential quality of feeling and thought.

Now, let us turn and ask ourselves why this fear is necessary spiritually. Each is aware of the nature of third density. It is a density of opposites. Where there is love, there is fear. Other terms for love and other terms for fear exist. Where there is good, there is evil. Where there is light, there is darkness. Where there is hope, there is despair. Where there is compassion, there is bigotry, prejudice. Where there is life-saving grace, there is life-killing brutality. The spiritual entity must face the fact that it always has a choice. It does not feel, seem, appear or look to the senses as though in many cases one had options. Examine any situation which seems without possible options for the feeling tones of fear, whether they be angry fear, frustrated fear, terrified fear, or the fairly purely perceived fear of helplessness and powerlessness. Lack of control is the basis for reaching out and pulling into the life experience this quality of fear. It is a simple choice. When fear is felt, and after it is recognized that the self is not fixed, and it does not have to fix fear to any object, it then is aware that it may proceed further, and gaze at the object of fear to find a positivity or affirmative quality which may be seen to be that which love offers in that same object of attention. You cannot blink when you gaze at the object which is causing you fear, because it is up to you to choose how you shall respect this object. Shall you respect it by fearing it, by bowing before it, by accommodating yourself to it regardless of the cost? Or shall you relate to this in love, offering it the respect of compassion, and, in many cases, the appreciation of, and respect for, opportunities that may seem very, very challenging?

It is not an easy process to balance the fear within the life pattern. At all times, the body which you enjoy will have its instinctual life to live. There are things of which it is appropriate to be afraid, unless one wishes to end an incarnation. These things are learned, enter into the automatic portion of the mind's clear memory, and before the mind can even think, that memory which is almost muscular moves one out of innumerable situations in which life, limb or some other quality would either be terminated or made very uncomfortable.

This is an acceptable portion of the instinctual, red ray energy, and not to be confused with fears which have an object which does not, in and of itself, cause all who observe it to be afraid. When an entity chooses to dwell in love and to accept all that is given without fear, the degree or quality of love which it is possible to perceive is greatly enhanced.

Like any other portion of a life in faith it is not the first determination alone to look at a fear which delivers one from fear, for fear may be attached to any number of objects. Consequently, it is to be expected in the life experience of one working spiritually that the evolving self will repeatedly experience a fear of something, and always the situation must be gazed at apart from the fear. It must be seen that fear, like love, is not something one can own, but is an energy, or a quality, or a vibration, which is allowed by the entity to move through the being of the entity and to radiate a certain kind of vibration.

The vibrations of negative emotion are most uncomfortable, especially to that portion of the self that is attempting to become more loving. But one cannot move from fear to love and expect love to overcome anything. This is a misunderstanding of the suggestion that love does cast out fear that is found in your holy works. Love is not aggressive. Love does not cast out. Anger may cast out, but that is not clear, openhearted love, but rather a blocked, and incorrectly or inexpertly expressed love, even if the one to whom you refer is known to you as Jesus, as the entity is recorded to have thrown over tables upon which lay money made by priests, not for the glory of the Creator, but for the betterment of the priests' pockets. It must be understood that this entity was capable of error. This entity acted out of a kind of fear called anger. It is a kind of moral or ethical feeling common to those with ideals when dealing with that which your peoples call politics.

Fear, and the expression of fear, can be balanced by looking at the object of the fear, and then allowing love to teach, from within, in its own time, amidst confusion and darkness, how to see that same object affirmatively. Thusly, love casts out fear when love is invoked as a quality which will modify the noun of that object. Fear is no noun; fear is not a thing. The self which fears is not a thing, but an experiencer of illusion. Learning spiritually involves moving beyond that illusion in blind faith, and invoking a higher truth, higher than can be comprehended by the mind within the illusion. One must trust one's heart for spiritual wisdom, for it is not within the mind. The mind overcomes, the heart loves, and when the heart is actively loving an object, fear does not have room to modify that same object, unless the love is not complete. And when one sees oneself in mixed feelings, one must once again face the object, for it is that catalyst to which you may choose your response. You may choose creatively, you may choose positively. You have these options at all times.

Before we leave this instrument we would like to express that it is understandable in the extreme that this concept is difficult to put into practice in the third-density life experience. It is the calling into action of higher truths, of non-word modifiers to word-type objects. You invoke a concept to modify a word. You invoke infinity to modify finity. The subtleties of this process are many, many layered. As you unearth one layer of a circle of fear within personality, you are not finished, for you will find a deeper layer, and a deeper, and a deeper, until finally you find yourself in the womb being forced out, and learning what it is to feel abandoned, helpless, and above all, completely alone. That is fear, and you are no longer helpless.

We thank this instrument, and would now transfer. We are known to you as Q'uo, and leave this instrument in love and light.

(Jim channeling)

I am Q'uo, and am with this instrument. We greet each in love and in light, and we would offer ourselves at this time to any who may have a query for us. Is there a query to which we may speak?

Carla: Not for me, thank you.

K: I'm going to have to look at that, and may have some questions at a later time. Thank you.

I am Q'uo, and we thank you, each of you, once again, for offering us this opportunity to speak to you and to offer that which we have found in our own experience to be helpful on the topic of fear. It is a topic which each of your entities has a close relationship to because of the very basic nature of those animal selves which we find you have been discussing somewhat within your own personal correspondence and thinking. It is a subject which can cause one consternation and confusion. We hope that we have been able to place it within a perspective so that you may observe it without undue distress.

We shall leave this group at this time, looking, as you say, forward, to that opportunity that we may have again in your future to join you actively. We are known to you as those of Q'uo, and we leave each in the love and in the light of the one infinite Creator. Adonai, my friends. Adonai. ✤

Intensive Meditation
January 31, 1991

Group question: The question for our intensive meditation is: Discuss the male and female relationship—why each of us is born with a desire for a committed love relationship with another person, yet why it is so difficult to obtain.

(Carla channeling)

Greetings to each of you this evening in the love and the light of the one infinite Creator of All. We are pleased, as always, to be asked to join this group for the purpose this evening of the exercising of the instrument. As you know, it is our service to work with you and you offer a service to us in allowing us this opportunity. For this, we thank you.

We would, as always, ask each to use the faculties of discrimination to the fullest extent to which they have been developed, in listening to our words this evening and at any other time. Indeed, we urge that this be the approach to all the information encountered by the seeker, as each is responsible only for the self, for the thoughts and words and deeds that proceed from the self and create the world about each. There is no other entity who knows you and your path, no other entity who is capable of judging what is appropriate for you. So you must each do it for yourselves and for no other.

You wish information this evening on what many view as the most central core relationship known to your peoples. We would agree that the relationship between man and woman is important in many ways, but we do not agree that it has the most central importance. The relationship of central importance is that of the self with the self. Information has been given on this and each is urged to consider this relationship first of all and to request additional information at a later time if so desired.

The next most important relationship is that of the self with the Creator, or in a sense, with all that there is. This, also, is a topic for discussion at another time if so desired.

After these two centrally important relationships have been worked with and balanced to some extent, then and only then is each individual ready to consider a relationship of importance in the sense of a committed life partnership relationship between a man and a woman.

Some of the advantages of this type of relationship for the seeker have been related previously. It has been said to this group before that a relationship between male and female is most advantageous in the polarization process and in the seeking process in general. Firstly, because the energy generated by two seeking together far surpasses that of each one's own; and secondly, because of the complimentary natures of the male and the female. For these reasons, this relationship is deemed to be most efficient in terms of the usefulness to the seeker. This is not to say that this is the only possibility available. It is certainly the most common type of partnership among your peoples. There are other partnerships that may be extremely successful, of between members of the same sex or between groups of more than two. However, in larger numbers, while the energy generated will be greater and if properly focused will be extremely effective in the polarization seeking processes, with greater numbers it is much more difficult to maintain the degree of harmony necessary for such focusing. Therefore, the partnership between one man and one woman is most often chosen, not because it has any particular moral preeminence, shall we say, over any other type of relationship; but because, in many senses, it is the simplest, even with all its many complexities.

The desire that most among your people feel for this type of relationship has its basis in the realization of the deep self that all are one. It is, therefore, a striving for unification. In this relation, you are aware primarily of separation rather than unity. The grossness of the physical bodies makes this unavoidably apparent to you in your lives and daily activities. Thus, the sexual union between male and female may be seen to be the greatest attempt that may be made to overcome this most obvious of barriers; and, as such, is also a symbolic permeating of them. The illusion of separateness evidences itself only in the other levels of the ways each views itself as a mind/body/spirit complex on whatever level of awareness each has, as being separate from an other such mind/body/spirit complex. *(Inaudible).*

The fact that each person's thoughts and feelings are not obvious to others except on a fairly surface level, and to a greater or lesser extent, depending on the intent to which such are broadcast and the receptibility of those perceived as such, also serves to perpetuate the illusion of separateness. This barrier, as you are aware, gradually is permeated as the social memory complex forms, and the thoughts of one are available to all as are the resources of all to all.

There are many efforts among your peoples at this time to attempt to share more of the self with others, and again, this is taking place on many levels. The giving of the self merely to another or to many others in the sexual energy sharing is one means by which this is attempted. The progress of your peoples in a technological sense of developing communication networks over your planet's surface is another way in which this is attempted. And in the sharing of self with self, as it takes place on an individual basis, is the most *(inaudible)* whereby this is accomplished. There are those among your peoples wherein the process of opening the self to another self seems natural and is fairly easy. For others, it is extremely difficult. There are many reasons for this. There are many wanderers on your planet at this time who know quite well this sense of unity and openness they shared elsewhere and have an innate sense of the appropriateness of this, and, therefore, attempt to manifest it in their lives. Likewise, there are many of third density on this planet who, in reaching toward fourth density characteristics, are becoming aware of this trend, shall we say, also in making the same attempt. These attempts are greeted sometimes with open arms and sometimes with hostility and violence, as there are still many, many of your people who are not open to this openness, shall we say. As each seeker attempts to know the self to a greater extent and to make connections with other selves, each must be aware of the possibilities of infringement in this area.

All these attempts at greater communication stem from that underlying awareness of the oneness of all, which is an *(inaudible)* for the committed relationship between male and female.

The strong attraction or compulsion when they feel for such a relationship stems from this awareness and also from the magnetic connection possible between male and female as being complimentary energies. The difficulties with this type of relationship are many. The causes stem from sources within the self and within their society's training process of each. The problems in this type of relationship or any other will stem from expectations which are held by the self which are not being met. Each, in feeling the strong attraction toward those types of relationships, will develop certain biases which are molded by the society to which each belongs; that is, the views of family, friends and culture. The expectations one has are deeply rooted so that one may not even be consciously aware of their existence. However, if at any time a difficulty arises, upon its examination there will always be found an expectation of some sort that is not being met. This is not to suggest that one should have no expectations, it is merely an analysis of how things work, shall we say. And that, therefore, to be aware of the expectations one has in a given situation, is the first step in dealing with whatever difficulties may arise. Once one is aware of one's expectations, this may be worked with and perhaps adjusted if found to be unsatisfactory.

The great difficulties with the committed relationship between the male and female, we would suggest, therefore, are due to the sometimes extremely stringent expectations placed upon such a relationship by the individual and the culture which the individual functions within. We would urge each to consider these factors and the question at a later time if additional or more specific information is desired. We feel that these thoughts are sufficient for a beginning of ponderance at this time.

We transfer at this time to the one known as Jim. This instrument was to take the [offer,] shall we say, and to continue with the contact we have made. We leave this instrument now in the love and the light and transfer to the one known as Jim. We are those of Q'uo.

(Jim channeling)

I am Q'uo and greet each again in love and in light through this instrument. We would ask if there may be any queries at this time to which we may speak.

Questioner: *(Inaudible).*

I am Q'uo, and am aware of your query, my sister. We also have observed that this particular session of working has been free of attempts of intrusion by those of negative polarization, and can only surmise that the continued strong desire of this group to seek and to provide itself with those aids to protection that it has learned to use have made this group *(inaudible)* of lesser interest to those of negative polarization, for if these entities are not able in some degree to control the proceedings of such a working, this lack of ability to control tends to depolarize and reduce the metaphysical power of such entities. Thus, they find the need for retreat and for the regathering of their polarity while keeping, shall we say, an eye on this group for any possible target of opportunity that might present itself and offer an easier entrance into the circle or any entity within it.

Is there another query, my sister?

Questioner: *(Inaudible).*

I am Q'uo, and we would agree that the conflict of which you speak is one situation which has attracted a great deal of interest of those of the negative polarization. For at such a time and in such a situation, entities of negative polarity may find a great many opportunities to enhance their own power by the manipulation of those energies which are already strongly biased in the direction of control and manipulation. However, those entities which have stationed themselves with this group in previous times are utilizing not only that means but others as well to regain the polarity that has been lost by the inability to control, in any sufficient degree, the workings of this group. If there were, present within this circle, an opening that allowed negative entry, this would be attempted, no matter what other conditions prevailed upon the surface of your planet, for negatively-oriented entities are quite willing and able to undertake more than one task, if you will, in any of your diurnal periods and would find it easy to participate in the depolarization of your group if this was possible, as well as utilizing any other avenues for the increasing of the negative polarity.

Is there any further query, my sister?

Questioner: *(Inaudible).*

I am Q'uo. And we are also grateful for this blessing, my sister. Is there another query at this time?

Questioner: *(Inaudible).*

I am Q'uo. And it appears that we have exhausted not only the instrument, but the queries for the nonce. We do not speak of this instrument. We are very happy to have been able to speak through the one known as K, and are aware that our exercising of this instrument may be somewhat wearing upon it as it is already quite fatigued. But we hope that the instrument will take heart and feel the joy of being exercised and working in a manner which continues to impress us with its dedication and its meticulous attention to detail.

The one known as K is working quite efficiently as an instrument and we do not feel it is any longer appropriate to describe her as a new instrument. This one is gaining experience *(inaudible)*.

At this time we shall take our leave of this instrument and group, leaving each, as always, in the love and in the light of the one infinite Creator. We are known to you as those of Q'uo. Adonai. Adonai. ❧

Sunday Meditation
February 3, 1991

Group question: The question this afternoon has to do with the concept of faith. It has been said during the Ra contact that the two qualities that the seeker of truth needs to develop, or does develop, as he or she goes through the various incarnational patterns, is the concept of faith and the concept of will. Does it help in the developing of the concept of faith to act as though you had faith in order to develop faith? Is there a better way, or are there other ways to develop the quality of faith that allows us to keep working on the spiritual path?

(Carla channeling)

I am Hatonn. Greetings in the love and in the light of the infinite Creator. We are most privileged to be among you and to be blending our vibrations with yours at this time. We thank you most humbly for asking us to share our opinions with you. It is our way of learning, to share with you, and to walk with you, and we cannot express our gratitude for the opportunity which you have given us of your free will. We ask only that you remember that as all expressed knowledge, our knowledge is incomplete. Therefore, we ask that you use your own discrimination, for those truths which are yours shall be remembered by you as you hear them, and you will recognize them, and those truths that are not yours, you will not recognize, and we ask you to leave them behind, for if they are not your personal truths at this time, then we would not be a stumbling block before you by asking you to believe or accept on authority anything that we have to say, for we are as you, pilgrims upon a path. It extends beyond us, and we are not yet perfect, or we would not have identity, for in identity there is imperfection.

We are most happy to consider the question of faith and how to attain its pleasant pastures of consciousness. First let us gaze at the fundamental dynamic which causes faith to be important. Let us look within; let us gaze at smaller and smaller things. Let us imagine ourselves to be studying, first, the things that can be studied about visible life forms. It is found that there seems to be in each cell of a life form the entire knowledge, history and consciousness of that life form, so that from one cell another being may be created to duplicate that one cell. How can knowledge and identity be so compressed? It is not known, it is only manipulated by your peoples without knowledge. Let us gaze at smaller things, at one of your atoms. Although your scientists have succeeded in breaking it, which was considered the ultimate particle of mass, into even smaller particles, yet has any science or system of measurement been able to see, weigh or deduce the reality of mass? No, this has not been done. All that has been done is finding instrumentation to observe the paths of energy left by these particles within the atom. Then if all is energy, energy and fields, energies interpenetrating other fields, how is it that fields exist? Again, your scientists can manipulate magnetism and electromagnetism, but they cannot explain it.

In the genuine sense, nothing is known. All is, if followed to its conclusion logically, a mystery. That which you may view is inevitably not that which it seems, for the entire nature of your experience is one of learning in a special classroom which was created specifically to confuse and baffle the intellectual mind, and thereby force the consciousness of humankind, because of the desperate hunger that it has for spiritual grace, to move from the mind to the heart, from intellectualization to love, and the wisdom of love. That is your situation. You are consciousness aware of yourself, but all the tools that you use within the illusion, beginning with the mind itself, are creatures of the illusion designed to operate within the illusion and doomed by birth itself to a life sentence ending in death. Shall you strut and fret, as your Shakespeare has said? Shall you watch that petty pace until the last tomorrow, and then cease? There is that within the human consciousness which, once awakened, is aware of but one thing, that whether or not there is survival without the physical body, the yearning for consideration of that continued existence is a real, vital and actual part of the nature of humankind.

Entities within your culture are fond of saying that humankind is made in the image and nature of the Creator. What image do we think of? What image comes to mind when one thinks of the Creator? That is a key question, and central to those who seek faith. For if a Creator is sought that is angry and punishing, righteous and full of justice, then we gaze at a part of ourselves, and if the Creator is gentle and nurturing and all embracing and unifying, then we gaze at a part of ourselves. Since there is a mystery, there is a choice to be made concerning one's attitude towards that mystery. Those who feel instinctively that the Creator is an unifying, loving and nurturing Creator are those which discover faith in one way, that is the positive path of polarization through service to the infinite One and to other selves, the images of the infinite One. Those who choose to see the creator of judgment, righteousness and law, are those who wish control, control over the life, control over the self, control over others, that there be no surprises, but that all be reckoned ahead of time, safe and tidy. This is the path of separation. We are aware that we speak to those upon the positive path of polarization, and so we will address faith in its positive sense, that is, that faith does not begin with faith in the self, but faith in the Creator.

Now, the faith that is so hungered for does not rise out of nothing. It begins with very simple faiths. Even as a young entity, one early begins to have faith that the sun will rise, and the sun will set, that the moon shall appear, and the stars, and then shall disappear in the blushing dawn of day. As your young ones grow in years, they find more and more things which may be trusted. These things are not often other entities, but more likely to be of your second density, the pets who love without reason, the trees which drop their leaves, root deep into the earth and then once again bloom in the yearly miracles of your springtime. Your entities learn gradually to work towards a faith in the conventional wisdom of the culture.

And there, all comes to a screeching halt, for unless one is not very observant, one soon discovers that absolute fidelity, that which one may have faith in regardless, when applied to humankind, will fail. Not always, but sometimes. There is always the risk and a gamble in trusting another entity or the self, for if entities are made in the nature and image of the Creator, that image would not seem to include absolute trustability, but could the Creator be capable of such capriciousness as humankind?

Let us gaze about at the creation for which it is responsible. Is the infinite intelligence which created the balance of the infinite universe, the planets in their courses, the stars in their long, slow expressions of love, the work of a capricious Creator? It would seem unlikely, for if one were to gaze upon one of your calculators, one would not mistake it for that which occurred in nature, for that which is random and perhaps came from a process of evolution. This calculator is obviously made for a purpose, to do a certain task accurately again and again. Yet, how simple is this calculator compared to the infinite accuracy of the clockwork universe whose steadiness your scientists so have faith in.

Once a seeker is aware that faith is not faith in the human self, one is then open to examine other possibilities of where to place faith. As one gazes up to the stars, one realizes the face of the Creator, as it is written in your holy works, moving across the face of the waters of your consciousness. And there is an intuition that says to this intelligence, far or near, I place and give my faith to this kindly, loving, nurturing Creator; I offer my trust.

Now, there is no proof that this is either a wholesome or wise consideration or conclusion. Why should entities think about faith? Why should they not simply enjoy what life they can and begrudge not leaving that life when it is time? Examine your hearts and see if you are satisfied with this life which is you, ending. Does this seem appropriate for consciousness? We certainly hope that this is not your opinion, for if it is, then you are caught in the net of mortality. You shall begin, and end, and that is all. The mind of the seeker rejects this null hypothesis as untrue. It moves beyond logic. What is beyond logic within the mind except utter chaos?

Now we have the stage set for an honest beginning in faith. The mist of chaos surrounds the entity as he stands upon the cliff, a sheer rock face with barely a foothold of human knowledge. Shall he ascend? Shall he descend? No, for he cannot climb sheer rock, there is no cleft, there is no comfort. That is your situation. Consequently, with the tiger above, the tiger below, of that which is not possible, those who choose to live a life in faith must choose to leave the cliff of human knowledge and embrace the mystery, willing to allow that mystery to teach them. At that point the seeker gathers itself together, centers its consciousness upon the next step, and begins its long and dusty road of seeking by leaping from the cliff into the thin mist of chaos, that chasm of unknowing which will forever separate time from eternity. Yet, the seeker knows that it does not know any way to proceed except to will itself to take that leap. The will is secondary. The feeling for faith is primary. However, it takes an application of will to leap into a chasm, and it is a right use of will, not to corral oneself into doing anything, but when one feels that the time metaphysically is correct to act. And so, the first expression of faith is very much, for most entities, that of acting as if there was faith within the heart already.

In all spiritual matters there is paradox, for all things are so at one time, and simultaneously. And to a world caught in space and time, there is no place for all things occurring at once. All things are, instead, linear, a road to be traveled. How can we tell you that it is a spiraling circle in one location? We cannot tell you these things, for they do not make sense. Thus, we speak of walking a dusty road, of narrow paths, of being a pilgrim and being upon a quest. However, the actual experience of developing faith is forged in midair in absolute unknowing, and often in fear and panic because of the step that has been taken and the dramatic unknowing of that step. In your holy works the one known as Thomas is said to have refused to believe until he could put his hands in the wounds of this teacher, and see that his teacher, though dead, was alive. And that teacher said at that time, "That is all very well Thomas, you see, and so you believe, but there are those who believe what they have not seen," and this may be a more intelligent way, a more skillful way, to perceive objects of faith, and to pursue the object of a life in faith.

So we say to you that, indeed, one must accept the utter vulnerability of unknowing, of, indeed, acting as if one were faithful, for only when one acts in this way do the processes of spiritual evolution accelerate so that one may eventually have immediate experiences of tabernacling with the Creator. It is this immediate experience of unity with deity which informs one's faith. These moments upon the mountain tops of your experiences within the incarnational pattern are precious gold, to be treasured within the memory and to be brought to remembrance again and again, for faith does not have its place upon the mountaintop, faith has its place in the valley of the shadow of death, if we may quote again from your holy works. Thusly, one acts as if one has faith, and in so doing is faithful, for nothing can be understood or known. This is very important to realize within your illusion.

If you wish any sort of knowledge, much that is supposed knowledge will be examined and ultimately abandoned until the spiritual and metaphysical quest centers upon all that is left when one strips away that which one has been told, and that is an instinct, a hunger, a yearning for something that is variously called love, or charity, or virtue, or beauty, or truth. Many entities among your people have no use for faith, any more than they have any clear perception of the truth. That is acceptable, for it is not those who are unripe that will be harvested, but those whose time of ripeness has come. Each of you has taken that leap of faith, but each is at an unique position within the heart regarding faithfulness. Thus, each experiences a continuing and often repetitive scenario of events and situations in which faith can be informed as one attempts to behave and express and manifest the self in a faithful and loving manner, attempting to glorify by imitation that which is conceived to be the nature of the Creator, that is, love itself, the energetic, original and absolute thought which is love.

Now, once one has had the immediate experience of joy in the presence of the infinite One, one is almost immediately cast back into the desert of the valley. Words can only muddy and distort that absolute experience of being one with the Creator. Therefore, one does not approach faith through words. One is content simply to live in faith a simple, wholehearted and single-minded faith that humankind expresses itself most truly when it expresses itself in fidelity to love and service.

How can one be a faithful servant of the Creator? Perhaps the most difficult thing, and the central thing that a faithful entity does, is to lay aside the human self, that endearing and much beloved outer shell personality, in order that one may experience the treasure that lies within, the treasure that can only be approached with love and trust and faith, for doubt and mistrust are distancing emotions, and when entities think in that mode they remove themselves further and further from the shining sinecure of grace. The life of faith is a life lived in the limelight. One who lives in faith stands with a light that is bright that others may see. It is a kind of public undressing of the self, metaphysically speaking, to live a life in faith, for when one who is faithful perceives that in the midst of the confusion of mundane living there is a spiritual principle which must needs be upheld in order to be faithful, one must then abandon so-called human wisdom and express foolishly faith that appearances are deceiving, and that all is truly well. The essence of faith is the simple feeling that all will be well, and all is well.

Now, let us look at one who faces a tiger, a lion, a predator. Is all truly well for one of faith as this predator comes to eat its chosen prey? How foolish can the prey be to have faith that there is something more than eating and being eaten, killing and being killed, striving against adversities? Such an entity must be quite foolish. Yet, it is those foolish entities who shine through the centuries of your recorded time and history, blazing off the pages of books and records into the human heart. Those who loved and gave themselves for others, no matter in what circumstances in the outer world, those who acted according to an absolute and perfect love, are those whose shining memory inspires all seekers still. Thus, when faith is young, and, indeed, faith shall always be the faith of the beginner for you, for in this illusion you enjoy faith only begins, and it is that choice of how to begin that you are making. As you make that initial choice, so you build a cornerstone upon which other choices may be erected one after another, act upon act, thought upon thought.

Now, what shall hinder the seeker from this faith? May we say to you, my children, that which hinders you most is your lack of faith in yourselves, for as you regard yourself, so you may be seen to regard all things. Gaze at yourself as you forgive others. It is easy, is it not? Now gaze at yourself as you look at yourself. Have you forgiven yourself, accepted yourself and loved yourself this day? Carefully, firmly, assertively? Or have you been upset with yourself, or frustrated at your limitations, or in many other ways less than peaceful within?

May we say that the failure of faith is a foregone conclusion. It will fail again and again. You will hold yourself accountable again and again, and must go through the pain of your own damnation. Yet always the handle of the door to faith is ready to be turned, but you as a spirit must turn it, and must go through that door into self-forgiveness and awareness of infinite redemption and newness, a resting place for all eternity. It takes very little faith to do very, very much, so you need not attempt to live entirely faithful lives when first you get the idea to live faithfully, but rather see yourself as one whose journey is one of learning, and whose way of learning is that of making the errors and correcting them, making the errors and correcting them. For in learning it would not be possible to be always correct, else one would not be learning, one would have nothing to learn. Thus, you may gaze at yourself with mercy, for you are learning, and you are a beginner.

But you can more and more set yourself free from this solidity of judgment, of expectation, of completely visualized goals, and instead turn the mind to a simple and terrifying thought, complete and absolute surrender to the object of faith, which is infinite, intelligent and unknowable. Do you dare be swept into the deep sea of faith when you know not the object of that faith except by immediate experience that cannot even be said in words? Yes, this is the situation. You can, indeed, choose this. And if you do choose this, again, and again, and again, then you are exercising your faith, using the will to aid that faith when you wish to intensify your seeking, to deepen …

(Side one of tape ends.)

(Carla channeling)

In living this life of faith one has the feeling that one is alone, and in the sense of being responsible for each choice that is made, this is so. But in the sense of ultimate aloneness, this is not at all so, for there are companions upon the way, there are energies which offer wisdom of various kinds to those who offer various calls for wisdom. And above all, as one lives faithfully, one more and more becomes aware of the interconnectedness and unity of all that there is. And in becoming aware of this, one is able more and more to rest in a peace which is due in large part to the surrender of the judgmental, nitpicking, detail-minded and critical intellectual portion of the self. When one lets go of judgment for the self, one finds that one is able to refrain from judging all that one meets, whether it be personalities or situations.

We feel that this has been a beginning upon this question, and if you wish to ask further upon it we would be glad to attempt further clarification. At this time we thank this instrument for allowing us to use it, and for its care in the tuning and the challenging. We would at this time transfer this contact. I am known to you as those of Hatonn. I leave this instrument in love and in light.

(Jim channeling)

I am Hatonn, and we greet each again in love and in light through this instrument. We realize that we have spoken for a lengthy portion of your time, and that there is some fatigue in the circle. However, we are desirous of offering ourselves for the potential response to any further queries which may be present upon the minds of those gathered here this afternoon. Is there a query to which we may speak?

Carla: I have a question, but I don't know if you want to deal with it in a short manner. I have had the impression more and more that there is a correlation between the pulling apart of the religious systems from the inside out into various factions of fundamentalism and *(inaudible)* and all that, and the ways of government upon planet Earth which make incorrect assumptions about the necessity of each entity to be for itself, for himself or herself, sort of against the world, that we are very far, at this point, from natural realms because we see so much separateness. Would you wish to comment upon this is a short way, or would you rather I asked the question for a group question?

I am Hatonn, and we are aware of your query, my sister. This is a query which may be spoken upon as the central query of an entire session, or, indeed, of a number of sessions of working, for there is much information here that is of importance to many of your peoples at this time. There is the quality of faith that is, as we have just spoken, inherent in the choice making that each seeker undergoes in a more and more intense fashion as the journey continues. As you find yourselves as a people and as many cultures on this planet reaching the culmination of the cycle of third density, there is an increasing effect that the action of faith has upon both the individual and the group decision making within all realms of your existence, most especially that which you call the religious or the spiritual, the political, the social, and the various interrelationships between peoples.

As there is also a greater activity of the planet itself toward the end of the cycle in the direction of releasing of those disharmonious energies that have been absorbed by it as a result of many thousands of years of bellicose actions, there is also, then, the testing of peoples, of cultures, and of the faith that binds each to each and each to a purpose for the life pattern. Thus, there is the potential for the splintering of peoples, of religions, of philosophies, and of that quality of faith which provides the foundation upon which all within your culture is built.

Thus, we would suggest that in order the give this particular query its just place and importance in the spiritual considerations, that it would be a good focus for a future working, if this is acceptable to you.

Carla: Yes, it is. Thank you very much.

I am Hatonn, and we thank you, my sister. Is there another query?

Carla: Not from me, thank you.

I am Hatonn, and it appears that we are without a query at this time, having spoken to those concerns which are most important to those here gathered. Therefore, we shall take this opportunity to again express our great gratitude at having been able to join this group which is close to our hearts, and has been so for a great portion of your time, though it has been a significant period of time since we have had the opportunity to join this group in meditation. We are very grateful to be able to utilize instruments within this circle, and we thank each for the work that has been done in this session of working.

We shall take our leave of this group at this time. We leave each of you in the love and in the light of the one infinite Creator. We are known to you as those of Hatonn. Adonai, my friends. Adonai. ✦

L/L Research

L/L Research is a subsidiary of Rock Creek Research & Development Laboratories, Inc.

P.O. Box 5195
Louisville, KY 40255-0195

www.llresearch.org

Rock Creek is a non-profit corporation dedicated to discovering and sharing information which may aid in the spiritual evolution of humankind.

ABOUT THE CONTENTS OF THIS TRANSCRIPT: This telepathic channeling has been taken from transcriptions of the weekly study and meditation meetings of the Rock Creek Research & Development Laboratories and L/L Research. It is offered in the hope that it may be useful to you. As the Confederation entities always make a point of saying, please use your discrimination and judgment in assessing this material. If something rings true to you, fine. If something does not resonate, please leave it behind, for neither we nor those of the Confederation would wish to be a stumbling block for any.

CAVEAT: This transcript is being published by L/L Research in a not yet final form. It has, however, been edited and any obvious errors have been corrected. When it is in a final form, this caveat will be removed.

© 2009 L/L Research

Intensive Meditation
February 8, 1991

Carla: … the concept of one religion out of many. Would that be better for you than coincidence?

Questioner: It doesn't matter.

Carla: Which one interests the group more?

Jim: One religion out of many.

Carla: One religion out of many.

(Unknown channeling)

Greetings in the love and in the light of the infinite Creator. I am Hatonn. We appreciate this instrument's low energy and will not use it for long, but we did wish to begin through this instrument as the configurations of energy within the group were much less regularized than usual because of the novelty of the situation experienced, that is, the strongest and purest channel asking not to be used, while being able to be used in a gentle manner. The one, who is, while experienced, less experienced than the others, being asked to discriminate without the solid backing of the trusted circle. The remaining channel desiring to aid, but not by opening the communication. Thus we open through this one and speak words of comfort and strength that the energies may be regularized, that it may be felt, that peace that descends upon those who focus their minds on a good and central purpose.

Whatever the discussion concerning moving towards an unified spiritual expression upon a global scale, such unity is easily seen to be that topic which cannot be discussed in a sensible manner. It is a large topic, a topic upon which one can only make a beginning.

The intent of these normal sessions, this instrument would call them, is that in the privacy of those who belong in a normal school that is teachers only, teachers may learn how better to teach, without yet having the responsibility of offering this information to others. It is a safe and protected environment created well by the intellectual reasoning of this instrument, but there are uses for the intellect, and analysis is one of them.

In analyzing the situation of one religion out of many, there are also obvious things: the difficulty of moving by law, the necessity of turning to spirit. These are intellectual and logical considerations. These are the givens.

We ask each instrument always to be unafraid, for if words appear wrong, they may simply be unspoken. It is the instrument's choice. We feel most privileged to be able to aid instruments in finding their voice, finding that voice which is the blend of concepts which are novel and expressing them as poetically, clearly and evocatively as possible. We know that each in this circle wishes to serve and to encourage each in their several services.

We thank this instrument for its willingness to alter its own planned behavior out of trust that we would not contact an instrument in order to cause it harm. We shall leave this instrument. We find the flow of energy much regularized and much quickened and that is precisely what we had hoped.

Thusly, we are most grateful to you for allowing us to work with you in this way, to give you more stability and peace, as you do the great work of service to others. We leave this instrument and each of you, though we are never gone from your hearts, as you are never gone from ours, in the love and in the light of the infinite One. Adonai. We are those of Hatonn.

(Pause)

(Unknown channeling)

(Inaudible) and greet each in this group once again in the love and in the light of the infinite Creator. We wish to offer thanks to our brothers and sisters of Hatonn for their willingness to participate in this working and make the way smooth, shall we say. We thank this group, as always, for its willingness to be of service and inviting us to work with each of its members.

You wish information this morning on the subject of one religion out of many. As each in this group is aware, the orientation of the Confederation of Planets in the Service of the Infinite Creator is that of conveying concepts of the Law of One, which we do not consider to be a religion, however, it is a unifying philosophy, shall we say, and as such, it is certainly applicable to all peoples at all times.

There is a growing tolerance among your peoples for the beliefs and religious preference of others. There are movements that you see now and that have been going on for some time among various groups to unite those of various faiths. There are certain criteria inherent in these movements. Some are restricted to the acknowledgment of the concept of God as created by the Judeo-Christian and Muslim traditions. There are others that are broader in their scope, that seek to encompass those religions and practices of your eastern cultures as well, and in these the criteria are less specific, perhaps being only the acknowledgment of some type of higher power or greater self and the desire for unity among your peoples. We laud these efforts and note that once again, this type of unification is the beginnings of the social memory complex function.

We feel that those who are dedicated to this purpose of unification of the preservation of the right of each individual to worship in whatever way is comfortable to each and yet, [there is] the desire for all to be able to share together as well. We feel that these shall discover in the process of such workings those means by which such joint worship is best accomplished for those involved. That is to say, we have no desire, nor do we feel it would be beneficial to offer another more all-encompassing religion, shall we say.

Indeed, we feel the concept of religion to be quite restrictive in nature and we leave such adherence to certain beliefs to the discrimination of those involved on each particular path. We do, as always, offer whatever information we feel able to provide of a more philosophical nature, shall we say and indeed such may be considered to be spiritual, though not specifically religious.

We feel that those involved in the process of unification of religions shall, in time, grow beyond the need for a religious sense, shall we say, and while various individuals will continue to find the particular path or story or religion that is most congruent with their perceived selves, the unifying concepts will be less and less considered to be religious, as many among your peoples are already discovering congruencies between ideas which have traditionally been held to be religious and new scientific, shall we say, discoveries regarding the nature of what you regard as the physical world or the universe.

From our perspective there is no difference, for all is one and your peoples are beginning to perceive this also. However, there has been such rigid training and differentiation, especially in your Western cultures, between the sacred and the mundane that many have much retraining work to do within themselves. Much of this is accomplished naturally as new realizations occur to people. For others this process will be more difficult and there are many who are, by choice, so steeped in their own religious traditions and beliefs that [they] will never allow themselves consciously to grasp the unity of the concepts. For these, all one who is attempting unification can do is to extend love and acceptance and acknowledgment of the ascendancy of free will within which these individuals have chosen to restrict their use of life. Individuals in such a position are, as are all others, on their own path and learning those lessons appropriate to themselves, and although it may be viewed by many that such restriction is unfortunate and perhaps even damaging to the efforts of those desiring unification, yet as in all such cases where events may be viewed to be unfortunate or even tragic, this is true only within the bounds of the illusion that you now operate within.

The true work of each is being done on much deeper levels and individuals that on a conscious, intentional level are most adamant about maintaining restrictions and divisions may on deeper levels be doing much more work toward true unification than those who, on a conscious, intentional level appear to be most open-minded and accepting. Therefore, we would remind each again not to attempt to judge any entity on the basis of what it sees, for you have no way of knowing what true processes are involved and the responsibility you are left with is simply to offer love and acceptance to each entity as the Creator. Such efforts indeed are, we feel, the most beneficial if an entity wishes to progress towards unity of all. The love and acceptance offered from one entity to another on an individual basis is the cornerstone for such work on a global basis and is a vital necessity to any such unification process, or if unification of religion were attained structurally and openly, and yet love and acceptance were not offered on an individual basis, where is the true progress?

The temptation in this situation, as in many others, is to desire tangible results. This is natural, my friends. It is most difficult to proceed in the dark with no way to see what has been accomplished. Yet this is the situation within your illusion because of the nature of the illusion. However, each entity will continue to desire to see results and to operate on such a basis. We do not mean to discourage such efforts but rather would encourage that the importance of the tangible results be de-emphasized and the focus be placed once again on the individual basis. We do encourage the efforts of those seeking on a more structural and tangible basis for these efforts are certainly not without merit and will achieve results and are greatly helpful to the process of unification and positive polarization. We would encourage each to examine the self, to place the focus first on an individual basis and then to proceed in whatever direction is made available for one.

Each is aware that opportunities do occur from time to time and that the nature of service is to do whatever is in front of your face to do. At times, whatever is in front of your face may be to speak to a person three feet away from you; at other times what is in front of your face may be to travel a great distance to speak to others. We do not mean to be restrictive ourselves, but merely to redirect the focus.

We feel that this information is sufficient for a beginning upon the subject and would be happy to provide further information at another time upon requesting either in general or with regard to a specific facet of this most interesting and appropriate topic.

We thank this instrument and at this time would transfer to the one known as Jim to complete the working of this moment. I am known to you as those of Q'uo, and leave this instrument in love and light.

(Jim channeling)

I am Q'uo, and greet each again in love and in light. We would ask at this time if there may be any comment or query which we may entertain and to which we may respond?

Carla: Could you suggest a strategy for making clearer *(inaudible)*.

I am Q'uo, and we are aware of your query, my sister. It is one which is important to many of your peoples at this time for there is the bellicose activity that is widespread upon your planet, that which takes up arms against brother and sister nations. We know that you ask this question in seriousness. There is the kind of adversary relationship that each feels for another at different times that is based upon the misunderstandings that can be intensified to the point of the delivering of violence of one form or another to those that are close within the circle of entities of a seeker. The resolving of difficulties is the great means by which each seeker shall learn the giving and receiving of understanding. For the seeker that wishes to be purely polarized, the paramount concern for any action, thought or word is how can I best serve others through this opportunity? It may be that one who feels very strongly that there should be no life taken will find itself, despite all of its efforts, to be in a situation which seems to allow no other course. For example, one who would be serving in the medical attending to those victims of war may at some point find itself near enough to the fighting that it would discover that if it were not able to injure or kill that described as an enemy soldier that many of its own kind would be destroyed as a result of its own indecision. This entity may then decide that the greatest service is to take up the arm and to kill the enemy that intrudes. The motivation of the action is that which is the greatest factor in determining the polarization of the entity.

We apologize. The instrument is distracted *(inaudible)* shall attempt to continue.

Jim: I'm sorry. I can't go on, Carla. There's too much going on over here. I lost your hand and that totally distracted me.

Carla: I couldn't hold on anymore.

Jim: Okay, I …

(Tape ends.) ❧

L/L Research

L/L Research is a subsidiary of Rock Creek Research & Development Laboratories, Inc.

P.O. Box 5195
Louisville, KY 40255-0195

www.llresearch.org

Rock Creek is a non-profit corporation dedicated to discovering and sharing information which may aid in the spiritual evolution of humankind.

ABOUT THE CONTENTS OF THIS TRANSCRIPT: This telepathic channeling has been taken from transcriptions of the weekly study and meditation meetings of the Rock Creek Research & Development Laboratories and L/L Research. It is offered in the hope that it may be useful to you. As the Confederation entities always make a point of saying, please use your discrimination and judgment in assessing this material. If something rings true to you, fine. If something does not resonate, please leave it behind, for neither we nor those of the Confederation would wish to be a stumbling block for any.

CAVEAT: This transcript is being published by L/L Research in a not yet final form. It has, however, been edited and any obvious errors have been corrected. When it is in a final form, this caveat will be removed.

© 2009 L/L Research

Sunday Meditation
February 24, 1991

Group question: How important is the knowledge of the self for a channel and for the contact? This is knowledge in the metaphysical sense, the knowledge of the essence of the self by which a channel may offer a challenge to any discarnate entity, and why, when such a challenge is offered, cannot a discarnate entity lie about who it is when it is thusly challenged. How does its knowledge of itself keep it from lying?

(Carla channeling)

I am Q'uo. Greetings to each in the love and in the light of the one infinite Creator. How tender is the mercy that allows us to come to you! How blessed the event of our joining! We greatly appreciate the opportunity to share our views with you and hope they may be helpful, for that is our service and your service to us is to ask for the teacher, who is still learning. We experience each of you as colleagues and the deepest blessing of all perhaps is the beauty we experience in sharing the vibrations of each of you and the group as a whole.

It is as a teacher, although one prone always to error, that we address the question of the importance to a channel of its knowledge of itself. Any person that experiences contact and channels it in an outward form that may be perused by others is responsible to the effect that information has upon those beings about it. Thusly, one who channels incomplete or outright false information does so in a situation that sets up for that entity an honor and responsibility to that body of teaching. Such an entity is responsible firstly for living the life promulgated by the information as being the most spiritually evolved. Further, if one is teaching, whether one can or cannot see that student which is also that colleague, one is still responsible to the results of the catalyst to others that has been offered.

Consequently, it is, while literally unnecessary, spiritually efficacious to have gained sufficient knowledge of the self to be able to be responsible stewards of the gift of channeling. It is sometimes felt, especially as many of your peoples are engaged in combat, that words, as this instrument's old time rhyme says, "cannot hurt one," whereas bullets and other destructive weapons can hurt one. This is indeed so. Within the relativistic illusion which you occupy, the round sphere upon which you live and abide seems to be one in which there are few true examples of the connective tissue between words and consequences. Certainly, words do not drill a hole in the body. However, metaphysically speaking, they do indeed carry a tremendous weight. Depending upon how listeners are able to have access to the information, whether a teacher is considered a spiritual teacher, an academic teacher or any other kind of teacher, the teacher's awareness that it is expressing itself with authority may be understood.

How, then, can one become responsible stewards of a gift, such as channeling?

As always, the answer lies within the self. Each of you, each of us, and indeed all of creation which is conscious of the self is imbued in a vast ocean of overlapping and various illusions, some of which are brighter than others. In order to be able to find words that are evocative of the truth, the channel is most well prepared who has deeply considered the nature of the self, for the depth of the channeling, in its most appropriate configuration, is equal to the depth of spiritual solidity within the channel.

Let us give you an example. Say that an entity discovers itself able to heal but not able to continue the healing. The entity whom the one who channels healing wished to help has been given the illusion of health, but it finds it must return to that fountain of health that exists within the healer. Insofar as this is so, the healer has become negatively oriented in that it is causing dependency in the illusion that one entity intrinsically knows more than another. Far better that the healer first ride the horse of ego, experience self-importance and generate sufficient hubris to create nemesis, surrender to that force which has given this gift.

In just the same way, if one who channels does so from even the dearest and sweetest hearts, but is not able to ground that channeling in self-knowledge, that entity will be unable to refrain from responding to any and all questions that are asked without discrimination. This is due to the fact that when personal and freedom-robbing questions are asked of one such as we who are merely messengers and not planetary entities, we become, in the inept channeler's mind, the same identity, subjectively, to the channel, but quite a different energy altogether in terms of the metaphysical qualities of the entity which is calling itself by the same name as did the positively oriented entity which it first contacted through this gift.

Thusly, the instrument takes it upon itself to claim that it is psychic. It does not shrink at prophecy or dream interpretation or information about Earth changes or any other of the myriad of phenomena which assaults any channel. In the same way as with the healer, the clumsy and inexpert use of this gift creates learners which are dependent upon the teacher, and increasingly so as time goes on. Thusly, instead of the channeler being able to aid those about it, it may well become, through infringement of the free will of the questing entity, a negative, controlling, authoritarian voice.

We do not come among your people in thought to be authorities, to give worldly advice or to contemplate out of the vast range of possibilities and probabilities events, situations and processes that are beyond the scope of a free will outer planes entity. Thusly, we may say that in our opinion it is extremely important that one who wishes to use the gift of discernment of spirits learn first to discern the nature of the self. Any channel which is not so grounded in self-knowledge is open to offering misinformation and thus creating far more folly than aid to humankind upon your globe.

We have materialized and attempted to work within your peoples face to face, and we have found that not one single experiment of this kind has added to the richness and the depth of third density experience. Indeed, the reverse is true, for there are, in the majority of entities in third-density, enormous desires to be secure, to be safe, to be invulnerable. Thusly, before a spiritual teacher may lead others beyond the illusions of time and space, that entity must first reckon with eternity within itself. Certainly, most entities have a vaguely ethical code by which it leads the little life of one incarnation, but this can be related to true spirituality as impulsivity created—we correct this instrument—compared to well thought out suggestions grounded in the best ideation, analysis, creativity and intuition of which that instrument is capable.

How, then, does one work upon knowing the self? Firstly, we would say that one does not work upon the self by the use of outward authority. For instance, this instrument is a devout Christian. However, this instrument also does not see Christianity as an authority, or, indeed, even the one known as Jesus. But rather, it sees the realized human entity living a life that is an exemplar for all peoples who are able to respond to this particular narrative of a life lived and lost in joy, love and charity. The instrument does not give authority to any but the Creator. Nor does it give it to itself, for it has done the great work to the point where it realizes that it is merely a steward harboring, abetting and polishing those gifts which are its own unique gifts.

One of an infinite array of paths is the correct path for each individual spirit. No two entities are able to come to self-knowledge in the same way. However, there are things with which one may begin to learn about the self. Simple observation of behavior is a good beginning. Allow the observer within the self to become stronger without hindering the spontaneous choices created by the catalyst of the present moment. You may observe yourself being angry and throwing an object against the wall to hear the satisfying sound of breakage. However, one is also observing just how the object is tossed, just precisely the feelings within and the expression upon another's face. If an entity finds it difficult to observe the self and act spontaneously, it is well—and this is for the most part tending towards a truth for the majority of entities—to refrain from analysis until the day has darkened into the sweet evening dusk, the work of the day is over and one is ready to lay the head upon the pillow and surrender to sleep. Then one is able to go over the behavior, the responses, the thoughts, the actions and inactions that were the harvest of that day.

It is well, in order to use a deeper source of information about the self, to work with the dreaming. There are no two who dream in the same symbology. Many generalizations are true in the majority of cases, but there are no images within dreams that are precisely and archetypically the same for any two entities. Consequently, when studying the dreams, as in studying behavior, it is well to allow a large portion of your time, which this instrument calls years, in order that this process may bear fruit.

There are other means of working upon knowledge of the self. One passive but extremely helpful way is meditation. Now, meditation has been greatly misunderstood among your peoples. It is thought that one is to make one's intelligence a blank tablet, a "tabula rasa." One is supposed to find silence within. Only then in that silence is the meditation considered successful. This is not our understanding of the helpful value of meditation. The intention of those who meditate is that they may be open to spiritual grace—not knowledge, for there is no such absolute within third density—but grace. Thusly, whatever thoughts come into the mind, even if they pelter one, moment by moment by moment, it is the resistance to this listening to the voices within that cannot be stilled that creates a poor meditation.

If one is simply mindful, and notes without emotion or condemnation each thought that moves through, allowing it to arise, allowing it to dissolve, then meditation has done that which it was intended for. It has allowed the entity to step back from the trees and see the forest. It has removed the tension of judgment and consideration and allowed a time that is truly free, a time in which the observer may simply watch thoughts arise and dissolve. Not turning them away, not holding onto them. One may plan an entire menu, a shopping list or any other thought whatsoever during meditation if it is observed without that feeling of necessity to solidify the intelligence of the mind around the shopping list or the menu.

Let this thought about meditation sink deeply within each, for when one judges oneself for having a poor meditation, one has just stripped oneself of the saving help which is available to the meditator. The key of meditation is a silent, accepting and nonjudgmental observer, not that "thing in itself" [*ding an sicht*]. Never judge, calibrate or measure in any way the spiritual work that you do. Firstly, that which is done out of fear—the fear of not being worthy or any other fear—is liable to catastrophe. It is far, far better to have what is subjectively called a bad meditation and find the self being able to accept the bad meditator.

Self-knowledge can also be called self-acceptance. Self-acceptance can also be called self-forgiveness. Self-forgiveness can also be called self-redemption. Within you lies all these things. Not because you are a wise and powerful being, but because the self is one with the Creator. Would you suggest to the Creator that It may be having a bad day? Would you berate the Creator for having roses grow from gravel? It is not likely that one who is not hit by outward catastrophe would find reasons to blame the Creator for that which is occurring to one. Thusly, as the realization begins to dawn through immediate experience that the Creator is truly within, that all lore and love flow through rather than from the self, the entity who wishes to channel is more and more able to invest in that tenuous quality called faith or trust.

Faith is quite important to any entity and to any channel. How can one then encourage faith? When the groundwork has been laid in knowledge of the self by observation of behavior, observation of the subjects and hints of dreams, and aware of the aid given in meditation, one is then beginning upon a long, long journey. As one walks upon the journey, observing the self, observing the dreaming self, and investing in meditation, one begins to collect to itself a floating sea or ocean of catalyst that is not necessarily chosen to solidify about the heart of the self. Just as thinking about food or seeing it in pictures can make one hungry, so entities are endlessly suggestible, and as they open themselves more and more to the resonances of the present moment the catalyst which occurs from that point ceases to become feared and begins to become appreciated.

Since the third density is rife with duality and confusion, if not downright chaos, on the part of the entities of humankind which dwell upon its surface, it is only to one who is doing the inner work that there ever appears even the thought of finding a positive choice in a seemingly impossible situation. Yet, that is what each incarnated to do, that is, to find positive choices where none seem to exist, to love the unlovable, to console the inconsolable, to accept the unacceptable and to allow its grip upon the consciousness to loosen little by little, until finally one's heart does not find it necessary to hold the armor of the past and the future over the vulnerable and naked self.

This instrument has said recently that history is relevant. This is quite true. All that happened before this present moment has been harvested and lies whole, intact and progressively healed within the deep mind. One who begins to know the self begins to lose fear, for gradually one becomes aware that if one believes not in the Creator, then one is liable to believe virtually anything, and one is then truly adrift in an abyss of unpolarized feelings and thoughts.

Another tool for inner work is the gazing at the kingdom of the Creator which is visible. All the beauties and balances and rhythms of life as you perceive it can be seen to be endlessly and over-generously beautiful. The more sensitive one is to the vast numbers of miracles which occur with regularity in blooming, in fruit and in harvest, the more one is able to perceive a love that created balance, harmony and rhythm. If the Creator created that which you can observe, then what has the Creator created in you? Would the Creator depart from Its basic nature in Its creation of anything? We think not. We find, rather, that the Creator has given to us a creative power and the freedom to make choices. The Creator has infinite faith in each entity, for It allows each entity complete freedom to believe, doubt or disbelieve any and all qualities and absolutes, all of which are invisible and unreachable by the measurement of your scientists.

Each pilgrim is on its own walk, but it certainly does behoove those who are going to have to be responsible for that which they have uttered or done, first, to know the abilities of the self so that one does not overstep those abilities, and, instead of being a voice of truth, becoming a voice of confusion. We would, however, broaden the scope of this answer to include all beings, for the essence of polarization in the positive sense …

(Side one of tape ends.)

(Carla channeling)

… experience the leaping into the abyss of unknowing to find that there is a rainbow bridge that faith creates. Once that bridge has been crossed the first time it stands slender, frail, but there. It has been erected. And each time the spirit moves to that bridge, to eternity, and crosses it, it becomes more and more aware that it is a citizen of eternity. We do not encourage, in those who are doing inner work, complete retreat from the world unless that be a specific and heartfelt calling. For, you see, each entity comes to this incarnation with gifts, and until the entity knows the self well enough to appreciate the gifts that have been given and to dedicate themselves to the right use of those gifts, such a person shall be forever unsure, forever dithering, dallying, sitting upon the fence, as this instrument would say.

We urge each to find the path that comforts him the most, to move off the fence and into the green and growing life that expresses itself within your nature as the grass, but which, in a metaphysical sense, is the healthful, healing and supportive ground upon which right knowledge stands firm and may be shared. We ask you to understand that whenever we use terms like knowledge or understanding that we are approximating that which is possible within third-density experience.

To know the self is to know the universe. An entity which does not know itself sees many things and believes them. An entity which starts upon the path of spiritual seeking finds one after another landmark disappearing. It realizes that it does not know anything, that it cannot depend upon its five senses or upon logical thought in order to make skillful choices within third density.

Perhaps the goal of knowing the self in the end is to find that one does not know and cannot understand, except within that great open and radiant energy which is called the heart. It is from heart wisdom that channeling springs, and it is well, when working at that level or any other within third density, to bring to the occasion the tools and resources of spiritual self-knowledge. Who are you? Who am I? Take this question which has been asked so often and ask yourself that question many times a day. In this way you shall discover just how scattered your identity may be and just how much you need to discover the true roots of your consciousness and being.

May the Creator become apparent to each of you. May clarity light your path and may you never judge yourself as you strive to learn, to love and to bear the fruit of your gift's bounteous tree. We apologize for speaking overlong, as usual, and we would at this time transfer with thanks to this instrument, to the one known as Jim, that this instrument may of its own gifts move towards the ending of a session which we have greatly enjoyed and are still enjoying. We are those of Q'uo. We would now transfer.

(Jim channeling)

I am Q'uo, and we greet each again in love and in light through this instrument. At this time it is our privilege to offer ourselves to those who may have queries for us. If there is another query at this time, may we begin with it now.

Questioner: Could you speak a little bit more on how one can accept the self?

I am Q'uo, and am aware of your query, my brother. The self that is to be accepted must first be known. This knowing of the self requires a careful observation upon a regular basis—daily, we would recommend—so that you have the opportunity to review those expressions and responses of the self to the catalyst that has come before you, and that in this observation you make careful note of those responses which are other than you would desire, which are other than the ideal by which you have chosen to live your life. This observation and notation of response may be accomplished in the meditative state, in the contemplative state or through prayer if that is a means by which you find nourishment.

When you have noted those deviations in thought, most importantly in word, secondarily and of least importance in deed, then within your inner room retire there to consider in meditation once again those deviations. Begin first with that which seems to you to be of most significance. See again the situation which brought it about. Relive in the mind this situation. Intensify in the mind the response that was the deviation from the ideal, until the response is ridiculously large and all encompassing as you can imagine. Then, without further conscious thought but remaining in that feeling state associated with the enlarged thought, allow the polar opposite response to grow within your conscious awareness. Allow that opposite response to grow until it is as large as was the first response with which you began. When you have felt this feeling for as long as you are able to hold your attention upon it, then see both as the means by which the one Creator has come to know Itself more fully and richly and with greater variety through you and through your experiences.

Continue in this manner until all deviations from your ideal have been considered, meditated upon and balanced with their opposite. This means of balancing is most effective when carried out, as we have said previously, upon a daily basis. This means of balancing is, in effect, a speeding up of the normal process which occurs in each life pattern, for if you will look in that which you call your past of this life and note those experiences that were of difficulty in whatever manner, you may with the perspective of the present moment see that within yourself there is more acceptance of the self at that time than there was acceptance of the self while the experience was occurring. Time and experiences within time tend to seat themselves in such a manner that the emotional charge one gives to a situation begins to dissipate and it is easier to forgive and accept the self for that which has passed than it is to forgive and accept the self for that which is currently being experienced as a distortion within the life pattern.

To balance the self in meditation upon a daily basis, then, is to intensify, to speed up the process which each entity finds itself within during the entire length of the incarnation.

Is there a further query, my brother?

Questioner: Q'uo, it has occurred to me that there have been not just one, but many exemplary lives lived on this planet which offer to spiritual seekers a kind of template by which to live their lives in such a way as to approach an immediate realization of infinite intelligence. Is it possible … or let me put this in another way. I have thought to myself that it is possible that Jesus, the Christ, as well as many other entities, are part of a social memory complex which at the so-called time of the end of fourth density, beginning of fifth, have chosen to offer themselves when the need is found for a new telling of the story of Love. Could you comment on this supposition: that there are many individuals who deserve *(inaudible)* and that Jesus is one of them but not all of them, but rather a social memory complex which we could call Christed has offered sacrificial entities in order to express the nature of love so the people can polarize and move into civilization. Could you comment?

I am Q'uo, and we are aware of your query, my sister. Your supposition, by itself, is correct, for many entities which have been both known and unknown to the majority of the population of your planet. There are many entities whom you call wanderers who have offered themselves in attempts to be of service along the same line or means of providing that which you have called the template to this planet's population, but who have done so in a manner which is far less well-known and observable. There are also many entities who have come from this planet's second density through graduation into third and what you might call the normal progression of evolution, who have been able to so balance and crystallize their own energy centers that there has been the contact with intelligent infinity and the resulting channeling forth of the intelligent energy of the one Creator in a manner which is also that which offers a viewpoint, a template once again, or a blue print, shall we say, or portions thereof for many entities upon this planet's surface.

There are those who have come to this planet from other third-density planets which have joined this third-density progression and who have accomplished this same feat, shall we say, for it is rare upon your planet but is that which is the goal of each entity which incarnates within the third-density experience, for within your experience there is the veil that covers so completely, it would seem, every hint of the trail that leads to the One, and each entity that finds itself a conscious seeker upon this path lends some assistance to others that also seek and receives assistance from others that have gone yet further ahead and who have turned back to offer the helping hand.

There are many entities who have reached that point in their own conscious development where they have been able to establish a stable contact with the one Creator and have been able to channel some form of intelligent energy as a result of this stable contact. These are those whom you have called the Christed Ones. They have attained a level of development which allows them to share, as the Creator shares, from Creator to Creator. There are those who have chosen to be more visible, shall we say, and to offer themselves to a larger portion of your planet's population. There are those who have chosen to remain hidden, and who seek to work upon the development of the planet itself and upon the development of the population of this planet as a whole by offering the love and healing vibrations in what you may call the magical means of visualization and the sending of love.

Is there a further query, my sister?

Questioner: No, my brother, you anticipated my follow-up by talking about different parts of entities working with planetary needs. Thank you.

I am Q'uo, and we thank you once again, my sister. Is there another query at this time?

(Pause)

I am Q'uo, and we are aware that we have spoken for a great portion of your time at this session of working and we are very grateful both for the call to join this group and for the patience to listen to our somewhat lengthy responses. We shall be with you in your future at your request. We look, as you say, forward to these gatherings with great joy and anticipation. We shall leave this group at this time. We are those of Q'uo, and we leave each in the love and the light of the one infinite Creator. Adonai, my friends. Adonai. ❧

L/L Research

L/L Research is a subsidiary of Rock Creek Research & Development Laboratories, Inc.

P.O. Box 5195
Louisville, KY 40255-0195

www.llresearch.org

Rock Creek is a non-profit corporation dedicated to discovering and sharing information which may aid in the spiritual evolution of humankind.

ABOUT THE CONTENTS OF THIS TRANSCRIPT: This telepathic channeling has been taken from transcriptions of the weekly study and meditation meetings of the Rock Creek Research & Development Laboratories and L/L Research. It is offered in the hope that it may be useful to you. As the Confederation entities always make a point of saying, please use your discrimination and judgment in assessing this material. If something rings true to you, fine. If something does not resonate, please leave it behind, for neither we nor those of the Confederation would wish to be a stumbling block for any.

© 2009 L/L Research

Introduction
February 28, 1991

The Aaron/Q'uo Dialogues are a series of co-channeling sessions done by Barbara Brodsky, channeling Aaron, and Carla L. Rueckert, channeling the Q'uo group. The material was received during a series of nine weekend gatherings, seven of them being held at L/L Research near Louisville, Kentucky and the other two being held at Deep Springs Center, Barbara's non-profit group, near Ann Arbor, Michigan. These gatherings spanned about a decade of time.

Our objectives in co-channeling were three. We wished to produce material helpful to spiritual seekers. We wished to demonstrate that positively oriented channels can work together without ego. And we wished to demonstrate that positive information harmonizes, even when the sources of that information seem to come from profoundly different traditions. Aaron, a Buddhist master in his final incarnation, 500 years ago, is now an inner-planes guide. The Q'uo group are an ET source, part of the Confederation of Planets in the Service of the Infinite Creator.

This material is now in the process of being edited for a printed book. Meanwhile, we felt it would be a good service to put the drafts of these sessions up so that you could use them. Aaron and Q'uo, Barbara and Carla all hope that you may read the material with as much enjoyment as we experienced in producing it.

With L/L – Barbara and Carla ☙

L/L Research

L/L Research is a subsidiary of Rock Creek Research & Development Laboratories, Inc.

P.O. Box 5195
Louisville, KY 40255-0195

www.llresearch.org

Rock Creek is a non-profit corporation dedicated to discovering and sharing information which may aid in the spiritual evolution of humankind.

ABOUT THE CONTENTS OF THIS TRANSCRIPT: This telepathic channeling has been taken from transcriptions of the weekly study and meditation meetings of the Rock Creek Research & Development Laboratories and L/L Research. It is offered in the hope that it may be useful to you. As the Confederation entities always make a point of saying, please use your discrimination and judgment in assessing this material. If something rings true to you, fine. If something does not resonate, please leave it behind, for neither we nor those of the Confederation would wish to be a stumbling block for any.

CAVEAT: This transcript is being published by L/L Research in a not yet final form. It has, however, been edited and any obvious errors have been corrected. When it is in a final form, this caveat will be removed.

© 2009 L/L Research

The Aaron/Q'uo Dialogues, Session 1
February 28, 1991

Barbara: We seek to know ourselves and the Creator but do not know how to do this, as we fear we are imperfect in ourselves and our understanding, and incapable of this. How can we proceed?

Q'uo: Be aware that the Creator is often blocked or banished by third-density entities due to lack of awareness of the journey each came to make. However, the earth is never away from the heart of unity, love and concord.

We would suggest that you again investigate yourself within this incarnational experience. Each entity is all that is lovely and all that is not. Yet each entity can make many choices which bias him or her towards being a loving, giving source of love; for in surrendering the life to serving, the entity becomes a miracle, a wonder. Let the self come to know, respect and love this entity more and more. Let this entity become the great comfort, protection and above all, companion. For when the self realizes its selfhood as a living testament to loving choices, the entity receives the greatest gift of all: true friendship, true companionship. This is not to say that an entity whose self is one's best friend will ever seem impeccable, but to say that friendship and trustful companionship must begin with the self with all of its self-perceived errors. In accepting this friendship, the pores of the spiritual skin open to drink in the elixir of felt, palpable love. When you are friends with yourself, you can relax into an aloneness which retains the comfort of true friendship.

May we speak further, my sister?

Barbara: We are eager to surrender to service, but we know how limited we are and have the fear that we cannot succeed, that we'll run out of the food of love and energy to serve. How can we address this?

Q'uo: As a spirit you need not food. As an entity in third density, respect for the incarnated self suggests an overwhelming love for that sheep which must be fed so that it may sit in perfect fullness of being and allow the voice of spirit to flow through without diminishing or exhausting the third-density, manifested self.

Is there a further question?

Barbara: How can I learn to love and accept myself fully when I see in myself so many imperfections?

Q'uo: I am Q'uo. We do not find it difficult to love your self. We gaze at your courage as you walk in spiritual darkness, making choices by faith alone. We are deeply moved by the bravery of those who choose to express manifestation when it seems risky and almost hopeless.

The solution to perceived lack of perfection is so simple that it escapes notice. This third-density experience was designed expressly so that perfection would be quite improbable. It is in the furnace that brittle steel is tempered until it becomes flexible, supple and strong. The third-density spirit learns in the furnace of self-perceived fire, the fire of ever ongoing, never decreasing imperfection. Were an entity to express perfection in this, your density, such an one would be responsible to all to whom that incarnation became known. Such a responsibility is beyond the intention of your Higher Self at this moment. The imperfections of which you speak are your links to those to whom you wish to offer heartfelt love.

There is one state in which perfection may be well realized, and that is the sitting in the presence of the infinite Creator, the great original Thought or logos that is love. That perfection does you great good. When you are in tabernacle with the Infinite One, there you may be fed the infinite perfection that is love. When you open your eyes, retain that sharing of perfection. Remember at each moment this infinite perfection, and allow it to make resonant, deep, wide and spacious your perceptions of the specifically limited and often misleading events, entities, relationships and occurrences of your relativistic time/space continuum. Perfection does not aid, except when embodied in third-density entities; that is, it does not aid the self or others. This furnace of incarnation is that which burns away the dross. Although the heart of self is always perfect, the incarnated manifestation of self is useful, more and more, as the self perceives the harsh but meaningful, halting steps of will led by faith alone.

We speak to you from a density wherein we approach what you might accept as perfection; however, were we in the third density, we would have become a gambler—nothing more, nothing less. Your self gambles that, in spite of all self-perceived failures, the self will not be afraid or bow to indecision but will choose to love—again, nothing more and nothing less. Whether you perceive the self as successful or unsuccessful, perfect or imperfect, the intention will burn away the dross of which you are so aware. If you can find the courage to proceed in hope of expressing love, then you shall be as perfect as one may hope to be within the dust-laden confusion of perceptions of your illusion. Do not be deceived by the perceptions of the senses or the intellect, both of which were designed to embrace the illusion to the exclusion of all things absolute.

May we answer further, my sister?

Barbara: Thank you very much, Q'uo. I have one more brief question. I need to wait. I think I will have further questions. I will go over what you said to me sometime tomorrow and then talk to you again, because I don't want to ask you to repeat. I have lost too much already.

I have one very brief question. As I relaxed and stopped trying to get all of K's words, as she is signing what Carla is channeling,[4] there were many times when I felt that I was getting the material without lip-reading and that it was coming in telepathically; not in words the way I channel Aaron, but picking up concepts telepathically. Is it possible that I was hearing the words, only telepathically, when I relaxed and stopped trying to lip-read?

Q'uo: I am Q'uo. You may perhaps hear our laughter. Yes, my sister, we are those known by many names, but above all, [as] messengers of love. As social memory complexes, we may speak to any entity which is tuned to our frequency. You are indeed a sensitive instrument, and we are having difficulty keeping this instrument [Carla] from grinning like a fool because we are so happy; we laugh in joy. We thank you, my sister, for the pleasure of communicating with your beloved self.

I am Q'uo. We feel that this is sufficient for this working, and at this moment would leave this instrument and this group in the love and the light of the one infinite Creator. We bid you Adonai. We are known to you as the principle, Q'uo.

Carla: I've been working to learn to value *being* as opposed to *doing*. It's very important to me because my physical abilities are more and more limited. Do you have suggestions on how I can best proceed in this line of seeking?

Aaron: I find it a great blessing to have the privilege of being with you tonight and to speak to your questions. I might remark before we start that the light emanating from this room is brilliant, and I find it very beautiful. I remarked to Barbara and Carla earlier that I am not hampered by restraints of time or space and truly can experience the light of this room at any time I choose, regardless of whether Barbara is using her senses. However, even though she perceives differently than I through her eyes and

---

[4] Barbara is deaf.

is not seeing the light but the faces, by experiencing *while* she experiences, I can perceive the effect of the energy of this room on her energy and have still deeper experience of the force of it. Thus, I can see this group without using Barbara's senses; but with her senses added, I profoundly feel the energy bursting forth.

Carla, we are looking at your question about being versus doing, and I'm afraid there's something you do not quite understand here. In being, you *are* doing. This comes back to this same truth I shared above. I see you as light—just that. Each of you radiates a very beautiful and unique pattern of light. When you are being in the most pure way possible for you, you allow that universal energy to flow through you and out so that you become charged with the love of the universe, with the love of God. Then the light that channels through you is enhanced by your own inner energy so that there are truly two sources of light. You are each a spark of God. Picture the small ember and picture the large bonfire. Yet this ember has so much power, is so unlimited, that it, itself, is its own source as well as a channel for the universal source. What more important thing can you do, what deeper way can you serve, than to magnify that love and light, simply to allow yourself to be a channel for that love and light by being? Do you imagine that you are more of a channel for that love when you are physically active than when you are physically quiet? So the distinction is not so clear as you are making it, not so strong as you are making it.

It does not work the other way. In doing you are not always channeling that love and light so clearly; rather, you are using your energy, feeling that something must be done, that you in yourself are not sufficient. In a sense, this is what Q'uo was just speaking to Barbara about: beginning to understand that you are unlimited and that anything that flows through you is enhanced. As you allow this energy flow, the doing becomes simply another way of being. But as long as it's doing just for doing's sake, much of the light is lost.

Would you like further clarification of this before I go on?

Carla: What different choices can I make? Can you clarify for me what you feel I have to choose between? I feel when people write me, I want to give them something they can hold and hear.

Aaron: There are two things happening here simultaneously, Carla. One is that you do find it a joy to be able to serve others in such a way, and yet at times you push yourself beyond your comfortable physical limits. There is a certain difference in giving out of joy and in feeling a very small sense of, "I should do this." Can you see all the judgment in that "should"? It does not negate that aspect of you that wants to serve, but both voices are speaking at the same time: the "I want to" and the "I should." Because of the historical associations within this incarnation for the "I should," there is a churning of the inner energy.

Barbara spoke to you earlier about my description last Thursday of the ways energy flows through you, the ways that you are channel for the energy of God, of the universe. As soon as that small "I should" comes into it, it is like a twisting of the energy within your body so that it becomes a tumult within and doesn't flow through in the same way. What I'm describing here is, very simply, the way I see the patterns of energy and light; but your experience of this non-flow is as a churning in the stomach, perhaps, or some increased physical pain. There is a sense of tension. Can you begin to separate the "I want to" and the joy of that intended service from the "I should"—to notice that very quiet "I should"? It's very quiet, just a whisper; but it's enough.

The more aware you become of that "I should," the more you can laugh at it and say, "Well, here comes the 'I should' again!" When you can laugh at it, you can greet it with so much less judgment, and then the energy continues to flow through you and there is no distortion of that energy. The "I should" is the doing, and the "I aspire to" is the being. Can you see that? The conflict is not in what to do, but in the way in which you do it. When the "I should" pushes you beyond your physical limits, there can develop the build-up of resentment and some accompanying pain.

You are human, and you are not expected to be perfect. While in a human form in this incarnation, there are emotions. To want to get rid of the emotional body is a non-acceptance of the self, because the emotional body is an essential part of the incarnate self. So what you are being given here is another opportunity to look at the emotional body and embrace it, not to hate that aspect of yourself. Each of you needs to purify yourself into that spiritual body and to move further along the spiritual path that you are on; and that's easy when you are not in an incarnation. The incarnation offers the opportunity to practice when such embracing is more challenging. Do you look at the physical body and say, "This is gross and I don't want it," or do you attempt to love it? And it's much harder to learn to love the emotional part of the body complex.

I speak here to all four of you. Can you each see the ways that you've learned to accept the physical body more completely than the emotional body? It is harder, but until you've learned to accept all of that emotional energy in yourselves, you cannot accept it in others. That is what you're feeling. I keep asking Barbara to honor the incarnation. You cannot learn unconditional love, compassion, and forgiveness as easily while as a spirit, because there is not the same force of the emotions on the spiritual plane. So here is the chance to learn.

Speaking again to you, Carla, can you see that it is not a choice of how to answer or whether to answer these readers' letters, but how to relate to that small "I should" more lovingly so that you can begin to relate from the full being, harmonizing all its four bodies? Once you have begun to do that—not getting rid of but accepting even the "I should"—you realize there is nothing of which to be gotten rid. When it is no longer necessary it falls away. That last idea is not original to me; I quote Q'uo. And that "I should" *will* fall away! It is still necessary now because you haven't learned to accept it. At that point when it falls away, you will understand that there is truly no difference between being and doing. The doing in its purest form is a way of being; and when you are being, you are always doing.

Do you have further questions?

Carla: Yes. I just don't know how best to serve. You say, "When you are being you are always doing," but I often can't *do* anything. Can you speak to this?

Aaron: I would ask one question before I answer this. Is your doubt based in not knowing in which way you would best serve then or in the physical pain that comes when you push yourself to respond, or is it in both?

Carla: The first.

Aaron: If it is acceptable to you, Carla, I will address both, as there is also a physical burden that is being put upon your body.

I ask you first to look very closely and see the places where the desire to serve another through giving them something to hold on to comes from a pure place of love within your heart, and where the desire to serve is to alleviate the sense of unworthiness. Both create a physical drain on your body by the sense of "I should" that I just spoke of, by any small feelings that create some resentment. Can you see that both exist?

I would like you all to visualize your energy as I see it. When you are feeling loving and allowing your own energy to be channeled to others without distortion, there is still minimal distortion, the distortion which is essential to the human form because as a human there could not be a complete absence of distortion. When you each allow that energy to be channeled within the distortion, the pattern of energy I see coming from the body looks like the concentric circles that appear when a pebble is thrown into a pond, each one of the circles radiating out. When there is any anger, greed, resentment, hate, visually what I see are sharp spikes like a child's image of the sun. When there is a mixture of love and resentment, I see both. This is why, when you are in a room with another being and feel the presence of that being's anger, that one need not be talking to you for you to know that anger. When you feel the presence of love, there need be no words. You simply walk into the room and you feel it. The anger and love are tangible. Now visualize, if you will, what happens when those spikes of anger or fear hit these concentric circles of love. The sharp tips are softened, gently, each time they make contact, until they slowly wear down and smooth out into a circle.

When I speak of being versus doing, one of the best ways that you can serve another being is simply in sending out those concentric circles of light which will soften another being's anger or fear. You are in a position, Carla, where people are writing to you, so it's very difficult to send that love out through the mail and feel assured that they will feel it. You can send it out and know some beings are capable of feeling it. But a simple few words from you, "I love you. Thank you for your letter. Thank you," would be felt by some beings but others would misunderstand it. You are right, there.

You must ask yourself two questions here: "What am I responding to? What is their need and what am I sending out?" When there is any feeling of resentment or pressure or even uncertainty about answering that letter, some of that is received not as a softening circle but as small spikes. I am not suggesting that your letters are not loving and skillful, but you must really look carefully for that small "I should" I just spoke of, or any physical exhaustion, so that this letter is created with a loving desire to serve.

The second question is, "What is their need?" You know that you cannot learn for another, yet that is a large part of your pain because you have so much wisdom. It frustrates you that you share that wisdom at times and others can't hear you because of their own fears.

You ask, is it unskillful to want to reach out in love to these souls that turn to you for help? First be sure that your response is purely that of love. If there is any resistance to replying, simply put it aside for later that day or for another day and then know that the response does come from that pure place of love within you—a desire to serve—and wears as minimal a distortion as you can manage. Ask yourself, "In what way am I trying to change them, to make them hear me? Am I speaking with a voice of love and reassurance? If I speak with love and they can't hear me, is that okay?" Remind yourself that you cannot learn for them. You can open a door but you can't push them through.

Carla, put quite simply, you have a tendency to want to solve others' problems for them; and this is one of the things you find most difficult, because you know that is not something you can do. Can you begin to relate to the source of that need to solve others' problems, to take away another's pain? Can you begin to make yourself so comfortable with your own pain, and here I don't mean physical pain, but with the pain of your own existence, that you no longer need to take away their pain? Can you see the lesson in this for you—that as you find a deeper acceptance for yourself, your response to others will become increasingly skillful; and that instead of needing to change things you will help them to find a deeper acceptance for themselves?

Do you understand and is there a further question?

Carla: Yes, but I have to think about it first.

Aaron: Is there a further question?

Carla: Yes. I have always had low physical and emotional energy. What do I need to learn and how can I work to heal that in myself and serve better? It makes me angry that I can't do everything I wish to do. Then I feel guilty because I'm angry. Help!

Aaron: I perceive a normal amount of energy within you but it is partially blocked below the heart chakra by the anger, so the energy flow is restricted. So let's talk about anger. There is the misunderstanding of assuming one has only two choices in dealing with anger, or any heavy emotion: that one express it and talk about it, or that one suppress it. There is a third choice, and that's just to notice it. When you notice something quietly and touch it with your gentleness, very often it dissolves. It simply doesn't have the same solidity, the same hold over you. It's not necessary to practice your anger, to express it verbally or through such a practice as throwing pillows. This practice, in a sense, enhances the anger. It does allow the being to recognize it; and for some beings who have a great deal of trouble recognizing it, it may be used as a useful first step. I prefer simply treating it as one treats the stubbed toe.

Will you try an experiment with me here? Picture yourself sitting on a mountaintop. It is a beautiful day. There is a clear view. The sun is shining with a lovely warmth, as a warm cloak on your shoulders, and a cool breeze touches your face. In the distance you see a cloud, and then turn your back to it and go back to enjoy the view. That cloud approaches, but you're totally unaware of its presence until suddenly it sweeps over the top of the mountaintop, enclosing you completely within it, shutting off the sun. You can't see your hands six inches in front of your face. The air feels cold and clammy. There is a sense of panic, thinking, "How will I find the path to get down?" There is a sense of anger, of wanting this cloud to go away. Can you feel that need to push it away, feel how hard it is to just sit there and let it be there? Can you feel how strong the aversion is to it?

Come back again to the sunny mountaintop and the same cloud in the distance. Enjoy the view and notice the cloud: "There's a cloud coming … umm, looks like it will be here in ten or fifteen minutes. Well, here it comes … another minute or two … It's a pretty big cloud, too, and very dense looking. I think it will be here for half an hour, maybe even more. Perhaps I should put my jacket on … and here it comes." And it encloses you completely again; and again you can't see your hands in front of your face, and you do miss the warm sun and the view, and it does feel cold and clammy. But you saw it coming and you know how long it will be there. Can you see how much easier it is to simply sit with it and allow its presence, that there is no longer a struggle with it; it's just a cloud. Can you all feel the difference?

Your anger is like that. It becomes solid when you struggle with it, when there's a sense of needing it or needing to make it go away or to do anything special with it. When you can simply allow it as a cloud passing through and let go of your struggle with it, then there's no need to react to it. Certain conditions prompt the anger to arise, it's noticed, and it dissolves and goes its way. It's not the anger that's a problem, it's your reaction to the anger. That is what solidifies the anger.

So how do you work with this? It is truly just a skill that may be developed, and it has two parts. One is noticing the arising of anger as quickly as you can, each time it comes, even beginning to notice the situations that may provoke anger and saying, "I wonder if anger will arise next?" And the second is noticing your reaction to the anger, asking, "Is there judgment against it? Is there hatred of it? Or can I simply hold it, holding myself in my arms as I would mentally with that stubbed toe? Can I respond to this anger the way I would respond to a child who came inside crying and saying, 'A bully pushed me down'? Would I tell that child, 'Well, don't be angry,' or would I more skillfully hold that child in my arms and say, 'I see how angry you're feeling,' and reassure it that it's still loved despite the anger, that the anger has nothing to do with its lovability, with its soul's perfection?"

It is so easy for all of you to have compassion for others but not for yourselves. So I ask you, can you begin to relate to this anger in a more open and loving way? I am not suggesting here that it's skillful to walk around angry; but anger does arise, just like clouds do come over. As long as you are here in a physical body, there are going to be feelings. Even the most highly evolved being incarnate in a human body still has feelings but there is no longer attachment or aversion to those feelings. There is no longer a need to get rid of them or to struggle with them. And it is through that relaxation of the struggle that one finds a deeper peacefulness. Anger and love are not mutually exclusive. It all depends on how you relate to the anger.

In purely practical terms, I would suggest that it would be useful to play a game with yourself to help you loosen up and relate more lovingly and openly to anger. Take a notebook with you, a small notebook, and for a day, or several days as seems practical to you, every time you see anger arise just jot down a line. Be a cat at a mouse-hole and think, "Aha! There's anger; I caught it; I see it this time. I'm getting faster. I can see it faster and faster." See if you can lighten up a little, "Oh my, here's anger!"

The second thing I would suggest that might be helpful is to begin to observe the pattern of how you relate to your anger—to start to note, every time you do note anger arise, that little voice that says, "I shouldn't be angry," and ask that voice, "Why shouldn't I?" There is a big difference [between] using your anger as a reason to act unskillfully toward another and in simply feeling anger.

Do you have further questions?

(There were no questions at this time.)

I thank you all for the opportunity to share your love and your light. Please know how much my love is with you, and that the love and courage that you bring to your work is truly a light and an inspiration to all beings on all planes. That is all. ❧

L/L Research is a subsidiary of
Rock Creek Research &
Development Laboratories, Inc.

P.O. Box 5195
Louisville, KY 40255-0195

L/L Research

www.llresearch.org

Rock Creek is a non-profit
corporation dedicated to
discovering and sharing
information which may aid in
the spiritual evolution of
humankind.

ABOUT THE CONTENTS OF THIS TRANSCRIPT: This telepathic channeling has been taken from transcriptions of the weekly study and meditation meetings of the Rock Creek Research & Development Laboratories and L/L Research. It is offered in the hope that it may be useful to you. As the Confederation entities always make a point of saying, please use your discrimination and judgment in assessing this material. If something rings true to you, fine. If something does not resonate, please leave it behind, for neither we nor those of the Confederation would wish to be a stumbling block for any.

© 2009 L/L Research

Introduction

The Aaron/Q'uo Dialogues are a series of co-channeling sessions done by Barbara Brodsky, channeling Aaron, and Carla L. Rueckert, channeling the Q'uo group. The material was received during a series of nine weekend gatherings, seven of them being held at L/L Research near Louisville, Kentucky and the other two being held at Deep Springs Center, Barbara's non-profit group, near Ann Arbor, Michigan. These gatherings spanned about a decade of time.

Our objectives in co-channeling were three. We wished to produce material helpful to spiritual seekers. We wished to demonstrate that positively oriented channels can work together without ego. And we wished to demonstrate that positive information harmonizes, even when the sources of that information seem to come from profoundly different traditions. Aaron, a Buddhist master in his final incarnation, 500 years ago, is now an inner-planes guide. The Q'uo group are an ET source, part of the Confederation of Planets in the Service of the Infinite Creator.

This material is now in the process of being edited for a printed book. Meanwhile, we felt it would be a good service to put the drafts of these sessions up so that you could use them. Aaron and Q'uo, Barbara and Carla all hope that you may read the material with as much enjoyment as we experienced in producing it.

With L/L – Barbara and Carla ☙

The Aaron/Q'uo Dialogues, Session 2
March 1, 1991

Barbara: Yesterday's talk from Q'uo didn't record on my tape recorder, and I got just what little I was able to lip-read. I had meditated on the content I'd gotten and felt Q'uo's presence, felt Q'uo knew what I did or didn't understand. I didn't want to ask Q'uo to take responsibility for me or my questions, but I also didn't want to ask for repetition. Would Q'uo reshare whatever they feel I missed, that they shared last night?

Q'uo: I am Q'uo. I greet you in the love and in the light of the one infinite Creator, Whose presence permeates all and is all that there is.

My sister, there is no such thing as repetition in responding to the needs of a consciousness, because each entity is at this moment a new and different person, unlike the entity of any other moment. This is why history, especially personal history, is largely irrelevant to the great work of living and loving in this moment, just this one moment.

We would speak of the saying of the one known as Jesus, that saying which he gave to his disciples: "Feed my sheep."[5] Many are the loving servants of the one Creator who are eager to feed other sheep but who do not realize that first they also need food, not the food of the earthly vehicle alone, but far more importantly, the bread and wine of spiritual companionship. There is a great companion which awaits all who heed her heart; that is, the first and second densities of your sphere. The very earth beneath your feet is alive and pulses with undiminished, infinite love. Each rock, each portion of grass, meadow, or pine needle beneath your feet connects a third-density entity with the heart of the Grandmother Earth. How this being loves you! The friendship of the elementals of earth, air, wind and fire; the devas of plants of all kinds; the ever-rising consciousness of animal forms, all wait to embrace the one who stops to pay attention and to take comfort in the cathedral of what you call nature. When an entity allows itself to admit the entrance of these divine and loving spirits, the air is filled with cherubim, the trees with the laughter of the seraphim, and angels ascend and descend in every fire, in every storm, in every calm, in all beams of living sunlight. Here lies food indeed for the spirit.

We would move further and speak of another very true and real companion. Many are aware of this entity as Jesus the Christ. Others find it helpful to think of this Christed energy as the living Holy Spirit of the Christ, which speaks to the world yesterday, today, and forever. Imagine the spirit form of the one known as Jesus beside you and mentally take the hand that is offered. Thus, palm to palm, heart to heart, love divine to love in manifestation—a companionship of infinite trust,

---
[5] *Holy Bible*, John 21: 16, 17.

infinite mercy, infinite kindness, and infinite love is born and forged anew every moment. The need for companions along the way seems to the third-density eye impossible to be met when one is alone in the way in which it has chosen to walk the path of love and service to others. Yet every zephyr of breeze, every silent bird, and all that the senses experience are your loving companions; and the fellowship of the Christ, however it is perceived, is nearer than your breathing, closer than your hands or feet, infinitely more intimate than any third-density companion. So, in any weather of life, in storm or calm, it is the third-density entity which must call to remembrance in each present moment the very present help and companionship that those who are yet asleep do not find themselves perceiving. The love and caring is always there. It is the entity who must remember to open the door to that friendship, reach out the hand to that love which is so palpable one could almost imagine the incarnative form of the Christed One.

Especially when outward circumstances seem murky and turgid with heavy cares, the seeker will find those cares lifted so easily away simply by remembering to reach out the hand to the friendship of the sanctified Christ. Now that sanctified presence is truly within each seeker, as is all the universe. You are the creator of your particular creation, and co-Creator with infinite Intelligence of that which is experienced and how it is experienced. Although you cannot be another's creation, you cannot help but be the creator of your own. So, in making the choices from moment to moment, do not let your heart flag or falter because you are alone; for there is companionship more real than the manifested forms of your density, ever waiting for your simple recognition and acceptance. How loved all entities are! Yet without the intention to reach out in trust for that love, an entity may walk forever in a fog of self-created solitude.

I am Q'uo, and would ask if there is a further question at this time.

Barbara: Thank you. Q'uo, I'm aware of a desire in myself to serve that seems to come from two places. When I sense that the desire to serve comes from any place of ego or self, it makes me pull back in fear that ego will distort the work. Then that fear touches and distorts the honest places of loving and worshipful desire to serve. It confuses me. When there's fear, although I hear Aaron, I doubt even that. Yet when there's love and the full experience of God and of that love from Aaron that surrounds me, I know no doubt. Aaron has talked about this at length with me, but I wonder if there's anything you would add that would help me to understand and balance these forces?

Q'uo: I am Q'uo. We would speak of two minds and two hearts. The first mind is the mental mind. In it there can only be mentally feared obstacles. For one who is an adventurer within its own mind, the barriers of fear do not arise. However, the mind that is mental deals almost exclusively with the relativistic illusion in which each now experiences and enjoys the dance of incarnation. Thusly, although one may be mentally curious, one cannot use that mentality to plunge into that abyss which must be accepted in order to reach the second mind.

The second mind is often called the heart. In the open heart is stored the true mind which begets wisdom and compassion, which is as infinite and effortless as the love of an open heart. Many things, however, occur during an incarnation which may tend to cause an entity to erect defensive barriers in order that this precious heart may not be wounded more than it already is. Thusly, in order to open the second heart—the heart of wisdom—one must first gaze at the erected barriers in acceptance and love for the self that needed those barriers, allowing them to remain until they are no longer needed. Then the heart may open, and wisdom may be fearlessly received and equally fearlessly manifested forth.

It is said in the holy work called the Bible by the one known as Jesus, "I am the vine, you are the branches."[6] Let us look at *I am*. I Am is the true name of the infinite One. I Am. Say this in your heart: "I Am. I Am with you always. I Am the way. I Am the truth. I Am the life."[7] Each is I Am. Thusly, each open heart receives, reveals and manifests the fruit of that great root of Consciousness, the I Am of all that there is. When the branches of the vine surrender their self-importance in an humble awareness that without the root I Am, their I Am would be dust and ashes, then the branches bloom, flower and bear fruit and seed to replenish the earth inexhaustibly.

---

[6] *Holy Bible*, John 15:5.

[7] *Holy Bible*, Matthew 28:20, John 14:6.

Let us now speak of the first and the second heart. This, too, is helpful in finding and allowing the release of fear; for in the first heart there is wisdom, but there is only the perceived awareness of the nurturing constancy that is love. The first heart often attempts to bloom, to nurture, and to give simply because it is full and those about it need replenishing and filling. The first heart, though wise, when full because of its unstinting compassion, is also foolish. This folly is beautiful to us, and a testament to the incredible generosity and power of the open heart. Yet there is a second heart, and that heart may be conceived to be—whether we speak of the male or female form—the womb of life. That heart moves in fullness with no need to serve, no need to do anything other than be full. The second heart is the womb, ever pregnant with love, ever giving birth out of fullness into that which is actually full. Thus, the second heart responds not because of the needs of others, but because it, like sunshine, must propagate its light and give birth ever and ever and ever to its own I Am, which—as the womb of this second heart is more and more maturely experienced—becomes more and more nearly the undistorted, uncreated logos, which is love.

I am Q'uo. Is there a further question, my sister?

Barbara: I have no further questions at this time. Thank you, Q'uo.

Q'uo: I am Q'uo. We thank you, my sister.

Now we would speak just a moment about that which is called patience. How boring to be patient, to wait and to watch, when the heart leaps like a deer and wishes to fly higher than the highest mountain in joy, in radiance, in awareness of perfect love! Yet the will of entities in incarnation is made perfect, not by its use, but by the surrender of its use to the will of the one infinite Creator. In your illusion it seems there is a passage of time. Outside of this illusion, all times are one, all times simultaneous. Yet within the illusion, darkness broods over the mind and over the heart, and sometimes the night watches seem to go on forever. Yet it is in the darkness of midnight that the messenger of realization, illumination, and love comes ever so quietly, walking on feet of I Am, I Am, I Am … silent feet that cannot be heard unless the heart is watching and praying and waiting.

This is the use of patience—not time to be spent quickly, but time to treasure that expectancy that the bride and bridegroom feel as they wait for the wedding day that has already been set. Within an incarnation, the spirit has many wedding days, many glorious feasts; but those feasts are punctuations—gifts, we may say—which give the commas and the periods to the long sentences of expectation. Thusly, it is well to give great respect to the practice of waiting, watching patiently in complete faith that, although the seeker does not know the next wedding day, yet it is known and it will come. In this joyful readiness lies a fearlessness which does not quail at the darkness of the hour or the solitude of the night watch. Rather, it waits in a patient faith, in a honed edge of will to listen, to surrender, and to be that I Am which is the wedding present of the consummation of the present moment.

We would leave this instrument at this time, thanking each for the beauty of your vibrations. It has been a great joy for us to be with you, to be called to your group by the intensity and beauty of your calling and your needs. We hope we may have offered helpful opinions, but as always, ask each to remember to cast aside anything that does not speak to the personal truth. We are of the principle known to you as Q'uo. Adonai. Adonai. I am Q'uo. I leave you in the love and in the light of the infinite Creator.

Barbara: Last week, Aaron, you spoke of promptings to serve coming from the emotional body. What comes to the mental body is a pure desire to love. You've previously spoken of imbalances between these two and of bringing them into harmony. This morning in meditation I began to see the opposite side of the above. I felt the mental body was the one blocking the true loving emotion, that when I enter that tabernacle it feels like the emotional body opens and any separation comes from the mind. Will you speak further about this?

Aaron: My greetings and love to you all. I am Aaron. It is a joy to be with you this morning, to feel the love and light that emerge from this group; and I thank the principle of Q'uo for that which has been shared. There is great comfort in hearing the same thing repeated by different voices. It is part of trust, because truly there is nothing I can say to any of you that you don't already know. But our words reassure you and help you trust the wisdom of your own hearts.

You ask about these bodies. You understood this morning, as you thought that question, that you were asking partially in reference to Kabir's powerful poem[8], where he makes the statement, "How hard it is to feel that love with all our four bodies. Those who try to be reasonable about it fail."

You are consciously aware of the concepts about which I speak and the experiences that underlay those concepts; but to some degree, perhaps, we don't share the same vocabulary. Let me speak first for a moment, simply establishing the vocabulary that I use so you can hear this without misunderstanding. Please feel free to substitute the labels with which you are familiar with the labels that I put on the experience.

There are four bodies: physical, emotional, mental and spiritual. In your incarnation you deal with all four of them. The astral body is that which you experience when you are not within this physical body but are in the spirit plane between lifetimes and experiencing only the emotional, mental and spiritual bodies. These two—the physical and astral bodies—are what you are used to referring to here as a third-density being.

Slowly the emotional body drops away. To say it in your terminology, you graduate from this third density. There is still somewhat of an emotional body, but there is no reaction to that body. It is merely felt as that cloud passing by that I spoke of last night; and you don't need to do anything but observe that emotional mass appear and disappear. As you move beyond the causal plane, the emotional body drops off completely and there are only the mental and spiritual bodies. Here the being is learning a sense of wisdom for which thought is still necessary.

Yes, there are two kinds of wisdom: that which comes from the heart and that which comes from the mind. As Q'uo has just pointed out, they are simply two levels of the same way of knowing. Slowly this mental body also drops away as it is no longer needed, as you move back into that core heart of the Creator of which Q'uo has just spoken. Thus, the being moving into what you refer to as seventh density moves more purely to being the pure spiritual body, which is the soul. That is all the soul is, the spiritual body with all the rest, not discarded, because that implies an aversion, but simply fallen away, as you shed your clothes when the sun is hot on a summer day.

Coming back to where you are now, in this third density, as you begin to understand, no one of these four bodies is more mature or less mature than another. Each body serves its purpose. What you experienced this morning when you felt the heart open so completely and then experienced fear of that opening was neither the isolated mental nor emotional body.

Fear is an emotion, and fear comes from many places. It is not that the emotional body is less mature but that the emotional body is less accepted; that while at some deep levels of meditation you are aware of the usefulness of moving beyond conceptual thought, you do not condemn yourself for thinking. But you condemn yourself so often for feeling, until habitually you build up a fear of the emotions. Essentially, you have backed yourself into that tunnel we've talked about so often.

I have talked in another channeling[9] of a tunnel, a very safe place; and you are comfortable in this womb. Perhaps you will wish to think of it as a cave with only one end open, and across that end you've put strands of cobwebs to protect yourself from that which you feel will harm you, to protect yourself from another's anger and also your own anger, to protect yourself from the pain of feeling separation, to protect yourself from grief. And each strand that you have put up has served a purpose, because you felt you needed that protection. And yet, it is dark in your tunnel and on the outside it is light; and you've reached a place where you want to allow in that light. Can you feel the brutality if one were to reach in a hand and tear out all of those cobwebs, all of those strands, and how you would cower in terror against tearing all of that protection away?

Yet gently and with full awareness, you can reach out, lift one strand at a time, and examine it. What is this fear? Have I still need of this? Whence is it arising? How long must I hold on to it? Seeing a strand, perhaps of anger or greed, one notes how that greed or anger arises out of fear and out of a sense of separation. One sees the ways that fear has enhanced the sense of separation. The self, which

---

[8] *The Kabir Book*, poem 43.

[9] November 21, 1990; unpublished; available from Deep Spring Center for Meditation and Spiritual Inquiry, 3455 Charing Cross Road, Ann Arbor, MI, 48108.

then perceives itself to be separate, feels a need to protect and allows the arising of anger or greed as its protection: "What if my needs are not met? What if I'm harmed?"

But this can only come from a sense of self and other self. Where there is no separation, there can be no anger. Can you begin to see how fear leads to that sense of separation which leads to the first distortion of self-awareness? This distortion provokes one not yet fully immersed in separation but experiencing a distinction between self and other self to cultivate that distortion which first allows fears. Observing, you can begin to understand how this process works in yourself. Then as fear or separation arise, you can gently lift that strand of anger from where it blocks the light, look at it, and ask yourself, "Do I still need this or am I able now to put it aside?" Always do this with gentleness and never with force, never asking the self to be what it is not ready to be, but accepting the self as it is so that the being will always be challenged, but always simultaneously accepted and loved. In this way the emotional body is not something with which one fights, but is part of your integral, harmonious self.

You asked me to speak further about the distortion of service-to-others that grows out of fear in the emotional body. When there is a sense of the self's not being adequate so that there comes a feeling of needing to do something to prove oneself adequate, to soothe that pain, then the service in itself becomes distorted. You experienced this morning the love of that spirit that was known in his last incarnation as Jesus, and you felt the strength of that loving energy flowing through with absolutely no distortion. Last night I said that in human form it is impossible to allow the energy to flow completely distortion-free. This is because as soon as there is a concept of service-to-others, there is a self and an other. And thus, we come back to that fact that self-awareness is a distortion. Ra calls it the first distortion and I would agree with this. Excuse me, Ra calls free will the first distortion—potentiation of an active Creator whose nature is Logos, or love.[10] But in order to love, there must be that which is loved; and that takes self-awareness, so in a sense we're saying the same thing in a different way.

If you will, picture a river flowing with an absolutely clean and sandy bed, and with a strong current. Somewhere down the stream place one stone, just large enough to break the surface, and see the ripples that break around it. Let's call that first stone self-awareness. The current flows around it with its full force, and yet there is a small distortion in that current. From self-awareness grow so many doubts and fears: comparisons; competitiveness; and thoughts like, "Am I good enough? Am I acceptable and loved?" Suddenly we have a whole load of stones thrown into this river, and now the water flows through in many ripples. There is still a current; but if you were to float a stick downstream of that very first stone, it would float smoothly down the stream. If you put a stick just upstream of that first stone and watch it, you see how it deviates around that stone and loses some of its direction and thrust. Now let that stick move downstream to where all these stones are and see how it swirls around in little whirlpools.

Thus, when you are lost in a distortion of any sort, your energy does not flow freely. In the meditation you felt that entity known as Jesus' energy flowing unimpeded and enhancing all energy that came into it. All separating emotions, even love, create distortion and turbulence. The mental body quiets that turbulence through reason, and yet that reason separates the entity from the strength of the river's flow. It is as if one, seeing all those rocks in the river's bed, erected a dam within the rocks, diverting the water so that there was no longer turbulence from the rocks but impeding the full flow of the water.

Each distortion must be worked with back and forth, always with gentleness and compassion, always asking the self, "What am I being offered to learn? How can I work with these fears, these forces within me, more skillfully? How can I gently begin to lift out each stone, to move to that perfect awareness that there is no separation, that this self that is aware is not a separate self but only part of the force of the universe?" The fully evolved soul returns to the fire whence it came; but it returns, not as the tiny ember that it began as, but as a brilliant sun in itself, enhancing and strengthening the power of that original sun.

Do you wish me to speak about this further, or are there other questions?

Barbara: I have no more questions about this, Aaron, thank you. I don't know if others do or not.

---

[10] *The Law of One, Book II*, pp. 2-3, 54.

K: With regard to working skillfully with anger, I understand the concept of noticing, feeling and allowing anger to pass as it comes up in the day-to-day life. I'm not sure what to do with the angers that have been there for many years—the angers that I can tap into at any moment just by recalling any of many situations. In each case, I suppose the anger has to do with my feeling that I have been wronged somehow; and I know that what I need to do is to be able to accept and forgive myself fully, as well as whatever other person is involved in the situation. But this seems to me to be the work of an entire lifetime, at least, and leaves me feeling pretty hopeless about dealing in any significant way with those long-term angers. Can you comment on this?

Aaron: You say that this seems to be the work of a lifetime, and that leaves you feeling hopeless; and yet, this is the healing for which you took birth, because in past lifetimes you have held anger in much the same way, learning slowly to let it go, reaching an understanding that anger is just anger. And now you've arrived at a point where you understand the usefulness of moving beyond that anger, of letting it drop away, and it *is* the work of a lifetime; and yet you are working on it and making progress. You are in that tunnel that I just spoke of with all these strands across. And when present anger arises, you've learned skillfully to look at that and not necessarily need to attach it across the entrance. But there are still all those strands from the past.

I suggest that it would be useful in meditation, as you feel the courage and readiness, to lift each strand and examine it. Don't start with the heaviest ones. Build up your strength with the lighter ones. As you recall some moment of intense anger where the self felt attacked in some way by another self and felt that it was wronged, just gently look at that strand and the feelings that came, asking yourself, "What is this anger? Why is it here? What was its function? Do I still need it, or am I ready to set it down?" Always know that if you feel vulnerable and afraid, you may put it back again [into place] if you need to, trusting that as you grow you will have less and less need to do that.

Each of you is here to learn to love yourself and others more fully, to learn faith and love. The anger is quite simply one of your learning tools. It's very easy to love unconditionally in a situation where there is nothing that arises to provoke any feeling but love. But how do you love when you are provoked to defend yourself, when that separation arises? Can you continue to love when noticing the fears, when noticing the separation and how anger arises from that? As you become more skillful with doing that with each small resentment that arises in your present life, you will find the faith and love to go back [to loving in the moments of larger resentment].

There is one more thing here. You say you know this is what you need to do. I feel a sense of judgment in that. There is some sense of your feeling that until you do, you are not quite adequate or there's something wrong with you that needs to be corrected. You do not need to do this; rather, as you grow you allow yourself to do this. Can you see the difference? Allow yourself to be where you are, always reaching for the next step, but reaching out of a sense of love, not out of a sense of despising that which is. It is essential to treat all of this within you with love, because your contempt will only further enhance the sense of separation and further fragment the self into what's acceptable and what's unacceptable.

Do you understand, and do you have further questions?

K: Thank you, Aaron, I think I understand. I may have more questions at a later time.

Aaron: I would like briefly to add one thing, which is to emphasize that I share the concern of what Q'uo has said about patience. Can you picture yourselves swimming up the stream in a river? You know that eventually you will come to the source of that river. But for now you are just enjoying the swimming, noticing the brightly colored fish that swim beneath you, feeling the coolness of the water and the sun on your back, stopping to rest when you need to and then swimming again. As you move further upstream the river begins to narrow a little, and suddenly you start to have a sense that this river is coming from someplace and that perhaps you will get to its source.

Now, you stop your strokes and look up, wondering how much further; but as you stop there, the current pushes you back and you lose your momentum. You start to swim again. The closer you get to the source, the fresher the water feels and the stronger the energy of that source. When you start to look around and say, "How much further? I can't wait to get there," you lose some of the joy that you had before of just enjoying the water, enjoying that life in the water, the sensations of it on your body. This happens to all beings as they come closer to the source. It is not a fault, simply something of which you must be aware so that you can begin to notice the impatience and allow yourself to return to the joy of this incarnation, knowing that yes, you do come closer and closer to moving beyond the need for rebirth, to knowing your true Self in a deeper sense and connecting with the source of that love and light in a deeper sense. But that will be when it will be, and this is now. Cherish this *now*. It will not come again.

As there are no more questions, I wish to thank you all for sharing your loving presence with me. I cherish each and every one of you, and wish for each of you that you could grow to cherish yourselves as those loving spirits and friends that surround you cherish you. That is all.

L/L Research is a subsidiary of Rock Creek Research & Development Laboratories, Inc.

P.O. Box 5195
Louisville, KY 40255-0195

L/L Research

www.llresearch.org

Rock Creek is a non-profit corporation dedicated to discovering and sharing information which may aid in the spiritual evolution of humankind.

ABOUT THE CONTENTS OF THIS TRANSCRIPT: This telepathic channeling has been taken from transcriptions of the weekly study and meditation meetings of the Rock Creek Research & Development Laboratories and L/L Research. It is offered in the hope that it may be useful to you. As the Confederation entities always make a point of saying, please use your discrimination and judgment in assessing this material. If something rings true to you, fine. If something does not resonate, please leave it behind, for neither we nor those of the Confederation would wish to be a stumbling block for any.

CAVEAT: This transcript is being published by L/L Research in a not yet final form. It has, however, been edited and any obvious errors have been corrected. When it is in a final form, this caveat will be removed.

© 2009 L/L Research

The Aaron/Q'uo Dialogues, Supplementary Session
March 1, 1991

Aaron: With greetings to you both. I am Aaron.

You ask why I am not content with the term "density." I have nothing against the label itself, but it is your misunderstanding of the label which I was trying to circumvent, to stir you beyond that misunderstanding.

When you were speaking of this on Thursday morning, K was thinking of it as specific grades that at a certain density of light, there is immediate movement into the next density. It doesn't work that way. You move back and forward to a certain degree. Yes, there is this harvest that Ra talks about. There is a time when you are ready for the next, for the lessons of the next density and yet, you may move back and forward as you need to. Sometimes you wish to repeat a class for certain reasons. We are speaking here of opacity of transparency *(inaudible)* and there is a general movement toward more transparency and yet on any plane there are times when the entity becomes stuck, in a way. Not that it's [not] moving forward, but that it needs frequent repetitions of the lesson.

As that happens that being may temporarily find they misunderstood, not because it is falling backwards, but because there is more to understand. It might help you here to picture a being climbing a mountain. At first, there is a gentle slope and not as much exertion is required. At some point, the being may come to a steep cliff and it begins to climb, seeking out footholds and handholds. And as it does, so its energy changes. It becomes more tired. It's sweating, perhaps. This does not mean it is not as skillful a climber as it was in the lower levels, where it was not sweating or exhausted, simply that the slope is steeper.

Yet, for many of you when you come to that steep slope and feel a sense of spiritual exhaustion there is a reaction to it. It is not the exhaustion that is the problem but the reaction. The reaction pulls the solutional body that we spoke of this morning into play and temporarily your light becomes more opaque. Yet, in a sense that cliff must be climbed to reach the plateau on top.

Barbara: Say that again, Aaron. You gave me a lot of images at once. This is Barbara speaking. Aaron, I'm seeing it as you see it, through your eyes, so to speak. Yes, I see, side by side, two beings: one has energy. Its own energy is flowing swiftly and it's very transparent and its aura is radiating with light. The one beside it is climbing up the steep cliff, I guess. *(Inaudible)* not nearly as transparent, but it's putting forth such a feeling of hope and love of reaching the top that it's radiating even more brilliantly.

So, Aaron, is what you're saying that a … (I can't begin to say how fast that is) transparency is not the only significant factor. *(Inaudible)*. Will you tell me if that is correct?

(Side one of tape ends.)

Aaron: Essentially, child. This density is only one factor. This is why I have preferred the word "dimension." Let us first define what I mean by dimension, as I don't know if Carla has read this in the transcripts.

Picture a ball of clay, trapped between your hands. Pressure is applied to it from both sides and as it squeezes together, most of the mass eases out from the top of your hands to form a new ball in another dimension. You still have the flat piece that went down between your hands, but now you have a piece that's erupted onto the top. Take that and squeeze it and allow it to move in a new direction.

You cross many thresholds within each of what you are accustomed to thinking of as a density and [also] from one density to another. Thus within each density are many of these thresholds and each time a meditation or *(inaudible)* experience takes you to a new perspective, your eyes are opened to some truth to which they have been shut before. You have a new way of understanding.

Now, there are larger thresholds and smaller thresholds. One might liken it to a flight of stairs with a landing, and then you are on to the next flight but it is all one stairwell. For the density of the being is generally moving toward transparency and there are certain limits of transparency or opacity within each of your labeled densities. This is only one factor.

Barbara is asking me here what are the other factors and I find it almost impossible to find words in your vocabulary which will express [our thoughts]. In a sense, I understand why Ra is using density because they all translate into light. And yet it is not enough to simply say, "This is light," or, "This is not light." When you have a deeper faith, you do meet more light.

As distortion is dissolved, you meet more light and allow more light to pass through you, but there is a level here where the distortion must be accepted as where that being is. In other words, Ra speaks of love as the first distortion.[11] That original energy that was flowing through this small spark of God cannot grow into a flaming sun without the distortion of love. Yet the distortion of love does create a *(inaudible)* and take one away from transparency. This is where the term density can be misleading. [There can be the] feeling that it is preferable to move toward transparency, but it is not that it is preferable, it is simply to be seen in the same way that as one walks down the path, one moves further down the path. It is inevitable. It is not something that you need to try to do.

Barbara: Say it again, please, Aaron.

Aaron: I am sorry, child. This is not the fault of your channeling. I am thinking two thoughts at once. I am thinking this through as I speak.

One must continually love and reach out toward that love that is other, giving and receiving and clarifying the connection between the self and the source of that love until the self is absorbed into the source and further separation ceases. The soul yearns for that but so does the love that draws one deeper back to love. It is love that overcomes the separation and yet love is the separation.

As I am trying to understand how to explain this to you, we are found to be thinking two thoughts. Firstly, that one must always be striving to love more fully, to live more wisely. Yet at the same time one must not be doing anything. And there is no paradox there.

Do you understand what I mean with this, or should I try to explain it further?

Barbara: I understand it Aaron. Do you, Carla?

Carla: Yes.

Aaron: So we come back to this original question about density and my preference for another term. Actually, I don't prefer another term, I prefer [that] there be no term, that you try to move yourself and your thinking beyond labels. Simply understand that you go through this progression, which can be roughly broken up into eight mutual parts, each with many smaller parts, but that they overlap. You are always in the space you need to be and that space truly needs not labels so much as your constantly being in that space, in that moment, and not striving to be anywhere else while still knowing the absolute desire to be fully merged with that love. Do you have questions?

---

[11] Actually, the Ra group speak of free will as the first distortion. But love or Logos is next!

Barbara: I don't have questions. Aaron. I understand what you are saying. Carla?

Carla: I would suggest the image of a stairway. Each step is more full of light. The spirit walks the stairway until it reaches the light that is comfortable. If it tries to go further it is uncomfortable, so it finds its place. That place may be in third density or fourth density but it only matters if you are comfortable.

Aaron: I thank you, Carla. That is a very clear illustration. I would add a bit to it. Let us put the stairway outdoors and allow you to visualize the light of the sun as shining brightly on it and, of course, as you come up from the world you move more and more into the sunshine. Picture it as a spiral staircase, perhaps, with small landings at different places. There are times when you move around and find yourself in the shadow for a bit. So you are both emerging up into the light and yet temporarily fully covered in shadow and will emerge back into the light as you move around, beyond that shadow.

Each shadow is a difficult place in your growth. [And this is so] in any density, because it is not only third density that has to learn, though learning is not as painful [in other densities.] Yet there are times when we feel ourselves to be in darkness. The difference is [that] when you feel yourself to be in darkness, it is as if there is total blackness and you lose sight of the stairs that wander round.

When a being of a higher density finds itself to be in darkness it is only a slight shadow, and one can still clearly see the staircase, but while it is a constant progression, into more and more light—and you are very accurate in saying that you only move as high as the light is pleasant and when it becomes intolerably hot, burning away that in you that is still too dense to meet that light, then you pause for a bit to work to a degree of transparency—so while you are moving toward this light, there are also moments of more brightness and moments of shadow.

I find this very accurate, Carla. May I suggest that the steps are such as you may have meant in what you call a funhouse, perhaps, where there are times they are firm, and times when you step up [where] they seem to sink down. So that the difference of one step, and the step that follows after, disappears and the next step looms very high above.

Each step is truly a universe unto itself. That is all.

Carla, I see a bit of confusion in your understanding of this. Yes, that happened to you, but it didn't happen to you by chance. Thus, first there was some energy blockages [in some] *(inaudible)* region of your body. Then there was your mother's action, which around your life is called your "retention tether," but the energy blockage existed in a sense of the potential for the energy blockage, let us say, before that choice of your mother's. I would suggest that this is related to a past life prior to this one. Do you wish me to speak further on this?

Carla: Yes.

It may be useful for you to know that there has been a past life in which there was severe brutality and mutilation to the bowel area of your body. I would suggest that this may be a defense, a protection, against that. I can give you more details on this life if it would be more useful to you but you [do not] really need to know *(inaudible)* what happened, so much as to become aware that you are creating some protection of some sort. You have released most of the karma between you and that being who did this disemboweling but the body is working in its own way, on a cellular level almost, to provide protection. It is not a matter of forgiving, which is why I feel you do not need to know the whole story behind it.

It is just a story. [To tell it] will pull you back into it. Rather [than going back into that story], understand the fear of the body itself against such violence to it. Hold that fear lovingly in your arms and relate to it compassionately, as I believe there has been more warfare than love with this area of your body, in this lifetime. Do you understand?

Carla: I think so.

You seem to be dealing remarkably [well] with learning of this incarnation without knowing about other incarnations. I believe you do know what you need to know at a certain level that is not conscious. But you do not need to know about something that simply happened to a being that you were that is not immediately relevant to this lifetime. All that is relevant here is that you are saying that the pattern your mother established has been carried through but the pattern was established long before your mother toilet-trained you in that way and in fact her choice of toilet-training in that way [served] to emphasize the pattern in this lifetime[12], to draw your attention to it, so you may heal that brutality from a past lifetime, not by needing to know the details of it but just to bring *(inaudible)* to that area of your body and understand the cellular level. Do you understand?

Carla: *(Inaudible).*

I understand that you have, Carla, but there is still another level here that you can begin to relate to more consciously as [we] speak about it. Perhaps just knowing this will be a help to bring the awareness more to the conscious level of mind.

I find it delightful that on my plane I have finally reached the point where I equate beauty with the light that shines from within and [has] nothing to with the physical. It is a pleasant stage to have reached. I would like to remind you both that when you choose to incarnate into a body, into a family, into a culture, you know the generalities of that body or family or culture, that for these that you have chosen to be parents, these have been the issues that they have come to work with and that you have shared with them in the past.

You know the basics of what that fetus will become, but you have no idea whether it is going to be beautiful or not. This is not one of the choices you make. Let me amend that to say you may know that it will be extremely unattractive as the parents are unattractive or that *(inaudible)*, but beyond those general limits, you have no idea whether it will very beautiful, or somewhat beautiful, or highly attractive or attractive or moderately unattractive, or so on.

This only becomes a concern to you on the physical plane and is of no concern to your spirit. That is all.

Barbara: [Aaron,] we are talking about densities. You've generally not been willing to say anything about what density you are and said it didn't matter. However, some time in the past few weeks in the Thursday group[13] we were talking about this spirit known as Jesus and in the Ra material it talked about him as being at fifth density and you said the spirit had nearly entered the seventh density and K was feeling upset about why there was a seeming contradiction. K said, "In the Ra material, Ra states the Jesus is currently in the fifth density and you say he's seventh." And Aaron said, "That spirit whom I understand as Jesus is far beyond the fifth density." K is questioning the density of Jesus, who Aaron says is at the seventh density. K showed me the related features of the Ra material. Aaron said, "K, I want to you to discuss this [with] Q'uo. I do not agree with it. I am what you would term fifth density and this being has evolved far beyond me. That is all."

And then you, [Aaron], went on to talk about what the term density means and about not thinking of it as a specific grade and that we are not fixed in place. So, Aaron, the question this is leading to is *(inaudible)* I don't know, are you feeling, Carla, that as *(inaudible)* what makes you *(inaudible)*. What need you *(inaudible)* feel Aaron has not talked to my knowledge about what density he was at before. The only thing he has ever told me before is that he is beyond the causal plane. What made you feel that he was third density? And Carla was saying, "Barbara saved his life 400 years ago. At that time he was a third-density being. So he must still be third density."

Aaron: Carla, here we are back to the *(inaudible)* more fixed notion, that a being must wait for this general harvest to go on. Immediately after the end of that lifetime there was no need for me to return to incarnation. I have been very close to that for many lifetimes. On the spiritual plane between many lifetimes and for several thousand years, I had learned many lessons that you would term fourth-density lessons and yet had felt a need to return to Earth for the clarification of *(inaudible)* that needed to be cleansed, thus, actually was moving between

---

[12] Carla's mother toilet-trained her from before the age of one year old by explaining to her that she needed to move her bowels, then putting her on the potty. Carla was too young to be able to perform as expected, although she spoke early and clearly understood what she was supposed to accomplish. She simply could not do it. This resulted in a perception that she was constipated. Therefore, she was given enemas at least once a week from babyhood.

This compromised her peristaltic health and throughout her life until 1991 she had difficulty absorbing and processing food. Ten months after this discussion with Aaron and Barbara was taped, half of her transverse colon was surgically removed, the "disemboweling" being necessary to preserve her life. Thusly, the pattern played out for Carla in this incarnation, but in a healing and helpful way which ensured her continued life and increased vitality. She used this opportunity to rededicate her life to service and also to her own care for herself. She radically improved and remains in greatly increased health to the present time (2005).

[13] Barbara is here speaking of a regular meeting of the Deep Spring Center for Meditation and Spiritual Inquiry in Ann Arbor, Michigan, where Barbara and Aaron teach.

these. Here again, I prefer to not use the word density for these levels of being, although density will do in a sense, because as a spiritual being, with an almost clear emotional body, I was far more transparent, but coming back to the *(inaudible)* final lifetimes, there was more opacity because of the presence of the emotional body …

Barbara, you need to reposition yourself. Your concentration is weak.

(Pause)

Following the final cleansing of that karma, there was no need to return to the earth plane, and yet I left behind me a beloved one whom I would *(inaudible)* through my guidance.

There is no need for me to do this work, karmically. There's no karma between me and the present being you know as Barbara that draws me back and so I have no present bonds to work through to need to be part of the earth plane. I do so purely out of love, and yet there is still this distortion of love, of the desire to serve this one whom I have loved through many lifetimes. Besides that there are lessons of both wisdom and compassion that are valuable for me as a spirit that may be deepened with recontact with those of you who walk this Earth.

So, as I emphasized many times, you teach me as much as I teach you. You have reminded me of what it was to be young. When I say I am presently of fifth density, I am not speaking of a place where I am, but am speaking purely in terms of the degree of clarity of my mind. If I did not choose to do what I am doing now, during which work I must assume a look of personality and consciousness as I have spoken of before, then, going back to our visualization of that staircase in the amount of light that the being can enjoy and tolerate and benefit by being, I would be at the beginnings …

(Tape ends.)

L/L Research

L/L Research is a subsidiary of Rock Creek Research & Development Laboratories, Inc.

P.O. Box 5195
Louisville, KY 40255-0195

www.llresearch.org

Rock Creek is a non-profit corporation dedicated to discovering and sharing information which may aid in the spiritual evolution of humankind.

ABOUT THE CONTENTS OF THIS TRANSCRIPT: This telepathic channeling has been taken from transcriptions of the weekly study and meditation meetings of the Rock Creek Research & Development Laboratories and L/L Research. It is offered in the hope that it may be useful to you. As the Confederation entities always make a point of saying, please use your discrimination and judgment in assessing this material. If something rings true to you, fine. If something does not resonate, please leave it behind, for neither we nor those of the Confederation would wish to be a stumbling block for any.

CAVEAT: This transcript is being published by L/L Research in a not yet final form. It has, however, been edited and any obvious errors have been corrected. When it is in a final form, this caveat will be removed.

© 2009 L/L Research

The Aaron/Q'uo Dialogues, Session 3
March 2, 1991

Group question: We all have questions about fear. Barbara has fear of responsibility she is not able to meet, fear of the unknown, and fear of going beyond her prior limits. Carla and J fear being unable to measure up to their own standards, ability and potential. K does not wish to rely on outer authority but fears she is not equal to the task of establishing her own inner authority. Would you please speak to these fears, or fear itself?

Aaron: I am Aaron. I think it would be useful for each of us to speak for some time, and then to relax from that rigidity a bit so that we can speak back and forth. This is almost a ritual form of communication. I do not wish to impose this on Q'uo. If that is acceptable to Q'uo it is acceptable to me. That is all.

(A pause while Aaron waits for any objection. There is none.)

I am Aaron. You are asking about fear, and I do prefer this idea of a dialogue to individual monologue. So, rather than trying to give you a half-hour, comprehensive view of the subject, I'm going to talk a bit about what seems to me to be your deepest issues, and then pass it on and let it return to me again. I feel we will learn more that way.

Each of you has different understandings about fear and questions that come from a different need, a different place, so that we start with a very basic question, "What is fear?" Not even, "How does it arise?" or, "Where does it come from?" but, "What is it?" Essentially it is an emotion that also touches on the physical and mental bodies, not just the emotional body; and finally it affects the spiritual body. So it is a feeling that totally enfolds you.

Fear is rather paralyzing to many of you. It distorts your way of seeing. It creates confusion and chaos within you. Because of the turbulence that it creates within you, it easily moves out of control. It is even harder than anger to step back from to get some perspective, because of the ways it paralyzes you. As with any emotion, it is not fear that is the problem but your reaction to it. Fear in itself is just a mind/body experience, but it does lead to all these reactions within the physical body and in the spiritual body as well.

I have left out the mental body in talking about reactions to fear, because fear does not provoke a reaction in the mental body so much as it grows out of both the emotional and mental bodies. The emotional body feels the fear. The mental body in a sense creates the fear, unless it is a purely physical fear in response to a physical stimulus, such as a fear of falling as you feel yourself falling.

The mental body originates the fear. It is then picked up by the emotional body. For example, when you are in a car about to crash, at that moment you are safe; but you move from that present moment to an image of what you perceive will happen in the future. You feel yourself skidding, and suddenly you envision yourself folded against that tree beside the road—an image which comes from the mental body—or you move back to the past, to your past experiences with a similar situation. Again, fear arises from the mental body; so the mind creates that situation where fear may enter by moving out of the present and into the past or future. Then the emotional body picks up on that fear. It then moves on to the physical body, this being such a quick process that I would not expect you to be able to break it down. But there is immediate physical tension, and at that moment the fear enters. Fear cannot coexist with love. Along with love I also place those experiences of faith and trust. At that moment when fear is that strong, the spiritual body loses all sense of trust that this will be okay.

Let us speak about this more specifically. Firstly, fear is never in this present moment, but always in the past or the future. Think about this. Put yourself again in that skidding car. It's just skidding. You may be fine. Can you see your mind moving to that tree and the collision with it, or your mind moving backwards to the last time you skidded? Can you see how you have moved out of the present moment?

Let's take a purely emotional situation. Somebody is walking toward you and his face looks very angry. The last time that you had an encounter with that person, he raged and snarled at you; he led you to feel small and humiliated, and so both anger and fear arise. The fear is not based on this present moment, but only on your past experience.

Let us move from this to both Carla's, J's and K's questions. Looking at K's question of fear of her own inner authority versus an outer authority, of trusting herself, I remind you again that there is no fear in the present moment. K, when you are feeling this, can you take a deep breath and ask yourself, "Where is this fear?" Begin to gain that perspective that allows you to know that you are creating an outcome if you act in a certain way or remembering an outcome when you did act in a certain way; but that each moment is fresh, and you are not the same being who was in that situation before. You have learned not to trust your own inner authority, and now you are trying to learn to trust. And yet there is a sense of wanting to know that you are right before you claim that authority; there is that in you which says, "Maybe I'm not right," and gets caught up in those fears and angers. Then it moves to resentment of that other being who feels more self-assurance that it is right. So you have fear and anger mixed together here: anger that you don't have that same self-assurance, resentment against that being for its assurance, and a fear that maybe you're not right. The fear itself diminishes the sense of inner knowing.

Carla, when you spoke about your concern that your work would be adversely affected by pain medicine tonight, you were not remembering that it is not the medicine that prevents clear channeling but a fear that the medicine might prevent clear channeling. Can you see that difference? You are perfectly capable of repeating the concepts you receive under almost any circumstance down to near unconsciousness, because you have trained yourself so well to do this. But you are capable of allowing it to flow through you only when there is love. Again, love and fear can't coexist. As soon as fear enters, and sense of doubt, of, "Can I do this?" it diminishes the ability to do it.

Here we come back to your question, Carla and J. (I know I have not answered the other question in depth, but I do want to avoid a long monologue here and would prefer that all six of us speak. I will gladly speak more on this upon request.) You fear you are not measuring up to your potential. Can you see how fear itself invites such perceived failure? I believe you understand; and the question is, How do you work with that fear? There is nothing special you need to do. You can't take that fear and fling it away from you. But you can notice it and reach out to it with love. This fear is the child that comes to you, saying, "There's a big dog outside and I'm afraid." And you open the door and pat the dog and see that it's friendly. You might reassure the child, saying, "The dog is friendly," but you don't belittle the child's fear; you don't say, "It's stupid to be afraid." But that's what you do to yourselves; and as soon as you do that, the fear solidifies.

When you embarrass the child into going back out, it may finally reach out and pat the dog, but it will not get over its fear. When you hug the child and say, "I see how afraid you are. It's okay to be afraid of big dogs. Would you like me to walk outside with you?"—this is not pushing the child to pat the dog or do anything special, just reassuring it with your love. The child will feel that calmness and begin to touch its own fear with love. As fear falls away enough, the child can naturally reach out and pat the dog.

Can you apply that to yourselves? Your dog here is your potential and all the ideas that you have for yourselves. As with the big dog, it may feel overwhelming! You are truly, each, unlimited; and there is no way that in human form you can achieve all that is possible for you. Can you accept that? You are not asked to be perfect, just to do the best you can do. But when you relate to that fear with criticism, saying, "I shouldn't feel afraid. I should know my unlimitedness. I should be able to do anything," you can see how that solidifies the fear and prevents you from acting.

You know this. You know that love is the answer, and yet in a sense it becomes an intellectual mantra: "Love is always the answer." But what does it mean to say that love is the answer when the heart is feeling fear? How much more lovingly can you relate to the fear?

There is much more that I could say about fear here. I would prefer that others speak and come back to me. If you have specific questions about what I have said, I would be glad to answer them. If Q'uo wishes to speak now, that is fine with me; or if any of you wish to share your own ideas about fear, that would also be appropriate. That is all.

Q'uo: I am Q'uo. It is with joy at the insights of the one known as Aaron, as well as in the love and in the light of the one infinite Creator, that we, known as Q'uo, greet you.

Let us look at fear from the perspective of deep generalization. This does not mean that the generalization always applies, but it may be a tool which the seeker may use. Fear is an intensification based on the illusion of separation. Were all beings aware that they were one, the motives and circumstances of behavior would be plain to see. If the Akashic Records[14] were known, people might well choose to enjoy themselves more, being courageous enough to accept death as an ending to an incarnation. Although death is inevitable, most entities do not reckon with this.

Much fear is caused by a need to control the environment in a way helpful to the physical animal which houses the consciousness of each of you. This animal has a need to survive, which predisposes consciousness in manifestation toward control over the environment in order to obtain comfort, relaxation, and a feeling of security. Thus, fear is a perfect example of that which we would call a negatively polarizing thought. It assumes separation and usually hinges upon gaining or keeping control of that situation.

Let us examine this instrument; for though it is not aware of fear, yet it acts in fear. The red-ray center of this instrument's body is very strong. However, the instrument feared it would not remember to be kind to its animal, as this instrument is always energetic emotionally, mentally and spiritually. Thus, through fear of a possible outcome, through fear of losing control of a vital piece of paraphernalia, this instrument restrained itself.[15] This can be called good judgment, or it can be seen to be the fear of losing control of a detail of behavior which is supposed or presumed to be a life-or-death matter. Consciously the instrument feels no fear, yet there is enough respect for probable outcomes that the entity does indeed fear, and reacts in as loving and helpful a way as possible to the animal which honors it by serving as its manifestation in form.

Look at fear and ask, "What am I trying to control?" It is well to know that it is only an illusion that we ever are in control of anything. Not that entities are not free to make choices, but that the reality which eludes the illusion you enjoy is that all are parts of one flowing fountainhead of an active, creative, beautiful and living ocean of light. All flow into each other, through each other, through the self; and always, whatever condition the flow experiences, it is experienced not only as harmonious or aesthetically beautiful, but perfect. Each of you, as a spark, perceives the self as imperfect and at risk. That stops your spark of light from joining in shared heart as one. The only control entities have is not in

---

[14] The Akashic Records are defined by the web site, www.themystica.com/mystica/articles/a/akashic_records.htm, as "A theosophical term referring to an universal filing system which records every occurring thought, word, and action. The records are impressed on a subtle substance called akasha (or Soniferous Ether). In Hindu mysticism this akasha is thought to be the primary principle of nature from which the other four natural principles, fire, air, earth, and water, are created. These five principles also represent the five senses of the human being."

[15] Carla was loosely tying her hands down so that she would not damage her shoulders by gesturing thoughtlessly, as they were very flared-up with arthritic pain.

circumstances, but in choosing skillful actions to deal with the catalyst which has been given. Thusly, if you see, hear and analyze mentally where the being is attempting to control and in what way, the start is made. However, it must be continually grounded in constant reaffirmation of faith and an awareness that one has no control except when one dedicates oneself to that highest and best occupation one may personally offer. We feel that we reach out to each other; but in reality we reach in to free ourselves from the fear of an unknown, only partially manifested other self or from a condition or substance with which one has experienced loss of control previously. The true freedom is that of the devoted and absolutely faithful seeker.

We are those of Q'uo, and open the sextalogue[16] once again. We leave this instrument in love and in light.

Aaron: I am Aaron. I find it wonderful to talk like this in that Q'uo's thoughts expand my own, and I would assume the reciprocal is true.

There are two things that Q'uo has spoken of that I'd like to take to a different space. One is the relationship between fear and separation. There is never fear in the spiritual body of a self in relation to that self. The fear is always of a perceived other self.

There are two kinds of separation that occur here. One is the illusion of being separate so that there is a self and an other, and one is the separation from the self. Let us address these separately. Let us firstly come back to that being approaching you with an angry face, and the sense of fear that perhaps that being will attack or harm you in some way. There is, of course, the need to protect the self. As Q'uo has pointed out, this physical body desires to continue itself; yet that being approaching you is not an other, it is just an aspect of the one heart and mind as you are, an aspect of the Creator as you are. Then this slips into fear because one perceives another about to harm it. One way to approach it in a more skillful and creative way would be to remind the self that this is an angry aspect of yourself and to treat that angry aspect that approaches you as you would treat your own anger. If you have learned to deal more skillfully with your own anger; [you know] that just as your own anger cannot harm you, another being's anger cannot harm you. It is the illusion of separation that creates the defensiveness that escalates the anger into a spectre of harm.

We come back here to the visualization I asked you to make yesterday morning of love as these concentric circles, of fear and anger as sharp points emerging. When you can see those sharp points emerging and know that this is not an other but simply an aspect of yourself, that it is not that being's anger or fear but just anger or fear, you can remain enfolded by those concentric circles and send them out to that angry being. Each sharp point hits these softening circles that you send out. As soon as you pull back and begin that sense of separation that allows you to feel attacked, then you begin to send out your own sharp points. From my point of view, I simply see a sword fight of light—sharp points are stabbing at each other and nothing exists to soften them.

Secondly, what about the separation from the self? The self, the deepest Self, is love. The pure spirit body can feel nothing other than love. When fear arises there is always a separation within the self. Here I am simply explaining more deeply what I introduced earlier in this evening's session—that separation from one's self creates a fragmentation, with the spirit body sending out love and the emotional and mental bodies feeling need. The feeling, then, is one of great distress to that self, because that of itself that knows oneness and knows love as the deepest truth is imprisoned in a way, torn out and separated. The being is cut asunder from its spiritual body. When you are separated from that sense of love, such strong doubt arises in you that it becomes very hard to get back to that love. You know what is happening within you, but it is so hard to stop it.

This, above any other time, is where the being must cherish itself. As soon as fear is noted, the first step must be to enfold that frightened being with love, thus reducing fragmentation so that the being can come back into the center of itself and begin to feel again its connection with the Creator and with all things, and know that it cannot be harmed.

Often you think of fear as being a useful emotion in that it protects you. You are crossing a street and suddenly see a truck coming toward you. There is that instant of terror, of, "What if it hits me?" And you move quickly. It's true that the physical body responds to that fear in a chemical manner that

---

[16] A sextalogue is a a talk between six people.

allows a fast reaction. But fear is not necessary and in fact works counter to the most appropriate reaction. Let me explain: While it is true that the being does move out of the way of the truck and that you would not want to stand there in the middle of the street and send love to that fear when the appropriate action is to move, the movement does not grow out of fear but out of love that respects the physical body enough to preserve it. Fear is paralyzing and love is enabling. You cannot take the time to analyze danger. The physical being must act to preserve itself in a certain way. But this does not need to be a matter of fear, simply a matter of wisdom; and here again, wisdom grows out of love.

Q'uo spoke of Carla's fear and the sense of separation. The attempt to preserve the physical body through a sense of separation enhances the separation. Will you look at this carefully, each of you, in some example that suits your own needs and see that it is not necessary to respond with fear to preserve the body? When you know your oneness with all things, truly know that there is no separate self, then each time that you see separation emerging, you can remind yourself that this is the voice of fear and allow that illusion of separateness to fall away. It is not expected that the incarnate entity will always be able to keep that in its mind; and yet the closer you can come to that, the less paralyzing your fear will be and the more freedom you will find.

There is one more thing that I would add, which is that fear can be balanced by loving-kindness to oneself and others. This is a quality in the self that can be nurtured. It is helpful to remind oneself each time one feels fear, that one is fearing a delusion when one sees part of the self as a separate self. You may acknowledge that delusion, and then send love not only to the self that is fearing but to that which is feared. Beyond that, begin to notice all the times one does not feel fear. When one is in a situation that is in some way threatening, often one responds with love to that situation. Truly, each of you do that far more than you respond with fear or anger or separation. And you don't notice that response; it goes by. But it is a small, tender sprout, that of loving-kindness; and it must be nurtured. Can you begin to bring your attention to each time you respond in a loving way to a situation that might goad you toward separation? You do this not to pat yourself pridefully on the back for that loving response but to nurture that sprout of love within you and encourage it to blossom.

There is more that I could say about fear, but would prefer to end here to allow Q'uo or any of the others of you to speak with either questions or comments, as you feel appropriate. That is all.

Q'uo: I am Q'uo, and greet each once again in joy, love and light.

And how shall seekers learn to bloom into adventurous and fearless citizens of the universe? One good resource is one's own imperfect memory; for fears upon the catalyst of an outer happenstance are merely the top layer, in most cases, of what could be seven or seventy times seven layers of similar and repetitive situations which ended in a perceptive judgment that this situation is frightening. The lines of genealogy of fear go back like the long listings of who sired whom in your holy works. The most recent fear can be worked with helpfully by assessing gracefully and accurately the present fear and all it connotes, and comparing it to previous similar experiences. The pile of repetitive experiences may eventually begin to be seen as a repeating pattern; and as one peels away the onionskin layers of memory, one comes at last to the initial occasion of fear.

We may not be able to forgive the self for its present fear; however, we surely may be able to gaze upon the helpless infant and see with compassion the utter and complete dependence of this helpless consciousness. The infants have chosen parents which shall offer them the fears; that is, the unmet desires which will not be met. Talking is out of the question. Writing is out of the question. Even independent movement is unthinkable to the newly born. It routinely experiences areas of sheer terror. Since the infant is in a very small universe within the illusion, the fear is deeply rooted because of the absoluteness of its lack of ability to control situations in order that it may be clean, full of nutrition, and comfortable.

We do not encourage the exercise of moving backwards to discover the root of a present fear as any kind of parlor game or diversion. When each fear is followed to its root, that root is as strong as a lifetime of distortion in recurrent patterns can make it.

When one has found the root of that fear, one is then able to become aware of the portion of the identity that has been lost. However, like wearing an old shoe that never fit, entities tend to accept fear stoically. There is far more use in full and clear communication of the self. Each self has an observer that is a portion of the self and integrated with it. It is an art to avoid doing violence to the beingness of the self when one is rooting out a portion of that identity. Thusly, it must be done courteously and honorably, as the one known as Aaron has said, as the gentle stripping away of any minuscule portion of the blockage which is no longer needed. Thusly, one is able to have spiritual cleansing without attendant violence to the integrated mind, body and spirit.

Perhaps the greatest anguish of all to each self is the inevitable iniquity which is part of the experience of being in what you call human manifestation.

I am Q'uo, and once again we leave this instrument in love and in light, that all others may feel free to collaborate upon this most important topic.

Aaron: With thanks to my spirit friend and brother/sister self, I would like to speak to this idea Q'uo has raised about the infant and the terror that it feels. It would seem that a sense of terror is inbuilt into the human experience, and one must then ask, "Why?" If one cannot avoid the experience of fear as a human, then one must assume there is a reason why that is given; and perhaps looking deeper into that reason will help one to accept fear in a more loving way. Come back here to the thought that it is not the fear that's the problem, but your relationship to the fear. The infant's relationship to fear is necessarily one of aversion. It has needs, and if those needs are not met immediately, as Q'uo pointed out, it has no way of expressing this pain beyond its crying. And so it learns to fear and also to perceive itself as separate, because as long as it is nurtured and never feels the rising of a need, there is no separation from the mother. But each time that need arises and is not met instantly, it begins to perceive itself in this illusion as a separate self; and that self solidifies.

Of course, my dear ones, this is necessary to the human experience or it wouldn't be given. If you incarnated and this veil that screens you out of full spiritual knowing did not drop into place, if this illusion of separation did not happen, then you wouldn't learn on this earthly plane. There would be no difference between this plane and the spirit plane except that you would be in a body. But to be here in a body with no illusion of separation and with full spiritual awareness would mean that you could not learn the lessons that this incarnation is meant to teach you. Can you see that?

So I would ask you to begin to embrace fear as a gift that is meant to teach you. When it arises, rather than struggling with it and hating it, say a small "Thank you" to it. Let your fear talk to you of oneness and not of separation. Let it be a reminder to come back to that core where you are part of the one heart and the one mind, rather than experiencing fear as a sword that severs you from your heart and mind. Treat your fear with love and gratitude for its teaching.

Are there specific questions that any of you have related to anything that has been said or has not been said? That is all.

Carla: Aaron, I see myself as a perfectionist, and see the fear that comes from not being able to live up to my own ideal. That would seem to suggest that being a perfectionist is not wise; however, I have found that unless one aims for the ideal, one never begins to approach it. I don't mean this in the sense of brutally urging myself to do what I obviously cannot. It is more an existential question, apart from any situation, as to the value of the perfectionism that is at once my greatest helper in living a godly life and certainly my most devastating vice: self-judgment. I see I am not flowing in the stream by asking continually to be my best, for I am always watching myself; yet this attitude has helped me tremendously in that in disciplining myself I seem to have been able to become accepting at a deeper and deeper level of compassion. Would you wish to comment upon this, Aaron? I would be glad to hear it. Thank you.

Aaron: My dear one, this quality that you call perfectionism can come from two different places. It can be a voice of fear or of love. As you have pointed out, it helps you to realize your ideal, to be all of what you can be, to hold that in front of you. What you are holding in front of you is the soul, which is unlimited and perfect. You see the image of that perfection and know that while the physical manifestation cannot reach that full perfection, yet in the true sense it has already reached it. You are already all that you will ever be, and always have been. Here we get into a question of simultaneous time, and I will not go deeply into that now. You are all familiar with the general concept of which I speak. But the self that holds that ideal in front of you is no different than the self that kneels down in prayer before an image of the Christ, understanding the depth of that being's love and compassion and ability to forgive, and knowing that one has the potential in oneself and can achieve that potential as it works at it through many lifetimes, to reach eventually—not in this density but further along the way—that level of pure, unconditional love.

Then there is that perfectionism that comes from the voice of fear. This doesn't hold an image up as our ideal, but rather, it is a derogatory voice. It speaks of non-acceptance. It speaks of the history of the being, both in that incarnation and in other incarnations where so many times there has been defeat, so many times there has been non-acceptance by the self and by perceived other selves.

A voice of perfection speaks of eventual success because it knows, fully knows, that it is already perfect. The other voice speaks of failure, because it sees all the places where the physical manifestation is limited. So, as with anything else in your life, it is not the quality of perfectionism that's the problem but where that is coming from, which voice is speaking.

This is not true just of perfectionism, but of any quality in your life. A desire to serve comes to mind here. We have spoken of the concept in the past few days that this desire can come from a voice of love or a voice of fear. It is the voice of fear that distorts the ability and fragments the self, and further enhances the sense of helplessness and limitedness. It is the voice of love that opens the self, that inspires, leading the being to be all it can be and touching the deep sense of acceptance and compassion when that human can do no more because it is human.

Would you have me speak further on this, or have I answered your question?

Carla: No, thank you, Aaron. This is sufficient.

Aaron: My friends, you each contain a great deal of wisdom within you. I understand that when there are these channeling sessions you are anxious to hear our thoughts, and yet your own thinking would prompt you to a greater depth as well. So, it is not only questions but also comments that are appropriate. That is all.

Q'uo: I am Q'uo. We dwell in love and light, and would sculpt the final thought of this extremely enjoyable session of working.

The ones known as Barbara and Carla this day were speaking about the concept of prayer pills. This concept was visualized as a simple recognition and respect for conditions perceived, the particular condition being the one known as Barbara's clear awareness of outer-plane contact which is unlike inner-plane contact, which is the privilege of only those teachers that have incarnated upon this planet at one time and which cannot harm the self, as it is within the energy web of that particular consciousness' field. At some level [inner-planes contact] has been accepted personally by the self or it would not come into manifestation.

There are many outer-plane influences upon entities. For instance, the astrology which many use is a way to become more aware of circumstances, although, because the exact moment when the soul enters the physical vehicle must remain unknown, astrology will remain inaccurate specifically and is only helpful in mapping out the topology or neighborhood where catalyst is now occurring.

No matter what the personal situation may be, the tools of prayer—contemplation, meditation, inspiration and all of those intuitional qualities—are of much aid. The outer-plane confluences are from stars, galaxies and in truth any external consciousness which has been perceived. When affirming and praying, one is able to experience fearlessness, for one is involved in worship; and all else may be put aside for that moment of worship. It has been suggested to pray without ceasing. This is excellent advice, for the outer-plane entities which speak through instruments such as this one are cosmic energies which influence the self. A continual "medication" of meditation in ceaseless remembrance, love and praise of the infinite One places one's conscious awareness in a state far more resonant with unity than an unprayerful state would be, in relation to its ability skillfully to perceive.

Respect and honor the need for heavenly food of the self. If positive and negative outer-plane entities rain upon all alike, like the cosmic influences that they are, and if free will is to be maintained, the self must be independent and thoughtful; for above all, fear is uninteresting.

May you each find the gentleness and tenderness to re-create and re-experience that helpless and brutalized infant whose space has been invaded again and again, whose needs are not often adequately met in some area or another. Be gentle with this and patient, and remember to remember the one infinite Creator, whose nature is limitless love and whose every manifestation is light. We greet you and offer benediction in all that there is—the love and the light of the one infinite Creator.

May we of Q'uo speak for the one known as Aaron in thanking each for the passionate love of the Creator and of service to others that has called us here and given us an incredible opportunity to triangulate upon a central question. We find working with Aaron a delight, and are humble before this entity. [We offer] our blessings and our love, our peace and our joy, our love, our light. All that there is, is that condition in which we leave you, never truly leaving, but merely receding so that the raindrops of our positivity may not fall upon the unprepared heart. Adonai. Adonai. I am Q'uo. ❧

L/L Research

L/L Research is a subsidiary of Rock Creek Research & Development Laboratories, Inc.

P.O. Box 5195
Louisville, KY 40255-0195

www.llresearch.org

Rock Creek is a non-profit corporation dedicated to discovering and sharing information which may aid in the spiritual evolution of humankind.

ABOUT THE CONTENTS OF THIS TRANSCRIPT: This telepathic channeling has been taken from transcriptions of the weekly study and meditation meetings of the Rock Creek Research & Development Laboratories and L/L Research. It is offered in the hope that it may be useful to you. As the Confederation entities always make a point of saying, please use your discrimination and judgment in assessing this material. If something rings true to you, fine. If something does not resonate, please leave it behind, for neither we nor those of the Confederation would wish to be a stumbling block for any.

CAVEAT: This transcript is being published by L/L Research in a not yet final form. It has, however, been edited and any obvious errors have been corrected. When it is in a final form, this caveat will be removed.

© 2009 L/L Research

The Aaron/Q'uo Dialogues, Session 4
March 3, 1991

Group question: Please talk about accepting and not judging the self, concepts of what we think we should do, and how this is involved in fear. How do we accept ourselves and avoid the "shoulds"?

Aaron: I am Aaron. I greet you each with my love in the beauty of this new day.

"I should" is a voice of fear. I would like to explain that further. We spoke of this last night: the ways in which the "I should," that sense of perfectionism, comes from a yearning toward the ideal; but it also may come from fear. When it comes from fear there is a sense of pushing the self, forcing the self, rather than allowing the self to express its own radiance. It is rather like bringing in a flower, a soft bud, and brutally pulling the petals open, as if one could force it to blossom in that way. But it cannot be forced. It must be allowed by leaving it in the nurturing sunshine of one's love.

Yesterday Barbara was reading some material by Ram Dass in one of your record albums. In it he tells the story of how he met with a Buddhist teacher who suggested that they do a meditation together, expanding outward. After a few minutes the teacher said to him, "You're still trying." And Ram Dass said, "Yes, I'm still trying to expand outward." The teacher said, "Don't try to expand outward, just expand outward." Do you see the difference? By trying, you create the conditions where it becomes very difficult to allow. This does not mean that no effort is required, but the effort is that which flows through the being in perfect harmony rather than the effort that comes from a distortion of self-will.

There is a piece of writing by the third Zen patriarch which speaks of quieting the mind. He notes that in your effort to become quiet, you simply generate more activity. I am sure this is clear to all of you. The question then becomes, "How does one quiet the mind, or move beyond the dualistic, conceptual mind to reach that state of total merging with the Eternal?" Why not allow it? Why have any "I should"s? You do not need to achieve or attain anything. There is nothing to attain. You are already there. What you are doing is allowing the perfect flow of energy through you until you come to that understanding of the knowledge that you are already there. You must begin to understand that you are not moving yourself from "this" to "that," but simply knowing that you have always been "that" and can be nothing else.

You have heard me say many times that love and fear cannot coexist at the point where you understand fully that you have always been "that"— even though sometimes you act as if you were not— in that place there is total harmony with all that is. When you are trying to become "that," there is disharmony and there is a state of fear. We spoke last night of the correlation between fear and separation, and why one outgrows that pattern. The first occurrence is a state that recognizes self-awareness, and out of that self-awareness comes the fear that there is something that one is not, something to be attained; and out of that fear arises a stronger sense of separation. Can you see that as long as there is something to be attained, the being feels some fear as to whether or not it is good enough, worthy enough of attaining that? But when the being fully trusts that it already is all that it has ever been and ever will be, then it allows that fragile bud to open so that the full beauty of the flower becomes visible.

Allow me to speak a bit more specifically here. It's fine to speak of knowing intellectually that you are "that," but how does one keep that faith that allows one to move beyond fear? You are always in connection with the Divine. Several months ago Barbara was singing a song many times, early in the morning. The words were, *"Seems like such a long time, Holy Spirit, waiting, since I've drawn your breath in, silent and all-pervading."* As she sang that song over and over, she began to have that deep understanding that the breath of the Holy Spirit is always present, that the Creator is always present, that it is she that chooses to draw that breath in or not to draw that breath in. Then she understood how fear had separated her from choosing of affirmation of holiness.

To make such a choice, to fully affirm that oneness, is a responsibility. At times you feel you are not ready to commit yourself quite that far, and in fact you're not because you are here to learn; and in a sense that fear, first learned by the infant, is a part of your learning. There is nothing wrong with fear. Yes, it does seem to prevent you in some ways from fully reaching your potential; but that is a bit of an illusion. If you did not choose that fear as a catalyst, it would not be there. Fear is just fear. Can it be met with kindness? So, as you are able to turn around and relate more lovingly to that fear, you move yourself further on this path, reducing what I have called the specks or shadows from the self so that that self becomes more transparent and is more nearly ready to reach into higher levels of light.

In essence, what I am suggesting here is that you learn to trust that when fear arises, that's okay, that you don't need to flee from that fear but just to greet it with an openheartedness that says, "Oh, here's fear," and relate lovingly to fear, allowing it to bring whatever lessons it brings.

As with last night, there is much more that I could say here, but would prefer to have Q'uo speak first and let us pass this back and forth. That is all.

Q'uo: I am Q'uo. I greet you in love, light and delight in the infinite Creator. We are most privileged to be called to your group once more, and are enabled and ennobled by the sharing of our fallible opinions with the beautiful one known as Aaron.

Fear and the "shoulds": Where do these "shoulds" first occur? The voice of "should" is learned before the small entity has gained enough experience to count as irrelevant all suggestions that do not fall upon the heart with the feeling of truth and love. Thusly, the original voice of fear does not take into account the nature of the self or of how the self might relate to these parental and authoritarian instructions toward behavior and values.

At some point within the incarnation, most entities realize that these voices of "should" are a relic of childhood teachings. These teachings are generally intended to benefit the child and create for it a knowledge of how to move through the intricate rituals of social behavior with the lubrication of appropriate, kindly thoughts, words and actions. Thusly, the "shoulds" are valuable in dealing skillfully with the societal group at large. It is within the self and the self's perception of the self that the "shoulds" become less than benign.

The voices of childhood come without volition of the self; however, the internalized voices of childhood, even though forgiven and no longer valid upon the outer, manifested entity's self, may well be internalized and become the voice that seems to the self as the voice of the self. Here we may see the ultimate separation of self from self. The self needs to be aware of its inner voices and to heal, by forgiveness and acceptance, those voices of the ultimate critic which gaze upon the self's manifested works with a jaundiced eye, an eye for not what is right with this picture but what is wrong with this picture. This is a form of self-torture, a denigration of the self which is done quite innocently. To become mature one does need to see those things within the self which are not innocent or authentic but rather judgmental and full of complex argumentation.

The amount of complexity experienced by the self is a good gauge of the authenticity of the self.

Authentic selfhood is simple, pure and full; not reaching, not grasping, but content to do the best one can, as one can, however one can, and where one can. These voices, then, that denigrate the self judgmentally need to be recognized, accepted, named and then forgiven. Yet how shall one forgive? The psychology, if you will, of redemption is the choosing of a perfect symbol which then is able to forgive the self because its very nature is love, which always accepts any gift that is given.

It is no error that the one you know as Jesus was born into a mystical Jewish tradition. This tradition is chock-full of "shoulds." It is into this milieu that the one known as Jesus chose its incarnation in order that it, a fully literate Jewish scholar, created the firm concept of constant redemption. How greatly does the Jewish tradition emphasize the positive value of fear. Concepts of kosher, of living ethically and humanely, flood the Hebrew personality. Thusly, when the one known as Jesus said, "Your sins are forgiven you,"[17] he was speaking out of a background quite full of "shoulds" and judgment. Thusly, you may see that if the one known as Jesus could gaze at iniquity and instantaneously forgive it, then how indeed can one fail to forgive the self?

This method of becoming aware of redemption is roundabout and makes use of the illusion of separation. The Jesus that forgives is easier to hear as an other self speaking from a great distance of time than if Jesus the Christ were considered to be within the self, a part of the self, and ultimately the self. So, although all religions and spiritual systems of faith have much to recommend them in terms of finding allegories between their experiences and one's own, one must at last meet the self upon the plane of inner awareness. Then when "shoulds" and guilt arise, one may experience redemption, not only from an imagined other self but in a hearty, earthy and substantive way as part of the process of love, which includes love itself and therefore a lack of judgment. As the one known as Aaron said, each must bloom in its own time, ripen according to its own rhythms.

Yet entities usually do not perceive themselves as either virtuous and godly seed or beautiful blossom. It seems to the self that the self is anything *but* that beautiful seed which grows and blooms as one sees flowers and living trees express. This creates an instant bias towards judgment. How can one learn to experience the self as beautiful, as godly, as perfect? We would let this question linger in the air as we allow the thread of this message to be elaborated by the one known as Aaron. We briefly leave you in love and light. We are those of Q'uo.

Aaron: I am Aaron. I would like to address the question of the fear of moving beyond one's perceived limits, how one perceives those limits in the first place, and how it presents one with a choice: to let go and proceed, or to hold on to the perceived safety of shore, to the delusion of limits.

We start with the reality that you are unlimited and that within the illusion you perceive yourself as limited. While it is incidental to my main direction, I would point out that the perception of the self as limited is not an accident, but is a gift to help you to understand that you are unlimited. If there is never a sense of being limited but only the full understanding of the reality of your limitlessness, there would not be any inspiration or provocation for growth. So you hold up that ideal and want nothing more than to reach that ideal, noting the standards of your own behavior as well as the ways that you manifest in your life.

Because you are human you constantly fall short of the ideal, and yet you constantly ask yourself to let go of that edge on to which you were you holding and strike out again to cross the sea of truth. It is a very courageous act, and yet you rarely give yourself notice of the courage. You perceive the fear that asks you to hold back and you miss the beautiful bravery and love exhibited each time you take a new step. Does a child learn to walk with a parent who says, "Don't take another step, you'll fall!"—or with a parent who applauds each new step and picks that child up and takes away the hurt from the inevitable fall? How can you learn to pick yourselves up in this way? I believe this is the question Q'uo raised at the end of the preceding talk. Can you learn to cherish that self who so bravely tries again and again? Know that in this physical manifestation you cannot reach that perfection toward which the self yearns and finally come to an acceptance that reaching that perfection is not necessary. Rather, the yearning is a tool to build the strength and faith so that one begins to understand one's inner perfection.

When you make a choice, and it turns out to be an unskillful choice and brings harm to another because there was fear or anger or greed as part of that

---
[17] *Holy Bible*, Luke 7:48.

choice, there is that in the being that declines responsibility for that choice, that says, "I couldn't help it." But as you evolve to the point that all in this group today have reached, you have learned that you are always responsible. Can you see how difficult this is? You used to be able to make your choices in a less judgmental way, though they were less skillful, and there was more anger and blame. But now you truly know that you are responsible; it feels like a burden and not a joy. The question, then, becomes how to make that sense of responsibility appear as it really is, a joy and a gift, so that even your unskillful choices can be met with love and not self-denigration.

This is where we come back to what I spoke of earlier, about allowing rather than forcing. When you come to a place of choice and understand the responsibility for making a skillful choice, and yet at times don't see the fear or greed or anger until it is too late, that distorts that choice so that another feels pain from it. When you come to that place and there is a sense of fear, of, "What if I make the wrong choice?"—that fear shuts out the flow of energy, shuts out the flow of knowledge within the spirit. When you can come to that place with a prayer, opening yourself to all the love coming from within the self and coming to the self from without, then the voices of fear or anger or greed are heard as voiceless echoes. Then there is a joyousness about that responsibility because you see that it is leading you into being a mature being, into blossoming into the light.

Q'uo spoke of the separation of self from self. All of you, at one time or another, fail to notice the positivity within the self, the generosity, the patience and loving-kindness; all of those beautiful qualities which are part of this beautiful being that you are. Then you judge yourself and focus on all of the qualities that you judge as negative: the impatience, the anger, the greed. I would suggest that two practices may be helpful for you. One is to begin to notice more and more carefully all those times when you are loving and patient and kind, to begin to allow this beautiful self to move into the sunshine of its own love. This is not pride. It is reality. Also, it is useful, when one perceives oneself as love and will not allow that this is so, to ask why you will not allow it. Why does one pay attention only to those qualities that are perceived as negative? One must then begin to see that there is something in the self that wants to cling to those qualities that are felt as negative, even while it begins to move on into the light. There is a yearning for that light and for the full knowing of oneness, and yet there is that within the self which feels unworthy. In the book with which I think most of you are familiar, called *Dark Night of the Soul*, St. John of the Cross suggests that the soul feels itself to be unworthy of God and yet yearns toward connection with God. And although it feels itself to be unworthy, the force of its love is what gives it the courage to seek that connection.

How can you allow the force of your love to come to the forefront of your awareness so that it can lead you into the full knowledge of all that you are and always have been, to lead you past that fear that calls the self unworthy? You are both. As long as you are human, you are not intended to be perfect. What you perceive as limitations are not limitations at all, but merely the teaching tools offered by this density. You do not have to get rid of fear or anger or greed. All you need to do is to allow what beauty is there to flourish and bloom. And the fear and anger and greed will fall away, because the knowledge that was gained from them is no longer needed.

The most important tool here is awareness: knowing always what is being felt; and if anger or greed are being felt, touching those, not with judgment but with an acceptance that allows the being not to need to act on those emotions. It is not the emotions themselves that are a problem. You don't harm another by feeling greed. You harm another by taking what belongs to another.

How much more lovingly can you begin to respond to all these forces within yourself? As you do that, the need for them will pass. It is as if you were swimming across a river and there were 100 floats to hold on to. Moving across the river, you swim to one of them and grab hold to keep you afloat. And yet as you look, you say, "They mar the beauty of this scene. I don't want them." But in one aspect of you, you know that if you get rid of them and your swimming ability is not yet refined enough, you will drown. So you leave them there, noticing that they mar the beauty, but also that they are useful until you have perfected your swimming so you do not need them anymore. At that time, they will simply drift away.

I believe that Q'uo has something to say here and would like to pass this to my brother/sister at this time. That is all.

Q'uo: I am Q'uo, and greet each again in love and light.

We are attempting to offer tools and resources to the third-density entity for working toward the state of allowing and accepting. A great resource for doing work in consciousness is creative visualization. The closer the visualization comes to resonating with the timbre of memory, the better the chance that it will aid the entity at deep levels of emotion, those levels of emotion which contain true wisdom. Such a visualization about the loving self might be such as this: Within you lies the small child which is attempting to do well, and [which] perceives the self constantly through the awkwardness of childhood as failing to be adequate to its own requests of the self. Picture, then, the loving self; and you are indeed all very loving entities as the nurturing parent. Would the parent within you turn to a child and scold it when it has acted in self-perceived error, or would the loving parent take the child into the cradle of its arms and place the child's head where it can again hear the heartbeat of the womb?

The child is afraid of the vampire which it has seen in a movie, and so it wakes to nightmare. The parent moves swiftly to the child's side and offers it a sense of proportion. It does not make fun of the child for having the nightmare. It is aware that each entity has its nightmares, its fears; but when the child is cradled upon the breast of the nurturing parent, it quickly becomes comforted as the parent says, "This was a true nightmare. There are truly portions of consciousness which are terrifying. That is the way that that is. But that is only a small portion of you, my child, my beloved one." As the parents rock and nurture this baby child, the feelings of safety, of security, and of being loved slowly and gently allow the child to accept its own vampire and to find that it is not so scary after all; that vampires, too, fall under love and care of the nurturing parent. Thus, one may invite into the self that vampire, realizing at last that although the vampire is a part of the self (and any other image is equally acceptable here), it is not the totality of the self. Thus, may your own lovingness be shined as the light that it is into the darkness of that child which is fearful.

When this inner child becomes stronger, it is, as children are, willful. Thusly, it is well for the visualization of the nurturing parent cradling the child to become more organic, more within a flowing process. The child, newly strong now, is willful. The loving parent is wise to advise the child to be silent, to let not the outer expression of new realizations become important.

It is not at all important that others know the insights one has gained, for these insights are fragile, just as the infant is fragile. They must be treasured and protected as they grow stronger. When the child is willful, the loving self gently reminds the child within that it may remember all the many times that willfulness has not been a skillful choice of attitude; for in willing from within the conscious mind, there is an ignoring of the greater will of the Higher Self which is lost in the Creator so that self and Creator are truly one. These tantrums of will may be gentled and healed by that nurturing parent until the child sees clearly that its will is likely not to have a very intelligent or spacious perspective.

It is not that it is incorrect to will or to use the faculty of will, but rather, that such will must be seen as sacramental so that one is aware when one uses the will, sees that volition for the choice it truly is, and surrenders that short-sighted will of self in the mundane sense, utterly and completely, moment by moment, to the will which speaks from a vast perspective of thousands of years, shall we say.

It is written in your holy works that the yoke of Christ, or the yoke of Christ Consciousness and acting according to that level of thinking, is easy, the burden is light. This may be examined as a deep truth. One within incarnation always carries baggage, always has something strapped upon its back to carry. For in finity, which the body expresses perfectly, there is always perceived effort; that is, effort perceived as effort by the self. It is the work of faith to enable that small child that is nurtured by the loving parent within to present to that child's eyes a view of an whole and unified process. It has learned that it can use its will; and if treated gently and with respect, it shall learn to choose that will which is most well informed, which has the spacious perspective. In this way of service, one approaches such a light burden, such an easy yoke, that one becomes free. In surrendering a small volition, one is able to hear, at last, the volitions of love itself.

Thus, one who does the will of the infinite Creator is simply listening more skillfully to the voices within. One of the many conversations one has endlessly with the self is a conversation with that Self which is the Creator. How splendid and glorious it is that that which is of the dust of the earth yet may speak with the Deity and be heard, and then hear also what the will of that Deity is. Then one is free to do the best one can, single-mindedly and with a full and generous heart.

One aspect of the self is well encouraged by the nurturing parent; that is, the sense of humor. One may perceive oneself without humor and thus become heavier and heavier with the weight of solemnity. Yet does not any play, even a tragedy, have its moment of heartfelt release and catharsis?

And how much of life may be seen by the self as the soap opera or the cartoon? This is not to denigrate the importance of the self or of service, but to allow the sense of humor to strip outer experiences of fearfulness. When one may undress the object of fear and see it, however allegorically, in its boxer shorts—preferably those sprinkled lavishly with hearts, frogs, or golf clubs—one then sees the vulnerability of that object of fear. It is only strong when it is dressed majestically. Thusly, in not accepting a solemn and heavy view of the present moment, one is allowing a sense of proportion, an ever-growing spaciousness of attitude. Humor is the beginning, in many ways, of full acceptance of self, which eventually very nearly silences the voice of fear within.

We would at this time move into the contributions of the one known as Aaron. We leave this instrument in love and light. We are those known to you as the principle, Q'uo.

Aaron: I am Aaron. It is a joy and delight to work in this way, with Q'uo and me stimulating each other through our ideas, and also with the sharings of each of your thoughts which you have sent to us. I wish to thank Q'uo especially for reminding me of the importance of humor and must stress my strong agreement with what Q'uo has said—that with humor comes the beginnings of acceptance. There is much more that could be said here; and yet in the interests of this session not becoming heavy, I would simply like to open myself to your questions rather than speaking on with my own thoughts. That is all.

Carla: How may one help another to begin to perceive this process? It is easier to work with the self, by far, than to create useful and persuasive inspiration for another seeker, which has its own journey, its own priorities, and its own keys. Perhaps in essence I am asking how one can serve as inspiration while completely observing free will.

Aaron: I am Aaron. In serving another in this way there are two factors of key importance. One is that you can only learn for yourself. You can open the door for another, but you cannot push him through. To attempt to do so is a violence against that being. Thus, if you see another's misunderstanding, you may gently and lovingly point out that misunderstanding while assuring the being that it has your full acceptance and love, whether it accepts that misunderstanding or not. That is fully its choice. You are concerned that even to state that the misunderstanding is seen could be a violence. It depends how you phrase it. If you say, "You're wrong. Look at this!" and reach out to shake another to make him understand, that's a violence. If you simply say, "We have a different perception of this, and I see it differently. Are you willing and interested to hear how I see it?"—and if that being then says, "No," of course that's it; and if that being says, "Yes, how do you see it?" then you can share the way you see it, and then it is his choice to select helpful thoughts and leave the rest behind. So that is one way you may be of service.

And the other and more important help is through the example of the self. Mistakes are corrected through constant work on oneself; and a deeper level of honesty with the self develops so that one becomes a shining example. But be ever mindful that this self that one offers as an example is also imperfect, that there will be errors. There will be unskillful choices. The example, then, is not to be perfect but to accept the imperfections in the self and in other selves with love.

Here I would like to stop, unless there is further specific question upon what I have said, and offer Q'uo the chance to speak.

Q'uo: I am Q'uo. We greet each in love and light once more and suggest that this be the final portion of this working, as this amount of material is sufficient for one, shall we say, meal for the heart and spirit to digest. We would not be heavy on the dumplings when offering you the good protein of thoughtful insight.

We would simply ask the self how powerful it thinks it truly is? The concept of being able to infringe upon free will by an opinion is deeply narcissistic, deeply aggrandizing the mundane self's power. Once again, there is the shadow of control, of fear. Why would this instrument be afraid of speaking honestly with its opinion or offering itself as channel for the opinion of one whose opinion the instrument values? Can this instrument or any other leap tall buildings at a single bound? Can this instrument or any other single-handedly destroy or create, or add height to the body or length to the life? Where is this notion of powerfulness?

You see, the true power is always in the Creator. Thus, as one stills that narcissistic concern, one allows oneself to become transparent; one becomes as that city upon the hill in your holy works, shining for all to see.

The very natural human tendency is to listen to a needy person, to accept that person's expression and then to say, "Yes, I respect that, *but …*" In that little word there lies the shadow of fear, of separation. Rather, can one not be humble enough to allow this entity to express and express until it is done?

And if it does not ask the opinion, or ask the opinion of an entity which one is channeling through one's instrument, that is perfectly all right. There need be no "Yes, but …" type communication. It is only if that other self invites either one's own opinion or the opinion of the contact that one may offer the opinion in a very righteous and feeling manner.

When one hears the question mark, one knows that the seeker's heart is ripe and ready for the picking, for the aid. When each hears itself say, "Yes, but …" to one who is vulnerable and needy, one may simply observe the fear of that, the fear for another being as foolish, and fear for the self. Thus, one is free to ignore. Nearly perfect expression of a life lived in faith with no "buts" but only a loving awareness of the flowing of all that is necessary to learn, moving to each one, through each one, and sweeping into infinity—that is the true nature of consciousness as an Infinite Intelligence.

Allow yourself to stop being a bubble and to become the ocean. Allow yourself the luxury of being asked before speaking, and of feeling no responsibility for those who do not ask questions. The skillful help one may give the entity who does not ask questions, but is suffering, is simply to allow the overwhelming compassion within and send, out of fullness of Self, that loving and healing energy of acceptance of that other self just as it is, with all of its self-perceived imperfections. This acceptance is as much a catalyst for another, although it is not aware of that, as is the verbal acceptance. Entities prefer verbal acceptance because they do not understand the depth of their own perceptive abilities. Honor this simple holding of another in compassion, acceptance and forgiveness. And honor, above all, that same attitude toward the one named self, that everlasting child within which is bound to make unskillful choices again and again.

We embrace you all, as does the one known as Aaron. It is indeed a privilege and a great deal of fun for us to dance together with these concepts. We delight in each other as one flowing stream. How beautiful is this service, and how grateful we both are to the dedication and love which allows this calling to come to us. We thank each as we participate in the great work which ever goes on, the work of learning to cease the striving, to still forever the child's fears. We leave you in the love and in the light of the one infinite Creator and recede from your consciousness at this time. We are those of Q'uo. Adonai. Adonai. ☙

The Aaron/Q'uo Dialogues, Session 5
March 3, 1991

C: I would like to know how to draw anger out of my son and reestablish a calm relationship with him. There is a lot of pent-up anger and it comes out in inappropriate behaviors. He is a very sensitive, bright child. He never felt that he fit in anywhere. He has never felt like he belonged anyplace that he's been. He's never been able to adapt to just functioning in the everyday world. He tends to be off in his own world quite a bit, and he can't reconcile the two and it comes out in anger which is expressed physically and that type of thing.

Aaron: With greetings and love to you all, I am Aaron. It is indeed a blessing and a gift to be invited to join you tonight and speak to your heartfelt concerns. Before we go any further, I want to make sure that Barbara is being heard above the computer hum, especially by Carla.

(Pause)

This question of working with anger in another, of helping another truly in any way, is a difficult one. You love your son and don't want to see him in pain. Each of you wants so much for your children, and yet each of you can only learn for yourself.

You cannot learn for him. It becomes useful to begin to differentiate where you hope to learn for yourself through your son's anger and where it becomes a matter of wanting to take away his anger because it is painful to you.

I am going to start here with something that you all know; but sometimes it is very hard to accept, especially when the one involved is one you love. You cannot take away another's pain. You cannot deprive them of the experience of that pain, nor can you know why they have moved into such experience. That knowing is for the wisdom of their own soul. You can create the learning situations and the loving and accepting environment that will allow that which is not angry in your son to flourish. You can nurture all that is not angry within him, but only he can work with his own anger. I don't mean that to sound hopeless. There is much that you can do. I only want to point out here that to try to take away his anger is a form of violence to him. You say he has always been very sensitive. He, in his wisdom, has created certain situations in his life, including choosing you to be his father so that he might work with that which most needs to be healed within the spirit.

First, try to separate your discomfort at his anger, knowing that that is work that needs to be done not on him but on you. In short, if he needs to be angry, can you simple let him be angry? Can you reach that place in yourself where he feels from you only complete acceptance, that there's not that within him that is unacceptable to you? This may help him more than anything else you can give him, because surely he already judges his own anger; and if he finds that unacceptable to you, it will increase the depth with which it is unacceptable to him.

How well do you accept your own anger? This is another way that you can teach him. I seem to be saying this a lot this weekend. There is nothing wrong with anger; there is nothing bad about the emotion of anger. It's just a feeling. When you use that anger as a reason to act in an unskillful way toward another, then you have a problem. Then you are creating disharmony and adhering karma. But the emotion of anger is simply the emotion of anger. It's not the anger that's a problem, but your relationship to the anger. Moving into yourself, then, are you totally loving and accepting when anger arises, not needing to get rid of it or do anything with it but just to watch it? So many of you feel that anger must either be suppressed or acted upon, but there is this third choice, just to observe it: "Here comes anger … I wonder how long it will stay … there it goes …"

One of the things that all of you are here to learn is to approach—not to attain but to approach—non-judgmental and unconditional love for yourself and what you perceive as other selves. As long as there is that within you which feels unacceptable, then you judge the same to be unacceptable in others. I am not denying that anger causes you pain or that your son's anger causes him pain. But he will need to work with that pain on his own. So, the best gift you can give him is first to begin to look closer into your own anger and to reach a point where you truly can accept your own anger. Then you can begin to accept his anger, so that when he is angry he still feels love from you. In this way, he can begin to let that anger drop away, to be honest with himself about it, and to understand it more clearly.

The second gift that you can give him is to nurture all those qualities that are beautiful in him and help him to nurture that in himself. How much has his anger or sensitivity made him see himself as different and feel himself to be unworthy? While assuring him that neither his anger nor anything in him is unworthy, can you also nurture what is beautiful in him, including that sensitivity you spoke of, letting yourself feel how much you cherish that in him so that he may begin to cherish it in himself?

There is one more issue here that needs to be looked at. Why does a being choose to incarnate into a situation where he will feel different in any way, where he will become angry? Why does he choose to subject himself to those catalysts? It would seem to me that it is likely that you both have this issue of self-acceptance. Sometimes one needs the catalyst of anger in order to be challenged to look at one's feelings more deeply, to uncover the love, and to nurture that.

There is a story told about a spiritual teacher named Gurdjieff. This Gurdjieff had a spiritual community in France; and living in that community was a man that was intensely disliked by all, including himself. He was slovenly in his personal habits. He was rude and abusive to others. He did not do his share of the work. Finally, feeling the dislike that surrounded him, he packed up and left. Gurdjieff went after him and begged him to come back. The man said, "No," at which point Gurdjieff offered to pay him to come back. The people in the community were aghast. They said, "How can you bring him back?" Gurdjieff said to them, "He is the yeast for the bread. How can you learn about compassion and forgiveness when you live here in a community of such perfect harmony—beyond this one man—that you have nothing to be compassionate about, nothing to forgive? You need him to help you learn compassion."

One who chooses to incarnate into a situation where one lives with anger is choosing that situation to prod oneself, one might say, to learn a deeper level of forgiveness and compassion. Of course, one starts with the self, finding acceptance for that anger in the self so that one may not judge that in others, but may love that, and all aspects of all beings. How does one love another's anger? It is not the anger that one is loving, it is the spirit of the being itself, which is pure and holy and beautiful. The being is not its anger nor its greed nor its fear. And yet you constantly create this duality, and so much of your work is to move beyond that.

There is one more specific thing I want to say about your son. Please remember that each being is always exactly where it needs to be, regardless of surface appearances. For a parent with a child, this idea takes a high level of trust. You can open doors for him, but you cannot push him through those doors. You can do nothing with his anger but to love him and to love yourself. As you create that doorway through your own power of love, when he is ready he will walk through it.

There is a great deal more that could be said on this subject of anger and the specific question about the son. We prefer to end this teaching and allow Q'uo to speak, and listen to your further questions about this. That is all.

Q'uo: I am Q'uo. We greet you in the love and in the light of the one infinite Creator through this instrument, with thankfulness that you have called us and the one known as Aaron to offer our opinions. Take what each feels is his own truth and please leave the rest behind.

The communications of a spiritual nature which promise that the result of spiritual seeking shall be a simplified, comfortable and easy existence are promising the direct opposite of that which is the inevitable outcome of living the life as a spiritual seeker that is eager to accelerate the rate of spiritual evolution. This situation is one good example of this truth. Spiritual awareness often brings pain, for one is now responsible for an enlarged grasp of the nature of illusory catalyst and its purpose. The more one accelerates this pace of learning, the more one is responsible for creating a way of living in faith that is the equal of the concepts which have enlightened one.

One such concept is the spiritual truth that all are one, and that within each one there is all of the universe of possibilities of attitudes and biases. Thusly, when one experiences another's anger, one is, in truth, in terms of one's spiritual growth, gazing at the self. What one has not come to forgive in one's self, one feels far more keenly when the mirrors of intimate family members and friends express in any way. The son's anger then becomes a mirror held ruthlessly and clearly up to the face of the parent. The parent, in assuming that the child is separated from the self, is cheating the self of the valuable, accurate mirroring of the self to the self through the catalyst of another.

Let us gaze at anger towards the self, for this is truly the spiritual situation. Has this seeker allowed an awareness of its own anger to ripen and mature until it can look at that anger it feels without judgment? If all entities possess in potentiation all qualities, should it surprise one when a seemingly negative quality appears in the mirror? Must you turn away from the mirror because it is too painful to see the self which is that behavior and painful experience of the other self? The best teacher of accepting the negative aspect of the self is the drawing of the attention, as the one known as Aaron has so rightly said, to those many times when one is experiencing, either in one's own mirror of self to self or in the mirror held up by another to the self, all the loving, compassionate, helpful and wise portions of the self. The beginning of the healing of self-judgment is the awareness that the mirror does not always show the negative or negatively perceived aspects of consciousness.

Intellectually it is easy to say we are each all things; we contain all that there is. But much circumnavigation and rationalization is practiced by most spiritual seekers in order to avoid gazing into the mirror when it shows that which is perceived as negative qualities which the self, of course, shares, as it contains all things and all qualities. Thusly, the focus is upon the healing of the self; and that healing begins not with the head-to-head confrontation of self with the disappointment in the self but simply of the self. Sit with the self. Watch what arises and departs within the mind, within the heart. Watch each transaction to discover, not how to change the self but simply [how] to identify the self more clearly within the self. For until the spiritual seeker accepts itself as it perceives itself—that is, in a state of considerable error—it cannot gaze in compassion at the mirrors which reflect that self to the self.

The injunction to "Know thyself"[18] is primary and fundamental to a life lived in faith. Again, we emphasize that as the student of spiritual principles moves further in assimilating material, the responsibility for living the spiritual principles involved in that material becomes ever more challenging. The critical observer-self seems biased toward noting not what is right but what is lacking and by this unhappy habit, many have come to the conclusion that they are unworthy and incapable of becoming that which they wish to be. This is not so. The road does not end. It is, however, occasionally very bumpy and stony. Yet the pilgrim, when it is rested, moves on as best it can, clambering over debris and stony paths with the eye always upon this precise moment, this particular resonance of infinity as it intersects with the life-stream, perceived within the illusion as linear.

---

[18] Inscription at the Delphic oracle, as reported by Plutarch in *Morals*.

Always, infinity is at the behest of one which chooses to remember the infinite Creator and the love the entity has experienced from this great source of love. Thusly, in healing the self-judgment, the parent is then able to express itself as an healed and whole entity, and is thus able to give whatever it may find possible to give out of a fullness of heart, a total and 360-degree acceptance of the self, knowing that the self is indeed all things, positive and negative, as is perceived within the illusion. When this healing is complete, then the entity may simply sit with this anger from another and see it as a catalyst which has done its job already.

There is eventually no self-perceived need to assign any quality to the other self, for that quality has clearly been seen within the self and forgiven within the self. It is in this acceptance and rest that the child may come to believe that it is possible to be miserable and yet to be hopeful, for the child knows well the parent and knows well the parent's version of this same negative trait, as perceived within the illusion. When the parent authentically establishes an healed awareness of self, when it is capable of saying, "Just as I am, just this much is perfect in a way I do not understand but perceive by faith alone," then compassion flows from that womb which is the true heart, which is ever pregnant with the fullness of love and ever propagating itself in seeds of fullness out of fullness that may rain upon those about it. Thus, in finding the peace and acceptance of the self, one finds the acceptance of the unquiet mirror offered by another self.

(Pause while the tape is turned over.)

I am Q'uo. We continue. When one is able fully to accept that self, one then becomes the healer who has healed the self first and is willing simply to act as catalyst, as the light upon the hill which gleams forth hope to those who are mired in pain.

So much between parent and child is a learning for the child based upon simple imitation. When two spirits with the same sort of areas of perceived weakness are parent and child, it may clearly be seen that each is the teacher of each. Thus, in allowing the self to heal, one by definition has allowed the entire creation to heal.

What is concern but a kind of fear, fear lest that loved one not be happy? We ask you, can any entity create happiness either for the self or for another? The answer, as far as we know, is that happiness is like a visitor that never stays long. It brings its gifts, it holds in its embrace the self, it shares in rejoicing and love; and quickly, perhaps before the self has even grasped the source of this happiness, the weather of the emotions becomes cloudy and the happiness is gone, leaving the self, perhaps, to brood overmuch on loss of happiness.

What baggage creates anger? What is it that is picked up and held and cherished that creates the anger of the self? Perhaps we may suggest that anger, at base, is anger at the lack of complete acceptance of the self. Thusly, to work upon one's own anger, it is well to perceive the benefits of not striving to become anything, not trying to advance, but simply trying to allow an awareness of the full nature of the self, to be held in the gentle arms of that nurturing portion of the self. Once one's own inner child, which is often angry because of lack of control, has been clearly perceived, then the attempts of a young soul—that is, young within this incarnation—to control the environment in order to make the self heard or in some way more secure can be accepted as the spiritual process it truly is.

Each of you sees the self, unless one is careful, as a solid object; that is, a solidified being which is such and such a way. However, the present moment insists that there is no solidity of being or of the qualities of being, either positive or negative, but rather that the present moment flows from present moment to present moment to present moment. To see oneself in process, and that the process is ongoing in far more large terms than one incarnation, is to allow oneself the perception of the enormous malleability and plasticity of the self in process: The Creator is not done with any. None is finished. All are in process. Let this sink into the heart [so] that it feels less and less judgment; and when it experiences judgment, it accepts that judgment also as a portion of the self. When all is seen clearly, choices may be made more skillfully. Once the element of fear is removed, the loving heart is content to offer itself without condition and without over-concern for the pain of a beloved other self.

Is there at this time a following query?

C: Both you and Aaron seem to have anticipated the further queries that I would have had. I thank you for your words, and hopefully I can begin further work upon myself. Thank you.

Q'uo: I am Q'uo. We thank you, my brother. We would at this time allow the vibration of the channeling to move to the one known as Aaron for any further question. We leave this instrument, briefly, in love and light. I am Q'uo.

T: I have just a short question. Most was answered by the previous channeling. My question is, in my life I am looking for love, for someone to be with and share my life with. I realize that I have to accept myself, and there are many things about myself that make me angry and that I cannot accept. I realize that I have to do this first. My question is, While I attempt to accept myself, am I being counterproductive in even attempting to find this love outside of myself?

Aaron: I am Aaron. I understand your question. It is never inappropriate for the heart to seek what it desires. Yet I believe the confusion here comes from not being certain what is desired. There is that part of you which finds itself to be lovable and loving, and wishes to share that love with another self. The fact that you have not yet been able to do that speaks to the fact that there is also that within the spirit that pushes away that intimacy. In short, when you think that you want something and yet hold yourself back from that, you must ask why.

I see a number of possibilities here, and would ask you to choose what seems most appropriate to yourself and discard what doesn't fit. One possibility is that while such intimacy is desired, there is also that in yourself which feels unworthy and is afraid to open itself so closely to another for fear that another would recognize that unworthiness. I spoke of this earlier today to a friend, saying that within each being there is what I call the *what-if-someone-found-out?* space. You see yourself as a loving being. You have work to do, yes, but [are] still a loving being, a spiritual seeker, and a good and caring person. And yet within the self there are so many emotions, so many forces that you can't accept, that each of you cannot accept. You are each like an iceberg with what is acceptable being that small bit that shows above the surface and so much buried that you have not been able to accept. As you progress on your path and become mature and responsible and more highly evolved, you become harder with yourself. When there is anger, rage, greed, jealousy, or fear, there is a strong "I shouldn't"; but you can't keep this separate from the self.

Q'uo and I have been speaking about fear and how it arises, and the point was made that the newborn infant experiences fear because its needs are not met. No matter how attentive the parents, there are times when that infant's needs are not met, and it knows that it cannot care for them itself. Q'uo pointed out that there is terror there.

One must then accept that fear and other emotions are meant to be, in some way, part of your experience, that one does experience emotions, and that these emotions are here to teach you. When you are incarnate in a physical form, you have both an emotional and a physical body which the being who goes beyond the astral plane does not possess. These are your tools for learning. This physical manifestation, this form, and the emotions are part of the complete being in this human form. You are never going to free yourself of emotion. It's impossible while you are a human. And it is not the emotion that's a problem, but how you relate to it. You see that rage or greed or whatever it may be, relate to it with hate, and say, "This doesn't fit with the being I want to see myself as or the self-concept that I want to impart to others. What if someone finds out?" I do not know to what degree this is true for you, but for many it becomes a strong factor in keeping them apart from a closeness with others, even when they long for that closeness. I would suggest that it would be worth exploring.

Another factor, that often enters into one's ambiguity as to whether there will be or there will not be a close relationship, is the learning about separation and oneness. So many beings incarnate on this earth to experience the strong sense of separation. It is a gift to teach you. When you feel the pain of that illusion of separateness, eventually it becomes painful enough that you must truly probe and study and investigate it. Then and only then do you begin to look at reality, which is that you are not and have never been separate. The sense of separation is painful; so are the heavy emotions that we just discussed.

I am not implying that your learning must be painful. Pain doesn't teach you anything. Pain is, if Carla will excuse a bad pun, a pain in the neck. But pain screams, "Pay attention!" and paying attention teaches you. When you can learn to pay attention without pain, you will need far less pain to learn. When you can pay attention to the ways in which you feel separate and move past that wall of pain and anger that enhances the sense of separation, finding acceptance and forgiveness for all of that in yourself which has created the illusion of separation, then you will no longer need that illusion.

There is one further thing I would say here. So often you seem to hear two voices within you. One, that comes from the heart, is a voice of love, and one, that we would call the voice of the brain or of reason, is often a voice of fear. You have one voice within you that asks you to trust yourself and trust others, to allow yourself to open, to cherish that beautiful self within as a bud, bringing it into the sunlight of your love. And then there is the voice of fear, and it says, "Well I have work to do on myself. Maybe I'm not ready for a relationship." Do you see the excuses there? Can you see the avoidance? There is always work to do on oneself, no matter how evolved you become. You are never complete but always in progress. Do you wait for perfection? Can you begin to see that it is the voice of fear that suggests that you wait and to ask yourself with some compassion, "What am I afraid of? What is this fear?"—not to track it down analytically as it grows out of this or that event of childhood, but to begin to see all the anger and lack of self-acceptance behind it and to relate to that with love and compassion?

It is so hard to have compassion for yourselves. Each of you here would respond with great love if someone else had told you your own story. But to yourselves you turn only judgment and contempt. It is not that you need to become more lovable before someone will be interested in you enough to have a relationship with you. It is not that you need to become more lovable, to have enough to offer to another so that it seems right to offer yourself; rather, it is that you need to love yourself enough and to trust.

Know that when you open and trust there may be pain. At times, the trust will not be met with the same level of love and trust. Begin to take everything in your life as a learning experience, to know that being alone and lonely is teaching you something, opening yourself and allowing yourself to be vulnerable to another is teaching you something. Finding a deep and loving relationship with another will teach you something. What is it that you need to learn? It is so hard to let go of the edge of one's current perceived illusory limitations and strike out across the vast sea of consciousness, letting go of the shore, of the safety of that shallow and safe beach, to move into deeper water, not knowing where one is going. Indeed, one often feels like those early explorers who wondered if the world was flat and if they would fall over the edge. That story appeals to many because of the depth it holds in one's own unconscious mind. How difficult to let go of the edge and proceed with faith and courage that one is always where one needs to be, and that the next learning offered, whether it is of loneliness of or love, is exactly what one needs. If one is able to accept that love that is offered and to move beyond the fears a bit, not getting rid of the fear but allowing it to fall away as it is no longer needed, then one finds that a world of love is offered.

I feel that you have specific questions about what I've said, but I would prefer to let Q'uo speak now; and if those questions are not answered in what my brother/sister says, we would be glad to return to them. That is all.

Q'uo: I am Q'uo. To continue this thought, we would bring the attention back to a fundamental concept regarding the nature and purpose of the third-density incarnational experience. Earlier this instrument was singing a phrase from your holy works, "for he is like a refiner's fire."[19] In this pioneer density, it is not expected that all the slag and dross of self shall be purified. It is expected, rather, that in the darkness of unknowing and by faith alone, one may see that the incarnational experience is a process, first of choosing the way that the self wishes to be distilled, of what essence it wishes to smell; and then having made that fundamental choice of how to love, opening oneself to the very painful process (to the self, which does not like to change) of distillation or refining. This instrument often sings a prayer which is, *"Temper my spirit, O Lord. Keep it long in the fire. Make me one with the flame. Let me share that upreaching desire. Grasp it Thyself, O my God, Swing me straighter and higher. Temper my spirit, O Lord. Temper my spirit, O Lord …"*[20]

The densities above your own are densities in which this refining process progresses from the point at which you are when you graduate from the third-

---

[19] *Holy Bible*, Malachi 3:2, and the text for a bass solo from Handel's oratorio, *Messiah*.

[20] A hymn often sung at camp in Carla's childhood. The hymn book used is no longer to be found.

density schoolroom. Shall we say that in third density, the Higher Self, which is the Creator, evaluates and grades, shall we say, using the curve, as this instrument would call it. There is not absolute perfection possible. Thusly, one is simply hoping in a relativistic way to approach nearer and nearer to a heartfelt dedication to begin the refining process in a conscious manner, not simply reacting to the stimuli in this thick darkness of unknowing but choosing rather to live a life in blind faith and to prosecute that first choice of service to others which does begin in love of self with every possible vehemence and passion.

There is always much to forgive when the self perceives the self. We suggest that each entity may helpfully see all the dross of self, not as shameful but as inevitable—as, to use the one known as Ram Dass's phrase, grist for the mill. Thus, one can refrain from fear of one's own fears, anger at one's angers, judgment at one's own unskillful judgments, so that the process may be seen mercifully, that the self may see that the self plunges into the furnace by choice. Yet we would suggest that loving-kindness and mercy be a portion of self-awareness, so that one is able to move into the refiner's fire only when it will not do violence to the young, precious spiritual self that was born immaculately within when the first decision was made of how to serve the infinite Creator. The choice to serve others is not a conclusion; it is the cornerstone or beginning of a process of distillation that will continue for a long, long time, as you understand time.

We would conclude with a comment about emotion. Entities over-value the intellect because it seems to the intellect that one has only the intellect with which to analyze situations. In the strict sense of analysis and linear thinking, this is so. Yet by depending upon that analytical ability, the attention is drawn from the true intelligence of the self, the true seat of wisdom, which is the mercy seat of purified emotion. It is not *your* lack of self-acceptance, it is *a* lack of self-acceptance, a quality which you now dip into and experience and use. It is not personal to you. It is an emotion felt by you and [by] many. In emotion one is never alone, for the emotions run like the underground waterways which bubble up in clear springs at their own time and season. One who wishes to dig a well to tap this underground or subconscious source of the water of spiritual refinement needs to go gently, to go deep carefully, so that one rather woos or courts the earth away which lies between it and the water of purified emotion, which is a portion of the deep wisdom of the self. Honor each emotion. Look at it as you would gaze at a gem, at a crystal. You may see it as imperfect, but it is your truth. As you turn that crystal, flawed as it is, you may see that though it refracts light unevenly, yet the refraction is full of beauty and color. Thusly, in honoring the emotions for the wisdom that they truly convey, one is able to bear the pain of self-revelation, which is the essence of conscious entrance into a safe and gentle refining fire, a fire that does not burn away that which you still need.

We would at this time allow the energy of the group to move back to the one known as Aaron. We leave this instrument, briefly, in love and light. I am Q'uo.

Aaron: I am Aaron, and it is with love and joy that I share this process of responding to your questions with the principle known as Q'uo. I speak for both of us when I say that it enhances our understanding as well to listen to each other and to your own thoughts, and to investigate these questions more fully. We have by no means exhausted any discussion of fear or anger; and yet, perhaps enough has been said for tonight.

Are there further questions that any wish to ask?

Questioner: R would like to know[21] if the work begun in healing the child within, and which was left undone after discovering it, plays a significant part in his current illness.

Aaron: I am Aaron. I am troubled by the question because of the place of self-judgment from which it comes. We have spoken with R and find much anger within him at the self. His assumption is correct, and yet, he must be helped to understand the desire within him to use that assumption to simply blame himself further; that it will become simply another object of anger, another source of that anger. Can you see how easily this is distorted? It is necessary to be truthful with him. And yet, if I were speaking to him in person, I would stress instead the healing that is needed, the opening more compassionately to the self. Rather than putting the focus of the attention on what has not been done, I would put the focus of the attention on what it is possible to do. Is this

---

[21] Offered in absentia for R.

answer sufficient, or would you prefer me to speak on it?

(The questioner indicated that this was sufficient.)

Are there further questions?

M: My question has to do with pain and the emotions that surround pain as a messenger. One technique that I've learned in looking at the pain is to be soft with the pain, to resist not. I wonder if you could elaborate on how one learns to soften more. I think that is enough.

Aaron: I am Aaron. I understand your question. As you know, this technique is a very valuable one. It would be useful to look deeper at why it works. What does softening around pain mean? I would like to suggest the value of investigating the difference between pain and suffering. Pain is just pain. That doesn't mean it's pleasant, but one can deal with a great amount of pain without its causing suffering. Suffering comes to your resistance to pain and is very different. We speak here both of physical and emotional pain and suffering. When you struggle with what is, wishing it away, hating it, you create suffering for yourselves because you cannot control what happens in your life. You've seen this countless times. You are happy and everything is beautiful, and suddenly it has been turned upside down. You are picnicking with your loved ones in the sunshine and it begins to pour. And you hate the rain! You are hiking on a beautiful trail with exquisite views and begin to rub a blister on your foot. How can you avoid pain?

Q'uo spoke earlier of happiness. As it comes and goes there is a much deeper level that one can reach than happiness. What is happiness? It's not something that comes from sunshine on a picnic or freedom from a blister on a hike. It comes from a place within that knows that whatever happens is okay. I would suggest the term equanimity here—a deep space of acceptance where one lets go of the need to control, where there is neither aversion to what is nor a grasping for what is not. This does not mean that one does not give energy to try to make things better. But there is a difference between preferring that something be a certain way and working toward that preference, and needing it to be that way. When you need it to be that way then you create suffering for yourselves, seeing suffering, then, as resistance to what is, even to the point of hating what is.

I would like you all to try an experiment with me. I would suggest that Carla not do this. Hold out an arm, just hold it up while I talk. I will go on to other things and allow this arm to become heavy, allow you to feel some pain.

What I want you to begin to look at is the difference between the pure physical sensation of discomfort that you call pain and that within you that hates the pain, that wants to put the arm down, that says, "This is enough"—the struggle to make it go away. As you begin to sense that struggle, whether it be with physical pain, with an emotional pain, with anything in your lives that brings intense discomfort, when you begin to see aversion to that discomfort, that fear is what you need to soften around. First, you notice the aversion, the wanting it to be different, the hating it the way it is, and you allow yourself permission to grieve for that which could not be. In its most simplistic terms, you wake up on the day of the picnic and see it pouring. You stub your toe and feel the pain, and know that because of that pain you won't be able to continue to walk, that your life will be uncomfortable for several weeks. Then you move into a space of anger and judgment. Finally, especially those of you who are more advanced spiritually, you say, "I shouldn't be judging; I shouldn't be angry," and that just increases the suffering.

I believe most of your arms are feeling heavy enough now to continue with this experiment. Can you begin to separate the physical discomfort from the suffering that comes from disliking that discomfort, allowing yourself the right to be uncomfortable? Experiment with this for a moment, and when you need to, put your arms down.

So there are two different things we're speaking about here. To soften around pain means to let go of the resistance to that pain. When you do that you are no longer suffering; then it is just pain, nothing else, and is far more easy to bear in that way. Second, when you notice the suffering, you begin to treat yourself with much more love. To honor the pain and respect it gives you a great deal of freedom from hating it.

There are many other techniques that can be used to soften around pain. Visualization is a great help here, especially when speaking of physical pain. Simply think of that being whose presence connotes love to one. It may be Jesus or whatever being of your choice. Visualize that being literally sending out love and light to that part of the body where there is pain, not lessening the pain, perhaps, because that may not be in its power nor may it be desirable that the pain be lessened, as it is there for a reason, but touching the heart that fights against the pain, the place of fear that says, "Will this pain never end?" because there is so much fear in pain.

Another thing that may help is remaining in this moment, because so much of the fear of pain is not that it's intolerable in this moment, but fear that it will continue till the next moment and the next and the next. When you can come back to this moment you can simply experience the pain with a far less intense need to get rid of it. What is pain? When you come back to this moment, you can begin to investigate it. You'll see that it's not solid as it feels at first. It comes and goes; it moves around. Sometimes it seems to peak, then to relax a bit, and then it returns. It is not a solid object with which you need to wage a war. How much more lovingly can you relate to it?

Finally, I would suggest a method whereby one visualize the blockage in that part of the body where the pain is concentrated. Visualize, if you will, your own inner energy as flowing through you and simply blocked at that point. A visualization that some have found helpful is to see themselves as lying in the bed of the stream … a hot sunny day and the water feels cool and refreshing; and it's flowing strongly, a stream with bubbling rapids. Lying with your head upstream, allow that water to flow in through the crown chakra, not forcing its way past any obstruction, as that would be a violence to the self, but allowing that gentle water to touch the obstruction with loving coolness, to remind the self where the obstruction exists so that the self may gently allow it to dissolve, not feeling any brutality at all but just the loving pressure of water that over a time erodes even the largest boulder. Allow that same loving presence gently to touch this obstruction, one sandy grain at a time, until the energy flow is restored. When there is an injury to some part of the body or a recurrent physical ailment, this continued use of this visualization may be helpful.

One of the things that may grow out of such a visualization is a clearer understanding of where the energy is blocked. When you experience a chronic illness, it will help you to understand why there is blockage in that area. I say this because you are each aware that you have certain weak points in your body; and when there is physical injury or loss, it seems to concentrate, for one in the head, for another in the stomach, for a third in the back, and so on. These are not by accident, but come from the cells' memories of past karma. One does not need to know the experience of the entire lifetime to have a brief glimpse that there was an injury there or violence to that area of the body, and that there is still holding or contraction there that needs your love and forgiveness to dissolve.

I believe that Q'uo has more to say to this, and rather than trying to answer it all myself, would prefer to share the answer. That is all.

Q'uo: I am Q'uo, and as we feel this amount of material is sufficient to engage the hearts and minds of those now sitting, this shall be the concluding response from Aaron and ourselves.

In parting, we would offer to each that which is not original or new, but that which seems at this particular moment to be helpful. We would preface this by saying that each entity is far more than it realizes itself to be, yet the ruthlessly literal nature of logical processes in which the mind is so often engaged creates a situation wherein the body is indeed the creature of the mind. But the body, in its literal hearing of the mind, expresses itself as literally as possible in response to catalyst that has not been used by the mind, thus expressing within the body in a very dogmatic and fundamentalist way, if one were to speak in terms of spirituality, those blockages or difficulties encountered by the mind as stimulus.

Thusly, we would ask each to perceive again that there are indeed, as we have been speaking of in these last few sessions, two hearts and two minds. The mental mind is shallow, but extremely useful for dealing with the illusion. The second mind is that heart or emotional self wherein lies deeper knowledge, deeper wisdom, and true awareness. Likewise, there is that heart which is the heart of wisdom and which would give anything and everything to ameliorate or palliate pain, either self-perceived or perceived by another who comes to the self for helpful advice. This first heart strives in its wisdom ever to become more wise, more purified in its emotions and its wisdoms. The second heart is indeed the heart which needs to be worked with in softening the self to "resist not evil,"[22] as the phrase goes.

This heart, whether male or female, can be imagined as a womb which is full, soft, and pregnant with unlimited fullness. Each time that one experiences the tightening of any portion of the physical vehicle, it is well to move gently, slowly, down this tree of mind and heart to the full heart, which gives a fullness without diminishing itself. Feel the tension in all of the body, but especially in this womb-heart and literally in the way the abdomen is tensed. One may even push at the abdomen to feel the degree of tension and explore this as a physical sensation. Then one may guide one's breath ever deeper, breathing in mercy and loving-kindness, allowing that rigid belly to be soft, literally soft. You will find that as soon as the attention wanders from the softness of that abdomen, of that womb, the belly begins once again to tense. The entire body, when facing the catalyst of pain, reacts quite literally in defense by tensing against a danger. Thus, it is very, very healing to work continually with patience at the unending task of relaxing that creature of mind which is the body, and especially allowing the breath to flow into the heart-womb, bringing its gentleness and its healing to dissolve tension, and breathing out all that tension in deep, spontaneous breathing, not to attempt to breath deeper than usual but simply to breath in visualized love, nurturing light, and spaciousness in which the self may relax.

In the case of a solidified pain due to illness, there are many, many layers of tension and tightness. Thus, it is not enough to do this exercise once or periodically, but rather to honor the self by paying the coin of attention and mindfulness that it deserves. Attend to the state of the tenseness of the body; and whenever it is perceived, in whatever company or circumstance, allow the mind to do its visualization of softening that heart-womb of fullness and allowing that fullness to give out of fullness into fullness at the cellular level for all of the body. Then, the feedback of body to mind becomes that which the mind cannot create; that is, mercy and merciful forgiveness.

May each respect its own striving to be more and more a channel for the love and the light of the infinite One, but may each also perceive the mercy and kindliness of a Creator which is love, and allow that love to inform ever more deeply the conscious being which often feels unloved.

You are all beautiful. The blending of your vibrations is that which gives us enormous aesthetic pleasure; and the joining of our hearts to yours in shared thought is a more precious gift than we can convey with mere words. So allow the love of the Creator which is channeled through us and through each other to rest upon you, now and in each moment. We would leave you in the love, the light, and the peace of the infinite One. We are known to you as those of the principle, Q'uo. Adonai. Adonai vasu borragus. ❧

---

[22] *Holy Bible*, Matthew 5:39.

L/L Research

L/L Research is a subsidiary of Rock Creek Research & Development Laboratories, Inc.

P.O. Box 5195
Louisville, KY 40255-0195

www.llresearch.org

Rock Creek is a non-profit corporation dedicated to discovering and sharing information which may aid in the spiritual evolution of humankind.

ABOUT THE CONTENTS OF THIS TRANSCRIPT: This telepathic channeling has been taken from transcriptions of the weekly study and meditation meetings of the Rock Creek Research & Development Laboratories and L/L Research. It is offered in the hope that it may be useful to you. As the Confederation entities always make a point of saying, please use your discrimination and judgment in assessing this material. If something rings true to you, fine. If something does not resonate, please leave it behind, for neither we nor those of the Confederation would wish to be a stumbling block for any.

CAVEAT: This transcript is being published by L/L Research in a not yet final form. It has, however, been edited and any obvious errors have been corrected. When it is in a final form, this caveat will be removed.

© 2009 L/L Research

Intensive Meditation
March 8, 1991

Group question: Dealing with the question this morning of why it seems to be that for each of us, throughout our lives, the mother and father relationship seems to be the most critical, the most important. The voice that we hear in our head when we do one thing or another and the voice to which we seem to respond in one pattern or another and why is it so critical as in criticizing?

(Carla channeling)

I am Q'uo and greet each of you this morning in the love and in the light of the infinite Creator. We are please to be called to your group, once again as it is a great joy to us to be able to share with you the great work in which we all collaborate. This being the work of attempting always to know more of the mystery of the Creator and in extending what aid we are able, to others in their attempts to do so, also.

As always, we ask that you consider our words carefully and accept for yourselves, only those words which resonate within the deepest self as true and to discard all others without a second thought. We would have you place no judgments on yourselves in considering our words.

You wish information this morning on the role each parent plays with the entity. You are aware that the relationship between each and its mother and father within this physical illusion is one which plays a central role in the life of each entity, beginning with the obvious fact that it is this relationship which allows each entity the opportunity for physical incarnation.

In addition, to this starting point, the mother and father are central teaching figures for most entities within your illusion for a significant portion of time of time the younger years of the entity and it is during this time that the basic personality of the entity is molded and formed and lessons desired in this incarnation are set up and well begun.

It is knowing the importance and centrality of this relationship that causes entities to set up these relationships before incarnation.

You wish to know why it is that these mothers and fathers, while playing, what would appear to be, a nurturing role in starting the young entity out upon its life path, so often have such a deeply, what you perceive to be negative effect upon the young entity which lasts throughout a great portion if not the entire lifetime.

You realize we must speak in some terms of overgeneraliztion as each relationship is most individualistic and specific and there are indeed many mothers and fathers who are perceived by their children to be adequate and loving nurturers however there are many who may, while attempting from their own perspective, to be as loving and nurturing as they know how, they yet, in the non-acceptance of the child entity in various matters which may be more or less perceived by them to be so, instill the child entity with the voice of criticism of which you spoke and indeed there are those mothers and fathers who do not find it in themselves to be nurturing and loving and find that all they have to offer is this voice of criticism.

"Why is this the case?" you ask. Many of your entities seem to have the bias of opinion that states that the role of the mother and father is properly that role of the all accepting, all nourishing, all loving parent and that whenever the parent entities fall short of this goal, they are then responsible for the damage incurred by the children.

This however, is not the case for as you are aware, the purpose for which third density entities have incarnated is in order that they might learn the lessons of love.

If each entity were born into a family where the only thing experienced was total love and acceptance, the experience of the entity would be similar to those entities who incarnated before the advent of the veil between the conscious and unconscious minds or before the availability of the choice between the positive and the negative paths, the result being that with no stimulus which is perceived as negative, very little growth takes place. Thusly, for one who incarnates for the purposes of learning the lessons of love, the perceived absence of love is essential in order that such learning may take place.

If the perception of love may be felt as total acceptance, then the perception of the absence of love may be felt by non-acceptance, which is manifested in the criticism of which you spoke.

The degree then, to which this criticism is perceived by the child entity from the parents may be seen as correlative to the lessons each entity wish to set up for itself, beginning with the infancy and early childhood. This relationship is by no means the only situation by which entities may learn these lessons of love, throughout the life, many other relationships and situations will be encountered in which again the non-acceptance or the criticism is experienced however, most entities will choose to set up these lessons early in the life pattern so that the patterns have got an attitude having been established at a very early age, have the opportunity to grow throughout the incarnation and interact with other situations that may be perceived similarly thus affording the entity multiplied, shall we say, opportunities for learning these lessons.

The learning of the lessons, of these lessons, as always with the lesson of love focuses again and again on the acceptance of the self and the other selves in the light

This group has done much work in this area, and these matters have been spoken of before. We would say at this time that we particularly enjoyed speaking with this group about these matters in what you see as your recent past and speaking and working also with the one known as Aaron and the one known as Barbara. We have been very pleased with the dedication of this group to such workings and feel that the interactions were of a great help to those present and a value to ourselves as well.

Thus the concepts of acceptance and forgiveness are those with which you are familiar.

We would reiterate only that in the dealing with the voice of criticism from the mother and the father that each entity may continue to feel and hear throughout the life pattern, that the purpose of the incarnation for the seeker is not to be comfortable and happy thus the goal of the seeker in dealing with this voice is not to make the voice go away, but to be able to accept it and continue to live the life. Gradually, becoming able to accept the self and the other self to greater extents and then becoming able to forgive the self and the other selves also to greater extents. This is not work which may be forced.

As the one known as Aaron has spoken about the need for the flower bud to be allowed to bloom.

We realize that it is a difficult process to proceed with a certain course of action in learning lessons and dealing with the self and at the same time not to judge ones progress. Yet this is what is necessary for the seeker, toward that end, we would encourage each in attempting to learn the acceptance. To focus on the present moment and not to attempt to swallow the entire life in a single bite, shall we say.

We feel that these words are sufficient at this time for this working and we'd be happy to respond further to any queries you may have at a later time. At this time we would transfer to the one known as Jim in order to close this working. We leave this instrument with thanks and in love and light. We are known to you as those of Q'uo.

(Jim channeling)

I am Q'uo, and greet each of you again in the love and in the light of the one infinite Creator. At this time, we would offer ourselves for the responding to any queries, which you may have for us. Is there a query at this time?

N: Not from me, Q'uo. I thank you for answering both of the questions that were *(inaudible)*.

I am Q'uo, and we thank each of you as well for your invitation to us to join your circle of seeking once again. We are most grateful for this opportunity and we cannot express our joy at these gatherings to a sufficient degree but can reaffirm that we feel a great peace and purpose is awakened each time we gather with your group. We are known to you as those of Q'uo and we leave you now in the love and in the light of the one infinite Creator. Adonai, my friends. Adonai.

Sunday Meditation
March 10, 1991

Group question: Some sources say that the Mayan culture was contacted by extraterrestrial entities and given information concerning this planet's transition to the fourth density. Is this information relatively accurate or should we look into other areas for a clear understanding of their culture? How can we use the information which has been left behind concerning their culture?

(Carla channeling)

We are those of Q'uo. We greet each of you in the love and in the light of the one infinite Creator. It is indeed a privilege to be here, to enjoy each energy as it blends into unity, the energy moving in such a rhythmic and lovely way about the circle of seeking. It is a blessing to share in your meditation, and we are most grateful to you for asking our opinion upon such an interesting subject of the ways entities might work to aid in the coming of the next age or series of experiences and lessons which shall be that which is suited to your planet in your future.

We encourage each to be aware of the oneness of the group and the energies of light that move about it, to allow them to flow through you to the next density, not moving or changing them but realizing that you are part of a whole which is greater than yourself, a beautiful group of people who, together, have much more power than any one separately might, power to ask, power to seek, power to hope. This is the greatest thing, we feel, that entities such as yourselves who seek to serve the planet at this time can possibly do. And that is to spend time in the seeking, in the being with the infinite One and those who seek the infinite One.

Let us begin with a few introductory remarks which we feel would make a good basis for the general message. We are aware that each within this circle has a different gift. This is so not only of each in the circle but of each entity that is ever created. Each of you is unique. No one has your gift or gifts. No one your talents but you, yourself. But if you sit thinking, "Well, I have gifts, but I also have difficulties," may we say that if you gaze at your difficulties you will find them to be the other side of the coin of your greatest virtues. This instrument, for example, spoke of its lack of memory. This is that which seems within the illusion to be thoughtless and rude. It is, however, that which allows us to fill this entity with our concepts, for this entity does not cling to the past nor think greatly on the future. It is within the present moment that each of you exists. Memory and prophecy are irrelevant to aiding the planet or to living in the most spiritually appropriate way of service to others that you can possibly devise.

We also realize that each has aspirations and hopes. Each hopes to be able to contribute and because of the culture in which you live you see these contributions as those which can be held, seen, measured and given to others as objects. Indeed, each of you may feel quite appropriate, wishing to serve in these ways. However, it is well to realize that that which is a creation of yours is that which has been given to you because you have honed your consciousness, begun the process of choice which more and more refines the self, the emotions, the self-images and the journey itself so that there is no outside authority that may say to you that "This and this is what you must do." Only you in your inner guidance may come to a sense of peace and creativity, a feeling that needs no outside affirmation, a feeling that this is right action. This occurs when the entity simply allows the Higher Self within to make known to the self the environment in which the gifts which each has are to be created and presented.

Behind all of these objects of creations, or may we say more accurately, co-creation with the infinite love and light of the Creator, is the infinity of Oneness, the primal beingness of which your consciousness is at this time an individuated field. Yes, each of you is unique. But each of you is created of Love, created with Love, created from Love, and within each of you is that which is pure, infinite, compassionate Love. Not the romantic love or a gentle sort of love, but a dynamic and creative love that burns away the dross within, that burns away the petty concerns so that you gently, quietly, allow that dross to be burned away, little by little, never judging the self, never allowing discouragement to last longer than is necessary to express it to the self.

When one feels discouragement, when one does not know what to do, one is generally used to blaming the self for this impasse. We would specifically encourage each to allow those feelings that are appropriate to a disappointment in the self, but to realize that they are but the disappointments of one who has made a mistake in spelling, and so the eraser is taken out, and the spelling corrected. There is no more weight to be given to such errors than errors of any kind. That which you have not yet learned you are not responsible for. It is only as you learn things that you do become discouraged. Yet the discouragement is predictable. Therefore, we ask you to cherish yourself and nourish yourself during these times of change, for as you seek you shall find that change has sped up, and change is painful to the mind that is distinct to the consciousness that all have in common.

You are asking your mind to refrain from being critical, whereas all intelligence is based upon the making of choices. You make choices each moment of each day. What you shall hear among all the things that come into the ear—when you are concentrating upon this instrument's voice you do not hear the cars, or the furnace, or the birdsong, or the gentle sound of the unpredictable wind. Yet your ears have heard them. You simply have chosen to focus the attention which is finite upon the most interesting thing in the environment. Each time that a seeker comes to the realization that it wishes a transformed experience, it is wishing for the pain of becoming the butterfly. The pain is left behind with the chrysalis in the cocoon and the butterfly is free and beautiful. This is the process of change. The change itself will seem to the physical vehicle and to the mind of the physical vehicle very painful and it is considered appropriate within your culture to allay or palliate any kind of pain or at least to be disgruntled because there is pain.

As spiritual beings we ask you to realize that your situation is that you are a field of consciousness. You are using a second-density creature which has offered itself up to you that you may use it for an incarnation. It does not have the same priorities of consciousness. It is more of a creature that is capable of fear than the consciousness, and that which is fear is also that which is desired. When one moves either in fear or in love to desire or to not desire, either is seen as a desiring. Thus, that which you desire positively comes to you, and we always remind each to be very careful of what you desire. However, that which you fear will also come to you, so we ask you also to be very careful about what you fear.

Now we shall begin with the question about specific ways of working in order to midwife the coming age, as it has been called. When one is dealing with a culture that is not one's own it may be seen in many different ways depending upon one's goal in aiding the planet as a whole to become more harmonious with the change taking place. If the desire is to be utterly accurate in detail then the requirements of both the mind of your physical vehicle and the requirements of your consciousness must needs be addressed. If a point is to be made in a completely fictional manner it matters only that the consciousness be allowed its intuitions and hunches.

Thus you may see that there are as many ways of determining the level of history compared to the level of intuition with which one shapes one's gifts as there are entities who may choose this form of service to others.

In the healing sense, also, there is the information which may be funneled into the mind from sources within the illusion which you share at this time; there is also the possibility of allowing intuition and intuition alone to aid one in finding one's own voice as a healer. Any combination of these two may again be considered appropriate by one's unique character, vibration or harmonics.

To one who wishes to use an object skillfully in order to aid in the birthing of the new age, again, one may go to those written words within your historical documents and find layers and layers of thought which have been crystallized in your writing. One may also simply sit with the object for it to offer that which it is and allow the intuition to arise to meet it. Any of these variations is acceptable. The place between one extreme and the other, between intuition and intellect, is equally acceptable as long as it is your true balance, that which you can stand behind and say, "This is I, this is the way I felt the need to do this."

Until you have settled upon that much it is well to ponder the self itself. For it is your self, your consciousness, that which is in the end in union with all that is, that will be the vehicle which is able to aid the planetary consciousness. All of the tools of the intellect are just that, tools which may be respected and used but only in ways which do not create fear. May we say that fear is indeed a denial of the oneness of consciousness and an acceptance of the illusion.

Now, each of you is aware that science describes this universe, this room in which you sit, to be specific, as a great emptiness within which, just as the night sky sparkles with stars near and far, the atoms and molecules of your bodies, of that upon which you sit, that of the air and of the floor, look back at you winking in the cosmic flow of energy. Each of you is galaxy upon galaxy, creation upon creation. There is in fact nothing but illusion and who you are is in the end that consciousness, that light being that is and was and shall ever more be, whether it is activated or has chosen to come once again into an awareness with the unpotentiated Creator. You are you. You are also all that you see and the Creator Itself. Within this illusion, however, each of you has made the vital choice that is the purpose of this entire density of learning, that choice being how to relate to the one infinite Creator. Shall you love the Creator by serving others, or shall you love the Creator by keeping others at a safe distance while you make yourself more powerful and thus more able to control your environment?

It may be seen that in one way you express unity, or that which is. In the way of separation you may see the acceptance of that which is not, the illusion that there is anything separate from anything whatsoever. There is in fact no separation at all. And as you rest back into this awareness you find no room or place for fear. It has never been a welcome visitor. We encourage you to bid it leave you when it wishes, not fearing fear, not judging fear, but simply saying, "This is fear. I know that voice." This allows you to become more and more skillful at making choices seemingly large and seemingly small. The greatest choices that you have to make are simply the choices of how you wish to be and this is indeed the heart of our simple message to you this day. No matter how you wish to be a midwife, no matter in what way you wish to assist the birth of a new vibratory rate of consciousness, the work that needs to be done is work within the self, for it is in your being, and not in those things that you do, that by far the majority of your service lies.

Think back to someone you have known. It may be a person of any age, sex or degree of estate in life, but that person, regardless of its race, intelligence, or color, or age, was lit up, illuminated from within. This entity somehow made you feel that hope was possible, that things were OK, that you were safe. That is because this entity had learned how to be a servant, had learned the hard lesson of disassembling the reliance on the rational thinking enough so that it was able to place more emphasis on the moment by moment considerations of the catalyst that it is being offered in every present moment.

It is in the present moment, as we have said, that one meets the infinite Creator, there and nowhere else. The present moment is always the intersection with eternity. You move in a river of time and space, and it is inexorable within your illusion. It is an excellent illusion. However, there is that x-axis and the y-axis, the x-axis being the inexorable movement of the river of illusion intersected by the y-axis of infinity so that each present moment has extravagant possibilities of resonance and of resonant, euphonious living and being. It is to those who dwell in the present moment in praise and thanksgiving regardless of the estate which they have within the illusion who are able to channel through themselves that infinite love that no humanity can ever engender.

For within the illusion you are indeed finite. The patience wears out. The temper snaps. The love is embittered by disappointment. It is only when one seeks to live a life in resonant faith—and this can be done only blindly and courageously—that one is able to tap into that endless love that rains upon each and wishes only to move through each and manifest within your illusion as only you with your specialness can do. No one else can bring this energy into manifestation but you. For although all light is one basic vibration, yet it is your choices through many, many lifetimes that have made you able to receive in just this way, and for just this way you may radiate it. When you come to the working of the various objects in order to produce a desired service for others then you are necessarily dealing with distortion and somewhat imperfect memory. We may say that a good deal of that which is written is written in so biased a way as to not only camouflage the spontaneous moment in which something is being described but even to change its nature in such a way that it seems like something else entirely. Thusly, when one does the research among those artifacts of your culture one must be prepared to deal continuously with those facts that seem to contradict or in some way modify that which you would wish to be the way you would wish to express to others that verity which you are seeking to express. In this we encourage each to use its special gifts by allowing them to do their work without interference of will, for when one has been hollowed out by this consciousness of fiery and creative love one is then precisely such and such a vessel, and that vessel more and more, as you allow it to be so, has its own wisdom, its own ways, and will be able to communicate those ways to you.

The allowing of a life in faith, then, is the primary resource which each entity may use regardless of its path of service in order to aid the infinite oneness which is more and more perceived as you enter a new area of the space and time river. This river has occasional bends in it, shall we say, occasional changes literally of the area of space through which the planet itself is traveling, this great spaceship, this island of yours you call Earth is rotating into a previously unpopulated vibratory pattern. It is doing this naturally and economically and the difficulties that you have spoken about are those difficulties of a difficult labor wherein the Earth itself must be able to continue its balance while receiving as the living being that it is these new cosmic influences and the new ways in which other cosmic influences from outside your sun system may come to you.

It is fortunate for those who wish to serve others upon this planet at this time that the most skillful way to serve is indeed by being. Each prayer, each moment in which you have thought of the one Creator becomes resonant and light-filled and the joy and light and peace of that contact with infinity moves through you along the x-axis of time and space and illusion, and beyond all illusion entities may be greatly touched and greatly helped simply because you are. Your consciousness is the greatest treasure which you hold within the hollowness of your Earthly, physical vehicle. Know it for its sanctity and purity and see that as these emotions and desires arise they arise repetitively again and again and each time you have the opportunity to move into resonance and into infinity and to make a more skillful choice, not out of fear, not out of worry that you may not be doing the right thing, but in perfect allowing of this moment to be this moment, of allowing that which you can never understand, that mystery which is the Creator to flow through you. Love flowing through Love into Love, fullness through fullness into fullness, all perfect, all beautiful and all one.

You may say to any who may say something like this, "This is not true. There are wars and rumors of wars. There is hunger. There is pain. Why are these things there, and how can we fix them?" that it is precisely for such experiences as these that you incarnated. It is precisely the forgetting of oneness that you wish to accomplish in your incarnation here. You did not want to remember the truth. You wanted to forget the truth and then find it again, for within an illusion where you cannot know even scientifically the root cause of anything you most certainly cannot know the root cause of those things which are invisible and which are immeasurable by the instrumentation of your peoples. You wished to be confused, chaotic and scared. Why did you wish this for yourself? Were you in some way mean to yourself? To the contrary. You were giving yourself an opportunity to live a life in faith alone. Nothing can be known, but you have all inside, each of you has all inside. And as one approaches the self, more gently, more quietly and more aware of the true nature of the self, one is able to see that one is indeed born again, as so many of your peoples have been distressed to hear the phrase. Born within as a self-aware, eternal light being, to aid the Earth that you so love, to aid the changes that must come. It is simply necessary to find who you are and then be who you are in the very most truthful way, the most honest way that you can. All else will follow.

When one accepts the higher wisdom of this mysterious love one is a servant, yet one is for the first time entirely free of the prison of flesh and bone, life and death. One has become a citizen of eternity. Give respect to that part of yourself that is being born with the so-called new age. Love that child within. Nurture it within your heart's womb. Talk to it. Cherish it. Nurture it. And as you cherish the growing awareness of who you truly are you open your eyes at the present moment and there is your service before you, precisely there. It may distress you. It may be a pile of dirty dishes. It may be a discipline problem with a child. It may be digging a hole. It may be anything whatsoever. If it is done in love and compassion and respect for this experience right now, it is the greatest service you could ever perform. For you are being an entity that approaches the illusion fearlessly and lovingly.

We would at this time transfer this contact to the one known as Jim. We thank this instrument and in love and light transfer. I am of those of Q'uo.

(Jim channeling)

I am Q'uo, and greet each again in love and light through this instrument. We realize that we have not spoken in a precise manner concerning some portions of your query for this evening and we would ask at this time if there are any questions whatsoever that remain upon your minds to which we may speak? We would also preface any responses by saying that we wish to give that which is helpful to you in your journeys of seeking, but we do not wish to be seen as those which are infallible, for, indeed, we are not infallible, and we give that information which we have found to be useful in our journeys. And we ask that you take that which is useful to you, leaving behind that which is not.

Is there a query at this time?

Questioner: I am still quite interested in the Mayan connection to the Pleiadians. Is this what was responsible for the beginnings of their peaceful culture?

I am Q'uo, and am aware of your question, my sister. As we look into that culture which has been called by many of your peoples the Mayan culture, we see that these entities through their desire to know more of that which you call the truth and their desire to progress as a people upon the evolutionary journey drew to themselves a variety of influences that were both of this planet and entities that had their location both within this solar system and beyond it.

(Tape ends.)

L/L Research

L/L Research is a subsidiary of Rock Creek Research & Development Laboratories, Inc.

P.O. Box 5195
Louisville, KY 40255-0195

www.llresearch.org

Rock Creek is a non-profit corporation dedicated to discovering and sharing information which may aid in the spiritual evolution of humankind.

ABOUT THE CONTENTS OF THIS TRANSCRIPT: This telepathic channeling has been taken from transcriptions of the weekly study and meditation meetings of the Rock Creek Research & Development Laboratories and L/L Research. It is offered in the hope that it may be useful to you. As the Confederation entities always make a point of saying, please use your discrimination and judgment in assessing this material. If something rings true to you, fine. If something does not resonate, please leave it behind, for neither we nor those of the Confederation would wish to be a stumbling block for any.

CAVEAT: This transcript is being published by L/L Research in a not yet final form. It has, however, been edited and any obvious errors have been corrected. When it is in a final form, this caveat will be removed.

© 2009 L/L Research

Special Meditation
March 20, 1991

Group question: Special Meditation for R and S in the area of long-term serious life-threatening illness. What does a person who is very much consciously aware of the necessity of maintaining balance in the life, of working out lessons, of facing the lessons, what does such a person do when there is an illness that continues to come back with various manifestations that puzzle doctors, that puzzle the person, that puzzle friends and family? What does such a person do in the way of realigning the thinking, the attitude, the being when everything has been exhausted, it would seem, in attempting to deal with the illness and the distortions of mind or emotions that have caused it? When all of the research into the childhood, the experiences of a traumatic nature during a life, and the lessons that one feels that are spiritually set before one have been explored in-depth and have been gone over very carefully? Is there a surrender and acceptance? Is it possible to push away the healing and the wholeness that we seek, by seeking too much? What would you say to such a person who is in need of the peace and the healing that comes with finding the wholeness and the integrity of the life pattern and how does such a person go about healing the mind/body/spirit complex?

(Carla channeling)

We are those of Q'uo. Greetings to each of you in the love and in the light of the one infinite Creator. It is a great privilege to be called to this group and we thank you for the intensity of your seeking and the harmony of your meditation. Both are great blessings to us and great teachers of us.

You ask concerning health and ill health. This is indeed a subject to which many approaches may be taken. If it is acceptable to each of you, we would find a somewhat different approach to be useful as long as it is acceptable to each that the material offered herein not be offered to other entities.[23] We will pause, while each considers this and if there is an objection, we shall speak in a more desired way. I am Q'uo.

Jim: No objection here, Q'uo. Continue.

I am Q'uo. Very well. We ask each to gaze upon that which has been accepted by each as a subjectively known truth. That is, that the experience of this particular density is not an experience which is the experience of a native of this density. It is, rather, the experience of one who moves into an incarnational experience in which the very vibrations of the entire culture are somewhat, shall we say, distressing subjectively to each. In other words, we are speaking to those whom the Confederation has often called "wanderers."

---

[23] We are grateful that S has granted permission to share this transcript with others.

Each of you knows a good deal about the transparency of third density illusion. To the various reflections, illuminations, and resources of the deep mind. Of the help available to and through the deep mind and of the continuing urgent necessity of being self-forgiven and self-accepting, being able to gaze, not only on all the world, in forgiveness and acceptance but upon the self. Because each of you has found this incarnational experience challenging, the aforementioned resources have been used to a great extent and we may simply go forward from there.

When a wanderer makes a decision to serve by moving into an incarnational experience amongst the people which it hopes to serve, it carries with it that desire for service which is beyond the description of normal desire. It is so deeply heartfelt that it is more of an instinct than a desire. Because this sort of service takes a very balanced structure or fundament, each within the group has agreed to have companions along the way, most especially, the companions called mates.

Thus, although each is equally sensitive, equally loving and equally willing, as the incarnational vibrations begin to wear away at the very fabric of the physical vehicle, this erosion is mirrored more by one than the other of the entities in the mated pair. It may be seen, for instance, that in the work that was the life desire of the one known as Don, the one who now acts as instrument acted not as the one who sacrificed, but as the strong right arm that could enable this wanderer to move through that ministry, that witness that unspoken evidence of love which each of you is not only capable of showing, but indeed does show. Without speech, without indication, without expression.

This entity, then, became polarized towards being that one which bore the vibrational difficulties in a more obvious way, and as the mated relationship with the one known as Jim occurred, there was more and more the polarization of the one who seems to serve physically and in a mundane way, and the one who seems to serve in a more directly communicative way. This may be seen also to be the case where, in the one known as R, there is the capacity for and the opportunity for much communication, while the one known as S balances this gift with the gift of sacrificial, physical, mundane responsibility. The more that is hoped for by the spirit that each of you is, the more intense will be this polarization so that each of the mated pair may experience as much of an extreme of difficulty as is possible while retaining an unbiased observational viewpoint whose nature is love.

It is to be reckoned with, with wanderers such as yourselves—and we are only able to say this to you because each of you has reckoned with and accepted that classification—that there is an additional burden that may be carried and that is carried by those who are able for as long as they are able and that is a far less personal, a far more planetary distress. Each entity in this room is an equal partner in a healing, not of one person, but in attempts to heal the planetary vibrations of those whom you came to serve. It is a great privilege, greatly treasured by each before this incarnation, to be offered the opportunity to carry not only a personal suffering, but also a deep, pure sorrow that is the pain of the planetary sphere which you came to love and to serve. It is well for each to realize that the one seems to be well and the other ill. This is, in fact, illusory and is an artifact of the masks which each chose to wear during this particular portion of the incarnational experience in order that a situation where there was love evidenced amidst difficulty could occur. Without the balancing mate, the vibrations of healing for the planet could in no way be carried by the one who has offered to take this part of the experiential catalyst which is, as we said, as artifact of each entities own high hopes and love as each gazed at this very difficult birthing upon the planet which you call Earth.

We are attempting to move each entity's mind from the concept of illness to the concept of suffering impersonally. We are aware that each questions how much suffering should be allowed; how much should it be fought; at what point shall it be completely accepted. To give each entity specific information would cross that fine line and move us into direct confrontation with the law of free will.

Therefore, there are those things which we cannot offer you. What we can offer you is a careful view of the situation which you are experiencing from the point of view of one who is not incarnate and not moving through the extreme physical experiences which are shaping and honing the faith and the will of those who came to aid planet Earth in the most direct and loving way possible. You may easily gaze upon the crucifixion scene and see not simply the two that seem ill, but the four to whom we speak upon the cross, gazing at the planet. Gazing upon the people. Seeing weddings and funerals and families from the perspective of the cross. Seeing with compassion the imperfections and iniquities of all entities in third density including that third-density self, which each of you must somehow manage to engineer a way through the incarnation for.

Yet, to grasp the nature of your situation it is necessary to move beyond the curtains of space and time. Move deeply within and touch the heart this is you. Find the I AM within the center of your being. Ask I AM, "How much shall I hurt?" and listen to the I AM for your I AM is true and that I AM says to you, "Sit. Feel. Listen." Become aware of the love that is the I AM. Know because you feel it, because you can touch it, that whether the physical body lives, dies, or does something in between, this I AM within you has only one ambition and that is to carry as much sacrificial love as is possible.

In order that the energies of the planet may be stabilized during what is indeed a fairly intense period of sorting out those who are harvestable, both positively and negatively, it should be no surprise to any that there are many very negative seeming events occurring at this time. There is also a negative harvest and there are those attempting to gain that harvestability.

We are aware that each wishes very much to ameliorate the illness, to become physically strong again, fit and seemingly far more ready to be a spiritual warrior. But the spirit has ever used those who seem weak in body, for the seeming weakness of body is instead a strength of spirit that does not wish to end the incarnation, that wishes always and in every place to give thanks for the opportunity to serve and like a true servant, hopes, no matter what the situation seems to be, to multiply the gifts and the talents of communication to those of this planet. To add a voice of compassion and humor and love and to subtract from this illusion as much judgment, prejudice and narrowness of view as possible, by picking that up too and carrying it into the light that wanderers are so aware of and feel with such reality.

My brothers and sisters, we are aware that this may not give you comfort, for we are not speaking of healing your bodies, but we ask you to look at this situation of healing. Gaze, not at the physical for a moment, but turn your gaze to the degree of "I AM" that has been expressed and experienced by each mate from the other.

Ask yourself how important that wholeness is? And how many entities of whom you are aware that have a whole, healed mated relationship? You see, each of you moves into relationship with a knowing. A knowing that is beyond explanation. A knowing that it is that natural way to grow and learn. This you cannot share with entities. This you can only celebrate with the mate. This is the spiritual health, the wholeness, this relationship, for with it you stand, yoked and pulling together and the ordeal of pulling this wagon of love and concern and care and treasuring and nurturing is pulled uphill and the more that it becomes steep, the more is the spirit fed with ever more refined fire, until there is actually a burning away of physical substance, the desire to help, to sacrifice, and to love is so very strong. An entity cannot do this alone. An entity can do many things alone but it cannot pull that wagon within which the Creator is the passenger. Thus, we ask each to respect the incarnational experience, which seems so hopeless. For each of you is indeed a living hope, a kind of sigil, the stamp of something far greater than you shall ever know that you are able to share.

We would say just one more introductory thing before we open to questions. The cooperation or lack of cooperation with an illness that is manifesting within the body is always a concern for those who wish to liven an impeccable life. We are able to say that at the point at which all speak to us this evening with their hopes and thoughts it is an acceptable and appropriate time to gaze at a cooperation with a destiny which you came to fulfill. Where is there fear? Examine that fear. Is there fear of loss? Move into your heart and sense what lies beyond fear and loss. Is there fear that one is not doing all that one could to work for health? Move into your heart. Touch that self and discover true weariness, true acceptance, and a readiness to be a consolation that is unspoken. This is not resignation. This is not giving up. This is not choosing death over life. This is choosing a present moment and determining that insofar as each is able, each shall appreciate, explore and care about the present moments that are the link betwixt the illusory bodies that your spirits now use and the eternity to which your spirits belong. Oh, how you yearn for the light of home, for the rest of eternity, for the peace of infinity, for the simple joy of living in truth when all about you in this incarnational experience is illusion upon illusion, all of it telling lie after lie after lie.

Be respectful of the duty you chose to shoulder in this incarnation. Realize that very few wanderers awaken to the extent that those present have awakened and then see that the illusion is going to seem for those who are this much awake ever less harmonious, ever more deleterious to the sensitized, physical vehicle.

Why this and not that mate? Why the illness here and not there? Think not upon that, for the mated entity, the "I AM" of the two, have this illness. It is manifesting partially by one entity seeming weak, partially by one entity seeming strong; by one entity seeming to be unable and the other seeming to be able. But we ask each who seems to be so able, how able do you feel? And at the same time, we ask each who seems to be so weak, how weak is your spirit, now?

We ask you simply to gaze upon the remainder of this incarnation in peace. The only thing you need ask of yourself is to work on harmony with the mate as first priority among all things. To ask of the self, not what the world would ask of you, but to touch the "I AM" within you and move in accordance with that wisdom, no matter where it seems to lead you. For your strength as wanderers is knowing, accepting and rejoicing in the opportunity for servanthood upon a planet that is dark and much in need of the light and the love that you convey beyond all words and actions.

We are aware we have not settled anyone's problems, but we cannot without infringing upon free will. We may say, however, that although we seldom experience an emotion, we do experience an emotion at this time and that is sympathy. Each of you has been very greedy. When you came to this incarnation, each of you chose to fill the plate full with every problem and difficulty you could imagine, because you wished to be a witness to the light and to the love that is the true reality, that is the infinite creative Thought. Now you are here and you are doing this. Sometimes better, sometimes subjectively, but so much better.

We ask you to cease judging and simply live in the moment without concern. When the incarnations of each are over, each will be so unbelievably pleased that the opportunity to express this kind of love and to communicate it in light and gentle ways has been taken and has been used. You will be saying, "What fun we had! What a wonderful time! Yes, it was tough. But, oh! What a time we had!"

For you see, you are warriors—old, old warriors. Not against anything, but for love, and the love that you offer in this incarnation is the love which this density needs to understand; that is, sacrificial love.

Gladly split yourself open and bless the splitting. Worry not [about] the outcome of this or that and insofar as you can, remain aware of the reason you came. Of the joy of service. Of the great sympathy you deserve from yourself as the animal, which has given itself as your vehicle, suffers because of the mismatch of spiritual vibrations betwixt the wanderer self, and the third-density vehicle.

We salute you, my brothers and sisters, and we do indeed express sympathy. May you encourage each other. May you express your love and faith for each other and in each other and may you bring each other ever more close to that awareness of the "I AM" that is the center of all that there is. That place that is closer to you than your heart or your mind. That temple within which your spirit sits, while upon the physical plane all sorts of things are happening. Rest there in peace. We bless each and we thank this instrument for the care it took in challenging and for the trust it showed when it was asked to channel that which was not to be offered to others.

At this time, we would transfer this contact to the one known as Jim. I am Q'uo, and leave this instrument in love and in light.

(Jim channeling)

I am Q'uo, and greet each again in love and light through this instrument. At this time, we would offer ourselves to those present in the capacity of attempting to speak to any queries which may be upon the minds. Is there a query at this time?

R: Yes, Q'uo. First off, for the message. There doesn't seem to be much left to say that you haven't said. I have one question. I'm wondering if my recent urge or compulsion to just let it go and let it happen, is it more a feeling of helplessness, or am I finally just realizing that I'm just here for the ride and then stop trying to control it, just let it happen. It's going to happen either way, whether I try to effect the outcome or not.

I'm just curious. I've recently been feeling almost lighter with the realization that I should just stop and let it happen. I'm sure you know what I'm trying to say, but I am having a hard time verbalizing it.

I am Q'uo, and am aware of your query, my brother. The ability to live one's incarnation in the present moment in the face of great discomfort is an ability which works its way to the conscious awareness by a circuitous path in many which find themselves in a situation such as that one which you now experience. Deep within one's subconscious mind and memory of that which encompasses this life pattern is the sure knowledge that all is well. As one lives the life and encounters the catalyst, this sure knowledge that all is well makes itself available in those ways which the entity is able …

(Side one of tape ends.)

(Jim channeling)

I am Q'uo, and am again with this instrument. The efforts that you make, seemingly in your own behalf, then, are those that extend in their effect to that environment which is this planet's third-density illusion. Thus, it is well to be of a light and accepting frame of mind and to offer oneself as that entity which gives light and love in whatever form is available to it.

Is there a further query, my brother?

R: I don't think so, Thank you, Q'uo.

I am Q'uo, and we thank you, my brother. Is there another query?

Carla: I'd sure like to follow up on that one. Then the thing to do is to go ahead and accept whatever and to realize the healing is taking place simply because of our love of the planet. Is that a fair paraphrase of which your *(inaudible)*?

I am Q'uo, and am aware of your query, my sister. We would agree that this is a relatively accurate interpretation of our intentions. We do not wish to place your feet for you upon your path or to choose those actions in which you shall engage or those actions in which you shall engage, or those actions which you shall not take part in. These choices are those which are of most importance to each entity.

However, the attitude in which any attitude—we correct this instrument—in which any action is taken, is that attitude of acceptance and that placement of the attention within the moment that is before one, allowing that moment and its own urgencies to direct the feet upon the path rather than placing the feet according to a future or past determination or approximation.

Is there a further query, my sister?

Carla: Yes. I have a couple of things I wanted to ask and I think they'll probably be pretty brief. One thing I've wanted to ask for a long time that I haven't felt the vibration *(inaudible)*, is that when Don Elkins died, I felt as if it would *(inaudible)* … but that was part of what we traded. I was learning wisdom and he was learning compassion and compassion killed him, and he didn't heal in this density.

It has been my feeling that's gotten surer, since I have been able to heal that *(inaudible)* been able to forgive myself for somehow not being able to keep him alive. That as I heal that mental image in myself, that *(inaudible)*. Could you confirm that?

I am Q'uo, and am aware of your query, my sister. Because of the nature of your own surety in this area of your own investigation we may confirm that the exchange of energies that occurred between the two of you, prior to the death, as you would call it, of the one known as Don, that the one known as Don transferred a portion of his personality to you so that it became necessary for you in your own evolution and attempt at balancing the lessons of your life pattern, to undergo the same manifestations of the mental complex as did the one known as Don. Because this entity's personality resided in some part within your own mental complex, this then was a necessity, if you were to find your own mental balance once again. Thus, that which you have surmised is in the large part correct.

Is there a further query, my sister?

Carla: Yes, I have one more. When … well, Jim and I have been calling it "ill spouse/well spouse." When the ill spouse is feeling rotten, it's not too difficult for the well spouse to do something to comfort. To touch, a cool washcloth, some words of encouragement, but I am puzzled about what the ill spouse can do to somehow ease the burden of the one who has to deal with *(inaudible)*. Is there a word? Is there a sentence? *(Inaudible)*.

I am Q'uo, and aware of your query, my sister. As you have correctly determined in your own query, a word, a touch, an expression of that love which is truly felt with the heart has a great transformative ability so that there need be no great display of gratitude other than the heartfelt offering of that love which truly resides within your heart.

Love is the great healer and enabler in all illusion. Call upon that quality of love that wells up from within you. Give it whatever form is possible.

Is there another query, my sister?

Carla: I do have one final one. I know that my systems are weak enough now that just about any illness could be fatal to me *(inaudible)* and it tears at me that I would be leaving somebody who would be *(inaudible)* quite devastated and devastated for the rest of the incarnation. How can I forgive myself for putting him in this position? I have no choice.

I am Q'uo, and am aware of your query, my sister. You can do only that which you can do, my sister. You cannot take another's burden, in most cases. You have borne much in your incarnation. Worry not about that which is projected from the present moment into that which shall be a future moment. Do and be in this moment and allow each succeeding moment to be created from the harmony of this moment. It is natural for entities within your third-density illusion to move from the present moment and to reminisce about those previous experiences and to project those that may occur in your future, for the present moment is that which is the most illusory and difficult to comfortably place oneself within, for all of one's life, then, is contained within that immediacy of experience which the present moment surrounds. And for most entities who have not consciously considered the purpose of the life pattern, the present moment is that which shall be escaped from. Thus, we would recommend that you share your love at each present moment when it is felt and allow the moment to be enough unto itself.

Is there a further query, my sister?

Carla: No, my brother, I thank you very much. And I guess we'll just *(inaudible)* memorial statement. *(Inaudible)*.

I am Q'uo, and we again thank you, my sister. Is there another query at this time?

S: Yes, Q'uo, I have a question. We've been doing a lot of discussing about the childhood and working those things out. And it seems that problems in the childhood that aren't worked out sometimes tend to contaminate the present moment and working things out, apparently, is going to be a very difficult and very painful process. My question is, is the clearing out and balancing of all of these painful experiences and feelings and dusting out cobwebs beneficial to allowing the present moment to be experienced with more purity or perhaps more clarity?

I am Q'uo, and am aware of your query, my sister. We feel that you have a good grasp of this concept, for it is the early experiences within each entity's incarnation that prepare the entity for those lessons that shall be laid out and those trails that shall be followed in order that an overall balance within the mind/body/spirit complex might be obtained. The clarity of vision of which you spoke is increased as one is able to see those factors and forces that have shaped one's attitudes and which yet echo within the present moment of each entity. A portion of one's efforts is well spent when one attempts to understand the formative years and their effect upon the perceptions and life pattern. The ability to enjoy each passing moment is enhanced, as one is able to balance the distortions that have been borne for these many years. This is not an escape into the past as one is attempting to enhance one's ability to express the truest nature of one's personality as the clearing of these early imprints is completed.

Is there a further query, my sister?

S: Not really. This was something I was concerned about and was having a hard time getting *(inaudible)* in the proper way. I would like to ask if there is anything that I can do help R better, to support him better to make this less difficult for him.

I am Q'uo, and am aware of your query, my sister. We realize that each entity present would wish to improve in the effort that is offered in service to others, especially to those that are the mated entities in the relationships and we look upon those efforts which are being made and see that there is little left for suggested improvements for each gives with an whole heart and would give any more that was asked, if only it could be described. We commend you, each of you, for your whole-hearted giving and receiving of love. It is important not only to give the love which you feel, but to receive the love which is offered as well. We would make one general suggestion to each entity in this regard and that is that when the effort has been made, that the worry that attends intensive opportunities for learning be discarded and that whatever efforts are made, be made with as light a heart as is possible, for the worrying, as you call it, the overconcern for any situation, tends to debilitate the offering of service and to drag, as it were, the air speed, if we may utilize the terminology for flight, for each present is indeed an entity that attempts to soar ever higher in the realms of love and service, therefore, be of good cheer, looking at the moment as that opportunity to share the love that is within, freely and creatively.

Is there a further query, my sister?

S: No, thank you very much.

I am Q'uo, and again we thank you, my sister. As we assess the energies of this gathering, we feel that we have spoken to those concerns which were the focus of this group and for the time being, would suggest the pondering of that which we have been honored to share with you. Take those thoughts that are of value to you and leave those that are not.

We should be happy to speak with you again upon your request. At this time, we shall take our leave of this group leaving each, as always, in the love and in the light of the one infinite Creator. We are known to you as those of Q'uo. Adonai, my friends. Adonai.

L/L Research

Intensive Meditation
March 22, 1991

Group question: Happy Spring! Could Q'uo describe the learning process … their learning process. Is there any regression in this learning process? Do we assist Q'uo's learning in our communication with them?

(Unknown channeling)

I greet each of you this day in the love and in the light of the infinite Creator. We thank you for calling us to be with your group and, as always, appreciate the opportunity to be of service in the humble sharing of our opinions with you. As always also, we enjoy being with this group. This level of purity of dedication to search for the truth, for the mystery, is high and we enjoy the feeling of blending our vibrations with yours. We also enjoy experiencing the awareness of your third density surrounding us, for it gives us not only stimulations of memories of our own third density experiences, but also enhances our understanding of the illusion in which you now work.

You wish information this morning on our own learning process. This process is no different from your own, my friends, for we seek the same mystery which ever recedes before us and our journey upon the path is but the placing of one foot in front of the other, no more, no less than your own.

We have but advanced a little further along this path, as you currently view your time/space continuum. For us, all times are the same. We realize this is perhaps a simplistic answer to your question and shall endeavor to give more information on the subject. However, we would say at this point, with regard to the question of regression in learning, that we feel there is no such thing as regression for each moment of time brings new learning experiences and the degree to which these experiences are incorporated into the life pattern perhaps measure the progress that is made. However, progress will always be made regardless of the efficiency, shall we say, of the learning.

You are aware that learning and progress cannot be measured on a conscious level although your peoples are greatly biased toward this opinion and constantly seek to monitor both themselves and others. In terms of progress on many levels, indeed, performance in your societies is certainly measured by certain achievements which are consciously measured and analyzed. It is therefore perhaps a natural tendency that this same process be applied to spiritual progress and the measuring of this.

However, spiritual progress can never be measured in this way and those who cling to such methods of measurement are merely buying into, shall we say, the illusion in which you dwell.

We realize it is a difficult thing for your peoples not to attempt to measure the progress made, especially in a spiritual sense. For the seeker who is devoted to the search for the mystery to continue to advance along the path, being aware only of the present moment, of the step that is taken now, not of the steps that were taken yesterday or those that may be taken tomorrow, or the mountain that is ahead, or the ravine or other such obstacle, but [focusing] only on the current step, [this] is a very difficult step for many. And yet, is this not the simplest step way, my friends?

You burden yourselves with so many things that are unnecessary to you. You burden yourselves with memories of the past, with anticipations and fears of the future. These do not belong to you in this present moment. We realize the difficulty of laying down these burdens. We would not mean to suggest that it is an easy thing. However, it can be done at any moment and the freedom known to one who has done so is unsurpassed by any thing.

We apologize for being shy of information with regard to our own learning process. Wherefore appearing to be so, however, it really is no different from your own. There are no techniques or pieces of advance knowledge we feel we can impart to you that would be of any help to you in your journey for each seeker will draw to itself those things that are compatible with the self that will aid the self in the learning process. These are unique to each and for one to share indiscriminately with another those things which are found to be helpful may often prove to be harmful to the one with whom they are sharing.

This may be done more beneficially between those who have walked a path together for some way, are familiar with the idiosyncrasies of each, and in these situations indeed the sharing of the learning experiences and of the companionship may be most beneficial and while we walk the same path that you do, we walk in a different location, shall we say, and what we find is helpful to us is simply that: it is helpful to us.

Each of you will find for yourselves that which is helpful to you. We have thanked this group often for the opportunity to work with you and have stated that you do us a great service in requesting our help for our service is our learning and our growth. Thus, by offering us the opportunity to be of service to you, you offer us the greater service that we may receive. For this we once again extend our thanks, our gratitude, and our love.

We feel these words are sufficient for a beginning treatment of this subject and would be happy to answer further questions on this or any other subject at a later time.

At this point, we would transfer to the one known as Jim for the purpose of answering any further questions which may be on the minds of those present. We leave this instrument with thanks, in love and light. We are known to you as those of Q'uo.

(Jim channeling)

I am Q'uo, and greet each of you again in love and light through this instrument. May we ask if there is a query to which we may speak?

Carla: *(Inaudible).*

I am Q'uo, and am aware of your query, my sister. We feel that we have shared what is the heart of the learning experience, not only for ourselves, but for any entities which yet seek the mystery and the unity of the one Creator and that is the interaction between entities. The opportunities for communication, for misunderstanding, for the wounding, for the healing, and for the transformation of entities in mind, body and spirit through the relationships that develop between entities. These means of learning are those which are most important. Not only to your own peoples, but to ourselves and all others of whom we are aware for the Creator shall learn from Itself. We, of course, as do other entities of those densities beyond your own third-density illusion, partake in individualized means of enhancing or working with this learning process.

Just as you utilize forms of meditation, visualization, prayer, ritual and so forth, so do we partake not only of these kinds of means of working with catalysts, but we also have developed other means which, though useful to us in our way of thinking and modes of perception, have little that may be offered from them to those of your people for there is enough difference in our personalities and our means of exploring our personalities that it would seem either incomprehensible to you, or seem that we were so different or other from you that the qualities that bind us as one and unite us as equal seekers of the one Creator would be overwhelming.

Thus, we do not find it is completely helpful to share in complete detail that which is our refining process. Rather, we have chosen to emphasize that we share with you the learning that is born of the interaction between portions of the one Creator that seek the identity of self, of each other, and of the one Creator.

Is there a further query, my sister?

Carla: Just a very small one that you might be able to answer. For the last two sessions I have been experiencing extreme heat. Can you comment on this?

I am Q'uo, and we aware of your query, my sister. As you have progressed in your process of the vocal channeling, the sensitivities that allow you to be aware of the conditioning vibration and of the narrow band transmission, you also are sensitive to this vibration in a way which affects your body's heating element, shall we say. You experience the light and love that we offer through you and through this contact even when it is being voiced by another instrument as a kind of heating or radiance that expresses itself in an analogous fashion in your physical vehicle and produces that heating of which you speak. This is simply an outgrowth, shall we say, or side effect of this contact and your increasing sensitivity to all stimuli.

Is there another query, my sister?

Carla: No, thank you very much.

I am Q'uo, and we thank you, my sister. Is there another query at this time?

Questioner: I have sort of a general one. I may have more specific formulations although I know that you can only answer generally. With regard to the situation with my parents and my brother, both that I experienced in greater depth just this weekend, I am beginning to be able to feel greater compassion and acceptance for my parents, where they are. At this point, I'm not able to feel that much for my brother and not feeling it a whole lot for my parents either. I know that this is a long process and there are things I am aware of that will aid that process.

My question is are there any general comments you can make or suggestions that you feel that would be helpful in being able to extend greater compassion and acceptance at this time?

I am Q'uo, and am aware of your query, my sister. We examine your recent memory and that which is your long-term memory regarding these entities that have offered themselves as your parents, as is the custom to describe such entities that bring or provide an entry into this illusion for others that they may learn and seek the One within third density.

We may suggest that insofar as it is possible for you that you take a, shall we say, an inventory of what you are able to remember of your experiences with them, and as you are the observer of these images passing through the mind, look first with that objective of the observer [and] record mentally that which is observed, and then attempt to enter into the experience from the perspective of the ones known as your parents on an individual basis. That is, gather that which you know has formed each entity, become that entity, participate in the experience that you remember as that entity, then feel those feelings that come to you as that entity in each experience.

This is a process which may take as much time and effort as you are willing to invest and which you feel is fruitful to invest and which can give you the beginning approximation of these entities' means of perceiving and of these entities' life pattern as a whole.

Then you may begin to perceive how these entities have chosen to learn various lessons, how these entities have found a difficulty or ease in various expressions in their selfhood and begin to understand and have compassion for that which is the heart of each entity and begin to explore how accessible or inaccessible is the journey that each entity makes from its heart to your heart and to any other heart by becoming these entities insofar as it is possible for you. Then you may begin to experience their reality, shall we say, or illusion, and through this experience have a bridge formed between the hearts of each of you, that you may travel mentally and/or emotionally at those times of your choosing so that this process may become internalized in a fashion that then is offered to the subconscious mind and may through the working with the subconscious mind provide those images to you through either your dreaming process or through meditation that may enhance and enable further compassion from you to them.

This is a means of experiencing the life pattern or flavor, the tone of another which may aid you in your overall understanding of any other entity.

Is there a further query, my sister?

Questioner: Not for now. Thank you very much.

I am Q'uo, and we thank you, my sister. Is there another query at this time?

Carla: *(Inaudible).*

I am Q'uo, and am aware of your query, my sister. Without moving past the boundary of infringement upon free will, we may suggest that there is a family of kindred souls that is well known to each of you, the combinations of which would provide the harmony that would enable those of our social memory complex and other contacts known to this group to work with this group in a fashion which would be helpful to the understandings of each entity, much as the harmony of the group now gathered provides a stable basis upon which we may construct various concept-complexes that may be more or less useful to you and to others who seek in the same general fashion as do you. Thus, there are many combinations of entities that would provide the kind of harmony that is necessary for a clear opening to be made into the group by entities such as ourselves.

Is there a further query, my sister?

Carla: No, Q'uo. Thank you very, very much.

I am Q'uo, and again we thank you, my sister. Is there another query at this time?

(No further queries.)

I am Q'uo, and we again thank each for yet another opportunity to blend our vibrations with yours and to speak from heart to heart those thoughts that are called by the desire to move ever closer to each other and to the one Creator. We move with you upon this journey and thank you for the opportunity of giving voice to our thoughts. We shall leave you at this time, though ever do we walk with you in the love and in the light of the one infinite Creator. Adonai, my friends. Adonai.

L/L Research

L/L Research is a subsidiary of Rock Creek Research & Development Laboratories, Inc.

P.O. Box 5195
Louisville, KY 40255-0195

www.llresearch.org

Rock Creek is a non-profit corporation dedicated to discovering and sharing information which may aid in the spiritual evolution of humankind.

ABOUT THE CONTENTS OF THIS TRANSCRIPT: This telepathic channeling has been taken from transcriptions of the weekly study and meditation meetings of the Rock Creek Research & Development Laboratories and L/L Research. It is offered in the hope that it may be useful to you. As the Confederation entities always make a point of saying, please use your discrimination and judgment in assessing this material. If something rings true to you, fine. If something does not resonate, please leave it behind, for neither we nor those of the Confederation would wish to be a stumbling block for any.

CAVEAT: This transcript is being published by L/L Research in a not yet final form. It has, however, been edited and any obvious errors have been corrected. When it is in a final form, this caveat will be removed.

© 2009 L/L Research

Sunday Meditation
March 24, 1991

Group question: The question this afternoon is: From the Ra contact we learned that there was a price to pay for each service-to-others opportunity that was in a direct ratio: the greater the purity of the desired service, the greater was the price to pay for it. As a related principle, we also learned in the Ra contact that the use of any gadget to enhance evolution, such as meditating in a pyramid or using biofeedback equipment to deepen the meditative state, or using marijuana to enhance the perspective, necessitated the seeker's use of the enhanced evolution for greater service to others, or the use of the gadget would become negative. This is the Law of Responsibility.

Would you speak to the fact that both an increased desire to serve more purely and the use of gadgets to enhance our own evolution bring about a greater price that the seeker will have to pay in the quantity and quality of energy expenditures? Would there be any other kind of price to pay other than an increase in the kind or quality of quantity of energy expenditures, the efforts on the part of the seeker as a result of utilizing either gadgets or finding an increased desire to be of service. What I am really wanting to know is, why there is a direct ratio that requires greater effort on the part of the seeker when the seeker either wants to serve more purely or uses some gadget to enhance the evolutionary progress?

(Carla channeling)

I am Q'uo. Greetings in the love and in the light of the one infinite Creator. It is a pleasure to join your meditation and to offer our very fallible opinions. We thank you very much for allowing us to be of service to you in this way, for it is in this way that we ourselves learn more of wisdom and compassion. We are especially pleased to address a question on service and the cost of service to others. Upon this day which is an holy day in the liturgy of your Christian church, that day called Palm Sunday, when a young man with dusty feet rode willingly to meet his passion, his false judgment, and his death, all counted as nothing in his consideration, when held against the privilege of doing the will of the Father.

Let us examine this portion of the story which Christianity tells about one man, a countryman, a peasant, a scholar, and depending upon whom you would ask at the time, a prophet, a savior, a political upstart, or a religious fanatic. This entity came into its incarnation with very little idea of the destiny it was to experience. Simply by following its own interests and disciplines it was able to unfold before its face those things which were important for this entity to be made aware of. He did not know, when he was studying the religious lore of his particular cultural group, that he would be an instrument of change for that group. He studied because he was in love, in love with the Creator that gave the law.

Through long years which are unrecorded in most history, this entity studied and journeyed in Africa, India and many places which now are called different names, Asia Minor, the northern portion of east Europe, and then back to the Galilean home from which he had sent himself in search of wisdom. There was a period during which this entity known to you as Jesus simply grounded himself in hard labor, working as his father had done before him as a carpenter and a worker in wood. His heart was at times full of love, full of romance, and full of an ever-increasing force within which began to guide this entity into the ways of an ideal which he could not find in the world about him, or in the testimony of his forefathers.

There was not one day when this entity awoke and said "Eureka, I now know what I must do, what my destiny is. I see every step and I am willing to take it." Rather, this entity was moved by a spirit and a voice that spoke not of the larger picture, but of that which was to be accomplished in the immediate present. It would be unwise and untrue to consider that the entity known as Jesus had a grand overview and simply observed the many changes and transformations which occurred during the entity's active ministry. This was not a god; this was a third-density human being, with every possible potential, both for the light and for the dark side of third-density human nature.

However, this entity had long loved his Lord. Day in and day out, year after year, beginning when he was but a child, he had turned every spare moment to the consideration of his own nature and the nature of the Lord he knew he loved, but wished very deeply to know how to serve. He received many, many guidances from the spirit that is with the Father, and, as his destiny came upon him, there was no Abraham to take him off the fire of sacrifice. In order to transfigure the written history of the Lord which he loved, the Father of which he knew he was the son, he found he must recreate a covenant, a spiritual covenant betwixt the Lord God and the people of the Lord.

Gazing at the strictures of the ten commandments given to Moses, he prayed for years to know the truths of what he found as shadows in those laws. And as he prayed, so did guidance come to him who prayed so deeply, so that he was able to say what he felt that new covenant was, not a list of things that were not to be done, the tale complex and infinitely separating one from another of the children of the Creator. This entity chose to place these same laws in a simpler and positively oriented perspective. The first commandment remained the same, to love the Creator with all of one's energies and talents, gifts and abilities. But in the second law, he erased a dark, gauze veil of warning and fear that had hung over spiritual teachings within his culture for a millennium and more. The second commandment dispensed with all the "do nots," and offered two things to do: to love the neighbor, be that neighbor a stranger, a friend, or an enemy, under all circumstances, just as an entity loved himself. He specifically said that these two commandments, love of God, and love of all other selves as the self, fulfilled and replaced all the law and the prophets.

He did not deny the history of his people, but when he felt, through intense years of prayer, the guidance of a voice which he trusted, he made himself available to do that which the Father had sent him to do. In the name of love, truth and life, he endured hate, lies and death itself. It was faith alone that allowed him to say, "Though these bones be dust, yet I shall be risen from the dead," a spirit clean at last before the Lord God, clean of humanity, clean of trouble, clean of the depth of confusion that the incarnational experience inevitably offers. And he did, indeed, keep the promise he had made in faith. In that story lies the path to eternity for many millions of your peoples. He created a life worth the telling by the purity of his desire to serve his Father, the Creator of all that there is.

Now, let us bring this discussion to all of third-density humankind. We may see that there is a certain percentage of those who, though alive within their bodies, are dead unto their spirits. These entities, because of their lack of desire to serve either themselves or others, experience the pleasant life insofar as it may be experienced, for life is always filled with loss and private anguish. Yet a simple, sunshiny day is enough for those who sleep to feel at one with all things, and the next day, if it rains and clouds and storms they should feel completely out of sorts and unhappy. Those who sleep blow with the wind and do not desire a path.

We speak to those who do desire to serve with excellence and purity. Gaze upon your desire. Do you burn? Do you hope? Do you desire more than anything within the illusion the opportunity to serve the one infinite Creator? There are many whose desire is simply to be with the infinite One. These are not lives which make great stories, although the light of those lives is very strong. There are others to whom we speak who desire not only to experience oneness with the Father, but who wish to follow that second request of the one known as Jesus, to love other selves as the self is loved by the self.

Now, you have asked why those who desire most keenly to serve purely experience difficult incarnations, and why those who use gadgets, such as pyramids, crystals and magical rituals, also run into a good deal of difficulty in the life experience as perceived subjectively.

Let us take the case of those who are using gadgets such as drugs, or shapes, or methods of focusing concentration, in order to aid their service to others, for their difficulties arise from a different level than others. Those who are willing to use a crutch in order to vault themselves upwards into the light, whether the crutch be drugs, or magical rituals, or whatever other occult science may be used as a gadget, have literally pulled themselves to a place for which they have not worked, and for which they well may not be ready. Whether or not they are ready to experience the wisdom and light, the love and compassion, of intercourse with the deity they must reckon with the falseness of their position in the light. Drugs wear off. The magical personality may crumble between the grocery store and gas station. Occult wisdom may leave one without resources when something occurs that is completely against that particular dogmatic method of perceiving the archetypical mind. And alone at last with itself, this entity who has no crutch now, finds itself committed to dispensing actions and words and the very beingness of its self in a way congruent with what it has learned. The crutch is gone, but the entity is responsible for the light that that crutch has gained.

Thus, it may be seen that those who by any means other than natural move themselves to transformation, must needs be responsible for that which has been gained long after the crutch has been thrown away. The more effective the use of the crutch has been to an entity, the greater will be the disparity between that entity's awareness of truth and that entity's ability to show it forth in the life experience.

Thusly, we have always encouraged entities who seek spiritually to do so honestly and naturally, having infinite patience for the wayward, conscious self. It is in fact a breach of the love of self to use any crutch whatsoever to gain knowledge of the most high, for it is an action of one who does not love or trust the self as much as it loves and trusts other selves. It finds itself quite unworthy, and must needs use this crutch to gain access to spiritual awareness. Entities, therefore, that have experienced difficulty because of using a crutch of any kind that alters the consciousness of the self, will find themselves in a difficult position, for they have attempted to serve others before they have learned to love themselves, and therefore to love others without stint.

Now, for those entities about which this question was asked, the path is honestly walked, the desire is felt within more and more the central portion of the activity of thought, intuition and action within the incarnational experience. Such an entity is hungry for good works. If it could be a fisherman, it would wish its nets to overflow, as with Jesus' aid the fishermen experienced the great catch. Even with meditating, focusing the self, learning to love all portions of the self, and wishing most intensely to serve others, to share with them the love and the light of the one infinite Creator, they will find that inevitably they have perhaps been too greedy for gain.

You see, gain is not only a gain of money or power. One who wishes to gain for the kingdom of truth and love as many entities as possible also has a very human third-density ambition that pushes that entity, causes that entity's orange and yellow rays often to become muddy with impatience, and the desire to save all of the planet's people, if possible, within the next twenty-four hours. While this ambition has in many cases been the foundation of a beautiful spiritual life which is of great aid and comfort to other seekers along the path of truth, it is far more common that seekers who have piled their plates full of intended good works shall find themselves full in the middle of the meal of incarnational life, that there is more to be done, more to be digested, more to break and bless and give, and for many the heart wavers, the soul stands aghast at the job before it, and it asks itself, "Why have I been given this guidance and these desires, only to find them the rose with the thorn, the bed of nails, the crucifixion as well as the resurrection?"

In the case of those who genuinely love themselves and wish to serve others, because of their understanding that they are of the light and love of the infinite One, they will be at some point within the lifetime in a position where there is seen what to do, and how to do it with the energy and joy of spiritual comfort, while the physical body, which has been inundated with the powerful experiences of spiritual transformation, begins to fail in one way or another because the energies that are being taken into the web of consciousness are those which are beautiful to the self which is infinite, but destructive as a fire would be to the physical animal which is the vehicle of each third-density field of consciousness.

It is important to note that the Creator allows an entity before incarnation, who has gained the right to choose incarnational patterns, to choose as many lessons to learn and services to offer as it wishes. Some entities have a beautiful simplicity about them, and are happy with an humble life, a simple witness, an ever-prevailing spirit of love and peace. You will find these saints in menial jobs, in highborn houses, and in all places in between. What marks them out is their peace of mind and their lack of ambition; they have desired only to witness to the Creator through the normal practices of living, raising children, having relationships and treasuring them, and moving to a peaceful incarnational death, in every expectation of eternal life.

These souls are rare because of the headlong impetuosity of young souls, and each soul is young no matter whence it comes when it enters into incarnation. By far the majority feel that they can handle the absolute utmost of personal lessons, and the absolute utmost use of the gifts and talents which have been given them. Is it any wonder, then, that when spiritual eyes are larger than the spiritual stomach, the physical vehicle which is finite begins to burn away because of the mismatching of vibrations between the incarnational, outer experience, and the inner vibrations of practicing the presence of the infinite One? Always, such an entity continues to burn with desire to serve regardless of circumstance, and it is quite usual for such entities to lose their health, and their incarnational lives, as they press forward ever onward to a more perfect use of their talents, a more perfect expression of the love of the Creator.

What shall we say to those who are experiencing this? We would suggest firstly that entities who are seeking spiritually begin to become aware of the power of humility. The greatest error made by those who wish so much to serve is that they are too impatient to listen to the guidance within. Thusly, they well may not note when their time has come to witness, and when it is time to remain silent, when it is time to burn with the glory of the infinite One, and when it is time to rest the physical vehicle from all the vigors of transformation that occur in the spiritually oriented life.

The spiritual polarity may be understood to be in direct proportion to the strength of the field of consciousness, that is the I AM of you. The more polarized and sacrificial the life, the stronger the field of consciousness, the greater the spiritual gravity, and the more appropriate and seemly appropriate rest shall be considered.

So, we ask those who are burning perhaps too quickly with the love of the Creator and of service to all to spend time, not asking what more they can do, but allowing the Creator to minister to them, for love from the Creator flows through them, why should it not include them? So many entities drive themselves as if their vehicles were used cars, unrespected and unloved. Consult the physical vehicle, all of you who seek. And when the physical vehicle, with its emotions, its thoughts, its fears and its plans, are crying out for rest, know that the one infinite Creator is guiding you to pay attention to that need to rest, for is not the primary service of those who love simply to be love? Is there not great virtue in resting in the tabernacle of the most high? In walking through second-density woodlands, exulting in the sheer majesty of the Creator? Would you not give even your worst enemy a rest when he is tired? Yet how you drive yourselves, those who seek, to accelerate the pace of their spiritual evolution, and how unnecessary it is for you to drive yourself.

Those who have caught fire from the love of the one infinite Creator will do their utmost, and cannot be accused of laziness because the physical vehicle must rest. We suggest that respect and love and compassion are not those gifts that you give only to others, but primarily and firstly to the self, for you must honor your physical vehicle. And if you have piled your plate too high, and feel quite unaccomplished because you have not been able to do everything you intended, cannot the spirit within you see that if you attempt your utmost when you are strong, that you may also attempt a quiet love that knows no surrender, and needs no ambition, while you are still? If you wish others to receive heavenly food, shall you then deny yourself that perfect rest, that gentle light, that fullness of being?

We ask those who have begun to burn out upon the spiritual path to quench that fire with the gentle water that slakes the spiritual thirst forever. Imagine the self standing beneath a waterfall of heavenly rain, rain that renews and refreshes, that honors and respects all that it touches, that connects the heavy chemical body back in appropriate working order to the desires of the field of consciousness that you are. In other words, there is no spiritual law which says that you must, at all times and under all circumstances, do one particular thing in service to others. How narrow would be the capabilities of the spirit of the living I AM if this were so. It is indeed not so, so we ask spiritual students to reckon honestly with their own spiritual ambitions. Ask yourself how do you wish to serve? What do you wish to learn? And how deep and full of grace is the consciousness that is doing these things? It is easy to reckon with the first two questions. Reckoning with the third tends to be seen upon the part of spiritual seekers as a way of admitting weakness, inadequacy or failure.

My brothers and sisters, you have given yourself a lifetime. You see before you the present moment. If you see in that moment a high ambition, and ideas upon how to serve, and what gifts to use, which are bouncing forth from you before any consultation with the spirit within, then it is that you must have compassion on yourself, and love yourself by letting ambition and service go for the moment, for to serve, and to hope to serve, are steps which are taken after reckoning with the self.

Have compassion on the clay that carries you. Have compassion on the soul which was not reckoning with the limitations of incarnation, who asked far too much. Know that there is not the one test given to all, the one body of service of knowledge that must be known by all. Know instead that insofar as you have trusted and have faith in yourself and hoarded yourself as a miser would, so that each gift and talent may be offered as directed by the spirit, so the seeker has learned to use more and more clear and lucid polarity, not asking that self be negated, but asking that the self be used to its utmost capacity.

If you can rest in the peace of stopping when you are tired, and starting when you are inspired, you shall be at all times learning as much as you can, transforming your field of awareness in positive ways to the utmost, and honoring the Creator of all. If there seems to be something that you wish to do that cannot be done, avoid frustration and judgment, and instead speak to yourself, this body that has carried you, in words of love and comfort and divine peace. In this way your sacrifices shall be those guided by the spirit of infinite wisdom, and you will know when your time is upon you, and when it is far better to rest and recoup your strength for the ordeals to come.

We would not in any way suggest that there is a way in which a spiritual life can be lived with particular ease. It is an increasing difficulty to change, and change again in the pursuit of positive polarity. The vibrational mismatch begins to take its toll upon the physical vehicle. Entities whom you love may no longer love you, and almost certainly will not understand you. And as you gaze upon your gifts you know that the stewardship of them is a great responsibility, ever greater as the gifts and talents are perceived as greater. And so the spiritual seeker strives, struggles, loves, breaks itself, and dies to the world, entering larger life as a warrior of peace and love, in a field of consciousness much transformed by the rigors of manifestation.

May all who seek and all who wish to minister to others ask first of the Creator, "What is Thy will for me?" This simple meditation will create a wealth of rest.

We are sorry that we have talked overlong, but felt that it was necessary to use as much time to express the complexity of the question in some way which seemed to us to focus on helpful answers. As always, we ask that you be aware that these are opinions, and to be taken as such. We would now close this working through the one known as Jim. I am Q'uo, and leave this instrument with thanks, in love and light.

(Jim channeling)

I am Q'uo, and great each of you again in love and in light. May we ask if there are any queries at this time to which we may speak further?

Carla: Did you wish to speak more on this topic at another time?

I am Q'uo. We feel that we have addressed this query as it was presented to us in sufficient detail at this time, and would reserve any further response to those further queries which you may have for us that would seek to refine your understanding.

Is there another query, my sister?

Carla: No, Q'uo, thank you.

I am Q'uo, and we are most thankful to you, my sister. Is there a query at this time?

Carla: Not from me.

I am Q'uo. Therefore, if we have exhausted the queries we shall extend again to each of you our extreme gratitude of the opportunity to join you in your meditation and to offer those words of information and inspiration which you may find useful in your journeys of seeking. We cannot thank you enough for this great service you offer to us. We hope that we have offered to you that which gladdens your hearts as ours are gladdened by your invitation. At this time we shall take our leave of this instrument and this group, leaving each, as always, in the love and in the light of the one glorious infinite Creator. We are known to you as those of Q'uo. Adonai, my friends. Adonai. ✺

Special Meditation
March 27, 1991

Question from S: Question dealing with the concept of what sort of effort to make of a novel that would incorporate the qualities of the wanderer entering this Earth's planetary sphere in order to be of service and how the development of identity using various concepts that have been put forth in metaphysical writings, how this would be accomplished to best get across the idea of an entity of light wishing to aid a planet that is in the process of being born. And then any words that Q'uo might have to say to S in greeting in general and specifically concerning her desire to be in contrast and in balance to the great amount of doing that she has been doing.

(Carla channeling)

I am Q'uo. Greetings to this group this day. May we express our extreme gratitude that you have in your own love and your own life in the name of the infinite Creator called us who are messengers of love and light to you. Together we praise the one infinite Creator, the mystery that is always [invented] and always mysterious and yet always the bedrock of the incarnational experience for those who have the hearts to understand.

We also would like to express that we of Q'uo is of a principle or combined energy offering consisting of the ones known as Latwii and the ones known as Ra. Each of us in our memory blesses, thanks and offers you love. We wish you to know as we wish all who would seek us to know that to experience our presence in your meditation you need only ask and you shall never be alone. We speak this to the one known as S especially, for it has been our privilege many times as Latwii to be with the one known as S.

Now we would say a few words about this principle, for these words are not those of Ra. The ones of Ra have been our teachers as well as your own. We are much more progressively guided by the ones of Ra than we would normally be in working with this group because the vibrations of this group are such that those less orthodox and introductory teachings are not the desire of this group but rather the desire is to explore further. And as that desire puts out a certain call and as both the ones known as Ra and the ones known as Latwii have permission from the Council which governs entering into your energies within this sphere we banded together, that we of Latwii might use more of the teachings of the one known as Ra.

So, we speak to you with Latwii's voice but with far more ability to have access to the teachings of the ones known as Ra. There is not a partnership here. You are listening to those of Latwii. It is simply that we have collaborated with those of Ra and we use our own discrimination in guarding the free will of each. It is indeed a blessing to do this work as we very much enjoy and love each other's social memory complexes.

Now, on to the questions at hand. When a body of work is being written concerning metaphysical truths it is completely up to the author as to whether to fictionalize information or to work with the highest and best information which you have, using it literally and without alteration. This would not be true if by such writing the free will of any would be infringed upon. However, it is impossible to infringe upon someone in book form, for there is no difficulty whatsoever in closing a book. Those who do not wish to see the information or the emotions therein within their own experience will simply find your book quite invisible.

Therefore, it depends completely upon the sensitivities of one who is attempting to become a carpenter in words, building with these structural members an area around those infinite concepts and possibilities that can never be put into words. There is another reason of why it is not necessary, unless it is simply desired to alter the truth of that which you know at this time. Entities who are not ready for this particular material, even if they find it helpful, will assume it to be fiction. For it is stranger than things that are created in the mind of man.

The peculiarities, shall we say, of a truly lived spiritual path are such as cannot be reduced to cliché without considerable practice. Consequently, we feel the issue that is truly being asked here is an issue concerning free will and the potential for an author infringing upon the free will of the reader. We do not feel that this is possible. Therefore, we encourage the one known as S to recruit her own inner wisdom, her own personal truth, and to write fearlessly, carefully and with absolute bravado. For all the tools that are placed within the reach of entities so that they may see them are those works of inestimable service.

In closing out this question, we would add that no matter what the physical fruits of a life lived in faith are, the life itself is a far greater gift to the planet and to the Creator than any artifact of this love and wisdom imparted in things which can be measured and seen. Higher gifts are always unseen.

This brings us to the question about being and doing. And in this question we find each within this group to have a poignant and deep confusion concerning the appropriate way to live a life in faith. We find in each case that each is by nature expressive and radiant, [each] one strongly polarized towards service to the Creator and to other selves. We find that each has been raised in a culture which praises the fruits of labor, whatever they may be, which finds virtue in such things as making money for the sake of making money. In other words, the concept of doing is not only corruptible but is constantly being corrupted. That is, positive polarity service to others is constantly moving into neutral or negative services which catch one upon, shall we say, the blind side. This is a matter of personal discrimination. We do not feel we have to talk about the doing except to express that in a metaphysical or spiritual sense the core of a realized action or doing is that expression of faith which is, "Not my will but [Thine.]" So that as you do that which you do you are grounded in a dedication of that doing to the love of the infinite One. It is said in your holy works, "I am the vine. You are the branches." In your doing realize that your roots are in the one infinite Creator and that the fruit that you bear is fruit that has come through the Creator like sap up to the inspiration of the self within and there it is fertilized by third-density catalyst so that it is unique to you and to your situation but in all ways beautiful and good to the taste.

Being, although it seems very simple, is very much put aside within your western culture. This culture is overstimulated, distracted, irritated at the extraordinarily close contact each must have with the other in most circumstances. How does one be when one is constantly being fed stimulus after stimulus after stimulus? One way to experience that being in a very vital way, and also in a very harsh way as concerns your physical vehicles habits, is simply to, as this instrument had suggested earlier, move to a retreat situation where there was the silence of the self to be explored with the companion that is also silent. This would entail a good deal of mental and emotional discomfort, for a desert experience, whether it is natural or contrived, is never particularly pleasant. In the desert, in the silence, one meets the self in all of its aspects. Yet it is in this desert and in this experience of the self that has both its light and its shadowed sides that the self learns finally to accept all of the self and thereby learns a compassion that cannot be learned in any other way. For when one sees oneself to be so far from what it wishes to be it is humbled with a good humility, a humility that realizes that within this density it is impossible not to err and be deceived repeatedly.

Beingness moves into the life experience as it is given space. The meditation is the beginning. Other tools which encourage being are those tools which also offer solitude or company with like-minded entities. In gardening, in hiking, in walking, in contemplation, in reading ideas are brought before the eye, the ear, and all the senses. And the being is allowed to expand beyond the quantity of flesh and bone until it is felt securely the nature, the essence of this field of consciousness that you are, each of you. What beingness does for this field of consciousness is to amplify the positive polarity of the entity who is being in a way that attempts to express with more and more compassion the self that is loved and accepted and forgiven and therefore is able to experience all entities as loved, accepted and forgiven.

The deep layers of being include purified emotion, worship, adoration, faithfulness and an unshakeable and unquenchable love for the one infinite Creator. None of this need be spoken. None of this need be obvious by word or deed for the work of beingness to be done. This offering that is directly to the infinite greatly aids the planetary consciousness for it has no object except simply to be, and by that being to channel love and light. Indeed, being is the most strenuous activity possible, for in being there is no past, there is no future, and there is no solidity to the form of the one who is. The strength of the field of consciousness is your strength. The nature of that field of consciousness is your identity. You cannot see results from things that are not actions unless you watch very carefully and then you shall see the power of authenticity in beingness.

We would at this time transfer this contact, with thanks, to this instrument, the one known as Jim. I am the principle known to you as Q'uo. Love and light to you.

(Jim channeling)

I am Q'uo, and greet each again in the love and the light of the one infinite Creator. At this time it is our privilege to offer ourselves in the attempt to speak to any queries which may be upon the minds of those present. It is with great joy that we offer ourselves in this sharing of that which we have found helpful upon our journeys and we desire that your journey may be enhanced to some degree.

Is there a query at which we may begin?

Carla: *(Inaudible).*

I am Q'uo, and am aware of your query, my sister. As we look at the entity that is your planet in its present state of transition we see that there is much confusion among a great many of your peoples who are more conscious of the process of growth and that of seeking which you might call the pilgrim's path. For many of these entities have become aware of how their own life patterns are evolving to the point where there is the necessity of giving greater and greater amounts of attention to what seem to be the tedious details of the day; that is, the very basic nature and level of living and continuing in this pattern in a manner which is stable and productive. Many find that there are difficulties which are more intensive and in need of attention than any previous time within the incarnation. This is [due] in large part to the current experience of the planetary sphere itself, as this may be seen to be the most critical period in this birthing process. We say critical in that there is movement towards polarization in both the positive and in the negative sense, so that those entities which are able to welcome and enjoy the more intensive vibrations of love and light are doing so in the manner which is helpful to each entity as an individual in that its choice of polarity begins to be apparent.

This choosing and polarization process, as it is reflected in your mundane world, is seen as that which is traumatic, for much of progress within your third-density illusion is the product of that which you call trauma. It is often the case that those who have been for a great period of time slumbering or nearing the wakeful period of their seeking will be nudged into greater polarity of seeking and consciousness of the process by that means of resolving the difficulty of, as you would say, dealing with the traumas that are increasingly a part of each entity's incarnation. If your illusion was less, shall we say, encumbered with the veils of forgetting there would not be the necessity for the loud and long ringing alarm to awaken those that wish to be awaken. However, this same nature of intensive veiling also allows greater progress in the spiritual journey. For each step is far more valuable and carries a great deal more weight within the total beingness as each step is taken with less surety and the need for greater will and faith to continue and even to begin this conscious journey of seeking.

Thus, we see upon this planetary sphere that there is the seeding of light in many places where light has not been in predominant expression, shall we say, but has only flickered briefly. And at this time we see that there is a great deal more light beginning to shine forth from many areas, entities and groupings of entities upon your planet. However, as with all transformations within the third density this is a process which must partake of the breaking or shedding of the older ways of perceiving, of thinking, and of doing so that there might be made a place for a new way of perceiving and of bringing forth that quality of compassion and understanding that has long been hidden within the hearts of many who have incarnated with the desire that they may show forth this energy of love that will aid, not only their own evolutionary growth, but will enhance the opportunity to be of service to others and will also lighten the planetary vibrations as a whole.

Thus, we see the difficulties that many have yet we see that this is the portion of this birthing process in which difficulties may be expected. Further polarizations, both towards that which you call positive or radiant and towards that which you call negative or that which absorbs the light, may be expected to continue so that there is as it would appear to be a movement in the mass consciousness of the planet in the direction of both of these poles with the great majority of entities remaining between these polarities yet also feeling this movement of polarization.

Thus, the time is critical. The time is that portion of the process during which the process gains what you may call a momentum and continues towards both the positive and the negative vibratory rates.

Is there a further query, my sister?

Carla: I am acutely aware of the wall being placed before me. Is this a point where I have to stop and wait for a teacher, although I am very suspicious of a physical teacher … I know I know that thought. Just wondering why I can't get past that wall.

I am Q'uo, and aware of your query, my sister. As the conscious seeker moves further upon its path using those tools which it feels are appropriate to continue the journey there is a process that occurs within each entity that may be likened to building the shell around the young that is to be born, seeing the seeker at any point in its journey being both the father or mother of that which shall be its new self as what you have learned is put into practice in your thinking and in your being. You find that there is constructed an area or field of reach which becomes more and more familiar to you as you construct the qualities, the concepts, the relationships, in short, the philosophy of your beingness and your relationship to the one Creator.

In its fullest flowering and expression this philosophy provides with a means by which you may move each step upon your journey up to a point which becomes increasingly difficult to approach with the existing philosophy, requiring, therefore, that there be a new means of penetrating the mystery which has again symbolically solidified around you in that form which you call the wall, which may also be seen as the egg through which the birthing entity will chip a new way through, a new path, a new perception as this entity is transformed by its own desire to seek and by its previous success in seeking.

Thus, you may experience the feeling of being before the wall for a significant portion of what you may call time. As there is then the necessity for that transformation which many have called initiation that will in some fashion allow the "new you" that is waiting to begin again at another level in this process to find the tools that will allow you to move through, around or to move beyond this wall which seems to restrain but which is more accurately a threshold that requires a greater degree of what we may call an intensity or increased desire to penetrate. There is often aid given by those whom you may call the guides or teachers. This aid may or may not take a form which is recognizable as that which would proceed from a guide or teacher. The aid in many cases is the inspirational dream or continuing series of dreams or line of thinking that develops within the prayerful, contemplative or meditative state so that a trail is laid and there is the accumulation in a step-by-step process of the tools necessary to penetrate the wall and begin again at a new level of understanding, shall we say.

Patience is that which is a paradoxical recommendation at a time when there is also the need for the renewal of inner determination to continue. Thus, if one is able to await patiently yet alertly and with firm intent one has prepared the self as well as one can for this time of a transformation.

Is there a further query, my sister?

Carla: *(Inaudible).*

I am Q'uo, and aware of your query, my sister. We walk carefully in this response, wishing not to step over the boundaries of infringement upon free will but we find that you are querying concerning you own powers of discrimination and we would advise you or any seeker on this journey inward to value highly the discrimination that is borne …

(Side one of tape ends.)

(Jim channeling)

I am Q'uo, and again with this instrument. We are pleased to make a time to pause so that those of Latwii may join you in your meditation. We shall pause at this time.

(Pause)

I am Q'uo, and am again with this instrument. Those of Latwii greet each in love and in light and wish to assure the one known as S that there is never a separation between us. We are always near and walk with joy upon the journey. Seeing the heart of love inspires each step however difficult the steps may become or however confused the process of thinking may become. There is always support. We are honored to be available in this manner and would be most happy to join you in any of your meditations for the purpose of deepening your meditation.

At this time we shall take our leave of this group and this instrument, leaving each, as always, in the love and in the light of the one infinite Creator. We are those known to you as Q'uo. Adonai, my friends. Adonai. ☥

www.ingramcontent.com/pod-product-compliance
Lightning Source LLC
Chambersburg PA
CBHW080420230426
43662CB00015B/2155